D0891481

DEC 1 - 1992
MAR 2 3 1993

MAR 2 8 1994

APR 2 4 1996

DEC - 9 2002

Trade and Structural Change in Pacific Asia

A National Bureau
of Economic Research
Conference Report

Trade and Structural Change in Pacific Asia

Edited by Colin I. Bradford, Jr., and William H. Branson

The University of Chicago Press

Chicago and London

Colin I. Bradford, Jr., is associate director of the Yale Center for International and Area Studies at Yale University. William H. Branson is professor of economics and international affairs at the Woodrow Wilson School of Public and International Affairs of Princeton University.

ERINDALE
COLLEGE
LIBRARY

The University of Chicago Press, Chicago 60637
The University of Chicago Press, Ltd., London

© 1987 by The National Bureau of Economic Research
All rights reserved. Published 1987
Printed in the United States of America
96 95 94 93 92 91 90 89 88 87   5 4 3 2 1

Library of Congress Cataloging in Publication Data

Trade and structural change in Pacific Asia.

(A National Bureau of Economic Research conference report)
Papers from a symposium entitled "Global implications of the trade patterns of East and Southeast Asia, held in Kuala Lumpur, Malaysia, Jan. 4–6, 1984 sponsored by the National Bureau of Economic Research and the Malaysian Economic Association.
Bibliography: p.
Includes index.
1. East Asia—Commerce—Congresses. 2. Asia, Southeastern—Commerce—Congresses. 3. East Asia—Commercial policy—Congresses. 4. Asia, Southeastern—Commercial policy—Congresses. 5. East Asia—Economic conditions—Congresses. 6. Asia, Southeastern—Economic conditions—Congresses. I. Bradford, Colin I. II. Branson, William H. III. National Bureau of Economic Research. IV. Persatuan Ekonomi Malaysia. V. Series: Conference report (National Bureau of Economic Research)
HF3820.5.A46T73   1987   382'.095   86-19293
ISBN 0-226-07025-5

National Bureau of Economic Research

Officers

Franklin A. Lindsay, *chairman*
Richard Rosett, *vice-chairman*
Martin Feldstein, *president*

Geoffrey Carliner, *executive director*
Charles A. Walworth, *treasurer*
Sam Parker, *director of finance and administration*

Directors at Large

Moses Abramovitz
Andrew Brimmer
Carl F. Christ
George T. Conklin, Jr.
Jean A. Crockett
Morton Ehrlich
Martin Feldstein
Edward L. Ginzton
David L. Grove

George Hatsopoulos
Walter W. Heller
Saul B. Klaman
Franklin A. Lindsay
Roy E. Moor
Geoffrey H. Moore
Michael H. Moskow
James J. O'Leary
Robert T. Parry

Peter G. Peterson
Robert V. Roosa
Richard N. Rosett
Bert Seidman
Eli Shapiro
Stephen Stamas
Donald S. Wasserman
Marina v.N. Whitman

Directors by University Appointment

Albert Ando, *Pennsylvania*
Marcus Alexis, *Northwestern*
Charles H. Berry, *Princeton*
James Duesenberry, *Harvard*
Ann F. Friedlaender, *Massachusetts Institute of Technology*
J. C. LaForce, *California, Los Angeles*
Paul McCracken, *Michigan*

James L. Pierce, *California, Berkeley*
Nathan Rosenberg, *Stanford*
James Simler, *Minnesota*
James Tobin, *Yale*
John Vernon, *Duke*
William S. Vickrey, *Columbia*
Burton A. Weisbrod, *Wisconsin*
Arnold Zellner, *Chicago*

Directors by Appointment of Other Organizations

Edgar Fiedler, *National Association of Business Economists*
Robert S. Hamada, *American Finance Association*
Robert C. Holland, *Committee for Economic Development*
James Houck, *American Agricultural Economics Association*
David Kendrick, *American Economic Association*
Douglass C. North, *Economic History Association*

Rudolph A. Oswald, *American Federation of Labor and Congress of Industrial Organizations*
Douglas D. Purvis, *Canadian Economics Association*
Albert T. Sommers, *The Conference Board*
Dudley Wallace, *American Statistical Association*
Charles A. Walworth, *American Institute of Certified Public Accountants*

Directors Emeriti

Arthur F. Burns
Emilio G. Collado
Solomon Fabricant

Frank W. Fetter
Thomas D. Flynn
Gottfried Haberler

George B. Roberts
Willard L. Thorp

Since this volume is a record of conference proceedings, it has been exempted from the rules governing critical review of manuscripts by the Board of Directors of the National Bureau (resolution adopted 8 June 1948, as revised 21 November 1949 and 20 April 1968).

Contents

Overview

During the period since the early 1970s, the newly industrializing countries (NICs) of East and Southeast Asia have become major factors in world trade in manufactures. First Japan and then the "Gang of Four"—South Korea, Taiwan, Hong Kong, and Singapore—emerged as major manufacturing centers. Japan during the seventies moved to the frontier of technology and joined the major Organization for Economic Cooperation and Development (OECD) countries as an industrial power. The Gang of Four expanded production and exports in a range of medium-technology products, from basic imports such as steel (Korea) to sophisticated electronics and financial services (Singapore). These countries have generally experienced rapid structural change in industrial composition and real income, and their export capacity is viewed as threatening to North America and Europe. An extensive literature has grown around the issue of the "secret" of the Gang of Four's success. Can they be imitated or are they sui generis? This is one issue addressed in this conference volume.

A second, and related, issue is the degree to which the resource-rich "ASEAN Four" (Association of South East Asian Nations)—Malaysia, Thailand, the Philippines, and Indonesia—will follow a similar path of development. Are they "next-tier NICs"? Manufacturing capacity has begun to grow rapidly in these countries, while their economies remain heavily based on resource endowments. The relations among the groups of countries at three levels of development in Pacific Asia—Japan, the Gang of Four, and the ASEAN Four—are also discussed in this volume. Do the industrializing countries further down the ladder displace those higher up as exporters to North America, Europe, and Latin America, or will those higher up the ladder themselves open to manufactured exports from those lower down? This is a third issue that runs through the papers in the volume.

The emergence of Pacific Asia as a center of manufacturing production and export and potentially as a major economic power is a phenomenon that we felt required some analysis in depth. Toward this end, with the financial support of the IBM World Trade Asia Corporation, we organized a conference, which was held 4–6 January, 1984 in Kuala Lumpur, Malaysia. The conference was jointly sponsored by the National Bureau of Economic Research and the Malaysian Economic Association and was (somewhat awkwardly) titled "Global Implications of the Trade Patterns of East and Southeast Asia." The volume includes the edited versions of the conference papers, plus an introductory chapter by the editors.

The conference program, reproduced as the appendix to this overview, included sixteen papers, eight of which discussed trade patterns of the eight developing countries mentioned above and eight of which covered international or comparative issues in world trade with Pacific Asia. Of the latter eight, three focused on patterns of trade of the United States, Europe, and Japan with the area. The conference program was organized as a mixture of overview and country papers. In the volume, we have reorganized the program into four cohesive parts plus our introduction in part I. Part II discusses the role of Pacific Asia in global trade patterns. Part III follows with papers on structural changes in the area. Then parts IV and V include the country papers on the Gang of Four and the ASEAN Four.

Our term *Pacific Asia* is meant to be descriptive of the countries at the Pacific edge of Asia running from Korea to Indonesia. This includes countries normally labeled East Asian and Southeast Asian. Strictly speaking, the term includes the eight economies of Parts IV and V plus Japan. Perhaps unfortunately, we omitted China from the project. Of course, some of the papers include a wider selection of Asian countries in their analysis, but Pacific Asia is the principal focus.

The first paper of part II, by William H. Branson, compares trade patterns of the United States, Europe, and Japan with the NICs in Asia and Latin America. He finds that the United States, the Latin American NICs, and the Far Eastern NICs form a trade triangle. The United States exports manufactures (mainly capital goods) to the Latin American NICs, who in turn sell raw materials on the world market, while the Far Eastern NICs import raw materials and export manufactures (mainly consumer goods) to the United States. These patterns show, on the one hand, the sensitivity of U.S. exports to the debt situation in Latin America and, on the other hand, the rapidity of change in the structure of U.S. industrial production. As the United States expands its exports of equipment to the developing countries and its imports of consumer goods from them, its economy becomes increasingly interdependent with them.

Using a new data set on production and trade in developed countries, Jean L. Waelbroeck's paper examines the pattern of trade in manufactured goods between developing countries and the European Community (EC, or Common Market). The first section examines the revealed comparative advantage and the geographic pattern of trade of the EC, the United States, and Japan. The second part is devoted to an in-depth study of trade between the EC and developing countries. Waelbroeck and Branson observe a similar "proximity effect" in trade patterns; the trade of Europe, the United States, and Japan is most intensive with African, Latin American, and Asian developing countries, respectively. Waelbroeck also concludes that while exports from Japan and the Gang of Four have put considerable pressure on Europe and North America, the export shares of the next-tier NICs are still small enough to permit significant expansion in their manufactured exports.

The third paper in part II, by Ippei Yamazawa, finds that Japanese manufacturers have been competing with manufacturers in the Asian NICs and other Asian developing countries: first, in their export markets in the United States and Western Europe and later, since the mid-1970s, in the Japanese market itself. This has created a deficit in trade in manufactured goods for the Asian less-developed countries (LDCs). Beyond this competition, strong complementarity has continued between Japan and her Asian neighbors through Japan's supplying capital and intermediate goods and importing labor-intensive consumer goods and primary products. However, the paper argues that in order to further this trade relationship, Japan would have to increase manufactured imports and improve the balance of trade with the Asian LDCs through structural adjustment and industrial cooperation as well as by eliminating "implicit barriers."

The paper by Robert E. Baldwin and J. David Richardson concludes that three basic economic and political influences explain most shifts in U.S. trade policy in the postwar period. They are (1) the emergence and subsequent decline of the United States as a hegemonic power, (2) the persistence during the entire period of a politically significant group of domestic industries that were opposed to duty cuts on competing import products, and (3) efforts by Congress to reduce the greatly increased power granted the president during the depression and World War II. In fact, the authors find that conflict has punctuated relations between branches of government more often than between political parties. They believe that leadership on U.S. trade policy is still potentially strong despite the decline in U.S. hegemony.

The last paper in part I, by Lawrence R. Klein, describes the role played by the Pacific Asian economies in Project LINK. There, the developing countries play an important role and are represented in four area models: Africa, Latin America, Middle East, and Southeast Asia/ Pacific Far East. Projections for 1983–88 indicate relatively poor prospects for these developing countries in the context of relatively moderate performance for the world as a whole. Within the developing areas of the world, there is great diversity. In the short run, the Asian countries are expected to do fairly well in contrast with Latin American countries, where activity levels are expected to be quite depressed. Over a longer period, until 1988, economic prospects appear to be good for the countries of Southeast Asia and the Pacific Far East. Similarly, among socialist countries, the People's Republic of China is expected to turn in an outstanding performance.

In the first paper of part III, Colin I. Bradford, Jr., examines the sources and manifestations of internal and external structural change in the NICs and next-tier NICs in East and Southeast Asia, comparing them with European and Latin American transitional economies. By compiling data on compositional shifts in exports, Bradford finds patterns that are broadly consistent with an explanation of structural changes in trade based on factor proportions. His paper also finds evidence of policies encouraging underpricing investment goods in rapidly industrializing countries, which appears to have been an important vehicle for countries becoming NICs in the 1970s but may have produced overinvestment in the NICs during the slower-growth 1980s. Bradford also presents data that relate the degree of price distortion to the degree of inward versus outward orientation of growth strategies. Getting prices right, while important, is not a sine qua non of economic growth, and the identification of correct prices with outward-oriented growth strategies has been overdrawn in some of the recent literature.

Lawrence B. Krause presents an empirical study of the structure of trade in manufactures within the Pacific Asian region. He concludes that, despite the world recession of the early 1980s, which reduced international trade, international specialization continued to progress. Moreover, LDCs continued to increase their share of world trade in manufactured goods. The developing countries in East and Southeast Asia were the star performers among the LDCs. The basis for the comparative advantage of these countries differed depending on whether they were NICs who moved from labor-intensive goods to more skill- and technology-intensive goods, or whether they were the other developing Asian countries who remained heavily involved in natural-resource-intensive development during the 1970s. The paper also examines the special case of textiles and clothing and, despite the Multi-Fiber Arrangement, finds increased scope for LDC trade in these commodities. Krause concludes that development in Pacific Asia has followed lines of comparative advantage.

In the last paper of part III, Laurence J. Kotlikoff and Edward E. Leamer examine the relationship between trade, growth, and factor prices in (1) the standard Heckscher-Ohlin (HO) model, with equal numbers of factors and goods; (2) the uneven HO model, with more goods than factors; and (3) a generalized HO model, with adjustment costs caused by immobility of physical capital in the short run. Preliminary statistical tests of the three models of transitional international growth in twenty-eight countries and twenty-eight industries provide some support for each view of the evolution of international trade and factor prices. This partial support for each of the models suggests that an uneven model with adjustment costs provides a better basis for discussing international trade than any of the three models on its own. Consistent with the results of Bradford and Krause, the more general conclusion of this analysis is support for a general factor endowment HO view of sources of comparative advantage and growth.

The first country study of part IV, on South Korea, is by Wontack Hong. His paper first sets out to analyze the relationship between the export-oriented growth strategy and the high-growth performance of the Korean economy, on the one hand, and Korea's shifting comparative advantage and pattern of trade in manufactured goods, on the other. He also looks at the impact of subsidized credit and the consequent rationing of credit on the pattern of trade in manufactured goods. The paper concludes that subsidization of credit favored capital-intensive industries and skewed Korea's exports toward capital-intensive goods, such as machinery. The Korean experience is contrasted with that of Taiwan, which subsidized credit less and had more labor-intensive exports.

The paper on Taiwan, by Chi Schive, argues that Taiwan's fast economic growth during the past two decades came mainly from the expansion of trade. Taiwan's trade pattern was determined by comparative advantage, with labor-intensive exports. The trade balance in Taiwan fluctuated widely in the 1970s, partly as a result of the inflexibility of the exchange rate in that period. When trade expansion created a potential market for intermediate and capital goods, local entrepreneurs responded to this signal to the extent that other conditions for the development of such industries were also met. Schive notes that Taiwan's exports in the 1970s were relatively labor-intensive, but that growth with rising real wages has ended this phase. He concludes that Taiwan's trade in the late 1980s will shift toward more capital-intensive exports and consumer-goods imports.

Edward K. Y. Chen's paper on Hong Kong begins by documenting that the rapid growth of the past twenty years has been based on manufactured exports. Chen shows that this growth was largely demand determined, with trade liberalization and growth in the industrial countries expanding demand for consumer goods, especially clothing. Hong Kong responded by diversifying production within industrial groups rather than undergoing fundamental structural change. Chen concludes that this period of demand-determined growth is ending and that Hong Kong will have to shift toward exports that are more skill- and technology-intensive. He believes that this shift will be hindered by the existing relatively low technological capability and by the political uncertainty related to the expiration of Hong Kong's British lease in 1997.

In the last paper in part IV, Chung Ming Wong examines the changes in Singapore's trade in manufactured goods in the last two decades. He relates these changes to domestic economic development and to shifts in government policies. Since the turn from import substitution to export promotion in the 1960s, Singapore has achieved high rates of industrial growth by rapid absorption of labor into labor-intensive industries. In view of the current shortage of labor, however, the government is following a deliberate policy of phasing out unskilled-labor-intensive industries and restructuring the economy to emphasize high-technology and skill-intensive activities.

The part IV papers on the Gang of Four all point to an anticipated shift toward less labor-intensive and more technology-intensive production. The authors tend to agree with Waelbroeck's assessment that there is ample room in the markets of the industrial economies to accommodate this shift.

Beginning the country studies of part V, the paper by Chee Peng Lim traces the changes in the Malaysian economy over the last twenty years and examines how these changes affected the product composition and direction of Malaysia's trade. He notes particularly the rapid growth in manufactured exports. The paper illustrates the tension between development of manufacturing and resource-based industry in the conclusion that Malaysia may move toward development of "high-value" machinery and resource-based exports. Lim sees Malaysia joining the NICs by the end of the 1980s.

In his paper on Thailand, Juanjai Ajanant asserts that the growth of Thailand's manufacturing sector during 1960–76, in terms of both production and exports, was stimulated by the moderate import substitution industrialization policy. While industrial activities were promoted, other sectors, such as agriculture, maintained steady growth in terms of both production and export value. This import substitution policy was replaced by a more export-oriented policy after 1976. Ajanant argues that a combination of supply and demand factors spurred manufactured export growth so that by 1980 30% of Thailand's exports were manufactures. Ajanant concludes that Thailand will experience further growth in exports of agriculture and manufactures, with the balance continuing to shift to the latter.

Florian A. Alburo examines the industrialization process in the Philippines and the role that trade has played in it. He points out that the country has begun a shift from an "inward-looking" path to an "outward-looking" strategy. He also presents evidence that the increasing exports of nontraditional manufactured goods in the 1970s have been associated with structural change that is consistent with the country's resource endowments and its comparative advantage. While Philippine development is currently hindered by the debt problem and political turbulence, Alburo finds the prospects for sustained structural change encouraging.

In the last paper in the volume, on Indonesia, Ralph E. Beals finds that despite progress toward industrialization since 1966 under the "New Order" government, exports have remained almost exclusively unprocessed mineral and agricultural products, with crude oil being the dominant export since 1974. Government policies—including protective tariffs and other barriers to trade, interest rate subsidies and credit controls, tax holidays and other investment subsidies, energy price controls, and investment in capital-intensive industry—have steered industrial growth away from areas of Indonesian comparative advantage and into import-competing sectors. Growth in these sectors has not provided satisfactory employment growth and, indeed, appears to be slowing down. Beals concludes that Indonesia's pattern of trade and industrialization is quite different from that of other countries under discussion in this volume. While the other three resourced-based ASEAN countries have moved toward manufacturing and an export-oriented growth strategy, Indonesia is still in the import substitution phase.

Our intent, in organizing the conference, was to generate a lively and wide-ranging discussion of the comparative patterns of trade and structural change in Pacific Asia and their implications for the world economy. Rather than record the discussion, we decided to write an introductory chapter that integrates the main points that emerged. This is the first chapter in the volume. It discusses issues such as whether the NICs exist as an ex ante category, patterns of trade and growth in the three tiers of Pacific Asia, the extent of government intervention in the growth process, the role of financial repression, and supply-led versus demand-led growth. The chapter is, in a sense, the research agenda that emerged from the conference.

We extend our thanks to the IBM World Trade Asia Corporation for providing financial support and to the Malaysian Economic Association for providing the local arrangements for the conference in Kuala Lumpur. We are particularly indebted to Kirsten Foss, the NBER organizer, and especially to Dr. Lim Lean Lun of the Malaysian Economic Association for her organizing efforts on the scene in Kuala Lumpur.

Appendix
Conference Program

On 4–6 January 1984, NBER's Program in International Studies held a conference in Kuala Lumpur, Malaysia, on the "Global Implications of the Trade Patterns of East and Southeast Asia." This conference, organized by NBER's William H. Branson of Princeton University and Colin I. Bradford, Jr., of Yale University, was supported in part by the IBM World Trade Asia Corporation and was jointly sponsored by the Malaysian Economic Association and NBER. The conference program included sixteen papers, eight of which discussed trade patterns and trends of developing countries in the region and eight of which covered relevant international or comparative issues in world trade with the area. The program was as follows:

Wednesday, January 4

Opening Address by Y. B. M. Tengku Ahmad Rithauddeen, Minister of Trade and Industry, Malaysia

William H. Branson, "Trade and Structural Interdependence between the United States and the NICs"

Jean L. Waelbroeck, Université Libre, Brussels, "Trade and Structural Interdependence: The European Community and the NICs: Their Trade in Manufactures"

Ippei Yamazawa, Hitotsubashi University, Tokyo, "Japan and Her Asian Neighbors in a Dynamic Perspective"

Discussants: Narongchai Akransanee, The Industrial Management Company, Bangkok; J. David Richardson, NBER and University of Wisconsin; and Lawrence B. Krause, Brookings Institution

Chee Peng Lim, University of Malaya, Kuala Lumpur, "Changes in the Malaysian Economy and Trade Trends and Prospects"

Florian Alburo, University of the Philippines, Manila, "Manufactured Exports and Industrialization: Trade Patterns and Trends of the Philippines"

Juanjai Ajanant, Chulalongkorn University, Bangkok, "Trade Patterns and Trends of Thailand"

Discussants: Robert E. Baldwin, NBER and University of Wisconsin; Chong Ngian Yet, Ministry of Trade and Industry, Malaysia; and David L. Grove, U.S. Council for International Business

Thursday, January 5

Lawrence B. Krause, "The Structure of Trade in Manufactured Goods in the East and Southeast Asian Region"

Lawrence R. Klein, University of Pennsylvania, "The South Asian and Pacific Far East Countries in Project LINK"
Discussants: William H. Branson and J. David Richardson

Edward Chen, University of Hong Kong, "Hong Kong's Trade Patterns and Trends"
Chung Ming Wong, National University of Singapore, "Trends and Patterns of Singapore's Trade in Manufactures"
Discussants: Dr. Fong Chan Onn, University of Malaya, and Jean L. Waelbroeck

Friday, January 6

Wontack Hong, Seoul University, Korea, "Export-oriented Growth and Trade Patterns of Korea"
Chi Schive, National Taiwan University, Taipei, "Trade Patterns and Trends of Taiwan"
Ralph Beals, Amherst College, "Trade Patterns and Trends of Indonesia"
Discussants: Gustav Ranis, Yale University; Dr. Tan Tat Wai, Bank Negara Malaysia; and Giuseppe Sacco, Free University of Rome
Colin I. Bradford, Jr., "The Role of the Industrializing Countries of East and Southeast Asia in World Trade: NICs and Next-Tier NICs as Transitional Economies"
Laurence J. Kotlikoff, NBER and Yale University, "Empirical Tests of Alternative Models of International Growth"
Robert E. Baldwin and J. David Richardson, "Recent U.S. Trade Policy and Its Global Implications"
Discussants: Ronald Findlay, Columbia University; Lawrence R. Klein; and Peter B. Kenen, Princeton University

I   Introduction

1 Patterns of Trade and Structural Change

Colin I. Bradford, Jr., and William H. Branson

1.1 Introduction: Definition and Characteristics of NICs

Because of its rapid economic growth over the last twenty years, Pacific Asia provides a fascinating laboratory for analyzing the dynamics of economic growth. The fact that growth in Pacific Asia has been export-led has added to the analytical interest in the area both because of the impact of exports from Pacific Asia on the rest of the world and because of the interaction between trade and growth characteristic of the Pacific Asian experience. Japan led the way to dynamic growth in the 1960s. If Japan had been the only country in the region to achieve high growth, Japan's unique qualities would have been seen as the main determinants of exceptional performance. In the 1970s, however, the East Asian newly industrializing countries (NICs)—South Korea, Taiwan, Hong Kong, and Singapore (often referred to as the Gang of Four)—became major exporters of manufactured goods on a global scale and achieved extraordinarily high rates of economic growth. The remaining developing countries in Pacific Asia, sometimes referred to as the ASEAN Four (Association of South East Asian Nations)—Malaysia, the Philippines, Thailand, and Indonesia—have shown strong, though not spectacular, economic performance in the late 1970s and early 1980s. (Although a member of ASEAN, Singapore is nevertheless in the Gang of Four; also, the conference on which this volume is based was organized before Brunei entered ASEAN.) The major Latin Amer-

Colin I. Bradford, Jr., is associate director of the Yale Center for International and Area Studies and is a research economist with the National Bureau of Economic Research. William H. Branson is professor of economics at the Woodrow Wilson School, Princeton University, and a research associate of the National Bureau of Economic Research.

ican countries—Argentina, Brazil, and Mexico—also manifested high growth and export performance in the 1970s, but they experienced enormous financial problems in the 1980s. The Mediterranean European countries—Greece, Yugoslavia, Spain, and Portugal—industrialized rapidly in the 1960s and exported manufactures at rapid rates in the 1970s without the financial crunch in the 1980s experienced by Latin America.

This diverse economic record among high-growth, trade-oriented industrializing countries raises broad questions regarding the relationship of trade, structural change, and economic growth. From a global perspective, the most immediate issue is whether the East Asian NICs are sui generis, unique cases unreplicable elsewhere because of their unusual conditions, circumstances, and characteristics, or whether the East Asian NICs represent models that not only can but should be emulated by other industrializing nations. This is an issue which is addressed comparatively in chapters 7 and 8, by Bradford and Krause, and which occupied a good deal of the discussions at the conference in Kuala Lumpur.

It becomes clear from such analyses and exchanges that defining the phenomenon of dynamic, trade-oriented growth is a challenging intellectual task. Most analysts would agree that the East Asian Gang of Four are NICs, if by the term *newly industrializing countries* is meant countries with exceptionally high GDP growth rates and unusually strong export performance, especially of manufactured goods exports. But beyond this, the issue gets more difficult; it goes to the heart of thinking and theorizing about growth and development and the relationship of trade to sectoral change and aggregate performance, about which there is great debate, discussion, and controversy. This issue will not be settled here, but its main contours will be explored as a framework for reading the other analyses in this volume.

The issue of uniqueness versus universality of dynamic development is an old one. While concerned principally about the limited spread of economic growth historically, Simon Kuznets wondered in 1965 "whether the restrictive locus of pioneering impact is an inherent characteristic of all revolutionary breakthroughs to a new economic epoch" (1966, 465). The time periods when such "breakthroughs," "turning points," or "takeoffs" occurred are as much matters of controversy as the nature of the dynamic surge itself. Differences between Kuznets's designation of the time periods for the "beginning of modern growth" in what are now advanced countries and Rostow's (1978, p. 778, table N-31, n. 2) "takeoff" periods are not substantial. However, Lloyd Reynolds's (1983) "turning points" to "a sustained rise in per capita income" differ greatly from Walt Rostow's takeoff periods. Reynolds and Rostow agree that Latin America preceded East Asia, but Reynolds's analysis points to turning points in the mid-to-late nineteenth century, whereas Rostow's takeoff periods are in the mid–twentieth century (see table 1.1).

The major studies of the recent spurts in industrialization, growth, and trade have varying criteria for establishing categories. The first major study of the NICs was published by the Organization for Economic Cooperation and Development (OECD) in 1979. While acknowledging that borderlines between categories were "bound to be arbitrary," ten countries were identified as NICs based on (a) their rapid penetration of world markets of manufactures, (b) a rising share of industrial employment, and (c) an increase in real GDP per capita relative to the more advanced industrial countries (OECD 1979, 18–22). These criteria established Greece, Portugal, Spain, Yugoslavia, Brazil, Mexico, and the Gang of Four in East Asia as NICs. The Chatham House study of the NICs published in 1982 focused on the Gang of Four plus Brazil, Mexico, Argentina, and India, all of which had achieved exports of manufactures in excess of $1 billion by 1976 (Turner and McMullen 1982, 6, 10, table 2.1). The Development Assistance Committee (DAC) in its 1982 *Review* examined "second tier" exporters and distinguished between NICs and potential NICs based on both the magnitude of manufactured exports in 1979 and their growth rate between 1972 and 1978, while maintaining the classification of the ten OECD-designated countries as NICs (OECD 1982, 123–32, esp. table XII-2 and n. 1 on p. 123). Interestingly, the only developing countries to have both more than $1 billion in manufactured exports in 1979 and average growth rates in manufactured exports between 1972 and 1978 above 13% are Taiwan, Korea, Singapore, and Brazil in the $3 billion and above range, and Malaysia, the Philippines, and Thailand in the $1–$2 billion range, Hong Kong was the only other country besides Taiwan and Korea to have above $10 billion in manufactured exports, but Hong Kong experienced a 1972–78 growth rate of exports

Table 1.1   **Transition Periods in Dynamic Developing Economies**

	Turning Points (Reynolds)	Takeoff (Rostow)
Korea	1910	1961–68 (p. 555)
Taiwan	1895	1953–60 (p. 540)
Brazil	1850	1933–50 (p. 486)
Mexico	1876	1940–60 (p. 493)
Argentina	1860	1933–50 (p. 474)
Thailand	1850	1960s (p. 551)
Colombia	1855	n.a.

Sources: Reynolds 1983, 941–80, esp. 943 and 958. Rostow 1978, pages indicated in table.

in the 7%–13% range. The World Bank and the International Monetary Fund (IMF) have a category they call "major exporters of manufacturers," the criteria for which are unspecified. This category excludes Taiwan for noneconomic reasons and also leaves out Spain (which is classified by the World Bank as an "industrial market economy") and Mexico (which is classified as a "middle income oil exporter"). The World Bank and the IMF category of major exporters of manufactures includes Greece, Yugoslavia, Portugal, Argentina, Brazil, Hong Kong, Singapore, and Korea as well as Israel and South Africa. The World Bank adds two additional countries: the Philippines and Thailand (World Bank 1985, p. xi; International Monetary Fund 1985, 201).

Development of a clear theory that would predict which countries will be the next NICs rather than establish criteria for the designation of NICs ex post is one of the central problems of the field of economic development. Rostow's analysis of takeoffs is an attempt at such a theory whose success is not universally acknowledged. While development theorists struggle with the problem, a more systematic empirical approach to the identification of NICs may be feasible. We have in mind the application of cluster analysis to a large body of data on developing countries, such as is contained in the World Bank data base.[1]

A clustering algorithm applied to such a data base would ascertain whether a group of countries that are generally considered NICs emerges as a separate cluster on the basis of the characteristics in the data base. This would identify a cluster of countries that are similar to each other relative to the entire group's dissimilarity to the rest of the countries. If such a cluster emerged, and if some non-NIC countries were also in it, they would share the characteristics of the already identified NICs. This type of analysis might provide a more systematic basis for identification of next-tier NICs. The entire procedure would test the validity of our current identifications of NICs as a meaningful economic category.

Despite all the limitations, qualifications, and differences in definitions, it is clear that the developing economies of Pacific Asia are of great interest in the study of dynamic trade and development performance. The East Asian Gang of Four qualify as NICs according to most classifications, even if the category either varies or is unclear; and Malaysia, Thailand, and the Philippines are of consequence in most studies as examples of potential NICs. There seems to be some convergence of analytical opinion that the relevant comparisons outside Pacific Asia are Greece, Yugoslavia, Spain, and Portugal in Europe, and Argentina, Brazil, and Mexico in Latin America. However, even though it seems to be clear which countries are NICs, it is not as clear what it means to be a NIC and, therefore, whether the NICs represent exceptional cases or replicable models. The fact that it is agreed that the category in the 1970s and early 1980s contains only a relatively few countries and that there is general agreement on the countries which should be identified as NICs does not provide the answer to the question, are the NICs sui generis?

The meaning of the NIC category explored most thoroughly in this volume is the relationship between exceptional export performance, especially in the growth of manufactured exports, and dynamic development, by which is meant some combination of rapid aggregate economic growth and structural change. The sectoral composition of output and trade, the rates of structural change in production and exports, and the relationship of rates of structural change to economic growth constitute continuing themes throughout the volume. The relationship between the sectoral composition of output and the composition of exports is of considerable interest in understanding the dynamics of growth and development. It raises a number of broad issues recurrent in the book, in particular the relationship of factor proportions to the composition of trade, the impact of abundant resource endowments on industrialization and manufactured exports, and the rapidity of adjustment of the patterns of trade and structures of production to dynamic growth in different "tiers" of countries. These are discussed more fully in the next section of this chapter. Also raised by these analyses are a set of issues related to the types of development strategies, styles, and regimes associated with varied economic outcomes. The nature of the mix between active government policies and market forces, the relative effectiveness of credit versus fiscal subsidies, and the balance between demand- versus supply-determined industrialization and exports are examined in the last section of this chapter.

1.2   Industrialization and Structural Change

The relationship between trade and structural change is brought to the fore by the dynamic performance of the transitional economies of Pacific Asia and their analogues in Mediterranean Europe and Latin America that have been identified as NICs. An index developed by the United Nations Industrial Development Organization (UNIDO) that measures the change in the value-added share of sixteen individual manufacturing sectors in total value added between 1965 and 1980 is a good measure of the rapidity of structural change in the manufacturing sector over the period in which there have been rapid exports of manufactures from the NICs and other transitional economies. This index is given in table 1.2 along with the average annual growth rate of manufacturing value added over 1965–80 for sixteen transitional economies in three major regions. (Again, no data are available for Taiwan.)

Overall, the figures in table 1.2 confirm the expected relationship between high rates of structural change within manufacturing and the dynamic performance in exports of manufactures and in aggregate

Table 1.2   Structural Change and Industrialization: 1965–80

Transitional Economies	Index of Structural Change in Manufacturing[a]	Average Growth Rate of Value Added in Manufacturing
European NICs		
Spain	24.73	6.78
Yugoslavia	12.01	6.94
Portugal	21.61	7.18
Greece	13.56	7.00
Asian NICs		
India	20.89	2.59
Korea	31.37	18.99
Taiwan	n.a.	n.a.
Hong Kong	9.87	6.05
Singapore	48.32	11.41
Next-tier NICs		
Philippines	10.95	5.45
Thailand	17.69	7.98
Malaysia	15.86	8.12
Colombia	10.90	6.36
Natural Resource NICs		
Brazil	30.03	9.50
Mexico	14.83	7.09
Argentina	15.90	3.12
Indonesia	19.52	10.20
Global Averages		
Developed countries	10.90	4.66
Developing countries	13.83	6.55
World	10.60	4.85

Source: United Nations Industrial Development Organization, *Industry and Development: Global Report 1985* (New York: United Nations, 1985), pp. 31–40 and country tables pp. 135ff.

[a]The index of structural change is derived from sixteen manufacturing branches. It is a measure of the degree of correlation between the value-added shares in 1965 and 1980. If the correlation is high, then there is little structural change and the index is low. But if the correlation is low, then there is a lot of structural change and the index is high. Both expanding and shrinking branches contribute to the index (UNIDO 1985, 39).

growth associated with the NICs. Of the total of thirty-two observations of the two variables in the table, only three are below the world averages and seven are substantially below the averages for developing countries, which are higher than the averages for developed countries. Of the sixteen economies, Korea, Singapore, and Brazil are in the top four according to measures of both structural change and value-added growth in manufacturing. One suspects that were there data for Taiwan, it would be in the high range of these measures as well. Hong Kong is the exception. Because of the dominance of textiles within the manufacturing sector and in the exports of manufactures of Hong Kong, dynamic growth in the 1965–80 period has been associated with this one subsector rather than with shifts in the sectoral composition of output and exports. Textiles was already a significant sector by 1965 in Hong Kong, so that the rate of structural change associated with its growth is relatively less compared with other transitional economies.

Indonesia is surprisingly high on both measures, the high rates of change deriving undoubtedly from low absolute levels of industrialization. The two measures for the next-tier NICs—the Philippines, Thailand, Malaysia, and Colombia—show relatively uniform rates among the four countries in the category, and averaged together they are almost exactly the average for the developing countries as a whole. Mexico and Argentina experienced rates of structural change above the average for developing countries, though half of that of Brazil. Mexico also had an above-average rate of growth in valued added in manufacturing, but Argentina's rate was below the world average. The European NICs experienced rates of growth in manufacturing value added slightly above the average for developing countries and well above that of the industrial countries. Rates of structural change in manufacturing vary among the European NICs, with Spain and Portugal having very high indexes and with Yugoslavia and Greece having indexes only slightly above the world average.

The association of unusually high rates of structural change in manufacturing with exceptionally high rates of growth in manufactured exports is a useful lens through which to view the country experience and trade patterns analyzed in this volume. Rapid industrialization, significant shifts in the sectoral composition of output and exports, and high rates of economic growth along with major surges in exports of manufactures constitute the dynamic development patterns now identified with the NICs. The policy experience of each country, the internal economic structure, and the trade relationships within Pacific Asia and between the region and the world economy provide material for further insight into the dynamics of rapid development and export growth.

1.3 Global and Regional Patterns of Trade

Patterns of trade have changed substantially between the OECD area (North America, Japan, Europe) and the developing world of Latin America, Africa, and Asia since the early 1960s. The United States and Japan have developed complementary trade with Latin America and Asia in manufactures, exchanging capital goods for final consumer goods. Europe's trade with Africa has remained more traditional, since the African developing countries below the Sahara are not yet exporters of manufactures.

Trade patterns *within* Pacific Asia have also changed substantially over the same period. We can distinguish three tiers of countries in the area, consisting of Japan, the Gang of Four, and the ASEAN Four.

Complex trade relations have developed among these three tiers, and currently tensions exist as the countries look toward the future. As the Gang of Four and the ASEAN Four move up the ladder of comparative advantage, to what extent will the markets of the Pacific Asian countries in the upper tiers open to the exports of the lower-tier countries, and to what extent will lower-tier countries have to supplant upper-tier countries in exporting to third markets, particularly the United States and Europe? These are important issues for economic relations within Pacific Asia.

In this section of the chapter we draw on the conference papers and comments to discuss the highlights of the changes in trade patterns between the OECD countries and Pacific Asia and within the latter, and we speculate on their implications for future developments. We begin by reviewing major findings on trade patterns between the OECD "Big Three"—the United States, Japan, and the European Community (EC)—and Pacific Asia. Here the overview papers by Branson, Waelbroeck, and Yamazawa (chaps. 2–4) are in surprising agreement. Then we discuss the *basis* for trade within Pacific Asia, drawing mainly on the papers by Bradford and Krause (chaps. 7–8). It is clear from all of these papers, as well as that of Kotlikoff and Leamer (chap. 9), that in a broad sense a factor-proportions model of comparative advantage is useful in understanding the patterns of trade of Pacific Asia. This impression is also generally confirmed by the country papers. Next we discuss briefly the potential problems of trade adjustment in the three tiers of Pacific Asia, as they move up the ladder of industrial and technological development. In a sense, the lower-tier economies are crowding up against the higher-tier ones; how are they each going to adjust? Finally, we will offer some observations on a point that comes up in several of the country papers and was a subject of considerable comment: the "problem" posed by natural resource endowments as the ASEAN Four industrialize. This discussion is reminiscent of the "Dutch disease" literature in northern Europe.

1.3.1   Trade between the OECD and Pacific Asia

The growth of manufacturing capacity in the developing countries, especially in Asia and Latin America since the 1960s, is changing the nature of north-south trade. As Riedel (1984) shows, only the sub-Saharan African countries now remain one-or-two-primary-commodity exporters. For many developing countries, the growth of manufactured exports has reduced the share of primary exports to well below 50% of total exports.

Growth in manufactured exports in the Latin American and Asian developing countries has been concentrated in labor-intensive goods, mainly consumer goods and assembly products. Textiles and simple electronics are good examples. To expand their manufacturing capacity, these economies must import capital equipment from the industrial countries. This has created an exchange of labor-intensive, somewhat lower-technology consumer goods for more capital-intensive (both physical and human) and technology-intensive goods. This exchange contributes at the margin to an increase in specialization within and complementarity between the economies involved.

The overview papers by Branson, Waelbroeck, and Yamazawa are in general agreement on the relevance of this analysis for trade between the countries of the OECD and Pacific Asia. At the broadest level, Branson's comparison of the patterns of trade in manufactures of the United States, Japan, and the EC finds a substantial expansion of this form of complementary trade between the United States and Latin America and between Japan and the rest of Pacific Asia. This proximity phenomenon is also noted by Waelbroeck: Europe's trade with the south is concentrated in Africa, the United States with Latin America, and Japan with Asia. The United States and Japan each compete in the other's "natural" market and have the second shares in these markets, with Europe third in both. Yamazawa's paper, concentrating on Japan and her Pacific neighbors, also notes the importance of complementary trade in manufactures. Thus, all three papers see the same general development in trade patterns.

This broad picture is complicated to some extent by the split in the direction of U.S. exports and imports of manufactures. The major source in the developing world of U.S. consumer goods imports is Pacific Asia, while the major destination of U.S. exports is Latin America. The latter remains relatively resource-rich, like the ASEAN Four, with their exports depending largely on world market conditions. While U.S. manufactured exports are more closely tied to economic developments in Latin America, U.S. imports of manufactures are linked to Pacific Asia.

The implications of these developing patterns of trade and interdependence between the United States, Japan, and Europe on the one hand and the major developing-country regions on the other can be the object of interesting speculation. It may be that Japan's trade is becoming relatively more complementary and integrated with the more "proximate" economies of Asia, while Europe's trade is more closely tied to Africa. This pattern is suggested by a joint reading of the three overview papers. The United States may be in an intermediate position. Its exports are more concentrated on Latin America, which has experienced midrange growth (between Africa and Asia). At the same time, the United States is increasingly integrated with Pacific Asia on the import side. This suggests that a broader Pacific concept (including Latin America) is now an important focal point for U.S. foreign economic policy.

1.3.2   Factor Proportions and Trade

The rise of new industrial powers in the world economy has been based on rapid structural transformation within these industrializing countries. This internal process of structural change has been characterized not only by the broad shift from primary production (mining and agriculture) to industry but also by sectoral shifts within manufacturing, as we have seen in the measure of structural change in table 1.2. The general pattern of development is for a gradual sectoral evolution to occur as the availability and the quality of factors of production evolve.

The industrialization process begins with natural resource based manufacturing. As the urban labor force increases, labor-intensive manufacturing grows more rapidly and eventually predominates. Per capita income growth based on the more dynamic industrial sector generates increased savings in the economy. This capital accumulation enables the economy to move into industrial sectors requiring more capital-intensive modes of production. Sophistication grows with industrial experience, and educational levels rise with economic growth. As a consequence, the economy eventually moves into skill- and technology-intensive industrial sectors.

These sectoral shifts within industry essentially respond to changing availabilities of inputs into the manufacturing process. Comparative advantage in trade is determined by the relative abundance of these factor inputs. Therefore, changes in the relative availability of labor, capital, skills, and technological innovation change not only the structure of industry but the composition of trade as well.

Countries at given moments in time can be thought of as being on a ladder of comparative advantage, tiered according to their standing in factor endowments. Data in the papers by Bradford and Krause confirm that the composition of exports from Pacific Asia reflects different factor intensities among countries and over time. Moving up the ladder of comparative advantage, natural-resource-intensive exports diminish continuously as a percentage of total exports, labor-intensive exports surge and fade, and physical and human capital-intensive exports increase their share.

The very substantial preponderance of labor-intensive exports from the Asian NICs is clearly manifested in the data in Bradford's paper as is the increase in physical and human capital exports. The nascent rise of labor-intensive exports from the next-tier NICs in the 1970s is also apparent. Accelerated structural change of exports is evident in the European NICs; structural change is more restrained in the Latin American NICs and Indonesia, where natural resource exports generate the foreign exchange required for growth.

The NICs, by definition, are on a divergent development path, outpacing other economies at similar stages of development. Their dynamism appears to have gone beyond that which follows naturally from changing factor endowments, though favorable factor conditions were important. Public policies and government promotion of export-oriented growth strategies also played a major role in the unusual success of the NICs. By the very nature of this process, the NICs posed adjustment challenges for the Pacific Basin, for the OECD economies, and for the entire world economy. This dynamic change in the composition of exports from Pacific Asia does not appear to have been accompanied thus far by changes in the composition of imports that would allow the absorption of export surges within the region. This pattern poses trade policy challenges for the future as factor endowments and export promotion policies play a continuing role in changing the composition of exports from dynamic economies that seek expanding markets for their exports.

1.3.3   Trade Adjustment among the Three Tiers of Pacific Asia

As the economies of Pacific Asia develop and grow, two alternative models of evolution of their trade patterns are likely to be relevant. The actual outcome will be some mixture of the two, but the distinction is useful analytically. In the first model, exports from the lower-tier countries displace those of upper-tier countries in world markets, particularly North America and Europe, as the upper-tier countries move on to higher levels of sophistication and technology. In this model, as Japan's export mix shifts toward high-technology items, such as computers and sophisticated machinery and electronics, the Gang of Four countries expand, for example, their exports of consumer manufactures, such as television receivers, to North America and Europe. As the Gang of Four moves gradually out of supplying textiles to these third markets, the ASEAN Four move in. A similar process could take place in electronics assembly. In this model, higher-tier economies in Pacific Asia do not open their own markets significantly to imports from lower-tier countries; instead they compete in external markets. In the conference, representatives of the lower-tier countries voiced opinions that seemed to reflect their view that this is the model favored by the upper-tier countries, particularly Japan and Korea. We might call this the "world integration" model.

The alternative has already been suggested. As the upper-tier countries grow and their industrial structures become more sophisticated, they open to imports from the lower-tier countries. The latter would find the direction of their manufactured exports more oriented toward the other Pacific Asian countries than to Europe or North America in this model, which we might call "regional integration." In the conference, lower-tier representatives seemed to prefer the regional integration model to world integration.

Which of these patterns seems more likely to develop? Manufactured imports were about $150 billion in Europe and in the United States in the early 1980s and $40 billion in Japan. Exports from the Asian NICs and the ASEAN Four were a relatively small share of the European market; in his paper Jean Waelbroeck argues that the Gang of Four and ASEAN Four shares of the European market can be expanded without meeting active resistance. The U.S. market remains relatively open with the exception of textiles, in which trade is governed by the international Multi-Fiber Arrangement. In textiles, the Pacific Asian countries face potentially serious competition from China. Nevertheless, the world integration model seems feasible in terms of potential expansion both of shares of North American and European manufactured imports and of their aggregate levels.

Japan's trade pattern is substantially different from that of the United States or Europe. Because of her need to import raw materials, Japan must run a sizable surplus on trade in manufactures just to maintain overall balance. Imports from the rest of Pacific Asia already occupy a substantial share of Japan's low level of manufactured imports, as shown in the papers by Branson and Yamazawa. This means that a significant further opening of Japan's market to exports of manufactures from Pacific Asia might require an expansion of her exports of manufactures to those countries. As Yamazawa shows, Japan already has established a complementary trade with the Gang of Four and the ASEAN Four, exporting capital goods while importing raw materials from the ASEAN Four and consumer goods from the Gang of Four. This is a pattern similar to trade between the United States and less-developed countries (LDCs) on a broader scale, with U.S. raw material imports coming largely from Latin America and consumer goods imports from Asia.

Thus expansion of trade along the regional integration model would probably involve growth in cross-trade in manufactures, with countries specializing further along lines of comparative advantage, as outlined in the paper by Krause. Cross-trade in manufactures would require a mutual openness of markets, rather than a unilateral opening by the upper-tier countries in Pacific Asia.

The implications of each outcome—world integration or regional integration—are still shadowy but are potentially important. The world integration model would bring the Pacific Asian countries, and perhaps China and South Asia as well, into a pattern of world complementarities, with a relatively high level of interdependence with the United States and possibly Latin America. The regional integration model would emphasize the interdependence *among* the Pacific Asian countries, with looser economic ties to the United States. The latter model could be an important element in the development of a regional power to rival the United States, Europe, and even the USSR, while the world integration model could tie the Pacific Asia economies individually more closely to the United States.

1.3.4 Natural Resources and Industrialization

The principal differences between the already-industrialized Asian NICs and the ASEAN Four are size and natural resource endowments. The Asian NICs industrialized on a base of skilled labor, a homogeneous population, good location, and perhaps a self-selected entrepreneurial class that was separated from China after the revolution. While to differing degrees the ASEAN Four also have a Chinese entrepreneurial class, they are much larger, more heterogeneous, and, most importantly, well-endowed with natural resources. Natural resources present a problem for development that is essentially the same as the now famous Dutch disease problem of deindustrialization in northern Europe.

In its simplest variant, the analysis runs as follows. The natural resource development boom pulls labor into that sector from agriculture and manufacturing, raising real wages throughout the economy. At the same time, export strength in the natural resource sector tends to appreciate the currency in real terms. Both the rise in the real wage and the currency appreciation squeeze profits in the incipient manufacturing sector, blocking its development. Thus, it is clear in an intuitive way that discovery and subsequent development of natural resources could dampen industrialization that would provide a more secure, longer-run basis for growth.

Considerations from models of trade theory add refinement to the standard Dutch disease analysis, as Ronald Findlay noted in a perceptive comment at the conference. The real wage will rise in the shrinking (or relatively slowly growing) manufacturing sector only if the natural resource boom pulls resources away from it in a way that increases labor-intensity in the manufacturing sector. In a simple two-factor Heckscher-Ohlin-Samuelson trade model, this would require that the shrinking manufacturing sector be capital-intensive relative to the expanding natural resource sector. In this standard case the capital-labor ratio would tend to fall in both sectors.

A more appropriate model, outlined by Findlay, would have three sectors—agricultural, manufacturing, resource extraction—each with a specific factor—land, capital, and resources—but all using labor. Then expansion of the resource sector, by pulling labor from agriculture and manufacturing, would raise both the land-labor and capital-labor ratios. This would raise the real wage in terms of both food and manufactures, yielding a strong Dutch disease result. This would be the model most applicable in the case of the ASEAN Four. It may also help to explain why the Latin American NICs have not achieved the same degree of specialization in manufactured exports as the East Asian NICs.

If this is the appropriate model, what policy can be followed to permit continued industrialization? Essentially, the problem is to shield the incipient manufacturing sector from the effects of the natural resource boom. Since the resource boom has both internal (rising real wages) and external (real exchange rate appreciation) effects, two measures might be useful. Taxation of wages in the resource sector could reduce the pressure on real wages in the manufacturing sector. Profits taxation or directed use of the budgetary surplus in a nationalized resource sector to invest abroad or to import capital goods could eliminate the effect on the exchange rate. Both policy measures are essentially ways to ensure that the proceeds of the resource boom are invested in growth in manufacturing by offsetting the real wage and exchange rate effects of a natural resource export boom.

1.4   Government Policy and Market Forces

The dynamic growth and export performance of the Pacific Asian developing countries raise the question of how these success stories were achieved. The relationship of cause and effect is an elusive one in economics generally and particularly so in analyzing aggregate performance. In a not dissimilar volume Arnold C. Harberger notes "the virtual impossibility of building a direct link of modern theory between the observed growth rate of a country and its overall economic policy" (1984, 6). The eight country studies in the present volume provide a sense of the variety of policy experience in Pacific Asia. As in the Harberger volume, which contains case studies of five developed and seven developing countries, the reader of the chapters in this book undoubtedly will conclude that "there is no magic formula" (Harberger 1984, 427).[2]

Nevertheless, economics would be a dull and probably less insightful enterprise without controversy. The East Asian NICs, in particular, have inspired a set of debates regarding the causes of their economic achievements. These debates concern the relative contribution of market forces and economic policies, of outward versus inward orientation, and of internal liberalization and export promotion; the effectiveness of fiscal versus credit subsidies; and whether exports are demand driven or supply determined.

The relative roles of markets and governments in dynamic growth is an old issue in economics. There has been a lively debate for decades in Latin America on what Albert O. Hirschman called in a widely read essay in 1961 "ideologies of economic development" (1961). More recently the issue has surfaced as a debate about getting prices right versus getting policies right. This version of the controversy was sparked by empirical research on price distortions undertaken by the World Bank which found that higher economic growth was associated with lower price distortions in thirty-one developing countries and that high price distortion was associated with low growth (World Bank 1983; Agarwala 1983). Later World Bank analyses showed that "big price distortions also lead to slower growth of exports and a greater likelihood of debt-servicing difficulties" (World Bank 1985, 54). Although Taiwan, Singapore, and Hong Kong were not included in the thirty-one countries analyzed by the World Bank, there has been a tendency to identify the Pacific Asian developing countries as market-oriented economies with low levels of price distortion. Indeed, Thailand, Korea, Malaysia, and the Philippines are among the six countries with the lowest price distortions as measured by the World Bank's composite index (World Bank 1983, table 6.1). As a result, the Pacific Asian experience has been at the center of the current controversy surrounding the efficacy of markets and governmental policies in promoting development.[3]

1.4.1   Inward versus Outward Orientation

The highly dynamic export performance of the Pacific Asian developing economies has given rise to a discussion about the virtues of inward- versus outward-oriented growth strategies (Streeten 1982; Balassa 1983). The East Asian and Latin American NICs have frequently been cited as contrasting examples of export orientation and import substitution respectively (Morgan Guaranty 1983). Part of the controversy undoubtedly derives from the use of loosely fashioned phrases which sound like dichotomous typologies when in fact more rigorous specification of meaning would reveal that they define different points along a spectrum of policy regimes rather than stark alternatives. What follows is an attempt to attach differentiated meaning to commonly used labels that are often used as substitutes for one another. The results are summarized in table 1.3 and reveal a continuum from autarky to export promotion that we hope captures a variety of configurations of elements defining development strategies. No attempt is made here to identify particular countries with specific development thrusts, but it is hoped that by differentiating the categories and conceptualizing them as elements of a spectrum, the varieties of policy experience analyzed in the case studies in this volume may be thought about more clearly than by applying the dichotomous framework conventionally used.

Inward versus outward orientation are helpful as the most general categories under which a variety of development strategies can be

Table 1.3   **Development Strategy Typologies: A Continuum**

Autarky	No trade "Delinking" Self-reliance	Dirigisme
Closed economy	Exports and imports less than 5% as a share of GDP	
Import Substitution	(a) Discriminates against all imports through controls: EERm $>$ EERx (b) Selective discrimination (c) Mild and limited applications ("left wing deviations")	
Inward orientation	Priority given to the domestic economy	Markets
Outward Orientation	Priority given to exports	Markets
Trade economy	Exports 15% or more as a share of GDP	
Open economy	Internal liberalization EERx = EERm (a) tradable goods (b) (a) + nontradable goods (c) (a) + (b) + macroeconomic variables	
Export promotion	(a) Uniform subsidies for all exports: EERx $>$ EERm (b) Selective subsidies: Industrial policy Import substitution ("right wing deviations")	Dirigisme

Note: EERx and EERm are the real effective exchange rates for exports and imports, respectively.

classified. They imply simply a difference in emphasis—as between the domestic market (not imports) and trade, and in particular exports, as the main sources of economic growth. They appear, then, at the midpoint of the spectrum between autarky and export promotion rather than necessarily being identified with the extremes in the type of development strategy.

Autarky means no trade and would derive from a severe government decision to "delink" from the world economy in order to achieve some measure of self-reliance or the appearance thereof (Diaz-Alejandro 1978). The terms *closed* and *open* are often used to describe the bias of policies toward import substitution or export promotion. In this rendering, it is helpful to have designations which empirically identify the importance of trade in the conomy. A closed economy is defined here as one in which trade (exports plus imports) as a share of GDP is low, that is, less than 5%. It may be that this ratio is low because of deliberate policies, but it may also be due to size, the abundance of natural resources, the similarity of country endowments to world endowments, or other factors. A closed economy is not autarkic but neither is it one in which trade is a major factor in the economy. By definition, closed economies are not of much interest in this volume. A "trade economy" is its opposite. It is a category in which exports are a large share of GDP, say above 15%. The phrases *export-led* or *open economy* are more frequently used. However, *export-led* implies some empirical substantiation of a cause-effect relationship *from* exports *to* economic growth, when in fact high GDP growth may drive exports by generating a supply surplus. The term *open economy* associates internal liberalization (the removal of import controls, tariffs, etc.) with trade as a large share of GDP. Abstracting for the moment the direction of the causality or the degree of this association, the phrase *trade economy* attempts to convey the importance of exports in an economy that is necessarily embodied in a high-export share of GDP. The term *trade economy* is meant to be policy neutral. The question of whether exports are driven by external demand and thereby induce internal growth or are supply determined is discussed briefly at the end of this chapter. Both the terms *closed economy* and *trade economy* identify endogenous economic outcomes rather than policy inputs.

An "import substitution" strategy is a set of deliberate policies that discriminates against those imports which compete with existing or nascent domestic sources of production. Import substitution does not necessarily imply a low volume of imports, as capital goods imports may be essential to establish the industries necessary to achieve self-sufficiency in the designated range of activities. Normally, import substitution strategies discriminate against imports through the use of import controls, tariffs, multiple exchange rate systems, or other policy devices (Findlay 1981, 30–33; Krause 1981, 597–611). But the scope and degree of the bias against imports may vary considerably. In the extreme case, it is the dominant policy, and hence, the development strategy is fundamentally determined by it. In a more limited case, policies may be applied only to selected sectors, with the bulk of the economy otherwise being relatively "open" in the sense that most activity is market determined. It is also possible that selective import substitution policies may be part of an industrial policy which in turn is part of an export promotion strategy.

The other large category of strategies is outward orientation, which means that priority is given to exports either in the economy or in the policy of the country. In its mildest manifestation, exports may be responsive to external demand and grow rapidly as a result of the intrinsic competitiveness of the economy or, at a minimum, of the tradable goods sectors. On the other hand, there may be a deliberate policy to liberalize the economy, ranging from a limited case of liberalization only in tradable goods sectors to a more inclusive case of liberalization across the economy as a whole, even incorporating macroeconomic variables such as interest rates. Internal liberalization is labeled here as an "open economy" strategy. In most of the literature, open economy is synonymous with outward orientation, and the two terms are used interchangeably as if they have identical and equally specific meanings.

In the formulation here, open economy is delineated as only one type of outward-oriented strategy, that associated with internal liberalization. The open economy–internal liberalization strategy implies that the incentives to export are equivalent to the incentives to import, or as Anne Krueger puts it, "there is as much incentive to earn as to save foreign exchange" (1985, 20). This in effect means, as Jagdish Bhagwati (1986a) has emphasized, that the effective exchange rate for exports "is not significantly different" from the effective exchange rate for imports. Curiously, Bhagwati labels this an export promotion strategy (EP), which has a potentially quite different meaning from the characterization of the term to be set forth here. In Bhagwati's formulation the absence of discrimination against exports is the major achievement and is seen to provide sufficient incentives for export "promotion." A policy of equivalent incentives for imports and exports would be a free trade optimality point in Ronald Findlay's (1981) ingenious formulation on the subject.

Finally, the most dirigisme form of outward orientation is designated here as export promotion. In this strategy category, the state plays a major role in goal setting and policy implementation to achieve the goals. Variation can exist under an export promotion strategy. A mild form, for example, would be illustrated by uniform export subsidies across the range of exports rather than favoring some export sectors over others (Krueger 1981, 18). A more interventionist form of export promotion would be linked to an industrial policy which sets sectoral priorities for investment, credit, foreign exchange, imports, and/or subsidy allocations to make the structure of production conform to the export strategy. It is in this more interventionist type of export strategy that the relative effectiveness of fiscal versus credit subsidies, discussed below, is of greatest interest. Import substitution policies could run simultaneously with and support this style of development strategy. Under this strategy category, it is highly possible that the effective exchange rate provides more incentives for exports than for imports, in effect subsidizing exports and shielding import-competing industries. As a result, exports are promoted beyond the range of optimality leading to what Findlay calls "right wing deviations" and Bhagwati now designates "ultra-EP strategy" (1986b).

These typologies of development strategies, while roughly hewn, at least differentiate among categories in the economic literature that are frequently lumped together. The often portrayed dichotomy between inward- versus outward-oriented growth strategies, in this framework, becomes more a gradual gradation of approaches to development composed of different clusters of elements. The eight transitional countries of Pacific Asia undoubtedly fall at different places on the continuum, as do their counterparts in Mediterranean Europe and Latin America. There is no reason to expect regional homogeneity. It may be hoped that the country experiences traced in this volume, as Alexander Gerschenkron's "journey" through the story of European industrialization in the nineteenth century, may, "by destroying what Bertrand Russell once called the 'dogmatism of the untravelled,' help in formulating a broader more enlightened view of the pertinent problems and in replacing the absolute notions of what is 'right' and what is 'wrong' by a more flexible and relativistic approach" (1982, 26–27).

1.4.2   Fiscal versus Credit Subsidies

The Asian NICs provide instructive contrasts between alternative policy measures to stimulate export-oriented industrialization. Two extremes are Korea, which essentially used a system of credit subsidies and financial repression, and Taiwan, which used fiscal subsidies with relatively free credit markets. The two cases are described in the papers by Wontack Hong and Chi Schive (chaps. 10–11).

The credit subsidy approach begins with the identification of favored export-oriented sectors to receive low-interest loans. Since these are provided below market rates, a queue forms and credit must be rationed. Unsuccessful applicants must turn to the curb market, where credit is available at a much higher interest rate. In general, the weighted average of the subsidized rate and the curb rate is an approximation of the shadow rate that would clear a free market.

With capital costs subsidized in the favored sector and effectively taxed in the curb market, the favored sector tends to become too capital-intensive, or "large-scale." The nonfavored sector becomes too labor-intensive, or "small-scale." This implies that when the system is ended and both interest rates move toward the shadow rate, the formerly favored sector will suffer capital losses and some bankruptcies, while the nonfavored sector will shed labor. Thus, ending a credit subsidy regime may entail a period of bankruptcies and unemployment. Hong suggests that this was the case in Korea.

In addition, the requirement that the banking sector provide loans at below-market rates, as well as a possible requirement to buy government debt at low rates, means that deposit rates must be suppressed if the banking system is to remain profitable. This will tend to discourage saving in the financial sector, shrinking the resource base for investment in industrialization. Thus, the credit subsidy route can reduce saving and misallocate it, creating a deepening distortion that can be expensive to eliminate. Again, Korea may be an example of the problem.

A fiscal subsidy on output or exports of the chosen industry can avoid these "side effects" without additional cost to the taxpayers. In the credit subsidy system, the cost is hidden in low deposit rates, while with fiscal subsidies it is explicit in the tax structure. To achieve equivalent incentives to invest in the chosen industries, the cost of fiscal subsidies should be less. They avoid the bias between factor inputs and the need for suppression of deposit interest rates. Further, the fiscal subsidies can be phased out without the twin difficulties of bankruptcy and unemployment threatening to reach unstable levels. Chi Schive's paper on Taiwan illustrates the case. Thus, Pacific Asia provides experiences with alternative forms of government intervention that can be instructive throughout the developing world.

1.4.3 Demand- versus Supply-Driven Export Growth

The trade and development literature contains discussions regarding the degree to which trade-related dynamic growth is externally driven or internally generated. James Riedel goes to quite some length to question the notion of trade as the "engine of growth" of developing countries, especially as this notion is put forward by Sir Arthur Lewis in his 1979 Nobel lecture. Nevertheless, Riedel concludes, after considerable statistical analysis, that "the evidence, therefore, suggests that supply rather than demand factors have principally determined LDC export performance in manufactures" (1984, 69). Curiously, this is not too distant from Lewis's own assertion in the Nobel lecture that "if a sufficient number of LDCs reach self-sustaining growth, we are into a new world. For this will mean that instead of trade determining the rate of growth of LDC production, it will be the growth of LDC production that determines LDC trade, and internal forces that will determine the rate of growth of production" (Lewis 1980, 562).

The focus in this volume on structural change and trade and the association of rapid structural change in industry with dynamic exports of manufactures highlights the issue of supply- versus demand-driven growth. The issue cannot be resolved here. However, evidence in the case studies in this book on the development strategies of Korea, Singapore, and Taiwan seems to fit, with some variation among them, within the "export promotion" category above (Bradford 1986). This evidence, along with the association of unusually rapid rates of structural change with transitional economies, leads toward the conclusion that supply push may have been more important than demand pull in driving the transition process. Rapid structural change in manufacturing and in exports seems to have been induced by a strategic sectoral design that was an integral part of export promotion and seems to have gone beyond the scale feasible based on responsiveness to international demand under conditions of favorable factor endowments. High export growth associated with unusually rapid rates of structural change in manufacturing and exports suggests that public policy played a role in continuously shifting the specialization of production toward exports. The identification of supply push and export promotion strategies as key elements that determine dynamic transitional growth is offered here as a central idea with which to approach the studies in this book.

Notes

1. See Hartigan 1975 for an introduction to cluster analysis. A special application is factor analysis. Algorithms exist, so our suggestion here would appear to be feasible.

2. The Harberger (1984) volume contains studies of the growth experience of twelve countries and explores "the connections between economic policy and economic growth" of Britain, Japan, Sweden, Germany, and the United States, and Tanzania, Ghana, Indonesia, Jamaica, Taiwan, Mexico, and Uruguay.

3. For critical views see Bradford 1984, 121–26, and chap. 7 in this volume; Fishlow 1985; and Evans and Alizadeh 1984, 22–43, 43–46.

References

Agarwala, Ramgopal. 1983. Price distortions and growth in developing countries. World Bank Staff Working Paper, no. 575.

Balassa, Bela. 1983. Outward versus inward orientation once again. *World Economy* 6, no. 2.

Bhagwati, Jagdish. 1986a. Rethinking trade strategy. In *Development strategies reconsidered,* ed. John P. Lewis. Overseas Development Council, U.S. Third World Policy Perspectives, no. 5. New Brunswick: Transaction Books.

———. 1986b. Export promoting trade strategy: Issues and evidence. World Bank Development Policy Issues Series, report VPERS 7.

Bradford, Colin I., Jr. 1984. The NICs: Confronting U.S. "autonomy." In *Adjustment crisis in the Third World,* ed. Richard E. Feinberg and Valeriana Kallab. Overseas Development Council, U.S. Third World Policy Perspectives, no. 1. New Brunswick: Transaction Books.

———. 1986. East Asian development strategies as models for development. In *Development strategies reconsidered,* ed. John P. Lewis. Overseas Development Council, U.S. Third World Policy Perspectives, no. 5. New Brunswick: Transaction Books.

Diaz-Alejandro, Carlos. 1978. Delinking north and south: Unshackled or unhinged? In *Rich and poor nations in the world economy,* Albert Fishlow et al. New York: McGraw-Hill.

Evans, David, and Parvin Alizadeh. 1984. Trade, industrialisation and the invisible hand. *Journal of Development Studies* 21, no. 1.

Findlay, Ronald. 1981. Comment. In *Trade and growth of the advanced developing countries in the Pacific Basin,* ed. Wontack Hong and Lawrence B. Krause. Seoul, Korea: Korean Development Institute Press.

Fishlow, Albert. 1985. The state of Latin American economics. *Economic and social progress in Latin America (External debt: Crisis and adjustment).* Washington, D.C.: Inter-American Development Bank.

Gerschenkron, Alexander. 1982. *Economic backwardness in historical perspective.* Cambridge: Harvard University Press.

Harberger, Arnold C. 1984. *World economic growth.* San Francisco: Institute for Contemporary Studies.

Hartigan, John A. 1975. *Clustering algorithms.* New York: Wiley.

Hirschman, Albert O. 1961. *Latin American issues: Essays and comments.* New York: Twentieth Century Fund.

International Monetary Fund. 1985. *World economic outlook.* Washington, D.C.

Krause, Lawrence B. 1981. Summary. In *Trade and growth of the advanced developing countries in the Pacific Basin,* ed. Wontack Hong and Lawrence B. Krause. Seoul, Korea: Korean Development Institute Press.

Krueger, Anne O. 1981. Export-led industrial growth reconsidered. In *Trade and growth of the advanced developing countries in the Pacific Basin,* ed. Wontack Hong and Lawrence B. Krause. Seoul, Korea: Korean Development Institute Press.

———. 1985. Import substitution versus export promotion. *Development and Finance* 22, no. 2.

Kuznets, Simon. 1966. *Modern economic growth: Rate, structure and growth.* New Haven and London: Yale University Press.

Lewis, W. Arthur. 1980. The slowing down of the engine of growth. *American Economic Review* 70, no. 4.

Morgan Guaranty Trust Company of New York. 1983. *World Financial Markets,* September. New York.

OECD. 1979. *The impact of the newly industrialising countries on production and trade in manufactures.* Paris: Organization for Economic Cooperation and Development.

———. 1982. *1982 review: Development co-operation.* Paris: Organization for Economic Cooperation and Development.

Reynolds, Lloyd G. 1983. The spread of economic growth to the Third World. *Journal of Economic Literature* 21, no. 3.

Riedel, James. 1984. Trade as the engine of growth in developing countries, revisited. *Economic Journal* 94, no. 373, 56–73.

Rostow, Walt Whitman. 1978. *The world economy: History and prospect.* Austin and London: University of Texas Press.

Streeten, Paul. 1982. A cool look at "outward-looking" strategies for development. *World Economy* 5, no. 2.

Turner, Louis, and Neil McMullen, eds. 1982. *The newly industrializing countries: Trade and adjustment.* London: George Allen and Unwin.

World Bank. 1983. *World development report, 1983.* London: Oxford University Press.

———. 1985. *World development report, 1985.* London: Oxford University Press.

II   Pacific Asia in Global Trade Patterns

2   # Trade and Structural Interdependence between the United States and the Newly Industrializing Countries

William H. Branson

2.1 Introduction and Summary

During the decade since 1973, the U.S. economy has become increasingly interdependent with the developing countries, and especially the newly industrializing countries (NICs) among them. (See table 2.2 for a list of identified NICs.) These countries have had high investment-to-GNP ratios, financed mainly by domestic saving but also partly by foreign borrowing. They have invested in manufacturing capacity, importing capital equipment. This increase in international demand for equipment has resulted in an increase of U.S. capital goods exports to over 50% of all U.S. manufactures; the twelve NICs enumerated in the tables in section 2 of this paper absorbed 22% of all U.S. capital goods exports in 1981.

In turn, exports of consumer manufactures by the NICs to the Organization for Economic Cooperation and Development (OECD) countries have expanded rapidly. The twelve NICs provided half of U.S. imports of consumer manufactures (non-food, non-auto) in 1981 and 40% of European imports. As the NICs grew during the 1970s, they imported capital goods from the United States and exported consumer manufactures to the United States.

This pattern of trade has strengthened the interdependence between the U.S. economy and the NICs. In section 2.3 below we show that U.S. exports of manufactures are less balanced across commodities than European or Japanese exports, with high shares in the United States for capital goods and chemicals. The NICs are a major market area for these U.S. exports.

William H. Branson is professor of economics and international affairs at the Woodrow Wilson School, Princeton University, and a research associate of the National Bureau of Economic Research.

The geographical pattern of U.S. trade with the NICs also shows some interesting asymmetries. In overall trade in manufactures, the United States has a large surplus ($12.2 billion in 1980) in trade with the Latin American NICs (Argentina, Brazil, Colombia, Mexico), a small surplus ($2.5 billion) with the ASEAN (Association of South East Asian Nations) countries, and a large deficit ($11.3 billion) with the Far Eastern NICs (Hong Kong, South Korea, Taiwan). Thus the United States exports capital goods to the NICs and imports consumer goods from them, following broad lines of comparative advantage. But the exports are relatively focused on Latin America, mainly Mexico, and imports on the Far Eastern NICs. In the data of sections 2.3–2.5 a trade triangle appears, with the United States exporting manufactures, mainly capital goods, to the Latin American NICs; who in turn sell raw materials on the world market. The Far Eastern NICs buy raw materials and sell manufactures, mainly consumer goods, to the United States.

The data presented in the next sections support this view of interdependence between the U.S. economy and the NICs, which differs from the relations of Europe or Japan with those countries. In section 2.2 we begin by describing investment- and manufacturing-led growth in the NICs since 1970 or so. This is part of a broader pattern of growth in manufacturing in the developing countries that has left only the African primary producers dependent on a single primary export. Growth of manufacturing capacity, particularly in the NICs, has provided a market for exports of capital equipment.

In sections 2.3 and 2.4 we compare the evolution of the geographical and commodity composition of manufactures exports and imports of the United States, Europe, and Japan. The NICs take a high proportion of U.S. and Japanese exports relative to European exports, with the United States relatively concentrated on capital goods and Latin America. The United States is the biggest market for NIC exports of manufactures, particularly consumer goods.

The pattern of U.S. trade with the industrial NICs, disaggregated by commodity, is examined in the last section. There we see the geographical imbalances mentioned above, which make growth in the U.S. economy interdependent with growth both in Latin America and in the Asian NICs.

2.2   The Rise of the NICs

2.2.1   Introduction

During the 1970s the relative size of the manufacturing sector expanded in a broad range of developing countries. In a subset of these countries in Latin America and Asia, this growth made them significant producers of manufactures on a world scale by the end of the decade. This group has been labeled the newly industrializing countries, or NICs. In this section we analyze some aspects of the rise of the NICs that are important for the later discussion of their trade interactions with the OECD countries.

Growth in manufacturing capacity and trade in the developing countries, which will be documented below, seems to have reduced their tight dependence on OECD growth. While there is still a strong correlation between growth rates of industrial countries and the average across all developing countries, the correlation is less tight when we look at groups of developing countries.

Growth rate data since 1973 are summarized in table 2.1 for areas of interest for the analysis below. The data for the industrial countries show the deepening stagnation in the OECD area, especially in Europe. For example, the West German economic institutes are forecasting a significant recovery in 1984, with real GDP growing at 2%–3% and *unemployment rising only slowly.* In Europe, recovery has been redefined to mean only a small increase in unemployment! The average growth pattern over all developing countries is roughly similar to that of the industrial countries, but there are important differences in timing. While the OECD countries, led by the United States, went deep into recession in 1982, growth was about the same as in 1981 in the developing countries.

The subgroups of developing countries in table 2.1 show a wide diversity of growth patterns relative to the industrial countries. The low-income and the Western Hemisphere countries show a rise in the

Table 2.1   **Growth Rates of Real GDP of Selected Groups of Countries**

| | Average Annual Percentage Growth | | | |
	1973–79	1980	1981	1982
Industrial countries[a]	2.8	1.3	1.0	−0.2
Developing countries	5.1	6.1	2.0	1.9
Low-income	5.1	6.1	3.7	3.7
Middle-income oil importers	5.5	4.2	1.1	1.1
East Asia and Pacific	8.5	3.6	6.9	4.2
Middle East and North Africa	2.9	4.7	0.1	2.7
Western Hemisphere	4.9	5.7	−2.4	−1.2
Major exporters of manufactures[b]	6.4	4.5	−0.2	0.2

Sources: World Bank 1983, table 2.1; IMF, *Annual Report, 1983,* table 2.

[a]All data are averages weighted by real GDP.

[b]International Monetary Fund (IMF) classification of major exporters of manufactures.

growth rate in 1980, and the East Asian and Pacific countries show a sharp rise in 1981. Middle East and North Africa and the major exporters of manufactures (the NICs) show an increase in the growth rate in 1982, when the OECD slump deepened. Thus the pattern of growth among the subgroups of table 2.1 does not mirror the movement in the industrial countries.

In the rest of this section of the paper, we will look in more detail at the structure of growth in the NICs, the development of the manufacturing sector in the NICs and in a broader sample of developing countries, and the financing of this growth. The facts to be presented are all well known by now; the point here is to present them in a way that will make clear the connection between these developments and the evolution of the structure of trade between the NICs and the OECD countries, especially the United States.

2.2.2   Growth in the NICs, 1970–81

There are about as many lists of which countries are NICs as there are authors on the topic of their emergence and growth. So we have an initial problem of identification of countries. There is also in the background of this literature a deeper question of whether the identification has not been done purely on an ex post basis by looking at a narrow set of indicators related to growth in manufacturing capacity. It is quite possible that the category "NICs" does not exist as measured by other characteristics of the economy. For example, on the "distortion index" of the World Bank, of the NICs listed in table 2.2, Thailand, Korea, Malaysia, the Philippines, and Colombia are in the low-distortion category; Indonesia, India, Brazil, and Mexico are middle-distortion countries; Argentina is the only high-distortion country (World Bank 1983, 60). Does this grouping imply that we can categorize NICs as relatively low distortion countries? The answer is not clear. An urgent topic for research in this area is an analysis using a clustering algorithm grouping countries by a wide range of economic indicators, such as the entire set of World Bank indicators, to see if a category "NICs" emerges statistically.

In the face of these reservations, we must proceed, so I have decided to adopt the list of NICs provided by Colin Bradford (1982), which includes countries which are on most lists. Bradford further introduces the subsets of existing NICs and potential NICs (or, as they are labeled in table 2.2, new NICs). The categories in table 2.2 are also broken down by the World Bank's groupings by income level. Taiwan is omitted because it no longer appears in the World Bank data; it is included later in the analysis of trade data.

The growth rates of real GDP, investment, and manufacturing output in the NICs are summarized in table 2.2 for the period of 1970–81.

Table 2.2   **Growth Rates of GDP, Investment, and Manufacturing Output,**
1970–81 (percentage per year)

	GDP	Gross Domestic Investment	Manufacturing Output
NICs			
Low income (average)[a]	3.6	3.7	2.8
India	3.6	4.9	5.0
Upper-middle income (average)	5.6	7.2	6.3
South Korea	9.1	12.2	15.6
Hong Kong	9.9	14.1	10.1
Singapore	8.5	7.2	9.7
Brazil	8.4	7.9	8.7
Mexico	6.5	9.0	7.1
Argentina	1.9	2.5	0.7
New NICs			
Lower-middle income (average)	5.6	8.2	5.8
Indonesia	7.8	14.0	13.9
Thailand	7.2	7.5	10.3
Philippines	6.2	10.1	6.9
Colombia	5.7	10.8	5.7
Upper-middle income			
Malaysia	7.8	10.4	11.1

Source: World Bank 1983, tables 2 and 4.

[a]Average for low-income economies other than China and India.

Among the NICs identified there, the only countries with lower growth rates than their income-group average were Argentina in all three categories and Thailand in investment growth. Comparing growth rates across columns, only Singapore and Brazil show slower investment growth than GDP growth, and only Argentina shows slower growth of manufacturing output than GDP growth.

The impression left by the data of table 2.2 is of investment-led growth in the NICs, with manufacturing output growing faster than GDP. Next we see the effects on the structure of output and exports, and how this growth was financed.

2.2.3   The Shift toward Manufacturing

The increase in the manufacturing sector as a fraction of GDP and, even more strikingly, in exports among the NICs is shown in table 2.3. The increase in the share of manufacturing in GDP from 1960 to 1981 was greater than the average for the income group in all of the identified NICs except Brazil and Argentina (it actually decreased in the latter).

The last two columns of table 2.3 show the increase in the share of manufactures in exports. Here the numbers are striking. Even in countries where the manufacturing share of output did not rise significantly,

Table 2.3   **Manufacturing Output and Exports in the NICs**

	Manufacturing Output as % of GDP		Manufactures Exports as % of Goods Exports	
	1960	1981	1960	1980
NICs				
Low income (average)[a]	9	10	9	29
India	14	18	45	59
Upper-middle income (average)	23	24	16	45
South Korea	14	28	14	90
Hong Kong	27	—	80	93
Singapore	12	30	26	54
Brazil	26	27	3	39
Mexico	19	22	12	38
Argentina	32	25	4	23
New NICs				
Lower-middle income (average)	15	17	4	18
Indonesia	(0)	12	0	2
Thailand	13	20	2	29
Philippines	20	25	4	37
Colombia	8	14	2	20
Upper-middle income				
Malaysia	9	18	6	19

Source: World Bank 1983.
[a]Average for low-income economies other than China and India.

Table 2.4   **Structure of Developing-Country Exports** (percentages)

Export Category	1955	1960	1970	1978
Total nonfuel exports	100	100	100	100
Food	49	47	40	35
Agricultural raw materials	28	25	15	10
Minerals, ores	13	15	18	10
Manufactures	10	13	27	45

Source: Riedel 1984a, table 1 (taken from UN Conference on Trade and Development, *Handbook of International Trade and Development Statistics* [New York, 1972, 1979, 1980]).

the export share did. Indonesia, whose exports came to be dominated by oil, in a mild version of the "Dutch disease," is the only country with a small increase in the manufacturing share.

This shift toward manufactures exports is not limited to the NICs, as we see in table 2.4 and figures 2.1–2.4, taken from James Riedel 1984a. Table 2.4 shows the evolution of the distribution of nonfuel

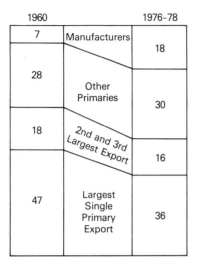

1960		1976-78
7	Manufacturers	18
28	Other Primaries	30
18	*2nd and 3rd Largest Export*	16
47	Largest Single Primary Export	36

Fig. 2.1 Average export structure for total sample of LDCs (fifty-four countries). *Source:* World Bank.

1960		1976-78
15	Manufacturers	39
30	Other Primaries	
12	*2nd and 3rd Largest Export*	29
		10
43	Largest Single Primary Export	22

Fig. 2.2 Average export structure for balanced exporters (eleven countries). *Source:* World Bank.

1960		1976-78
4	Manufacturers	7
28	Other Primaries	31
20	2nd and 3rd Largest Export	16
49	Largest Single Primary Export	46

Fig. 2.3 Average export structure for African primary exports (twenty countries). *Source:* World Bank.

1960		1976-78
4	Manufacturers	16
28	Other Primaries	32
23	*2nd and 3rd Largest Export*	20
46	Largest Single Primary Export	32

Fig. 2.4 Average export structure for non-African primary exporters (twenty-three countries). *Source:* World Bank.

exports of the developing countries from 1955 to 1978. Over that period, manufactures increased from 10% to 45% of developing-country exports. Noting that four Asian NICs—Hong Kong, South Korea, Singapore, and Taiwan—account for over 60% of developing-country manufactures exports, Riedel went on to study a 54-country sample that excludes those four. The sample was divided into 11 "balanced exporters," 23 non-African primary exporters, and 20 African primary exporters. The evolution of the average export structure of the entire sample is shown in figure 2.1. The increase in the share of manufactures from 7% in 1960 to 18% in 1976–78 is balanced by the decrease in the share of the largest single primary export from 47% to 36%. The experience of the "balanced exporters," which include Brazil, India, and Mexico from our list of NICs, is shown in figure 2.2. The share of manufactures rises from 15% to 39%, and the share of the largest single primary export falls from 43% to 22%. In figure 2.4 we see that the non-African primary producers, which include Argentina, Malaysia, Philippines, and Thailand from our list, increased their manufactures exports from 4% to 16% and reduced the largest single primary exports from 46% to 32%. Only the African primary producers, shown in figure 2.3, remain heavily dependent on the largest single primary export. These trends in the structure of developing-country exports continued to 1980, as is shown in Riedel 1984b.

The developing countries on average, and especially the NICs, grew rapidly in the 1970s, even in the face of stagnation in the OECD area. Investment and manufacturing output grew faster than GDP in the NICs, and the manufacturing share of output and exports increased substantially. In later sections of the paper we link this growth in manufacturing output to demand for capital goods exports from the OECD countries, particularly the United States.

2.2.4   Investment, Saving, and Foreign Borrowing

Rapid growth in investment in the NICs has been associated with relatively high shares of investment in GDP, financed partly by high domestic saving rates and partly by foreign borrowing. The data for 1981 are summarized in table 2.5. Among the identified NICs, only Brazil and Indonesia had investment rates lower than their group averages. The 25% investment share for middle-income developing countries is itself high by international standards.

The last two columns in table 2.5 show how investment in 1981 was financed. The upper-middle-income NICs, including Malaysia, have saving rates not much different from the group average of 24%. Singapore is higher and Brazil lower. So this group experienced a higher-than-average foreign capital inflow, as shown in the last column of table 2.5. On the other hand, the lower-income NICs, including India, all

Table 2.5   **Investment and Savings in NICs, 1981** (percentage of GDP)

	Gross Investment	Gross Domestic Saving	Foreign Borrowing or Transfer
NICs			
Low income (average)[a]	14	7	7
India	23	20	3
Upper-middle income (average)	25	24	1
South Korea	26	22	4
Hong Kong	30	24	6
Singapore	42	33	9
Brazil	20	19	1
Mexico	25	23	2
Argentina	26	23	3
New NICs			
Lower-middle income (average)	25	19	6
Indonesia	21	23	− 2
Thailand	28	23	5
Philippines	30	25	5
Colombia	28	24	4
Upper-middle income			
Malaysia	32	26	6

Source: World Bank 1983.
[a]Average for low-income economies other than China and India.

have saving rates much higher than their group average and lower-than-average capital inflow.

The data of table 2.5 confirm the impression that the NICs have experienced high saving rates, around 23% or 24%, and even higher investment rates, grouped around 28% or so. The difference has been financed by foreign investment of around 5% of GDP. The main exceptions are Indonesia, which has on balance been investing abroad, and Brazil, with lower rates of investment and saving. Thus the NICs are good examples of international capital flowing toward countries with high investment rates, financed mainly by domestic saving.

The consequences of this pattern of investment-led growth partly financed by foreign borrowing are summarized in the debt and debt service data of table 2.6. The first two columns show external public and publicly guaranteed debt in billions of dollars in 1970 and 1981. The middle two columns show this debt as a fraction of GNP. The last two columns show the ratio of debt service to export earnings. Since the data cover public debt only, they seriously understate total national foreign debt in countries with extensive borrowing by the private sector, such as Brazil and Mexico.

Table 2.6   External Public Debt and Debt Service Ratios

	External Public Debt				Debt Service Ratio	
	Billions of $		% of GNP			
	1970	1981	1970	1981	1970	1981
NICs						
Low income (average)[a]	—	—	22.0	28.3	12.5	8.8
India	7.9	18.0	14.9	10.8	20.9	8.6
Upper-middle income (average)	—	—	12.4	17.8	10.1	15.4
South Korea	1.8	20.0	20.8	32.1	19.4	13.1
Hong Kong	(0)	0.3	0.1	1.2	(0)	0.7
Singapore	0.1	1.3	7.9	10.2	0.6	0.8
Brazil	3.2	43.8	7.1	16.0	12.5	31.9
Mexico	3.2	42.7	9.1	18.5	23.6	28.2
Argentina	1.9	10.5	8.2	8.7	21.5	18.2
New NICs						
Lower-middle income (average)	—	—	15.6	23.2	9.3	12.5
Indonesia	2.4	15.5	27.1	19.0	6.9	8.2
Thailand	0.3	5.2	4.9	14.4	3.4	6.7
Philippines	0.6	7.4	9.0	19.3	7.4	9.9
Colombia	0.5	3.2	38.2	38.0	17.5	13.9
Upper-middle income						
Malaysia	0.4	4.6	10.0	19.2	3.6	3.1

Source: World Bank 1983, table 16.
[a]Average for low-income economies other than China and India.

While Brazil, Mexico, and Argentina do not stand out in the columns showing debt-GNP ratios, they do stand out in the debt service data, reflecting their lower levels of exports relative to GNP. All of the upper-middle-income NICs show increases in the debt-GNP ratio from 1970 to 1981. Among them, Hong Kong and Singapore have markedly low debt-GNP and especially debt service ratios. Thailand and the Philippines also show increases in both ratios from 1970 to 1981. The exceptions are India (with a marked decrease in both ratios), Colombia (with debt and GNP growing at the same rate from 1970 to 1981 and the debt service ratio falling), and Indonesia (with a falling debt-GNP ratio and a rising debt service ratio).

It is clear from the data of table 2.6 that while in general the NICs have grown with foreign borrowing, their debt positions in the early 1980s varied significantly, from the low-exposure positions of Hong Kong, Singapore, and Malaysia, to the crisis conditions of Argentina, Brazil, and Mexico. As we see below, U.S. exports are relatively more oriented toward the Latin American NICs, and Japan's toward the

Asian NICs. Thus while the U.S. economy has become more inter-dependent with the NICs through trade, the Latin American orientation of its exports leaves it more sensitive than Europe or Japan to a Latin American debt squeeze.

2.3   The Structure of OECD Exports

2.3.1   Introduction

During the past two decades, the share of U.S. exports going to the NICs has increased substantially, while the NICs' share of Japanese exports has remained constant, and the NICs' share of European exports has decreased. In the U.S. case, the NICs' share of each one-digit SITC category of manufactures exports has risen. By 1981 the NICs absorbed 31% of U.S. exports of chemicals and 22% of U.S. exports of capital goods, the two biggest single U.S. export categories. Overall, by 1981 24% of Japan's manufactured exports went to NICs; comparative figures are 21% for the United States, 12% for OECD Europe, and 9% for the European Community (EC). These data reflect one aspect of the increasing interdependence of the U.S. and Japanese economies with the rapidly growing developing countries, especially as compared with Europe.

In this section we summarize the comparative data on U.S., Japanese, and European exports to the NICs, especially the Asian NICs. We begin by looking at the data disaggregated by one-digit SITC group and destination, and then we look at the distribution across commodity groups of the exports of manufactures of each of the three main OECD areas.

2.3.2   Distribution of Total Exports and Total Manufactures Exports by Destination

The evolution of exports and their fraction going to the NICs and the Asian NICs from 1964 to 1981 are shown for OECD Europe, the EC, the United States, and Japan in table 2.7 for total exports and table 2.8 for total manufactures exports. Intra-area trade has been excluded from the European data to make them comparable with the U.S. and Japanese data. Thus EC exports can be larger than OECD Europe exports because of the exclusion of EC exports to other European countries from the OECD Europe data. The EC here is the community of nine countries, before the accession of Greece.

In table 2.7 we see that U.S. total exports grew a little less rapidly than Europe's from 1964 to 1981. In 1964 the totals for the United States and OECD Europe are nearly equal, but in 1981 U.S. exports were 84% of OECD Europe's. The differential growth is the result of

Table 2.7   **Distribution of Total Exports**

	1964		1973		1981	
	Billions of $	%	Billions of $	%	Billions of $	%
OECD Europe						
World	25.0	100.0	81.0	100.0	268.3	100.0
NICs	3.3	13.4	9.6	11.8	32.6	12.1
Asian NICs	2.1	8.2	5.2	6.4	20.1	7.5
EC						
World	30.4	100.0	98.1	100.0	295.6	100.0
NICs	2.9	9.4	7.8	7.9	26.3	8.9
Asian NICs	1.9	6.1	4.4	4.5	16.8	5.7
United States						
World	26.1	100.0	70.2	100.0	225.8	100.0
NICs	4.0	15.2	11.1	15.9	46.6	20.7
Asian NICs	2.1	7.9	5.4	7.8	21.7	9.6
Japan						
World	6.7	100.0	36.8	100.0	151.9	100.0
NICs	1.5	23.0	9.6	26.1	37.0	24.4
Asian NICs	1.4	21.3	8.5	23.1	32.7	21.5

Source: OECD Foreign Trade Data Bank.
Note: Percentages are calculated on values in million dollars in all tables.

Table 2.8   **Distribution of Exports of Manufactures[a]**

	1964		1973		1981	
	Billions of $	%	Billions of $	%	Billions of $	%
OECD Europe						
World	21.0	100.0	69.5	100.0	219.5	100.0
NICs	3.1	14.6	8.8	12.7	30.2	13.8
Asian NICs	1.9	8.9	4.8	6.9	18.4	8.4
EC						
World	25.6	100.0	84.4	100.0	241.4	100.0
NICs	2.6	10.2	7.2	8.5	24.4	10.1
Asian NICs	1.7	6.5	4.0	4.8	15.4	6.4
United States						
World	17.2	100.0	46.5	100.0	160.1	100.0
NICs	2.6	15.0	7.5	16.1	34.8	21.7
Asian NICs	1.1	6.4	3.1	6.8	14.6	9.1
Japan						
World	5.9	100.0	33.9	100.0	144.9	100.0
NICs	1.4	23.6	8.8	26.1	35.0	24.1
Asian NICs	1.3	22.0	7.7	22.8	30.7	21.2

Source: OECD Foreign Trade Data Bank.
Note: Percentages are calculated on values in million dollars.
[a]SITC sections 5–9.

rapid European growth during 1964–73; the ratio of U.S. exports to European exports has stayed constant at about 85% since 1973. Japan's total exports have grown much faster than Europe's or those of the United States, as is well known. In 1964 Japan's exports were about 25% of the U.S. total; this ratio rose to 52% in 1973 and 67% in 1981. This growth of Japanese and European exports relative to the United States was a natural result of recovery and development in Europe and Japan, as discussed in Branson 1981.

More interesting here is the *distribution* of exports by destination. The NIC share of OECD Europe and EC exports fell from 1964 to 1973, and then rose a bit to 12.7% for OECD Europe and 9.3% for the EC by 1981. The NIC share of Japanese exports has remained at about 25% from 1964 to 1981. The NIC share of U.S. exports was about 16% in 1964 and 1973 but grew to 21% by 1981. Three initial observations can be made from the data of table 2.7. First, the shares of European and Japanese exports going to the NICs have remained roughly constant, low for Europe and high for Japan. Second, the NIC share of U.S. exports has increased markedly since 1973. Third, about half of the 21% of U.S. exports to the NICs go to Asia, and the other half go to Latin America.

The *distributional* pattern of total *manufactures* exports, shown in table 2.8, is similar to the pattern in table 2.7. Comparison of the two tables shows that in 1981 manufactures account for 95% of Japanese exports, 82% of OECD exports, and 71% of U.S. exports. Agriculture and raw materials account for a higher fraction of U.S. exports than they do in Europe or Japan.

The share of European and EC manufactures exports going to the NICs fell from 1964 to 1973 and then rose a bit by 1981. The NIC share of Japanese manufactures exports increased slightly from 24% to 26% from 1964 to 1973 and fell back to 24% in 1981. The NIC share of U.S. exports of manufactures increased a bit from 1964 to 1973 but then rose sharply to nearly 22% by 1981, with nearly half going to the Asian NICs.

The fraction of U.S. manufactures exports going to the incipient NICs in 1964 was the same as OECD Europe's. But as the NICs grew, the share of U.S. manufactures exports to them also grew. By 1981 this share was similar to the NIC share of Japanese manufactures exports, with the United States relatively more concentrated in Latin America and Japan in Asia.

2.3.3   Disaggregation of the Distribution of Manufactures Exports
         by Destination

The distribution of manufactures exports by (approximately) one-digit SITC code is shown in tables 2.9–2.14 for Europe, Japan, and the United States. The SITC codes are defined in the Appendix. Rather

Table 2.9   Distribution of Exports of Chemicals and Related Products, N.E.S.[a]

	1964		1973		1981	
	Billions of $	%	Billions of $	%	Billions of $	%
OECD Europe						
World	2.8	100.0	9.2	100.0	30.2	100.0
NICs	0.5	17.3	1.6	17.9	4.7	15.4
Asian NICs	0.3	9.1	0.8	8.8	3.0	9.9
EC						
World	3.3	100.0	11.3	100.0	34.4	100.0
NICs	0.4	12.9	1.4	12.3	3.9	11.3
Asian NICs	0.2	7.0	0.7	6.2	2.6	7.5
United States						
World	2.4	100.0	5.7	100.0	23.3	100.0
NICs	0.4	18.1	1.2	21.4	7.1	30.5
Asian NICs	0.2	6.9	0.5	7.9	4.1	17.5
Japan						
World	0.4	100.0	2.1	100.0	6.8	100.0
NICs	0.2	40.2	1.0	47.2	3.1	45.1
Asian NICs	0.1	38.1	0.9	44.2	2.9	42.9

Source: OECD Foreign Trade Data Bank.
Note: Percentages are calculated on values in million dollars.
[a]SITC section 5.

than discuss each table exhaustively, I will mention only the major points.

Beginning with *chemicals* in table 2.9, we see that the United States and Europe are major exporters, and Japan is not. The NIC share of U.S. chemicals exports is twice that of OECD Europe, at 30.5%, and Japanese exports are highly concentrated on the Asian NICs. In table 2.10 we see that Europe is the biggest exporter of *industrial materials,* with Japan second and the United States third. The NIC share of Japan's exports is high, and its share of Europe's is low, with both concentrated on the Asian NICs. The NIC share of U.S. exports is intermediate and is concentrated on Latin America.

The important category of *capital goods* is shown in table 2.11. As the NICs industrialize, they import capital goods. In 1981, U.S. and European exports of capital goods were about the same—$82.2 billion for the United States and $84.7 billion for Europe—and Japanese exports were $51.7 billion.

Both the growth since 1973 and the distribution of these exports are interesting. As we see in table 2.15, capital goods were 51.3% of U.S., 38.6% of European, and 35.7% of Japanese manufactures exports in 1981. First, let us compare OECD Europe and the United States. In 1973 European total capital goods exports were 13% greater than those

Table 2.10   **Distribution of Exports of Industrial Supplies and Materials other than Fuel[a]**

	1964		1973		1981	
	Billions of $	%	Billions of $	%	Billions of $	%
OECD Europe						
World	5.8	100.0	18.0	100.0	52.5	100.0
NICs	0.6	11.2	1.6	8.9	6.1	11.7
Asian NICs	0.4	7.1	0.9	5.0	3.9	7.5
EC						
World	6.9	100.0	21.7	100.0	55.0	100.0
NICs	0.5	7.8	1.3	6.0	4.8	8.8
Asian NICs	0.4	5.2	0.8	3.7	3.2	5.9
United States						
World	3.0	100.0	6.8	100.0	20.2	100.0
NICs	0.4	14.1	1.1	15.5	4.3	21.3
Asian NICs	0.3	8.7	0.5	7.2	1.4	6.9
Japan						
World	2.7	100.0	10.4	100.0	32.7	100.0
NICs	0.7	24.7	3.5	33.3	10.0	30.7
Asian NICs	0.6	23.0	3.0	29.1	9.1	27.8

Source: OECD Foreign Trade Data Bank.

Note: Percentages are calculated on values in million dollars.

[a]SITC section 6 minus SITC (Revision 1) groups 676, 692, and 695. See Appendix for code descriptions.

of the United States, and European exports to the NICs were slightly greater than U.S. exports to the NICs. By 1981 European exports were 3% greater than those of the United States, and the NIC share of U.S. exports was significantly larger than that of European exports, with more of the U.S. exports going to Latin America.

Now, let us compare Japan and the United States. In 1973 Japanese exports of capital goods were 53% of those of the United States; by 1981 this ratio rose to 63%. Japan's exports remained highly concentrated on the Asian NICs. The NIC share of U.S. capital goods exports grew faster than its share of Japan's capital goods exports, but the United States also grew more concentrated on Latin America.

Thus in capital goods exports, U.S. total growth from 1973 to 1981 was slower than Japan's but faster than Europe's. The growth of U.S. exports to the NICs was about the same as that of Japan but is significantly greater than that of Europe. This suggests that the United States was maintaining its competitive position vis-à-vis Japan, and both were improving relative to Europe in capital goods. But the concentration of the United States on the Latin American NICs, combined with the debt crisis of Argentina, Brazil, and especially Mexico, pro-

Table 2.11   **Distribution of Exports of Capital Goods**[a]

	1964		1973		1981	
	Billions of $	%	Billions of $	%	Billions of $	%
OECD Europe						
World	7.1	100.0	25.5	100.0	84.7	100.0
NICs	1.4	19.6	4.2	16.6	14.6	17.2
Asian NICs	0.8	11.8	2.2	8.5	8.5	10.1
EC						
World	8.7	100.0	30.1	100.0	89.9	100.0
NICs	1.2	14.2	3.5	11.6	12.0	13.3
Asian NICs	0.8	8.8	1.8	6.1	7.3	8.2
United States						
World	7.9	100.0	22.6	100.0	82.2	100.0
NICs	1.2	14.5	4.0	17.5	18.0	21.9
Asian NICs	0.5	6.5	1.8	8.2	7.8	9.5
Japan						
World	1.5	100.0	11.9	100.0	51.7	100.0
NICs	0.4	25.3	3.0	25.3	14.1	27.3
Asian NICs	0.3	23.1	2.5	21.3	11.8	22.8

Source: OECD Foreign Trade Data Bank.

Note: Percentages are calculated on values in million dollars.

[a]SITC section 7 minus the SITC (Revision 1) groups 7232, 7241, 7242, 725, 7292, 7294, 732, 733, and 7358 plus groups 676, 692, 695, 8121, and 861 (less 8612). See Appendix for code descriptions.

vides a serious short-run threat to this otherwise optimistic assessment of the U.S. position.

Exports of *autos* are shown in table 2.12. Here the rise of Japan as a major exporter is clear. What may be surprising is the maintenance of the U.S. position vis-à-vis OECD Europe. U.S. total exports were about 70% of Europe's in 1964 and in 1981. U.S. and Japanese automotive exports to the NICs are heavily concentrated in Latin America and Asia, respectively, while Europe's go half to each area.

Exports of *consumer goods* are shown in table 2.13. The United States was a major exporter after World War II but returned to its normal position of net importer as the economies of Europe and Japan grew. This restoration of the prewar pattern of trade is described in Branson 1981, 1983. By 1981 Europe was the largest exporter, Japan second, and the United States third. The NIC share of U.S. exports was close to its share of Japanese exports (and much higher than its share of European exports), with the United States concentrated on Latin American and Japan on Asia.

Finally, exports of other manufactured products are shown in table 2.14. These include *military equipment*. Here Europe is the largest

Table 2.12   **Distribution of Exports of Autos[a]**

	1964		1973		1981	
	Billions of $	%	Billions of $	%	Billions of $	%
OECD Europe						
World	2.4	100.0	7.9	100.0	22.5	100.0
NICs	0.3	10.4	0.6	8.2	1.9	8.3
Asian NICs	0.2	7.2	0.4	5.0	0.9	4.0
EC						
World	3.3	100.0	10.2	100.0	26.8	100.0
NICs	0.2	7.1	0.6	6.0	1.7	6.4
Asian NICs	0.2	5.0	0.4	3.8	0.8	3.1
United States						
World	1.7	100.0	6.0	100.0	15.9	100.0
NICs	0.3	20.1	0.5	8.5	2.3	14.3
Asian NICs	0.1	3.8	0.1	1.6	0.3	1.9
Japan						
World	0.3	100.0	4.9	100.0	33.2	100.0
NICs	0.1	29.1	0.6	11.7	3.6	11.0
Asian NICs	0.1	27.4	0.5	10.9	3.2	9.6

Source: OECD Foreign Trade Data Bank.

Note: Percentages are calculated on values in million dollars.

[a]SITC (Revision 1) group 732, road motor vehicles.

exporter, followed by the United States and Japan. The Asian NICs take 19% of Japanese exports, and the Latin American NICs take 11% of U.S. exports, about the same as the total NICs share of European exports.

2.3.4   Distribution of Manufactures Exports by Commodity Group

The evolution of the distribution of each area's exports of manufactures across commodity group is shown in table 2.15. This table gives the distribution of the totals from table 2.7 across the SITC one-digit categories of tables 2.9–2.14.

The main impression one gets from table 2.15 is the relatively static composition of OECD Europe's and the EC's manufactures exports from 1964 to 1981, compared especially with the large changes in this composition for Japan, with the United States in between. The share of industrial materials (SITC 6) in OECD exports fell from 27.5% in 1964 to 23.9% in 1981, while the share of capital goods (SITC 7) rose from 34.1% to 38.6%. The other categories remained roughly constant.

The composition of U.S. manufactures exports is dominated by a high and rising share of capital goods (SITC 7), from 46.1% in 1964 to 51.3% in 1981. The shares of industrial materials (SITC 6) and consumer goods (SITC 8) fell during this period, while the share of autos (SITC

Table 2.13   **Distribution of Exports of Consumer Goods** (except Autos)[a]

	1964		1973		1981	
	Billions of $	%	Billions of $	%	Billions of $	%
OECD Europe						
World	2.0	100.0	6.4	100.0	20.1	100.0
NICs	0.2	9.1	0.6	8.8	2.0	9.8
Asian NICs	0.1	5.4	0.4	5.7	1.3	6.7
EC						
World	2.3	100.0	7.7	100.0	23.5	100.0
NICs	0.1	4.2	0.3	3.7	1.2	4.9
Asian NICs	0.1	3.0	0.2	2.6	0.8	3.6
United States						
World	1.3	100.0	2.7	100.0	10.0	100.0
NICs	0.1	8.6	0.4	13.9	1.7	17.4
Asian NICs	0.0	3.5	0.1	5.2	0.6	6.1
Japan						
World	0.8	100.0	2.9	100.0	14.5	100.0
NICs	0.1	7.3	0.5	15.8	2.8	19.4
Asian NICs	0.1	6.8	0.4	13.6	2.6	17.7

Source: OECD Foreign Trade Data Bank.

Note: Percentages are calculated on values in million dollars.

[a]SITC section 8 minus SITC (Revision 1) groups 8121 and 861 (less 8612). See Appendix for code descriptions.

732) increased from 9.7% to 13.0% from 1964 to 1973 and then fell to 9.9% in 1981.

The structure of Japanese manufactures exports shows major changes in all categories from 1964 to 1981. The biggest changes are the continuous rise in the share of autos (SITC 732), the jump in the share of capital goods (SITC 7) from 25.5% in 1964 to 35.0% in 1973, with virtually no change after 1973, and the continuous decrease in the share of industrial materials, which dominated the distribution in 1964.

Comparison of the structure of manufactures exports in 1981 across the three major areas shows Japan with a significantly lower share in chemicals (SITC 5) and a higher share in autos (SITC 732) than the United States or Europe, and the United States with a significantly higher share in capital goods (SITC 7) than Europe or Japan. In a sense, relative to the other geographical areas, Japan seemed to be specializing in autos and the United States in capital goods, with no single commodity group standing out in OECD Europe or the EC.

2.3.5 Conclusion

In table 2.11 we saw that a high and rising share of U.S. capital goods exports goes to the NICs. This share reached 22% in 1981, with 9.5%

Table 2.14   **Distribution of Exports of Other Manufactures**[a]

	1964		1973		1981	
	Billions of $	%	Billions of $	%	Billions of $	%
OECD Europe						
World	0.8	100.0	2.6	100.0	9.6	100.0
NICs	0.1	10.5	0.2	6.1	1.0	10.7
Asian NICs	0.1	8.2	0.1	3.9	0.7	7.0
EC						
World	1.1	100.0	3.4	100.0	11.8	100.0
NICs	0.1	8.3	0.1	4.0	0.9	7.4
Asian NICs	0.1	6.7	0.1	2.5	0.3	2.8
United States						
World	0.9	100.0	2.6	100.0	8.5	100.0
NICs	0.1	14.5	0.4	13.6	1.3	15.8
Asian NICs	0.1	5.7	0.1	4.5	0.4	4.7
Japan						
World	0.2	100.0	1.7	100.0	5.9	100.0
NICs	0.0	23.3	0.3	20.0	1.3	21.7
Asian NICs	0.0	21.7	0.3	18.6	1.1	19.0

Source: OECD Foreign Trade Data Bank.

Note: Percentages are calculated on values in million dollars.

[a]SITC (Revision 1) section 9 plus groups 7232, 7241, 7242, 725, 7292, 7294, 7358, and 733. See Appendix for code descriptions.

going to the Asian NICs and 12.4% to Latin America. Then in table 2.15 we saw that U.S. exports of manufactures are dominated by capital goods exports to a degree that no one-digit commodity reaches in Europe or Japan. By 1981 over half of U.S. exports of manufactures were capital goods.

Thus rapid growth and high levels of investment in the NICs have been associated with rapid growth and concentration in U.S. exports of capital goods, and this association is strongest with the Latin American NICs. This has contributed to an increasing interdependence of the U.S. economy with the NICs, especially in Latin America.

2.4 The Structure of OECD Imports

2.4.1 Introduction

There have been two striking developments (aside from OPEC) in the structure of OECD imports from the leading developing countries in the two decades since 1964. The first has been the change in the structure of European and U.S. imports of manufactured goods, mainly away from industrial supplies and materials and toward consumer goods,

Table 2.15   **Distribution of Manufactures Exports by Commodity Group[a]**

	1964		1973		1981	
	Billions of $	%	Billions of $	%	Billions of $	%
OECD Europe						
Total	21.0	100.0	69.5	100.0	219.5	100.0
5	2.8	13.2	9.2	13.2	30.2	13.8
6	5.8	27.5	18.0	25.9	52.5	23.9
7	7.1	34.1	25.5	36.7	84.7	38.6
732	2.4	11.6	7.9	11.4	22.5	10.2
8	2.0	9.5	6.4	9.2	20.1	9.2
9	0.8	4.0	2.6	3.7	9.6	4.4
EC						
Total	25.6	100.0	84.4	100.0	241.4	100.0
5	3.3	12.8	11.3	13.4	34.4	14.2
6	6.9	26.9	21.7	25.7	55.0	22.8
7	8.7	34.0	30.1	35.6	89.9	37.2
732	3.3	12.8	10.2	12.0	26.8	11.1
8	2.3	9.1	7.7	9.1	23.5	9.8
9	1.1	4.4	3.4	4.1	11.8	4.9
United States						
Total	17.2	100.0	46.5	100.0	160.1	100.0
5	2.4	13.8	5.7	12.4	23.3	14.6
6	3.0	17.6	6.8	14.6	20.2	12.6
7	7.9	46.1	22.6	48.6	82.2	51.3
732	1.7	9.7	6.0	13.0	15.9	9.9
8	1.3	7.6	2.7	5.9	10.0	6.3
9	0.9	5.2	2.7	5.7	8.5	5.3
Japan						
Total	5.9	100.0	33.8	100.0	144.9	100.0
5	0.4	6.5	2.1	6.3	6.8	4.7
6	2.7	45.7	10.4	30.7	32.7	22.6
7	1.5	25.5	11.9	35.0	51.7	35.7
732	0.3	5.1	4.9	14.4	33.2	22.9
8	0.8	13.9	2.9	8.7	14.5	10.0
9	0.2	3.2	1.7	4.9	5.9	4.1

Source: OECD Foreign Trade Data Bank.

Note: Percentages may not total to 100, because of rounding error. Percentages are calculated on values in million dollars.

[a]*Commodity groupings have been made as follows:*
   5 = SITC section 5.
   6 = SITC section 6 minus the following SITC (Revision 1) groups: 676, 692, and 695.
   7 = SITC section 7 minus the following SITC (Revision 1) groups: 7232, 7241, 7242, 725, 7292, 7294, 732, 733, and 7358; plus the following SITC (Revision 1) groups: 676, 692, 695, 8121, and 861-8612.
732 = SITC (Revision 1) commodity group 732.
   8 = SITC section 8 minus SITC (Revision 1) 8121 and 861 (less 8612).
   9 = SITC section 9 plus 7232, 7241, 7242, 725, 7292, 7294, 733, and 7358.
See Appendix for descriptions of SITC codes.

capital goods, and automotive products. The other has been the rise of the NICs, especially since 1970, as the source of manufactured imports to Europe and the United States. This has been most striking in consumer goods, where the NICs provided nearly 40% of European imports and 50% of U.S. imports by 1980.

As is well known, the level of Japanese manufactures imports remain low relative to the United States and Europe. Basically, the Japanese economy exports manufactures and imports nonmanufactures, because of its relatively poor resource base. Fully 95% of Japanese exports are manufactures, but only 21% of Japanese imports are. Comparable numbers for the United States are 70% on the export side and 55% on the import side. However, the fraction of Japanese and U.S. total manufactures imports coming from the NICs are almost the same, a bit over 20%. As on the export side, the proportion of European manufactures imports coming from the NICs is smaller, under 15% in 1980.

The evolution of total imports, total imports less fuel, and total manufactures imports and their distribution by source are shown in tables 2.16–2.18 for OECD Europe, the EC, the United States and Japan. The date on total imports are sufficiently influenced by oil prices since 1973 that we will begin by focusing on table 2.17, which gives total imports less fuel.

In table 2.17, we see that U.S. and Japanese imports grew much faster than European imports from 1964 to 1973. Then from 1973 to

Table 2.16   **Distribution of Total Imports**

	1964		1973		1981	
	Billions of $	%	Billions of $	%	Billions of $	%
OECD Europe						
World	35.4	100.0	98.2	100.0	331.8	100.0
NICs	4.0	11.4	11.7	11.9	38.4	11.6
Asian NICs	1.9	3.5	5.8	6.0	22.8	6.9
EC						
World	37.4	100.0	104.5	100.0	332.8	100.0
NICs	3.5	9.4	9.8	9.4	31.0	9.3
Asian NICs	1.8	4.7	5.2	5.0	19.7	5.9
United States						
World	18.6	100.0	69.5	100.0	271.2	100.0
NICs	2.9	15.8	11.0	15.8	56.1	20.7
Asian NICs	1.4	7.6	6.8	9.8	35.2	13.0
Japan						
World	7.9	100.0	38.1	100.0	140.8	100.0
NICs	1.4	17.1	8.6	22.5	32.0	22.7
Asian NICs	1.1	14.1	7.6	20.0	28.6	20.3

Source: OECD Foreign Trade Data Bank.

Note: Percentages are calculated on values in million dollars.

Table 2.17 **Distribution of Total Imports less Fuels**[a]

	1964		1973		1981	
	Billions of $	%	Billions of $	%	Billions of $	%
OECD Europe						
World	28.7	100.0	75.2	100.0	189.0	100.0
NICs	4.0	13.9	11.7	15.6	34.3	18.1
Asian NICs	1.9	6.7	5.8	7.8	22.5	11.9
EC						
World	31.6	100.0	84.6	100.0	212.5	100.0
NICs	3.5	11.0	9.8	11.6	28.8	13.5
Asian NICs	1.7	5.4	5.2	6.1	19.5	9.2
United States						
World	16.6	100.0	61.3	100.0	187.0	100.0
NICs	2.8	17.0	10.7	17.4	42.5	22.7
Asian NICs	1.3	8.2	6.6	10.7	29.2	15.6
Japan						
World	6.5	100.0	29.8	100.0	68.2	100.0
NICs	1.2	19.1	6.7	22.5	16.4	24.0
Asian NICs	1.0	15.5	5.8	19.4	13.9	20.4

Source: OECD Foreign Trade Data Bank.

Note: Percentages are calculated on values in million dollars.

[a]SITC section 3 (mineral fuels, lubricants, and related materials) was subtracted from total imports.

1981 growth rates were much more equal, with U.S. imports growing fastest and the Japanese slowest. The fraction of European nonfuel imports coming from the identified NICs rose slowly throughout the period to 18% in 1981. The share of the NICs in U.S. imports was constant for 1964 to 1973 and then increased significantly to 23% by 1981. The share of the NICs in Japanese nonfuel imports increased gradually over the entire period, reaching 24% by 1981.

The data on total manufacturing imports are summarized in table 2.18. There we see the difference between the levels of imports of Europe, the United States, and Japan. However, from 1964 to 1981, Japanese manufactures imports grew at the same rate as those of the United States; in 1964 and in 1981 their ratio was 0.21. European manufactures imports grew more slowly, however. The ratio of European to U.S. manufactures imports fell from 1.09 in 1964 to 0.84 in 1973 and then to 0.78 in 1981.

The proportion of manufactures imports coming from the NICs has increased over time in all three areas, with the biggest increase in Japan, especially from 1964 to 1973, and the smallest in Europe. By 1981 roughly 21% of U.S. and Japanese manufactured imports came from the NICs, as compared with 15% of European imports. In contrast to

Table 2.18   **Distribution of Imports of Manufactures**[a]

	1964		1973		1981	
	Billions of $	%	Billions of $	%	Billions of $	%
OECD Europe						
World	10.5	100.0	38.8	100.0	119.8	100.0
NICs	0.7	6.9	3.9	10.1	18.3	15.3
Asian NICs	0.6	5.9	3.3	8.5	16.0	13.4
EC						
World	12.6	100.0	47.3	100.0	144.6	100.0
NICs	0.7	5.2	3.4	7.3	15.7	10.9
Asian NICs	0.6	4.5	2.9	6.1	13.8	9.6
United States						
World	9.6	100.0	46.0	100.0	153.1	100.0
NICs	0.8	8.7	6.8	14.8	32.6	21.3
Asian NICs	0.6	6.7	5.0	10.8	25.0	16.3
Japan						
World	2.0	100.0	11.6	100.0	32.2	100.0
NICs	0.1	3.8	2.2	18.9	6.7	20.8
Asian NICs	0.1	3.5	2.0	16.9	6.0	18.7

Source: OECD Foreign Trade Data Bank.

Note: Percentages are calculated on values in million dollars.

[a]Sum of SITC sections 5–9.

the export pattern, all three areas' imports of manufactures from the NICs are concentrated in Asia rather than Latin America.

2.4.2   Disaggregation of the Distribution of Manufactures Imports by Origin

The distributions of manufactures imports for the one-digit SITC categories are shown in tables 2.19–2.24. The categories are the same as for exports; details are given in the Appendix.

Chemical imports (table 2.19) are small; the largest total is $14.2 billion for Europe in 1981. Relative to the other areas, the United States has a higher proportion coming from the Latin American NICs, and Japan from the Asian NICs, but the numbers are small. Imports of industrial supplies are summarized in table 2.20. There we see low numbers for Japan relative to the other areas, with a high concentration on the Asian NICs. By 1981 the United States was a bigger importer than Europe, but they had similar imports from the NICs. Table 2.21 summarizes the distribution of imports of capital goods. OECD Europe imports in 1981 were $43.6 billion, compared with $40.2 billion for the United States, and $9.4 billion for Japan. There is a significant difference in the distribution by source however. In 1981, 23% of U.S. imports of capital goods came from the NICs, 16% from Asia. The

Table 2.19   **Distribution of Total Exports**

	1964		1973		1981	
	Billions of $	%	Billions of $	%	Billions of $	%
OECD Europe						
World	1.4	100.0	4.2	100.0	14.2	100.0
NICs	0.0	2.8	0.1	3.3	0.5	3.6
Asian NICs	0.0	0.9	0.0	1.0	0.2	1.2
EC						
World	1.5	100.0	4.7	100.0	10.7	100.0
NICs	0.0	2.3	0.1	2.6	0.4	2.3
Asian NICs	0.0	1.6	0.0	0.7	0.1	0.8
United States						
World	0.7	100.0	2.5	100.0	10.7	100.0
NICs	0.0	5.5	0.1	4.5	0.8	7.2
Asian NICs	0.0	0.6	0.0	1.2	0.2	2.1
Japan						
World	0.5	100.0	1.9	100.0	6.5	100.0
NICs	—	1.5	0.1	5.4	0.8	11.8
Asian NICs	—	1.1	0.1	4.5	0.6	9.4

Source: OECD Foreign Trade Data Bank.

Note: Percentages are calculated on values in million dollars.

[a]SITC section 5.

proportions for Europe and Japan are much smaller. The United States is a much bigger importer of capital goods from the NICs, especially those in Asia, than are Europe or Japan.

The distribution of imports of autos is shown in table 2.22. The obvious fact that stands out is the emergence of the United States as a major importer in the period from 1973 to 1981. The NICs still had very small shares of the auto market of the OECD countries by 1981; mainly Japan exported to the United States and, to a lesser extent, Europe.

There is less importation of consumer goods (table 2.23) than industrial supplies or capital goods, but the concentration on the NICs, especially in Asia, is much stronger. Out of roughly equal total consumer goods imports of $24–$27 billion in 1981, over half of U.S. imports and just under 40% of European imports come from the NICs, mostly from Asia. The U.S. share has risen much more rapidly over time than the European share. U.S. and European imports of consumer goods from the NICs are greater than the imports of any of the other one-digit categories as a result of this concentration. Japan also has a relatively high share of consumer goods imports from the Asian NICs, but out of a very small total.

Imports of other manufactured products, including arms, are summarized in table 2.24. Here the numbers are small, with relatively low

Table 2.20   **Distribution of Imports of Industrial Supplies and Materials other than Fuel[a]**

	1964		1973		1981	
	Billions of $	%	Billions of $	%	Billions of $	%
OECD Europe						
World	4.3	100.0	14.1	100.0	24.9	100.0
NICs	0.4	8.8	1.6	11.0	4.8	19.3
Asian NICs	0.3	7.4	1.2	8.3	3.9	15.6
EC						
World	5.6	100.0	18.6	100.0	39.5	100.0
NICs	0.3	6.2	1.4	7.4	4.2	10.6
Asian NICs	0.3	5.3	1.1	5.7	3.4	8.7
United States						
World	4.5	100.0	13.0	100.0	38.6	100.0
NICs	0.5	10.9	1.8	13.7	6.4	16.7
Asian NICs	0.4	8.3	1.2	9.5	4.7	12.2
Japan						
World	0.6	100.0	4.5	100.0	10.0	100.0
NICs	0.1	11.4	1.2	27.7	2.6	25.5
Asian NICs	0.1	10.8	1.1	23.8	2.2	21.9

Source: OECD Foreign Trade Data Bank.

Note: Percentages are calculated on values in million dollars.

[a]SITC section 6 minus SITC (Revision 1) groups 676, 692, and 695.

concentration on imports from the NICs in Europe. As usual, U.S. imports from the NICs are mostly from Latin America and Japan's from Asia. NIC exports of manufactures to the OECD countries are concentrated in industrial supplies, capital goods, and especially consumer goods, with very small NIC export participation in chemicals, autos, and arms.

2.4.3   Distribution of Manufactures Imports by Commodity Group

The distributions across commodity groups are given in table 2.25. Here one impression is of change in the structure of manufactures imports over time in Europe and stability in the United States and Japan, at least since 1973. By 1981 the U.S. structure was more "balanced" than that of Europe or Japan. The distributional peaks are 36% for European capital goods imports, and 31% for industrial supplies and 29% for capital goods in Japan. (Remember that in all cases the Japanese totals are relatively small.)

In Europe, the major movement has been away from imports of industrial supplies, with a share falling from 40.8% in 1964 to 20.8% in 1981, and toward consumer goods, with a share rising from 8.8% in 1964 to 20.2% in 1981. Smaller but significant increases came in their shares of capital goods and auto imports.

Table 2.21   **Distribution of Imports of Capital Goods**[a]

	1964		1973		1981	
	Billions of $	%	Billions of $	%	Billions of $	%
OECD Europe						
World	3.1	100.0	12.4	100.0	43.6	100.0
NICs	—	0.9	0.4	3.0	2.8	6.3
Asian NICs	—	0.6	0.3	2.5	2.3	5.2
EC						
World	3.5	100.0	13.9	100.0	45.9	100.0
NICs	0.0	0.7	0.3	2.5	2.4	5.3
Asian NICs	0.0	0.5	0.3	2.1	2.0	4.3
United States						
World	1.4	100.0	9.7	100.0	40.2	100.0
NICs	—	0.9	1.4	14.9	9.3	23.0
Asian NICs	—	0.7	0.9	9.1	6.5	16.1
Japan						
World	0.8	100.0	3.1	100.0	9.4	100.0
NICs	—	—	0.2	6.0	1.0	10.9
Asian NICs	—	—	0.2	5.2	0.9	9.4

Source: OECD Foreign Trade Data Bank.

Note: Percentages are calculated on values in million dollars.

[a]See table 2.15, note a (SITC section 7), for description of this group.

In the United States, the main shifts in the structure of manufactures imports came between 1964 and 1973. In this period the share of industrial supplies fell from 46.9% to 28.3%, while the share of capital goods rose from 14.3% to 21.0%, and that of autos rose from 8.2% to 21.8%. Since 1973 the composition of U.S. manufactured imports has been relatively stable and more balanced across categories than in Europe or Japan.

2.4.4   Conclusion

Among the OECD areas, Europe and the United States are the major importers of manufactured goods and thus are the principal potential markets for the NICs. U.S. imports from both Latin American and Asian NICs—$7.6 and $25.0 billion respectively—are greater than those of Europe (table 2.18). The United States is the largest importer of manufactures from the NICs, especially those in Asia, of the three main OECD areas.

Despite the relatively balanced structure of U.S. imports across commodities, there is a concentration on the NICs as a source, especially in consumer goods but also in capital goods. In 1981 U.S. and European consumer goods imports were 17.5% and 20.2%, respectively, of their total manufactures imports. But the U.S. concentration on the NICs,

Table 2.22   **Distribution of Imports of Autos[a]**

	1964		1973		1981	
	Billions of $	%	Billions of $	%	Billions of $	%
OECD Europe						
World	0.3	100.0	1.5	100.0	7.9	100.0
NICs	—	—	0.0	0.9	0.3	3.9
Asian NICs	—	—	—	—	0.1	0.9
EC						
World	0.2	100.0	1.8	100.0	9.5	100.0
NICs	—	—	0.0	0.7	0.3	3.1
Asian NICs	—	—	—	—	0.1	0.7
United States						
World	0.8	100.0	10.0	100.0	29.3	100.0
NICs	0.0	0.0	0.1	0.6	0.4	1.3
Asian NICs	0.0	0.0	0.0	0.1	0.1	0.2
Japan						
World	—	—	0.2	100.0	0.5	100.0
NICs	—	—	0.0	0.5	0.0	3.1
Asian NICs	—	—	—	—	0.0	2.9

Source: OECD Foreign Trade Data Bank.

Note: Percentages are calculated on values in million dollars.

[a]SITC (Revision 1) group 732, road motor vehicles.

who had a 51.2% share of the U.S. market, compared with 38.2% in Europe, resulted in U.S. imports from the NICs of $13.7 billion in consumer goods. This was the largest single NIC export category to an OECD area in 1981. The $12.0 billion of Asian NIC consumer goods exports to the United States was the largest single category for that subgroup in 1980.

The imbalance in U.S. imports in favor of the NICs as a source adds to the impression of a growing interdependence of the U.S. economy with the NICs, as an exporter of capital goods, mainly to Latin America, and as an importer of consumer goods, mainly from Asia.

2.5 U.S. Trade with the NICs

The previous sections of this paper have compared the trade patterns of the United States, Japan, and Europe with the NICs, both Asian and Latin American. Here we focus in more detail on the structure of U.S. trade, by one-digit SITC category, with the individual NICs.

First, in table 2.26, we show the evolution of total U.S. manufactures trade by commodity group from 1973 to 1981. The data in nominal terms can be seen in tables 2.15 and 2.25. In 1973 U.S. manufactures exports were $46.5 billion and imports were $46.0 billion—almost ex-

Table 2.23   **Distribution of Imports of Consumer Goods** (less Autos)[a]

	1964		1973		1981	
	Billions of $	%	Billions of $	%	Billions of $	%
OECD Europe						
World	0.9	100.0	5.3	100.0	24.2	100.0
NICs	0.3	29.4	1.8	33.9	9.3	38.2
Asian NICs	0.3	29.1	1.7	32.4	9.0	37.3
EC						
World	1.1	100.0	6.3	100.0	26.0	100.0
NICs	0.2	20.8	1.5	24.2	7.8	30.2
Asian NICs	0.2	20.8	1.5	23.2	7.7	29.5
United States						
World	1.5	100.0	7.6	100.0	26.7	100.0
NICs	0.2	15.7	2.7	35.8	13.7	51.2
Asian NICs	0.2	15.2	2.3	30.6	12.0	45.1
Japan						
World	0.1	100.0	1.8	100.0	4.7	100.0
NICs	0.0	3.4	0.6	34.4	2.0	43.9
Asian NICs	0.0	3.4	0.6	34.2	2.0	43.8

Source: OECD Foreign Trade Data Bank.

Note: Percentages are calculated on values in million dollars.

[a]SITC section 8 minus SITC (Revision 1) groups 8121 and 861 (less 8612).

actly balanced. In 1981 exports had increased to $160.1 billion and imports to $153.1 billion, for a surplus of $7.0 billion. But much of that increase was inflation, so in table 2.26 we show the data deflated to 1973 prices. The surplus on overall manufactures exports, in real terms, went from $0.5 to $2.8 billion (1973 prices) by 1981. Over a period when the U.S. economy grew by about 2.5% per year (on average) in real terms, manufactures exports grew by 8.4% a year, and manufactures imports grew by 8.2% per year. This is hardly a picture of a "deindustrializing" economy; rather it reflects a rapid change in the structure of U.S. industrial production, with export sectors drawing resources from shrinking, import-competing sectors.

The structure of U.S. trade in manufactures with the NICs in 1981 is shown in table 2.27. There the countries are separated between the Asian and Latin American NICs, and within each group, the NICs and the "new NICs." At the bottom we present an ASEAN aggregate— Singapore, Indonesia, Malaysia, the Philippines, and Thailand. Data are given for each of the one-digit SITC categories, and for the total. The balance on the upper-right-hand corner of the table is the $7.0 billion surplus for 1981 already mentioned. The first row shows the structure of U.S. world trade in manufactures: surpluses in chemicals and capital goods, deficits in industrial materials, consumer goods, and autos, and approximate balance in "other."

Table 2.24   **Distribution of Imports of Other Manufactures**[a]

	1964		1973		1981	
	Billions of $	%	Billions of $	%	Billions of $	%
OECD Europe						
World	0.6	100.0	1.4	100.0	5.1	100.0
NICs	0.0	2.0	0.1	4.1	0.7	13.2
Asian NICs	0.0	1.0	0.0	3.3	0.6	12.1
EC						
World	0.7	100.0	1.9	100.0	7.4	100.0
NICs	0.0	1.7	0.1	2.7	0.6	8.5
Asian NICs	0.0	0.8	0.0	2.1	0.6	7.7
United States						
World	0.7	100.0	3.2	100.0	7.6	100.0
NICs	0.1	8.3	0.7	20.6	2.0	26.7
Asian NICs	0.0	3.7	0.5	15.1	1.4	18.8
Japan						
World	0.0	—	0.2	100.0	1.2	100.0
NICs	—	—	0.1	23.5	0.3	24.7
Asian NICs	—	—	0.1	22.3	0.3	23.8

Source: OECD Foreign Trade Data Bank.

Note: Percentages are calculated on values in million dollars.

[a]SITC section 9 plus SITC (Revision 1) groups 7232, 7241, 7242, 725, 7292, 733, 7294, and 7358.

Let us focus first on the differences in trade patterns with the Latin American and Asian NICs. In aggregate, U.S. trade with the Asian NICs follows the broad pattern of U.S. world trade, except for balance in autos, with little trade either way. But with the Latin American NICs, the United States has a surplus in every category except consumer goods, where trade was roughly balanced. Overall, the United States had a deficit in manufactures trade of $10.3 billion with the Asian NICs and a surplus of $12.6 billion with the Latin Americans in 1981. Mexico alone provided an $8.8 billion surplus to the United States in 1981, the largest component being capital goods. This highlights the exposure of U.S. trade to the debt situation in Latin America.

Another interesting distinction appears when we separate the Asian NICs into ASEAN and the Far Eastern countries of Hong Kong, South Korea, and Taiwan. In 1981 the Far Eastern NICs had an aggregate surplus of $11.8 billion in trade in manufactures with the U.S., while ASEAN had a $1.3 billion deficit, compared with the Latin American deficit of $12.6 billion. On balance, the U.S. exports manufactures to Latin America, the Latin American NICs sell nonmanufactures (especially Mexican oil) in the world market, the Far Eastern NICs buy nonmanufactures in the world market and sell manufactures to the United States. A similar triangle could be drawn between the United States, ASEAN, and the Far Eastern NICs, with Indonesian oil re-

Table 2.25   **Distribution of Manufactures Imports by Commodity Group[a]**

	1964		1973		1981	
	Billions of $	%	Billions of $	%	Billions of $	%
OECD Europe						
Total	10.5	100.0	38.8	100.0	119.8	100.0
5	1.4	12.8	4.1	10.6	14.2	11.8
6	4.3	40.8	14.1	36.4	24.9	20.8
7	3.1	29.3	12.4	32.1	43.6	36.4
732	0.3	2.5	1.5	3.8	7.9	6.6
8	0.9	8.8	5.3	13.6	24.2	20.2
9	0.6	5.8	1.4	3.6	5.1	4.2
EC						
Total	12.6	100.0	47.3	100.0	144.6	100.0
5	1.5	11.7	4.7	9.9	16.3	11.3
6	5.6	44.1	18.6	39.4	39.5	27.3
7	3.5	27.7	13.9	29.4	45.9	31.8
732	0.2	1.9	1.8	3.8	9.5	6.6
8	1.1	9.0	6.3	13.4	26.0	18.0
9	0.7	5.7	1.9	4.0	7.4	5.1
United States						
Total	9.6	100.0	46.0	100.0	153.1	100.0
5	0.7	7.4	2.5	5.4	10.7	7.0
6	4.5	46.9	13.0	28.3	38.6	25.2
7	1.4	14.3	9.7	21.0	40.2	26.2
732	0.8	8.2	10.0	21.8	29.3	19.1
8	1.5	15.8	7.6	16.6	26.7	17.5
9	0.7	7.4	3.2	6.9	7.6	4.9
Japan						
Total	2.0	100.0	11.6	100.0	32.2	100.0
5	0.5	22.4	1.9	16.0	6.5	20.1
6	0.6	28.7	4.5	38.3	10.0	31.1
7	0.8	40.5	3.1	26.7	9.4	29.0
732	0.0	1.5	0.2	1.6	0.5	1.5
8	0.1	5.7	1.8	15.5	4.7	14.4
9	0.0	1.1	0.2	2.0	1.2	3.8

Source: OECD Foreign Trade Data Bank.

Note: Percentages may not total to 100, because of rounding error. Percentages are calculated on values in million dollars.

[a]See table 2.15, note a, for definitions of categories of goods.

placing Mexican. These trade patterns highlight the importance of Latin America and ASEAN as U.S. export markets and the U.S. as an export market for the Far Eastern NICs.

The data of table 2.27 thus show interesting patterns of imbalance in U.S. manufactures trade across both commodities and geography. Following its lines of comparative advantage, the United States is a major exporter of capital goods, chemicals, and military equipment,

Table 2.26 **U.S. Trade in Manufactures in Constant 1973 Dollars** (Billions)

Commodity[a]	1973		1981	
	Exports	Imports	Exports	Imports
Chemicals	5.7	2.5	13.2	6.0
Industrial supplies	6.8	13.0	11.4	21.8
Capital goods	22.6	9.7	46.5	22.8
Autos	6.0	10.0	9.5	17.5
Consumer goods	2.7	7.6	6.1	16.2
Other	2.7	3.2	4.7	4.3
Total	46.5	46.0	91.4	88.6

Sources: See OECD Foreign Trade Data Bank and the OECD foreign trade publication *Trade by Commodities, Series C,* for trade data in current dollars. See Council of Economic Advisers, *Annual Report, 1983,* for price indexes as follows: chemicals and industrial materials and "other," see Total Goods Deflator, tables B-6 and B-7; capital goods, see Deflator for Producers' Durable Equipment, table B-3; autos, see Auto Product Deflator, tables B-6 and B-7; consumer goods, see Deflator for Consumer Expenditure on Durables, table B-3.

[a]See table 2.15, note a, for detailed descriptions of individual categories.

and is an importer of industrial materials, consumer goods, and autos. Net exports to the NICs alone provide half the U.S. surplus on chemicals and one-quarter on capital goods; the Asian NICs, mainly in the Far East, supply three-quarters of the U.S. deficit on consumer goods. U.S. trade in manufactures has become increasingly interdependent with the three groups of NICs—Latin America, ASEAN (plus India), and the Far East. The patterns of interdependence are complicated and will require increasing attention from U.S. foreign economic policy.

Table 2.27   **U.S. Trade in Manufactures with the NICs, 1981** (in billions of dollars)

	Chemicals (5)[a]			Industrial Materials (6)			Capital Goods (7)		
	E	I	E − I	E	I	E − I	E	I	E − I
World	23.3	10.7	12.6	20.2	38.6	− 18.4	82.2	40.2	42.0
Asian NICs	4.1	0.2	3.9	1.4	4.7	− 3.3	7.8	6.5	1.4
Hong Kong	0.4	—	0.4	0.4	0.4	− 0.0	0.8	1.0	− 0.1
India	0.4	—	0.3	0.1	0.6	− 0.5	0.6	0.1	0.5
Singapore	0.6	—	0.6	0.2	0.1	0.1	1.6	1.2	0.4
South Korea	0.5	—	0.5	0.2	1.5	− 1.2	1.4	0.6	0.8
Taiwan	0.5	0.1	0.4	0.2	1.2	− 1.0	1.6	1.9	− 0.3
Asian new NICs									
Indonesia	0.2	—	0.2	—	0.2	− 0.1	0.4	0.1	0.4
Malaysia	0.6	—	0.6	—	0.2	− 0.2	0.6	1.0	− 0.4
Philippines	0.5	—	0.5	0.1	0.2	− 0.1	0.6	0.5	—
Thailand	0.3	—	0.3	0.1	0.3	− 0.3	0.3	0.1	0.2
Latin American NICs	3.0	0.5	2.5	2.9	1.7	1.2	10.2	2.8	7.4
Argentina	0.3	0.1	0.2	0.2	0.2	—	1.1	—	1.1
Brazil	0.7	0.2	0.6	0.2	0.7	− 0.5	1.6	0.4	1.3
Mexico	1.7	0.2	1.4	2.3	0.8	1.6	6.7	2.4	4.3
Latin American new NIC	0.3	—	0.3	0.2	0.1	0.1	0.7	—	0.7
ASEAN[b]	2.3	—	2.3	0.5	1.0	− 0.5	3.4	3.0	0.4

Source: OECD Foreign Trade Data Bank. (See the OECD foreign trade publication, *Trade by Commodities, Series C.*)

[a]See table 2.15, note a, for definitions of categories of goods.

[b]Singapore, Indonesia, Malaysia, Philippines, Thailand.

Appendix
Standard International Trade Classification Revision 1; Product Classifications

3 Mineral fuels, lubricants, and related materials

5 Chemicals

6 Manufactured goods classified chiefly by material
   676 Rails and railway track construction material or iron or steel
   692 Metal containers for storage or transport
   695 Tools for use in the hand or in machines

7 Machinery and transport equipment
   7232 Electrical insulating equipment
   7241 Television broadcast receivers, whether or not combined with gramophone or radio
   7242 Radio broadcast receivers, whether or not combined with gramophone or radio

Consumer Goods (8)			Road Motor Vehicles (732)			Other (9)			Total		
E	I	E − I	E	I	E − I	E	I	E − I	E	I	E − I
10.0	26.7	− 16.7	15.9	29.3	− 13.4	8.5	7.6	0.9	160.1	153.1	7.0
0.6	12.0	− 11.4	0.3	0.1	0.2	0.4	1.4	− 1.0	14.6	25.0	− 10.3
0.2	3.7	− 3.5	—	—	—	0.1	0.3	− 0.2	1.9	5.4	− 3.5
—	0.3	− 0.2	—	—	—	—	—	—	1.1	1.0	0.1
0.1	0.3	− 0.2	0.1	—	0.1	0.1	0.2	− 0.1	2.5	1.8	0.7
—	2.6	− 2.6	—	—	—	—	0.3	− 0.3	2.3	5.1	− 2.8
0.1	4.3	− 4.2	—	—	− 0.0	0.1	0.5	− 0.4	2.5	8.0	− 5.5
—	—	− 0.0	—	—	—	—	—	—	0.8	0.3	0.5
—	0.1	− 0.1	—	—	—	—	—	− 0.0	1.3	1.4	− 0.1
0.1	0.6	− 0.5	—	—	—	—	—	—	1.4	1.3	—
—	0.1	− 0.1	—	—	—	—	—	—	0.8	0.6	0.1
1.1	1.6	− 0.5	2.0	0.3	1.6	0.9	0.6	0.3	20.2	7.6	12.6
0.1	—	0.1	0.1	—	0.1	0.1	—	—	2.0	0.4	1.5
0.1	0.5	− 0.4	0.1	0.1	− 0.0	—	0.1	− 0.0	2.8	1.9	0.9
0.8	1.1	− 0.3	1.7	0.2	1.5	0.8	0.5	0.3	14.0	5.1	8.8
0.1	0.1	—	0.1	—	0.1	0.1	—	—	1.5	0.2	1.3
0.2	1.1	− 0.9	0.2	—	0.2	0.2	0.3	− 0.1	6.8	5.4	1.3

725   Domestic electrical equipment
7292   Electric lamps
7294   Automotive electrical equipment
732   Road motor vehicles
733   Road vehicles other than motor vehicles
7358   Ships, boats, and other vessels for breaking up

8   Miscellaneous manufactured articles
    8121   Central heating apparatus
    861   Scientific, medical, optical, measuring, and controlling instruments and apparatus
    8612   Spectacles and spectacle frames

9   Commodities and transactions not classified according to kind

References

Bradford, C. I., Jr. 1982. The NICs and world economic adjustment, In *The newly industrializing countries: Trade and adjustment,* ed. Louis Turner and Neil McMullen. London: George Allen and Unwin.

Branson, W. H. 1981. Trends in U.S. trade and investment since World War II. In *The American economy in transition,* ed. M. Feldstein. Chicago: University of Chicago Press.

———. 1983. The myth of deindustrialization. *Regulation* 7, no. 5: 23–29, 53–54.

Riedel, J. 1984a. Trade as the engine of growth in developing countries, revisited. *Economic Journal* 94 (March): 56–73.

———. 1984b. The external constraint to long-term growth in developing countries. Trade Policy Research Centre, London. Mimeo.

World Bank. 1983. *World development report, 1983*. London: Oxford University Press.

3 Exports of Manufactures from Developing Countries to the European Community

Jean Waelbroeck

This paper discusses the prospects for manufactured exports from developing countries (the South) to the European Community (EC). Can and will the EC absorb the additional goods which these countries need to export to pay for the imports required for their development? What kinds of products will they sell? What are the commodity groups for which rising Southern exports may cause trade tension?

To investigate these issues, the paper uses a recently developed data bank, created at the initiative of the World Bank. By converting trade and production to a single classification, it is possible to calculate apparent consumption of the various goods and to calculate "market penetration rates" (the ratio of imports to that consumption).

The paper first describes this data base. To provide a comparative setting and to highlight the connection between market shares and protection, the second section compares the trade data of the "Big Three" trading nations: the United States, Japan, and the European Community. (The EC is a "nation" in this paper for linguistic simplicity.) That section examines some large shifts that have occurred in world trade, which have motivated the major trade disputes of recent years. The third section provides evidence that, although the EC is in principle a single trading area with a unified system of protection, countries have managed in practice to retain a good deal of autonomy in trade policy and have quite different degrees of openness to imports from developing countries. The fourth section describes trends in trade for different groups of commodities and assesses the implications of these trends for the future. The paper closes with conclusions.

Jean Waelbroeck is a professor of economics at the Center for Econometrics and Mathematical Economics at the Free University of Brussels, Brussels, Belgium.

3.1 The Data Base

The data base, constructed in the framework of a World Bank research project,[1] provides comparable data on production and trade in eleven developed countries (Sweden, the Federal Republic of Germany, the Netherlands, Belgium-Luxembourg, the United Kingdom, France, Italy, Japan, Australia, Canada, and the United States). The "EC" of the tables accordingly describes the European Community minus Ireland and Denmark.

The figures are obtained by converting all data to the international standard industrial classification (ISIC). For production data, this was done by economists in each country, who processed data organized according to the country's national classification to convert it to the international classification. The trade data were developed by the World Bank's staff by aggregating data from the United Nations' trade tapes to an ISIC basis, organized according to the standard international trade classification (SITC).

In each country, the person responsible used his own judgment and unofficial correspondences that might be available to establish the mode of conversion from the national to the international basis. (In Sweden, the statistical office produces production data on an ISIC basis.) For the trade data, the World Bank used the concordance established by the United Nations (1958) which converts the five-digit SITC to the four-digit ISIC. A number of five-digit ISIC items were created to highlight products that are of particular importance to developing countries, and the United Nations concordance was extended appropriately. This work is currently being transferred to the Organization for Economic Cooperation and Development (OECD).

3.2 The Big Three Trading Nations in the 1970s and Their Trade

To set the South's exports of manufactures to the EC in the right perspective, this section brings together the main facts concerning the exports and imports of these goods by the Big Three trading nations: the United States, Japan, and the EC. A more detailed discussion of the trade of the first two is to be found in the contributions of Branson and Yamazawa in this volume (chaps. 2 and 4).

3.2.1 Market Size and Openness

In 1980 the United States was the largest producer and consumer of manufactures, by a small margin over the EC; the rise of the dollar and the economic recovery in that country since that year have widened the gap. Japan's consumption is roughly half as large as that of the other two (table 3.1).

Table 3.1 Geographic Patterns of Trade in Manufactures of the EC, the United States, and Japan (billions of U.S. Dollars)

	1970						1980					
	EC		U.S.		Japan		EC		U.S.		Japan	
	M	E	M	E	M	E	M	E	M	E	M	E
Total	37.0[a]	53.9[a]	33.1	34.8	8.5	18.9	221.1[a]	295.9[a]	162.0	167.5	48.6	127.4
Southern Europe	2.0	6.0	0.6	1.3	0.1	0.6	19.5	30.8	3.0	4.8	0.5	2.1
East Asian NICs	0.8	1.0	1.8	1.1	0.5	2.6	11.6	7.3	18.2	10.9	6.1	18.6
Latin America	3.0	4.0	3.9	5.7	0.3	1.1	14.1	17.8	22.8	32.2	2.4	8.3
Other developing countries	4.9	10.5	1.4	4.6	1.6	4.5	24.3	87.1	10.5	25.7	10.0	36.2
Developing countries (except S. Eur.)	8.7	15.6	7.2	11.4	2.4	8.2	50.0	112.2	51.4	68.9	18.5	63.1
All developed countries	24.0	28.8	25.1	21.8	5.8	9.8	134.7	132.1	106.2	92.5	28.7	58.8
Socialist countries	2.3	3.4	0.2	0.3	0.3	0.4	16.8	20.9	1.4	1.3	1.0	3.4
EC	46.2	46.2	8.2	8.6	1.4	1.7	275.2	278.2	32.3	38.8	6.8	15.6
ASEAN	0.4	1.2	0.7	0.9	0.2	1.6	5.9	7.0	6.8	7.7	4.0	10.8
	C	P	C	P	C	P	C	P	C	P	C	P
Consumption	403.8		595.9		179.1		1,526.7		1,869.6		7,722.0	
Production		420.7		597.6		189.5		1,601.5		1,875.2		851.0
Imports/consumption	9.16		5.56		4.72		14.48[a]		8.66		6.29	
Exports/production		12.81		5.82		9.99		18.48[a]		8.93		14.97

Note: M = imports; E = exports; C = Consumption; P = Production.

[a]Excluding intra-EC trade.

Trade in manufactures of the United States is nearly in balance, whereas the EC and Japan earn surpluses, which are needed to pay for their large net imports of primary commodities and, in the case of Japan, of services. The European and Japanese surpluses would be even larger if resource-intensive manufactures such as timber and wood products, nonferrous metals, and manufactured foods were excluded from the total.

The EC is the most open of the three "big traders" to imports of manufactures, by a comfortable margin. The United States comes next, and Japan is not as far behind as is sometimes said; it is, however, true that, as a smaller economy, that country would be expected to trade more than the others in relation to its size.

Judging from recent figures on world trade, the gap in openness to trade between the EC and the United States has shrunk since 1980, but this reflects to a large extent the rising American trade deficit. The deficit is due to the unorthodox policies pursued by that country recently. This deficit is in any event not sustainable and reflects temporary factors: strong recovery in the United States at a time when unemployment is still rising in Europe and the overvaluation of the dollar. A return to a more normal balance of trade, which will eventually take place, will reduce imports.

Because Japan's imports of manufactures are low, the trade figures look lopsided, with exports far larger than imports. Although in dollar terms, the EC and Japanese surpluses in manufactures are roughly equal, the ratios of those surpluses to imports are sharply different. The ratio was 162% in Japan in 1980, a year in which the surplus in the EC amounted to 34% of imports.

3.2.2 The Geographical Pattern of Trade

Table 3.1 illustrates the polarization of trade according to proximity. Latin America trades predominantly with the United States; southern Europe and the European centrally planned economies (CPE) with the EC; and the Asian newly industrializing countries (NICs) and the Association of South East Asian Nations (ASEAN) with Japan. A curious "backyard effect" is to be noted in each case. With the exception of the EC's trade with the CPEs, which is subject to agreements prescribing bilateral balance, trade of the Big Three with their hinterlands yields exceptionally large surpluses.

A striking feature is the growing trading strength of developing countries. Both their exports to and their imports from the Big Three have been rising rapidly. Trade of the South with the Big Three rose from being equivalent to 46% of the latter's trade with developed countries in 1970 to 66% of that total ten years later. The developing countries remain large net importers of manufactures. These net imports grew with trade: the ratio of imports to exports did not change markedly. In net terms, the South has continued to be a net creator of manufacturing jobs in the developed countries: its import needs have helped to slow down deindustrialization.

The countries of East Asia have played a significant but by no means exclusive role in bringing about this change. In terms of fractions of the Big Three's trade with developed countries, the trade of the East Asian NICs and ASEAN grew from 6.8% and 5.0% to 13.1% and 7.6%, respectively.

As noted by Branson in chapter 2 of this volume, U.S. trade with the NICs of Latin America and Asia has increased considerably. These countries have built up strong industrial sectors and have become significant exporters of manufactures. The EC's trade is oriented quite differently. The countries of Africa and OPEC, which make up most of the category "other developing countries" in table 3.1, play the dominant role. Such an orientation is easy to understand in terms of geography and past colonial links. Because of this, however, the EC trades mainly with countries which are not yet significant exporters of manufactured goods.

These is much vague talk in Europe about the NICs and the problems which they will cause, but the figures show that at present they do not matter much to the EC. This situation will not last. The NICs are growing fast, and they are being joined by the "new NICs" in Asia and in the Mediterranean area, for example. The EC cannot escape from their trade dynamism and its consequences and should begin to think with care about issues of reciprocity in trade, which are a critical element of present policy debate in the United States. More active discussion is needed about the best ways for the EC to both adjust to and benefit from the rapid economic growth of the NICs.

3.2.3 Patterns of Specialization in International Trade

There is not much difference in production patterns in the three countries (tables 3.2–3.4). Patterns of apparent consumption are even more similar.

With respect to trade, the large share of steel and other metal goods in Japanese exports is to be noted. These goods are energy-intensive, and the energy embodied in these exports is another reason why Japan has such a strong need to earn an export surplus in manufactures.

The EC is a larger net exporter of metal goods, though the magnitude is no larger than Japan's. The chemical industry is the EC's other major net earner of foreign exchange. Net exports of steel remain considerable. They have, however, ceased to have a rationale in terms of comparative advantage and remain high only thanks to the extremely heavy subsidies which member country governments grant to EC producers

Table 3.2   **Patterns of Production and Trade in the European Community**
(1980, billions of U.S. dollars, intra-EC trade excluded)

	1970			1980		
	P	M	E	P	M	E
31 Food, drink, tobacco	72.4	7.6	3.1	271.2	27.8	20.1
32 Textiles, clothing, leather	43.0	2.7	4.9	113.7	24.8	18.8
321 Textiles	26.2	1.5	3.1	66.2	10.1	10.3
322 Clothing	10.6	0.8	0.9	30.6	10.7	4.8
324 Shoes	3.9	0.1	0.6	9.8	1.8	2.0
33 Wood	11.8	1.9	0.4	47.8	10.1	3.1
34 Pulp paper	23.0	2.8	1.1	83.9	11.9	5.2
35 Chemicals	66.4	4.2	9.5	337.8	38.3	62.3
36 Nonmetallic products	15.9	0.4	0.3	57.9	2.5	2.1
371 Steel	32.6	1.8	4.1	99.7	7.3	17.8
372 Nonferrous metals	10.8	4.8	1.4	34.4	15.2	7.7
38 Metal products	141.1	9.9	27.2	541.4	73.2	144.2
382 Nonelectrical machinery	42.5	3.9	10.6	156.3	22.5	54.2
383 Electrical machinery	29.2	1.9	4.3	109.5	16.2	23.4
384 Transport equipment	38.1	2.0	8.9	174.0	20.7	45.5
39 Other manufactures	3.6	1.0	1.2	13.9	10.1	9.7
3 All manufactures	420.7	37.0	53.9	1,601.9	221.1	295.9

Note: P = production; M = imports; E = exports.

Table 3.3   **Patterns of Production and Trade in the United States**
(1980, billions of U.S. dollars)

	1970			1980		
	P	M	E	P	M	E
31 Food, drink, tobacco	97.0	4.8	2.6	292.3	15.6	12.5
32 Textiles, clothing, leather	49.6	3.2	1.0	105.7	13.0	5.7
321 Textiles	26.1	1.2	0.7	61.9	2.6	3.9
322 Clothing	18.6	1.3	0.2	35.8	7.0	1.2
324 Shoes	1.7	0.2	0.1	3.7	1.1	0.5
33 Wood	17.1	1.1	0.4	51.1	4.9	2.4
34 Pulp paper	49.0	1.7	1.5	140.0	6.1	5.9
35 Chemicals	87.5	3.8	5.2	457.0	26.5	29.7
36 Nonmetallic products	16.0	0.5	0.4	44.0	2.3	1.9
371 Steel	28.9	2.1	1.3	95.1	8.6	3.3
372 Nonferrous metals	16.6	1.8	1.0	48.2	8.0	5.5
38 Metal products	228.0	13.1	21.0	662.7	72.0	97.9
382 Nonelectrical machinery	59.2	2.6	8.2	159.8	14.6	38.7
383 Electrical machinery	43.8	2.5	2.6	94.8	15.4	13.0
384 Transport equipment	76.8	6.6	7.4	221.4	33.5	32.4
39 Other manufactures	8.0	1.0	0.4	19.2	4.9	2.8
3 All manufactures	597.6	33.1	34.8	1,875.2	162.0	167.5

Note: P = production; M = imports; E = exports.

Table 3.4   **Patterns of Production and Trade in Japan**
(1980, billions of U.S. dollars)

	1970			1980		
	P	M	E	P	M	E
31 Food, drink, tobacco	22.2	1.1	0.5	116.9	7.2	1.4
32 Textiles, clothing, leather	14.2	0.5	2.4	50.2	4.2	6.0
321 Textiles	11.0	0.4	1.8	32.6	2.2	5.2
322 Clothing	2.3	0.0	0.4	13.0	1.5	0.5
324 Shoes	0.4	0.0	0.1	2.1	0.2	0.0
33 Wood	8.5	0.3	0.2	32.6	2.6	0.3
34 Paper	10.6	0.3	0.2	48.0	1.8	1.0
35 Chemicals	26.1	1.8	2.0	16.3	13.7	11.2
36 Nonmetallic products	6.8	0.1	0.4	31.4	0.4	1.9
371 Steel	17.3	0.3	2.9	64.1	0.9	15.8
372 Nonferrous metals	5.3	1.0	0.3	12.8	5.0	2.0
38 Metal products	76.3	2.8	9.6	320.2	11.5	85.6
382 Nonelectrical machinery	19.2	1.2	1.9	70.8	3.5	17.3
383 Electrical machinery	19.5	0.4	2.7	76.0	2.3	21.6
384 Transport equipment	19.5	0.5	3.6	98.6	2.6	35.7
39 Other manufactures	2.4	0.2	0.5	12.1	1.2	2.2
3 All manufactures	189.5	8.5	18.9	851.0	48.6	127.4

Note: P = production; M = imports; E = exports.

and to the strict import restrictions which the European Commission administers. These exports are bound to dwindle. Will the EC allow itself to become one day a large net importer of steel, as the United States has done?

For textile and clothing products, a sensitive item in trade, the EC is more open than the United States. This may be due to the fact that the EC tightened its control of these exports only in 1977, several years later than the United States.

The United States of America is in balance for chemicals and in deficit for everything else except metal goods and electrical equipment, the net exports of which cover the other deficits.

3.2.4   Changes in Trade Shares and International Economic Conflicts

There have been important changes in the trade profiles of the Big Three in the 1970s, which have motivated trade tensions. Tables 3.2–3.4 reveal two such changes. Similar shifts in the future will bring about equally strong pressures for protection.

One such change has been the extraordinary expansion of Japanese exports of capital goods, in particular of steel, metal goods, and transport equipment. Other countries have reacted to this by demanding that Japan agree to implement voluntary export restraints (VER). The other is the sharp deterioration of the three major trading countries' trade balances for textiles and even more for clothing, which reflects the surge of exports by NICs; this led the developed countries to impose on the developing countries the Multi-Fiber Arrangement (MFA).

Even Japan's trade reflects this shift in international specialization, though it is interesting to note that as late as 1980, there was still a textiles and clothing export surplus, a surplus which has provided that country with foreign exchange throughout much of its recent history (in fact, as late as 1984, Japan was still being "called" by the United States to reduce exports of particular types of textiles, and as late as 1982, Japan was a larger net exporter of textiles and clothing than Hong Kong). The surplus for "other manufactures" is another reminder of a pattern of comparative advantage which prevailed when Japan was still a low-wage country.

3.2.5 Bilateral Balances and Trade Bargaining

The imbalance in Japan's trade in manufactures has evoked a good deal of criticism and has often been quoted as proof that this country operates an occult system of trade protection. It has contributed in this way to the trade tensions of the decade.

Why should this be considered a problem? Economics tells us that there is no reason to demand that trade balance bilaterally for goods and services overall, and even less that it should achieve this for one category of goods, such as manufactures. Two hundred years after Adam Smith, however, the mercantilist illusion is still strong in the minds of both the public and trade negotiators, who tend to feel that partners with whom their countries have unfavorable trade balances are somehow causing harm. It also happens to be true that when two countries trade together, the one which is in deficit has a bargaining edge, because it can credibly threaten to limit imports from its partner, confident that its partner will not be able to inflict upon it equivalent harm by retaliating. Japan's lopsided trade with other developed countries has for this reason weakened its bargaining position and helped to maintain that country in something of a pariah status in the international trading community. The Japanese export surplus with developing countries is even larger of course; it causes considerable resentment in the more advanced ones and even brought about a small trade war with Taiwan.

Could the situation be changed by appropriate Japanese policies? There is no quick remedy. As indicated, that country needs its export surplus in manufactures. What could be envisaged would at best be a parallel rise of both exports and imports of manufactures. This increase would have to be very large to bring the import/export ratio close to the kind of rough balance registered by the EC, for example. Japan's partners, however, would probably be content with a rapid and matching growth of both exports and imports, which has not been taking place.

The East Asian NICs also have been building up a large surplus in their manufactures trade with the EC and the United States. This weakens their bargaining power for the same reason. This bargaining power is also affected by such political factors as the uncertain international position of Taiwan, South Korea's dependence on U.S. military aid, Hong Kong's status as a British colony that will be ruled by China in 1997.

Other developing countries are fortunately in a better position from the point of view of bargaining, as nearly all of them import much more manufactures from developed countries than they export to them. As they begin to export manufactures, they are confronting partners who need the outlets which they offer; countries such as Thailand and Indonesia have begun to use the threat of cutting down access to their markets to fend off protectionist threats to key exports; the current debt situation has been used as an argument for moderate protection in the United States.

3.2.6 Are Exports from the South Reaching Market Limits?

It is frequently asserted that, although the manufactured exports of developing countries grew spectacularly in the past, they are now reaching limits which will slow their progress in the future. Table 3.5 examines changes of rates of market penetration by developing countries into the EC, the United States of America, and Japan. The striking finding is that these rates are still very low, except for textiles and clothing and miscellaneous manufactured goods. The table suggests that developing countries are still far from having reached what could reasonably be thought of as a market ceiling to their exports to the developed countries; the room for further expansion appears to be enormous if they can increase and diversify supply.[2]

The figures also do away with the widespread idea that competition from the NICs has been a major cause of unemployment: the market penetration rates are so low that the gross number of workers displaced cannot have amounted to a significant fraction of the labor force (as explained above, in net terms developing countries have created industrial jobs).

It could be argued that the low level of market penetration rates by developing countries into the Big Three traders is an artifact reflecting undue aggregation of the data in the tables. It could be true that those countries are competitive only for a limited number of products, spread over a broad range of SITC items. Market penetration rates would then

Table 3.5 Trade of the EC, the United States, and Japan with Less-developed Countries, excluding Southern Europe (billions of U.S. dollars)

		1970						1980					
		Imports			Penetration Rate[a]			Imports			Penetration Rate[a]		
		EC	U.S.	Japan	EC	U.S.	Japan	EC	U.S.	Japan	EC	U.S.	Japan
31	Food, drink, tobacco	3.5	2.5	0.5	4.4	2.5	2.2	12.6	8.7	2.6	4.5	2.9	2.2
32	Textiles, clothing, leather	1.0	1.1	0.3	2.5	2.1	2.3	11.2	9.5	2.6	9.4	8.4	5.4
321	Textiles	0.5	0.4	0.2	2.1	1.3	2.1	3.8	1.3	1.3	5.7	2.1	4.3
322	Clothing	0.3	0.6	0.1	3.1	3.3	3.1	5.6	6.1	1.1	15.3	14.7	7.6
324	Shoes	0.0	0.0	0.0	1.1	1.0	0.7	0.7	1.3	0.2	7.0	20.4	6.9
33	Wood	0.3	0.3	0.1	1.9	1.5	1.0	2.1	1.4	0.7	3.8	2.7	1.0
34	Paper	0.0	0.0	0.0	0.1	0.0	0.1	0.47	0.3	0.2	0.5	0.2	0.4
35	Chemicals, petroleum, rubber	0.6	1.7	0.7	0.9	2.0	2.6	10.3	13.7	7.4	3.3	3.0	4.5
3511	Base chemicals	0.2	0.1	0.0	1.3	0.9	0.8	1.5	0.7	0.5	2.9	1.0	2.1
353	Refined petroleum	0.2	1.3	0.6	1.5	5.4	12.4	7.6	10.9	6.4	6.8	5.1	10.6
356	Plastic goods	0.0	0.2	0.0	0.7	2.4	0.1	0.5	1.1	0.3	1.8	3.1	0.4
36	Nonmetallic products	0.0	0.0	0.0	0.0	0.3	0.1	0.3	0.4	0.1	0.5	0.9	0.3
371	Steel	0.2	0.07	0.07	0.6	0.2	0.5	0.8	1.0	0.5	0.9	1.0	1.1
372	Nonferrous metals	2.2	0.5	0.6	15.8	3.0	9.7	5.2	2.6	2.3	12.4	5.1	14.4
38	Metal products	0.5	0.7	0.1	0.4	0.3	0.1	8.7	11.8	1.5	1.8	2.0	0.6
39	Other manufactures	0.6	0.3	0.1	16.9	3.8	2.8	6.2	2.1	0.5	41.2	10.0	4.5
3	All manufactures	3.7	7.2	2.4	2.2	1.2	1.3	50.0	51.4	18.5	3.3	2.8	2.4

[a]Imports as percentage of apparent consumption.

be low for the aggregates just discussed and yet be quite high for the products which developing countries are capable of exporting. It is worthwhile to look at more detailed data. Table 3.6 lists the goods for which the rate of market penetration is 10% or more, at the finest level of disaggregation available (four or five digits ISIC).

The detailed table confirms the earlier conclusions. More than half the items are textiles and clothing products, a group where the market penetration rate is high at an aggregated level. Three are food products, which are vulnerable to the agricultural protectionism that is rampant throughout the world. Others (nonferrous metals, jewelry including diamonds, and leather) are largely raw materials. These have usually been subjected to protection only to a limited extent; as such products tend to have rather perfect markets and the developing-countries' share is not high in most cases, they are not threatened by market saturation constraints (the case of diamonds, subject to marketing decisions of the Diamond Trading Corporation cartel, is discussed below). The table does not reveal any unsuspected danger points: the conclusion stands that there is a good deal of room for increase of exports of manufactures from developing to developed countries provided that developing countries, as they have managed to do up to now, are flexible enough to shift to new products as some existing markets close up.

3.3   The EC Common Commercial Policy, the Trade Policies of Member Countries of the EC, and the Design of Trade Policies for Developing Countries

Does the EC offer to developing countries a unified market? Does the EC have a trade policy of its own? Given the threat of protection, it is important for developing countries to give thought to identifying the most effective negotiating strategy in dealing with the EC.

In principle, what the EC offers to developing countries is indeed a common market. There is a common external tariff. Most of the overt quantitative restrictions which existed in 1958 when the Rome Treaty was signed have been abolished. The European Commission represents member country governments in negotiations. To regard the Community as an entity for purposes of trade negotiations would seem the right basis for policy thinking.

A closer look reveals, however, that member countries retain a good deal of freedom to control access to their markets. Of the few import quotas which these countries still administer, some are important, for example, those for automobiles in Italy and for consumer electronics in some countries. Even the Multi-Fiber Arrangement and the steel import restraints administered by the commission under Article 58 of the Rome Treaty provide for national import quotas and leave to the

Table 3.6 **High Market Penetration Items in Developed-Country Imports* from Developing Countries** (imports as percentage of apparent consumption)

	EC		United States		Japan	
	1970	1980	1970	1980	1970	1980
3115 Vegetable and animal oils and fats	17.8	20.3	2.6	2.2	6.4	5.5
3116 Grain products	21.5	24.0	20.0	18.6	7.3	8.7
3118 Sugar products	9.9	11.5	23.1	18.4	18.6	39.4
3211-1 Cotton fabrics	6.1	14.3	2.5	7.3	1.8	5.0
3211-7 Fiber for textile use	13.0	21.9	10.0	31.5	7.5	7.3
3214-1 Knotted carpets	56.8	59.2	6.7	59.1	0.4	2.2
3215 Cordage, rope, twine	0.7	12.6	10.0	17.3	0.5	1.8
3220-2 Women's, girls', infants' apparel	1.6	14.1	1.4	9.9	1.6	3.1
3220-3 Underwear	4.0	15.0	4.9	19.3	2.1	9.9
3220-4 Leather apparel	5.3	32.7	6.5	31.7	1.4	22.6
3220-5 Headgear	3.7	13.3	2.2	20.1	3.3	5.6
3220-6 Knitted apparel	17.9	50.3	33.7	77.1	37.8	36.0
3231 Tanned, finished leather	9.5	13.9	3.7	7.6	4.7	7.3
3232 Furs	7.3	21.1	1.2	4.1	16.6	9.8
3233 Manufactured leather	1.4	17.3	4.8	26.0	1.5	1.6
3240 Footwear	1.0	7.0	1.0	20.4	0.7	6.9
3720-3 Other nonferrous metals	33.7	28.3	3.9	6.3	23.5	29.5
3853 Watches and clocks	0.5	23.6	0.6	17.9	0.4	5.1
3901 Jewelry	79.6	111.8	3.0	11.7	11.7	18.1
3909-2 Toys, ornaments	5.2	16.9	2.0	16.3	1.6	4.8

Note: Southern Europe is not included in the developing world.

discretion of member countries some important decisions about imports. Subsidies to producers are a very important form of "nonborder protection"; except for agricultural products, they are granted almost exclusively at the discretion of individual governments, though the commission can and does try to limit them, to the extent that "political realities" make this feasible.

It should also be remembered that it is the member countries who, in the EC Council, set down the instructions which define the commission's bargaining stance on such occasions as the renewal of the MFA. These terms of reference, often agreed to after an excruciatingly slow debate in the EC Council, tend to be so rigid that there is little choice for the other party: they must agree or face the risk of a trade war.

All of this suggests that if developing countries are to be successful in increasing exports at the rate which their development requires, they should start from the premise that the effective decision makers for trade policy remain member country governments. The EC procedures are basically a convenient way of pooling the member countries' bargaining power. It is to the task of persuading these governments to accept their exports that they should devote their main efforts.

The figures provided in table 3.7 in fact suggest that twenty-six years after the Rome Treaty was signed, the various national markets in the EC are not yet equally open to developing nations. It will be argued here that these differences reflect structural factors only to a limited extent. The main reason for the differences in openness is the control which governments continue to exercise on accesss to domestic markets.

We start with a discussion of differences which reflect structural factors. The Dutch and Belgian figures for imports of textiles and clothing are a clear example of this. Benelux is a single trading area from the point of view of the administration of the EC MFA regulations, yet developing countries have achieved much higher penetration of the Dutch than of the Belgian market. This is because of the greater strength of the Belgian industry. The large United Kingdom and Belgian imports of "other manufactures" are dominated by diamonds, which the former redistributes to diamond cutters throughout the world, while the latter does the processing itself. Belgium's imports of nonferrous metals reflect historical links with Zaire, which are gradually getting weaker. The Netherlands, a large producer of animal feeds and products made from vegetable oils, imports for this reason large quantities of cassava pellets, oilseed cakes, and oils, which account for its large imports of "food, drink, and tobacco."

Country trade policies are clearly also at work however: the remarkable match between the figures on openness of different markets

Table 3.7   Openness of Different EC Countries to Imports from developing Countries (imports as % of apparent consumption)

	Federal Republic of Germany		Belgium		Netherlands		France		United Kingdom		Italy	
	1970	1980	1970	1980	1970	1980	1970	1980	1970	1980	1970	1980
31 Food, drink, tobacco	5.4	5.5	6.4	5.1	8.3	8.3	4.1	4.2	3.5	2.9	3.4	4.3
32 Textiles, clothing, leather (including shoes)	2.6	11.2	2.5	9.9	3.3	15.2	1.1	5.7	4.1	10.4	1.9	7.9
35 Chemicals	0.5	2.5	0.8	5.4	3.9	9.3	3.9	2.8	1.9	1.6	9.6	5.3
372 Nonferrous metals	9.8	10.9	138.9	44.6	9.4	9.8	10.3	7.8	14.6	12.6	21.3	14.6
38 Metal products	0.2	2.2	0.4	1.2	2.4	2.1	0.1	1.0	0.6	3.0	0.2	1.1
39 Other manufactures	7.3	8.8	300	34.5	111.1	12.3	2.2	7.5	69.3	160.0	2.2	28.3
3 All manufactures	1.8	3.4	5.2	5.1	4.3	6.0	1.6	2	2.8	2.5	1.6	3.6

Note: Southern Europe is not included in the developing world.

in table 3.7 and what is known of the underlying trade policy stance of different countries cannot be accidental.

Who the protectionist and nonprotectionist members of the EC are is not difficult to find out: the EC Council alignment in debates of trade policy for manufactures never varies. The Netherlands, the Federal Republic of Germany, and Denmark are for free trade, and the United Kingdom, France, and Italy for a restrictive policy, with Belgium liking protection instinctively but held back by Benelux loyalties. These attitudes are remarkably immune to political shifts. It had been feared that France would become even more protectionist when a popular-front government was elected which advocated "reconquest of the domestic market," but this did not happen; the liberal convictions of Britain's Mrs. Thatcher should have tilted that country's attitude in favor of free trade, but this turned out not to be true. Trade policy appears to reflect a kind of modus vivendi between interest groups, the bureaucracy, and what in France is called the "political class," which does not depend very much on the changing fortunes of parties.

The match between openness and trade policy preference is quite apparent in the figures for imports of "textiles, clothing, leather." These imports are influenced by key decisions on administration of the MFA, which individual governments continue to control, and are also affected by the VER agreements for shoes which some governments have negotiated outside the EC framework. France is by a substantial margin the most closed country, while the Federal Republic of Germany and the Netherlands are very open.

It is particularly interesting to notice that the United Kingdom, which was relatively open to imports from the South in 1970, became relatively closed ten years later. In the early postwar years, that country accepted very liberally imports of manufactures from the Commonwealth members of the developing world, but its import policy has gradually become more restrictive. In recent years, it has been exercising to the fullest possible extent its rights to limit imports under the EC version of the MFA and has in addition pressured low-wage suppliers into accepting VER agreements for such goods as television sets and shoes. The low growth of U.K. imports in the table reflects this gradual policy shift.

The key to success in trade negotiations is to apply diplomacy at the right time and to the right target. Developing countries feel that they have so far been doing poorly in disputes with the EC. Perhaps they would do better if they used their power of persuasion and bargaining strength to deal with the true source of their problems: the countries who in the EC Council argue most strongly in favor of restrictions to their exports.

3.4 The Comparative Advantage of the South in the EC Market: An Attempt at a Diagnosis

This section examines in detail the export performance of developing countries with respect to the EC market. An attempt is made to identify the products for which developing countries have a comparative advantage and to assess the risk that exploitation of this advantage will be thwarted by protection. The judgment will draw on the work of the European Group for Research on Protection, organized in the framework of the World Bank research project on which this paper is based.[3]

The largest group of the manufactured exports from developing countries to the EC has traditionally consisted of resource-intensive products, a consequence of Europe's lack of natural resources. Most of the other exports consist of unskilled-labor-intensive products, again reflecting the relative conditions in developing countries and in Europe. Physical capital intensity, on the other hand, does appear to have a clear-cut impact on the competitiveness of the South. Perhaps, in contrast to the human sort, this capital is mobile enough to equalize returns across countries, so that the amount available does not influence costs of production to an appreciable extent.[4]

There have been indications in recent years that the more advanced of the NICs have been acquiring a comparative advantage for the products of yet a third group of industries. These are sectors characterized by large-scale production, mature technology (which is thus more readily acquired than that of other sectors), and automation (which has made irrelevant labor skills that used to be vital to production). The chief examples are the shipbuilding, steel, and automobile industries. The main constraint is that a high level of industrial competence is required for competitive production—the developing world is strewn with inefficient steel mills, which were built for national pride or because it was believed that they would turn out to be poles of growth for other industries.

These three industries require quite a bit of capital but also much labor. The large size of plants has meant that, in developed countries, unions are very strong and in these plants, which have far above average wage levels and/or a great deal of job padding; these "endogenous distortions," as Bhagwati's (1971) well-known classification labels them, have provided countries where unions are not so powerful or where, as in Japan, they cooperate better with employers with a clear-cut comparative advantage in these industries.

Most of the discussion in this section is devoted to the first two sources of comparative advantage. A brief subsection is devoted to the third.

3.4.1   Simply Transformed Primary Products

About half of developing-countries' exports of manufactures to the developed countries have traditionally been made up of primary products, exported after simple processing, which in most cases added little value to the goods. Such products are manufactures only statistically. (This of course does not mean that their export is less worthwhile than that of "true manufactured goods.") Table 3.8 provides data on these exports.

This category is dominated by three categories of products—vegetable oils and fats, nonferrous metals, and jewelry (largely diamonds)—which together account for two-thirds of the total. Imports of forest products have been growing particularly quickly, a trend which can be expected to continue as more and more developing countries decide to prohibit export of timber in the round. Basic chemicals are included in the table because developing countries tend to sell largely crude or barely elaborated products. Basic chemical sales have tended to grow quite quickly, and there exists a potential for quite a lot more growth if developing countries are quick to seize market opportunities.

The table suggests that the share of crudely elaborated materials in the South's exports of manufactures has not been decreasing. This category accounted for 55% of developing-countries' exports to the EC in 1970; by 1980 the proportion was 53%, a negligible drop.

This apparent stability is misleading, however. Refined petroleum should be considered separately. Here the extremely quick growth of

Table 3.8   **"Barely Transformed Primary Products" in EC Imports of Manufactures from Developing Countries**
(millions of U.S. Dollars)

		Imports		Penetration Rate[a]	
		1970	1980	1970	1980
3115	Vegetable and animal oils and fats	842	3,183	17.8	20.3
3118	Sugar products	284	1,084	9.9	11.5
3211-7	Fiber for textile use	94	380	13.0	21.9
3231	Tanned, finished leather	114	572	9.5	13.9
3311-1	Sawn lumber, etc.	167	1,208	6.1	11.9
3311-2	Veneer plywood, etc.	62	461	5.4	10.4
3511	Basic chemicals	196	1,527	2.0	2.9
353	Refined petroleum	220	7,596	1.5	6.8
3720	Nonferrous metals	2,223	5,175	15.8	12.4
3901	Jewelry	559	5,284	79.6	111.8
Total		4,761	26,470		

Note: Southern Europe is not included in the developing world.
[a]Imports as percentage of apparent consumption.

oil exports is to a large extent a price phenomenon. The efforts of oil-exporting countries to refine their own oil were another contributing factor. Removing oil from the total focuses attention on the products which are of interest mainly to oil-importing developing countries. When this is done, the proportion of crudely elaborated materials in developing-country exports to the EC changes to 52% in 1970 and to 38% in 1980, a substantial drop. Resource-based manufactures have thus accounted for a steadily falling fraction of the South's exports of manufactured goods to the EC.

Sales of most of those commodities are supply, rather than demand, determined. An exceptions is sugar, the export of which is narrowly restricted by the EC's Common Agricultural Policy and by the Lome Agreement, which allow a limited number of African and Caribbean countries to export to the EC fixed quantities of a good of which the EC is a very large net exporter: this is an artificial trade which will not expand. For diamonds, sales are controlled by the Diamond Trading Corporation cartel, but countries that find new deposits have always obtained quotas for the newly obtained output: here supply is what determines exports. Protection of vegetable oils may increase as the EC seeks to find room for Spanish olive oil after that country joins the EC—but a long transition period will postpone the problem for quite a few years. Here the United States is both a powerful competitor of developing-country vegetable oil exporters and a strong ally, which has so far been able to use its bargaining power to prevent higher protection.

3.4.2   Unskilled-Labor-Intensive Products

Textiles, Clothing, Shoes

Exports of textiles, clothing, and shoes account for a fifth of the exports of manufactures by developing countries to the developed countries and have been another mainstay of their export drive. These are the exports hit hardest by protection. The system of restriction contained in the MFA for textiles and clothing is very elaborate. In addition, the EC has concluded agreements outside the MFA with Mediterranean countries and with prospective EC entrants; these have been somewhat more generous, especially the agreements with the latter countries. Lome countries (former colonies in Africa and islands in the Caribbean and the Pacific) are also treated separately. They are not yet significant exporters, and in most cases the EC has not bothered to impose elaborate agreements. They do not enjoy a privileged market access, however. As soon as Mauritius, a Lome country, managed to develop small exports of some textiles and clothing articles, it found that it had to limit its exports to the EC.

How watertight is the system? It is in principle very restrictive, but there are loopholes and safety valves.

The VER agreements define ceilings to the quantities that may be exported. However, countries may increase the value of their exports by exporting higher-quality or more highly processed goods, a shift that can increase the unit value of exports severalfold.

Also, the smaller and newer exporters of textiles and clothing are less tightly controlled than Korea, Taiwan and Hong Kong, the so-called textile NICs. Most of the secondary exporters do not use their quotas fully—India is notorious as a country that is not competitive enough to use its quotas, in spite of wages that are among the lowest in the world. Fairly rapid growth is possible for such secondary exporters if they find ways of exporting successfully on a world market where competition is very hard; an easy way to do so is to invite foreign direct investment from the textile NICs, as Sri Lanka and Mauritius have done, for example.

The EC's agreements with Mediterranean countries are not as watertight as the others, and those countries have benefited from higher permitted growth rates of exports and from looser agreements. Turkey—a prospective entrant—has refused quite successfully to sign any general agreement and has gone on to build up exports using every trick in the rule book and some which the book does not describe. Of course, a good deal of cheating goes on, only a small fraction of which is detected.

An interesting way of viewing the MFA is to regard it as a kind of customs union that shelters the developed market economies behind a common wall of protection. The situation is quite clear-cut. There are special cases as always. Japan is one: it is a "developed country" that does not make use of its MFA rights and is "called," like a developing country, to restrict exports to the United States. Switzerland does not protect its market by quotas or VER agreements, though it does nmake use of more informal protective devices. Apart from such cases, the customs union interpretation is valid. The world is indeed split between a protected market sheltered by discriminatory protection and an "open" market elsewhere, where tariff walls may be very high but are not discriminatory.

Trade theory leads us to expect that such a union should affect trade in well-defined ways. If the discriminatory protection is effective, exports of the customs union producers to third countries should drop if protection increases, as it raises prices on the protected market above the world level; union producers should obtain a rising share of the union's imports as trade diversion occurs. Has this happened?

MFA protection was tightened a great deal during the 1970s: the "customs union of rich countries" has become more closed to the outside world. Yet table 3.9 does not reveal the strong changes in the orientation of trade flows that would be expected. There was a swift growth of imports from low-wage countries into the EC but also of

Table 3.9   EC Trade in MFA Goods (millions of U.S. dollars)

	1970				1980			
	Textiles		Clothing		Textiles		Clothing	
	User	Source	User	Source	User	Source	User	Source
Exports/imports								
Developed countries[a]	1,823	740	625	220	5,079	4,363	3,246	1,615
Developing countries[b]	1,261	770	237	550	5,237	5,780	1,516	9,129
Total	3,084	1,510	862	770	10,336	10,143	4,762	10,744
Apparent consumption of respective product	24,602	26,179	10,487	10,579	66,007	66,200	36,541	30,559

[a]Developed countries, excluding southern Europe and intra-EC trade, as users of EC textile and clothing exports and source of textile and clothing imports into the EC.

[b]Developing countries, including southern Europe and CPEs, as users of EC textile and clothing exports and source of textile and clothing imports into the EC.

exports to that part of the world. For textiles, in fact, EC exports to the "open" market grew even faster than exports to the protected one. The latter result is especially surprising: it implies that even today, EC producers remain able to compete on world markets for many products: adaptation to a more open trading system should be possible and perhaps not difficult for these firms. It is true that for the so-called highly sensitive goods, the competitive edge of the textile NICs remains overwhelming. But the rates of market penetration for these goods are quite high already: much of the adjustment that would result from more open trade has already taken place.

There is a good deal of "water" in the MFA system, therefore; some of the protection that a busy and politically powerful industry lobby has won is not really needed.

It is interesting to speculate that the lack of impact of protection on trade flows also reflects a decline in the comparative advantage of the textile NICs for their traditional products. This would be the result of both technological and economic changes. The textiles industry has been undergoing extraordinary technological change, which has slowly turned it into an industry that is quite capital-intensive, thanks to automation, which made it possible for workers to supervise even greater numbers of spinning and weaving looms. Cheap labor is less important for competitiveness than it used to be. A similar revolution is beginning today in the clothing industry (especially for the standardized products, where the competitive strength of low-wage producers has been greatest) as computer-controlled devices begin to be widespread.

Very swift economic change is reinforcing the effect of this technological revolution. Wages in the textile NICs have risen dramatically: the wage rate in Korea, a country that was as poor as India thirty-five years ago, exceeded that in Portugal by 50% in 1983; the wage rate in the other textile NICs was similar. Yet Portugal has been accepted as a member of the EC—though not without a transition period that shields other EC producers from its exports.

From an economic point of view, the present time seems to offer a unique opportunity to experiment with liberalization of textiles and clothing imports. The next renegotiation of the MFA would be the right time for this. The textiles and clothing lobby has acquired such political power over the years, however, that it would be risky to plan on even limited trade liberalization in textiles and clothing.

Table 3.10 provides more detailed information on the pattern of EC trade for textiles, clothing, and shoes. A first question is inspired by Balassa's (1979) concept of "stages of comparative advantage," according to which countries that start on the road to development begin by exporting simple unskilled-labor-intensive goods and then shift to products that embody more human and physical capital as development

Table 3.10   **Percentage of Imports in Apparent Consumption in the EC**

	Textiles			Clothing			Shoes		
	1970	1975	1980	1970	1975	1980	1970	1975	1980
East Asian NICs	0.43	0.85	0.99	2.70	7.01	9.32	0.72	1.25	4.01
Other developing countries[a]	1.67	2.59	4.74	0.40	1.98	6.02	0.27	1.13	2.98
Southern Europe	0.70	1.39	2.40	1.34	4.57	7.07	0.83	3.59	5.85
Italy	1.99	2.98	3.88	5.19	6.05	8.42	6.88	15.13	21.50
Japan	0.30	0.24	0.50	0.24	0.13	1.65	0.14	0.10	0.04
Other suppliers	94.91	91.95	87.49	90.13	80.26	67.52	91.16	78.79	65.62

[a]Excluding southern Europe.

increases their endowment of those factors. This opens the way for countries that begin to develop later to take over the markets relinquished by their seniors.

Has the process been working? For the EC market, at least, the answer so far is negative. Even today the textile NICs can produce textiles and clothing at lower cost than other developing countries, the very great majority of which have not managed to exploit the competitive edge that their lower wage levels might provide. That the exports of the textile NICs grew less than those of other developing countries is due to stricter protection.

Could it be that when they began to enter world markets, their own success was eased by a conveniently timed withdrawal of Japan, which by that time was ceasing to be a low-wage country? The figures do not suggest this. The Japanese withdrawal from the European market was complete in 1970, whereas the major increase in developing-country exports of textile and clothing articles took place after that date.

The hypothesis might perhaps be vindicated by a more disaggregated look. Both Japan and the textile NICs have shifted to higher-quality goods as their industrial skills grew; they have been encouraged to do so both by the working of market forces and by the fact that trade restrictions have been specified in quantities, so that it was profitable to export goods with higher unit values. It is possible that this strategy is leaving open easy "beginners' markets," facilitating the market entry of less experienced exporters today, such as China for instance. The low unit values of Chinese exports would suggest this. Verifying this conjecture would constitute an interesting research project.

Another question on which the table is designed to shed light is the degree to which trade diversion may have been caused by trade restraints. The tightening of MFA controls by the EC in 1977 was a boon to Italy, the lowest-wage country in the EC and an efficient producer of textiles and clothing. Table 3.10 illustrates the sharp export gains achieved by that country between 1975 and 1980. Trade diversion to low-wage member countries can be expected to increase with the entry of Greece, Portugal, and Spain into the EC. Greece, which conducted a very protectionist trade policy before it entered the EC, had not felt it necessary to impose MFA-type controls on imports of textiles and clothing from the South; this shows how competitively it is able to produce these goods. The competitiveness of Portugal is better known.

Again, the point should not be overstressed. The shift in the pattern of Italian trade was not only due to trade diversion; another structural distortion was at work. In the 1970s, large-scale industry in that country was heavily handicapped by social legislation, which enabled trade unions to block measures of rationalization and to force enterprises to retain excess labor almost indefinitely; the large state-run sector went through a management crisis. This shifted the pattern of comparative advantage in favor of small-scale industries. Many small firms within the so-called submerged economy have in addition managed to escape paying taxes and social security contributions. Similar distortions exist in Spain and Portugal, which will strengthen the tendency of these countries to take over markets for textiles, clothing, and shoes.

Japan remains competitive enough to make it hard for the NICs to breach its domestic market. That country does not make use of the VER agreements of the MFA, though it has used the threat of anti-dumping duties to convince Korea and Pakistan, for instance, to restrict exports of some sensitive products. The very rapid rise of its wage level should have led Japan to lose competitiveness rapidly in textiles, clothing, and shoes, and a high rate of increase of the rate of market penetration should have taken place. Interestingly, the increase of market penetration for these products has been lower than in Korea and Pakistan; but only for shoes is this obviously a result of protection.

The competitiveness of domestic producers again explains why the rate of market penetration into the EC domestic market for shoes is much lower than into the U.S. market. There are VER agreements between some countries of the EC and the main developing-country exporters of shoes, but these are not tight enough to have much effect: what has limited imports is the competitiveness of Italian shoe producers, who are so efficient that, like East Asian producers, they were subjected at times by the United States to VERs.

The most striking finding is, however, that everywhere both exports and imports of these goods rose much faster than production. This striking shift to greater openness to trade must be seen as one of the most important structural changes of the 1970s, to which many producers must have found it difficult to adjust. This must have increased pressures for protection.

In ten years, clothing and shoes switched from being goods that were little traded to goods that are very open to trade. A sophisticated trading system has also come into being, encouraged by lower transportation and communication costs as well as by General Agreement on Tariffs and Trade (GATT) tariff reductions. Even the MFA has stimulated the growth of this network, because the system of regulations which the MFA defines is so complex that it places a premium on the acquisition of specialized trading skills. This paradoxical situation in which discriminatory protection can increase trade could be interpreted in a second-best framework.

Miscellaneous Light Manufactures

In the future, protection will limit the growth of developing-countries' exports of textiles and clothing, and possibly also of shoes. These countries will have to identify other products, the markets for which remain open. What other goods are there for which developing countries have demonstrated a comparative advantage? Is there room for further growth of their exports? Does the list of such goods tell us something about the markets which they are likely to enter in coming years?

Table 3.11 provides figures that are relevant. The goods listed are light industrial goods whose exports were significant in 1980.

What is striking is the wide range of items listed in the table, from brooms and brushes to computers. Exports of each type of such goods are not large, but the aggregate volume is impressive: $7,387 million,

Table 3.11   **Minor Exports of Manufactures from Developing Countries to the EC** (millions of U.S. dollars)

		EC Imports		Penetration Rate[a]	
		1970	1980	1970	1980
3113	Fruit and vegetable preserves	159	712	4.4	26.2
3114	Fish preservers	71	418	6.3	10.2
3119	Cocoa, chocolate, confectionery	80	455	2.7	3.7
3232	Furs prepared, not sewn	13	108	7.3	21.1
3319	Miscellaneous goods from wood	8	138	1.3	6.7
3320	Nonmetallic furniture	4	114	0.1	0.5
3420-2	Printing, etc.	7	139	0.1	0.5
3551	Tires	3	109	0.1	1.4
3559	Other rubber goods	7	89	0.3	1.0
356	Miscellaneous plastic goods	41	484	0.7	1.8
3610	Porcelain, ceramics, etc.	3	172	0.2	2.6
3811-1	Cutlery	5	74	2.2	11.0
3811-2	Hand tools, other hardware	18	193	0.9	2.9
3819-2	Metal containers	16	256	0.2	1.3
3825-1	Office equipment except computers	7	94	0.3	3.7
3825-2	Computers	16	166	0.9	1.4
3829	Miscellaneous nonelectrical machinery	83	620	0.6	1.1
3832-1	Radio and TV equipment	24	1,087	0.6	8.7
3833	Electrical household durables	1	64	0.0	0.5
3839	Batteries, lamps, etc.	9	190	0.2	1.2
3852-3	Photographic equipment	6	174	1.2	7.3
3853	Watches and clocks	3	557	0.5	23.6
3902	Music instruments	1	42	0.7	4.9
3903	Sport goods	7	224	2.4	14.5
3909-2	Toys	32	480	5.2	16.9
3909-4	Brooms, brushes	1	20	0.3	3.4
3909-5	Umbrellas, pipes, etc.	75	206	18.4	22.8
Total		700	7,387		

Note: Excluding southern Europe.
[a]Imports as percentage of apparent consumption.

half the value of clothing exports. In quite a few instances, exports were negligible fifteen years ago: these exports were "invented" quite recently, as entrepreneurs identified items that could be produced at low cost given the cost structure of developing countries.

The list is made up entirely of unskilled-labor-intensive goods, as economic theory would predict. In some cases, the exports were "invented" by multinationals, who saw that it was profitable to shift to low-wage countries for the unskilled-labor-intensive stages of the production process. Examples are computers and television sets (in the more advanced NICs there are also local companies producing television sets and other consumer electronics items, and even [copied] microcomputers). In the majority of cases, however, it is the local entrepreneurs who have developed the new exports.

As often happens, this neoclassical interpretation of the list of successful exports can be replaced by a neotechnological interpretation. Production of most of the items in the table requires only a limited industrial competence (Westphal, Rhee, and Pursell 1981): the apparent exceptions are largely produced by multinationals, which provide the skilled staff and know-how and locate the unskilled-labor-intensive stages of production in developing countries. Proponents of a neotechnological view of international trade could stress that the goods developing countries are able to produce efficiently are those whose production does not require hard-to-obtain technology or the organizational skills required for large-scale production and which can be marketed without needing to set up an elaborate international marketing network. To the extent that building up human capital is necessary to the acquisition of industrial competence, it is not surprising that the neotechnological and neoclassical interpretations are hard to distinguish. They are not equivalent of course: sending young people to school does not suffice to procure the industrial competence which a country may need. (Westphal, Rhee, and Purcell make the interesting point that an outward-oriented strategy, which introduces the challenge of competition on world markets, is crucial to achieving industrial competence.)

For a few products, the rate of market penetration has become rather high, and exports could encounter absorption limits and possibly new protection barriers (preserves, furs, cutlery, radios and television equipment, watches and clocks, sporting goods, umbrellas, for instance). The econometric work of the European Group for Research on Protection suggests, however, that these minor industries find that the tight protection obtained by larger and more politically powerful sectors (like textiles and agriculture) is difficult to extract from policy makers for themselves. This warrants optimism about the continued openness of markets for these goods. There are import restrictions in

France for quite a few of these goods, but access to other EC markets is quite free (and smuggling into France is easy).

The list should, however, be looked on mainly as indicating the products in which developing countries potentially have a comparative advantage. Many of these exports were only recently "invented"; there will be more such discoveries. Industrial competence has been a limiting factor, but its acquisition is a cumulative process: the range of goods which developing countries are able to produce efficiently will become even broader, enabling further diversification of exports.

3.4.3   The Troubled Mature Trade-Union-Intensive Industries

Finally we will discuss the participation of developing countries in the troubled "new mature industries": shipbuilding, automobiles, and steel (see table 3.12). Production of these goods requires complex technology and skill in running complex industrial operations, which quite a few of the more advanced NICs have acquired by now. Technology for steel and shipbuilding is available fairly freely. Efficient producers of automobiles in the developing world are subsidiaries of multinationals. They are beginning to export to a greater extent as their owners pursue "world car strategies"; one of the two large Korean industrial groups has been able to develop a model and to produce it fairly effectively. Other countries, such as India, are starting to develop automobile industries. They are acquiring the right to produce models developed elsewhere and are obtaining assistance and some capital funds for building the necessary plants. (The CPEs were pioneers in this development but have had only moderate success. The number of cars exported by the CPEs to the EC is of the same order of magnitude as the Japanese total, but the quality is very poor and unit prices are low.)

Exports of these three categories of goods by developing countries were negligible in 1980. For steel, the situation is not likely to change fast. Imports from third countries into the EC are limited by VER agreements, which are not likely to be lifted soon; trading partners who have refused to conclude such agreements have been hit by an-

Table 3.12   **EC Imports from Developing Countries** (millions of U.S. dollars)

	Imports		Penetration Rate	
	1970	1980	1970	1980
371 Steel	195	815	0.6	0.9
3841 Shipbuilding	10	762	0.4	7.6
3843 Automobiles	8	449	0.0	0.4

Note: Excluding southern Europe.

tidumping duties. Meanwhile the EC, which itself resorts to dumping on world markets, is a competitor to be reckoned with on third countries' markets, as is Japan's highly efficient steel industry.

Union power in the EC has had a disastrous effect on the steel industry by preventing adjustment of the labor force and of capacity, but it has also forced member country governments and the EC Council to grant very large subsidies and to virtually close the domestic market to imports. The "endogenous distortion" has been offset by an equally endogenous tariff, which negates the comparative advantage of the foreign producers. Such a situation cannot continue indefinitely, and often-postponed capacity cuts of over thirty million tons were finally agreed to in 1983.

In the long run, there will be no surge of import demand for steel in the Common Market and no sudden decrease in the low-priced exports of EC producers to the rest of the world, unless the business cycle situation improves a good deal more than now seems probable. But over time, the most developed of the NICs are likely to become gradually significant exporters of steel. The world market is very large: the steel exports of the Big Three traders amounted to nearly $35 billion in 1980; even if access to their domestic markets is denied by protection, Europe's steel producers will be slowly displaced from their export markets.

The EC shipbuilding industry is dying rapidly; more than half of the jobs which existed in 1973 have been shed during the recession, and the contraction of the industry continues steadily. Here also the true competitor of developing countries is Japan. Korea, a small producer until a few years ago, has been winning a fifth of world new orders in recent months; there is reason to think that this "infant export" has had a high cost in covert subsidies. Protection in the EC is of little avail to Europe's shipyards. Since shipping is a world industry, tariffs would not be effective. And EC shipyards, which in some recent instances have quoted prices that were three times as high as the Korean ones, can be kept going only by subsidies that are so prohibitive that governments are not willing to continue to give them indefinitely. The industry, which is much smaller than steel, does not have the political weight required to win the protection which it needs to survive.

For automobiles also, prospects depend on a complex interplay among trade unions, multinationals, and the governments of both developed and developing countries. The world market is extremely large, and enormous export opportunities would be created for the developing countries by breaking into the automobile market—of course, this would entail severe competition with Japan. In the developed world tariff walls are of the same order of magnitude as for textiles; in developing-country markets, auto imports are limited by tariffs and domestic content regulations.

In contrast with the situation for steel and shipbuilding, there is no unified lobby arguing for protection of the automobile industry. Automobile companies have found it advantageous to produce the same car in different places, in part to make themselves less vulnerable to trade union pressures but also to amortize the extremely high setting-up costs which launching a new model entails. A good deal of the exports of developing countries is short term in nature; for example, the recession in Brazil has led to substantial exports of cars that could not be disposed of domestically. Another part reflects commitments by producers to earn foreign exchange in return for the grant of a privileged market access. The fact that so much of the trade between the developed and the developing countries will consist of intrafirm trade will check the rise of protection. However, except for Korea, there is as yet no growth of production in the South that is both clearly export-oriented and successful.

In conclusion, there will be no breakthrough in the three industries to match that which the South (and in particular the Far Eastern NICs) achieved for clothing in the 1970s. The coming years should, however, witness steady growth of exports of these products. These markets are so large that the winning of even only small fractions of them could yield substantial amounts of foreign exchange.

3.5   Conclusion

Using a new data set, this paper has discussed export trends for manufactures from the South to the European Community and has drawn implications for future prospects and for policy.

Comparison of the Big Three trading nations (the United States, Japan, and the EC) reveals the United States as the biggest producer and consumer of manufactures. As a trader, the EC makes up for this by being more open to imports, both globally and from developing countries. Japan has a more closed market. The figures reveal clearly the market shifts that have caused tensions in the 1970s: the swift gains in shares by the East Asian NICs, in particular, for textiles and clothing and by Japan for steel, automobiles, and some other metal goods. Both Japan and the East Asian NICs have a large export surplus with the United States of America and Europe, and this has lessened their ability to seek arrangements that might check the increase of protection. The so-called new NICs, the developing countries which are beginning to export manufactures today, are in a more favorable position from this point of view and are net creators of manufacturing jobs on quite a large scale. Their situation is advantageous because trade negotiators and the interest groups which push for protectionism have a tendency to think of primary products as the unambiguously desirable category of imports while imports of manufactures are thought of as needing to be watched. Market penetration levels are quite low: developing countries are far from having reached any upper bound to their exports to the three trading nations. However, export growth depends on their ability to diversify exports as their export volume rises, an ability they have so far demonstrated.

The figures also reveal the impact of proximity on the intensity of trade, with each of the Big Three trading intensively with nearby developing countries. There is also a curious "backyard effect," where their trade with these countries yields an exceptionally large surplus.

Study of the EC market suggests that member countries retain much tighter control over their domestic markets than is usually thought. Perhaps the EC should be thought of not as a maker of policy in the usual sense but rather as an institutional device which softens economic aggression between its members and enables them to pool their bargaining power in dealing with the outside world. This suggests that influencing member country governments should be the main task of the trade diplomacy of developing countries rather than maintaining links with the EC in Brussels. Such an approach might in fact be more fruitful for all concerned since, by the time that the European Commission comes to the bargaining table, it has usually been assigned so tight a negotiating brief that it is hardly able to take account of unexpected negotiating opportunities that might come up and to seek the deal that is truly most advantageous to all concerned.

The composition of developing-country exports of manufactures to the EC confirms that the primary components of their comparative advantage are the natural-resource and unskilled-labor content of the exported goods. Setting apart refined oil, the share of natural-resource-intensive goods in these countries' exports of manufactures has been falling rapidly, a trend which reflects some missed opportunities that have been lost to natural-resource-rich countries such as Australia, Canada, and the United States. A very large share of other exports consists of unskilled-labor-intensive goods.

The latter goods have been hit by protection, but the EC market continues to be very open. Trade restrictions for textiles and clothing are the strictest of all, but even there, loopholes and safety valves built into the protection system have so far permitted an import growth that is far from negligible. Apart from a few exceptions, any protection for other goods is casual.

For miscellaneous light manufactures, developing countries have shown much inventiveness in spotting opportunities to produce and to export goods which they are able to produce efficiently, given their factor costs and industrial experience; the list of such products is widening as there become more of such "inventions" and as the industrial expertise of developing countries increases.

The last topic discussed in this paper, that of the opportunities that might arise in the troubled "new mature industries" (steel, shipbuilding, and automobiles), is somewhat more speculative. The markets for their products are huge. Exports of their goods from developing countries were very small in 1980. These industries are handicapped both in Europe and in the United States by adversary relations between employers and very powerful trade unions, which keep costs a good deal higher than they should be (an endogenous trade distortion valuable to competitors). The more advanced NICs have shown themselves to be able to master the relevant technology. A breakthrough for these goods is unlikely to be as swift and decisive as that which developing countries achieved for textiles and clothing in the 1970s, because of both the competitiveness of Japanese producers and the protection which these politically powerful industries are able to obtain. But the markets for those goods are so large that, even though market shares remain low, exports of these goods could make quite a large contribution to the foreign exchange receipts of the South.

Notes

1. The project was coordinated by H. Hughes and J. Waelbroeck. A note by V. Panoutsopoulos, presenting the concordances between national production statistics and the ISIC, will be available in the near future. The detailed SITC/ISIC concordance is available on request from the author.

2. Thus figures have to be looked at carefully. "Other manufactures' include diamonds, and because transit trade in diamonds is hard to separate from imports for further processing, some market penetration rates exceed 100%. Refined petroleum has a large weight in group 35, and this accounts for the high penetration rate in that row of the table.

3. For econometric studies of the determinants of protectionism, see Cable and Rebelo 1980; Glisman and Weiss 1980; Grilli and La Noce 1983; Koekkoek, Kol, and Mennes 1981, Lundberg 1981; Messerlin 1982; and Tharakan 1980.

4. For econometric work of the World Bank group on comparative advantage of EC countries, see Cable and Rebelo 1980 and Tharakan 1980. In addition, F. D. Weiss has provided a survey of German research on that country's comparative advantage (1983), while a detailed discussion of Sweden's comparative advantage is given in Ohlsson 1982.

References

Balassa, B. 1979. A stages approach to comparative advantage. In *Economic growth and resources,* vol. 4, ed. I. Adelman. National and International Issues. London: Macmillan.

Bhagwati, J. N. 1971. The generalized theory of distortions and welfare. In *Trade, balance of payments, and growth,* ed. J. N. Bhagwati, R. W. Jones, R. A. Mundell, and J. Vanek. Papers in International Economics in Honour of Charles P. Kindleberger. Amsterdam: North-Holland.

Cable, V., and I. Rebelo. 1980. Britain's pattern of specialization in manufactured goods with developing countries and trade protection. World Bank Staff Working Paper, no. 425.

Glisman, H. H., and F. D. Weiss. On the political economy of protection in Germany. World Bank Staff Working Paper, no. 427.

Grilli, E., and M. La Noce. 1983. The political economy of protection in Italy. World Bank Staff Working Paper, no. 567.

Koekkoek, V. A., J. Kol, and L. B. M. Mennes. 1981. On protectionism in the Netherlands. World Bank Staff Working Paper, no. 493.

Lundberg, L. 1981. Patterns of trade barriers in Sweden. World Bank Staff Working Paper, no. 424.

Messerlin, P. A. 1982. Groupes de pression et choix protectionnistes. In *Economie et finance internationales,* ed. J. L. Reiffers. Paris: Dunod.

Ohlsson, L. 1982. Sweden's trade with developing countries: Comparative advantage and barriers to adjustment. Forthcoming as World Bank Staff Working Paper.

Tharakan, P. K. M. 1980. The political economy of protection in Belgium. World Bank Staff Working Paper, no. 431.

United Nations. 1958. *Classification of commodities by industries of origin.* Statistical Papers, series M, no. 4, rev. 1. New York: United Nations.

Weiss, F. D. 1983. The structure of Germany's international competitiveness. World Bank Staff Working Paper, no. 571.

Westphal, L., Y. W. Rhee, and G. Pursell. 1981. Korean industrial competence: Where it came from. World Bank Staff Working Paper, no. 469.

4 Japan and Her Asian Neighbors in a Dynamic Perspective

Ippei Yamazawa

4.1 Introduction

The Asian newly industrializing countries (NICs) and the countries belonging to the Association of South East Asian Nations (ASEAN) recorded an economic growth rate of 6%–10% during the 1970s, a rate matched by no other group of countries in the world. Japan's growth rate of 5.2% during 1976–80, while much higher than that of other developed countries, fell far short of the growth performance of her Asian neighbors.

The rapid growth of the Asian NICs and ASEAN countries in the 1970s has been outward-looking, based on the rapid expansion of production and exports of manufactured goods, whose ultimate destination has been predominantly the developed countries. North America and Western Europe absorbed 37% and 23% respectively of the industrial exports from the NICs during the years 1969–79. They also absorbed 25% and 21% of those from ASEAN. Japan's share of the industrial exports from the NICs was 11%, and its share from ASEAN was 8%.

After the second oil shock, however, developed-country markets were depressed considerably in 1981 and 1982, and the export growth of the NICs and ASEAN decelerated. They each suffered from foreign exchange shortages and were forced to slow down their development programs, resulting in their economic growth rate dropping by 2–5 percentage points. Economic recovery began in early 1983, originating from the revived import expansion of the United States. It is likely that the industrial exports from the NICs and ASEAN will continue to flow into the developed-country markets. This reflects the basic com-

Ippei Yamazawa is professor of international economics at Hitotsubashi University, Tokyo, Japan.

plementarity of the industrial structures of the two groups; however, the trade pattern involved presents some problems.

First, the growth of the economies of the NICs and ASEAN will be disrupted again by a setback to developed-country economies. Secondly, growth of their exports to those markets will be limited in the long run, because the growth of those markets, especially that of Western Europe, has decelerated and the recent expansion of the NICs' exports has aggravated the adjustment difficulty of import-competing industries there and has provoked import restriction. Diversification of their export markets is desirable to avoid the vulnerability of their exports in both the short and the long run. During the 1970s the number of their export markets was expanded to include the Middle East, Japan, and China, but considering the growth potential of the NICs and ASEAN countries, their own markets deserve more attention as promising demand sources.

It is often suggested that Japan should absorb more industrial exports from the NICs and ASEAN countries. If primary products are included, Japan has absorbed 27% of the ASEAN exports, far exceeding the absorption by North American (18%) and Western Europe (16%). But her importation of industrial products from the NICs and ASEAN still remains a smaller share, and the possibility of its expansion is yet to be explored.

This paper examines Japan's economic relationship with the Asian NICs and ASEAN countries from a global perspective.[1] The trade matrices in tables 4.1–4.3 show the trade flows of Japan, the Asian NICs, and the ASEAN countries, both among themselves and with the rest of the world, at three different levels of commodity aggregation—all commodities, industrial goods, and textiles and clothing. Singapore is duly regarded as a NIC given its stage of industrial development, but in our analysis it is included in the ASEAN group because of the effect of geographical location on its trade pattern.

Although primary commodities still composed 75% of Japan's imports, 36% of the NICs' imports, and 74% of ASEAN exports in 1979, it is industrial goods trade that receives attention in this paper. The catching up of the NICs and ASEAN has been most prominent in the production and export of textiles and clothing.

The trade of Mainland China is represented as an independent entry in our trade matrices. It absorbed 3.6% of Japan's industrial goods exports and supplied 11.7% of Japan's textile and clothing imports in 1979. It is widely anticipated that Japan will be further involved in trade and other forms of international division of labor with China in the 1980s. But the unpredictability of China's future course confines our discussion to Japan's relationship with her Asian neighbors that are characterized by a market economy system.

4.2   The Spread of Industrialization

In the Far East industrialization has spread sequentially from Japan to the NICs and finally to the ASEAN countries. Changes in the comparative advantage structure of individual countries have corresponded to the spread of industrialization.

Let us give a brief overview. In the prewar period, Japan was the only industrialized country in the region, and the trade pattern was a simple complementary manufactures/primary commodities exchange between Japan and other countries. The present-day NICs completed import substitution of light manufactures in the 1950s and started exporting them to the United States and Europe in the 1960s. There then emerged a competitive aspect to the trade relations between the NICs and Japan and a complementary relationship between the NICs and ASEAN. Following this new development, the 1970s saw the development of ASEAN light industrialization and the start of a competitive relationship between ASEAN and the NICs. The NICs, in turn, proceeded with heavy industrialization and in some commodities began to compete with Japan.

It should not be ignored that at present Japan still supplies heavy industrial products, such as capital and intermediate goods, on a large scale to these countries, and about 80% of ASEAN exports consist of primary commodities. There is a growing tendency in Japan, however, to import from the NICs and ASEAN low-price light manufactures instead of producing them domestically; this is expected to continue. Therefore, in summary, the present trade relationship among Japan, the NICs, and ASEAN is a complex structure consisting of both competitive and complementary elements. This of course reflects the economic differences among the three groups, such as their varying levels of industrialization and the different sizes of their domestic markets.

The achievement of industrial development and trade expansion by the Asian NICs and ASEAN countries can be attributed to the activities of the private sector. Direct investment by U.S. and Japanese firms and technology transfer through their activities played an important role in the spreading of industrialization to the present NICs and the ASEAN countries. Leading local enterprises have evolved in response to the growth of demand both at home and abroad. The commercial activities of overseas Chinese also had a role in creating the division of labor within the region.

However, government policies of both the NICs and the ASEAN countries have affected private business activities and are partly responsible for the present structure of extra- and intraregional trade. Foreign investment and protection policies of the governments of the NICs and the ASEAN countries contributed by paving the way for

Table 4.1   **Trade Matrix of All Commodities, 1969 and 1979** (millions of U.S. $)

	1.	2.	3.	4.	5.	6.	7.
1. Japan		606*	767*	615	313*	138*	434
		4,365	6,245	3,675	2,665	1,506	1,714
2. Taiwan	158*		22*	93*	26*	9*	27*
	2,260		171	1,131	422	130	185
3. Korea	133*	13*		24*	12*	2*	6*
	3,352	160		531	197	86	110
4. Hong Kong	141	35	18		90	26	26
	530	185	41		282	86	64
5. Singapore	110*	10*	11*	47*		85*	58*
	1,365	112	230	961		2,037	607
6. Malaysia	305*	—*	37	18*	352		11*
	2,590	193	209	188	1,931		149
7. Thailand	153*	31	1*	56	57*	55	
	1,112	64	50	247	427	228	
8. Philippines	337	15	26	8*	5*	1*	4
	1,201	61	141	158	66	57	19
9. Indonesia	252*	6*	4*	7*	141*	50	7
	7,192	407	387	99	1,964	66	38
10. South Asia	331*	2*	8*	55	45	6*	10
	3,426	209	237	276	168	71	53
11. Australia/New Zealand	1,160	36*	16*	64	84	73*	31
	5,849	409	570	377	486	442	158
12. North America	4,040	333*	506*	375	154*	71*	155
	20,695	3,239	4,153	2,106	2,333	981	914
13. Western Europe	1,340*	99*	198*	553	278*	231	282
	8,328	1,313	2,073	3,163	2,218	1,349	1,217
14. Middle East	1,730*	a*	24*	44	4*	46*	10*
	27,563	1,900	2,863	95	3,399	606	899
15. China	245*	—	—*	401*	123	72	—
	2,968	—	5	2,719	370	199	218
16. Rest of the world	2,055	29*	3*	66*	48*	12*	8*
	7,887	688	901	673	416	263	470
17. World total	12,490*	1,215*	1,642*	2,425*	1,729*	878*	1,068*
	96,318	13,305	18,276	16,399	17,343	8,107	6,815

Sources: Institute of Developing Economies, *Computerized Trade Statistics Search System* (AIDXT) (Tokyo), supplemented by United Nations, *Monthly Bulletin of Statistics* (New York), and individual country trade statistics. See Yamazawa, Hirata, and Taniguchi 1983 for details of the compilation.

Notes: The numbers making up the headings across the top of the table indicate the importing countries and regions. In the body of the table, the upper figure indicates the

8.	9.	10.	11.	12.	13.	14.	15.	16.	17.
476	237*	184*	579	5,498	2,052*	207*	391*	3,495	15,990*
1,620	2,124	2,189	3,191	28,336	16,524	9,610	4,115	15,154	103,032
15*	13*	1*	16*	440*	104*	7*	—	118*	1,050*
201	399	61	448	6,092	2,306	902	—	1,370	16,078
1*	2*	1*	6*	327*	55*	2*	—	37*	623*
109	195	248	181	4,777	2,841	1,366	—	900	15,052
17*	62	11	72	827	557*	23*	6*	266	2,178
115	42	56	417	4,079	3,915	434	120	793	11,160
6*	36*	24*	50*	186*	250*	15*	57	605	1,549*
237	483	709	718	2,088	2,209	482	170	1,825	14,233
25	16*	11*	50	274*	293*	13*	45	200	1,650*
118	235	328	264	1,988	2,133	199	182	361	11,068
3	13*	31	4*	104	139*	12*	—*	50*	707*
11	188	86	59	613	1,372	261	77	412	5,207
	1*	1*	5*	324	77*	a*	—*	19*	823
	46	8	97	1,434	1,001	50	52	211	4,601
25*		a*	62	120*	123*	a*	a	3*	800*
165		64	241	3,199	1,230	62	—	475	15,590
4	9*	1,097	80	576	841	274*	82*	142*	3,562
13	182	2,025	264	1,890	4,317	2,194	581	2,461	18,366
67	27*	69	250	860	1,700	59*	125*	491	5,110
251	331	357	1,445	3,353	4,284	974	914	2,814	23,014
394	201	1,500	1,140	18,760	14,320	1,289*	115*	7,856	51,210
1,607	1,021	3,126	4,677	68,736	56,161	9,985	2,243	46,785	228,762
252	192*	1,296	1,800	11,900	78,310*	3,220*	520*	18,250	118,720
974	1,304	5,886	5,954	47,240	478,278	33,910	3,941	104,098	701,246
13*	1*	507*	215*	481	4,530*	660*	19*	1,095*	9,380*
863	328	5,639	1,760	18,637	59,178	8,395	202	18,108	150,435
—	39	126*	36	27*	405	85*		692	2,250*
109	119	958	216	707	2,149	749		3,772	15,258
13*	25*	1,471	135	7,034*	19,753	1,225*	1,190	26,892	56,960
241	400	1,195	614	57,578	100,576	7,753	4,965	120,579	305,200
4,311	873*	6,329	4,500	47,740	123,510	7,090*	2,550*	57,210	272,560
5,634	7,397	22,935	20,546	250,747	738,474	77,326	17,561	320,119	1,638,302

trade value (f.o.b.) in 1969 and the lower figure the value in 1979. * = the growth rate is higher than the world average; a = the trade value is less than U.S. \$1 million; — = no record in the basic data. The years 1969 and 1979 were chosen in order to highlight the increase in world export. Since 1979 was a peak year before the adverse effects of the second oil shock emerged, the 1969–79 period will reveal the fastest growth in world export.

Table 4.2   **Trade Matrix of All Industrial Goods, 1969 and 1979**
(millions of U.S. $)

	1.	2.	3.	4.	5.	6.	7.
1. Japan		561*	584*	569*	294*	132*	422
		4,056	5,787	3,450	2,576	1,453	1,652
2. Taiwan	31*		2*	76*	19*	7*	25*
	1,379		94	1,052	387	122	156
3. Korea	57*	8*		20*	11*	1*	5*
	2,360	122		484	182	83	104
4. Hong Kong	96	25*	16		73	18	22
	421	173	35		241	72	46
5. Singapore	3*	1*	1*	15*		30*	11*
	248	52	43	328		1,325	280
6. Malaysia	87	—*	1*	4*	35*		5
	377	28	52	137	352		25
7. Thailand	8*	a*	a*	3*	4*	1*	
	215	6	13	98	163	37	
8. Philippines	3*	1*	a*	2*	1*	1*	3
	155	19	10	115	22	16	18
9. Indonesia	4*	—*	a	a*	108	1*	a*
	114	3	a	43	275	28	15
10. South Asia	58*	a*	5	37	26	2*	9
	592	34	18	193	57	49	32
11. Australia/New	93	10*	a*	34*	27*	29	18
Zealand	520	123	62	230	281	123	105
12. North America	1,657	200*	198*	292	132*	53*	110*
	7,519	1,844	1,872	1,574	2,146	873	679
13. Western Europe	1,148	88*	193*	494	239*	193*	256
	6,713	1,174	1,942	2,921	2,006	1,227	1,081
14. Middle East	30*	a*	2*	34	3	8	1*
	425	48	28	19	3	6	13
15. China	51*	—	—*	169*	73	30	—*
	700	—	3	1,470	216	71	61
16. Rest of the world	595	1*	1*	9*	2*	1*	1*
	2,359	73	448	427	164	55	14
17. World total	3,920*	895*	1,005*	1,757*	1,045*	507*	888
	24,098	7,756	10,406	12,544	9,072	5,539	4,281

Sources: Institute of Developing Economies, *Computerized Trade Statistics Search System* (AIDXT) (Tokyo), supplemented by United Nations, *Monthly Bulletin of Statistics* (New York), and individual country trade statistics. See Yamazawa, Hirata, and Taniguchi 1983 for details of the compilation.

Notes: The numbers making up the headings across the top of the table indicate the importing countries and regions. In the body of the table, the upper figure indicates the

8.	9.	10.	11.	12.	13.	14.	15.	16.	17.
432	226*	174*	548	5,273	1,848*	198*	382*	3,328	14,970*
1,532	1,975	1,883	3,113	27,679	15,866	9,345	3,587	15,086	99,041
13*	12*	1*	15*	387*	46*	6*	—	95*	734*
176	266	45	432	5,903	2,105	657	—	1,304	14,077
a*	2*	1*	5*	306*	33*	1*	—	29*	479*
104	176	237	173	4,595	2,673	1,287	—	843	13,428
14*	58	10	66*	815	542*	22*	2*	234	2,01015
112	41	47	410	4,001	3,879	432	103	720	10,734
3*	30	9*	7*	38*	22*	4*	a*	192	365*
135	135	267	158	1,532	1,056	464	72	620	6,715
5	11	4*	3*	153*	49*	1*	—*	43	401*
23	16	36	95	991	686	33	2	157	3,009
a*	3	1*	1*	63	29*	a*	—*	5	117*
5	13	35	35	357	599	83	11	13	1,683
	a*	1*	2*	43*	4*	a*	—*	6*	67*
	10	26	48	430	146	24	2	44	1,085
a*		—*	1*	21	34*	a*	a	3*	173
17		27	9	23	231	32	—	16	832
3	8	53*	46	329	314*	50*	2*	472	1,414*
7	24	1,666	208	1,171	3,021	1,063	326	655	9,171
43	17*	13*	192	180	210	2*	5*	213	1,088
124	131	180	970	525	807	72	218	871	5,343
293	99*	273	919	14,257	8,626	422*	a*	7,740	35,271
1,246	643	1,426	3,970	49,631	34,590	7,265	758	31,582	147,618
212	163*	632*	1,672	10,104	57,876*	1,545*	427*	17,825	93,070
868	1,198	5,140	5,395	39,829	357,792	29,303	3,616	85,143	545,349
1	a*	2*	5*	151	251*	6*	a*	127	619*
3	4	228	31	108	1,585	2,406	21	671	5,599
—*	33	28*	30	15*	147*	1*		83*	660*
15	99	212	171	460	1,126	509		2,382	7,495
1*	5*	2,265	37*	1,267*	6,819	2,805	771	9,989*	24,568
59	80	1,176	269	8,643	23,752	3,948	3,248	62,415	107,166
1,020	667*	3,466	3,550	33,400	76,850	5,065*	1,590*	40,284	176,010
4,425	4,813	12,632	15,487	145,878	449,914	56,976	12,000	202,523	978,345

trade value (f.o.b.) in 1969 and the lower figure the value in 1979. Industrial goods represent SITC sections 5–8. * = the growth rate is higher than the world average; a = the trade value is less than U.S. $1 million; — = no record in the basic data. The years 1969 and 1979 were chosen in order to highlight the increase in world export. Since 1979 was a peak year before the adverse effects of the second oil shock emerged, the 1969–79 period will reveal the fastest growth in world export.

Table 4.3   Trade Matrix of Textiles and Clothing 1969 and 1979
(millions of U.S. $)

	1.	2.	3.	4.	5.	6.	7.
1. Japan		51	103	220	107	11	47
		140	296	568	173	41	47
2. Taiwan	10*		a*	39*	10*	1*	7
	449		23	473	128	30	18
3. Korea	36*	a*		11*	9*	1*	3
	1,242	41		204	85	14	17
4. Hong Kong	11*	6	1*		26	7	3*
	188	23	15		90	20	18
5. Singapore	a*	a*	a*	2*		2*	1
	20	2	3	14		97	5
6. Malaysia	a*	a	—*	a*	1*		a
	21	a	2	6	11		a
7. Thailand	2*	a*	a*	a*	2*	a*	
	51	2	3	36	37	10	
8. Philippines	a*	a	—*	a*	a*	a*	—*
	20	a	a	27	11	1	a
9. Indonesia	a*	a	—	a*	a*	a*	—
	10	1	—	15	45	1	—
10. South Asia	11*	a*	—*	24	19	2	1
	114	6	2	118	27	1	1
11. Australia/New Zealand	1*	a*	a*	3	1	a	a*
	24	23	3	14	4	2	2
12. North America	15*	3*	3*	20	3*	1	3
	210	19	26	66	19	5	5
13. Western Europe	84*	a*	1*	62	16	9	7
	780	15	24	219	63	20	9
14. Middle East	a*	a*	a	a	a*	—*	a
	11	15	—	1	1	a	—
15. China	23*	a	—*	79*	38	9	—*
	426	—	2	752	92	13	12
16. Rest of the world	1*	a*	a*	a*	a*	a*	a*
	59	60	3	20	5	2	1
17. World total	198*	62	109	462	235	45	71
	3,627	347	402	2,533	791	258	135

Sources: Institute of Developing Economies, *Computerized Trade Statistics Search System* (AIDXT) (Tokyo), supplemented by United Nations, *Monthly Bulletin of Statistics* (New York), and individual country trade statistics. See Yamazawa, Hirata, and Taniguchi 1983 for details of the compilation.

Notes: The numbers making up the headings across the top of the table indicate the importing countries and regions. In the body of the table, the upper figure indicates the

8.	9.	10.	11.	12.	13.	14.	15.	16.	17.
44	27	21*	118	635	147	57*	14*	495	2,097
77	88	174	215	593	328	430	112	1,060	4,343
3*	4*	a*	8*	114*	24*	4*	—	38*	263*
46	54	16	115	1,121	488	134	—	440	3,535
a*	2*	a*	1*	120*	26*	1*	—	15*	226*
11	27	63	71	1,234	1,106	170	—	378	4,664
1*	22	6	40	318	319*	6*	a*	108	874
52	6	29	201	1,681	2,055	162	41	247	4,829
a*	4	2*	1*	15*	7*	2*	a*	49	85*
3	2	79	25	155	195	30	2	102	733
a	a	a*	a*	5*	1*	a*	—*	1*	10*
1	1	3	25	36	129	5	1	22	263
—*	2	—*	a*	1*	2*	a*	—*	a*	11*
2	4	20	17	84	214	61	5	6	551
	a	—*	a*	3*	a*	a*	—	a*	5*
	a	a	10	81	110	6	—	5	273
—*		—*	a*	a*	a*	a*	—	a*	1*
1		a	3	8	18	14	—	3	118
a	5	25*	39	284	141	23*	2*	240	817
a	1	336	107	543	1,488	533	92	236	3,584
1	a*	a*	19*	5	4*	a*	a*	5	41*
3	1	5	118	21	114	6	5	9	251
19	23	3	32*	217	294	10*	a*	288	935
47	4	9	211	818	1,618	132	34	1,333	4,556
4	4	10	126	773	6,643	126*	10	1,306	9,183
13	6	45	303	1,545	34,702	1,327	36	3,697	42,804
—	—	a	2	36	72*	4*	a	31	146*
—	—	—	5	61	760	154	—	40	1,048
—*	18	8	23	12*	54*	a*	—	46*	311*
a	16	31	122	296	477	222	—	1,301	3,763
a	a*	7*	2*	76*	189*	23*	1*	417*	717*
—	a	64	38	784	3,298	737	121	3,414	8,606
73	111	83*	412	2,614	7,923	256*	27*	3,037	15,720
256	211	873	1,586	9,061	46,958	4,123	449	12,310	83,921

trade value (f.o.b.) in 1969 and the lower figure the value in 1979. Textiles represent SITC sections 65 and 84. * = the growth rate is higher than the world average; a = the trade value is less than U.S. $1 million; — = no record in the basic data. The years 1969 and 1979 were chosen in order to highlight the increase in world export. Since 1979 was a peak year before the adverse effects of the second oil shock emerged, the 1969–79 period will reveal the fastest growth in world export.

industrialization. The change of their development strategy from an inward- to an outward-looking one has accelerated the export expansion of manufactures from these countries. However, it has tended to increase the extraregional concentration of their exports while leaving their intraregional division of labor lagging behind.

4.3   Competition with the NICs and ASEAN in the Export Market

Japan trades with the global market, and her trade with the NICs and ASEAN represents only slightly more than one-fifth of her total exports and imports. These statistics, however, underestimate Japan's close competitive/complementary relations with these countries. Competition between their products has been occurring more often in third-country markets than in their own.

In table 4.4 the trade matrices of tables 4.1–4.3 are rearranged to illustrate competition among Japan, the NICs, and ASEAN in their major export markets. For all industrial goods, each of the three increased its share in both North America and Western Europe. Although Japan still retains much larger shares, the NICS and the ASEAN countries more than doubled their shares. In the NICs' and ASEAN markets the decline of Japanese shares was matched by increases in the NICs' and ASEAN shares. In textile competition this is more visible. While Japan lost half of its shares in all markets, the NICs gained an amount equal to the Japanese loss. It is clear that textile exports from the NICs and the ASEAN countries were very competitive with Japan's products and succeeded in replacing them at the low-quality end of the product line.

4.4   Japan's Industrial Imports from the NICs and ASEAN

Japanese imports of manufactures from the NICs and ASEAN countries started in the late 1950s but reached a significant level only in the latter half of the 1970s. The basic reason for the recent increase is the rise in wage costs in Japan, but the following factors also contributed to Japan's import expansion: (1) substantial tariff cuts in 1967–72 in the Kennedy Round, the Unilateral Tariff Reduction, and the Generalized System of Preferences to developing-country exports; (2) repeated, rapid yen appreciation during the 1970s; (3) some products of Japanese multinational companies and procurements by government trading companies flowed back to Japan (boomerang phenomenon); and (4) the NICs' efforts to diversify their export markets to the Middle East and Japan in response to the rise of protectionism in the United States and Western Europe.

Table 4.2 shows that Japan's imports of manufactures rose sixfold, from $4 billion in 1969 to $24 billion in 1979. Especially notable in this is the rise of the NICs' share. Textile imports, according to table 4.4, show an even more sharp increase and in value terms increased eighteen times in the same period; more than half of it from the NICs. The share of imports from ASEAN countries shows a rising trend but is still small. Japan's imports of textiles from the NICs and ASEAN became comparable in size to those of the United States and Western Europe combined, although Japan imports much more from Korea and Taiwan than from the others.

Detailed analysis of individual commodity items will be worthwhile. The combined share of the NICs and ASEAN in Japan's manufactured imports averaged 22% in 1979, but many individual commodity items exceeded this figure. Table 4.5 lists the twenty groups (out of 102 SITC three-digit level categories) in which the Asian NICs and ASEAN countries held the largest shares of Japan's import market, in order of the size of the share. More than half of the Japanese imports in these twenty categories were supplied by the NICs and ASEAN countries. Tin (concentrates and metal) has been included in the table although it may be classified as a primary commodity. Cement, watches, radios and televisions, and five products from SITC division 67 (iron and steel) are new exports which had only very small shares, if any, in the 1960s but grew to be major export commodities of these countries in the 1970s. The last three columns of the table identify the major exporters and their shares. It is remarkable that for seventeen commodities either Korea or Taiwan held the largest share, followed by Hong Kong, which led in two items (see table 4.5). On the other hand, the ASEAN countries had shares of more than 5% only in eight commodity groups (textiles, miscellaneous products, and indigenous products; see table 4.6).

4.5 Japan's Exports of Intermediate and Investment Goods to the NICs and ASEAN

An examination of the competitive aspect of trade does not tell the whole story. Although the NICs, and to a lesser degree the ASEAN countries, have substantially increased their exports of consumer goods, they cannot yet domestically supply many needed intermediate and investment goods and have to import them from Japan and other developed countries. Every aspect of competition and complementarity in trade relations can be observed in trade matrices, in the change of market shares, and in the expansion of imports. But the coexistence of both can be established only with an international input-output table.

An international I/O table has been completed recently by the Institute of Developing Economies, Japan. It links the I/O tables of Japan,

Table 4.4 **Competition in Major Markets** (millions of U.S. $)

	Japan	NICs	ASEAN	North America	Western Europe	Australia and N. Z.	Middle East
				All Commodities			
Japan	3.5	37.6	27.3	11.5	1.7	12.9	2.9
NICs	6.4	29.8	20.8	11.3	2.2	15.5	12.4
	9.3	3.9	5.7	3.3	0.6	2.1	0.5
ASEAN	14.0	4.6	5.7	6.0	1.2	5.1	3.5
		5.2	16.2	2.5	0.7	3.8	0.6
		7.3	24.2	3.7	1.1	6.7	1.4
Total	100.0%	100.0%	100.0%	100.0%	100.0%	100.0%	100.0%
	(12,490)	(5,281)	(5,860)	(47,740)	(123,510)	(4,500)	(7,090)
	100.0%	100.0%	100.0%	100.0%	100.0%	100.0%	100.0%
	(96,318)	(47,980)	(46,296)	(250,747)	(738,474)	(20,546)	(77,326)

Industrial Goods

Japan	4.7	46.9	36.5	15.8	2.4	15.4	3.9
NICs	17.3	43.3	32.7	18.9	3.5	20.1	16.4
ASEAN	2.7	4.0	6.8	4.5	0.8	2.4	0.6
	4.6	6.4	8.1	9.9	1.9	6.6	4.2
		0.7	6.1	1.0	0.2	0.4	0.1
		3.1	10.3	2.2	0.6	2.2	1.1
Total	100.0%	100.0%	100.0%	100.0%	100.0%	100.0%	100.0%
	(3,920)	(3,657)	(4,128)	(33,400)	(76,850)	(3,550)	(5,065)
	100.0%	100.0%	100.0%	100.0%	100.0%	100.0%	100.0%
	(24.098)	(30,707)	(28,130)	(145,878)	(449,914)	(15,487)	(56,976)

Textiles and Clothing

Japan	28.8	59.1	44.1	24.1	1.9	28.6	22.3
NICs	51.8	30.6	25.8	6.5	0.7	13.6	10.4
ASEAN	1.5	9.1	18.3	21.1	4.6	12.1	4.3
	3.4	23.7	37.4	44.5	7.8	24.4	11.3
		0.5	2.8	0.9	0.1	0.5	0.8
		3.4	14.1	4.0	1.4	5.0	2.8
Total	100.0%	100.0%	100.0%	100.0%	100.0%	100.0%	100.0%
	(198)	(634)	(535)	(2,614)	(7,923)	(412)	(256)
	100.0%	100.0%	100.0%	100.0%	100.0%	100.0%	100.0%
	(3,627)	(3,282)	(1,651)	(9,061)	(46,958)	(1,586)	(4,123)

Source: Tables 4.1–4.3.
Note: See notes to table 4.1.

Table 4.5   Japan's Imports of Manufactured Goods from Asian NICs and ASEAN

SITC Code No.	Commodity	Japan's Total Imports 1979 (U.S. $1,000)	Eight Countries' Combined Share 1979 (%)	1970 (%)	Individual Countries' Share (1979, %)		
687	Tin	452,413	98.6	98.0	ML (57.9)	IN (20.9)	TH (19.7)
679	Iron and steel castings	1,989	87.1	51.5	KR (57.1)	TW (30.0)	
632	Wood manufactures	141,127	77.4	61.9	TW (55.6)	TH (7.6)	KP (6.8)
					PH (3.5)	ML (1.7)	SP (1.0)
674	Iron and steel plates	224,109	70.8	0.5	KR (41.4)	TW (29.2)	
851	Footwear	288,709	68.1	22.6	KR (42.0)	TW (25.6)	
673	Iron and steel bars	26,329	63.4	19.7	KR (39.4)	TW (23.4)	
841	Clothing	1,650,406	63.3	54.5	KR (39.6)	TW (16.1)	HK (5.7)
					PH (1.1)		
651	Textile yarn and thread	592,608	61.9	40.3	KR (45.7)	TW (10.6)	HK (2.6)
693	Wire products of metal	8,733	61.8	0.2	KR (54.5)	TW (3.6)	HK (2.3)
821	Furniture	231,910	61.2	10.9	TW (40.2)	KR (6.8)	HK (6.4)
					TH (2.6)	PH (2.2)	ML (1.4)
					SP (1.0)		

Code	Item	Value				
661	Cement and building materials	94,477	59.5	12.2	KR (47.8)	TW (11.6)
677	Iron and steel wire	9,911	57.8	0.7	KR (55.8)	TW (2.0)
521	Mineral tar	67,605	57.4	18.9	KR (56.8)	
899	Other manufactured articles	258,284	56.1	39.7	TW (26.6) PH (2.1)	KR (14.5) IN (1.8) HK (8.6) ML (1.4)
842	Fur clothing	150,820	55.5	8.0	HK (49.9)	KR (5.5)
864	Watches and clocks	209,571	50.5	5.6	HK (20.5) KR (6.2)	TW (9.7) PH (5.9) SP (7.2)
654	Tulle, lace, embroidery, etc.	63,790	48.1	9.7	KR (43.6)	TW (3.9)
672	Ingots of steel	165,584	47.0	18.4	TW (25.4)	KR (21.6)
612	Manufactures of leather	40,159	45.5	23.7	KR (39.0)	TW (6.2)
724	Radios and TVs	320,713	45.3	7.6	TW (23.2) SP (3.3)	KR (15.6) HK (2.4)
	Total (20 items)	4,999,265				

Source: Compiled and computed by H. Kohama using the AIDXT program of the Institute of Developing Economies.

Notes: All percentages in parentheses indicate the proportions of Japan's total imports from individual countries. KR = Republic of Korea; TW = Taiwan; HK = Hong Kong; SP = Singapore; ML = Malaysia; TH = Thailand; PH = Philippines; IN = Indonesia.

Table 4.6   Japan's Other Major Imports from ASEAN

Commodity	Exporter	(%)
611 Leather	PH	(10.1)
897 Jewelry	TH	(9.7)
621 Materials of rubber	ML	(7.9)
656 Made-up textile articles	TH	(7.6)
655 Special textile fabrics	SP	(6.6)
667 Precious stones	TH	(6.6)
541 Medical products	SP	(6.5)
683 Nickel	PH	(5.0)

Source: Compiled and computed by H. Kohama using the AIDXT program of the Institute of Developing Economies.

Notes: Percentages indicate the proportions of Japan's total imports from individual countries.

SP = Singapore; ML = Malaysia; TH = Thailand; PH = Philippines.

the United States, Korea, and the five ASEAN countries by means of trade matrices and enables us to trace both direct and indirect effects of an increase in a country's final demand on the trade and production of all countries.

Table 4.7 is an excerpt from the inverse matrix computed from the international I/O table (IDE 1982). It gives the induced manufacturing output generated by a million U.S. dollar increase of final demand for the manufacturing output in each country. It includes the expansion of manufacturing output both directly and indirectly required for induced export expansion.

For example, a million dollar increase in demand for manufacturing output from Indonesia induces the expansion of manufacturing output not only in Indonesia but also in other countries (in the form of imports). It includes both direct inducement of the product demand and indirect inducement of intermediate input into the production. It amounts to a $1,155,300 increase in manufacturing output for Indonesia, $600 for Malaysia, and so on. The induced manufacturing output for the other seven countries combined totals $131,900 and that for all eight countries totals $1,287,200.

Even with constant exogenous demand for each individual country, the different composition of final output of each country, that is, the different structure of production of intermediate inputs, results in different amounts of induced expansion of output. Japan has the largest amount of induced domestic output, $1,782,000, reflecting the high degree of intermediate production characteristic of her industrial structure. On the other hand, induced expansion of foreign output reflects

Table 4.7   Interdependence of Manufacturing Production among Asia-Pacific Countries: Output Induced by $1 Million Increase in Demand for Manufacturing Output in the Importing Country (thousands of U.S. $)

Importing Country	Exporting Country							
	Ind.	Mal.	Phil.	Sing.	Thai.	Korea	Japan	U.S.
Indonesia	1,155.3	1.0	0.2	27.2	0.2	1.2	1.1	0.2
Malaysia	0.6	1,219.1	0.4	26.1	0.8	5.4	0.8	0.7
Philippines	0.3	0.3	1,257.5	0.9	0.4	1.1	2.0	0.5
Singapore	9.0	16.0	0.4	1,210.2	1.9	0.5	1.0	0.4
Thailand	0.6	6.0	0.3	4.7	1,277.2	1.3	1.6	0.2
Korea	1.7	1.5	0.8	3.9	2.3	1,459.1	2.5	1.2
Japan	97.2	65.0	71.1	122.8	82.9	143.4	1,782.0	16.6
U.S.	17.1	25.1	36.6	67.9	11.2	69.2	22.0	1,626.2
Total induced output abroad	131.9	114.9	109.8	253.5	99.7	222.1	31.0	19.8
Total induced output both at home and abroad	1,287.2	1,334.0	1,367.3	1,463.7	1,376.9	1,681.2	1,813.0	1,646.0

Source: Rearranged from the inverse matrix of the twenty-four-sector international I-O table (Institute of Developing Economies 1982).

import dependence. Singapore has the highest figure, $253,500 in output induced abroad per million dollars of exogenous demand in Singapore.

A detailed examination of the table establishes the unique role of Japan in providing Korea and ASEAN countries with the intermediate inputs needed for their manufacturing production. The induced expansion for Japan is on the order of U.S. $70–$140 thousand and far exceeds those for other countries, which are on the order of $200–$2,000 except in the case of Singapore, with its closer ties to Indonesia, Malaysia, and Thailand ($2–$26 thousand).

Let us take as an example the Japan-Korea relationship. The replacement of a million dollars' worth of Japanese products by Korean ones (a million dollar increase in Korean exports and a corresponding decrease of Japanese exports, say, to North America) generates $140 thousand in Japanese output, resulting in a net $840 thousand decrease in Japan's manufacturing output. The figure $140 thousand is the induced effect for all manufacturing on average, but the amount is much larger for some manufactures ($290 thousand for textiles, $400 thousand for machinery, and $530 thousand for metals) because the intermediate inputs needed for such heavy manufacturing are less available at home.[2]

How will further heavy industrialization of Korean industry affect this complementary relationship with Japan? Indeed, the import substitution in the heavy industries would reduce complementarity; however, since Korea cannot promote heavy industrialization in many product lines at the same time because of its limited market and capacity size, it is more likely that Korean heavy industrialization will increase both complementarity and competition with Japan. A similar competition/complementarity relationship exists between the ASEAN countries and Japan, although to a lesser extent.

Japan's export growth continued at a reasonable speed in the latter half of the 1970s. Partly, this was because of the steady export expansion of automobiles, electronics, machinery, etc., to the major markets of the United States and Europe and to the new market of the Middle East. Industrialization in the NICs and the ASEAN countries, on the other hand, through its inducement effect, promoted Japan's export of intermediate and investment goods to these countries.

Incidentally, the intermediate induced expansion to Korea and Singapore from the other four ASEAN countries reflects the emerging dependence of the latter on the former for the supply of intermediate and investment goods. It is presumed that this dependence has increased since 1975, considering the recent export expansion of those commodities from Korea and Singapore.

4.6 Japan's Trade Balance with the NICs and ASEAN

The trade matrix of all commodities (table 4.1) shows the regional structure of the balance of trade. Comparison of figures in the cells at symmetrical positions using the diagonal line as an axis enables us to obtain each country or region's balance of trade with others. Table 4.8 provides data on the balance of trade for Japan, the Asian NICs, and the ASEAN countries. Japan and the Asian NICs together, all of which are industrial goods exporters, incur deficits with such resource-rich countries as Australia, Indonesia, Malaysia, and the Middle East, and maintain trade surpluses with North America and Western Europe. And all Asian NICs and the less-resource-rich ASEAN countries (Thailand and the Philippines) incur big trade deficits with Japan, offsetting much of their surplus with other countries, from which stem the present complaints of these countries against Japan. It goes without saying that individual bilateral trade should not necessarily be balanced in a world of multilateral trade. So long as Japan imports raw materials and exports in processed form, a surplus in industrial goods trade is needed to pay for her imports of primary products.

However, Japan experienced big surpluses in current accounts in 1977–78 and 1981–83. The surplus of U.S. $27.5 billion in 1977 -78

Table 4.8   **Regional Structure of the Balance of Trade, 1969 and 1979**
(millions of U.S. $)

| | | | | | Austr. | | |
| | | | Asian | | and | North | Western |
	World	Japan	NICs	ASEAN	N.Z.	America	Europe
Japan	+3,500		+1,556	+441	−581	+1,458	+712
Asian NICs	+6,714		+8,143	−3,831	−2,658	+7,641	+8,196
Taiwan	−165	−448	+67	+28	−20	+107	+5
	+2,773	−2,105	+957	+500	+39	+2,853	+993
Korea	−1,019	−634	−3	−56	−10	−179	−143
	−3,224	−2,893	+479	−320	−389	+624	+768
Hong Kong	−247	−474	−64	+85	+8	+452	+4
	−5,239	−3,145	−1,436	−1,064	+40	+1,973	+752
	−1,431	−1,556	0	+57	−22	+380	−134
Total	−5,690	−8,143	0	−884	−310	+5,450	+2,513
ASEAN							
Singapore	−180	−203	−60	−870	−34	+32	−23
	−3,110	−1,300	+402	−1,024	+232	−245	−9
Malaysia	+772	+167	+18	+213	−23	+203	+62
	+2,961	+1,084	+288	+45	−178	+1,007	+784
Thailand	−361	−281	+29	+48	−27	−51	−143
	−1,608	−602	+2	+41	−99	−301	+155
Philippines	−488	−139	+16	−48	−62	−70	−175
	−2,033	−419	−65	−343	−154	−173	+27
Indonesia	−73	+15	−60	+175	+35	−81	−69
	+8,193	+5,068	+257	+1,281	−90	+2,178	−74
Total	−330	−441	−57	0	−111	+33	−348
	+4,403	+3,831	+884	0	−289	+2,466	+883

Source: Rearranged from table 4.1.
Note: The upper figures are for 1969 and the lower for 1979.

was resolved through various channels, partly through the appreciation of the yen, partly through capital outflow, partly by means of expansionary monetary and fiscal policies, and finally by the second oil price hike. The surplus of U.S. $32.4 billion in 1981–83 has not yet been followed by the appreciation of the yen but has been matched mainly by short-term capital outflow in response to higher interest rates in the United States. Capital flow of a longer-term nature (direct investment, long-term export credit, etc.) has also contributed to the capital account deficit, which offset the big current account surplus. Furthermore, fiscal and monetary expansion has been implemented, though insufficiently, being constrained by the accumulation of government debt and the fear of further depreciation of the yen.

Because of Japan's increasing surplus in her overall current account, complaints about trade with Japan have been leveled by the United States and the European Economic Community as well as by her Asian neighbors, all of them demanding the "opening of the Japanese market" to their products. However, Japan's overall imbalance should be distinguished from her bilateral trade imbalance with her Asian neighbors. The overall imbalance itself needs to be resolved by proper macroeconomic measures. The "Economic Policy Package" should have been implemented earlier than June 1983 and should have provided greater stimulus to aggregate economic activities. Many Japanese economists have been embarrassed by the cheaper yen rates and wish to see the capital outflow discouraged by the closing of the interest rate differential and by the appreciation of the yen rate to a level reflecting Japan's "fundamentals." It is expected that the overall imbalance will be improved to generate a surplus reflecting the normal level of her investment-savings gap. However, Japan's bilateral trade surplus with her Asian neighbors will remain, even after her overall imbalance is resolved.

In spite of the standard economic reasoning arguing that bilateral trade should not necessarily be balanced, the complaints of the NICs and ASEAN about their bilateral trade deficits with Japan will be examined to determine the extent of their validity. The preference for industrial production and industrial employment cannot be denied, and mutual exports of industrial products are needed to satisfy this preference. Free trade will not be maintained unless both parties are satisfied with gains from trade. What, then, affects Japan's imports of manufactures from the Asian NICs and the ASEAN countries?

4.7 Factors Affecting Japan's Imports of Manufactures

In spite of the recent increases in Japan's imports of manufactures from the Asian NICs, Japan is still strongly criticized abroad for importing insufficient amounts; only 11% of NICs' manufactured exports and 8% of ASEAN's manufactured exports go to Japan. It cannot be denied that Japan does not import enough manufactures, even after taking into account the smaller size of her market relative to those of the United States and Europe. This reflects the lack of complementarity in manufacturing production between Japan and the NICs and the ASEAN countries as depicted in table 4.7. Balanced growth of manufactures trade in this region requires further expansion of Japan's imports of manufactures.

Why does Japan import at such a low level? Tariffs and import quotas, implicit import restrictions (such as voluntary export restraints and administrative guidance to importers), and a complicated distribution channel are often mentioned, but they do not seem to be very important in affecting the long-run trend of imports.

Japan's tariffs on manufacturing have been lowered below those of Europe and the United States through a series of trade liberalization moves, i.e., the Kennedy Round Tariff Reduction (1967–72), the Unilateral Trade Reduction (1972), and the Tokyo Round Tariff Reduction (1980–87). Furthermore, imports under the Generalized System of Preferences (exempting 50%–100% of the duties on manufactured imports from developing countries) have increased steadily since 1971, and NICs and the ASEAN countries have been the major beneficiaries. Import quotas on manufactures have been almost totally abolished, leaving only those on raw silk, silk fabrics, and leather goods. Japan has not yet resorted to quota restriction of textile imports under the bilateral agreement of the Multi-Fiber Arrangement, Article 4.

What about voluntary export restraints and the infamous administrative guidance to importers? Voluntary restraint was requested only at a private business level from exporters of a few commodities: from Korea and Pakistan for cotton yarns, from China for cotton fabrics, and from Korea for certain steel products. All of them took place in cases of import surge into the Japanese market. Their import-restricting effect, however, was rather dubious, but the Korean Spinner's Association agreed on voluntary restraint of cotton yarn exports when a dumping case was brought up by its Japanese counterpart.

An import surveillance system and administrative guidance were introduced for textiles and clothing by the government in 1973–74 after the import surge motivated by speculation. The former is no more than an early-warning system based on import contract statistics. A record of all import contracts was collected from individual importers and circulated to all importers in order to avoid import without deficit market prospects. The latter is conducted by officials of the Ministry of International Trade and Industry, who telephone major importers in order to discourage further increase of import contracts in case of an import surge. There were a few cases when this scheme was attempted to discourage an increase of imports of cotton yarn, but it was not very effective since importation continued by minor importers. This tactic is seldom attempted for imports of such differentiated products as fabrics and clothing, where small-lot transactions are handled by many traders and thus high administrative costs would be incurred. It may well be concluded that administrative guidance can prevent import surges caused by speculation but not import increases caused by market forces.

Conventional import procedures and complicated distribution channels are often referred to as barriers to penetration into the Japanese market by foreign exporters. The import procedure, however, will be improved considerably by an overall amendment of the Import Law proposed in December 1982. The complicated distribution channels reflect the major role of Japanese wholesalers in providing small-and medium-sized manufacturers with merchandizing and financing facilities. A recent MIPRO report (1983) pointed out that the distribution channels for imported products are shorter and more simplified than those for their domestic competitors, thereby giving a competitive edge to importers. Direct imports of cheap consumer manufactures have been increased by department stores and supermarkets.

The same report listed around fifty European and American firms which have succeeded in establishing their distribution channels in Japan either independently or in cooperation with Japanese agents. Moreover, the alleged "lack of acquaintance" of foreign exporters with the Japanese market is much less important for Korean and Taiwanese exporters, who have had close contact with the Japanese market.

4.8 Structural Adjustment of Domestic Production

The slow expansion of Japan's imports of manufactures has been affected by such structural factors as adjustment of domestic production, competition within the Japanese market, and the business behavior of Japanese firms. We need to investigate how Japanese manufacturing industries have been adjusting to the increased export capability of the NICs and ASEAN. The data in table 4.9 show the change over time (1965–80) in export-output and self-sufficiency ratios for forty major industries. The two ratios are defined as E/X and $(X - E) / (X + M - E)$, where X, E, and M refer to domestic production, export, and import respectively. We expect the two ratios to decline in an industry in which Japan is losing comparative advantage.

For the manufacturing total (row 41) a slow adjustment is depicted. The export-output ratio increased by 4%, while the self-sufficiency ratio declined by 2% between 1965 and 1980. But more distinct adjustment is observed at less aggregated levels. For textiles and miscellaneous products (rows 16–20, 22) the self-sufficiency ratio showed a greater decline (10%–15% for natural fiber yarn and leather products); the export-output ratio also declined for many of them. Among processed foodstuffs (rows 10–15), meat, dairy, and fishery products showed distinct declines in the two ratios, while small amounts of exports and high self-sufficiency continued for others.

On the other hand, the export-output ratios increased greatly for machinery (rows 37–40), while their self-sufficiency ratios remained unchanged at 95–99% (except for precision instruments). For chemicals and metals, the self-sufficiency ratios declined slightly, and their high export-output ratios remained unchanged. The declining shares of the first two groups in total output and the increasing shares in machinery obscure the progress of structural adjustment when looking at the manufacturing industry as a whole.

Primary industries except fisheries (rows 1–3, 5–9) had insignificant export performance. The self-sufficiency ratios of forestry, coal, and non-ferrous-metal ores declined rapidly, while those for other minerals had been very low from the beginning. The increased self-sufficiency of livestock and the small decline of the same ratio for agriculture reflected partly the increase in domestic prices in the two sectors, since the ratio is calculated on the basis of current price data. Primary production contributed only 8% to the total output.

Competition has increased in textiles and miscellaneous products, for which both export-output and self-sufficiency ratios declined. The decrease in the two ratios will be more distinct when certain industrial activities, such as cotton yarn, fabrics, and lumber products, are disaggregated, while the two ratios will remain as high for others, such as synthetic fiber yarn and fabrics. This difference attributed to revived competitiveness in the latter industrial activities in Japan.

The products of the textile and other consumer goods industries have been diversified and upgraded in the face of increased competition with cheap imports from Asian developing countries, and their competitive edge has been strengthened significantly by changes in consumption patterns at home. It seems to be understood only insufficiently by economists that revitalization has resulted from the successful response of textile firms to changes in consumer taste in developed countries and also from the change in emphasis of firms from quantity to quality, and that microelectronic technology is geared well to efficient production of assorted items in small lots.

A recent General Agreement on Tariffs and Trade report (GATT 1983) criticized the current research efforts in automatic clothing production in developed countries as a waste of capital and suggested that the same supply of clothing could be obtained through trade with developing countries. However, the report misses the point that the constant change in taste and the preference for diversity are major characteristics of this industry. As a matter of fact, textile businessmen in developing countries, recognizing the current demand change in their export markets and expecting similar changes in their domestic markets in the near future, have started to upgrade the quality of their products.

However, the combined share of textile, miscellaneous products, and processed foodstuffs declined to 10% of the total output in 1980. The decline in self-sufficiency is needed in machinery and chemical-metal

Table 4.9   Structural Adjustment of Japanese Industries

	Share in Total Output (%)				Export-output Ratio (%)				Self-sufficiency Ratio (%)			
	1965	1970	1975	1980	1965	1970	1975	1980	1965	1970	1975	1980
1. Cultivation agriculture	6.4	4.1	4.3	3.0	0.5	1.6	0.2	0.6	80.7	78.8	77.9	76.4
2. Livestock	2.0	1.5	1.7	1.4	0.4	0.2	0.1	0.0	86.5	90.9	94.8	96.4
3. Forestry	2.1	1.2	0.9	0.7	0.5	0.6	0.8	1.0	83.3	67.8	67.1	57.9
4. Fishery	1.4	1.1	1.2	1.1	10.0	4.0	1.6	1.4	97.6	95.5	91.7	91.7
5. Coal	0.5	0.2	0.1	0.1	0.2	0.1	0.3	0.7	66.1	30.5	13.9	18.8
6. Iron ore	0	0	0	0	0	0	0	0	6.2	1.9	0.7	0
7. Non-ferrous-metal ore	0.1	0.1	0.1	0	0.3	0.2	1.5	2.3	36.3	17.8	14.7	11.6
8. Crude petroleum and natural gas	0	0	0	0	0.7	2.1	0.1	0	4.3	2.9	1.0	0.9
9. Other nonmetallic minerals	0.6	0.8	0.8	0.9	1.0	1.0	1.0	1.0	77.9	82.4	82.0	84.4
10. Meat and dairy products	1.7	1.4	1.7	1.4	0.9	0.5	0.2	0.4	92.2	91.6	89.1	86.8
11. Fishery products	1.1	0.9	1.1	1.2	10.0	10.8	7.2	5.8	95.5	92.0	88.0	85.0
12. Grain, milled and flour	3.3	2.0	1.8	1.4	0.3	1.1	0.1	0.8	95.5	99.5	99.6	99.6
13. Other processed foods	5.1	4.0	4.8	4.7	1.9	1.4	0.9	0.5	93.8	93.5	91.5	94.5
14. Beverages	2.2	1.9	1.8	1.6	0.5	0.4	0.4	0.8	99.7	99.3	98.6	97.9
15. Tobacco	1.2	0.9	0.9	0.8	0.4	0.1	0	0	99.6	99.6	99.3	99.4
16. Natural fiber yarn	1.4	0.7	0.5	0.4	6.2	6.1	3.0	2.3	98.0	92.7	87.8	83.1
17. Man-made fiber yarn	0.6	0.5	0.3	0.2	5.6	9.7	12.6	14.2	100.0	99.8	99.3	97.4
18. Fabrics and other textile products	5.2	4.1	3.3	2.6	17.4	14.5	14.0	14.1	99.0	97.2	94.8	93.3
19. Wearing apparel	1.6	1.6	1.8	1.5	13.6	8.8	2.5	2.2	99.6	98.9	96.6	93.6
20. Leather and leather products	0.3	0.2	0.2	0.2	12.6	12.9	14.7	14.2	95.7	93.3	89.8	86.6

	Share in Total Output (%)				Export-output Ratio (%)				Self-sufficiency Ratio (%)			
	1965	1970	1975	1980	1965	1970	1975	1980	1965	1970	1975	1980
21. Rubber products	1.0	0.8	0.9	0.9	17.5	16.7	16.1	16.5	99.5	99.1	96.1	95.3
22. Miscellaneous products	2.2	2.5	2.7	3.0	19.0	12.7	7.8	8.7	97.0	96.3	96.3	96.3
23. Lumber and wooden products	2.7	2.6	2.1	1.8	4.0	2.3	1.1	0.8	98.5	95.3	92.8	89.2
24. Furniture	1.1	1.3	1.3	1.1	1.3	1.0	0.7	1.3	99.9	99.8	99.1	98.2
25. Printing and publishing	2.0	2.1	2.4	2.3	0.8	0.9	0.5	0.6	99.2	99.9	99.1	99.3
26. Pulp and paper	3.1	3.0	3.0	3.1	2.2	2.5	3.1	2.7	97.3	97.2	96.8	95.5
27. Basic industrial chemicals	3.7	3.3	3.8	4.3	8.5	9.2	12.6	8.4	94.6	95.2	95.3	93.6
28. Chemical fiber materials	1.2	1.0	0.6	0.5	14.9	16.6	28.3	25.7	99.6	99.3	99.4	97.1
29. Other chemical products	2.4	2.3	2.6	2.7	4.1	6.1	8.8	9.4	93.1	89.9	91.0	89.7
30. Petroleum products	2.8	2.7	4.9	6.0	4.0	2.3	3.8	2.4	89.8	89.9	90.4	86.9
31. Coal products	0.8	0.9	1.4	1.3	0.2	0.2	0.8	1.4	99.8	99.8	99.7	99.9
32. Ceramic and other nonmetallic mineral products	2.6	3.0	3.1	3.2	8.3	5.5	5.8	6.3	99.4	99.3	99.2	98.9
33. Pig iron and crude steel	4.3	4.9	5.2	4.4	0.3	0.2	0.9	0.2	94.3	95.2	98.2	98.1
34. Primary steel products	6.7	8.2	7.2	7.5	16.8	13.8	25.5	17.9	99.9	99.8	99.9	99.4
35. Primary non-ferrous-metal products	1.7	2.2	2.0	2.5	6.8	5.0	7.7	11.4	85.1	82.3	86.8	79.9
36. Other metal products	3.6	4.2	3.9	3.8	7.9	7.4	9.7	10.2	99.3	99.3	99.0	98.9
37. Industrial machinery	6.7	9.4	8.5	8.1	8.3	8.9	14.7	19.4	95.0	95.7	96.3	96.5
38. Electrical machinery	5.9	8.6	6.7	8.7	12.7	13.2	18.4	23.0	97.2	94.4	95.5	95.6
39. Transport equipment	7.7	8.6	9.5	10.2	15.7	17.3	29.7	30.3	97.7	97.3	97.2	96.8
40. Precision instruments	1.2	1.3	1.0	1.3	19.5	23.6	32.3	38.4	93.5	89.8	84.9	84.3
41. Manufacturing total (rows 10–40)	86.9	91.1	90.9	92.8	8.7	8.6	11.6	12.3	96.5	96.0	95.5	94.5
42. Total (rows 1–40)	100.0	100.0	100.0	100.0	7.7	8.0	10.6	11.5	92.7	92.3	89.1	87.6

Source: Compiled by Takeshi Suzuki with data from the Economic Planning Agency.

Note: The two ratios are defined as follows. The export-output ratio and self-sufficiency ratio are defined as E/X and $(X - E)/(X + M - E)$, where X, E, and M refer to domestic output, exports, and imports respectively.

groups in order to increase Japan's import of manufactures. Although Japan still retains international competitiveness in these activities, the NICs have been promoting domestic production and export of these products, and they have a competitive edge in the labor-intensive, standardized portions of the production process.

It is typical for Japanese firms to procure some parts and intermediate inputs from affiliated suppliers within Japan. This type of firm behavior has been fostered for a long time by Japan's import substitution strategy to offset her persistent balance-of-payments deficits in her development process. It is also related to the well-developed system of subcontracting and the high technology and skill level of subcontracting firms. If, however, they modify their policy and extend their procurement sources to include their Asian neighbors, intraregional trade in parts and intermediate products will in the long run be as prevalent between Japan and the NICs as it is between the countries of Western Europe.

Japan's Asian neighbors need improved skills and technology to promote intraregional trade in both consumer goods and intermediate products.

4.9   Toward a Harmonious Division of Labor

Many Japanese economists welcome the catching up of NICs and ASEAN countries in various sectors of industrial activities. These countries have the highest potential for growth in the world, and Japan must cooperate with them for mutual prosperity. These economists recognize the need for promoting industrial development in the region at the cost of increasing competition with some Japanese sectors. There are of course strong objections from businessmen in import-competing sectors, and their demand for protection has increased recently. However, the Japanese government maintains a free trading position, and Japan has remained the last major developed country refraining from a policy of restraining textile imports under the MFA. Its industrial policies for adjustment assistance to the manufacturing sector are generally consistent with the idea of positive adjustment policies.

The promotion of industrial cooperation, however, should be consistent with the market forces and initiatives of private enterprises and individuals. The government can arrange a favorable atmosphere for technical transfer and upgrading of skills only through a joint venture with the private sector. An increasing number of Japanese businessmen have been regarding the East and Southeast Asia as an integrated area to which the supply of their parts and intermediate inputs may freely be relocated from the "traditional" domestic sources. But there still remains room for host governments to improve their rules and regulations that have been discouraging these private business activities beyond the national borders of Japan.

The promotion of a harmonious division of labor between Japan and her Asian neighbors requires modification of conventional governmental and firm behavior on both sides.

Notes

1. The first five sections of this paper are based on the joint research of the author and two of his colleagues. For details of the analysis and statistical information, refer to Yamazawa, Hirata, and Taniguchi 1983.
2. These figures are obtained from the original inverse matrix of the twenty-four-sector I-O table in Institute of Developing Economies 1982.

References

GATT. 1983. *Prospects for international trade: Main conclusions of GATT study for 1982–83*. Geneva.

Institute of Developing Economies. 1982. *International input-output tables for ASEAN countries 1975*. IDE Statistical Data Series, no. 39. Tokyo.

MIPRO (Manufactured Import Promotion Committee of the International Trade Conference). 1983. *An analysis of and recommendations regarding the Japanese distribution system and business practices*.

Yamazawa, I. 1983. Renewal of the textile industry in developed countries and world textile trade. *Hitotsubashi Journal of Economics* 24, no. 1.

Yamazawa, I., A. Hirata, and K. Taniguchi. 1983. Trade and industrial adjustment in Pacific Asia. *Developing Economies* 21, no. 4. Tokyo.

5   Recent U.S. Trade Policy and Its Global Implications

Robert E. Baldwin and J. David Richardson

5.1   Introduction and Summary

The purpose of this paper is to describe U.S. trade policy since World War II and to highlight some of its implications for Japan and her more recently industrializing neighbors in East and Southeast Asia. As such, it is aimed at filling the void that Lawrence B. Krause (1982, 72) observed in his recent essay on U.S.-Japanese competition in members of the Association of South East Asian Nations (ASEAN):

> In formulating and executing foreign policy, the United States must recognize that its form of government is difficult for foreigners to understand. Even close European allies have trouble following the meaning behind every policy swing in Washington and responding appropriately to it. The difficulty arises in part from U.S. policy mistakes. Also, foreigners are frequently unable to distinguish those American policies that stem from fundamental American interests and thus are constant from one administration (and Congress) to the next from those policies that are subject to reversal. Developing countries with short institutional memories must be forgiven if they confuse the American policies that should not be taken too seriously with those that should.

Robert E. Baldwin is a professor of economics at the University of Wisconsin and a research associate of the National Bureau of Economic Research. J. David Richardson is a professor of economics at the University of Wisconsin and a research associate of the National Bureau of Economic Research.

The authors are indebted to Peter B. Kenen for insightful criticism. Parts of the paper have been supported by National Science Foundation grant PRA-8116459 to the National Bureau of Economic Research. The entire paper is part of the NBER's research program in international studies. Any opinions expressed are our own, however, and not those of the NBER or of the National Science Foundation.

Filling this void has grown even more important as trade with East and Southeast Asia has grown. The region supplied 40% of all U.S. imports in 1982, almost doubling its 1962 share of 21% (Reagan 1984, fig. 10). And the region purchased 16% of all U.S. exports in 1982, up from 10% in 1962. Without Japan, the growth is proportionally even more dramatic: the region's share of U.S. imports more than tripled (from 5% to 16%), and its share of U.S. exports purchased doubled (from 5% to 10%).

U.S. trade policy over this period was fairly consistently liberal. In fact future economic historians will undoubtedly stress trade liberalization as the most distinctive feature of U.S. commercial policy over the past fifty years. As table 5.1 indicates, through a series of thirty bilateral agreements and eight multilateral negotiations, tariffs have been steadily cut to only about 20% of their 1930 average level.[1] The increased use in recent years of nontariff measures modifies this liberalization picture somewhat, but the trend in protection over the period has clearly been downward.

Although tariff reduction has been the dominant thrust of U.S. trade policy since the early 1930s, there have been important shifts in the

Table 5.1   **Duty Reduction since 1934 under the U.S. Trade Agreements Program**

GATT Conference	Proportion of Dutiable Imports Subject to Reductions (%)	Average Cut in Reduced Tariffs (%)	Average Cut in All Duties (%)	Remaining Duties as Proportions of 1930 Tariffs[a] (%)
Pre-Gatt, 1934–47	63.9	44.0	33.2	66.8
First Round, Geneva, 1947	53.6	35.0	21.1	52.7
Second Round, Annecy, 1949	5.6	35.1	1.9	51.7
Third Round, Torquay, 1950–51	11.7	26.0	3.0	50.1
Fourth Round, Geneva, 1955–56	16.0	15.6	3.5	48.9
Dillon Round, Geneva, 1961–62	20.0	12.0	2.4	47.7
Kennedy Round, 1964–67	79.2	45.5	36.0	30.5
Tokyo Round, 1974–79	n.a.	n.a.	29.6	21.2

Source: Real Philippe Laverge, "The Political Economy of U.S. Tariffs" (Ph.D. thesis, University of Toronto, 1981).

[a]These percentages do not take account of the effects of structural changes in trade or inflation on the average tariff level.

nature and extent of U.S. support for this trade liberalization. Underlying the different shifts in postwar U.S. trade policy are three basic economic and political influences: first, and most important, the emergence and subsequent decline of the United States as a hegemonic power; second, the persistence during the entire period of a politically significant group of domestic industries (whose composition changed somewhat over time) that were opposed to duty cuts on the import products with which they competed; and, finally, the efforts by Congress to reduce the enhanced powers granted the president during the economic emergency of the 1930s and the political emergency of World War II.

A number of important conclusions can be drawn from the following discussion that are important for industrializing developing countries. First, U.S. trade policy has shown remarkable consistency since World War II. It has never been as purely free-trade-focused as some commentators suggest, but it has not recently shifted toward isolationism as dramatically as alarmists fear. It has almost always been best described as "open but fair," with injury to import competitors being the measure of "fairness."

U.S. import relief policy is perhaps of greater interest to East and Southeast Asian nations than any other aspect of U.S. trade policy, since it is in U.S. imports from the region that the most dramatic growth has taken place. U.S. import relief policy also shows great consistency, although different vehicles for delivering it have been selected at different times from among the escape clause, unfair trade remedies, adjustment assistance, and orderly marketing agreements. For the first two vehicles, different mixes of tariff and nontariff instruments have been employed at various times also. The choice of tariff or nontariff instrument has importance because it affects the complexity and predictability of U.S. trade policy, and because it determines the division of implicit revenues between the United States and its export suppliers.

The general consistency of U.S. trade policy over time is all the more remarkable given the frequent change of political party in power, especially in the executive branch but also in the Congress. Party affiliation, in fact, seems no longer to be a useful predictor of U.S. trade initiative. A more useful predictor appears to be some measure of executive versus congressional control. The two branches of U.S. government have different outlooks on trade policy because of differences in constituencies. Conflict has punctuated relations between branches of government much more often than between political parties. Platform attempts by parties to distinguish themselves from each other on trade policy turn out more often than not to be sheer posturing.

U.S. trade policy leadership is still potentially strong despite the decline in U.S. hegemony. It is clearly strong in a protectionist direction. Any shift in U.S. trade policy toward aggressive insularity justifies parallel trade policy aggression in the eyes of its trading partners. It is arguably strong in a liberalizing direction as well. The United States seems ideally poised for aggressive trade policy peacemaking: perhaps multilaterally but perhaps also bilaterally; perhaps with its traditional industrial trading partners but perhaps also with Japan and newly industrializing Asian countries that play so important a role in U.S. trade and that, on many matters, may be closer in spirit to U.S. economic philosophy than Europe, Canada, or Latin America.

5.2   U.S. Trade Policy, 1945–1980[2]

5.2.1   Gaining Domestic Support for a Liberal International Trading Regime

Well before the end of World War II the foreign policy leaders of the Democratic party had concluded that the lack of an open world economy during the 1930s was a major contributory cause of the war (Gardner 1980). They had also concluded that the United States must take the lead after the end of hostilities in establishing an open international trading system in order to make "the economic foundations of peace . . . as secure as the political foundation" (from a 26 March 1945 statement to Congress by President Roosevelt). Thus, even before the war had ended the Roosevelt administration had drafted a proposal for a multilateral trade organization. It had also requested substantial new tariff-reducing powers from Congress.

A desire on the part of political leaders for a new international regime is quite different from actually bringing about such a change, especially when—as in this case—there was a lack of strong direct pressure for the change from either the country's electorate or other governments. The most important reason for the success of the Democratic leadership in first gaining and then maintaining domestic support for a liberal posture was the hegemonic trade and payments position that the United States assumed in the immediate postwar period.[3] The United States emerged from World War II with its economic base greatly expanded, while the economic structures of both its enemies and its industrial allies were in ruins. Except for Great Britain's position at the outset of the industrial revolution, economic dominance of this extent is unique in the history of the industrial nations. Even as late as 1952 the U.S. share of total exports of the ten most important industrial countries was 35%, whereas it had been only 26% and 28% in 1938 and 1928, respectively (Baldwin 1958). The 1952 U.S. export share of manufactures was also 35%, in contrast to only 21% in both 1938 and 1928. There was an export surplus in every major industrial group. These abnormally favorable export opportunities, together with the vigorous postwar economic recovery, vitiated protectionist pressure from industries whose underlying comparative cost position was deteriorating and built support for liberal trade policies on the part of those sectors whose international competitive policy was strong.

The ability of U.S. leaders to obtain domestic support for trade liberalization was further enhanced by the emergence of the cold war in the late 1940s. The public generally accepted the governmental view that the Communist countries represented a serious economic and political threat to the United States, its allies, and the rest of the market-oriented economic world. There was thus widespread support for the argument that the United States should mount a vigorous program of trying to offset the Communist threat by providing not only military aid to friendly nations but assistance in the form of economic grants and lower U.S. tariffs.

The fact that implementing an open international trading system did not involve any significant new increase in the powers of the president also was important in gaining domestic support for the regime change. Almost all commentators had regarded as excessive the use of logrolling during enactment of the Smoot-Hawley Tariff of 1930. This, coupled with the sense of crisis created by the depression that followed shortly thereafter, had led Congress in 1934 to give the president authority to lower (or raise) tariffs by up to 50%. Consequently, the 1945 request for another 50% duty-cutting authorization in order to enable the United States to take a leadership role in international trade liberalization did not entail any basic changes in existing presidential powers.

There was still considerable opposition to trade liberalization in the immediate postwar period, however. As in the 1930s a long list of industries testified during the 1940s and 1950s against giving the president the power to cut duties on imports competing with domestically produced goods. The products covered include textiles and apparel, coal, petroleum, watches, bicycles, pottery and tiles, toys, cutlery, ball bearings, glass, cheese, lead and zinc, copper, leather, and umbrellas. Pressures from these industries to halt further tariff cutting because of their belief that they would be seriously injured were further strengthened by the opposition of many Republicans to liberalization on doctrinaire grounds. Republican advocacy of protection on the grounds that this policy promoted domestic economic development had an even longer tradition than the Democratic position in favor of liberalization, which was based on the belief that low tariffs reduced monopoly profits and the prices of popular consumer goods.

From the outset of the trade agreements program, the Roosevelt administration assured Congress that no duty cuts would be made that seriously injured any domestic industry. However, in 1945 the administration, recognizing the possibility that such injury might occur, agreed to include in all future trade agreements an escape clause permitting the modification or withdrawal of tariff reductions if increased imports resulting from a concession caused or threatened to cause serious injury to an industry. Furthermore, under prodding from Republican members of Congress, President Truman in 1947 issued an executive order establishing formal procedures for escape clause actions whereby the International Trade Commission (ITC) would advise the president whether such a modification was warranted.[4]

These developments indicate that the U.S. trade policy commitment at the beginning of the postwar period was to a policy of liberal trade rather than to a policy of free trade. It was recognized at the outset that protection to particular industries would be permitted if these sectors would otherwise be seriously injured by increased imports.

The failure of the U.S. Congress to ratify the International Trade Organization (ITO) proposed to the Havana Conference of 1947–48, or even to approve the General Agreement on Tariffs and Trade (GATT) (the commercial policy provisions of the ITO) as an executive agreement, is another indication of the early concerns of domestic political interests for import-sensitive U.S. industries (Diebold 1952). Among other concerns, Congress was fearful that establishing a strong international organization to deal with trade matters would lead to the destruction of many U.S. industries as a result of increased imports. Numerous members of Congress and some of the groups they represented were also concerned about the increase in presidential power that the approval of such an organization might involve. They believed that the division of political powers among the legislative, executive, and judicial branches of government had shifted excessively in favor of the executive branch as a result of the unusual problems created by the depression and World War II; they were, consequently, reluctant to extend new authority to the president, especially in an area specifically reserved for Congress under the Constitution.

5.2.2   Gaining International Support for a Liberal International Trading Regime

The implementation of the change from an inward-looking to an open international trading regime required the support of other countries as well as of the U.S. electorate. The hegemonic model is the major explanation put forth by political scientists to account for this support. The reasoning behind this model is as follows.

An open international trading (and payments) system has elements of a public good. For example, adopting a mercantilistic viewpoint, if one country reduces its tariffs under the most-favored-nation principle, other countries benefit from the improved export opportunities this action creates even if they do not make reciprocal duty cuts themselves. Consequently, there is an incentive for any individual country to "free ride" by hoping that others will reduce their trade barriers. The net result may often be failure to secure a balanced, multilateral set of duty reductions even though they would benefit all participants. But as Olson (1965) and other writers on collective goods have pointed out, it is less likely that the public good will be underproduced if one member of the concerned group is very large compared with the others. The dominant member is so large that the cost to it of free rides by other members is small compared with its own gain. Furthermore, the large member may be able to use its power to force smaller members to practice reciprocity. Proponents of the hegemonic theory of regime change point to the dominant trading position of Great Britain in the nineteenth century to account for the creation of an open world trading regime then.

In similar fashion, in the immediate postwar period the United States was willing and able to bear most of the costs of establishing a liberal international economic order (Vernon 1983, 8–10). The other major industrial countries were plagued by balance-of-payments problems and rationed their meager supplies of dollars in order to maximize their reconstruction efforts. The tariff concessions they made in the early multilateral negotiations were not very meaningful in terms of increasing U.S. exports. U.S. negotiators were fully aware of this point. They nevertheless offered greater tariff concessions than they would have received even on the basis of the usual measures of reciprocity (Meyer 1978, 138). In effect what the United States did was to redistribute to other countries part of the economic surplus reaped from its unusually favorable export opportunities in order to enable those countries to support the establishment of an open trading regime.

5.2.3   Shifts in Domestic Support for Liberalization

When the Republicans gained both the presidency and control of Congress in 1952, some commentators expected a return to traditional protectionist policies. However, President Eisenhower and his main advisers believed that trade liberalization was an important foreign policy instrument, and Republican business leaders—especially those in the large corporations—also concluded that a liberal trading order was desirable from their own economic viewpoint. Thus, after a stand-off period in 1953 and 1954 during which protectionist Republicans in the House blocked any further tariff cutting, the liberalization trend was renewed. In 1955, with the help of a Democratic Congress, President Eisenhower succeeded in obtaining a further 15% duty-cutting authority. In 1958 he was granted an additional 20% duty-cutting authority.

Just as more and more Republicans came to accept the desirability of a liberal trade policy as a general principle, more and more Democrats began to press for special exceptions to this principle. In the late 1940s the industries requesting import protection tended to be economically and politically small. By the mid-1950s the politically powerful cotton textile, coal, and domestic petroleum industries, whose employees tended to vote Democratic, were asking for protection. In 1955 the Eisenhower administration, as part of its efforts to obtain the support of the Democrats for its liberalization efforts, pressured the Japanese into voluntarily restricting their exports of cotton textiles to the United States. In 1962 President Kennedy agreed to negotiate an international agreement permitting quantitative import restrictions on cotton textiles as part of his efforts to gain the support of southern Democrats from textile areas for the Trade Expansion Act of 1962.[5] The coal and oil industries succeeded in obtaining a national security clause in the 1955 trade act that permitted quantitative import restrictions if imports of a product threatened "to impair" the national security. Voluntary oil import quotas were introduced on these grounds in 1958 and made mandatory in 1959.

The most significant change in the nature of support for protectionism occurred in the late 1960s when the AFL-CIO abandoned its long-held belief in the desirability of a liberal trade policy and supported a general quota bill. The shift in labor's position was related to several developments. One was the rapid rise in import penetration ratios (and thus a rapid rise in competitive pressures) that occurred in many manufacturing sectors in the late 1960s. Another was labor's disappointment with the operation of the Trade Adjustment Assistance (TAA) program under the Trade Expansion Act of 1962.

As would be expected, this change in organized labor's position was reflected in the trade policy votes of Democratic members of Congress. Several protectionist initiatives progressed quite far in Congress during this period and created great uncertainty regarding the direction of U.S. trade policy. It is doubtful, furthermore, that the Trade Act of 1974 would have been approved had not the president made concessions to both organized labor and particular industries subject to import pressure. The criteria for obtaining adjustment assistance were made much more lenient to meet labor's objections, and the multilateral arrangement on textiles was extended to cover textile and apparel products manufactured from man-made material and wool as well as cotton. In addition, the voluntary export restraints agreed upon in 1968 by Japanese and European steel producers were extended in the early 1970s.

Although the pattern of congressional voting on trade policy measures in the early 1970s shows that Republicans favored and Democrats opposed liberalization, it is probably not correct to conclude that this represents a permanent shift in party positions. A more accurate description of what seems to have happened is that liberalization versus protectionism is no longer a significant party issue. The vote of individual members of Congress on trade policy is now more influenced by economic conditions in their district or state and by the pressures on them from the president (if they are both in the same party) rather than by party affiliation. Regression analysis of the voting patterns on the Trade Expansion Act of 1962 and the Trade Act of 1974 (Baldwin 1976, 1981) indicates that party affiliation was significant in 1962 but not in 1974.

5.2.4 Congressional Restraints on the President

From the outset of the trade agreements program many members of Congress felt that the president was too willing to reduce tariffs in import-sensitive sectors and—along with the ITC—too reluctant to raise them for import-injured industries. Furthermore, they believed that the executive branch was not sufficiently "tough" in administering U.S. laws dealing with the fairness of international trading practices. Consequently, Congress frequently took the occasion of the program's renewal to introduce provisions designed to force the president and the ITC to comply more closely with these congressional views. Much of the pressure for these provisions came from import-sensitive domestic industries and labor groups. However, some of the pressure seemed to stem from a belief that Congress had given the president too much of its constitutional responsibility "to regulate commerce with foreign nations" and to levy import duties.

In the Trade Expansion Act of 1962, Congress insisted on shifting the chairmanship of the interagency committee established to recommend tariff cuts to the president from the State Department (long regarded by Congress as being insufficiently sensitive to the import-injury problems of U.S. industry) to a new agency, the Office of the United States Trade Representative (USTR). The requirement of the Trade Act in 1974 that an elaborate private advisory system be established has further restricted the degree of independence that the president has in selecting items on which cuts are to be made and in determining the depth of these cuts. The creation and subsequent strengthening of congressional delegations to trade negotiations under the 1962 and 1974 laws have had the same effect. Since 1954, the president has been specifically directed not to decrease duties on any article if he finds that doing so would threaten to impair the national security. Furthermore, in granting the president authority in 1974 to permit duty-free imports from developing countries, Congress specifically excluded certain articles, e.g., watches and footwear, from preferential tariff treatment.

Congress tried to pressure the president into accepting the affirmative recommendations of the ITC on escape-clause cases when this provision was first introduced into law in 1951 by requiring the president to submit an explanatory report to Congress if these recommendations were rejected. Since this seemed to have little effect on the president, Congress included a provision in the 1958 renewal act that enabled the president's disapproval of any affirmative ITC finding to be overridden by a two-thirds vote of both the House and the Senate. This was eased in 1962 to a majority of the authorized membership of both houses and then in 1974 to only a majority of members present and voting.

Congress has also included numerous provisions in postwar trade laws to increase the proportion of affirmative import-relief decisions on the part of the ITC. The most obvious way of trying to accomplish this has been to change the criteria for granting increases in protection when an industry is threatened with or is actually being seriously injured because of increased imports. For example, the requirement that increased imports be related to a previously granted tariff concession was eliminated in 1974. Less obvious ways that Congress used in trying to make the ITC more responsive to its views included utilizing its confirmation powers to try to ensure that commission members were sympathetic to its views (Baldwin 1984c). In a further effort to weaken the influence of the president over the commission, Congress in 1974 removed all controls of the executive branch over the commission's budget and eliminated the power of the president to appoint the chairperson. This latter change was modified in 1977, but the president still cannot appoint his two most recent appointees to the commission as chairperson.

Similar steps were taken by Congress to try to ensure stricter enforcement of U.S. trade laws relating to unfair foreign practices. For example, for many years many members of Congress felt that the Treasury Department was too lax in administering U.S. antidumping and countervailing-duty legislation. One step designed to change this was to transfer the determination of injury (but not the determination of dumping) from the Treasury Department to the ITC in 1954. In 1979 Congress completely removed the authority to determine dumping and subsidization from the Treasury and gave these powers to the Commerce Department—an agency that it believed would carry out the intent of Congress more closely.

Perhaps the most significant reduction in the president's authority over trade policy concerns his ability to negotiate agreements with other countries covering nontariff measures. When Congress directed the president to seek such agreements under the Trade Act of 1974, it stipulated that any agreements must be approved by a majority vote in both the House and the Senate—unlike tariff agreements. This provision was extended in the Trade Agreements Act of 1979. It gives Congress much greater control over the nature of any agreement and increases its control over the pattern of tariff cuts undertaken by the president in a multilateral trade negotiation, since tariff and nontariff concessions made by participants are closely linked. These constraints notwithstanding, Congress fully supported the efforts of the president to negotiate new nontariff codes in the Tokyo Round, and the set of codes eventually agreed upon was approved without difficulty by the Congress.

5.2.5 Nontariff Instruments of U.S. Trade Policy

Efforts increased during the 1970s to negotiate agreements that would mitigate the adverse effects of foreign nontariff barriers (NTB). U.S. producers were pressuring government officials for the stricter enforcement of existing U.S. "fair trade" legislation, such as the antidumping and countervailing laws, and were seeking import protection under these laws to a greater extent than in the past.[6] Furthermore, domestic industries were demanding the greater use of quantitative restrictions (as compared with higher import duties) in protecting against injurious import increases.

One factor accounting for the greater number of less-than-fair-value cases has been the difficulty of obtaining protection by the traditional provisions pertaining to injury caused by import competition. Despite the 1974 easing of the criteria for determining whether import relief should be granted, only thirty-eight cases were decided by the ITC between 1975 and 1979, and in all but nineteen of these a negative decision was reached. Furthermore, the president rejected import protection in all but seven of the nineteen cases. The likelihood that the routine acceptance of affirmative ITC decisions would be interpreted by foreign governments as an abandonment of U.S. international economic leadership appears to have made the president willing to accept only a few of these decisions. Even the Congress has been hesitant on similar grounds to weaken the import relief criteria much beyond what they had been in the 1950s.

Providing protection to offset alleged unfair trade practices is much less likely to be interpreted as representing a basic shift in policy either by other governments or by domestic interests supporting a liberal trading order. Thus, within reasonable bounds a president can support efforts to achieve "fair trade" through measures that protect domestic products while still being regarded as a proponent of liberal trade policies.

A better understanding of this point has given domestic industries an incentive to utilize U.S. fair trade legislation more extensively in seeking import protection. The incentive has been further increased by legislative and administrative changes in this area. Congress, though diluting the president's power to reduce trade barriers and to set aside ITC decisions, has at the same time given him new authority to limit imports on fairness grounds. The 1922 and 1930 tariff acts granted the president the authority to impose new or additional duties on imports (or even to exclude imports) from countries that impose unreasonable regulations on U.S. products or discriminate against U.S. commerce. The 1962 trade act further directed the president to take all appropriate and feasible steps to eliminate "unjustifiable" foreign import restrictions and to suspend or withdraw previously granted concessions where other countries maintain trade restrictions that "substantially burden" U.S. commerce or engage in discriminating acts. The Trade Act of 1974 restates these provisions and also gives the president the authority to take similar actions in response to "subsidies [or other incentives having the effect of subsidies] on its [a foreign country's] exports . . . to the United States or to other foreign markets which have the effect of substantially reducing sales of the competitive United States product or products in the United States or in foreign markets" and "unjustifiable or unreasonable restrictions on access to supplies of food, raw materials, or manufactured or semi-manufactured products which burden or restrict United States commerce." In amending this provision, the 1979 trade act stressed the president's responsibility for enforcing U.S. rights under any trade agreement and simplified the list of foreign practices against which he is directed to take action.

Another legislative change that encouraged the use of fair trade legislation to gain protection was the extension of the definition of dumping in the Trade Act of 1974. Dumping was declared to encompass not only sales abroad at lower prices than charged at home but also sales of substantial quantities below cost over an extended period (even if domestic and foreign prices are the same). In 1977 the steel industry filed dumping charges covering nearly $1 billion of steel imports from Japan, all the major industrial countries, and India under this provision. As Finger, Hall, and Nelson (1982) point out, fair trade cases of this magnitude in such a key sector attract so much political opposition (both domestic and foreign) that they cannot be disposed of at the technical level and consequently spill over into the political arena. In this instance, the steel industry was successful in convincing President Carter that their claims were justified, and the so-called trigger-price system was worked out as an alternative to pursuing the antidumping charges to the final stage.

A similarly political solution was reached in 1982 when the steel industry filed charges that European steel producers were receiving extensive subsidies and therefore should be subject to countervailing duties. The possibility of countervailing duties had such significant economic and political implications that the governments of the parties involved did not wish the matter to be settled on technical grounds and sought a solution at the political level. Eventually the Europeans agreed to voluntary export restraints on a wide range of steel products to the United States.

Other important U.S. sectors have been protected in recent years by nontariff barriers. They include the footwear, television, and auto industries. Voluntary export restraints were negotiated by the president in the first two cases after affirmative injury findings by the ITC. Although the ITC rejected the auto industry's petition for import relief, the industry was nevertheless successful in persuading the administration of the need for import controls, and the Japanese eventually agreed to restrict their sales to the United States.

The increased use of nontariff trade-distorting measures has weakened the liberal thrust of U.S. trade policy. This is true not only because NTBs represent a move toward protectionism but because most of them have been applied in a discriminatory manner and are negotiated outside the GATT framework. Some of the political decisions reached at the presidential level have also occurred without the opportunity for all interested parties to be heard, as would be the case if a technical route such as an import injury petition before the ITC was being followed or even if a political route at the congressional level was being pursued.

5.3   U.S. Trade Policy under the Reagan Administration

President Reagan took office with an unusually well-defined set of domestic and international policy objectives, and his vigorous efforts to implement them have significantly affected certain aspects of U.S. trade policy over the last three years.[7] As often happens, however, conflicts and unexpected interactions among policy goals, difficult-to-resist domestic and international political pressures, and unforeseen events have combined to produce actual trade policies that only imperfectly reflect the administration's initial objectives. On an overall assessment, trade policy under the Reagan administration has been perhaps only somewhat more liberal than that of previous Republican and Democratic administrations.

5.3.1   The Administration's Trade Policy Objectives and Their
          Relation to Its Other Goals

Although all post–World War II presidents have supported the market system, none has been as firm in his belief in its economic efficacy as President Reagan. The administration's stance on trade issues was officially set forth by the United States Trade Representative, William Brock, before the Senate Finance Committee in July 1981. In this

"Statement on U.S. Trade Policy" Ambassador Brock maintained that liberal trade is essential to the pursuit of the goal of a strong U.S. economy. At the same time, however, he emphasized that the Reagan administration would strictly enforce U.S. laws and international agreements relating to such unfair practices as foreign dumping and government subsidization.

An important implication of the market approach is that when other nations "have a natural competitive advantage, U.S. industry must either find a way of upgrading its own capabilities or shift its resources to other activities." Primary reliance was to be placed on market forces rather than on adjustment assistance or safeguard measures to facilitate adjustment in affected industries. With respect to export credit subsidies, the objective was "to substantially reduce, if not eliminate, the subsidy element, and to conform credit rates to market rates." Along with cutting back on measures that artificially stimulate exports, the administration pledged to reduce or eliminate laws and regulations that needlessly retard exports. Three types of policies with export-disincentive effects were singled out: the taxation of Americans employed abroad, the Foreign Corrupt Practices Act, and export regulations and controls.

Several negotiating initiatives were outlined in the paper. Most significant were those aimed at reducing government barriers and subsidies to services that are internationally traded and at negotiating new international rules dealing with trade-related investment issues (export performance and local content requirements) and government interventions that affect trade in high-technology products.

With regard to developing countries, the stated goal was to ensure that the more advanced developing countries undertake greater trade obligations and that the benefits of differential trade treatment go increasingly to the poorer members of this group. Efforts to encourage greater conformity on the part of nonmarket economies with accepted principles of the international trading system were also promised.

The Reagan administration expected its macroeconomic policies to facilitate the implementation of its trade policies. The reverse was in fact the case. The basic reason was the failure to stimulate strong real rates of growth. Money remained tight; favorable supply-side effects of fiscal policy were insignificant; interest rates rose and then fell much more sluggishly than expected; and the dollar appreciated to near-record levels. The failure of interest rates to fall as much as expected is usually attributed to very high current and prospective government deficits related to high levels of defense spending, an inability to control spending on social programs, and the relatively lower tax revenues associated with the cut in tax rates. Interest rate developments put upward pressure on the dollar as did, apparently, political and economic uncertainties in many countries, which increased the dollar's attractiveness for safekeeping purposes.

The real appreciation of the dollar has had a significantly adverse effect on both U.S. export- and import-competing industries. Exporters have found it increasingly difficult to compete abroad with foreign producers, and import-sensitive sectors have had to contend with both the sales-depressing effects of the recession and increased import pressures as U.S. purchasers shift to cheaper foreign products. The U.S. trade deficit has significantly worsened. Export industries have also been hurt by the effects of the debt crisis in a number of developing countries. As the recession spread abroad and the volume of world trade declined, those countries that had borrowed abroad heavily in the latter part of the 1970s found themselves in a situation where their exports were falling at the same time that their debt burden had risen because of high international interest rates. The restrictive monetary and fiscal policies imposed on these countries by the International Monetary Fund as the price for agreeing to a rescheduling of their debt payments then had the effect of curtailing their imports and further compounding the export problems of U.S. industries.

5.3.2   Export-Promoting Policies

The adverse effects of the overvalued dollar and the debt crisis on U.S. exporters appear to have been important factors in causing the Reagan administration to modify its skeptical views on export-promoting policies. Under considerable prodding from Congress, the administration reversed its early intentions to reduce activities of the Export-Import Bank and to repeal legislation allowing domestic international sales corporations (DISCs). In 1983 the administration requested Congress to increase the loan guarantee authority of the Export-Import Bank and also to provide the bank with a sizable standby fund to match the export-financing activities of other countries. Furthermore, instead of scrapping DISCs, the executive branch has drafted new legislation that will provide the same tax benefits for exporters, yet be consistent with GATT rules.

The administration has delivered on most of its promises to reduce self-imposed export disincentives. The 1981 tax act eased the U.S. tax burden on Americans residing abroad for at least eleven out of twelve months. In the fall of 1982 Congress passed and the president signed the Export Trading Company Act. This important legislation permits bank holding companies and certain types of banks to take an equity interest in export trading companies and also permits a partial exemption from the antitrust laws for specified export activities that do not substantially lessen competition within the United States.

Another export-promoting measure proposed by the administration is the Business Accounting and Foreign Trade Simplification Act, which modifies certain provisions in the Foreign Corrupt Practices Act of 1977. Advocates of the changes claim that the Foreign Corrupt Practices Act has brought about a situation where American businessmen often do not even bother to compete abroad for contracts, for fear that payments regarded as legal and customary in foreign countries will be regarded as illegal under U.S. law. (Krause [1982, 82–84] discusses these effects in the context on ASEAN countries.) As one example of the type of change being proposed, the new act stipulates that a U.S. firm would be liable under the law only if it "directs or authorizes, expressedly or by course of conduct," that an illegal payment be made by its foreign agent, instead of being liable, as under the 1977 act, simply because it had "reason to know" such a payment was being made. The revised measure also explicitly permits payments to officials of foreign governments that are lawful under the local law and payments aimed at expediting or securing the performance of routine official action. The Senate passed the bill in 1982, but opposition to it has developed in the House.

5.3.3 Import Relief Policy

Most of the Reagan administration's import relief policies have been shaped by a complex mixture of free trade ideology, practical politics, and unanticipated events. On the basis of its "Statement on U.S. Trade Policy," one would have expected the administration to follow a very tough stance against import protection. However, on the surface at least, the administration's actual performance in granting import relief does not seem to differ significantly from the varied record of other recent administrations.

In 1981, for example, the administration pressured the Japanese into voluntarily limiting their exports of autos to the United States, even though the ITC had earlier rejected the industry's petition for import relief. In the same year the president introduced sugar quotas and supported an extension and tightening of the Multi-Fiber Arrangement. More recently, he accepted the affirmative import injury determinations of the ITC in the motorcycle and specialty steel cases. Duties were sharply raised on certain imported motorcycles, and a combination of increased import duties and quotas were used to restrict imports of specialty steel items.

In contrast, on the side of liberal trade policy actions, the president permitted the 1981 expiration of orderly marketing agreements on non-rubber footwear with Korea and Taiwan, despite an ITC recommendation that the Taiwanese agreement be extended for another two years. Furthermore, he has actively opposed "domestic content" legislation covering the automotive industry.

One policy dealing with increased competition on which there is a clear difference in performance between this and other recent administrations is trade adjustment assistance for workers. Prompted not only by a desire to reduce government intervention in the adjustment process but by the goal of reducing inflationary pressures by cutting government expenditures, the administration secured new legislation in 1981 that sharply curtailed the TAA program. It introduced more stringent qualifying requirements and reduced financial benefits. Legislation in 1982 restored the qualifying requirements of the Trade Act of 1974, but the Labor Department has interpreted the criteria in a strict manner so that the program still remains small. The administration has proposed a "voucher" system whereby workers displaced for whatever reason would search for suitable education or training and use vouchers issued to them by the government to pay for on-the-job training or for the costs of training at various schools.

It can be argued that the Reagan administration's overall import relief record is a reasonably liberal one. In speculating about what another administration might have done under similar circumstances, it should be stressed that today even a strong president shares policy-making powers in the trade field with Congress, as outlined above. Congress is much more responsive to the immediate economic problems of various industries and groups than the executive branch. Consider, for example, the auto case. In early 1981 Congress held hearings to publicize the plight of the industry, and Senator Danforth, the chairman of the Subcommittee on International Trade of the Senate Finance Committee, introduced a bill that would have imposed quantitative restrictions on Japanese auto imports. He and his colleagues preferred that the president negotiate a voluntary export restraint agreement with Japan, but apparently they were prepared to push the bill through Congress (with little opposition expected) unless such an agreement was reached. Faced with this prospect and the fact that he had made a campaign speech arguing for a cutback in exports by the Japanese, the president eventually put pressure on the Japanese government for voluntary export restraints. The president might have held to a strong liberal trade position and threatened to veto any restrictive bill emerging from Congress, but it would have been politically difficult to do so in view of his own stated position and the generally recognized fact that increased Japanese imports were an important cause of injury in this politically powerful industry.

The failure to follow the ITC's recommendation to extend footwear quotas against Taiwan was probably a consequence of the president's decision on autos, as Cohen and Meltzer (1982, 111) point out. The administration feared that approval of the ITC recommendation would send an undesirable protectionist signal to the rest of the world. Moreover, from a domestic political viewpoint the fact that the footwear industry is much less politically powerful than the auto, steel, or textile industries and had already been given five years of import protection made it much easier to reject the recommendation.

The proposed domestic content legislation for the auto industry presents still a different set of circumstances for the president. This legislation is clearly inconsistent with the trading rules of the GATT and is likely to lead to an outpouring of protectionist charges by other countries as well as retaliation against U.S. exports. The United States would jeopardize its traditional role as the international leader of a liberal international trading order. Domestic political support—even within the auto industry—is also not nearly as strong as in the Japanese voluntary-export-restraint case, especially as auto sales pick up in response to economic recovery. Thus, the president is able to adopt a much stronger liberal trade position without high political costs.

Finally, the administration's policy position during the international negotiations in the fall of 1981 on the renewal of the Multi-Fiber Arrangement further illustrates the complexity of trade policy decisions. The president had previously expressed sympathy for the view that textile imports should expand only at the same rate as the domestic market. He also needed the support of members of Congress from southern textile districts to pass the budgetary changes he proposed, and which he viewed as more important than import policy with regard to textiles. Moreover, the European Community (EC) strongly favored a more restrictive international agreement, and it would have been difficult to oppose their position.

5.3.4   In Pursuit of "Fair Trade"

While there is scope for disagreement concerning just how liberal the Reagan administration's import relief record is compared with that of other administrations, there seems little doubt that the current administration has pursued the goal of "fair trade" more vigorously than any previous administration. Two efforts in this regard are especially noteworthy for Asian trade: the enforcement of existing U.S. fair trade laws and the opening of the Japanese market to a greater extent. (For Europe the major U.S. initiative against unfair trade practices has been the attempt to reduce EC agricultural subsidies.)

The main push for stricter enforcement of U.S. laws relating to dumping, subsidization, patent infringements, and unjustifiable, unreasonable, or discriminatory foreign trade actions has come from Congress over the last several years, as outlined above. It was due to congressional initiative that the enforcement of the fair trade laws was transferred in 1979 from the Treasury Department to the Commerce Department. However, the Reagan administration has had ample incentive for its own initiative on this front.

The initiation by the Commerce Department of a countervailing-duty investigation into certain steel exports by six European countries is a good example of the administration's aggressive stance toward unfair trade practices. The case was significant for the large volume of trade involved, for the fact that it was the first time that the government had initiated such an investigation, and for the careful manner in which the Commerce Department tried to measure the subsidies.

The case was settled, however, not by imposing countervailing duties equal to the subsidies, as provided by the law, but by an agreement with the subsidizing EC countries. The agreement quantitatively limited the majority of EC steel mill exports to the United States for a three-year period. It is surprising that an administration committed to "free but fair" trade settled its major fair trade case with an arrangement that was not carefully designed to just offset the alleged subsidies and is regarded as the worst form of protection by liberal traders.

There has also been a greater use of section 301 of the Trade Act of 1974, which deals with unjustifiable, unreasonable, or discriminatory trade practices by foreign countries. Prior to 1981, only three presidential determinations supporting the petitioners had been made, whereas in 1981 and 1982 there were five such determinations. Furthermore, at the urging of Congress the Reagan administration has agreed to a strengthening of section 301's provisions. Specifically, the administration supports an amendment that would explicitly extend the president's authority to retaliate against unfair practices affecting trade in services and foreign direct investment.[8]

A case brought by Houdaille Industries in May 1982 under section 103 of the Revenue Act of 1971 further illustrates the increased concern with unfair trade practices. This law permits the president to deny investment tax credit on imported goods if the exporting country "engages in discriminatory or other acts (including tolerance of international cartels) or policies unjustifiably restricting United States commerce." Houdaille requested indefinite suspension of the investment tax credit on certain numerically controlled machines imported from Japan, on the grounds that the Japanese government had for many years fostered and encouraged a cartel among its domestic machine tool manufacturers, which had given them an unfair advantage. Although the Senate passed a resolution urging prompt retaliation, after a ten-month investigation the administration denied the request. However, at the same time, it announced that the U.S. and Japanese governments would hold talks on the issue and that there may be future action on the matter.

A second area where administration officials have vigorously pushed the notion of fairness relates to U.S.-Japanese trade more generally. There is no other trade topic that generates more heated discussion in Congress and within the administration than the U.S. trade deficit with Japan. This deficit increased from $7 billion to $18 billion between 1979 and 1982. It has become standard doctrine in parts of the government to attribute much of the deficit to unfair trading practices on the part of the Japanese. On the export side these allegedly take the form of industrial targeting—a practice whereby the Japanese government selects certain product lines for export emphasis and then facilitates their development by coordinating research, by helping firms secure low-cost finance, by encouraging specialization among potential competitors, by providing marketing assistance, etc. On the import side it is claimed that the unfair use of such nontariff measures as standards certification procedures, customs procedures, preferential government purchasing policies, and discriminatory distribution arrangements excludes a significant volume of U.S. goods from the Japanese market. (The average level of industrial tariffs in Japan is only about 3%, a figure lower than that for the United States or the EC.)

Since the fall of 1981 top administration officials including the president himself have pressed the Japanese to remove these unfair barriers, as well as to enlarge agricultural quotas and reduce tariff rates still further. Some success has been achieved along these lines, but there is still widespread dissatisfaction with Japan's response. The reciprocity bill insisted upon by Congress is largely a manifestation of this dissatisfaction. Recently, trade officials have begun to focus more closely on the industrial targeting practices of Japan. It is quite possible that the United States will take some form of trade policy actions to offset the effects of these practices.

The soundness of the case against Japan is difficult to determine. On the one hand, U.S. firms have documented numerous instances of practices that seem to restrict U.S. exports to Japan unfairly. More and more is also becoming known about the export-promoting policies of the Japanese government. On the other hand, an increase in the trade deficit for this reason would have required an increase in unfair practices, and there seems little evidence of increased unfairness. Writers such as Saxonhouse (1983) and even the president's own Council of Economic Advisers (1983; Reagan 1983) have further argued that Japan's trade pattern (a significant trade surplus for manufactured goods that is more than balanced by a significant trade deficit for primary products) is consistent with the country's human and physical resource endowments. While the Council of Economic Advisers believes that major trade liberalization by Japan would do much to relieve the political strains between the two countries, they state that "Japanese trade policy does not play a central role in causing the bilateral imbalance with the United States." (1983, 56).

5.4   The Key Question: How Much Opportunity for U.S. Trade Policy Leadership?[9]

5.4.1   The General Issue

U.S. trade policy since World War II has enjoyed unique liberties and been subject to unique limitations. It has enjoyed the early postwar liberty of serving international and national security goals without unduly serious domestic consequences. Those goals remain, with universal expectations that the United States will design trade policy at least in part to attain them. The expectations have, however, recently become a unique limitation on U.S. trade policy, which is increasingly subject to familiar domestic political pressures.

U.S. trade policy has always served two masters, a domestic and a foreign constituency. U.S. leadership has become more difficult in recent years as the relative strength of the domestic constituency has grown. Some have described this as the "domestication" of U.S. trade policy. Domestication causes tensions, especially for a U.S. president, whose trade initiatives must somehow continue to serve both masters. Congress has become, by contrast, much more narrowly focused. Ahearn and Reifman (1984) comment on "its continuing disinclination to sacrifice U.S. commercial interests for foreign-policy objectives."

Because of both domestic and foreign constituencies, no modern U.S. president feels able to promote openly a general policy of import protection. The United States is still viewed by the other major industrial nations as the leader of the liberal international trading order. These countries still basically support this regime and believe that if the United States adopts general protectionism, it will rapidly spread throughout the trading world along with beggar-thy-neighbor exchange rate policies. It is a widely accepted view that the result of this collapse of the existing trade and financial order would be extensive job losses in export sectors and massive financial losses in industries with export and foreign direct investment interests. Because of the great political and economic power of these sectors, together with the considerable pressures foreign constituencies can bring to bear, a president would run significant political risks if he openly pursued a policy of general protectionism.

At the same time, it is also very difficult politically for a president to resist granting protection to specific industries that are politically significant in voting and/or financial terms and that also seem to have a good case in U.S. and international import relief or fair trade laws. If, for example, the ITC had rendered an affirmative decision in the recent auto case and President Reagan had rejected this decision, it seems likely that Congress would have vetoed his action, as it could have at that time with a simple majority vote. Moreover, Congress probably would have blocked other legislation desired by the president in retaliation for his decision. Even without the congressional veto a president runs this risk when he takes actions against a strongly held congressional view. It is not politically rational to turn down "good" cases for protection—unless a president regards resistance to import relief for a politically powerful industry considered to be deserving of such relief by many members of Congress as dominant over his other political goals.

Difficulties and trade policy tensions are, of course, predictable results of growing U.S. dependence on international markets and of decline in U.S. influence in them. Growing U.S. trade dependence increases the effect of the country's trade policy on domestic economic variables. The responsiveness (elasticity) of sectoral output, employment, and profit with respect to trade policy rises as import and export shares rise. When trade shares were small, even export and import embargoes had only modest impacts on domestic industries. As trade shares have grown, so has the attractiveness of trade policy to attain domestic goals and to defend against "unfair" trade practices of foreign firms that are no longer just token competitors for U.S. giants.

In contrast, as the rest of the world has grown relative to the United States since World War II, its trade dependence on the U.S. has declined. Responsiveness (elasticity) of global output, employment, and profit with respect to U.S. trade policy has become smaller. U.S. ability to influence world economic prosperity has therefore declined, and so has the claim of this goal to priority in shaping U.S. trade policy. The important, but nonvoting, foreign constituents of U.S. trade policy have taken careful note of its reduced influence on them; at the same time, voting U.S. constituents have awakened to its growing influence on them.

5.4.2   U.S. Leadership Internationally: Hegemony, Oligarchy

If the tensions and trends described above are identified with the decline of U.S. hegemony, the natural question is whether they undermine the international leadership of the United States in establishing liberal trade policy. Several answers are possible.

The hegemonic model of regime change not only predicts openness in world trading arrangements when a hegemonic state is in its ascendency but a shift toward a closed system if this nation declines in power and is not replaced by another dominant state. Although this model is consistent with the early part of the postwar period, there is general agreement (Krasner 1976; Goldstein 1981; Lipson 1982) that the model does not perform very well as an explanation of regime change for more recent years.

Despite a shift in power from a situation where one country dominated the economic scene to one where there are now three major
economic blocs (the United States, the European Community, and
Japan), most observers agree that the trade and payments regime continues to be essentially an open and liberal one. The tariff cuts made
in the 1960s and 1970s were actually much deeper than those made in
the 1940s and 1950s (see table 5.1). Furthermore, the new nontariff
codes negotiated during the Tokyo Round, though often very general
in their wording, do represent a significant accomplishment. The GATT
ministerial meeting in November 1982 and the leadership role that the
United States played in establishing the agenda are additional indications of the continued commitment of the major industrial nations to
a liberal international economic order.

A consideration of the economic theory of either market behavior
or the production of collective goods suggests why the hegemonic
model fails to predict the continuation of an open system. A single firm
that dominates a market is likely to stabilize its price at a monopolistic
level while still tolerating some price cutting by the smaller firms making
up the rest of the industry. However, oligopolistic market theory suggests that the same result is possible if two or three large firms dominate
an industry. Similarly, as Olson (1965) pointed out, the free-rider problem associated with collective action by an industry can be overcome
if a small number of firms (as well as just one firm) produce a significant
share of the industry's output. Bargaining and enforcement costs may
then be sufficiently low that property rights to collective goods can be
established along with fees and penalties for cheating. Thus, the continued support for a stable, open trading order as the distribution of
power changed from an almost monopolistic situation to an oligopolistic
one is quite consistent with market behavior theory.

The shift from a hegemonic position to one in which the country
shares its previous economic and political power with a small number
of other nations is, however, likely to alter the country's own international behavior somewhat, just as the change in the status of a firm
from a monopolist to an oligopolist is likely to change the firm's market
behavior. In the United States, the nature of the change has been to
initiate trade negotiations mainly to achieve domestic economic benefits rather than to further international political and national security
goals.

As might be expected, the less altruistic behavior on the part of the
United States has resulted in an increased number of trade disputes.
Many who support a liberal trading order are concerned that these
disputes will become so numerous and difficult that the system will
collapse, with each of the major trading powers pursuing inward-looking
trade policies. This is of course a possibility and is discussed further

below. It is significant, however, that most of the trading frictions do not arise because of disagreements on the principles of an open trading system but on matters of interpretation within these principles. For example, the key parties in the system have always agreed that it was proper to shield an industry from injurious increases in imports. Consequently, when the United States protects the auto and steel industries from import competition, or when the Europeans subsidize industries as a means of retaining their domestic market shares, this is not regarded by most countries as a departure from the basic liberal trading rules. Disagreements sometimes arise, however, over whether a country is going beyond the intent of the rules and engaging in what are in effect beggar-thy-neighbor policies. The settlement of major disputes at a high political level and the continuing efforts to improve the GATT dispute-settlement mechanism are a recognition by the major trading nations of the damage to the system that could occur from such disagreements.

Krasner (1976) argues in his amendment to the hegemonic model that the abandonment of commitment to a liberal trading order is likely to occur only when some major external crisis forces leaders to pursue a dramatic new policy initiative. It may be that the existing power-sharing arrangement between the United States, the EC, and Japan reduces the likelihood of this outcome compared with the case of a declining hegemony in the midst of many smaller states. In this latter situation the dominant power is tempted in a crisis to take advantage of its monopoly power over the terms of trade. When power is shared, however, the recognition that a country's market power is quite limited and that retaliation is likely to be swift and significant tends to discourage such adventurism.

It is worth considering less sanguine outlooks, however, since major crises may occur, and since developing countries in particular may not enjoy the benefits of the countervailing trade policy power described above. A familiar American image may help to flesh out what could happen if some crisis prompted U.S. trade policy to become openly aggressive and nationalistic. "Frontier justice" might increasingly order trade and policy. Under frontier justice, if any government could "get away with it," it would "do it." Strong governments would survive prosperously; weak governments, tenuously. The economic problem with frontier justice is unpredictability. More organized systems of justice regularize economic exchange, establishing boundaries for what qualify as voluntary transactions, rules governing the exploitation of market advantage, and sanctions to guarantee the enforcement of contracts. Frontier justice, by contrast, could destabilize economic exchange, becoming an irritant to the market rather than its lubricant.

U.S. hegemony, undesirable though it was in some ways, clearly checked the scope for policy aggression, much as the frontier sheriff or U.S. marshal checked the scope for frontier justice. The awkward question that a crisis might raise is what happens on the frontier when the sheriff not only grows weaker but begins to act aggressively, "just like everyone else"?

Aggressive trade policies are to be feared more for their potential to *disorder* resource allocation than to *misorder* it. The law of the jungle is as haphazard a way of ordering policy transactions as it is of ordering market transactions. Even laissez-faire economists have in mind some particular legal structure of common-law conventions when they favor "free" markets and liberal trade policy. The threat is that a crisis might cause long-standing legal structures and conventions controlling government behavior to be abandoned. Uncertainty at best and chaos at worst could be the consequence for international trade and investment. The danger of the worst case can be appreciated by considering what happens to everyday commerce during civil disorder, when legal systems crumble and vigilantism waxes strong.

U.S. leadership in trade policy to minimize the chance of this worst-case scenario is still probably quite strong. The United States would seem the logical initiator in what Blackhurst (1981, 369–73) has described as a return toward "conventions" in trade policy. Blackhurst has in mind conventions that would at least order, but not bind, trade policy. Governments themselves should be the constituents. Mutually agreed conventions protect governments from each other and also from domestic political constituents in narrow pursuit of trade policies that serve their special interest at the expense of other constituents.

There are three important practical challenges in any such return toward conventions. One is to avoid overambitious promulgation of "rules" which, when broken, breed the unpredictability that disorders resource allocation. A second is to keep the resource and time costs of negotiation in check so as to increase chances for a cooperative outcome. A third is to increase the participation of developing countries in the negotiations and decision-making processes.

Thus it is worth evaluating the multilateral negotiating approach very carefully. In view of significant differences among countries concerning trade policies, multilateral negotiations may now be too cumbersome and costly in terms of what can be achieved. Negotiations among a small number of countries on selected issues of particular concern to the group may be more productive. This would represent a return to the negotiating technique followed so successfully in the 1930s under the Trade Agreement Act of 1934. The group is small enough and sufficiently concerned for the negotiations to be efficient, yet the collective benefits reaped from the most-favored-nation principle need not be sacrificed.

What this may suggest practically for the United States is aggressive bilateral peacemaking—the formation of mutually advantageous coalitions with like-minded governments.[10] For example, the United States and Japan seem likely partners for a bilateral trade agreement that would order trade along lines that both deem important.

5.4.3   U.S. Leadership Domestically: Potential for the Reagan Administration

A president's ability to reconcile the trade policy conflicts between domestic and foreign constituencies depends on many factors—his political strength among voters, his economic and political goals, his effectiveness in dealing with Congress and the public, the extent to which his own party controls Congress, etc. President Reagan thus far has not exhibited special interest in international economic matters. His policy decisions in this field have been mainly reactive. While he has been guided in these responses by a strong preference for the market mechanism, he has also shown a willingness to compromise in the face of strong domestic or international political opposition to a clear-cut market solution.

A president *can* make a significant difference domestically in the nature of trade policy. This is most likely to occur when he initiates major trade policy actions himself as well as responding to well-taken pressures. In this way he is often able to transcend the narrow, short-run concerns that dominate most political decision making and gain support among legislators and the public based on their concerns for the long-run economic and political welfare of the country. An initiative in this spirit is President Reagan's recent proposal to create a cabinet-level Department of International Trade and Industry. Yet in many ways this proposal may be premature. Clarification of U.S. trade strategy and policy instruments seems needful beforehand, along with credible actions underwriting such initiatives. We turn to these clarifying initiatives after a brief discussion of the proposal for a new department.

The proposed Department of International Trade and Industry would be created by merging the Office of the United States Trade Representative, which is in the Executive Office of the president, and parts of the Commerce Department. The new department would allegedly "provide a strong, unified voice for trade and industrial matters." There are sound arguments both for and against such a merger. With the 1979 transfer to the Commerce Department of responsibility for administering the basic fair trade laws and with the greater emphasis under the Reagan administration on enforcement of these laws, significant parts of trade policy administration are divided between the USTR and the Commerce Department. Conflicts between the two agencies weaken international effectiveness in trade disputes and sometimes result in sending conflicting signals to domestic producers. Yet such conflicts are inevitable under the present arrangement and would presumably be reduced with the new agency. Bringing together the economic staff of the Commerce Department and the trade officials of the USTR would also stimulate the kind of in-depth economic studies that are so badly needed to prepare U.S. negotiators adequately as well as to undertake long-range trade policy planning.

A possible drawback of the new department is that the interagency aspect of trade policy formation that has existed since the 1930s could be lost or seriously weakened. Trade policies affect matters over which most of the major federal departments have some control, and decisions on most issues are now reached through interagency meetings chaired by the USTR and involving such agencies as State, Treasury, Commerce, Labor, Agriculture, Interior, ITC, and Defense. Some individuals fear that the current process of balancing the diverse views of representatives from these agencies would be lost and instead be replaced by a process in which the business-oriented views of the Commerce Department become dominant. There is also some concern that trade policy may end up being downgraded in importance, since it will no longer be directed from the Executive Office of the president.

The merger issue is not likely to be resolved soon, since there is significant opposition to it in Congress. In the meantime, the debate over the new department could be informed greatly by initiatives to clarify the strategy and instruments of U.S. trade policy.

Strategy

Recent U.S. trade initiatives, especially from Congress, reveal an anomalous division of opinion concerning the proper trade strategy for the United States. Some initiatives attempt to export U.S. policy tradition to the rest of the world. Others attempt to import policy tradition abroad to the United States. Illustrating the first are new conceptions of "reciprocity"—notions that policy abroad must provide U.S. firms with the same market opportunities as our policies provide to their firms, or else! Illustrating the second are new conceptions of trade policy as active industrial policy—notions that U.S. trade policy should be marshaled as an important tool in striving for an optimum industrial structure.

The two strategies above are not inconsistent of course—trade policy abroad could become like "ours" at the same time as "ours" became like others'. The result of both strategies would be policy convergence. Thus both represent a departure from the historical U.S. approach, which is aptly characterized as policy tolerance—accept policy differences in general and at the margins exchange policy concessions for mutual gain. The appeal of policy convergence over policy tolerance appears to rest in the suspicion of unfairness discussed above. One might typify it as follows: "If only they would stop cheating on the system and play like we do, then the field would be more level; if only we would 'wise up' and play like they do, we could share all their advantages." In this light, the traditional tolerance approach may appear unappealing, "the same old thing again, just chipping away at the margin." The reality may, however, be otherwise than the appearance. Chipping away at the margin of policy differences may ultimately be more fruitful than a full frontal attack on them. The strategy of U.S. trade policy needs careful scrutiny.

The issue of rules versus discretion in trade policy is closely related. U.S. tradition is based on rules and thus ultimately on litigation. Tradition abroad is much more discretionary—flexible, managerial, and administrative. Negotiation rather than litigation is the vehicle for resolving differences. Here there is a genuine conflict for U.S. trade policy. Movement toward an even greater use of rules can satisfy domestic constituencies but isolate the United States still further in international negotiations. The changes in countervailing-duty law and its administration, described by Shuman and Verrill (1984), provide a good example. Although the rules are now clearer than ever, there is still marked sensitivity in the executive branch to foreign objections when countervailing-duty cases are aggressively pursued. Negotiations with industry and foreign governments may ensue, with the result that the admittedly clear rules are bypassed by discretionary negotiation among the participants.

Movement away from rules toward discretion may, however, aggravate the widespread sense that the U.S. government is not actively pursuing American interests and may undermine domestic support for all U.S. trade policy. It is curious in view of this to see the strength of U.S. support for active trade policy as industrial policy. Such active policy would almost surely necessitate fewer rules-centered policy decisions and more discretionary, technocratic, and unpredictable policy directives.

Finally, U.S. policy decisions are much needed on the adjustment issue of how to respond to sectoral policy abroad. Such policy in due time encourages U.S. sectoral adjustment in an opposite direction, with attendant adjustment costs. Should U.S. trade policy attempt to attenuate the adjustment, accelerate it, or remain passive? And what if the policy abroad appeared likely to fail? Should U.S. trade policy attempt to avoid the doubling of adjustment costs as industrial resources move to and fro? Should active adjustment-centered trade policy be bilateral or most-favored-nation?

Instruments

It may be timely for the United States to initiate the restoration of tariffs and other taxes as the chief instruments of trade policy. The increased reliance on administrative policy for exports and imports is well known. Yet some of the unfortunate by-products of this are not widely appreciated.

One result of the greater use of administrative policies is intricacy. It becomes harder to identify foreign policies, much less their effects. It also becomes harder to implement one's own trade objectives. Intricacy raises the resource cost of estimating and monitoring trade policy, no matter who initiates it. Intricacy also slows down trade policy-making. Administrative trade policy, unlike tariffs, invades the turfs of regulatory agencies, congressional oversight committees, and sometimes even the judiciary.

Intricacy increases allegations of unfairness and discrimination. This is because administrative trade policy is inherently opaque compared with tariffs or explicit export subsidies. Opaqueness tends to heighten suspicions that something discriminatory and unfair is going on below surface appearances. Opaqueness leads naturally to the increased pursuit of unfair trade cases. Furthermore, opaqueness invites Congress to respond to perceived inequity with comparably opaque initiatives. Administrative trade policy has made it increasingly difficult for the United States to maintain the balance in its historical position that trade should be "free but fair."

A closely related result from greater use of administrative policies is unpredictability. Unpredictability undermines the ability of the market system to function, especially impeding those markets that allocate resources over time for investment, education, and research. This in turn aggravates adjustment problems.

For example, in recent years many initiatives in U.S. trade policy have been nontax rules with discretionary overrides. Orderly marketing arrangements in footwear and television equipment can be described in this way, as can the Tokyo Round codes on subsidization, dumping, and government procurement. Unpredictability is an unfortunate by-product because these initiatives unwholesomely mingle policing with policy responsibility. The same authorities who are charged with predictably enforcing the rules are also charged with using their discretion to revise them sensibly. The two responsibilities are in conflict. Tariffs and other tax-based trade policy provide a sharp contrast. Enforcement of the rules is the clear responsibility of the Customs Service or the Internal Revenue Service. Discretionary revision of the rules is the clear responsibility of the Congress with the Executive's cooperation, featuring relatively predictable procedures for dissemination of information, expressing opinions, etc. There is no conflict since policing and policy are vested in different groups.

Economists who applaud the benefits of price competition but are chary of nonprice competition (advertising, etc.) might consider the trade policy analogue. There may be much clearer benefits from "tariff competition" (negotiating concessions in the traditional way, threatening tax-based retaliation, etc.) than from competition among governments in administrative protection.

Deregulation in the United States accentuates these tendencies. The removal of regulations, most of which are nontax directives, forces a trade policy question: should the regulations be removed for all agents or only for domestic agents? Taking the latter route implies special treatment for foreign sellers or buyers and is by its discriminatory nature a trade policy. But the initiating authority may be none of the traditional trade policy centers. It may be rather the Department of Energy, the Federal Communications Commission, or the Senate Committee on Commerce, Science, and Transportation. U.S. initiative is needed to clarify jurisdiction over these questions.

Implicit revenue provides, however, a possibly important counterweight for preferring the continuation of U.S. reliance on nontax policies. Orderly marketing agreements may transfer to exporting countries enough market power, related revenues, and terms-of-trade advantage to compensate them for injury caused by reducing shipments to the United States. Developing-country exporters of potentially differentiable goods, such as the newly industrializing countries of East and Southeast Asia, may have especially strong preferences for these nontax agreements. Even U.S. policymakers might defend them as an instrument of international compensation for what would otherwise be a clear beggar-thy-neighbor barrier to trade.

5.4.4   U.S. Leadership: Entries on an Agenda for "Aggressive Peacemaking"

U.S. trade policy initiative in "aggressive peacemaking" requires consensus building at home and abroad. Domestic and foreign constituents of U.S. trade policy are alike in their fragmentation over the best ways of ordering international exchange. "Disequilibrium" is the word that best describes their shifting and disparate views on trade policy.

For example, there are valid national reasons why countries may wish to introduce industrial policies or behave strategically in competing for international markets. However, in the absence of well-defined international conventions concerning just what constitutes acceptable international behavior and setting forth workable dispute settlement mechanisms, there are also dangers with a strategic policy approach. When each country actively pursues this approach and retaliates against others who do so, it is possible that all trading nations end up with lower employment and income levels than otherwise, as the sequence of actions may constitute a negative sum game.

These potential costs[11] need to be described clearly to the American public and internationally. The description needs to be rooted in current fact and recent history. U.S. leadership seems natural in this task, given U.S. comparative advantage in economic education and research and the still strong tradition of independence and objectivity among U.S. analysts and commentators.

A cooperative international approach worked quite well for many years after World War II. However, fundamental changes in the distribution of economic power among countries, including the growth of newly industrializing countries, coupled with differences among countries in the extent to which they have pursued active and reactive trade policies, have all served to lessen the effectiveness of the rules under which the postwar trading regime has operated. What is needed now is aggressive peacemaking aimed at establishing a new cooperative approach.

Any new cooperative approach is likely to require bilateral or multilateral agreements on several key elements of trade policy. One of the most important of these concerns the types of government intervention, especially public subsidization, that should and should not be countered with offsetting actions by other governments. Present GATT rules and practices are not sufficiently precise in this area. National laws on countervailing are also too simplistic to deal with modern conditions. In particular, there is insufficient recognition of the character of activist trade policies. By no means are all such policies aimed at gaining at the expense of others. Some can bring gains to all trading parties. Yet these are not sufficiently delineated in either GATT or national conventions. Nor are the procedures for settling disputes in this area sufficiently effective. Nor are the advantages and disadvantages of special treatment for developing-country subsidies carefully thought out.

Greater agreement among the industrial and the newly industrializing countries concerning temporary assistance to sectors faced with severe adjustment problems is also needed. Countries claiming that their subsidies are strictly for adjustment purposes sometimes find their adjustment problems made worse by countervailing duties imposed by others. The need for a new safeguards code has also been recognized for several years. Integration of a new safeguards code with preferential treatment, if any, for developing countries might be the next step.

Bilateral and multilateral agreements relating to competition policy seem necessary. When international markets are imperfect, the abnormal profits that are available are tempting targets of government trade policies.[12] However, if international understandings can be developed that discourage cartel-like behavior, abuse of dominant market positions, and attempts to monopolize, much of the incentive for such profit-shifting trade policies may be eliminated. It is unlikely that competition policy can be dealt with adequately without also strengthening existing agreements relating to foreign direct investment.

Aggressive peacemaking through cooperation may also be needed in the areas of exchange rate, monetary, and fiscal policies. Independent actions by some nations in these policy areas have created serious income and employment problems in others, especially when compounded with international debt problems. Without cooperative efforts to mitigate these problems, agreements in such areas as subsidization may not be meaningful or effective.

Notes

1. If the effects of structural shifts in trade and of inflation on specific duties are included along with the negotiated tariff cuts, the average tariff on dutiable imports drops from a 1931 level of 53% to about 5% after completion of the Tokyo Round cuts.

2. Additional detail on matters discussed in this section can be found in Baldwin 1984a.

3. Authors of this explanation for the postwar establishment of a liberal international economic order under U.S. leadership include Kindleberger (1973, 1981), Gilpin (1975, 1977), and Krasner (1976). See Lipson 1982 for a succinct statement and analysis of the hegemonic model.

4. See Leddy and Norwood 1963 for a detailed discussion of the escape clause, as well as the peril-point provision. The peril-point provision directed the president to submit to the ITC a list of all articles being considered for tariff negotiations and required the commission to determine the limits to which each duty could be reduced without causing or threatening serious injury to import-competing domestic industries. This provision was a part of U.S. trade law from 1948 through 1962, except for a brief repeal in 1949 and 1950.

5. For a description of the protectionist pressures from the cotton textile as well as the oil and coal industries during the 1950s and early 1960s, see Bauer, Pool, and Dexter 1963, chap. 25.

6. Between 1955 and 1972 the number of antidumping reports issued by the ITC averaged less than six per year. This rate increased to thirteen between 1974 and 1979. Similarly, the number of countervailing-duty investigations completed by the ITC between 1962 and 1973 was twelve, while the number rose to thirty-seven between 1974 and the end of 1978.

7. Additional detail on matters discussed in this section can be found in Baldwin 1984b.

8. This so-called reciprocity bill also requires an annual report of foreign trade barriers and what is being done to reduce them. Congress actually preferred a considerably stronger version of the bill but accepted this compromise at the urging of the administration.

9. Additional detail on some matters discussed in this section can be found in Baldwin 1984a, b, and Richardson 1984a, b.

10. See Aho and Bayard 1983 and Vernon 1983, 40–41, passim, for more detailed consideration of such proposals, including some that would abandon

most-favored-nation treatment. The EC has been essentially following this route as its membership expands and in its preferential arrangements with nonmember countries. See Camps and Diebold 1983 and Greenway 1984 for arguments in favor of renewed aggressive *multilateral* negotiating strategies.

11. "Would any of you think of building a tower without first sitting down and calculating the cost, to see whether he could afford to finish it? . . . Or what king will march to battle against another king, without first sitting down to consider whether with ten thousand men he can face an enemy coming to meet him with twenty thousand? If he cannot, then, long before the enemy approaches, he sends envoys, and asks for terms" (Luke 14:28, 31–32, *New English Bible*).

12. See Grossman and Richardson 1984 for a summary of the literature on this matter.

References

Ahearn, R. J., and A. Reifman. 1984. Trade policy making in the Congress. In Baldwin 1984b.

Aho, C. M., and T. O. Bayard. 1983. U.S. trade policy: Where do we go from here? Processed.

Baldwin, R. E. 1958. The commodity composition of trade: Selected industrial countries, 1900–1954. *Review of Economics and Statistics* 40:50–68, Supplement.

———. 1976. The political economy of postwar U.S. trade policy. *The Bulletin,* no. 4.

———. 1981. The political economy of U.S. import policy. Unpublished monograph.

———. 1984a. The changing nature of U.S. trade policy since World War II. In Baldwin and Krueger 1984.

———. 1984b. Trade policies under the Reagan administration. In Baldwin 1984c.

———. ed., 1984c. *Recent issues and initiatives in U.S. trade policy.* NBER Conference Report. Cambridge: National Bureau of Economic Research.

Baldwin, R. E., and A. O. Krueger, eds. 1984. *The structure and evolution of recent U.S. trade policy.* Chicago: University of Chicago Press for the National Bureau of Economic Research.

Bauer, R. A., J. Pool, and L. Dexter. 1963. *American business and public policy: The politics of foreign trade.* Chicago: Aldine-Atherton.

Blackhurst, R. 1981. The twilight of domestic economic policies. *World Economy* 4 (December): 357–73.

Camps, M., and W. Diebold, Jr. 1983. *The new multilateralism: Can the world trading system be saved?* New York: Council on Foreign Relations.

Cohen, S. D., and R. I. Meltzer. 1982. *United States international economic policy in action.* New York: Praeger.

Council of Economic Advisers. 1983. *Report of the Council of Economic Advisers.* Washington, D.C.: GPO.

Diebold, W., Jr. 1952. The end of the I.T.O. *Essays in International Finance,* no. 16 (Princeton: Princeton University).

Dobson, J. M. 1976. *Two centuries of tariffs: The background and emergence of the U.S. international trade commission.* Washington, D.C.: United States International Trade Commission.

Finger, J. M., H. K. Hall, and D. R. Nelson. 1982. The political economy of administered protection. *American Economic Review* 72:452–66.

Gardner, R. N. 1980. *Sterling-dollar diplomacy in current perspective.* New York: Columbia University Press.

Gilpin, R. 1975. *U.S. power and the multinational corporation.* New York: Basic Books.

———. 1977. Economic interdependence and national security in historical perspective. In *Economic issues and national security,* ed. K. Knorr and F. N. Trager. Lawrence, Kan.: Regents Press of Kansas.

Goldstein, J. L. 1981. The state, industrial interests and foreign economic policy: American commercial policy in the postwar period. Paper prepared for the National Science Foundation Conference on the Politics and Economics of Trade Policy, Minneapolis, 29–31 October.

Greenway, D. 1984. Multilateral trade policy in the 1980s. *Lloyds Bank Review* 151 (January): 30–44.

Grossman, G. M., and J. D. Richardson. 1984. Strategic U.S. trade policy: A survey of issues and early analysis. Forthcoming as a National Bureau of Economic Research *Research Progress Report.*

Hull, C. 1948. *The memoirs of Cordell Hull.* New York: Macmillan.

Kindleberger, C. P. 1973. *The world depression: 1929–1939.* Berkeley: University of California Press.

———. 1981. Cominance and leadership in the international economy: Exploitation, public goods and free rides. *International Studies Quarterly* 25:242–54.

Krasner, S. D. 1976. State power and the structure of international trade. *World Politics* 28:317–47.

———. 1979. The Tokyo Round: Particularistic interests and prospects for stability in the global trading system. *International Studies Quarterly* 23:491–531.

Krause, L. B. 1982. *U.S. economic policy toward the Association of Southeast Asian Nations: Meeting the Japanese challenge.* Washington, D.C.: Brookings Institution.

Leddy, J. M., and J. Norwood. 1963. The escape clause and peril points under the Trade Agreements Program. In *Studies in United States commercial policy,* ed. W. B. Kelly, Jr. Chapel Hill: University of North Carolina Press.

Lipson, C. 1982. The transformation of trade: The sources and effects of regime changes. *International Organization* 36:417–55.

Meyer, F. V. 1978. *International trade policy.* New York: St. Martin's.

Nordlinger, E. A. 1981. *On the autonomy of the democratic state.* Cambridge: Cambridge University Press.

Olson, M. 1965. *The logic of collective action.* Cambridge: Harvard University.

Reagan, R. 1983. *Economic report of the president.* Washington, D.C.: GPO.

———. 1984. *Twenty-seventh annual report of the president of the United States on the Trade Agreements Program, 1982–1983.* Washington, D.C.: Office of the United States Trade Representative.

Richardson, J. D. 1984a. Currents and cross-currents in the flow of U.S. trade policy. In Baldwin 1984c.

———. 1984b. U.S. international trade policies in a world of industrial change. In *Industrial change and public policy,* Federal Reserve Bank of Kansas City. Kansas City.

Saxonhouse, G. R. 1983. The micro- and macroeconomics of foreign sales to Japan. In *Trade policy in the 1980s,* ed. W. R. Cline. Washington, D.C.: Institute for International Economics and MIT Press.

Shuman, S. S., and C. O. Verrill, Jr. 1984. Recent developments in countervailing duty law and policy. In Baldwin 1984c.

Vernon, R. 1983. Old rules and new players: GATT in the world trading system. Processed May 11.

Wilkinson, J. R. 1960. *Politics and trade policy.* Washington, D.C.: Public Affairs Press.

6 The South Asian and Pacific Far East Countries in Project LINK

Lawrence R. Klein

6.1 Models for Developing Countries in the LINK System

The international model-building effort known as Project LINK was initiated some fifteen years ago with the objective of studying the international transmission mechanism. In effect, that meant model building for tracing trade flows and their effects on domestic economies of the major industrial nations. But virtually from the beginning, the project investigators realized that full world coverage would be necessary in order to obtain a meaningful assessment of trade flows in the industrial world. In order to extend coverage, in a model-building sense, to the entire world, models for developing countries and for centrally planned economies had to be introduced. This rounded out world coverage.

The specific treatment of developing countries within the LINK system has been stylized. In order to cover the vast number of developing countries, area models were introduced: (1) Africa, (2) Asia (South Asia and the Pacific Far East), (3) Latin America, and (4) Middle East.

An area model aggregates main economic variables measured in a common unit, 1963 U.S. dollars, and estimates behavioral, technical, and accounting relationships among the area totals in much the same way that it is done for individual countries. The only difference is that a country does not trade (exports or imports) with itself; an area, however, does. The intratrade for the area consists of the bilateral flows between country pairs within the area.[1]

A central feature of the LINK system is the passing of flows between countries and areas through the world trade matrix, which is a tabu-

Lawrence R. Klein is Benjamin Franklin Professor of Economics at the University of Pennsylvania.

lation of bilateral flows between exporting and importing pairs, measured in current U.S. dollars. The elements of the matrix are normalized into coefficients by dividing entries in each column by the column sum, which is total imports for the country or area designated in the column. The trade matrices are constructed for one-digit SITC groups and regrouped for LINK purposes into four merchandise classes: 0 and 1 = food, beverages, and tobacco, 2 and 4 = primary materials, 3 = mineral fuels, 5–9 = manufactures and miscellaneous.

In the manufacturing category, the coefficient matrix is not held constant but is changed, from year to year, on the basis of relative price movements, combined with RAS adjustments.

It would be natural to have separate (four in all) rows and columns of the world trade matrix devoted to each developing region, but at the present time they are grouped together into a single row and column for the developing world as a whole. In the LINK algorithm for solving the world model in the form of an accounting-balanced solution, the imports of each region $[M\$]^i$ (i = 1, 2, 3, 4) are estimated from the four regional models. Then a regional sum is formed:

$$[M(\$)]_{\text{LDC}} = \sum_{i=1}^{4} [M(\$)]_{\text{LDC}}^{(i)}.$$

This sum is placed in an entire import vector for a given category, together with the imports of OECD countries and centrally planned economies. The exports for the whole developing world are estimated from the standard equation:

$$[X(\$)]_{\text{LDC}} = \sum_{j=1}^{n} a_{ij}[M(\$)]_j,$$

where n is the total number of rows or columns in the trade matrix (individual countries and some areas), and i denotes LDC (less-developed country) in the present context. This export total is then adjusted for relative price change and by an RAS balancing calculation for the entire matrix.

This is the explicit treatment of export and import values. In effect it states that a country's or area's exports are a row-weighted average of partners' imports. The row weights are from the matrix of trade coefficients. Similarly, import prices are computed as a column-weighted average of partners' export prices.

The total exports so calculated from the trade matrix in country models in Project LINK override any calculations from country export equations that are separately estimated. This is done in order to achieve world consistency. In the case of the whole developing region, a different procedure is followed. The above estimate of $[X(\$)]_{\text{LDC}}$ comes from the first iteration of a world solution to the equation system. In the next iteration, country or area models are solved once again with the newly generated export values (also with generated import prices) to get a new import vector (also a vector of export prices), and the next iteration is formed.

But before the export values obtained on the first iteration can be used in a successive iteration, they must be disaggregated into four separate regional totals, one for each of the main regions of the developing world. This procedure is not necessary for individual countries who occupy individual rows and columns of the world trade matrix. It would not be necessary for the developing countries if their four regions were individually entered into four separate rows and columns of the trade matrix. At present, in Project LINK developing-countries' trade is treated only in a single row and column of a given matrix.

In order to make the area disaggregation, we must solve each of the regional models with their own export equations, estimated as functions of total world trade. This gives ratios among the exports of the four regions, and the developing-world total obtained from the first iteration is split into four regional values on the basis of the ratios computed from the explicit export equation. Import prices are disaggregated on the basis of their ratios before linkage.

The treatment of centrally planned economies within Project LINK is similar to that of the developing countries. For the CMEA (Council for Mutual Economic Assistance) group (six Eastern European countries plus the USSR), there is one row and column in the trade matrix, and the individual country models for the seven CMEA countries are used just as we use the four regional models of developing areas in successive LINK iterations. The People's Republic of China is treated as a separate row and column of the trade matrix and is handled in the same way that models of the OECD countries are handled. In some respects the PRC is most closely allied with the centrally planned economies and in some ways with the developing countries, especially the Asian group. Since it is separately treated, there is no special problem as far as consistent trade linkage is concerned; it is only a question of model specification.

All the regional models of developing countries in the LINK system are designed in a similar way. Output from the supply side is a function of accumulated capital and of imports (machinery, equipment, and raw materials). Consumption, investment, and exports minus imports are all estimated as functions of real income levels and relative prices, with some special allowance for financial capital inflows. The components of GDP add to the total; so goods and services imported and exported must be estimated as well as separate types of merchandise. Invisibles are determined from the difference between total trade and merchandise trade. Also, inventory investment is obtained as a residual from the GDP identity. Prices of exports in specific nonmanufacturing lines of activity are determined as weighted functions of key world commodity prices, where these key prices are generated by world market conditions or fixed marketing agreements.

The LINK system is based on the concept of completeness in world coverage and in accounting balance. The world totals of merchandise exports and imports are fully balanced by commodity groups. Since invisibles are determined in a way that is consistent with the GDP identity of each country or region, we have not allocated these flows on a complete bilateral basis and do not face up to the question of dealing with the discrepancy now prevalent in the amount of some $100 billion in the world's current account balance. But in order to achieve balance some countries or areas must be treated as residuals. For some time there has been a significant rest-of-the-world residual sector among OECD countries. Because Norway, Denmark, Greece, Switzerland, Spain, Ireland, New Zealand, and others have formally joined the LINK system, there are explicit models for virtually every OECD country, and the residual item is minimal. Within the developing and socialist worlds some difficult problems remain for dealing with Malta, Cyprus, Israel, Albania, Cuba, North Korea, and Vietnam. They are all treated in residual groups. The centrally planned economies of Asia and the Pacific (apart from the PRC, which is explicitly treated in its own model framework) are not investigated in any depth and are not part of the geographical model of Asia and the Pacific Far East. The regional model for the Asian group in LINK does distinguish, however, between OPEC and non-OPEC nations. Totals for Indonesia and Brunei, which are distinguished from the rest of the regional group, are tabulated separately.

6.2   Some Results for Asia and the Pacific Basin Group

With this methodological backdrop in mind, let us illustrate how the LINK model works by examining some results. The overall world outlook from Project LINK is for a continuing, moderate recovery from the 1980–82 recession (see table 6.1). Recovery begins during 1983, but the first full year of recovery is 1984. In projections through 1988, we look for about 2% or 3% growth in the world as a whole after 1984. This is decidedly slower than the good performances of the 1950s and 1960s. During the turbulent decade of the 1970s there was great variability among country and regional performances, but on average, it was a fair growth period, especially for the developing and centrally planned economies. The OECD countries experienced a setback as far as growth was concerned, and it was also a period of high unemployment with strong inflation.

Table 6.1   **The World Series** (percentages)

				Forecast[a]							
	1950–60	1960–70	1970–80	1981	1982	1983	1984	1985	1986	1987	1988
GDP:											
World total	4.9	5.3	4.3	1.7	0.9	2.3	3.7	3.0	2.7	2.3	2.9
OECD	4.1	5.3	3.5	1.5	−0.3	2.4	4.0	2.7	2.3	1.8	2.6
Developing	4.9	5.6	5.7	1.8	1.1	0.3	2.7	4.2	3.9	3.2	3.1
CPEs[b]	6.0	5.0	5.5	2.1	3.6	3.1	3.2	3.2	3.2	3.3	3.4
World trade volume	7.2	8.3	5.6	1.1	−1.0	1.0	4.7	5.1	3.6	3.3	3.4
Inflation in OECD	2.9	4.6	8.2	12.2	10.0	8.4	8.6	9.1	9.1	8.5	8.0

[a]These forecasts were prepared for LINK meetings in September 1983. New forecasts made in April 1984, based on March meetings of LINK, were somewhat higher for growth in most regions but lower for inflation in the OECD area. The patterns are basically similar, however.

[b]CPEs = centrally planned economics.

A principal feature of this forecast is the projected downgrading of the performance of the developing countries. Chronically low rates of growth in Africa and temporarily disturbed rates in Latin America, as a result of political instability and debt burdens, hold down the overall statistics for the developing countries. The Middle East is upset by the weakened oil market. However, the Pacific Far East has a promising economic outlook. Although they may complain and make nostalgic comparisons with results of a few years back, when many of these economies grew at double-digit rates, they are presently outstanding both at the world level and among developing countries (see table 6.2).

Price data are hard to obtain for developing countries, yet in the Far East some countries have good estimates, and it is remarkable that many of these economies have inflation rates well below 10% annually, and some are well under 5%. For the world as a whole these are excellent records, but among developing countries, particularly developing countries who are oil importers, they are truly extraordinary. That is not to say that these are trouble-free economies, but as a group they show excellent prospects as well as excellent present performance, with a great deal of self-discipline.

Indonesia is hurt by weak oil and other commodity markets; Hong Kong has to endure the insecurity worries vis-à-vis the Mainland; South Korea carries a very large debt (well over $30 billion); and the Philippines is experiencing serious political uncertainty, as well as debt and export problems.

As far as LINK results are concerned, the outlook is promising for the Asian and Pacific areas. In addition, general economic analysis of each country indicates a relatively favorable situation.

As far west as India and Pakistan growth has been occurring comparatively unnoticed, and there is a long way to go, but 3%–5% growth without undue inflation is a reasonable forecast. A softening of attitudes toward foreign capital in India may open the way for a new wave of expansion. Coming eastward, Bangladesh and Burma do not have an

Table 6.2   **GDP Growth Predictions for Developing Countries**
(for percentages)

	1983	1984	1985	1986	1987	1988
Africa	−0.7	0.7	0.8	0.6	1.5	1.8
Asia	3.9	4.3	5.4	5.3	4.0	4.6
Latin America	−2.6	1.4	3.9	3.2	2.4	1.2
Middle East	−1.9	2.6	3.4	3.5	4.0	4.6
Developing-countries total	0.3	2.7	4.2	3.9	3.2	3.1

Note: See note to table 6.1.

impressive record or outlook, but what might be called the Pacific Basin developing countries (Thailand, Malaysia, Singapore, Indonesia, Hong Kong, the Philippines, Taiwan, and South Korea) are in the best overall situation in the developing world. It is also a well-integrated and balanced grouping containing many primary producers, a major oil exporter, and some strong manufacturing countries. They are generally oriented toward the United States and Japan, with a fair amount of interaction with Australia and Canada.

The populations are well educated, highly motivated, and very productive and aggressive in world services. They produce quality merchandise and services. The LINK results mainly reflect the underlying strengths of this region.

The principal LINK model characteristics that account for the good growth of the South Asian and Pacific area countries are the sensitivity of GDP growth to exports and good export growth through competitive price advantage. These characteristics are built into the model and are produced by the fitting of parameters to historical data.

The reasons why these economies have more favorable projections than the Latin American countries, for example, is that the latter are saddled with large debt service burdens—*initial conditions*—and their domestic policy reactions to financial difficulties have been to restrict imports severly. Mexico cut back imports in 1982 by about 40% through foreign exchange rationing. Low imports and an exogenous cutoff in financial capital inflows lead to low investment activity, which, in turn, leads to low GDP growth, in both *potential* and *actual* GDP. This reaction is part of model structure.

An additional impact is being felt in Latin American through shortfalls in raw material exports. The direct productivity effects of raw material imports are not well reflected in the LINK models of developing countries.

Africa fares less well than Asia in LINK projections because the export mix is unfavorable. Asian countries have higher proportions of fast-growing manufactured exports. This is part of model structure.

Middle East growth, being highly dependent on oil trade, does not look impressive in a period when oil prices are restrained because of world conditions. Also, we have exogenously held back Middle East growth because of military disturbances in the projection period.

The acceptance of wage flexibility for downward adjustment of growth of nominal wage rates in recent years, both in Japan and in many of the developing countries of the Pacific, has contributed significantly to a good price adjustment to the second oil shock. That is a good part of the reason why the record on inflation is so favorable. Of course, estimated productivity growth is another part of the explanation.

6.3 Some Individual Country Results

A major research thrust of Project LINK is to improve the methodological treatment of the developing countries, by introducing separate models for many of the larger countries and treating them on a par, as much as possible, with the industrial countries and the centrally planned economies. To this end, a number of individual country models have been prepared at Project LINK for developing countries. They are presently being simulated by themselves, using LINK inputs for projections of world trade volume and world inflation. Work is underway, and far along, to build an enlarged trade matrix with separate rows and columns for individual developing countries—some twenty-five to thirty cases. Even before the full integration takes place, it is worthwhile looking at single country results that are projected consistently with LINK world results, but without feedback effect from the developing countries to OECD countries or centrally planned economies. We are thus looking at individual developing countries in a satellite mode.

For purposes of our present investigations it is noteworthy that a large number of Pacific Basin countries are included indirectly in the first batch of estimates of LDC models. There are estimates for South Korea, Taiwan, the Philippines, Indonesia, Singapore, Malaysia, and Thailand. In addition there are results for India.

Each model has been fitted to data for the period 1960–78. Data from the United Nations on national income and product accounts, maintained on a uniform basis, have been used for the estimation of each model. They have then been extrapolated beyond the sample for the period 1979–82 and compared with the data available on the indicators to see if the model is functioning well outside the sample and if corrective factors can be devised which would improve model performance in this postsample observation period. In some cases, more recent data acquired from a country itself were used for monitoring the dynamic evolution of the model to 1981 or 1982. The models were then extrapolated to 1985 using LINK inputs when relevant.

It should be mentioned that the preparation of models on a uniform basis and using uniform data prepared by a third party (UN) is not necessarily an optimal method for proceeding. It is, however, feasible and efficient. In the next phase, individual country models maintained within a country will be substituted, where possible, for the first approximation prepared at LINK headquarters. This is in keeping with the basic philosophy of Project LINK, which maintains that resident model builders know their own countries best and that we are well advised to use their models, if made available to LINK. The departure from uniformity in model structure and design may be occasionally a handicap, but it is compensated for by the richness of results. Uniformity, as with OECD countries in LINK, can be achieved through the trading relations.

Models are being made ready for use in LINK in South Korea, Taiwan, Hong Kong, India, Pakistan, and some countries in Latin America and Africa. These will be maintained on site in the countries mentioned. The project will use a mixture of small uniform models prepared at LINK headquarters and some models submitted on a regular and maintained basis from country research centers.

At the present time, I can report on preliminary results obtained by using the models built at LINK headquarters and cited above, using materials in LINK files. The results for Asian and Pacific Far East countries are given in table 6.3.

There is no country in this group that can be said to be doing poorly, in a macroeconomic sense. Some may have very high aspirations and be dissatisfied with these results, but from an outside view, they look quite favorable. South Korea has already outperformed the figure predicted for 1983, with about 9% growth, and they may be able to maintain a better pace than indicated in table 6.3 for 1985 although there could well be some degree of slowdown from their heated growth pace. The Philippines will be hard pressed to meet the good growth rates predicted for 1984–85, especially in view of the political situation, which is bound to create uncertainty in people's minds, including both business investors and household consumers.

Table 6.3   **Forecasts of Main Economic Indicators for Asian and Pacific Far East Countries** (percentages)

	1983	1984	1985
India GDP	2.8	4.9	5.7
Inflation	9.6	7.4	6.1
South Korea GDP	6.4	7.6	3.9
Inflation	7.9	5.6	4.3
Taiwan GDP	4.5	6.0	7.1
Inflation	5.2	5.3	6.0
Philippines GDP	3.2	5.2	5.6
Inflation	10.4	9.4	8.7
Indonesia GDP	3.0	4.7	7.4
Inflation	14.1	14.5	9.6
Singapore GDP	6.3	7.6	8.6
Inflation	4.3	5.4	6.4
Malaysia GDP	4.6	6.6	6.7
Inflation	5.6	5.8	6.1
Thailand GDP	6.1	6.4	7.2
Inflation	4.4	4.9	4.9

The inflation numbers projected in table 6.3 are outstanding for developing countries and would be the envy of several OECD countries. The Philippines, because of political uncertainty, and Indonesia, because of the poor balance-of-payments situation, have relatively high inflation rates in this group, but it was estimated that they will be brought under control by 1985.

It must be emphasized that the preliminary models used to generate these estimates are inadequately developed on the supply side and are not yet fitted out with debt simulators. These are being introduced on the next research round.

Some estimates from LINK participants who maintain country models on site or with area institutions should be considered alongside the results reported in table 6.3. These estimates are given in table 6.4. For the most part they are in line with the model estimates of table 6.3. Most of the estimates are a bit stronger on growth or better for inflation except for the Philippines, Indonesia, and Thailand (inflation only). The associated current balances are generally sound except for the Philippines and Indonesia. As mentioned in connection with table 6.3, the Phillipines should have poorer growth and more inflation. Taiwan should have stronger growth.

Table 6.4	Forecasts of Main Economic Indicators from a LINK Conference Held in Tsukuba, Japan, September 1983 (percentages)		
	1983	1984	1985
South Korea GDP	8.2	9.0	7.3
Inflation	3.5	7.0	7.8
Taiwan GNP	5.9	6.6	6.0
Inflation	4.3	5.9	3.8
Philippines GDP	2.0	4.2	5.6
Inflation	11.8	10.7	10.0
Indonesia GDP	2.0	5.0	6.8
Inflation	19.8	16.0	12.0
Singapore GDP	7.5	7.5	8.0
Inflation	3.5	5.4	7.0
Malaysia GDP	5.5	6.8	7.0
Inflation	5.3	5.2	5.8
Thailand GDP	6.0	6.4	7.0
Inflation	5.6	6.5	7.0
Hong Kong GDP	4.0	6.1	6.8
Inflation	8.5	8.0	8.0

Source: Vincent Su, City University of New York (Ministry of Education, Taiwan, summers of 1982 and 1983), made the estimates for Taiwan. The estimates for all the other countries are from Y. K. Wang, Chung Ang University, Seoul, and Asian Development Bank.

To get an idea of the sensitivity of the countries in this region to external shocks either from an increase in exports or from an increase in import prices, we have simulated each model and computed long-run elasticity responses for GDP and price with respect to shifts in exports or import prices (see tables 6.5 and 6.6). In the case of GDP sensitivity, the Asian countries respond positively to an increase in exports, generally with elasticity values between 0.4 and 1.0. The responses in the Philippines and Indonesia are surprisingly weaker than in the other countries of the area. The Indonesian response should be significantly positive. Import price rises sometimes depress domestic activity. In some cases they make home production and exports sufficiently more competitive that they lead to increases in production.

With two exceptions (Malaysia and Indonesia) export increases lead to upward price sensitivity, and without fail, import price increases show up in domestic price increases. The price sensitivities, expressed in elasticity form, are generally small.

These elasticities are expressed as reactions to general changes in exports and import prices, but we can be more specific about the changes. An export increase or decrease could be interpreted, both quantitatively and qualitatively, as the result of a change in protec-

Table 6.5   **GDP Elasticity**

	Change in Exports	Change in Import Price
India	0.69	−0.01
Indonesia	0.00	0.03
South Korea	0.26	0.02
Malaysia	0.47	0.28
Philippines	0.18	−0.16
Singapore	0.78	0.12
Taiwan	0.45	−0.01
Thailand	0.40	0.28

Table 6.6   **Demand Price Elasticity**

	Change in Exports	Change in Import Price
India	0.06	0.80
Indonesia	0.00	0.14
South Korea	0.28	0.25
Malaysia	−0.31	0.38
Philippines	0.09	0.10
Singapore	0.14	0.78
Taiwan	0.15	0.65
Thailand	0.16	0.39

tionism. Also, general import price changes could come about from oil or raw material price changes as well as from overall changes. By relating, in a quantitative sense, the changes in aggregate totals (shown in tables 6.5 and 6.6) to specific changes, we can study a variety of policy issues with these models in an elementary way.

This discussion would not be complete without some specific reference to the outlook for the People's Republic of China. As indicated above, the PRC is given separate treatment in the LINK system as a model on its own footing, with a separate row and column in the world trade matrix. Model building for this largest country in the world is in its infancy. Even the data base is enormously in need of development. It is both a developing and a centrally planned economy. Within the system, it is represented by a model constructed and maintained at Stanford University by Lawrence J. Lau. Many of the data series are smooth trends, and good price, employment, and labor force statistics are not available. Yet we do as much as can be done toward model building for this important country and monitor data of production and trade closely.

At the present time, projections by Professor Lau for LINK are quite favorable, similar to those for Pacific area countries and the other centrally planned economies. GDP growth is projected at 6%–7% for the next three years by Professor Lau, and good rates in this range have been estimated, ex post, for many of the past few years, since normalization of relationships. A slow steady growth for agriculture at about 4.0% is projected; stronger growth is predicted for industry. Exports are projected to grow as fast as GDP, while imports are more erratic, sometimes up by a wide margin and sometimes down, but there is no sign of prolonged imbalances or the carrying of an excessive external burden. Foreign economic relations appear to be very prudent.

6.4 Conclusion

There is no doubt that the Asian-Pacific countries are star performers in the present LINK system for the near and intermediate term. Some of the economies in the region have problems, but none appears to be on the verge of collapse or bankruptcy. Other developing areas have had similar bright outlooks—the Middle East in the mid-1970s and Latin America somewhat later—only to undergo rapid deterioration. But the foundation looks favorable in the Pacific area because it is based on good workmanship, intelligence, and high productivity. It is not based in a single-minded way on good terms of trade for one community alone.

India appears to be a solid economy but not as dazzling as the Pacific Basin countries. The other countries of South Asia who are not among those denoted as Pacific Basin countries are less well off economically, and they hold the averages down, but with some years of peace with political stability, they too could show a great deal of improvement.

Note

1. A trade matrix analysis of flows within the Asian area is given in L. Klein and V. Su, "Trade Linkages within the Pacific Far East" (paper presented at a conference at Rutgers University, 16 April 1981).

III Structural Change and Transitional Growth in Pacific Asia

7 NICs and the Next-Tier NICs as Transitional Economies

Colin I. Bradford, Jr.

7.1 Introduction

A focus of this volume is the degree of linkage between the performance of the domestic economies of the industrializing developing countries of East and Southeast Asia and their external performance as exporters of manufactures. Some of the economic literature in recent years dealing with the newly industrializing countries (NICs) and outward-oriented growth strategies has emphasized the degree to which trade has driven development through demand. The country studies in this volume have included a focus on the evolution of the internal structure of production in its supply dimension as facilitating if not indeed determining the volume and composition of manufactured exports of specific countries. This chapter examines various aspects of this focus in a comparative context that includes European and Latin American NICs and next-tier NICs.

There is a continuing debate in economics about the relative efficacy of policies and markets in influencing economic outcomes. This debate has particular poignancy today in relation to the role of developing-country economic policies and price systems in causing and resolving world debt and international trade problems. The NICs and next-tier NICs are of particular interest because of their emergence (or potential emergence) as exporters of manufactured goods on a global scale and because of their generally high level of debt financing. These new roles

Colin I. Bradford, Jr., teaches international economics at Yale University, where he directs a two-year masters program in international relations and is associate director of the Yale Center for International and Area Studies.

The author is particularly grateful to Ronald Findlay for written comments on an earlier draft and to William H. Branson for stimulating discussions of these issues. The author remains responsible for whatever rough edges still remain.

of the NICs in world trade and finance raise a number of broad issues which will be examined in this chapter.

One issue is the degree to which the NICs are part of a general process of economic development which yields relatively predictable patterns of internal structural change (in the Hollis Chenery tradition) and of changes in the product composition of exports according to Heckscher-Ohlin trade based on factor proportions. The next section examines data on the structure and changes in composition of fifteen leading exports in sixteen transitional economies according to changing factor proportions over time and as incomes increase. The evidence from these data has a bearing on the degree to which trade pressures are alleviated by countries moving along a spectrum of factor intensities of export composition or are exacerbated by competition from new exporters in existing, relatively static markets. To the extent that the cross-sectional and inter-temporal data are consistent with the factor proportions explanation of structural change in trade, they provide some evidence that the development process contains within it its own source of relief from transitional trade pressures. These sources of relief tend to be supported by market forces affecting factors of production and final goods, though government policies can enhance or impede them.

If changes in the composition of trade are linked to changes in the internal structure of production, the expectation would be that the NICs, with above-average rates of export growth and economic growth, would be countries with accelerated rates of structural change facilitated by high rates of capital formation. Section 7.3 examines comparative data on investment at international prices among the transitional economies to ascertain the importance of domestic policies affecting interest rates and credit allocations in distinguishing the NICs from other developing economies. Data supporting these notions reveal the importance of policies in determining export performance and add domestic monetary and fiscal policies to the emphasis given in earlier literature (Krueger 1978; Balassa 1978; Bhagwati and Srinivasan 1979; and Bradford 1982b) to trade and exchange rate policies as important variables explaining the NIC phenomenon.

The above inquiry leads to an examination of price distortions and the relationship between price distortions and the implementation of successful outward-oriented growth strategies. There is some literature which attempts to equate outward-oriented growth strategies with reliance on market forces and price signals. There is a tendency in these analyses to stereotype the market liberalization and outward-oriented approaches supposedly adopted by the Asian NICs and the more interventionist and inward-oriented approaches identified with Latin America. In section 7.4 price distortion data are compared for inward-

and outward-looking developing countries from Asia and Latin America to ascertain how clear-cut the stylized dichotomy is in reality.

7.2 Factor Intensities and Structural Change in Exports

The rise of NIC exports of manufactures can be seen as Heckscher-Ohlin trade based on changing factor proportions over time which results in shifts in the structure of trade. In the tradition of Colin Clark, economies are seen to move from primary product production to manufacturing to services in domestic output and from natural-resource-intensive to unskilled-labor-intensive to physical- and human-capital-intensive in the product composition of exports.

This view of the development process yields a concomitant view of trade adjustment in which countries move through different "stages" of comparative advantage (Balassa 1977) as the product composition of exports shifts along a spectrum of factor intensities. Since all countries are moving along the same spectrum, movement by countries further along the scale makes room for countries down the scale.[1] The source of the problems of trade tensions, in this view, is simultaneously the source of trade adjustment (see Balassa 1977, 26–27).[2] The only caveat—and it is an important one in the current circumstances—is that world trade adjustment depends heavily on continued economic growth in the major blocs of countries. Slow growth in one tier of countries slows growth in the next tier, dampening structural change in both tiers and worsening trade adjustment.

The analysis in this section will examine the NICs as countries experiencing transitional growth, that is, transformation from low-income, low-growth economies to more advanced industrial countries. The nature of the dynamic underlying NIC export growth can be most effectively understood in a perspective which compares them with the next-tier NICs and with industrial countries. We are interested less in the NICs than in the NIC phenomenon as a transition process which is best understood in comparative perspective. This analysis will be in the "half-way house" mode between general theories of patterns of development à la Chenery and the more historical approaches emphasizing countries' unique experiences (Ranis 1983, 5; Ohkawa, Fei, and Ranis, 1983, 2). "What clearly seems to be evolving is the recognition that we all are looking for some sort of half-way house between an ever-elusive general theory of development and the unacceptable notion that every country differs so fundamentally from every other at every point in time that nothing can be said which is of generalized value" (Ranis 1983, 5).

The NIC phenomenon is essentially one of a surge in manufactured exports (Bradford 1982b). The trade adjustment problems posed by the

NICs arise from high-volume exports in particular kinds of goods. Hence, we limit the analysis of the changes in the composition of exports of the high-exporting transitional economies to the fifteen leading exports at the three-digit SITC level. This focus on the fifteen leading exports is due to the fact that from a global economy perspective, we are interested in those exports which by virtue of volume make a difference in world markets. It is not Korean exports in general, for example, which are pressuring Organization for Economic Cooperation and Development (OECD) import markets but specific high-volume, high-growth exports from Korea. The advantage of using the United Nations Conference on Trade and Development (UNCTAD) data on the top fifteen exports is that it not only identifies these high-volume, high-growth exports but also shows the degree to which changes in factor proportions manifest themselves in shifts in the composition of the important exports in terms of volume.

The countries designated as NICs are drawn from classifications of earlier studies. In particular, the NICs are those identified as such in the Chatham House study based on manufactured exports of $1 billion or more in 1976 (Turner and McMullen 1982, 12–13). These NICs are South Korea, Taiwan, Hong Kong, and Singapore in East Asia; Brazil, Mexico, and Argentina in Latin America; and India. The OECD in an earlier study of the NICs (1979) included the southern European NICs (Spain, Portugal, Greece, and Yugoslavia), which are also incorporated here. The next-tier NICs are the other developing countries of East and Southeast Asia (Thailand, the Philippines, Malaysia, and Indonesia) and Colombia in Latin America.

To gain an understanding of the influence of factor proportions on the structure of exports of transitional economies in recent years, I have classified each of the top fifteen exports (SITC three-digit level) as natural-resource-intensive (NR), unskilled-labor-intensive (USL), and physical- and human-capital-intensive (P/HK), using the commodity classifications of Blejer (1978), which are based on Lary (1968) value added per man.

Tables 7.1 and 7.2 show the trade shares by factor intensity of the fifteen leading exports for the sixteen transitional economies as well as the United States as a benchmark advanced industrial country. The cross-sectional results for 1978 are arrayed in table 7.1, and the changes over time for 1967–78 are given in table 7.2. The countries with high natural resource endowments (Brazil, Mexico, Argentina, Indonesia) are at the beginning of the ladder. High natural resource endowments remove some of the impetus for an export-oriented growth strategy based on manufactured goods because foreign exchange requirements are more easily satisfied by natural-resource-intensive exports. In addition to the reduced foreign exchange incentive, there is the "Dutch

Table 7.1   **Factor Intensities of Fifteen Leading Export Sectors of Sixteen Industrializing Countries (cross section, 1978; percentage of total exports)**

	Intensities		
	Natural Resource	Unskilled Labor	Physical or Human Capital
Benchmark			
United States	11.08	8.08	36.38
European NICs			
Spain	16.44	15.01	18.96
Yugoslavia	4.50	24.82	19.65
Portugal	8.98	41.29	10.54
Greece	36.55	22.08	7.96
Asian NICs			
India	31.32	30.27	0.0
Korea	8.61	43.75	18.72
Taiwan	—	—	—
Hong Kong	0.0	72.05	13.44
Singapore	42.30	12.50	16.31
Next-Tier NICs			
Philippines	54.83	26.66	0.0
Thailand	66.01	13.68	0.0
Malaysia	72.46	9.12	7.52
Colombia	79.51	5.77	1.88
Natural Resource NICs			
Brazil	53.82	5.05	8.59
Mexico	63.20	1.95	8.36
Argentina	64.65	0.0	4.19
Indonesia (next-tier)	96.25	0.74	0.0

Sources: Commodity classification is based on Lary (1968) in Blejer (1978). Data are from UNCTAD 1982, table 4.4, SITC (three digits).

disease'' condition, where successful natural-resource-intensive exports drive up the real wage in manufacturing, reducing the competitiveness of labor-intensive manufactured exports. Hong Kong represents the opposite case, where the complete absence of natural resource endowments compels a manufactured-export thrust.

Another pattern noticeable in these figures that has been attributed by Ranis (1983, 25–26) to natural resource abundance is the skipping of what Ranis and others call ''the primary export substitution subphase'' in which labor-intensive nondurable consumer goods are exported. The figures show almost no exports of unskilled-labor-intensive goods for Brazil, Mexico, and Argentina and a larger proportion of physical- or human-capital-intensive exports. This indicates that import substitution has taken place in labor-intensive goods, but exports have not been forthcoming to any significant extent. The export stage for

Table 7.2   **Changes in Factor Intensities of Fifteen Leading Export Sectors of Sixteen Industrializing Countries** (percentage of total exports)

	1967	1978
Benchmark		
United States		
NR	8.52	11.08 +
USL	7.10	8.09 0
H/PK	28.74	36.38 +
European NICs		
Spain		
NR	39.82	16.44 − −
USL	8.61	15.01 +
H/PK	5.30	18.96 +
Yugoslavia		
NR	8.25	4.50 −
USL	20.49	24.82 +
H/PK	10.15	19.65 +
Portugal		
NR	22.21	8.98 −
USL	37.31	41.29 −
H/PK	5.04	10.54 +
Greece		
NR	57.61	36.55 − −
USL	4.16	22.08 + +
H/PK	6.21	7.96 +
Asian NICs		
India		
NR	37.94	31.42 slight −
USL	30.44	30.27 0
H/PK	0.0	0.0
Korea		
NR	31.95	8.61 −
USL	40.03	43.75 0
H/PK	2.00	18.72 +
Taiwan	—	—
Hong Kong		
NR	0	0 0
USL	73.85	72.05 0
H/PK	8.36	13.44 +
Singapore		
NR	52.96	42.30 −
USL	6.28	12.50 +
H/PK	3.78	16.31 +
Next-Tier NICs		
Philippines		
NR	84.04	54.83 −
USL	6.65	26.66 +
H/PK	0	0 0

Table 7.2   (continued)

	1967	1978	
Thailand			
NR	75.45	66.01	−
USL	2.11	13.68	+
H/PK	0	0	0
Malaysia			
NR	81.71	72.46	−
USL	5.82	9.12	+
H/PK	0	7.52	+
Colombia			
NR	90.90	79.51	−
USL	1.39	5.77	+
H/PK	0.0	1.88	+
Natural Resource NICs			
Brazil			
NR	66.43	53.82	−
USL	0.22	5.05	+
H/PK	0.08	8.59	+
Mexico			
NR	43.78	63.20	+
USL	2.36	1.95	0
H/PK	1.16	8.36	+
Argentina			
NR	79.03	64.65	−
USL	0.0	0.0	
H/PK	1.41	4.19	+
Indonesia (next-tier)			
NR	89.04	96.25	
USL	0	0.74	+
H/PK	0	0	+

Sources: Commodity classification is based on Blejer 1978. Data are from UNCTAD 1976, table 4.4; and UNCTAD 1982, table 4.4, SITC (three digits)

Note: NR = natural-resource-intensive,   USL = unskilled-labor-intensive,   H/PK = human- and/or physical-capital-intensive; +, 0, − = change from 1967 to 1978.

these goods has been skipped, and the countries have moved on to exports of goods higher on the factor intensity scale.

This contrasts with the countries further up the country ladder (the next-tier NICs), which seem to be moving from natural-resource-intensive to labor-intensive exports; and in the case of Malaysia and Colombia, on to P/HK-intensive exports without skipping labor-intensive consumer goods exports. Nevertheless, the abundance of natural resource endowments appears to continue to be a constraint on more substantial shifts in the structure of exports for these countries, as it is for the natural resource NICs.

The Asian NICs, on the other hand, less endowed with or constrained by, as the case may be, natural resource endowments, show substantial concentration in labor-intensive exports and increasingly in P/HK-intensive exports. The Asian NICs are closest in static structure to the European NICs. India and Greece have somewhat similar export structures, which, compared to the East Asian and other European NICs, show some constraints on movement into P/HK-intensive exports. Spain and Yugoslavia, among the sixteen transitional economies, manifest the furthest movement along the factor intensity spectrum. The United States serves as a benchmark advanced industrial country with a more diversified export structure (only 56% of U.S. exports are accounted for by the leading fifteen exports) and the largest concentration in P/HK- intensive exports (36%).

Table 7.2 presents the same kind of data on the structure of exports by factor intensity but, in this instance, over time for the period 1967–78. World export growth was quite high during this period compared with the 1980s. The European NICs show the most accelerated shifts in export structure, with very substantial reductions in the share of natural-resource-intensive exports and equally large increases in both labor-intensive and P/HK-intensive exports. Greece, in this perspective, manifests a very different pattern from India, which is relatively stagnant in terms of structural change. A still more interesting result of this intertemporal perspective is that Korea and Hong Kong had achieved high labor-intensive shares of exports by 1967. Singapore, with a very much lower labor share in 1967, doubled its labor share while quadrupling its P/HK share by 1978.

One wonders whether the Philippines, Thailand, and India are simply further down the scale with less physical and human capital formation or whether they are "stuck" in a high labor-intensive stage and having difficulty diversifying upscale to P/HK-intensive exports.

The next-tier NICs exhibit the expected patterns further down the scale, with declining natural resource shares and increasing labor shares, but except for Malaysia, they have not reached the point where P/HK-intensive exports have been forthcoming. The natural resource NICs of Mexico and Indonesia actually show *increasing* natural resource shares over time as oil exports become more important.

The data in tables 7.1 and 7.2 manifest patterns which are broadly consistent with a factor proportions explanation of structural change in trade. As one observes countries along the ladder of countries, or individual or sets of countries over time, the compositional shifts in exports confirm one's expectations that, as economies develop, their factor endowments will change to an emphasis on physical and human capital, which in turn will change not only the basket of commodities produced but also shift the comparative advantage of the country's leading exports. This general conclusion is also drawn by Lawrence Krause in chapter 8 of this volume, based on data for total exports.

Some of these countries are noteworthy because of their unusually rapid industrialization and highly dynamic export growth, especially of manufactures. The question is, can we identify causal variables that explain the reason(s) for the unusual growth and high export performance of the NICs as compared with other transitional economies and nontransitional economies. The NICs have been distinguished by the relatively accelerated rates of structural change, both internally and in their export shares. As Ranis puts it, the purpose of this sort of analysis is to discover "reasons for inter-country divergence of performance" (1983, 3).

7.3   Capital Formation and Structural Change

Up until now most of the literature dealing with the NICs has found that trade and exchange rate policies have been the principal policy regimes that seem to have played a key role in promoting the surge in manufactured exports from the NICs in the 1960s and 1970s (Balassa 1978; Krueger 1978; Bradford 1982b). Indeed, the term *NIC* is meant to designate that set of developing countries that has been sufficiently successful in implementing an export-oriented growth strategy to have become significant exporters of manufactures on a global scale.

As we have seen, countries identified in earlier studies as NICs because of the surge in the volume of their manufactured exports also manifest dynamic change (with the exception of India) in the composition of their exports. This implies that the unusual export performance of the NICs is based upon an internal process of economic transformation and structural change. Chapter 1 and the country studies in this volume provide further insight into the dimensions of this internal process and its connection with export performance. If the NICs are countries which have achieved exceptional rates of change in the structure of their exports and in their internal productive structure, then it seems likely that they may be distinctive in their domestic macroeconomic policies as well as in their trade and exchange rate policies. Indeed, if it is true that the single most important explanation of NIC export expansion is a historic national commitment to an outward-oriented growth strategy which forces an unusually high degree of consistency in trade and exchange rate policies (Bradford 1982b), then it seems reasonable to suppose that macroeconomic policies would also be brought into line with the basic national strategy. Furthermore, given the relationship between dynamic internal structural change and external export performance shown in chapter 1, it would be expected that investment would be the key macroeconomic variable facilitating structural change in both its internal and its external manifestations.

This section will examine the relationship between capital formation and structural change among transitional economies and in other economies in an effort to ascertain the degree to which the NICs are characterized by distinctive performance. The nature of the analysis is such that it is intended to be suggestive of general patterns that seem to prevail rather than to be highly conclusive.

The data used here have been generated by the United Nations International Price Comparison Project (ICP) led by Irving Kravis, Alan Heston, and Robert Summers (Kravis, Heston, and Summers 1982). The purpose of this work was to obtain real GDP comparisons based on international prices rather than real exchange rates. This was done by constructing a matrix of national expenditures on 151 commodities for thirty-four countries. "Real" quantities were derived by dividing expenditures by national prices at purchasing-power parity. The "real" quantities, in turn, were multiplied by international prices which were generated separately. Sets of commodities at international prices were aggregated into GDP components so that ratios of investment in international prices to national prices could be calculated. Each country's ratio of prices for GDP as a whole to international prices was taken as unity so that an index, or ratio, of national to international prices for investment higher than one indicates relatively higher national prices for investment goods and an index of less than one indicates lower national prices for investment goods vis-à-vis international prices.

The Kravis et al. work includes data on ten of the sixteen countries designated here as transitional economies. Table 7.3 shows the index of national to international prices for different types of countries (top panel) and for the transitional economies (bottom panel) for the consumption, investment, and government components of GDP. The pattern that Kravis et al. observe is that investment goods are more expensive in lower-income countries than in higher-income countries. The index for investment goods declines steadily as one moves up the country ladder from group I (lower-income countries) to group VI (the United States). The exception is group II, which shows a substantially lower index (0.96) for investment goods than is consistent with the overall trend. Group II consists of six countries, four of which are transitional economies (Korea, Malaysia, Colombia, and Brazil) with very low investment indices and two of which are nontransitional economies (Jamaica and Syria) with indices for investment goods well above 1.00. This suggests that one of the key characteristics accounting for the above-trend-line pattern of structural change in transitional economies is lower costs associated with capital formation.

Table 7.4 examines the relationship between this index of investment prices and various measures of structural change for the ten transitional economies for which the Kravis et al. study has figures. Since invest-

Table 7.3   **Relation of National Price Structure to International Price Structure: 1975**

	Consumption Goods	Investment Goods	Government	GDP
Types of countries (averages)				
Group VI	1.03	0.81	1.11	1.00
Group V	1.00	0.91	1.31	1.00
Group IV	0.97	1.05	1.04	1.00
Group III	0.96	1.13	0.93	1.00
Group II	1.01	0.96	0.86	1.00
Group I	1.04	1.19	0.66	1.00
Jamaica (group II)	0.96	1.12	1.08	1.00
Syria (group II)	0.93	1.08	1.28	1.00
Transitional economies				
Spain	0.98	1.03	1.48	1.00
Yugoslavia	0.91	1.25	1.01	1.00
India	1.00	1.29	0.61	1.00
Korea (group II)	1.05	0.92	0.86	1.00
Philippines	0.94	1.64	0.55	1.00
Thailand	0.98	1.16	0.86	1.00
Malaysia (group II)	1.04	0.87	1.05	1.00
Colombia (group II)	1.00	1.01	0.85	1.00
Brazil (group II)	1.06	0.93	0.73	1.00
Mexico	1.02	0.94	1.00	1.00
Advanced economies				
United States	1.03	0.81	1.11	1.00
Germany	1.03	0.83	1.38	1.00
Japan	1.04	0.90	1.31	1.00

Source: Kravis, Heston, and Summers 1982, table 1-8.

Note: "A value of more than 1 for a given country in a given category indicates that relative to the relationship of the country's prices to international prices for its GDP as a whole, its prices for that particular category are high" (Kravis, Heston, and Summers 1982, 193).

Group VI = United States; group V = United Kingdom, Japan, Austria, Netherlands, Belgium, France, Luxembourg, Denmark, and Germany; group IV = Hungary, Poland, Italy, and Spain; group III = Romania, Mexico, Yugoslavia, Iran, Uruguay, and Ireland; group II = Korea, Malaysia, Columbia, Brazil, Jamaica, and Syria; group I = Malawi, Kenya, India, Pakistan, Sri Lanka, Zambia, Thailand, and the Philippines.

ment is the key variable, the table is organized in terms of gross domestic investment (GDI) as a share of GDP. In nominal terms, eight of the ten countries have nominal GDI/GDP shares between 20.0% and 24.0%. Exceptions are Yugoslavia (29.4%) and Colombia (18.4%). Investment as a share of GDP based on international prices generates a different set of numbers. The table is set up in descending order based on the real GDI/GDP shares, from Malaysia (27%) to the Philippines (15%). There is a break in the rank ordering between those with shares of 22% or higher and those with shares of 18% or less.

Table 7.4   Capital Formation and Structural Change in Ten Transitional Economies

	Nominal GDI/GDP, 1975[a] (%) (1)	GDI/GDP, International Prices, 1975[a] (%) (2)	Investment Goods Ratio: National/International Prices, 1975[a] (3)	Per Capita Index based on International Prices 1975[a] (U.S. = 1.00) Total Invest. (4)	Producer Goods (5)	Share of Manufacturing in GDP[b] (%) 1960 (6)	1980	% Change in Structure of Total Exports 1967–78[c] (7)	P/HK as % of Total Exports, 1978[d] (8)	Debt Outstanding in 1981 (in millions of U.S. $)[e] (9)
Rapid structural change (average)	23.1	23.3	0.99	36.8	28.4	20.8	29.7	29.7	13.63	
Malaysia	23.8	27	0.87	28.8	15.1	9	23	20	7.52	4,627 (23)
Yugoslavia	29.4	24	1.25	41.8	36.3	36	30	18	19.65	5,266 (18)
Brazil	21.4	23	0.93	28.4	32.1	26	34	26	8.59	43,999 (1)
Korea	20.2	22	0.92	22.3	18.4	14	28	44	18.72	19,964 (3)
Mexico	20.9	22	0.94	37.9	18.7	19	26	27	8.36	42,642 (2)
Spain	22.6	22	1.03	61.8	48.9	—	37	43	18.96	—
Slower structural change (average)	20.7	16.5	1.28	11.5	6.1	16	21.5	23.0		
Colombia	18.4	18	1.01	20.0	6.5	17	22	16	1.88	5,026 (20)
Thailand	20.0	17	1.16	11.0	8.1	13	20	20	0.0	5,169 (19)
India	20.3	16	1.29	5.0	1.9	14	18	6	0.0	17,903 (4)
Philippines	24.1	15	1.64	9.5	7.8	20	26	50	0.0	7,388 (14)

[a]Kravis, Heston, and Summers 1982, tables 1-6, 1-7, 1-8, and 6-4.

[b]World Bank 1982; World Bank 1983, table 3.

[c]Rounded from table 7.2.

[d]From table 7.1.

[e]Lee 1983. World rank is shown in parentheses.

There is a reasonably scalar inverse relationship between prices of investment goods and real GDI/GDP shares (columns 2 and 3). The lower the price of investment goods, the higher the real GDI/GDP share and the higher the investment goods price, the lower the real GDI/GDP share. Yugoslavia is the only serious exception to the pattern. To be sure, the national to international price ratio has been used to generate the GDI/GDP ratios in real terms, but the correspondence is more than arithmetic. Lower real investment prices would be expected to induce high rates of capital formation. In turn, the countries with the lower-cost investment goods and the higher GDI/GDP ratios would be expected to be the countries with more rapid rates of structural change.

By and large this is the case; the countries above the break in investment shares are the Asian, Latin American, and European NICs, except for Malaysia, which appears to be the most promising next-tier NIC. The countries below the break are the next-tier NICs and India, which, as was pointed out above, has had a static export structure over time.

Further measures are consistent with these findings. The per capita indexes of total investment based on international prices (with the index for the United States being 1.00) and of producer goods prices are both decidedly larger in the countries with low investment goods prices, as would be expected (columns 4 and 5). The share of GDP accounted for by manufacturing in 1980 is generally higher for the countries with the lower-cost capital goods and higher GDI/GDP ratios than for Colombia, Thailand, India, and the Philippines (column 6) and is well above the average for the middle-income countries as well (19% in 1980). The Philippines had a surprisingly high manufacturing GDP share in 1980 (26%).

The absolute percentage point changes (positive and negative) in the shares of exports from 1967 to 1978 shifting from natural-resource to unskilled-labor and from unskilled-labor to physical- and human-capital-intensive categories (table 7.2) is taken as a measure of structural change in column 7. Brazil, Korea, Mexico, Spain, and again, curiously, the Philippines are more advanced according to these measures than Malaysia, Yugoslavia, Colombia, and Thailand. India, as we know, scores very low in these measures. While these data seem less markedly consistent with anticipated patterns, recall that the countries have been scaled on the ladder of countries (tables 7.1 and 7.2) according to the *size* of export shares in more advanced factor intensities, whereas these measures show *rates* of change in export shares. Column 8 shows quite clearly that India and the next-tier NICs have not yet reached physical and human capital intensity in their top fifteen exports, whereas the NICs and Malaysia have quite substantial percentages of their top fifteen exports in the P/HK-intensive category.

The evidence found here suggests that one of the significant factors explaining the high performance of the NICs is the relatively lower cost of investment goods in the domestic price structure of these economies. Whereas the general trend found by Kravis, Heston, and Summers is for investment goods to be more expensive relative to consumption and government GDP components the poorer the country, the transitional economies stand out as having lower-cost investment goods than would be expected relative to their place on the ladder of countries based on per capita income. Furthermore, there seems to be a reasonably consistent relationship between lower-cost investment goods and higher ratios of gross domestic investment to gross domestic product, higher per capita indexes of investment goods and producer goods, and higher shares of manufacturing in GDP among the ten transitional economies for which data were available. These patterns are more loosely associated with but still broadly consistent with the degree of structural change in the composition of exports by factor intensity and are highly consistent with the share of exports in the P/HK-intensive category. There is a clear difference in the average outcomes between the NICs and Malaysia, on the one hand, and India and the next-tier NICs, on the other.

These patterns would seem to indicate that NIC growth and export performance in manufactures have been accelerated by public policies that have lowered the cost of investment goods. These policies could have been in the form of domestic monetary policy affecting interest rates and credit allocations to industrial investors and borrowers or in the form of direct subsidies affecting the price of domestically produced investment goods. These monetary and fiscal policies have the effect of stimulating both the demand and the supply of investment goods, which in turn spurs capital accumulation, industrialization, and structural change.

These policies favoring domestic investment have been complemented by extraordinarily high levels of foreign borrowing by the NICs during the 1970s (table 7.4, column 9) at low if not negative real rates of interest. Hence, domestic monetary and fiscal policies affecting interest rates, credit allocations, and subsidies, together with foreign borrowing at low international interest rates to supplement domestic savings, appear to have been integral and consistent parts of an overall strategy of export-oriented growth based on trade in manufactures that help explain the unusually high performance characteristic of the NICs. It would appear that the focus of earlier studies of the NICs on trade and exchange rate policies should be broadened to include domestic economic policies and foreign borrowing.

These general conclusions can be highlighted by comparing the ten transitional economies with other economies in the Kravis, Heston, and

Summers study. Leaving out the United States (group VI), the eight Western European countries and Japan (group V), and Italy and Ireland, the other twenty-two countries in the Kravis study can be arranged in four groups. (See table 7.5.) Two of the groups are from table 7.4, except that Yugoslavia has been removed from the group of transitional economies experiencing rapid structural change and put with Poland, Hungary, Romania, and Iran, countries which probably experienced "forced" structural change. They are characterized by high real GDI/GDP shares despite high ratios of national prices to international prices for investment. This suggests investment allocation through direct government intervention and planning and state enterprises rather than indirectly through interest rates or price subsidies or through the market. In addition, there are eight nonindustrial, nontransitional economies in the Kravis et al. study (see Appendix), which constitute the fourth group.

There are two broad patterns that can be seen in this table. The first is the basic difference between the rapid and forced structural change countries, on the one hand, and the slower structural change and nontransitional developing economies, on the other. It appears that the first two groups have been successful in either inducing or forcing high rates of capital formation and industrialization through lower relative prices for investment or through direct government action. The second pattern is the similarity between the slower structural change countries (India and the next-tier NICs) and the eight nontransitional developing economies included in the Kravis et al. study (Uruguay, Syria, Jamaica, Zambia, Sri Lanka, Pakistan, Kenya, and Malawi). While one would like a larger sample in both categories, the similarity in the variables for these two groups of countries and their large differences from the NICs and the planned economies cast doubt on the degree to which there is a real difference between India and the next-tier NICs and the nontransitional economies. That is, it can be questioned whether Colombia, Thailand, India, and the Philippines are in fact in the process of becoming NICs. The evidence here is not conclusive, but it suggests they are not. From the figures in this section, Malaysia appears to be the only next-tier NIC that is on the NIC path rather than on the general development path, and the other next-tier NICs seem to have more in common with the nontransitional economies than with the NICs.

An examination of average annual growth rates in the 1970s and changes between 1970 and 1981 in GDP shares of investment, manufacturing, and exports and in "other" manufactured exports as a share of total exports of twenty potential NICs and the eight nontransitional economies in the Kravis et al. study sheds some further light on the issue. The figures for these twenty-eight countries are compared with the average growth rates and shares for the 100 countries in the World Bank's middle-income country category (MIC) in tables 7.6 and 7.7.

Table 7.5   Summary Table

Country Groups (averages)	Investment Goods Ratio: National/International Prices, 1975	GDI/GDP (real) (%)	Per Capita Index Based on International Prices, 1975 (U.S. = 1.00)		Share of Manufacturing in GDP, 1980 (%)
			Total Investment	Producer Goods	
Rapid structural change[a]	93.8	23.2	35.8	26.8	28
Forced structural change[b]	1.25	30.0	60.5	45.0	—
Slower structural change[c]	1.28	16.5	11.4	6.1	21.5
Nontransitional LDCs[d]	1.15	11.5	8.5	10.2	18.0

Source: Kravis, Heston, and Summers 1982.

[a]Malaysia, Brazil, Korea, Mexico, and Spain.

[b]Yugoslavia, Poland, Hungary, Romania, and Iran.

[c]Colombia, Thailand, India, and the Philippines.

[d]Uruguay, Syria, Jamaica, Zambia, Sri Lanka, Pakistan, Kenya, and Malawi.

Table 7.6   **Average Annual Growth Rates, 1970–81** (percentages)

	GDP	GDI	Manufacturing	Exports
MICs (average)	5.5	7.5	7.4	6.6
NICs				
Korea	9.0	12.1	20.9	20.5
Taiwan	9.0	12.1	20.9	20.5
Hong Kong	10.0	14.2	10.4	10.3
Singapore	8.6	8.0	10.6	11.9
Brazil	7.7	8.0[a]	7.4	7.3[a]
Mexico	6.5	9.0	6.0	8.2
Argentina	1.9	2.5	0.3	6.8
Spain	3.4	1.2	4.8	6.6
Portugal	4.2	2.2	3.2	2.5
Greece	4.3	1.3	6.1	10.0
Yugoslavia	5.8	5.9	7.4	4.0
Poland	5.8	5.9	10.7	4.0
Hungary	5.0	4.9	5.2	7.9
Romania	5.0	4.9	5.2	7.9
Iran	7.4[b]	22.0[b]	16.0	2.3[b]
Potential NICs				
Malaysia	7.8	10.4	11.0	8.2
Colombia	5.6	6.6	5.7	5.3
Thailand	7.2	7.6	10.4	9.4
India	3.6	5.2	4.3	8.4
Philippines	6.2	10.0	4.2	7.2
Nontransitional LDCs				
Uruguay	3.1	10.6	3.4	9.2
Syria	9.4	15.1	4.3	0.0[a]
Jamaica	− 1.1	− 9.6	− 2.7	− 1.0
Zambia	0.4	− 2.6[c]	0.3	− 0.9
Sri Lanka	4.7	10.3	2.1	− 1.7
Pakistan	5.0	3.2	3.8	2.2
Kenya	6.2	1.9	10.4[d]	0.7
Malawi	5.6	2.8[a]	8.3	5.8[a]

Source: World Bank, *World Tables,* vol. 1, *Economic Data,* 3d ed. (Baltimore and London: Johns Hopkin University Press, 1984).
[a]1970–80.
[b]1970–77.
[c]1970–79.
[d]1970–78.

Both in terms of growth rates and shares the East Asian NICs clearly exceed the averages for the middle-incomes countries as a whole, and the nontransitional economies generally fall well below these averages. Argentina consistently manifests below-average growth rates and shares. Brazil and Mexico, on the other hand, are above average in GDP, GDI, and export growth rates for the 1970s. Whereas the real spurt in in-

Table 7.7   **GDP Shares, 1970–81** (percentages)

	GDI		Manufacturing		Exports		Other Manufacturing Exports/Total Exports[a]	
	1970	1981	1970	1981	1970	1981	1970	1980
MICs (average)	22.7	27.0	21.3	20.7	17.7	28.4	18.5	24.9
NICs								
Korea[b]	26.9	27.4	20.9	28.5	14.3	39.9	69.3	70.2
Taiwan	26.9	27.4	20.9	28.5	14.3	39.9	69.3	70.2
Hong Kong	18.6	29.6	32.6	28.5	101.1	109.2	84.1	79.0
Singapore[b]	38.7	44.9	20.4	30.0	113.2	207.6	19.5	27.6
Brazil	22.7	19.5	26.7	30.0	6.5	8.7	10.6	21.7
Mexico[b]	22.7	28.9	23.7	22.3	7.7	11.9	21.9	20.5
Argentina[b]	21.1	28.9	30.0	22.3	9.2	11.9	10.2	16.7
Spain	24.4	20.1	25.4	27.3[c]	13.5	17.4	34.0	45.5
Portugal	23.5	26.7	33.3	34.7	23.4	26.7	55.5	58.4
Greece	28.1	24.5	19.1	19.5	10.0	19.6	33.1	44.4
Yugoslavia	32.3	31.7	25.7[d]	30.4[d]	18.4	22.6	37.0	44.8
Poland	24.5	31.7	54.6	30.4[d]	18.4	22.6	37.0	44.8
Hungary	33.6	30.2	38.7[c,d]	38.1[c,d]	30.1	39.2	35.3	33.7
Romania	33.6	30.2	38.7[c,d]	38.1[c,d]	30.1	39.2	35.3	33.7
Iran	18.9	33.4[f]	13.8[e]	12.0[e,f]	23.9	33.9[f]	3.9	33.7

Potential NICs								
Malaysia[b]	20.7	32.3	13.4	21.3	43.8	52.9	5.8	7.6
Colombia	22.0	27.7	17.5	21.4	14.1	12.1	7.3	18.0
Thailand[b]	26.2	26.7	16.0	19.9	16.7	24.4	7.9	22.2
India	17.3	25.1	14.2	17.2	4.4	6.8	47.3	51.7
Philippines[b]	21.2	29.7	22.6	24.7	19.1	19.0	7.5	34.7
Nontransitional LDCs								
Uruguay	11.3	14.7	24.3[d]	26.3[d]	11.9	14.6	19.7	34.1
Syria[b]	13.7	22.4	22.8[c,d]	25.6[c,d]	17.4	14.6	10.8	6.2
Jamaica[b]	31.5	21.1	15.7	14.8	33.2	48.0	45.9	62.0
Zambia[b]	28.4	23.2	10.2	18.1	54.0	35.6	0.2	62.0
Sri Lanka	18.9	27.8	16.7	16.2	25.5	30.5	1.4	18.2
Pakistan	15.8	16.5	16.1	16.9	7.8	12.9	56.8	47.2
Kenya	24.4	24.9	12.0	13.3	29.8	24.8	12.4	11.6
Malawi	26.1	24.9	12.7	13.3	22.7	24.8	3.5	6.6

Source: World Bank, *World Tables*, vol. 1, *Economic Data*, 3d ed. (Baltimore and London: Johns Hopkins University Press, 1984).

[a]"Other" is manufactured goods exports other than machinery and equipment (i.e., Other = SITC sections 5, 6 (excluding group 68), 8, and 9.

[b]GDP at market prices for manufacturing shares; all other GDP at factor cost.

[c]Includes gas, electricity, and water.

[d]Includes mining and quarrying.

[e]Includes mining other than oil.

[f]1977.

dustrialization in the East Asian NICs occurred in the 1960s and 1970s, the manufacturing sector of the three large Latin American countries had achieved manufacturing shares of 25% of GDP by 1955 and then leveled off until the 1970s. The European NICs (Spain, Portugal, and Greece) also reached a leveling off of manufacturing as a share of GDP prior to the 1970s, because of a jump in the GDI/GDP ratio in the 1960s. These industrialization trends in the 1950s and 1960s facilitated high-volume, high-growth manufactured exports from the Latin American and southern European NICs in the 1970s. By 1980, machinery and equipment exports as a percentage of total exports from Brazil, Mexico, Spain, and Portugal were almost double the middle-income country average, matching the export shares for these goods of the East Asian NICs.

Data for the group in the forced structural change category (four Eastern European countries and Iran) are spotty and in some cases not strictly comparable with the other countries. Yugoslavia and Hungary have registered shares in the 1970s well above the MIC averages, but growth rates were less than spectacular.

Colombia and India seem to fall below the MIC averages for both growth rates and shares more often than they exceed them. Malaysia, on the other hand, emerges as well above average both in growth rates in the 1970s and in shares by 1980–81. These trends for Malaysia coincide with the earlier conclusion that Malaysia is a strong candidate as a potential NIC. Thailand and the Philippines experienced consistently higher than average growth rates in the 1970s. By 1980–81 the Philippines had achieved above average GDP shares for investment and manufacturing and a higher than average share of total exports for "other" manufactured exports, while Thailand was consistently below average in GDP and export shares.

Apart from the Philippines and Argentina, then, the data on economic performance during the 1970s for these twenty-eight countries are broadly consistent with the patterns and conclusions derived from the analyses in the previous two sections. The East Asian, Latin American, and southern European NICs seem to be a select group of high-performance economies that have experienced accelerated investment, rapid industrialization, high export growth, especially in manufactures, and changes in the composition of their exports based on changing factor proportions. Policies encouraging investment appear to have played an important role in facilitating the dynamic structural change demonstrated by these newly industrializing countries, since high investment shares seem to be associated with the rapid industrialization and surges in manufactured exports of the NICs. Other aspects of NIC development strategies and performance are examined in the next section.

7.4   Outward-oriented Growth Strategies and Price Distortions

The success of the NICs in the 1970s in achieving dynamic export expansion, accelerated investment and industrialization, and higher than average rates of economic growth elevated their adoption of outward-oriented growth strategies to the category of a "new orthodoxy" (Williamson 1983, 269). The policies which seemed to be successful in implementing such a strategy were unification and devaluation of the exchange rate, liberalization of imports, and export promotion measures (Balassa 1978). There was at the time a mistaken identification of export-oriented growth strategies with free market policies and fears of the "Hong Kong–ization" of the Third World with the diffusion of the new orthodoxy, based on the perceived preeminence of the Asian NICs. More detailed case studies of the Asian NICs (Hong and Krause 1981) and more thoughtful reflection revealed the heterogeneity of the policy mix in the successful exporters of manufactures (Fajnzylber 1981). Indeed, there was considerable government intervention in the successful NICs. Public policy is now understood by most observers to play a fundamental role in achieving an outward-oriented economic thrust quite apart from the degree of reliance on the market involved in each instance. "In no case has government assumed a laissez faire posture" (Marsden 1982).

Nevertheless, the debate over the degree of bias involved in export and import substitution promotion continues (Streeten 1982; Balassa 1983b). Furthermore, as the debt adjustment problem of the NICs in the 1980s came to overshadow the trade adjustment problem posed by the NICs in the 1970s, there has been a resurgence of the view that government intervention is inimical to achieving adequate adjustment. In addition, the stereotypical contrast has been reasserted between Latin American interventionist import substitution biases and the Asian free market and export orientation biases (*Economist,* 24 September 1983, based on World Bank 1983, chap. 6). *The Economist* stated it crisply: "Increasingly, the two institutions [the IMF and the World Bank] have found themselves embroiled in the same set of policy issues: how can economies grow even when the international climate is unfavorable? The answer that the Fund and Bank give can be summed up in four words: get the prices right" (p. 39).

Morgan Guaranty has drawn the same basic picture: "a profound reordering of priorities" is necessary, especially in Latin America, requiring "a basic reassessment of the role of the state" (*World Financial Markets,* September 1983). The widely read newsletter goes on: "Strategies based on import substitution alone, which entail an anti-export bias, do not deliver enduring economic dynamism—as can be seen in the contrasting records of Asia and Latin America" (p. 11).

It also asserts a divergence in economic adjustment performance: "These trends [in Latin America toward protectionism] contrast with the adjustment strategies of most Asian economies, where liberalization (as in Korea, the Philippines and Thailand) has continued even in the face of balance of payments pressures" (p. 7).

There is a tendency in the literature to overdraw the contrasts not only regionally but in terms of the kinds of policy regimes which lead to success. There is an effort to link strategies, policies, and politics to each other so that pure forms tend to merge from the analysis, while reality is indeed more mixed. Export-oriented growth strategies are seen to be linked to realistic policies on exchange rates and interest rates and a reduced role for the state, thereby getting prices right and letting markets work. Import substitution strategies are seen to lead to a larger role for the state and more intervention in markets, thereby distorting prices and generating more severe external imbalances. In reality, the coherence of the different elements of a policy regime are rarely so clear-cut. The connections between strategy, policies, and politics are hardly pure or perfectly consistent. Reality is, alas, more mixed.

Nevertheless, consistency among the different elements is found in some of the literature on inward versus outward development strategies and on adjustment in developing countries. Bela Balassa concludes a summary work on the subject based on the 1974–78 period by writing: "Outward oriented economies provided, on average, similar incentives to exports and import substitution and to primary production and manufacturing, which inward oriented economies discriminated against exports and favored manufacturing over primary activities. Outward oriented economies also placed less reliance on price controls and on interest rate ceilings than inward oriented economies. More generally, they gave greater scope to the market mechanism. . . . Apart from affecting the efficiency of resource allocation, interest rates also influenced the amount saved. . . . By and large, outward oriented regimes were willing to accept lower rates of economic growth in the wake of the quadrupling of oil prices and the world recession in order to stabilize their economies and to avoid large foreign indebtedness. In turn, in inward oriented economies, except for those experiencing internal shocks, foreign borrowing was used to accelerate economic growth" (Balassa 1983a, 172–73).

If one goes back to the research work on price distortions mentioned in chapter 1 that underlie the *World Development Report* (Agarwala 1983) and the Balassa article (1981), it is possible to examine the degree of linkage among these elements and the assertions made about them. Tables 7.8 and 7.9 take the NICs and the less-developed countries (LDCs) identified as outward and inward oriented in the Balassa work

Table 7.8   **Outward versus Inward Orientation and Price Distortions in the 1970s**

	Exchange Rate	Interest Rate (%)	Distortion Index
	Outward Oriented		
NICs			
Korea	95	−5.0	1.57
Chile	n.a.	−38.6	2.43
Uruguay	106	−20.6	2.29
LDCs			
Kenya	101	−4.1	1.71
Thailand	92	0.5	1.43
Tunisia	88	−2.7	1.57
Average	96.4	−11.8	1.83
	Inward Oriented		
NICs			
Brazil	89	−8.0	1.86
Yugoslavia	122	−8.5	1.71
Argentina ($I > E$)	128	−31.2	2.43
Mexico ($I > E$)	101	−10.7	1.86
Turkey	104	−14.5	2.14
LDCs			
Egypt	89	−4.4	2.14
India	81	−0.3	1.86
Philippines	99	−4.9	1.57
Average	101.6	−10.3	1.94
$I > E$			
Jamaica	108	−7.5	2.29
Peru	84	−11.1	2.29
Tanzania	103	−7.7	2.57

Source: Agarwala 1983, 20, 23, and 40.

Notes: The exchange rate is the annual average appreciation of the real exchange rate during 1974–80 from the base exchange rate in 1972–73 (= 100). The interest rate is the average real interest rate for the 1970–80 period. The distortion index is a composite index including seven measures of distortion: protection of manufacturing, underpricing of agriculture, the exchange rate, the cost of credit, the cost of labor, the pricing of infrastructural services, and inflation. $I > E$ means internal shocks are greater than external shocks. Country classifications according to Balassa 1981.

and array the data for these countries from the research work on price distortions. Whereas the basic conclusion of the price distortion research is that countries with high price distortions are found to have low growth rates and vice versa, table 7.8 shows that on the average there is no fundamental difference between the six outward-oriented developing economies and the eight inward-oriented countries in the

Table 7.9   **Outward versus Inward Orientation and Country Savings, Growth, and Export Experience in the 1970s**

	Domestic Savings	GDP Growth	Export Growth
	Outward Oriented		
NICs			
Korea	22	9.5	23.0
Chile	14	2.4	10.9
Uruguay	14	3.5	4.8
LDCs			
Kenya	19	6.5	−1.0
Thailand	21	7.2	11.8
Tunisia	27	7.5	4.8
Average	19.5	6.1	9.1
	Inward Oriented		
NICs			
Brazil	22	8.4	7.5
Yugoslavia	27	5.8	3.9
Argentina $(I > E)$	22	2.2	9.3
Mexico $(I > E)$	22	5.2	13.4
Turkey	17	5.9	1.7
LDCs			
Egypt	12	7.4	−0.7
India	20	3.6	3.7
Philippines	24	6.3	7.0
Average	20.8	5.6	5.7
$I > E$			
Jamaica	16	−1.1	−6.8
Peru	21	3.0	3.9
Tanzania	12	4.9	−7.3

Source: Agarwala 1983, 40.

Notes: Domestic savings is the average domestic saving income ratio for the 1970s; GDP and export growth are average annual rates for the 1970s. $I > E$ means internal shocks are greater than external shocks.

degree of price distortion (1.83 versus 1.94). The degree of price distortion is small compared with the average price distortion index of 2.44 for the twelve developing countries in the high-distortion category in the World Bank study by Agarwala (1983).

Secondly, whereas there is a strong correlation between exchange rates and economic growth performance—stronger than any other price distortion examined in the study—there is not a strong association between the annual average appreciation of the real exchange rate and inward versus outward orientation (96.4% versus 101.6%). These averages stand in contrast to the averages for the twenty-seven countries in the study clearly designated as having low, medium, and high exchange rate appreciation of 94.3, 110, and 142 respectively.

Thirdly, the outward-oriented countries on average have a slightly more negative real interest rate than the inward-oriented countries (− 11.8% versus − 10.3%). This pales in comparison to the difference in the averages for the countries in the Agarwala study that have medium and high interest rate distortions of − 3.4% and − 14.8% respectively. While there is only a small difference in the averages between the outward- and the inward-oriented countries, the difference in the average is in the opposite direction of that anticipated by Balassa (1983a).

Hence, on the average, there is no association between outward versus inward orientation and general price distortion or distortion in the two key variables, the exchange rate and the real interest rate. There are individual countries for which there is an association; Korea, Tunisia, and Thailand in the outward-oriented group show relatively low indices for all three price distortion variables. However, India, the Philippines, and Brazil, in the inward-oriented group, show roughly the same order of magnitude for these three measures. It is regrettable that the price distortion research did not include Hong Kong, Singapore, and Taiwan, because their inclusion in the outward-oriented group would have undoubtedly helped substantiate the new-orthodoxy view. Nevertheless, even if the addition of these three countries did change the overall averages substantially, their addition would only further prove the unusual character of the three NICs and not enhance the generality of the claim. The general point drawn from tables 7.8 and 7.9 would still stand: there is a great deal of heterogeneity and complexity in the real world; we do ourselves ill by trying to simplify for the sake of providing a coherent policy framework. Ex ante advocacy of consistency does not mean that consistency can be found in country experience ex post.

Contrary to the expectations of the new orthodoxy, there is almost no difference between either the average GDP growth rates or the savings ratios of the outward-oriented versus the inward-oriented developing countries. The savings ratios are actually slightly higher for the inward-oriented than for the outward-oriented economies, and the growth rates were higher in the outward-oriented countries despite their greater presumed internal adjustment. But these differences in the opposite direction are not significant. The important conclusion is that there is no systematic difference when groups of countries are taken together; therefore, general policy conclusions should be drawn cautiously.

This cautionary note is confirmed when the average price distortion index is calculated for the four groups of countries in the previous section. (See table 7.10.) Compared with the averages calculated by the World Bank for the countries with low, medium, and high distortions (1.56, 1.95, and 2.44 respectively), the differences between the four groups of countries in this study are within a narrower range (1.64, 1.71, 1.71, and 1.93). This, again, opposes any sweeping conclusions regarding the relationship of the degree of price distortion and the pace of structural change. It should be noted that the average real interest rate figures for the 1970–80 period given in the World Bank study roughly correspond to those implied by the analysis of real prices of investment in the previous section. Uruguay and Jamaica are the only exceptions. Countries with rapid and forced structural change have relatively lower real interest rates than India, the next-tier NICs, and the nontransitional economies with slower structural change. (Uruguay is the exception.)

Table 7.10   **Price Distortions, Real Interest Rates, and Structural Change**

	Price Distortion Index	Real Interest Rate (%)	
I. Rapid structural change (average)	*1.71*	*– 7.9*	
Malaysia	1.57		
Brazil	1.86	– 8.0	
Korea	1.57	– 5.0	
Mexico	1.86	– 10.7	
Spain			
II. Forced structural change[a]			
Yugoslavia	1.71	– 8.5	
III. Slower structural change (average)	*1.64*	*– 1.7*	
Colombia	1.71	– 2.0	
Thailand	1.43	+ 0.5	
India	1.86	– 0.3	
Philippines	1.57	– 4.9	
IV. Nontransitional LDCs (average)	*1.93*	*– 7.3*	
Uruguay	2.29	– 20.6	
Syria			
Jamaica	2.29	– 7.5	
Zambia			
Sri Lanka	1.86	– 4.0	= 4.7 average
Pakistan	2.29	– 4.3	
Kenya	1.71	– 4.1	
Malawi	1.14	– 3.4	

Source: Agarwala 1983.

[a]No data for Poland, Hungary, Romania, and Iran.

7.5   Conclusion

This chapter has dealt with a number of issues relating to the NICs as high-performance economies distinguished from other developing economies by their accelerated pace of internal structural change, high export growth, especially in manufactures, and high economic growth in the 1970s. The chapter explored various aspects of the salience of markets and prices, on the one hand, and economic policies and government actions, on the other, in affecting economic performance. The nature of the evidence and the analysis are suggestive rather than conclusive.

The thrust of the evidence, the analysis, and the argument in this chapter is of the same order as the World Bank research on price distortions but is in the opposite direction. The World Bank research concluded that "prices matter for growth, though not only prices." This research leads in the direction of concluding that policies matter for growth, though not only policies. It is difficult to see how the NICs could have achieved the unusual economic and export performance that distinguishes and defines them as NICs without the crucial input of government policies.

Public policy commitment to export-oriented growth is the key element in achieving global status as an exporter of manufactures. Earlier research of mine and others has emphasized NIC trade and exchange rate policies as determinants of their success. The inquiry and evidence here suggest that monetary and fiscal policies affecting the real price of investment should be added to the set of policies considered as elements of export-oriented growth strategies. The Korea case study in this volume illustrates the point (chap. 10). The inclusion of these domestic policies further substantiates the importance of national commitment in NIC strategies for integrating diverse policy instruments into a coherent thrust.

However, in the same spirit of the World Bank research, it cannot be concluded that only public policies matter. The World Bank research states: "The findings reported here are a case for 'getting the prices right' and should not necessarily be interpreted as an argument for a laissez faire approach" (Agarwala 1983, 46). Similarly, the findings reported in this chapter are a case for getting policies right and should not be interpreted as an argument for price distortions or, indeed, against getting prices right. The argument here does assert that getting prices right is not the sine qua non of economic growth and that the identification of correct prices with outward-oriented growth strategies is misleading. Part of the business of getting policies right is to provide ample scope for prices and markets to work as well. But it is surely not the only business of public policy. Indeed, some of the evidence here suggests that underpricing investment goods for a time through deliberate policies may be an important means of accelerating structural change and a key instrument in the strategy for becoming a NIC. It is also true, however, that subsidization of investment, while effective in facilitating structural change for a phase in the development process, can be overdone, leading to excessively capital-intensive industries, underutilization of labor, and overinvestment, if not judiciously managed (chap. 10, this volume).

From the analysis presented here and in chapter 1, it seems clear that rapid structural change internally and in the composition of exports is central to successful development. There is a danger that, in circumstances in which the world economy is experiencing trade and financial pressures (some of which have their origin in the new role of the NICs), the power of changing factor endowments to alleviate pressure through structural change will be underestimated. There is also a danger, however, that the capacity of outward-oriented strategies to resolve the problems of slow growth, inflation, export stagnation, and debt may be overstated when these strategies are wrongly seen as the embodiment of free market pricing. Curiously, it seems more likely in trade policy that interventionist protection measures will be resorted to in order to shield industries from imports, when more rapid structural change would alleviate the fundamental problem. It also seems likely that market-oriented policies will be adopted when government-led export promotion policies might be more effective precisely because they accelerate structural change. The international economic policy debate is preoccupied with protectionism and orthodoxy when the more positive focus would be structural change and export promotion.

Table 7.A.1 Capital Formation and Structural Change in Nontransitional and Nonindustrial Economies

	Investment Goods Ratio: National/International Prices, 1975	GDI/GDP, International Prices, 1975 (%)	Per Capita Index Based on International Prices, 1975[a]		Share of Manufacturing in GDP (%)	
			Total Investment	Producer Goods	1960	1980
Group IV						
Italy	0.89	21	56.5	45.8	31	29
Poland	1.11	32	78.5	67.2	—	—
Hungary	1.16	27	65.7	58.1	—	—
Group III						
Ireland	1.01	15	31.9	41.8	—	—
Uruguay	1.55	6	12.1	7.2	21	26
Iran	1.55	33	61.0	31.3	11	—
Romania	1.19	34	55.6	32.1	—	—
Group II						
Syria	1.08	13	16.0	25.3	—	26
Jamaica	1.12	14	15.9	27.3	15	15
Group I						
Zambia	1.08	19	9.7	12.2	4	18
Sri Lanka	0.67	11	5.0	1.7	15	16
Pakistan	1.08	9	3.7	2.2	12	17
Kenya	1.31	10	3.3	2.6	9	13
Malawi	1.28	10	2.4	2.8	6	13

Sources: See table 7.5. (Groupings according to Kravis, Heston, and Summers 1982.)
[a]U.S. = 1.00.

Notes

1. A similar concept of transitional growth for technology-based trade where economies move up a "ladder of countries" and a "scale of goods" is contained in Krugman 1982.

2. "The stages approach to comparative advantage also permits one to dispel certain misapprehensions as regards the foreign demand constraint under which developing countries are said to operate. With countries progressing on the comparative advantage scale, their exports can supplant the exports of countries that graduate to a higher level. Now, to the extent that one developing country replaces another in the imports of particular commodities by the developed countries, the problem of adjustment in the latter group of countries does not arise. . . .

"A case in point is Japan whose comparative advantage has shifted towards highly capital-intensive exports. In turn, developing countries with a relatively high human capital endowment, such as Korea and Taiwan, can take Japan's place in exporting relatively human capital-intensive products, and countries with a relatively high physical capital endowment, such as Brazil and Mexico, can take Japan's place in exporting relatively physical capital-intensive products. Finally, countries at lower levels of development can supplant the middle-level countries in exporting unskilled labor intensive commodities" (Balassa 1977, 26–27).

References

Agarwala, Ramgopal. 1983. Price distortions and growth in developing countries. World Bank Staff Working Paper, no. 575.

Asian Development Review 1983. Manila: Asian Development Bank, Vol. 1, No. 1.

Balassa, Bela 1977. A "stages" approach to comparative advantage. World Bank Staff Working Paper, no. 256.

———. 1978. Export incentives and export performance in developing countries: A comparative analysis. *Weltwirtschaftliches Archiv* 114: 24ff.

———. 1981. Structural adjustment policies in developing economies. World Bank Staff Working Paper, no. 464.

———. 1983a. The adjustment experience of developing economies after 1973. In *IMF conditionality,* ed. John Williamson. Washington, D.C.: Institute for International Economics.

———. 1983b. Outward versus inward orientation once again. *World Economy* 6, no. 2: 215–18.

Bhagwati, Jagdish N., and T. N. Srinivasan. 1979. Trade policy and development. In *International economic policy,* ed. Rudiger Dornbusch and Jacob A. Frenkel. Baltimore and London: Johns Hopkins University Press.

Bitar, Sergio. 1983. Commercial relations between the United States and Latin America: Changes in the decade of the seventies. The Wilson Center, The Smithsonian Institution, Washington, D.C. April. Manuscript.

Blejer, Mario I. 1978. "Income per capita and the structure of industrial exports: An empirical study." *Review of Economics and Statistis,* November, 555–61.

Bradford, Colin I., Jr. 1982a. The NICs and world economic adjustment. In Turner and McMullen 1982.

———. 1982b. Rise of the NICs as exporters on a global scale. In Turner and McMullen 1982.

———. 1983. International debt and the world economy: Global integration on trial. In *Hearings before the Subcommittee on International Trade, Investment and Monetary Policy to increase the U.S. quota in the International Monetary Fund and related matters,* Committee on Banking, Finance and Urban Affairs, U.S. House of Representatives, pp. 666–98. 3 May 1983. Serial no. 98-17.

Branson, William H. 1981. The OPEC surplus and U.S.-LDC trade. National Bureau of Economic Research Working Paper, no. 791.

Deardorff, Alan V. 1983. Trade policy and factor prices in Krueger's model of developing country trade. Paper presented at a research seminar in international economics, University of Michigan, 29 April.

Fajnzylber, Fernando. 1981. Reflexiones sobre la industrializacion exportadora de Sudeste Asiatica. *Revista de la CEPAL* (Naciones Unidas, Comision Economica Para America Latina, Santiago, Chile), December, 117–38.

Havrylyshyn, Oli. 1983. The increasing integration of newly industrialized countries in world trade: A quantitative analysis of intra-industry trade. Paper presented at Symposium on Intra-Industry Trade, European Institute for Advanced Studies in Management, Brussels, Belgium, April.

Havrylyshyn, O., and E. Civan. Intra-industry trade and the stage of development. Discussion Paper 8301, Centre d'Economie Mathematique et d'Econometrie, Université Libre de Bruxelles.

Hiemenz, Ulrich, and Seiji Naya. 1983. Changing trade patterns and policy issues: The prospects for East and Southeast Asian developing countries. Paper presented at East-West Center Conference on Patterns of Growth and Structural Change in Asia's NICs and near NICs in the Context of Economic Interdependence, Hawaii, April.

Hong, Wontack, and Lawrence B. Krause, eds. 1981. *Trade and growth of the advanced developing countries in the Pacific Basin.* Seoul: Korean Development Institute Press.

Hufbauer, Gary C. 1970. The impact of national characteristics and technology on the commodity composition of trade in manufactured goods. In *The technology factor in international trade.* ed. Raymond Vernon. Universities National Bureau Conference Series, no. 22. New York: Columbia University Press.

Institute of Developing Economies, Economic Growth Department, ed. 1980. *New directions of Asia's development strategies.* Tokyo: East-West Publications.

Kotlikoff, Laurence J., Edward E. Leamer, and Jeffrey Sachs. 1982. The international economics of transitional growth—The case of the United States. National Bureau of Economic Research Working Paper, no. 773.

Krause, Lawrence B. 1982. *U.S. economic policy toward the Association of Southeast Asian Nations: Meeting the Japanese challenge.* Washington, D.C.: Brookings Institution.

Kravis, Irving B., Alan Heston, and Robert Summers. 1982. *World product and income: International comparisons of real gross product.* Baltimore: Johns Hopkins University Press.

Krueger, Anne O. 1977. *Growth, distortions and patterns of trade among many countries.* Princeton Studies in International Finance, no. 40. Princeton: International Finance Section, Dept. of Economics, Princeton University.

————. 1978. *Foreign trade regimes and economic development: Liberalization attempts and consequences.* Cambridge, Mass.: Ballinger, for National Bureau of Economic Research.

————. 1983. The developing countries' role in the world economy. Lecture given at ITT Key Issues Lecture Series: "The World Economic System: Performance and Prospects," University of Chicago, March.

Krugman, Paul. 1982. Technology gaps, technology transfers, and the changing character of U.S. trade. Paper presented at the NBER Conference on U.S. Trade Policy, February.

Lary, H. B. 1968. *Imports of manufactures from less developed countries.* New York: National Bureau of Economic Research and Columbia University Press.

Lee, Jungsoo. 1983a. Long-run debt servicing capacity of Asian developing countries: An application of critical interest rate approach. Asian Development Bank Economic Staff Paper, no. 16. Manila, Philippines.

————. 1983b. Relative external debt situation of Asian developing countries— An application of ranking method. Asian Development Bank, Economics Office Report Series, no. 19. Manila, Philippines.

Marsden, Keith. 1982. Trade and employment policies for industrial development. World Bank. Typescript.

Morgan Guaranty Trust Company of New York. 1983. International debt: Progress report and the task ahead. *World Financial Markets,* September.

Ohkawa, Kazuski, John C. H. Fei, and Gustav Ranis. 1983. Economic development of Korea, Taiwan and Japan in historical perspective. Manuscript.

OECD. 1979. *The impact of the newly industrializing countries on production and trade in manufactures.* Paris: OECD.

————. 1982. Developing countries' exports of manufactured products: Experience of the "second tier" countries. In *1982 review: Development cooperation.* Paris: OECD.

Rahman, A. H. M. Mahfuzer. 1973. *Exports of manufactures from developing countries: A study in comparative advantage.* Rotterdam: Rotterdam University Press.

Ranis, Gustav. 1983. Typology in development theory: Retrospective and prospects. Yale Economic Growth Center Paper, no. 435, February.

Sherk, Donald R. 1969. The new international trade models and their relevance for developing Asia. *Malaysian Economic Review* 24, no. 2.

Streeten, Paul. 1982. A cool look at "outward-looking" strategies for development. *World Economy* 5, no. 2.

Strout, Alan M. 1983. Estimating energy consumption from cross-country relationships. Study prepared for the World Bank. February.

Turner, Louis, and Neil McMullen, eds. 1982. *The newly industrializing countries: Trade and adjustment.* London: George Allen and Unwin.

UNCTAD (United Nations Conference on Trade and Development). 1976. *Handbook of international trade and development statistics 1976.* New York: UN.

————. 1982. *Handbook of international trade and development statistics, supplement 1981.* New York: UN.

Williamson, John. 1983. *The open economy and the world economy.* New York: Basic Books.

World Bank. 1982. *World development report, 1982.* London: Oxford University Press.

————. 1983. *World development report, 1983.* London: Oxford University Press.

8 The Structure of Trade in Manufactured Goods in the East and Southeast Asian Region

Lawrence B. Krause

8.1 Introduction

In 1983–84 the world economy recovered from the longest and deepest recession in the postwar period. One notable consequence of the recession was that world trade rose only 1.5% in 1980, had no growth in 1981, and declined by 2% in 1982 (GATT 1983). Thus trade, rather than being the handmaiden of growth, has been the transmitter of stagnation and recession.

Critics of an open trading regime might try to find lessons from this experience in an attempt to promote a protectionist point of view. They will be disappointed. International trade during this period made the recession less burdensome than it would have been with a less liberal regime in place. This is seen most clearly by concentrating on manufactured goods alone. In 1980 world production of manufactured goods increased 1.5% but exports of manufactures increased 5%; in 1981 manufacturing production increased only 0.5%, but its trade increased 3.5%; and in 1982 manufacturing production decreased 2% percent, but its trade declined only 1.5%. Thus, the presumption is established that international specialization continued to make headway and that efficiency was gained even during the recession. Looking at the difficult decade from 1973 to 1982, when aggregate growth and productivity declined in all industrial countries, production of manufactures increased at an annual rate of 2.5%, and trade of manufactures grew at the larger annual rate of 4.5%. In trade in manufactures, the handmaiden still lives.

Lawrence B. Krause is a senior fellow at the Brookings Institution. The views expressed in this paper are those of the author and should not be attributed to other staff members, officers, or trustees of the Brookings Institution.

From 1973 to 1982, the value of world trade grew at an annual rate of 13.8% (reflecting a great deal of inflation). The value of world exports of manufactures grew at a slightly lower rate of 13.0% (the lower rate entirely the result of the slower rise of prices). In table 8.1 the trade of manufactured goods is broken down into major subdivisions, and the growth rates between 1973 and 1982 are shown. Export growth of office and telecommunications equipment was particularly fast (15.7%), along with chemicals (14.6%). On the other hand, exports of textiles grew only 9.2%, and iron and steel, 10.3%.

During this same period, total exports from the developing countries (excluding traditional oil exporters) grew at a 15.8% annual rate, and their manufactures exports at a 18.6% annual rate. Thus, in 1973, only

Table 8.1   **Exports by Commodity Groups**

Commodity Group	Compound Annual World Growth Rate, 1973–82 (%)	Share of Exports from LDCs[a] (%)	
		1973	1981
Food	10.28	25.52	26.20
Raw materials	6.79	22.22	20.09
Ores and minerals	9.59	27.63	31.37
Fuels	23.45	9.42	13.70
Nonferrous metals	7.81	25.46	16.90
Total primary products	15.04	20.42	18.50
Iron and steel	10.34	13.18	6.91
Chemicals	14.62	4.37	6.96
Other semimanufactures	11.64	11.71	13.31
Engineering products	13.47	3.14	6.40
Machinery for specialized industries	12.21	1.54	3.25
Office and telecommunications equipment	15.71	7.44	15.01
Road motor vehicles	13.18	0.93	1.95
Other machinery and transport equipment	14.02	2.90	6.40
Household appliances	13.19	10.75	17.94
Textiles	9.19	17.35	23.05
Clothing	14.08	30.34	40.68
Other consumer goods	14.26	13.11	18.64
Total manufactures	13.04	6.66	10.14
Total exports	13.83	11.89	13.70

Source: GATT 1983.

[a]Excluding traditional oil exporters, defined as members of OPEC: Algeria, Ecuador, Gabon, Indonesia, Iraq, Islamic Republic of Iran, Kuwait, Libyan Arab Jamahiriya, Nigeria, Qatar, Saudi Arabia, United Arab Emirates, and Venezuela.

6.7% of world exports of manufactures originated in less-developed countries (LDCs), but by 1982, 10.2% was coming from LDCs (10.1% in 1981). In other words, the penetration ratio of LDCs in world markets of manufactures had increased by half. The LDC share was greatest for traditional labor-intensive products, and by 1981 LDCs were providing 40.7% of world exports of clothing, 23.1% of textiles, and 18.6% of other consumer goods. For each of these categories the LDC share had risen since 1973. However, the rate of growth of LDC penetration was greater for many other categories, including all subgroups of engineering products. Of course, some of these products were only assembled in LDCs and, therefore, represent a continuation of labor-intensive specialization. However, a pattern has been noted in several studies that foreign-owned assembly operations over time evolve into more local production of parts and thus create a great deal more domestic value added (Galenson 1985).

The only category of manufactured exports where the LDC share was reduced was in iron and steel, which declined from 13.2% to 6.9%. These capital- and skill-intensive products are still mainly the preserve of industrial countries. However, certain advanced developing countries such as Korea, Taiwan, and Brazil have already established international competitiveness in steel and probably strengthened their position in recent years through major new investments. Therefore, the declining LDC share may be due not to a lack of competitiveness but rather to either shortage of capacity or growing protectionism (Jones 1983). Protectionism probably also played a role in limiting the rise in the LDC share of textiles, clothing, and footwear.

8.2 East and Southeast Asian Countries as Exporters

The developing countries of East and Southeast Asia reflect, indeed exaggerate, world trends. As seen in table 8.2, the growth of exports of every country in the region from 1973 to 1982 was greater than world totals. Indonesia and Korea stand out among these countries as having the largest growth in their value of exports: Indonesia primarily because of the rise of oil prices and Korea because of increases in manufactured exports. All of the others had approximately the same rate of export success. The recession years of 1979–82 saw great differentiation among the countries; however, all the countries in this region outperformed the world as a whole in export growth.

What can explain the relative export success of these countries? One factor is the Pacific Basin region itself. For over two decades, the countries of this region have been the fastest growing countries in the world. While the 1979–82 recession has had a negative impact on them, they have nevertheless been able to sustain moderate growth rates.

Table 8.2   **Exports of Asian NICs and ASEAN Countries**

Country	Compound Growth Rate of Exports (%)		Share of Manufactures in Exports, 1980 (%)	Share of Textiles and Clothing in Exports, 1980 (%)
	1973–82	1979–1982		
NICs				
Hong Kong	17.1	11.3	93	34
Korea	32.3	29.7	90	29
Singapore	19.6	12.9	54	4
Taiwan	19.8	14.3	97	23
ASEAN Four				
Indonesia	32.3	19.1	2	1
Malaysia	16.1	5.1	19	2
Philippines	14.3	8.0	37	6
Thailand	19.5	13.9	29	9

Sources: International Monetary Fund, *International Financial Statistics* (Washington, D.C.); Ministry of Finance, Republic of China, *Monthly Statistics of Exports and Imports*, 20 August 1983; World Bank, *World Development Report 1983* (London: Oxford University Press).

Furthermore, compared with other developing countries in other regions, the LDCs in East and Southeast Asia have introduced more outward-oriented policies. Singapore and Hong Kong are at the extreme of completely free trade. Since the early 1960s in Taiwan and the mid-1960s in Korea, these two countries have been liberalizing imports as an ingredient of their export-led growth strategy. The natural-resource-exporting countries of the Association of South East Asian Nations (ASEAN) have some protection for manufactures, ranging from moderate in Malaysia to fairly restrictive in Indonesia. However, in every case, the protection is less than that of other LDCs with similar economic structures and at similar stages of development. The important point is that none of these countries envision their development within a context of self-sufficiency but rather have an outward orientation.

A third factor that helps explain the export success of these countries is the pattern of trade within the Pacific Basin. All of these countries sell more than half their exports to other countries within the Pacific Basin, and on average more than 60% (table 8.3). There are two distinct patterns of trade involved. There are the newly industrializing countries (NICs) that specialize in manufactured goods and sell between 50% and 70% of their exports within the Pacific Basin. For them the United States is by far the largest market. The other LDCs are primarily exporters of natural resources and sell between 50% and 81% of their

Table 8.3   **Exports of Pacific Basin Countries**

	1982 Total Value of Exports (tens of billions of U.S. $)	1981 Export Shares (% of total)			
		Pacific Basin	ASEAN	Japan	United States
ASEAN Four					
Indonesia	2.53	81.33	12.04	47.32	18.32
Malaysia	1.21	68.36	27.52	22.06	10.41
Philippines	0.50	71.23	7.22	21.79	31.01
Thailand	0.70	50.46	14.65	14.22	12.93
NICs					
Hong Kong	2.09	50.53	11.45	4.68	27.76
Korea	2.18	57.64	5.16	16.47	26.74
Singapore	2.08	61.63	21.11	10.13	13.21
Taiwan	2.22	69.67[a]	7.48	10.96	36.10
Papua New Guinea	0.07	60.37	2.67	37.70	4.82
Advanced					
Japan	13.84	48.98	10.00		
Australia	2.21	62.62	8.56	28.15	25.67
Canada	7.11	71.45	0.64	5.02	11.19
New Zealand	0.56	51.89	6.40	13.00	63.98
United States	21.23	36.89	3.77	9.88	12.51

Sources: IMF, Direction of Trade Statistics tapes; Ministry of Finance, Republic of China, *Monthly Statistics of Exports and Imports,* 20 August 1983.
[a]Excludes New Zealand and Papua New Guinea.

exports within the Pacific Basin. For them Japan is the largest market. Thus, the Pacific Basin provides a major market regardless of specialization—manufactures to the United States and raw materials to Japan.

Another factor of importance has been the burgeoning trade among the LDCs within the Pacific Basin. Because five of the countries are institutionally linked to one another through ASEAN, intra-LDC trade has been given a boost. About 17% of the exports of ASEAN countries (including Singapore) are to other ASEAN countries, ranging from 7% for the Philippines to 27.5% for Malaysia. What is also noticeable is the importance of the ASEAN market for the non-ASEAN LDCs of the Pacific. For Hong Kong, 11.5% of its exports find a market in ASEAN. That makes ASEAN almost three times more important to Hong Kong than Japan.

Thus, the answer to the question of why the LDCs of the Pacific Basin have had relatively good export success seems to be threefold; first, the countries in the Pacific Basin have grown faster than other countries; second, these LDCs have had more outward-oriented economic policies than other LDCs; and third, they had a ready market for their exports in other Pacific Basin countries.

8.3 Comparative Advantage in the Pacific Basin

As noted earlier, the countries of the Pacific Basin have sustained their economic growth better than countries in other regions. One of the reasons for this result is that countries in this region adjust better to shocks such as the two oil crises and the world recession. However, rapid adjustment also implies changing comparative advantages in international trade. Some empirical work was undertaken to summarize the nature of these changes.

A four-factor model was developed for this purpose. Goods were classified as either natural-resource-intensive, unskilled-labor-intensive, human-capital-intensive (skilled-labor-intensive), and technology-labor-intensive. Physical capital was dropped as a classification because it is so internationally mobile as to provide little guidance to the location of production.[1] A superior approach would be to measure the inputs of the various factors by product, but as the data were not available, an approximate method was employed. The results are shown in tables 8.4–8.7 for twelve countries of the Pacific Basin grouped into developed countries, NICs, and ASEAN.[2]

Table 8.4 shows the percentage of each country's exports that is made up of natural-resource-intensive products. Seven of the twelve countries had more than half of their exports in this category. One other country, Canada, was just about at the 50% mark. This illustrates the obvious fact that natural resources are the basis for much of the trade of the Pacific Basin for most of the countries. In the case of Singapore, this results from its role as an entrepôt for natural resource production of neighboring countries and from its own position as a large refiner of petroleum. All of the other countries are producers and processors of raw materials, which constitute the mainstay of their export basket. It is also evident that there was a general tendency for natural resource goods to become slightly less important during the decade of the 1970s. The trend is most noticeable for Malaysia, the Philippines, and Thailand—the group of countries that are considered to be directly behind the NICs in moving into manufactured production and manufactures exports. The NICs themselves also reduced their shares of natural resource goods, with the declines for Korea and Singapore being the most sharp.

Table 8.5 shows the trends during the 1970s of the share of labor-intensive goods in the exports of the Pacific Basin countries. At the beginning of the decade, three-quarters of the exports of Hong Kong, over half of Korea's exports, about one-quarter of Japanese exports,

Table 8.4 Exports of Natural-Resource-Intensive Commodities by Pacific Basin Countries (percentage of total)

	1970	1971	1972	1973	1974	1975	1976	1977	1978	1979	1980	1981
Developed												
Australia	83.22	82.59	82.77	81.25	80.86	82.94	82.41	81.89	79.22	82.62	79.38	79.07
Canada	49.82	48.98	49.54	53.55	56.66	54.59	52.01	50.13	48.01	51.47	n.a.	n.a.
Japan	8.41	7.57	6.99	6.72	7.52	5.83	5.23	4.96	4.83	5.19	n.a.	n.a.
New Zealand	89.69	90.28	89.82	91.27	89.05	87.37	85.91	84.75	84.14	83.60	n.a.	n.a.
United States	31.19	29.23	30.73	36.91	34.88	32.40	31.47	31.06	31.69	32.83	n.a.	n.a.
NICs												
Hong Kong	4.24	4.03	3.79	3.83	3.88	3.48	3.29	3.69	3.69	3.53	n.a.	n.a.
Korea	34.93	31.17	28.00	26.31	20.91	24.70	19.15	21.67	17.19	15.86	n.a.	n.a.
Singapore	72.59	66.67	59.61	57.27	60.77	59.17	56.44	58.28	56.22	53.37	n.a.	n.a.
ASEAN Four												
Indonesia	99.25	99.17	99.16	99.05	99.34	98.83	98.68	98.57	98.62	n.a.	n.a.	n.a.
Malaysia	95.34	94.85	93.31	92.34	89.51	84.90	87.45	87.09	n.a.	n.a.	n.a.	n.a.
Philippines	96.87	96.84	95.94	94.51	95.30	92.22	88.40	86.82	81.52	n.a.	n.a.	n.a.
Thailand	97.18	95.69	92.94	88.38	90.11	89.18	86.57	86.48	82.00	n.a.	n.a.	n.a.

Source: UN Commodity Trade tapes.

Note: Figures are rounded; n.a. = not available.

Table 8.5   **Exports of Unskilled-Labor-Intensive Commodities by Pacific Basin Countries** (percentage of total)

	1970	1971	1972	1973	1974	1975	1976	1977	1978	1979	1980	1981
Developed												
Australia	1.47	1.29	1.31	2.11	1.64	1.25	1.06	0.97	1.50	1.69	2.11	1.87
Canada	2.16	2.09	2.03	2.14	1.79	1.51	1.40	1.40	1.66	1.76	n.a.	n.a.
Japan	24.08	22.94	21.85	21.51	18.73	18.95	18.60	18.03	14.25	10.33	n.a.	n.a.
New Zealand	2.01	2.22	2.13	2.11	2.19	2.87	3.77	4.26	4.15	3.84	n.a.	n.a.
United States	5.76	5.88	5.95	5.29	5.40	5.25	5.66	5.91	5.80	5.69	n.a.	n.a.
NICs												
Hong Kong	76.15	75.89	73.79	71.75	68.93	70.52	69.83	66.05	64.64	63.08	n.a.	n.a.
Korea	52.82	54.53	50.10	47.64	45.12	49.49	51.71	48.54	51.17	45.86	n.a.	n.a.
Singapore	8.18	9.59	10.98	10.35	7.62	8.54	11.03	9.28	9.25	9.93	n.a.	n.a.
ASEAN Four												
Indonesia	0.18	0.16	0.18	0.16	0.14	0.10	0.12	0.12	0.24	n.a.	n.a.	n.a.
Malaysia	0.94	1.40	2.26	2.00	2.12	2.97	2.96	2.89	n.a.	n.a.	n.a.	n.a.
Philippines	1.39	1.52	2.48	3.99	3.46	5.83	8.85	8.82	12.37	n.a.	n.a.	n.a.
Thailand	1.59	3.06	5.12	9.05	6.71	7.29	9.30	9.03	12.01	n.a.	n.a.	n.a.

Source: UN Commodity Trade tapes.

Note: Figures are rounded; n.a. = not available.

Table 8.6   Exports of Human-Capital-Intensive Commodities by Pacific Basin Countries (percentage of total)

	1970	1971	1972	1973	1974	1975	1976	1977	1978	1979	1980	1981
Developed												
Australia	7.94	7.61	8.33	7.88	7.91	7.55	6.09	6.34	7.27	6.83	6.31	6.37
Canada	32.87	34.09	33.33	30.56	28.48	29.48	32.11	33.61	35.77	31.37	n.a.	n.a.
Japan	42.50	45.53	45.71	45.26	47.67	47.59	48.62	48.57	49.56	51.36	n.a.	n.a.
New Zealand	3.78	3.97	4.38	3.66	5.08	6.11	6.33	6.09	6.95	7.21	n.a.	n.a.
United States	19.56	20.25	20.40	18.31	19.03	19.81	19.71	19.77	18.59	17.40	n.a.	n.a.
NICs												
Hong Kong	12.67	13.58	15.05	15.98	17.64	17.83	18.65	21.23	22.32	23.72	n.a.	n.a.
Korea	4.31	5.90	10.86	14.33	20.61	15.19	16.93	18.32	19.42	23.90	n.a.	n.a.
Singapore	8.60	10.27	11.16	10.49	10.11	11.23	11.38	11.72	13.18	12.04	n.a.	n.a.
ASEAN Four												
Indonesia	0.29	0.54	0.40	0.59	0.35	0.35	0.34	0.24	0.21	n.a.	n.a.	n.a.
Malaysia	2.01	1.88	2.19	1.62	1.83	2.51	2.20	2.45	n.a.	n.a.	n.a.	n.a.
Philippines	1.21	0.97	0.65	0.88	0.56	0.74	1.30	1.61	2.80	n.a.	n.a.	n.a.
Thailand	0.91	0.90	1.45	1.88	2.00	1.76	1.69	1.63	2.17	n.a.	n.a.	n.a.

Source: UN Commodity Trade tapes.

Note: Figures are rounded; n.a. = not available.

Table 8.7   **Exports of Technology-Intensive Commodities by Pacific Basin Countries** (percentage of total)

	1970	1971	1972	1973	1974	1975	1976	1977	1978	1979	1980	1981
Developed												
Australia	7.37	8.51	7.59	8.75	9.59	8.27	10.45	10.80	12.02	8.86	12.20	12.69
Canada	15.15	14.84	15.10	13.75	13.07	14.42	14.48	14.87	14.56	15.40	n.a.	n.a.
Japan	25.02	23.97	25.45	26.51	26.08	27.62	27.54	28.43	31.35	33.12	n.a.	n.a.
New Zealand	4.52	3.54	3.67	2.97	3.69	3.65	4.00	4.90	4.76	5.35	n.a.	n.a.
United States	43.49	44.64	42.92	39.49	40.69	42.53	43.17	43.25	43.92	44.09	n.a.	n.a.
NICs												
Hong Kong	6.94	6.51	7.37	8.44	9.55	8.17	8.23	9.03	9.35	9.67	n.a.	n.a.
Korea	7.95	8.40	11.05	11.72	13.36	10.63	12.22	11.47	12.23	14.38	n.a.	n.a.
Singapore	10.64	13.47	18.26	21.89	21.50	21.06	21.15	20.72	21.35	24.65	n.a.	n.a.
ASEAN Four												
Indonesia	0.29	0.13	0.26	0.21	0.16	0.72	0.86	1.07	0.93	n.a.	n.a.	n.a.
Malaysia	1.72	1.87	2.24	4.04	6.54	9.63	7.40	7.58	n.a.	n.a.	n.a.	n.a.
Philippines	0.53	0.67	0.94	0.63	0.68	1.22	1.45	2.75	3.31	n.a.	n.a.	n.a.
Thailand	0.32	0.34	0.49	0.69	1.19	1.77	2.44	2.87	3.82	n.a.	n.a.	n.a.

Source: UN Commodity Trade tapes.

Note: Figures are rounded; n.a. = not available.

8% of Singapore's exports, and 6% of U.S. exports were labor-intensive goods. The exports of all of the other countries were 2% or less of those goods. During the 1970s, the share of labor-intensive goods dropped noticeably in Hong Kong and Korea, reaching 63% and 46% respectively, dropped sharply in Japan to only 10%, and remained unchanged in the United States. Singapore, New Zealand, and Malaysia had marginal increases in their shares. However, the Philippines and Thailand had significant increases. The rapid rise of wages in Japan, Hong Kong, and Korea no doubt explains why these countries became less competitive in exporting labor-intensive products. Wages also went up in the Philippines and Thailand but from a much lower base and by a lesser amount. These countries are at an earlier stage of development in which large gains in productivity are possible in labor-intensive products, giving them a new comparative advantage.

The measurement of the share of exports of human-capital-intensive products is shown in table 8.6. At the beginning of the 1970s, Japan had the largest share of its exports in human-capital-intensive products, followed by Canada and the United States. Several other countries had significant shares, especially Hong Kong, Singapore, and Australia. During the 1970s, Japan's export share of human-capital goods rose to over 50%. An even larger rise was recorded in Korea and Hong Kong, which both reached 24% by 1979. Singapore's exports of human-capital-intensive goods rose to 12%, and New Zealand's to 7%. The other countries that had high shares at the start of the decade, such as Canada, the United States, and Australia, each experienced a small diminution. The ASEAN Four had only slight increases. Thus the main trend was an increasing share in countries with few natural resources and in moderate or advanced stages of industrialization (such as Japan and the NICs) and a slightly decreasing share in advanced industrial countries that also have abundant natural resources. It should be noted that human-capital-intensive goods include some products such as steel and road motor vehicles which, under different models, would be considered capital-intensive. Thus, the accumulation of capital in the NICs might provide a partial explanation for their increasing shares.

Technology-intensive commodities are covered in table 8.7. The United States has the largest share of its exports made up of technology-intensive goods. Japan was the second largest at the beginning of the decade, with one-quarter of its exports technology-intensive goods, and its share rose to one-third by 1979. Canada had a rather high share of technology-intensive goods at the start of the decade (15%), but it grew no further. Singapore started below Canada at 11%, but its share grew rapidly so that by 1979 almost one-quarter of its exports were technology-intensive goods. Korea and Australia also increased their shares. The ASEAN Four had few technology-intensive exports at the start of the decade; however, Malaysia and, to a lesser extent, the Philippines and Thailand all saw some growth. Comparative advantage in technology goods results from relatively large expenditures on research and development, which explains why the shares are so high in the United States and rising in Japan. However, technology can also be transferred between countries, usually as part of investments by multinational corporations (MNC). This explains much of the export success in these products by the developing countries of the Pacific Basin. Singapore is the most notable in this regard. It has welcomed foreign investment by MNCs, and in recent years the MNCs have promoted the transference of technology to Singapore, resulting in production for domestic use and export of technology-intensive products.

To summarize the story presented in tables 8.4–8.7, natural resource commodity exports are very important for many countries of the Pacific Basin, but they have tended to decline as a share of total exports for most of them. Indonesia is the exception, and it remains almost totally a natural resource exporter. Exports of labor-intensive commodities were very important for Japan and the NICs, but they have declined as a share of exports. Two ASEAN countries, the Philippines and Thailand, for the first time became significant exporters of labor-intensive goods during the 1970s. Japan and the NICs increased their export shares of both human-capital-intensive and technology-intensive goods. The higher-income developed countries (Australia, Canada, and the United States) had a slight decrease in shares of human-capital-intensive goods and increases in shares of technology-intensive goods.

These tables map out some of the major shifts in comparative advantage, but it is important not to exaggerate these changes into inevitable stages. It is not necessarily true that, just because all countries start out as natural resource exporters, when they begin to industrialize, they will export labor-intensive goods, develop further, and export human capital-intensive goods, and eventually become rich, do R&D, and export nothing but technology goods.[3] Especially in the case of natural resources, the bases for some comparative advantages are permanent or very long lasting, as seen in many Pacific Basin countries. Natural resources may set such a high reservation price for labor that a country might never specialize in labor-intensive commodities or do so only briefly. Futhermore, there is no obvious necessity for shifting from human-capital goods to technology-intensive goods. Nevertheless, the patterns exhibited by the twelve Pacific Basin countries over the last decade in the factor content of their exports are broadly consistent with trends we would expect in fast-growing economies from traditional theory of comparative advantage. These patterns are strikingly similar to those for the sixteen transitional economies whose fifteen leading exports (based on United Nations Conference on Trade and Development data) were examined by Bradford in chapter 7 of this volume.

8.4   The Special Case of Textiles and Clothing

As already noted, major shifts have occurred in export shares of labor-intensive products in the Pacific Basin, particularly for the developing countries. Within the labor-intensive category, the most important product group is textiles and clothing. Therefore it merits some special attention. As seen in table 8.2, fully 34% of Hong Kong's exports in 1980 were textiles and clothing; these items constituted 29% of Korea's and 23% of Taiwan's exports. In fact, it was the dominant product group for the NICs (other than Singapore). It also had become an important part of Thailand's exports, reaching 9%.

Textiles and clothing are very sensitive to cyclical factors, more so than, for example, certain new electronic products for which there is a widening of the market in addition to replacement demand. Thus, during the 1979–82 recession, Hong Kong's export growth suffered from its heavy dependency on these goods. However, the vigorous recovery that began in the United States at the end of 1982 displayed the positive effects of cyclical sensitivity. In 1973, U.S. imports of textiles and clothing have risen rapidly, and the NICs have increased their exports to the United States.

A second factor that distinguishes textiles and clothing trade is that it is among the most restricted of any product group entering international trade. The long history of multilateral restrictions going back to the temporary agreement on cotton textiles is now enshrined in the all-encompassing Multi-Fiber Arrangement (MFA). Under pressures from the European Community, the last renewal of the MFA was even more restrictive and provided for little market growth. However, textiles restraints often work in unexpected ways. For example, witness the contrast between the United States and Japan; the former is part of the MFA and the latter is not.

Few importing countries ever evaluate or make known to their consumers the economic costs of their restrictions on textiles and clothing. Australia, however, in an exception. Through the excellent work of the Australian Industries Assistance Commission (IAC), the amount of assistance to the industry is measured and published (IAC 1983). Australia imposes high nominal tariff rates on textiles (25%) and clothing (81%) and in addition imposes quantitative restrictions on imports. Thus, the effective rate of assistance for textiles is 54%, having risen from 43% in 1968–69, and for clothing it is 213%, having risen from 108% in the earlier years. By way of contrast, the average effective rate of assistance to Australian manufacturing from 1968–69 to 1981–82 was reduced from 36% to 26%. Hence, textiles and clothing received above-average assistance in 1968–69, which was sharply increased in contrast to other manufacturing industries. However, the results of this rise of protection are not exactly what one would expect. Unsurprisingly, exports as a share of Australian output, especially of clothing, were reduced as expected since protection generally reduces international competitiveness. Significantly, however, employment in these industries declined sharply and at a faster rate than in other manufacturing industries. Furthermore, imports continued to rise, no doubt at a slower rate than would have been the case with less assistance. Thus, despite these policy efforts to thwart the workings of the market, comparative advantage was still operative.

In table 8.8 the trade in textiles and clothing for some countries in the Pacific Basin for 1973 and 1980–82 is shown. The misleading appearance of protective schemes is evident in the contrast between the imports of the United States and Japan. By appearance, the United States by being a participant in the MFA is more restrictive than Japan. However, the import statistics prove that the opposite is true. The United States imported 2.2 times as much as Japan in 1973, that is, $3.8 billion versus $1.7 billion.[4] By 1982, U.S. imports had grown to $11.6 billion and Japan's to only $3.4 billion. In fact, U.S. imports were 3.4 times that of Japan, and this occurred before the economic recovery pushed U.S. imports even higher.

The probable reason for this is that the U.S. restraints do permit imports to grow and the quality of goods to be upgraded. Japanese restraints may be both less visible and more restrictive. Japan does impose some overt quotas on silk and silk products. It also forces voluntary restraints on foreign producers of cotton thread. However, most of the restraints are exercised through MITI's (Ministry of International Trade and Industry) reorganization of the industry. In 1973–74, in response to rapidly rising imports and the distress of the first oil crisis, MITI designed a reorganization of the industry primarily by promoting vertical integration. Trading firms were urged to limit imports to promote the reorganization. This was particularly effective in clothing, since international trade in garments is initiated by the buyers and goods are produced to importers' specifications. If the Japanese will not initiate the purchase, there is no way to effectively export to them. Those imports that did increase are believed to be mainly from foreign joint ventures of Japanese firms.

The MFA has several unfortunate quirks. Quotas apply only to developing countries and Japan and are allocated by historical share of the market. New entrants are permitted without restraint until they reach significant amounts, at which time they are brought under the

Table 8.8   Trade in Textiles and Clothing in Some Pacific Basin Countries (in billions of U.S. $)

	Textiles				Clothing				Total			
	1973	1980	1981	1982	1973	1980	1981	1982	1973	1980	1981	1982
Exports												
Advanced												
Australia[a]	0.04	0.13	0.14	n.a.	0.02	0.02	0.02	n.a.	0.06	0.15	0.16	n.a.
Canada[a]	0.15	0.31	0.33	0.29	0.12	0.21	0.23	0.21	0.27	0.52	0.56	0.50
Japan	2.45	5.10	5.85	5.09	0.37	0.50	0.58	0.55	2.82	5.60	6.43	5.64
New Zealand	0.03	0.10	0.10	n.a.	0.00	0.04	0.04	n.a.	0.03	0.14	0.14	n.a.
United States	1.22	3.62	3.61	2.77	0.29	1.22	1.26	0.99	1.51	4.84	4.87	3.76
NICs												
Hong Kong	0.46	0.91	0.94	0.83	1.39	4.64	4.73	5.01	1.85	5.55	5.95	5.56
Korea	0.44	2.20	2.45	n.a.	0.75	2.95	3.86	n.a.	1.19	5.15	6.31	n.a.
Singapore	0.14	0.37	0.34	0.34	0.13	0.43	0.47	0.46	0.27	0.80	0.81	0.80
Imports												
Advanced												
Australia[a]	0.62	1.10	1.15	n.a.	0.11	0.34	0.42	n.a.	0.73	1.44	1.57	n.a.
Canada[a]	0.78	1.28	1.41	1.13	0.33	0.71	0.84	0.84	1.11	1.99	2.25	1.97
Japan	1.13	1.65	1.63	1.60	0.57	1.53	1.80	1.83	1.70	3.18	3.43	3.43
New Zealand	0.20	0.32	0.33	n.a.	0.01	0.02	0.02	n.a.	0.21	0.34	0.35	n.a.
United States	1.58[a]	2.54	3.07	2.85	2.17[a]	6.94	8.12	8.79	3.75[a]	9.48	11.19	11.64
NICs												
Hong Kong	0.94	2.97	3.43	2.97	0.12	0.69	0.93	1.06	1.06	3.66	4.36	4.03
Korea	0.30	0.41	0.49	n.a.	0.01	0.01	0.01	n.a.	0.31	0.42	0.50	n.a.
Singapore	0.42	0.85	0.88	0.88	0.04	0.15	0.21	0.27	0.46	1.00	1.09	1.15

Source: GATT 1983.

Note: n.a. = not available.

[a]Exports and imports f.o.b.

quota. Thus, the quota encourages investment in new capacity in new countries which might not be competitive by a market test. Second, trade among developed countries may be artificially stimulated. For example, the largest percentage growth of imports into the United States in 1983 came from the European Community. Third, old suppliers with large historic shares are protected from the competition of new countries. Thus, Japan is unable to fill its quota in the United States but still exports more than it would by market test. Hence, it is not unusual for mature supplier countries to lobby for the continuance of a quota system.[5]

Table 8.8 also indicates a difference in the textile policies among the NICs. Hong Kong, which has a liberal trade regime, imports considerable amounts of textiles and exports even larger amounts of clothing. Korea, with a more restrictive import regime, imports very little textiles or clothing.

8.5   Protectionism and Trade Patterns in the Pacific Basin

Exports of manufactured goods by Pacific Basin countries continued to make progress in the 1970s and early 1980s despite the recession and rising protectionism. This was true even for textiles and clothing, the most seriously constrained group of manufactures. This should provide no grounds for complacency concerning protection. The factors that have increased protection still exist. Secondly, exchange rates were for many years very far out of line with purchasing power values, with the U.S. dollar greatly overvalued and the Japanese yen greatly undervalued. Thirdly, a new round of trade negotiations may not provide enough impetus to liberalize trade to offset the drift toward protectionism.

World trade problems center around Japan. Japan is the second largest industrial country, and none of Japan's trade partners are satisfied with their access to the Japanese market. Japan has benefited from four years of export-led growth during the worst recession in the postwar period. This, in effect, constitutes a beggar-thy-neighbor policy. Japanese exports have risen but imports have not. No country can export without importing. Although Japan does import the raw materials it needs, the problem lies in insufficient imports of manufactures and competitive agricultural commodities. Presumably, Japanese leaders believe they can manage trade tensions by exercising selective voluntary export controls. Already more than half of Japan's exports to Europe are under such controls. However, the rest of the world may not be willing to let Japan use voluntary controls, because they create windfalls for Japanese producers at the expense of foreign consumers.

Somehow Japan's imbalance with the rest of the world will be corrected. A possible way might be an exaggerated appreciation of the yen. A less desirable solution would be worldwide discrimination against Japan. From its own self-interest, one would think that Japan would overcome its inertia and propose a solution based on an increase in Japanese imports rather than trade contraction.

Clearly the world needs a new round of negotiations to liberalize trade. In such a negotiation, the developing countries should be prepared to be full and equal participants. In the past, the developing countries have appealed to their status and have asked for special treatment. The developed countries have treated them as special and, on average, worse than they treat each other; witness the MFA. The developing countries should be willing to bargain away their special privileges such as preferences (Generalized System of Preferences) in return for ending their special penalties. Generalized liberalization of trade barriers by developing countries would also encourage more intra-LDC trade, which is already growing rapidly.

Optimally, the negotiations should be global in scope. However, in the event that Europe and/or Latin America are unwilling to take part, then a second-best solution might well be a regional freeing of trade within the Pacific Basin.

Appendix
Commodity Classification System

International trade in commodities is classified by the United Nations into ten broad groups, labeled by the numbers 0 to 9 (standard international trade classification, or SITC). The categories, when finally disaggregated, number approximately 1,300 basic items, each of which is identified by a four-digit—or, in some cases, a five-digit—code. These basic items, when summed, compose total commodity trade for a given reporting country and partner country.[6]

To create a manageable data bank, the UN trade data were initially aggregated into 106 commodity groups, which taken together represent total trade. For the purposes of this study, the category "goods, not elsewhere specified" (SITC 9, less 951) was then excluded because it is composed of goods without any common traits.

The 105 commodities were classified into four groups according to their relative factor intensities. These groups are natural-resource-intensive, unskilled-labor-intensive, technology-intensive, and human-capital-intensive goods (table 8.A.1).

The commodity classification procedure was performed sequentially by initially categorizing the commodities whose factor intensities are most apparent. First, the natural-resource-based goods were identified. This group consists of all commodities within SITC sections 0–4 (that is, food and live animals, beverages and tobacco, crude materials, mineral fuels, and animal and vegetable oils) and SITC classes 61 (leather), 63 (plywood), 68 (nonferrous metals), 661–63 (mineral manufactures), and 667 (diamonds). There were forty-two commodities in this group.

Second, by using the groupings of commodities according to their respective value added per worker, as presented by Garnaut and Anderson (1980, 141),[7] eleven goods were classified as unskilled-labor-intensive. These commodities, representing those with the lowest value added per worker, are the same goods appearing in Garnaut and Anderson, except where the commodity aggregations precluded separating goods further. Included in this group are such SITC classes as 65 (textiles and fabrics), 664–66 (glass), 735 (ships and boats), 81–85, 893–95, 899 (miscellaneous consumer goods, furniture, clothing, footwear, and toys), and 951 (firearms).

The remaining commodities were divided into technology-intensive and human-capital-intensive categories by selecting as technology-intensive those goods with the highest ratios of research and development expenditures to value added.[8] Ratios were calculated by industry, classified according to two- and three-digit standard industrial classifications (SIC), for the average of the years 1967–68 and 1975–76. The SIC classes were then cross-classified by using Balassa's system correlating SIC and SITC (1977, Appendix table 2). There are thirty commodities in the technology-intensive category, including SITC divisions 51 (chemical elements), 54 (medicine), 56 (fertilizer), 58 (plastics), 52, 57, 59 (other chemicals), 71 less 7199 (machinery), 7249 (telecommunications equipment), 726 (electrical apparatus, not elsewhere specified), 734 (aircraft), 861 (scientific, medical, and optical measuring apparatus), and 862–63 (photographic supplies).

Human-capital-intensive goods are those that have relatively lower ratios of research and development expenditures to value added than technology-intensive goods. Among the twenty-two commodities falling under the human-capital-intensive rubric are SITC groups 53 (paints), 55 (perfumes), 62 (rubber), 64 (paper), 672–79 (steel), 69 (manufactures of metal, not elsewhere specified), 7199 (machine parts), 7241 (televisions), 7242 (radios), 725 (domestic electrical apparatus), 7294 (automotive electrical equipment), 731 (trains), 733 (trailers), 864 (watches), 891 (phonographs), 892 (books), and 896–97 (jewelry).

Table 8.A.1 **SITC Designations for Products in International Trade**

Commodity	SITC, Rev.	Commodity	SITC, Rev.
Natural Resource Intensive		Diamonds	667
		Pig iron	671
Meat	00, 01	Unwrought	
Dairy	02	nonferrous	
Fish	03	metals	681, 6831, 6851,
Wheat	041		6861, 6871
Rice	042	Unwrought	
Other cerals	043, 045–47	copper	6821
Corn	046	Copper	
Prepared foods	048, 0713, 09	manufactures	6822
Fruit	051–53	Nonferrous	
Vegetables	054–55	manufactures	6832, 6852, 6862,
Sugar	06		6872, 688–89
Coffee	0711–12	Unwrought	
Cacao	072–75	aluminum	6841
Feed	08	Aluminum	
Beverages	11	manufactures	6842
Tobacco	12		
Hides	21	Unskilled Labor Intensive	
Soybeans	22		
Crude rubber	23	Yarn	651
Wood	24	Fabrics	652–53
Pulp	25	Textile products	654–57
Cotton	263	Glass	664–66
Fibers	261–62, 264–69	Ships	7353, 7358–59
Iron ore	281–82	Firearms	7351, 951
Nonferrous ore	283–86	Furniture	82
Crude materials,		Clothing	82
not elsewhere		Footwear	85
specified	29	Misc. consumer	
Coal	32	products	81, 83, 893, 895,
Gas, natural &			899
manuf., & elec.		Toys	894
current	34–35		
Crude petroleum	331	Technology Intensive	
Petroleum prod.	332		
Animal and veg.		Chemical	
oils	4	elements	51
Leather	61	Medicine	54
Plywood	63	Fertilizer	56
Mineral		Plastics	58
manufactures	661–63	Other chemicals	52, 57, 59
		Power-generating	
		equipment	7111–13, 7116–
			18

(*continued*)

Table 8.A.1 (continued)

Commodity	SITC, Rev.	Commodity	SITC, Rev.
Jet engines	7114	Aircraft	734
Car engines	7115	Cameras	8614–16
Tractors	7125	Film	
Agricultural		(photographic	
machinery	7121–23, 7129	supplies)	862–63
Office machinery	7141, 7149		
Computers	7142–43	Human Capital Intensive	
Metal-working		Paints	53
machinery	715	Perfumes	55
Textile machinery	717	Rubber	62
Mining machinery	7184	Paper	64
Other industrial		Steel	672–79
machinery	718, 7194–98	Metal	
Heating and		manufacturing	691–94, 698
cooling equip.	7191	Cutlery	696–97
Pumps	7192	Hand tools	695
Fork lifts	7193	Machine parts	7199
Electric power		Televisions	7241
machinery	722	Radios	7242
Telecomm.		Domestic elec.	
equipment	7249	apparatus	725
Elec. apparatus		Trains	731
for medical		Cars	7321
purposes	726	Trucks	7322–25
Transistors	7293	Road motor	
Elec. measuring		vehicle parts	7236–38, 7294
equipment	7295	Motorcycles	7329
Electrical		Trailers	733
apparatus	723, 7291–92,	Watches	864
	7296–97, 7299	Phonographs	891
Scientific		Books	892
equipment	8617–19	Jewelry	896–97
Optical equipment	8611–13		

Source: SITC numbers from United Nations 1961. This classification scheme was in effect from 1960 to 1975.

Notes

1. The classification method is described in the Appendix.

2. The exclusion of Taiwan from the United Nations commodity trade tapes prevents the extension of the analysis to that country.

3. However, technology goods are rising as a share of world trade, and therefore, the share of technology goods in the exports of all countries could increase.

4. Since the U.S. figure is f.o.b. and Japan's is c.i.f., the contrast would be greater if comparably measured.

5. In the case of U.S. quotas on stainless steel flatwear, only Japanese producers wanted them continued, but the quota was ended.

6. A detailed listing of the classification system used in this study is presented in United Nations 1961.

7. The presentation in Garnaut and Anderson is based on the work of Bela Balassa (1977, Appendix table 1).

8. Research and development figures were taken from National Science Foundation 1980; value added figures were from Bureau of the Census, *Annual Survey of Manufactures,* various years.

References

Balassa, Bela. 1977. A "stages approach" to comparative advantage. World Bank Staff Working Paper, no. 256.

Galenson, Walter, ed. 1986. *Foreign trade and investment: Economic development in the newly industrializing Asian countries.* Madison: University of Wisconsin Press.

Garnaut, Ross, and Kym Anderson. 1980. ASEAN export specialization and the evolution of comparative advantage in the Western Pacific region. In *ASEAN in a changing Pacific and world economy,* ed. Ross Garnaut. Miami: Australian National University Press.

GATT (General Agreement on Tariffs and Trade). 1983. *International trade 1982/83. Genva.*

Industries Assistance Commission (Australia). 1983. Annual report 1982–83. (Gives latest estimates of rates of assistance to specific industries.)

Jones, Kent. 1983. *Impasse and crisis in steel trade policy.* Thames Essay no. 35. London: Trade Policy Research Centre.

Krause, Lawrence B. 1982. *U.S. Economic Policy toward the Association of Southeast Asian Nations: Meeting the Japanese challenge.* Washington, D.C.: Brookings Institute.

National Science Foundation. 1980. *Research and development in industry, 1978.* Washington, D.C.: National Science Foundation.

United Nations. 1961. *Standard international trade classification, revised.* Series M, no. 34. New York: UN Statistical Office.

U.S. Bureau of the Census. Various years. *Annual Survey of Manufactures.*

9   Empirical Tests of Alternative Models of International Growth

Laurence J. Kotlikoff and Edward E. Leamer

9.1 Introduction

Recent changes in patterns of international trade and growth have rekindled interest in the relationships among trade, growth, and the international distribution of income. Three alternative models can serve as a theoretical foundation for an empirical analysis of these relationships. The first is the standard Heckscher-Ohlin-Samuelson (HO) trade model with equal numbers of factors and goods and incomplete specialization. The second model allows complete specialization and more goods than factors. The third model posits short-run capital immobility. Each of these models has quite different implications for the determination of wage levels and growth rates.

The traditional even ($n \times$ n) HO model with incomplete specialization predicts instantaneous factor price equalization and equivalent growth rates of wages across countries. In contrast, altering the standard HO model to permit specialization of production potentially eliminates factor price equalization and allows growth rates of wages to differ, both in the short and in the long run. The third model, which assumes short-run costs to adjusting capital intensity, predicts short-run differences in the levels and growth rates of factor returns but long-run equalization of these variables.

Because these three models can have very different policy consequences, it is important to make an attempt to determine which is the most accurate approximation of the real world. Unfortunately, many observations can be rationalized within the context of any one of these

Laurence J. Kotlikoff is a professor of economics at Boston University and a research associate of the National Bureau of Economic Research. Edward E. Leamer is a professor of economics at the University of California, Los Angeles.

models, and it is therefore difficult to determine which is the most accurate. Take, for example, the data reported in table 9.1 that show vast international differences in wages. If the even HO model is taken as the maintained hypothesis, then these data must be regarded to be wages averaged across skill groups. Wages within a given skill group are regarded to be the same in every country, and a country that has a relatively low reported wage is interpreted only to have a relatively

Table 9.1   **Ratio of Foreign to U.S. Annual Earnings per Worker**

	1958	1959	1960	1975	1976	1977	1978	1979
Western Europe								
Austria	—	—	—	0.63	0.59	0.65	0.74	0.78
Denmark	—	—	—	1.01	1.00	1.02	1.12	1.19
Finland	0.30	0.30	0.31	0.63	0.63	0.61	0.61	0.67
Ireland	0.03	0.03	0.03	0.10	0.13	0.15	—	—
Italy	—	—	—	0.51	0.45	0.49	0.54	0.61
Spain	—	—	—	0.46	0.46	0.49	—	—
Sweden	—	—	—	0.95	0.93	0.89	0.90	0.95
United Kingdom	—	—	—	0.51	0.44	0.45	0.51	0.61
West Germany	—	—	—	0.87	0.87	0.93	1.34	1.16
Pacific								
Australia		0.33	0.35	0.48	0.55	0.63	0.58	0.64
New Zealand	0.34	0.22	0.23	0.44	0.54	—	—	—
	0.22							
Asian								
Japan	0.13	0.14	—	0.54	0.61	0.19	0.87	0.87
Korea	—	—	—	0.08	0.10	0.12	0.16	0.19
South America								
Brazil	0.12	0.13	—	—	0.19	0.20	—	—
Chile	—	—	—	0.14	0.17	0.20	0.21	—
Colombia	0.13	0.13	0.14	0.11	0.11	0.17	0.20	0.16
Dominican Republic	0.09	0.09	0.09	0.13	0.14	0.12	0.12	0.12
Ecuador	—	—	0.15	0.16	0.17	0.17	—	—
El Salvador	—	—	—	0.13	0.14	0.13	—	—
Southeast Asia								
Hong Kong	—	—	—	—	0.19	0.19	0.22	—
Indonesia	—	—	—	0.04	0.04	0.05	0.05	—
Philippines	—	—	—	0.07	0.06	0.07	—	—
Singapore	—	—	—	0.23	0.21	0.21	0.22	0.24
Mideast								
Afghanistan	—	—	—	0.04	0.04	0.03	0.03	0.03
India	—	0.06	0.06	0.06	0.05	0.05	0.05	—
Israel	0.37	0.38	0.39	0.39	0.42	0.40	0.35	0.41
Jordan	—	—	—	0.13	0.14	0.14	0.18	0.23
Syria	—	—	—	0.07	0.06	0.08	—	—
Turkey	0.29	0.32	0.23	0.25	0.25	0.32	0.33	0.37

Sources: United Nations, *Yearbook of Industrial Statistics* (New York), various annual issues; and International Monetary Fund, *International Financial Statistics* (Washington, D.C.), various annual issues.

large supply of low-skilled workers. As a matter of fact, Krueger (1968) shows that a surprisingly large amount of the differences in gross wage rates can be accounted for by a bit of disaggregation.

On the other hand, if the uneven HO model is taken as a guide, the wage differences in table 9.1 are suggestive of countries with factor endowment vectors sufficiently different that they fall in different cones of specialization; in this case the increasing similarity of wages over time is regarded either as evidence of increasing similarity of factor endowments or as evidence of the blurring of the differences among the specialization cones associated, for example, with product price changes. These wage data can also be rationalized within the context of the third model—the even HO model with adjustment costs. Here the differences in wages are attributed to differences in initial conditions; and the tendency of wages to equalize over time is thought to be a consequence of increased domestic factor mobility over time.

Although the wage data can be rationalized within the framework of any one of these models, each model has very different implications concerning policies to raise wages in low-wage countries. In the even HO model the route to increased wages is increased training or, more generally, increased human capital. Physical capital deepening can have no effect on wages of a specific skill group, because the accumulation of physical capital leads only to an adjustment of the output mix and no change in capital per man within a given industry. For the uneven model, on the other hand, accumulation of physical capital can move a country from one cone of specialization to another and can raise wages paid to each of the skill groups. Policies to promote wage increases implied by the third model (the even model with adjustment costs) aim at reducing the effective adjustment costs, including policies that alter the path of net foreign investment.

The paper proceeds in the next three sections by briefly describing each of the models, pointing out in the process their different testable implications. Section 9.4 describes the data used to test the three models. Section 9.5 presents regressions of value added, factor demands, and factor returns on country-specific as well as industry-specific inputs. These regressions permit more formal tests of the three models. The final section summarizes the findings and suggests additional areas of research.

The conclusions that we draw from this research are rather mixed. Each of the models performs well on certain criteria and poorly on others. While the standard HO model clearly fails to satisfy certain cross-equation constraints, national endowments are remarkably good predictors of the locus of international production. There are, however, significant nonlinearities in the relationship between factor allocations and national endowments. Such nonlinearities are predicted by the uneven version of the HO model. At odds with both of these models is our finding that lagged values of inputs provide an important explanation of current factor demands. Such correlations are suggested by the adjustment cost model.

The inability to clearly discriminate among the three models leaves open the issue of long- as well as short-run wage equalization. The partial support for each of the models offered here suggests that an un–even HO model with adjustment costs provides a better basis for discussing international trade than any of the three models on their own.

9.2   The Even Heckscher-Ohlin-Samuelson General Equilibrium Model

The traditional general equilibrium theory of production describes a country with a fixed endowment of a set of resources, facing commodity prices that are completely determined in international markets. Competition for scarce resources determines their allocation among industries and their rates of remuneration. The notation which we will use to describe this model is the following:

X = vector of outputs of m commodities,
V = vector of endowments of n resources,
p = vector of prices of m commodities,
w = vector of factor rents of n resources,
A = $n \times n$ matrix of factor input coefficients with elements equal to the amount of factor k used to produce one unit of commodity j.

The factor input matrix, the vector of outputs, and the vector of endowments necessarily satisfy the relationship

$$(1) \qquad\qquad AX = V.$$

With a suitable list of assumptions, including identical linear homogeneous production functions for all countries, equal numbers of commodities and resources, and incomplete specialization, it can be shown that the matrix A is the same for all countries and, in particular, is independent of V. Under these conditions equation (1) may be inverted to obtain

$$(2) \qquad\qquad X = A^{-1}V,$$

which expresses outputs as linear functions of the endowments, with X and V varying among countries but A^{-1} constant.

Equation (2), which maps factor endowments into commodities produced, also implicitly allocates the factors among the industries. The amount of factor k used to produce X_j of commodity j is $A_{kj}X_j$, where

A_{kj} is the (k, j) element of the input-output matrix. Thus, the allocation of factor k to a particular industry is proportional to output and can be described by an equation which is linear in the factor endowments V. This equation can be estimated by regressing factor allocation data on factor endowment data. To clarify this regression model, consider the system for the simple case of two factors, labor (L) and capital (K):

$$(3a) \qquad X_{ij} = a^{L_j} L_i + a^{K_j} K_i,$$

$$(3b) \qquad L_{ij} = A_{L_j} X_{ij} = A_{Lj} a^{L_j} L_i + A_{Lj} a^{K_j} K_i,$$

$$(3c) \qquad K_{ij} = A_{Kj} X_{ij} = A_{Kj} a^{L_j} L_i + A_{Kj} a^{K_j} K_i,$$

where a^{Lj} and a^{Kj} are elements of A^{-1} and i denotes the country. Because of the constancy across countries of output per man, X_{ij}/L_{ij}, and capital per man, K_{ij}/L_{ij}, in industry j, these three equations are proportional to each other. Linearity and proportionality are two strong implications of the even HO model. In addition, the assumption of costless interindustry factor mobility rules out any influence of past history. However, higher-order functions of national endowments, lagged values of national endowments, and lagged values of factor allocations do influence current factor allocations in the uneven HO model and the adjustment cost model in ways described below.

The factor demand system, equation (3), can be transformed into a factor expenditure system by multiplying each factor demand by its rental rate. Multiplying the L_{ij} equation by the wage, w, and the K_{ij} equation by the rental rate, r, on capital gives

$$(4a) \qquad E_{ij} = wL_{ij} = wA_{Lj} a^{L_j} L_i + wA_{Lj} a^{K_j} K_i,$$

$$(4b) \qquad R_{ij} = rK_{ij} = r A_{Kj} a^{L_j} L_i + r A_{Kj} a^{K_j} K_i,$$

where E_{ij} is the labor earnings in country i and industry j, and R_{ij} is the corresponding payment for capital services. Summing equations (4a) and (4b) yields the following expression for value added in country i, industry $j (V_{ij})$:

$$(5) \qquad V_{ij} = (wA_{Lj} + rA_{Kj}) a^{L_j} L_i + (wA_{Lj} + rA_{Kj}) a^{K_j} K_i.$$

Equations (4) and (5) indicate that factor payments as well as value added are each linear functions of national endowments. In addition, equations (3), (4), and (5) are proportional to each other.

Estimation of the factor payments and value-added relations may be less subject to bias from measurement error than estimation of factor demands. Consider, for example, labor effort, which is ideally measured as total effective hours worked but in our data is proxied by total employment. Assume that effective hours worked, L_{ij}, and employment, $\hat{L}_{ij}$, differ by a country-specific factor λ_i; i.e., $L_{ij} = \lambda_i \hat{L}_{ij}$, and $L_i = \lambda_i L_i$. The term λ_i may reflect cross-country differences in hours worked per employee, the intensity of work effort, or the effectiveness of work effort due to training and ability. It is likely that $\hat{L}_{ij}$ and λ_i are positively correlated, because larger countries, with several notable exceptions, have higher per capita income; the workers in these countries are typically better educated and better trained. If this description of the relationship between effective hours and employment is correct, the use of $\hat{L}_{ij}$ rather than L_{ij} will introduce complex biases in estimating equations (3). These biases will contaminate tests of the cross-equation restrictions in equations (3), although the estimated R^2 of the $\hat{L}_{ij}$ regression are likely to remain high if the R^2 from the unbiased L_{ij} regressions are also large.

The earnings equation (eq. [4a]) may be less sensitive to this bias. In principle, measured E_{ij} equals true E_{ij}, since factor payments to labor are for effective hours worked rather than payments for simply coming to work. In addition, wL_i in equation (4a) can be replaced by E_i, total national labor earnings, thus eliminating the problem of mismeasuring total national labor input. A straightforward test of the constant proportionality properties of this model that do not involve measurement of the labor input is to determine whether the ratios E_{ij}/K_i, E_{ij}/R_{ij}, and E_{ij}/V_{ij} are roughly constant across all countries i. This is equivalent to asking whether profit rates and factor shares are equal across industry.

9.3   The Uneven Heckscher-Ohlin General Equilibrium Model

The simplest uneven model has many goods and two factors. A possible equilibrium of such a model has countries with sufficiently different factor supplies producing different subsets of the commodities and having different factor returns. Roughly speaking, the relatively capital-abundant countries produce the relatively capital-intensive commodities and have the higher wage rates and the lower returns to capital. This is illustrated in figure 9.1, where the first panel contains the unit value isoquants and expansion paths of three commodities: automobiles, textiles, and clothing. The second panel illustrates the levels of factor returns as a function of capital per man, and the third panel contains the corresponding outputs per man.

In the first panel, there are two unit isocost lines, each of which is consistent with the production of two of the three commodities. The hypothetical endowments of three countries are also indicated in this figure. The United States, which is capital abundant, has high wage rates and produces the two capital-intensive products—autos and textiles. Japan, which is less well-endowed in capitol relative to labor has lower wage rates and produces the two less capital-intensive products—

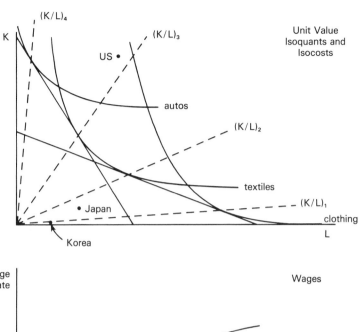

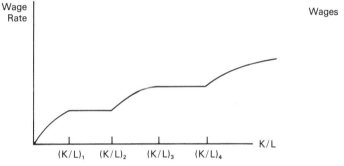

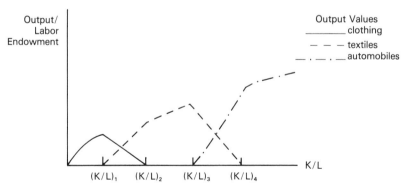

Fig. 9.1   The 3 × 2 Heckscher-Ohlin-Samuelson model

textiles and clothing. Korea, which is still less well endowed in capital, specializes in the least capital-intensive product (clothing) and has the very lowest wages. Note that although both the United States and Japan are producing textiles, the United States uses the more capital-intensive technique.

This figure provides a stylized picture of the situation in the 1950s and early 1960s. Figure 9.2 then represents the current situation and differs from figure 9.1 in two ways. First, both Japan and Korea have accumulated capital at a more rapid rate than the United States. Japan has moved into the same cone as the United States. Korea has moved into the cone where both textiles and clothing are produced. The other change that is evident in figure 9.2 is that the spread in wages between the two cones of diversification is less than in figure 9.1. What accounts for this change are the shifts in the world supply curves induced by the rapid accumulation of capital in Japan and Korea and the consequent change in the relative prices of the three goods. In figure 9.2 it is assumed that the relative supply of textiles increased and that of clothing decreased, and consequently, the price of textiles fell, and the price of clothing rose. This change is depicted in figure 9.2 by a shift outward of the textile unit value isoquant and a shift inward of the

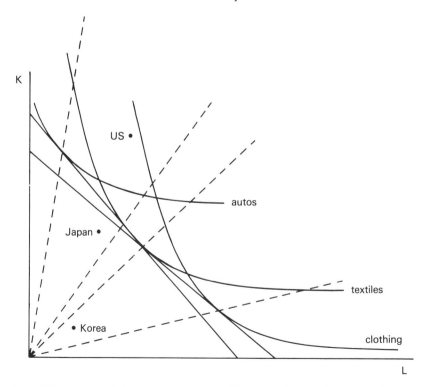

Fig. 9.2   Unit value isoquants and isocosts after product price changes

clothing unit value isoquant. This shift is accompanied by (1) a reduction in the wage in the United States, (2) a shift toward more labor-intensive techniques in the United States and a reduction in labor productivity, (3) an increase in the Korean wage rate, and (4) a shift toward more capital-intensive techniques in Korea and an attendant increase in labor productivity.

Worldwide accumulation of capital has generally the same effect in the even and the uneven model. Namely, supply curves of the relatively capital-intensive commodities shift outward, and as is indicated by the Rybczynski theorem, supply curves of the labor-intensive commodities shift inward. This will lead to a fall in the relative price of capital-intensive products and a general rise in wage rates. In the uneven model, however, wage rates of the most capital-abundant countries will fall if the supply curves of the most capital-intensive products shift outward less than the next most capital-intensive products. In terms of our stylized diagrams, this occurs if the supply of textiles increases more rapidly than the supply of automobiles.

Evidence in support of the uneven model would be wage, employment, or output data that conformed in a general sense to the second two panels of figure 9.1. Namely, wages depend on national endowments, and industry output and employment are nonlinear functions of the national endowments. Since the output and employment functions are linear within cones of diversification, a theoretically appealing data analysis would estimate linear models based on different subsets of the countries, possibly selected on the basis of similarity in factor returns.

A word of caution is in order here about aggregation effects. First it may appear that wage rates increase with capital abundance only because earnings include a return to human capital which naturally increases along with physical capital. On the other hand, the output and employment function may exhibit no clear nonlinearities because commodities with very dissimilar factor requirements are combined in a single aggregate. The textiles aggregate, for example, includes both capital- and labor-intensive products. Countries that are capital scarce produce the labor-intensive textiles, and countries that are capital abundant produce the capital-intensive textiles. As a result, there is relatively little variation in output of textiles overall associated with capital accumulation.

9.4   A Generalized Heckscher-Ohlin Model of Economic Growth with Adjustment Costs

The key feature that differentiates the adjustment cost model described here from the standard Heckscher-Ohlin model of international trade is the assumption that firms incur costs for altering their level of capital in any finite period of time. The adjustment cost technology we consider expresses adjustment costs as an increasing function of the rate of investment (or disinvestment). Since the rate of investment depends on both the absolute level of the firm's (industry's) existing capital stock and the absolute level of new investment, a firm's investment decision today will affect its capital stock tomorrow and, therefore, its marginal adjustment costs tomorrow. This formulation of the problem links the production and investment decisions of the firm at one point in time to these decisions at other points in time. Rather than equate the marginal product of capital to a common rental rate, as in the standard static trade model, firms in this environment alter their capital stocks over time to maximize the present value of profits where profits are net of adjustment costs. The relative immobility of physical capital does not preclude perfect national and international mobility of financial capital. In addition, the standard trade theory assumption of costless, domestic, interindustry labor mobility is maintained.

The assumption that altering levels of industry-specific capital is costly in the short run has several important implications. First, wage rates will differ across countries in the short run despite the facts that countries have identical technologies and are incompletely specialized in production and that financial capital is internationally mobile. The world relative price of the two commodities is not sufficient here to determine wage rates. In the short run, marginal revenue products of labor are equated across domestic industries, but marginal revenue products of capital are not. It is the satisfaction of both of these sets of conditions plus the assumption of identical constant returns to scale technologies that leads to factor price equalization. However, both conditions are satisfied in the long run when the economy has converged to a steady state characterized by incomplete specialization. Hence, if the economy converges to such a steady state, wage rates across different countries must converge as well.

A second feature of this model is that positive investment may take place even in those industries exhibiting low marginal revenue products of capital. The reason is simply that concentrating substantial levels of new investment in any given industry or set of industries within any year entails increasing adjustment costs; this will prove unprofitable relative to investing in low marginal revenue product, but low marginal adjustment cost, industries.

Even if disinvestment occurs, the rate of disinvestment will be slow, again because of the assumption of increasing costs to that activity. A consequence of this is that specialization in production will occur gradually if at all.

The supply relationships of this model are derived by noting that firms maximize the present value of profits. In country i, industry j, profits π_{ij} are given by

(6) $\quad \pi_{ij} = \int_0^\infty [P_{jt}F(K_{ijt}, L_{ijt}) - w_{it}L_{ijt} - I_{ijt}] \exp\left(-\int_0^t r_s ds\right) dt \, j = 1, 2.$

In equation (6) P_{jt} is the period t price of output j, K_{ijt} and L_{ijt} are country i, industry j, year t capital and labor demands, r_s is the interest rate prevailing in period s, and $w_{it}L_{ijt}$ equals payments to labor in year t. The quantity I_{ijt} equals country i, industry j's total investment in year t inclusive of adjustment costs. Letting J_{ijt} stand for the actual installation of new units of capital, we parameterize the investment relationship in equation (7):

(7) $\quad\quad\quad\quad\quad I_{ijt} = J_{ijt} + \frac{\gamma}{2}\left(\frac{J_{ijt}}{K_{ijt}}\right) J_{ijt}.$

The second term on the right-hand side of equation (7) reflects the costs of varying the level of industry's capital stock and exhibits increasing marginal costs to such activity. Ignoring depreciation, the industry increases its net capital stock according to formula (8):

(8) $\quad\quad\quad\quad\quad\quad \dot{K}_{ijt} = J_{ijt}.$

Maximization of equation (6) subject to equations (7) and (8) leads to the following first-order conditions:

(9) $\quad\quad\quad\quad\quad\quad \frac{J_{ijt}}{K_{ijt}} = \frac{q_{ijt} - 1}{\gamma},$

(10) $\quad\quad\quad\quad\quad\quad P_{jt} F_{Lijt} = w_{it},$

(11) $\quad\quad\quad\quad\quad\quad P_{jt} F_{Kijt} = r_t q_{ijt} + \dot{q}_{ijt},$

where q_{ijt} is the market value of capital relative to its replacement cost in country i, industry j, in year t.

In the steady state, $\dot{q}_{ijt} = 0$, $q_{ijt} = 1$, and

(12) $P_{jt} F_{Kijt} = r.$

In the steady state, equations (10) and (12) provide the standard HO relationship between marginal revenue products and factor prices. These relations hold for $j = 1, 2$, and suffice to determine factor returns, given constant returns to scale in production and output prices. Hence, assuming identical technologies in the foreign country, factor price equalization is satisfied in the long run.

In the short run, equations (10) and (11) together determine wage rates given the time path of q_{ijt}, the world interest rate, r_t, and the output prices P_{it}. Since the q_{ijt}'s differ, in the short run, across countries, short-run wage rates will also differ across countries.

According to equation (10) labor demand in the adjustment cost model depends on the fixed amount of capital in place at a point in time as well as the country's wage rate. In contrast to the HO model, the amount of capital in the rest of the economy should have no influence on labor demand. Hence, one test that can potentially discriminate between these models is to determine whether the economy's total capital endowment as opposed to the amount of capital in place in particular industries influences industry-specific labor demand. The economy's wage is another variable, whose inclusion in industry-specific labor demand regression is predicted by the HO model with adjustment costs but not by the non–adjustment cost model.

9.5 Data Descriptions

Data on number of workers, earnings, value of output, and investment expenditures for twenty-eight three-digit ISIC industries are compiled by the United Nations and published in the *Growth of World Industry*. The coverage of years and countries is very haphazard. The end years, 1963 and 1978, and the twenty-eight countries listed in the notes to table 9.2 were selected to assure a complete matrix of data. Even for this relatively short list of countries there are very substantial problems caused by the fact that various countries intermittently choose to aggregate two or more of the commodity classes together. In such cases, we split the reported number among the components in proportion to the size of the components in adjacent years. The capital stocks in 1978 were estimated from investment flow data beginning in 1963 using the perpetual inventory method (e.g., Leamer 1984). Missing intermediate investment data were imputed with straight-line interpolation methods. As a consequence of these imputation schemes, we are not altogether comfortable with the econometric analysis that follows, since it inappropriately ignores the possibility of gross or chronic measurement errors in the data.

Features of our data set are reported in tables 9.2–9.5. The first four columns of table 9.2 contain the total number of workers in each of the industries in each of the years and the share of these industries' workers in the total world work force included in our data. Over this period of time there was a 15% increase in employment in these industries, but the composition of world employment across industries did not change much. The one major exception to this statement is that employment in textiles dropped substantially, both as a share of

Table 9.2 **Labor Allocation Data** (in thousands)

| | World Totals | | | | Shares of World Totals | | | | | |
| | | | Shares | | U.S. | | Developed | | Other | |
ISIC	1963	1978	1963	1978	1963	1978	1963	1978	1963	1978
311 Food	5,372	6,261	.094	.094	.27	.21	.47	.42	.26	.36
313 Beverages	878	870	.015	.013	.22	.22	.58	.5	.19	.28
314 Tobacco	461	661	.008	.010	.16	.09	.37	.2	.46	.71
321 Textiles	6,512	5,918	.114	.089	.16	.18	.47	.31	.37	.51
322 Apparel	2,776	3,252	.048	.049	.41	.35	.51	.38	.08	.26
323 Leather	388	380	.007	.006	.23	.23	.53	.38	.23	.4
324 Footwear	668	640	.012	.010	.33	.24	.5	.33	.16	.43
331 Wood	1,983	2,077	.035	.031	.26	.26	.6	.51	.14	.23
332 Furniture	993	1,333	.017	.020	.31	.33	.49	.41	.19	.26
341 Paper	1,859	1,972	.032	.030	.31	.32	.57	.49	.11	.18
342 Printing	2,505	2,942	.044	.044	.36	.39	.5	.45	.13	.15
351 Ind. chem.	1,585	1,771	.028	.027	.27	.27	.56	.49	.16	.24
352 Other chem.	1,564	1,815	.027	.027	.29	.25	.51	.47	.19	.27
353 Petro. refin.	254	268	.004	.004	.46	.38	.37	.39	.17	.23
354 Petro., coal prod.	123	155	.002	.002	.28	.3	.53	.36	.2	.34
355 Rubber prod.	891	1,003	.016	.015	.28	.26	.54	.43	.18	.31
356 Plastics	642	1,521	.011	.023	.26	.32	.61	.5	.13	.18
361 Pottery	450	419	.008	.006	.09	.1	.59	.48	.32	.42

(*continued*)

Table 9.2 (continued)

| ISIC | World Totals | | Shares | | Shares of World Totals | | | | | |
| | | | | | U.S. | | Developed | | Other | |
	1963	1978	1963	1978	1963	1978	1963	1978	1963	1978
362 Glass	577	641	.010	.010	.25	.29	.49	.38	.26	.33
369 Nonmetal prod.	1,640	1,960	.029	.029	.23	.21	.53	.43	.24	.35
371 Iron and steel	3,266	3,213	.057	.048	.24	.25	.58	.5	.17	.25
372 Nonferrous metals	831	935	.014	.014	.3	.31	.58	.51	.12	.18
381 Metal prod.	3,925	4,750	.068	.071	.31	.31	.56	.5	.13	.19
382 Machinery	5,380	6,926	.094	.104	.3	.34	.61	.52	.09	.15
383 Electrical mach.	4,813	6,124	.084	.092	.3	.31	.62	.53	.07	.16
384 Transport equip.	5,140	6,328	.090	.095	.3	.32	.54	.51	.16	.17
385 Professional goods	946	1,409	.016	.021	.38	.42	.54	.43	.08	.15
390 Other	945	1,136	.016	.017	.38	.38	.53	.41	.08	.21
Total	57,367	66,680			.25	.29	.54	.46	.18	.25

Note: Developed countries are Australia, Canada, Denmark, Finland, Germany, Israel, Japan, Netherlands, Norway, Sweden, and the United Kingdom. Other countries are Brazil, Chile, Colombia, Cyprus, Ecuador, Greece, India, Ireland, Korea, Malta, Panama, Philippines, Portugal, Singapore, Spain, and Turkey. The "World" refers to these twenty-seven countries plus the United States.

Table 9.3   **Labor Earnings Data** (in thousands of dollars)

| | World Totals | | Shares | | Shares of World Totals | | | | | |
| | | | | | U.S. | | Developed | | Other | |
ISIC	1963	1978	1963	1978	1963	1978	1963	1978	1963	1978
311 Food	11,972	46,258	.077	.070	.62	.37	.32	.55	.05	.08
313 Beverages	2,302	9,163	.015	.014	.51	.24	.43	.57	.06	.1
314 Tobacco	736	3,276	.005	.005	.45	.24	.44	.57	.11	.18
321 Textiles	8,916	30,795	.057	.047	.45	.34	.42	.5	.12	.16
322 Apparel	5,805	18,297	.037	.028	.67	.46	.31	.45	.02	.09
323 Leather	785	2,369	.005	.004	.51	.33	.42	.51	.07	.16
324 Footwear	1,470	3,621	.009	.005	.55	.32	.39	.47	.06	.2
331 Wood	4,012	17,752	.026	.027	.53	.35	.43	.6	.03	.05
332 Furniture	2,292	10,679	.015	.016	.59	.42	.35	.49	.05	.09
341 Paper	5,831	22,394	.037	.034	.6	.44	.37	.51	.03	.05
342 Printing	8,387	33,659	.054	.051	.66	.46	.32	.5	.03	.04
351 Ind. chem.	5,255	24,099	.034	.036	.57	.36	.39	.57	.04	.07
352 Other chem.	5,335	19,798	.034	.030	.64	.37	.32	.55	.04	.08
353 Petro. refin.	1,284	4,643	.008	.007	.72	.48	.24	.43	.04	.09
354 Petro., coal prod.	367	1,625	.002	.002	.57	.47	.37	.44	.06	.09
355 Rubber prod.	2,520	9,700	.016	.015	.61	.39	.52	.05	.09	
356 Plastics	1,439	14,430	.009	.022	.58	.39	.55	.03	.06	
361 Pottery	630	2,747	.004	.004	.33	.17	.56	.64	.1	.19

(*continued*)

Table 9.3 (continued)

| | World Totals | | Shares | | Shares of World Totals | | | | | |
| | | | | | U.S. | | Developed | | Other | |
ISIC	1963	1978	1963	1978	1963	1978	1963	1978	1963	1978
362 Glass	1,487	6,377	.010	.010	.57	.43	.37	.48	.06	.1
369 Nonmetal prod.	3,990	17,224	.026	.026	.54	.34	.41	.56	.06	.1
371 Iron and steel	10,074	39,731	.065	.060	.56	.4	.4	.54	.04	.06
372 Nonferrous metals	3,284	11,610	.021	.018	.5	.42	.48	.53	.02	.06
381 Metal prod.	11,933	50,260	.077	.076	.61	.41	.35	.53	.03	.06
382 Machinery	17,355	84,638	.111	.128	.6	.44	.38	.52	.02	.04
383 Electrical mach.	14,596	66,770	.094	.101	.62	.39	.36	.56	.02	.05
384 Transport equip.	18,231	83,787	.117	.127	.63	.45	.34	.5	.03	.05
385 Professional goods	3,169	15,610	.020	.024	.71	.54	.27	.42	.02	.04
390 Other	2,336	9,207	.015	.014	.71	.49	.27	.45	.02	.06
Total	1.6e5	6.6e5			.60	.41	.36	.52	.04	.07

Note: Developed countries are Australia, Canada, Denmark, Finland, Germany, Israel, Japan, Netherlands, Norway, Sweden, and the United Kingdom. Other countries are Brazil, Chile, Colombia, Cyprus, Ecuador, Greece, India, Ireland, Korea, Malta, Panama, Philippines, Portugal, Singapore, Spain, and Turkey. The "World" refers to these twenty-seven countries plus the United States.

Table 9.4   **Value of Output** (in billions of dollars)

| | World Totals | | Shares | | Shares of World Totals | | | | | |
| | | | | | U.S. | | Developed | | Other | |
ISIC	1963	1978	1963	1978	1963	1978	1963	1978	1963	1978
311 Food	111.6	493.8	.145	.127	.56	.39	.34	.47	.10	.13
313 Beverages	15.44	79.83	.020	.021	.40	.30	.52	.60	.09	.11
314 Tobacco	13.02	41.71	.017	.011	.34	.23	.55	.59	.11	.17
321 Textiles	47.33	167.5	.061	.043	.39	.31	.45	.46	.16	.23
322 Apparel	23.33	76.85	.030	.020	.63	.45	.33	.42	.04	.13
323 Leather	3.756	13.79	.005	.004	.40	.26	.46	.48	.14	.25
324 Footwear	5.129	15.22	.007	.004	.51	.30	.41	.46	.08	.24
331 Wood	17.78	97.44	.023	.025	.46	.36	.48	.57	.05	.07
332 Furniture	8.099	44.17	.010	.011	.57	.39	.36	.50	.07	.11
341 Paper	30.45	133.9	.039	.035	.54	.43	.42	.50	.04	.08
342 Printing	25.92	123.8	.034	.032	.62	.45	.34	.49	.04	.05
351 Ind. chem.	34.57	207.9	.045	.054	.54	.38	.40	.50	.06	.12
352 Other chem.	28.79	125.1	.037	.032	.57	.42	.36	.46	.07	.12
353 Petro. refin.	26.09	221.0	.034	.057	.63	.44	.31	.43	.05	.13
354 Petro., coal prod.	3.36	21.68	.004	.006	.45	.33	.47	.49	.08	.18
355 Rubber prod.	11.12	45.33	.014	.012	.54	.37	.36	.47	.11	.16
356 Plastics	6.391	74.91	.008	.019	.50	.36	.48	.56	.05	.08
361 Pottery	1.715	8.123	.002	.002	.29	.17	.59	.61	.12	.22

(*continued*)

Table 9.4 (continued)

| ISIC | World Totals | | Shares | | Shares of World Totals | | | | | |
| | 1963 | 1978 | 1963 | 1978 | U.S. | | Developed | | Other | |
					1963	1978	1963	1978	1963	1978
362 Glass	5.276	26.20	.007	.007	.54	.41	.38	.47	.08	.12
369 Nonmetal prod.	17.41	93.62	.023	.024	.52	.32	.41	.55	.07	.14
371 Iron and steel	48.01	230.0	.062	.059	.47	.33	.46	.54	.06	.13
372 Nonferrous steel	19.32	93.01	.025	.024	.52	.41	.43	.49	.05	.10
381 Metal prod.	46.49	225.9	.060	.058	.58	.41	.38	.51	.04	.09
382 Machinery	60.65	354.2	.079	.091	.57	.43	.40	.51	.02	.06
383 Electrical mach.	53.41	294.8	.069	.076	.55	.36	.42	.57	.04	.08
384 Transport equip.	86.77	458.0	.112	.118	.61	.45	.34	.49	.04	.07
385 Professional goods	10.26	62.28	.013	.016	.69	.55	.28	.41	.03	.04
390 Other	10.05	43.03	.013	.011	.59	.46	.39	.48	.03	.06
Total	771.5	3,873.			.54	.40	.39	.50	.06	.10

Note: Developed countries are Australia, Canada, Denmark, Finland, Germany, Israel, Japan, Netherlands, Norway, Sweden, and the United Kingdom. Other countries are Brazil, Chile, Colombia, Cyprus, Ecuador, Greece, India, Ireland, Korea, Malta, Panama, Philippines, Portugal, Singapore, Spain, and Turkey. The "World" refers to these twenty-seven countries plus the United States.

Table 9.5 Value of Capital, 1978

ISIC	World		Shares			Capital-Labor Ratios			
	Total[a]	Share	U.S.	Dev.	Oth.	World	U.S.	Dev.	Oth.
311 Food	66,019	.076	.33	.50	.17	10.54	16.57	12.52	4.98
313 Beverages	21,661	.025	.28	.58	.13	24.90	31.69	28.88	11.56
314 Tobacco	10,310	.012	.12	.82	.06	15.60	20.80	6.95	1.32
321 Textiles	37,292	.043	.29	.42	.29	6.30	10.15	8.54	3.58
322 Apparel	7,280	.088	.35	.43	.22	2.24	2.24	2.53	3.24
323 Leather	1,540	.002	.24	.43	.32	4.05	4.23	4.59	1.52
324 Footwear	1,490	.002	.26	.46	.28	2.33	2.52	3.25	4.90
331 Wood	19,496	.023	.38	.50	.12	9.39	13.72	9.22	2.41
332 Furniture	6,959	.008	.34	.54	.12	5.22	5.38	6.86	9.68
341 Paper	49,099	.057	.41	.51	.07	24.90	31.90	25.86	4.37
342 Printing	24,129	.028	.47	.45	.08	8.20	9.88	8.24	22.08
351 Ind. chem.	97,149	.112	.37	.52	.10	54.86	75.17	58.44	6.18
352 Other chem.	25,220	.029	.37	.50	.12	13.90	20.57	14.84	60.25
353 Petro. refin.	33,763	.039	.43	.46	.11	125.98	142.56	148.59	15.62
354 Petro., coal prod.	6,381	.007	.17	.71	.13	41.17	23.33	81.19	5.42
355 Rubber prod.	11,859	.014	.37	.48	.14	11.82	16.83	13.20	5.42
356 Plastics	17,577	.020	.40	.48	.12	11.56	14.48	11.09	7.90
361 Pottery	2,802	.003	.12	.56	.31	6.69	8.16	7.80	4.97
362 Glass	9,875	.011	.37	.51	.12	15.41	19.66	20.68	5.70
369 Nonmetal prod.	40,344	.047	.23	.63	.14	20.58	22.54	30.16	8.23

(*continued*)

Table 9.5 (continued)

ISIC	World		Shares			Capital-Labor Ratios			
	Total[a]	Share	U.S.	Dev.	Oth.	World	U.S.	Dev.	Oth.
371 Iron and steel	83,022	.096	.27	.63	.10	25.84	27.91	32.56	9.82
372 Nonferrous metals	24,023	.028	.34	.54	.13	25.69	28.18	27.20	17.84
381 Metal prod.	39,886	.046	.40	.50	.10	8.40	10.86	8.38	4.46
382 Machinery	71,347	.083	.40	.51	.09	10.30	12.00	10.10	6.18
383 Electrical mach.	56,765	.083	.36	.54	.10	9.26	10.73	9.44	5.62
384 Transport equip.	80,913	.094	.36	.55	.09	12.79	14.34	13.79	6.84
385 Professional goods	11,847	.014	.53	.36	.12	8.41	10.53	6.96	6.50
390 Other	6,763	.008	.45	.42	.13	5.95	7.10	6.05	3.63
Total			.35	.53	.12	12.97	15.89	14.99	5.98

Note: Developed countries are Australia, Canada, Denmark, Finland, Germany, Israel, Japan, Netherlands, Norway, Sweden, and the United Kingdom. Other countries are Brazil, Chile, Colombia, Cyprus, Ecuador, Greece, India, Ireland, Korea, Malta, Panama, Philippines, Portugal, Singapore, Spain, and Turkey. The "World" refers to these twenty-seven countries plus the United States.

[a]In billions of dollars.

total employment and in absolute numbers. Iron and steel experienced less extreme employment declines. On the other side of the ledger, plastics had very substantial growth, as did machinery.

The last six columns of table 9.2 contain the shares of the industrial employment located in each of three regions: the United States, other developed countries, and the rest of the world. The other developed countries are the eleven countries with the highest overall capital per man, as measured in our resource data set. Generally speaking, the large changes in the distribution of employment across these regions involve shifts in favor of the "rest of the world" and, to some extent, the U.S. at the expense of the other developed (Organization for Economic Cooperation and Development) countries. There were very substantial increases in the employment share of the "rest of the world" in tobacco and in the more labor-intensive products of textiles, apparel, and footwear. The U.S. share generally fell for these industries, though textiles is an interesting exception.

The industrial distribution of world labor earnings (table 9.3) also remained remarkably constant over the fifteen-year period 1963–78. Though the U.S. share of total employment rose roughly from .25 to .29 (table 9.2), the U.S. share of total earnings fell substantially from .60 to .41. In fact, the U.S. share of total world industrial earnings has fallen in every industry, reflecting the faster growth rate of wages over the fifteen-year period in the rest of the world relative to the United States. Developed countries other than the United States account for most of the gain in the non-U.S. world earnings share despite their decline in employment shares documented in table 9.2. These data thus conform to the data in table 9.1 in the sense of revealing much faster wage growth rate in these countries relative to the United States and less-developed countries.

The data in table 9.4 indicate little change over time in the industrial composition of world output just as the previous tables reveal slight changes in employment and earnings. In food, textiles, and apparel there is more than a one percentage point drop over the fifteen-year period in the share of world output. Industries whose output share rose by over one percentage point are industrial chemicals, petroleum refining, plastics, and machinery.

The capital data summarized in table 9.5 indicate that there are great differences in the capital intensity of production in the three regions, both overall and at the industry level. These suggest that in a few industries current U.S. production techniques may be less capital-intensive than those in the other developed countries (tobacco, furniture, petroleum refining, petroleum and coal production, nonmetal manufactured products, and iron and steel). While the high rates of investment in many of the countries in the developed-country aggregate are well documented, it is surprising that the U.S. advantage in capital per worker may have been eroded in many industries as early as 1978. There are, on the other hand, twelve industries out of the twenty-eight for which measured 1978 U.S. capital intensity is more than one-third larger than that for those industries in the other developed countries. These industries are food, textiles, wood, printing, industrial chemicals, other chemicals, rubber products, plastics, metal products, machinery, professional goods, and other industries. These capital-intensity figures must be viewed with great skepticism because of the unknown quality of the available investment data and their intermittent nature, and also because of the capital depreciation method which is used. In particular, (1) investment occurring before 1963 does not contribute to the measured 1978 capital stock, (2) the depreciation rate is taken to be the same in all countries, and (3) nominal exchange rates are used to convert foreign investment expenditures into dollar units.

With these caveats in mind it is interesting to note that the measured share of output in the United States (table 9.14) exceeds the measured share of both capital and labor. One may suspect that the proper inclusion of pre-1963 investment would raise the U.S. share considerably.

The similarity in relative capital intensities by industry among the three country groups is remarkably high, particularly given the great differences in these numbers across country groups. For each region, petroleum refining, beverages, petroleum and coal products, and industrial chemicals rank among the top industries in terms of capital intensity. The correlation coefficients between industrial capital intensities are .89 for the United States and the other developed countries, .96 for the United States and the less-developed countries, and .87 for the other developed and the less-developed countries. There are also several anomalies. Tobacco has a quite high ratio of capital to labor in the United States and a quite low ratio in the less-developed country group. A second example is the apparel industry; while the U.S. capital-labor ratio is 2.6 times that of the less-developed countries, it is only .2 times greater in apparel.

Assuming that the capital-intensity figures of table 9.5 are fairly accurate measures, the data provide strong evidence against the even HO model. The similarity in relative capital intensities across industries suggests, however, that systematic measurement error (in particular, in the measurement of human capital) could account for much of the disparity between the services. Similar evidence casting doubt on the even HO model appears in table 9.6, which presents correlation coefficients between each country's capital per worker and its industry-specific capital per man, value added per man, and earnings per man. While the even HO model predicts zero correlation coefficients between these variables, seventy-five of the eighty-four coefficients exceed .5, and thirty-three exceed .8.

Table 9.6   **Correlation of Capital per Worker with Industrial**
                  Characteristics, 1978

ISIC	Capital per Man	Value Added per Man	Earnings per Man
311 Food	.65	.84	.91
313 Beverages	.80	.72	.89
314 Tobacco	.38	.49	.85
321 Textiles	.55	.85	.92
322 Apparel	.67	.79	.92
323 Leather	.44	.79	.92
324 Footwear	.65	.82	.91
331 Wood	.74	.90	.92
332 Furniture	.80	.89	.94
341 Paper	.66	.80	.89
342 Printing	.61	.85	.89
351 Industrial chemicals	.70	.69	.88
352 Other chemicals	.44	.67	.91
353 Petroleum refining	.54	.51	.66
354 Petroleum and coal production	.62	.51	.52
355 Rubber products	.69	.47	.89
356 Plastics	.66	.77	.93
361 Pottery	− .04	.83	.92
362 Glass	.57	.84	.89
369 Nonmetal products	.39	.87	.90
371 Iron and Steel	.60	.53	.84
372 Nonferrous metals	− .05	.66	.87
381 Metal products	.75	.81	.90
382 Machinery	.73	.83	.92
383 Electrical machinery	.79	.79	.90
384 Transport equipment	.63	.59	.87
385 Professional goods	.48	.82	.92
390 Other	.70	.83	.89

9.6   Regression Analysis

Table 9.7 reports industry-specific cross country results using 1978 data for four of the equations described in (3), (4), and (5). The four dependent variables are the industrial employment of capital and labor, factor payments to labor, and output. The explanatory variables are country endowments of capital, high-, medium-, and low-skilled labor (labor 1, labor 2, and labor 3, respectively), and land. Leamer (1980) describes the construction of these variables. National endowments are strikingly significant explanatory variables in each of the four regres-

Table 9.7　　Regressions on Five Endowments, 1978

	Capital		Labor		Earnings		Output	
	Coef.	t-Value	Coef.	t-Value	Coef.	t-Value	Coef.	t-Value
311 Food								
Capital	1.95	2.4	0.02	0.2	3.7	6.6	20.68	3.8
Labor 1	1,146.7	7.1	-4.4	-0.2	835	7.8	11,166.	10.4
Labor 2	-13.51	-0.5	15.9	4.7	-54	-2	-7,324.9	-1.7
Labor 3	-5.25	-5.3	-1.5	-1.3	-21	-3.1	-389.7	-5.9
Land	1.15	2.6	0.022	0.4	0.3	0.7	4.01	1.4
313 Beverages								
Capital	0.666	0.8	-0.03	-1	0.6	2.1	5.02	2.3
Labor 1	509.67	2.9	8.6	1.6	231	4.2	438.5	1
Labor 2	-23.43	-0.7	1.8	2	-19	-1.9	100.15	1.3
Labor 3	-16.32	-1.5	-1.07	-3.4	-3.5	-1.1	-62.9	-2.4
Land	-0.427	-0.9	-0.01	-0.9	-0.1	-0.7	-2.2	-2
314 Tobacco								
Capital	4.1	5.7	-0.008	-0.7	0.4	3.7	1.18	0.74
Labor 1	-1,241.	-9	2.14	0.9	-35	-1.9	-26.26	-0.1
Labor 2	108.6	4.4	0.669	1.6	5.6	1.6	116.5	2.1
Labor 3	14.7	1.7	1.52	11	-0.3	-0.3	-40.3	-2.1
Land	-0.283	-0.7	-0.011	-1.8	0	-1.2	-1.7	2
321 Textiles								
Capital	-0.101	-0.1	-0.121	-1.5	2.4	7.9	11.13	5.6
Labor 1	214.9	1.4	-27.7	-1.7	184	3.1	-867.4	-2.2
Labor 2	92	3.4	21.2	7.2	24	2.2	427.3	6.1
Labor 3	-44.98	-4.9	0.876	0.9	-14	-3.9	-87.3	-3.7
Land	-0.228	-0.6	-0.08	-1.8	-0.5	-3.2	-0.4	-0.3

322 Apparel								
Capital	−0.09	−0.6	−0.187	−4.1	0.7	2	1.237	0.9
Labor 1	171.8	5.1	55.7	6.2	636	10	2,377.4	8.6
Labor 2	2.94	0.5	8.99	5.6	−30	−2.5	−51.6	−1
Labor 3	−9.67	−4.7	−6.1	−11.	−19	−4.7	−94.5	−5.6
Land	0.036	0.4	0.006	0.3	0	0.1	0.739	1
323 Leather								
Capital	−0.075	−1.2	−0.025	−2.3	0.12	2	0.3507	1
Labor 1	23.7	2	1.3	0.6	37	3.2	3.782	0.1
Labor 2	2.59	1.2	1.51	4	0	0	35.19	3
Labor 3	−2.14	2.9	−0.54	−4.2	−1.8	−2.5	−12.36	−3
Land	0.019	0.6	5.5	0.1	−0.04	−1.3	−0.154	−0.8
324 Footwear								
Capital	−0.028	−0.4	−0.085	−3.4	−0.08	−0.6	−0.187	−0.4
Labor 1	33.15	2.5	9.2	1.8	106	−4.1	238.5	2.3
Labor 2	−0.193	−0.1	2.5	2.8	−1.3	−0.3	17.69	0.9
Labor 3	−1.6	−2	−1.37	−4.5	−4.7	−2.9	−19.05	−3
Land	0.004	0.1	0.025	1.8	−0.006	−0.1	0.19	0.7
331 Wood								
Capital	0.808	1.5	0.137	4.6	2.8	9.2	13.27	9.1
Labor 1	530.8	5.1	−28.4	−4.8	84	1.5	−32.06	−0.1
Labor 2	−38.7	−2.1	6.4	6.1	−26	−2.5	1.15	0
Labor 3	−12.5	−1.9	−1.13	−3.1	4	1.2	8.52	−0.5
Land	0.808	2.8	0.055	3.4	0.4	2.3	1.49	1.9
332 Furniture								
Capital	0.408	1.6	−0.048	−1.5	0.5	2.6	2.65	4.8
Labor 1	187.1	3.7	19.4	3	330	10	801.6	7.4
Labor 2	−14.9	−1.7	2.99	2.5	−16	−2.8	−12.95	−.7
Labor 3	−3.5	−1.1	−2.18	−5.4	−10	−4.7	−35.73	−5.4
Land	−0.016	−0.1	0.022	1.2	−0.04	−0.4	0.163	0.5

(*continued*)

Table 9.7 (continued)

	Capital		Labor		Earnings		Output	
	Coef.	t-Value	Coef.	t-Value	Coef.	t-Value	Coef.	t-Value
341 Paper								
Capital	2.95	1.7	0.012	0.5	1.3	2.9	8.26	2.9
Labor 1	1,398.7	4.1	36.5	6.1	762	8.7	3,059.3	5.5
Labor 2	-110.6	-1.8	0.873	0.8	-58	-3.6	-126.8	-1.3
Labor 3	-27.9	-1.3	-1.74	-4.8	-15	-2.7	-101.0	-3
Land	1.55	1.7	0.007	0.4	0.3	1.3	1.67	1.1
342 Printing								
Capital	0.445	1.1	-0.0004	0	2	3	8.22	2.8
Labor 1	947	11.5	73.57	7.4	987	7.7	2,619	4.5
Labor 2	-44.2	-3	0.933	0	-47	-2	-37.37	-0.4
Labor 3	-28.2	-5.6	-3.34	-5.5	-29	-3.7	-111.8	-3.2
Land	-0.06	-0.3	-0.014	-0.5	-0.2	-0.6	-0.632	-0.4
351 Ind. chem.								
Capital	5.59	4.2	-0.0299	-0.5	2.2	2.4	10.35	2.8
Labor 1	2,238.1	8.6	29.87	2.7	636	3.5	3,818.5	5.3
Labor 2	-104.4	-2.2	2.19	1.1	-58	-1.7	16.5	0.1
Labor 3	-66	-4.1	-1.72	-2.5	-7	-0.6	-176.1	-4
Land	0.086	-0.1	-0.035	-1.1	-0.8	-1.6	-1.84	-0.9
352 Other chem.								
Capital	1.25	4.8	0.036	0.6	2	2.8	5.92	3
Labor 1	571.2	11.2	30.7	2.8	519	3.7	2,335.2	6
Labor 2	-18.4	-2	-0.148	-0.1	-55	-2.2	34.47	0.5
Labor 3	-19.5	-6.3	-0.42	-0.6	-2.9	-0.3	-108.8	-4.6
Land	-0.417	-3	-0.045	-1.5	-0.4	-1.2	-0.778	-0.7

353 Petro. ref.								
Capital	2.2	3.3	−0.003	−0.5	0.22	1.6	7.7	1.6
Labor 1	869.6	6.7	6.96	7.2	190	7.1	6,570.7	6.8
Labor 2	−53.8	−2.3	−0.054	−0.3	−14	−3	−244.1	−1.4
Labor 3	−22.5	−2.8	−0.302	−5.1	−3.5	−2.1	−211.6	−3.6
Land	0.66	1.9	0.01	3.9	0.1	1.5	0.243	0.1
354 Petro./coal								
Capital	0.593	1.5	−0.009	−2.8	0	0.1	1.58	3.8
Labor 1	−64	−.8	3.22	4.9	72	11.8	−0.953	0
Labor 2	11.1	0.8	0.293	2.5	−3.1	−2.8	38.74	2.7
Labor 3	0.064	0	−0.162	−4	−2	−5.5	−12.37	−2.5
Land	−0.326	−1.5	−0.002	−1	−0.04	−2.2	−0.22	−1
355 Rubber prod.								
Capital	0.487	2.9	−0.05	−1.9	0.5	3.6	1.85	4
Labor 1	207.8	6.3	8.5	1.6	249	8.7	633.2	7
Labor 2	2.4	0.4	3.32	3.5	−11	−2.1	33.33	2
Labor 3	−11.1	−5.6	−1.4	−4.4	−8	−4.2	−40.31	−7.1
Land	0.0005	0	−0.019	−1.4	−0.1	−2.3	−0.033	−0.1
356 Plastics								
Capital	1.27	5.1	0.093	5.1	2	9.4	12.17	20.3
Labor 1	280.2	5.7	2.297	0.6	154	3.8	−696.5	−5.9
Labor 2	−3.62	−0.4	2.71	4.2	−17	−2.3	84.93	4
Labor 3	−12.8	−4.2	−1.19	−5.4	−1	−0.5	−4.4	−0.6
Land	−0.04	−0.3	−0.008	−0.8	−0.2	−2	−0.99	−3
361 Pottery								
Capital	0.084	0.5	−0.013	−0.6	3	2	0.775	2.3
Labor 1	−26.9	−0.9	−9.91	−2.2	−49	−1.9	−237.7	−3.6
Labor 2	6.9	1.2	2.74	3.4	8.4	1.8	38.9	3.3
Labor 3	−1.8	−0.9	−0.511	−1.9	−1	−0.7	−4.23	−1.1
Land	−0.01	−0.1	−0.009	−0.8	−0.1	−2.1	−0.29	−1.7

(continued)

Table 9.7 (continued)

	Capital		Labor		Earnings		Output	
	Coef.	t-Value	Coef.	t-Value	Coef.	t-Value	Coef.	t-Value
362 Glass								
Capital	0.44	1.9	−0.0129	−1.9	2.8	2	1.44	4.6
Labor 1	238.6	5.1	11.3	3.7	230	8.5	531.6	8.6
Labor 2	−10.6	−1.3	1.11	2	−13	−2.8	−4.3	−0.4
Labor 3	−7.7	−2.7	−731	−3.9	−5.5	−3.2	−23.3	−6.1
Land	−0.01	−0.1	0.003	0.4	−0.1	−1.6	−0.183	−1.1
369 Nonmetal								
Capital	3.7	1.3	0.05	1.3	2.1	11.8	11.07	12.7
Labor 1	308	0.5	−23.6	−3.1	87	2.6	−872.4	−5.1
Labor 2	−52.7	−0.5	7.24	5.3	−5.8	−0.9	171.2	5.6
Labor 3	2.2	0.1	−0.837	−1.8	−3	−1.3	−27.35	−2.6
Land	−0.25	−0.2	0.026	1.2	−0.2	0 −1.7	0.017	0
371 Iron, steel								
Capital	13.9	7	0.114	1.1	4.1	4	31.28	11.8
Labor 1	−2,253	−5.8	34.98	1.8	933	4.8	−2,828	−5.4
Labor 2	254.4	3.7	1.485	0.4	−80	−2.3	472.12	5
Labor 3	3.76	0.2	−0.31	−0.3	−12	−0.99	−38.1	−1.2
Land	−0.45	−0.4	−0.053	−0.9	−0.8	−1.4	−2.54	−1.8
372 Nonfer. met.								
Capital	2.45	8.7	0.022	1.3	1	6.5	6.898	6.7
Labor 1	29.7	0.5	13.67	4.2	291	9.8	1,428	7.1
Labor 2	7.2	0.7	0.52	0.9	−23	−4.2	−16.11	−0.4
Labor 3	−7.06	−2.1	−0.726	−3.6	−6	−3.0	−64.1	−5.2
Land	0.932	6.1	0.004	0.5	0.07	0.9	1.36	2.4

381 Metal prod.								
Capital	2.2	5.8	0.051	0.6	3.7	6.3	16.75	13.2
Labor 1	959.4	12.8	62.4	3.9	1,299	11.6	3,632	14.5
Labor 2	−42.3	−3.1	6.36	2.2	−81	−4	29.45	−0.7
Labor 3	−31.04	−6.8	−4.93	−5	−31	−4.5	−166.4	−11
Land	0.032	0.2	−0.053	−1.2	−0.7	−2.3	−0.75	−1.1
382 Machinery								
Capital	4.9	2.6	0.172	1.1	7.6	3.7	29.54	6.3
Labor 1	1,701.5	4.6	138.5	4.3	2,611	6.7	7,688	8.3
Labor 2	−82.3	−1.2	1.67	0.3	−206	−2.9	−302.1	−1.8
Labor 3	−48.98	−2.1	−5.89	−3	−43	−1.7	−236.1	−4.2
Land	−1.26	−1.2	−0.129	−1.5	−2	−1.9	−6.14	−2.4
383 Elect. mach.								
Capital	5.73	4.9	0.333	2.7	8.1	5.3	42.95	13.3
Labor 1	579.2	2.5	35.94	1.5	1,252	4.3	−1,342	−2.1
Labor 2	−12.5	−0.3	8.72	2	−120	−2.2	271	2.4
Labor 3	−26.3	−1.8	−6.43	−3.7	−70	−4	−305.9	−4.4
Land	−0.533	−0.8	−0.144	−1.8	−1.5	−2	1	0.3

(continued)

Table 9.7 (continued)

	Capital		Labor		Earnings		Output	
	Coef.	t-Value	Coef.	t-Value	Coef.	t-Value	Coef.	t-Value
384 Trans eq.								
Capital	8.9	7.4	−0.035	−0.2	4.4	3	39.81	7
Labor 1	363.5	1.5	155.05	5.4	3,240	11.7	8,880	7.9
Labor 2	26.6	6 0.6	1.39	0.3	−215	−4.2	−316.3	−1.6
Labor 3	−26.3	−1.8	−6.43	−3.7	−70	−4	−305.9	−4.4
Land	−0.533	−0.8	−0.144	−1.8	−1.5	−2	1	0.3
385 Prof. goods								
Capital	−0.15	−0.5	−0.027	−1.2	0.5	1.25	2.71	1.7
Labor 1	491.5	7.7	39.88	8.7	739	10.6	2,412	7.9
Labor 2	−8.88	−0.8	1.17	1.4	−38	−3	−91.2	−1.7
Labor 3	−19.8	−5.1	−2.218	−7.9	−19	−4.4	−76.8	−4.1
Land	0.117	0.7	−0.01	−0.8	−0.2	−1.2	−0.85	−1
390 Other								
Capital	0.008	0.1	−0.018	−0.7	0.6	2.5	3.3	2.8
Labor 1	1,620.8	5.6	8.18	1.6	204	4.4	498.9	2.2
Labor 2	6.11	1.2	3.97	4.3	−0.9	−0.1	48.42	1.2
Labor 3	−10.4	−5.8	−1.87	−6	−9.6	−3.3	−42.95	−3
Land	0.13	1.6	0.007	0.5	0	−0.03	−0.3	−0.5

sions for each of the twenty-eight industries. All but two of the 112 R^2-values equal or exceed .8; eighty-seven equal or exceed .95. The large values of R^2 may, however, simply reflect scale effects. Table 9.8 presents these R^2-values as well as R^2-values adjusted for scale effects. The adjusted R^2-values computed here are one minus the ratio of the error sum of squares of the table 9.7 regression to the error sum of squares resulting from regressions including only national capital endowment as an explanatory variable. Hence the adjusted R^2-values

Table 9.8   **R^2-Values: Regressions on Five Endowments, 1978**

	Including Scale Effects				Excluding Scale Effects			
	Out.	Lab.	Cap.	Wage	Out.	Lab.	Cap.	Wage
311 Food	.99	.97	.99	.99	.88	.89	.83	.78
313 Beverages	.95	.88	.87	.93	.24	.38	.30	.46
314 Tobacco	.88	.99	.90	.93	.26	.99	.82	.25
321 Textiles	.99	.98	.96	.99	.73	.97	.56	.63
322 Apparel	.98	.98	.96	.99	.84	.89	.71	.86
323 Leather	.95	.90	.82	.96	.36	.63	.40	.41
324 Footwear	.90	.83	.80	.90	.44	.64	.33	.54
331 Wood	.99	.98	.95	.98	.10	.68	.70	.41
332 Furniture	.99	.95	.91	.99	.80	.68	.42	.85
341 Paper	.98	.98	.93	.98	.68	.78	.56	.82
342 Printing	.98	.98	.99	.98	.57	.82	.89	.77
351 Ind. chem.	.98	.91	.99	.92	.65	.48	.81	.37
352 Other chem.	.99	.90	.99	.99	.74	.54	.87	.39
353 Petro. refin.	.98	.98	.98	.99	.74	.86	.76	.76
354 Petro., coal prod.	.98	.96	.68	.98	.31	.85	.17	.88
355 Rubber prod.	.99	.93	.99	.99	.83	.62	.76	.80
356 Plastics	.99	.99	.99	.99	.74	.54	.69	.45
361 Pottery	.86	.62	.55	.81	.50	.38	.07	.36
362 Glass	.99	.94	.96	.98	.83	.72	.60	.79
369 Nonmetal prod.	.99	.95	.56	.99	.58	.75	.01	.33
371 Iron and steel	.99	.91	.97	.97	.64	.55	.63	.52
372 Nonferrous metals	.99	.97	.99	.99	.82	.65	.68	.85
381 Metal prod.	.99	.98	.99	.99	.94	.66	.91	.87
382 Machinery	.99	.96	.97	.98	.78	.58	.51	.68
383 Electrical mach.	.99	.97	.98	.98	.47	.40	.26	.48
384 Transport equip.	.99	.96	.99	.99	.80	.68	.09	.87
385 Professional goods	.98	.99	.97	.98	.78	.87	.81	.86
390 Other	.97	.97	.98	.98	.37	.69	.79	.59

represent the fraction of the variance of the dependent variable explained by national endowments after controlling for scale effects. These scale-adjusted R^2-values are also quite large; eighty-one of these 112 R^2-values equal or exceed .5, and ninety-four exceed .4.

The coefficients in the rows labeled capital, labor 1, labor 2, labor 3, and land indicate the impact on the various dependent variables of raising these national endowments by specific amounts. As described above, the even HO model predicts that the coefficients of each of the four regressions of table 9.7 have the same sign. In addition the ratio of any two coefficients in any of the four industry regressions should equal the ratios of the corresponding coefficients of the same exogenous variables in each of the other three industry regressions. These predictions of the even HO model are sustained by many of the findings in table 9.7. Consider, for example, the twenty-eight pairs of capital and labor demand regressions. Of the 140 (28 times 5) pairs of coefficients, only forty-two pairs are opposite in sign, and only fourteen of these pairs of coefficients that violate the prediction about equal sign have corresponding pairs of t-values that are each greater than one in absolute value. In addition there are seven industries (nonferrous metals, food, beverages, tobacco, apparel, leather, and other chemicals) in which each of the pairs of capital and labor coefficients agree in sign. Note that the probability of five equal-sign coefficient pairs is 1/32 assuming an equal independent probability of each coefficient being positive or negative. In this case, the expected number of regressions with identical coefficient pairs in twenty-eight trials is .875, well below the seven actually observed.

The regressions of factor payments and output are potentially less plagued by systematic measurement error. Of the 140 pairs of coefficients in these two regressions only twenty-five exhibit opposite signs, and only thirteen of these coefficient pairs have t-values greater than one. Thirteen of the twenty-eight pairs of earnings and output regressions have pairs of coefficients each of which agree in sign.

As indicated, tests of proportionality of the four regressions may fail because of mismeasurement of both the endogenous and right-hand side variables. The nature of this mismeasure is, however, likely to be roughly constant in the two sets of results; the method of estimating industry-specific capital stocks as well as national endowments is quite similar for the two periods. As a consequence, differences in estimated coefficients across the two periods may provide more reliable evidence of changes in underlying production technologies and/or world relative commodity prices, either of which would alter the coefficients in equations (3), (4), or (5). Table 9.9 presents labor input and earnings regressions using 1963 data. A comparison of the estimated coefficients of this table with those for the corresponding 1978 regressions suggests

Table 9.9   Regressions on Five Endowments, 1963

ISIC	Labor		Earnings	
	Coef.	t-Value	Coef.	t-Value
311 Food				
Capital	− 2.7	− 3.1	1.3	0.6
Labor 1	257.1	3.3	199	1.2
Labor 2	12.6	4.6	− 5.3	− 1.1
Labor 3	− 6.6	− 5.9	− 3	− 1.2
Land	0.07	1.9	0	1.3
313 Beverages				
Capital	− 1	− 3.5	0	− 0.1
Labor 1	85.6	3.3	889	1.3
Labor 2	1.5	1.7	− 1.8	− 1
Labor 3	− 2.5	− 6.7	− 1.7	− 1.7
Land	0	.3	0	− 0.2
314 Tobacco				
Capital	− 0.2	− 1.8	0.6	1
Labor 1	21.2	2.1	− 41	− 1
Labor 2	0.4	1.1	1.7	1.4
Labor 3	0.17	1.1	0.5	0.7
Land	0	− 0.8	0	− 0.2
321 Textiles				
Capital	− 3.9	− 3.4	11.6	10.1
Labor 1	175.9	1.7	− 245	− 3.1
Labor 2	31	8.7	4	1.8
Labor	− 5.5	− 3.8	5.8	4.9
9t9b 3	0	0.1	0	− 6.2
Land				
322 Apparel				
Capital	− 1.8	− 3.3	0.5	0.7
Labor 1	290	5.9	82.1	1.5
Labor 2	− 4.6	− 2.7	− 2.4	− 1.6
Labor 3	− 5.5	− 7.8	− 1.4	− 1.7
Land	0	− 0.3	0	− 1.8
323 Leather				
Capital	− 0.3	− 1.7	0.64	3.8
Labor 1	30.4	1.9	8.1	0.7
Labor 2	0.3	0.5	− 0.5	− 1.4
Labor 3	− 0.7	− 2.9	− 0.1	− 0.8
Land	0	0.2	0	− 3.8
324 Footwear				
Capital	− 0.8	− 3	1.1	3.6
Labor 1	100	4.2	32	1.4
Labor 2	− 2.4	− 2.9	− 1.2	− 2
Labor 3	− 1.5	− 4.5	− 0.6	− 1.8
Land	0	0.1	0	− 6.5
331 Wood				
Capital	1.5	2	0.3	0.9
Labor 1	− 183	− 2.8	44.6	1.8
Labor 2	19	8.3	− 0.3	− 0.5
Labor 3	− 2	− 2.2	− 1.1	− 2.9
Land	0	0.6	0	1.2

(*continued*)

Table 9.9 (continued)

ISIC	Labor		Earnings	
	Coef.	*t*-Value	Coef.	*t*-Value
332 Furniture				
Capital	−0.5	−2.1	2.3	4.5
Labor 1	59.2	2.7	17.3	0.5
Labor 2	1.7	2.2	−1.1	−1.1
Labor 3	−1.9	−5.9	−0.5	0.8
Land	0	0.9	0	−6.6
341 Paper				
Capital	−1	−2.6	1.8	5.9
Labor 1	114.1	3.3	−10.2	−0.5
Labor 2	3.2	2.6	0	−0.1
Labor 3	−3.5	−7	0	0.3
Land	0	0.5	0	−1.9
342 Printing				
Capital	−2	−5.3	1.4	1.9
Labor 1	240	7.3	74	1.4
Labor 2	0.4	0.3	−2	−1.5
Labor 3	−4.9	−11	−1.1	−1.5
Land	0	−0.3	0	−2.5
351 Ind. chem.				
Capital	−1.5	−3.6	2.6	6.5
Labor 1	133	3.6	4	0.1
Labor 2	4	2.8	−0.3	−0.4
Labor 3	−4	−7	−0.2	−0.5
Land	0	−0.8	0	−0.7
352 Other chem.				
Capital	−0.8	−1.4	2.6	6.5
Labor 1	100	2	4.4	0.2
Labor 2	1.6	0.9	−0.4	−0.5
Labor 3	−2.3	−3.1	−0.2	−0.5
Land	0	−0.4	0	−0.3
353 Petro. ref.				
Capital	0.1	2.5	0.3	2.1
Labor 1	5.2	1.3	−12.2	−1.5
Labor 2	−0.09	−0.7	0.5	2.3
Labor 3	−0.8	0.1	0.9	0.9
Land	0	2	0	7
354 Petro./coal				
Capital	−0.3	−8.2	0.4	7.3
Labor 1	25.5	8.7	−6.2	−1.6
Labor 2	−0.3	−3.1	0.1	1.3
Labor 3	−0.5	−11	0	0.8
Land	0	0.7	0	−7.7
355 Rubber prod.				
Capital	−0.5	−2.7	1	2.5
Labor 1	46.2	3	0.8	0.03
Labor 2	2.5	4.5	0.2	0.2
Labor 3	−1.6	−7.1	0	−0.2
Land	0	−0.9	0	−2.8

Table 9.9   (continued)

ISIC	Labor		Earnings	
	Coef.	t-Value	Coef.	t-Value
356 Plastics				
Capital	0	0.02	0.9	6.6
Labor 1	−7.4	−0.4	2.2	0.2
Labor 2	4	6.6	−0.3	−1.3
Labor 3	−1	−4.2	0	−0.4
Land	0	−1.6	0	−10
361 Pottery				
Capital	−0.4	−1.5	2.1	6.3
Labor 1	15.3	0.7	−18.3	−0.8
Labor 2	2.4	3.1	0	−0.1
Labor 3	−0.9	−2.8	0.2	0.5
Land	0	−0.6	0	−11
362 Glass				
Capital	−0.3	−1.7	1.3	7
Labor 1	35.7	2	−12	0.1
Labor 2	0.8	1.3	0	0.1
Labor 3	−0.8	−3	0.2	0.8
Land	0	−0.1	0	−4.2
369 Nonmetal				
Capital	−0.9	−2.3	2.8	6.6
Labor 1	58	2	−15.5	−0.5
Labor 2	5.9	5.7	−0.2	−0.3
Labor 3	−2.5	−6	0.2	0.4
Land	0	0.2	0	−4.6
371 Iron, steel				
Capital	−2.5	−1.4	5.9	5.1
Labor 1	235	1.5	−15	−0.2
Labor 2	6.5	1.2	−1.7	−0.8
Labor 3	−5.6	−2.5	1	8
Land	0	−0.8	0	−5.7
372 Nonfer. met.				
Capital	−1	−4.3	1.3	7.7
Labor 1	281.6	3.6	−33.3	−0.6
Labor 2	0.2	0.3	0.2	0.7
Labor 3	−2	−7.4	0.3	2
Land	0	1.1	0	2.5
381 Metal prod.				
Capital	−2.7	−3	6.8	9.1
Labor 1	281.6	3.6	−33.3	−0.6
Labor 2	8	2.7	−0.6	−0.4
Labor 3	−8	−7.4	0	0.1
Land	0	−1	0	−9.4
382 Machinery				
Capital	−5	−2.2	3.7	4.8
Labor 1	520	2.5	6	0.1
Labor 2	11.7	1.9	−2.1	−1.6
Labor 3	−12	−4.7	−0.7	−0.9
Land	−0.1	−1.2	0	−4.6

(*continued*)

Table 9.9   (continued)

ISIC	Labor		Earnings	
	Coef.	t-Value	Coef.	t-Value
383 Elect. mach.				
Capital	− 3.7	− 1.9	2.7	3.9
Labor 1	365	2.1	55.3	1.2
Labor 2	11.7	1.9	− 2.1	− 1.6
Labor 3	− 12	− 4.7	− 0.7	− 0.9
Land	− 0.1	− 1.2	0	− 3.3
384 Trans. eq.				
Capital	− 9.5	− 7	5.6	4.1
Labor 1	928	8	26.8	0.3
Labor 2	− 11.7	− 2.8	− 3	− 1
Labor 3	− 14.6	− 8.7	0.5	0.3
Land	0	− 0.1	0	− 5
385 Prof. goods				
Capital	− 0.8	− 3.2	0.3	1.7
Labor 1	101	4.4	14.8	1.1
Labor 2	0.3	4	− 0.5	− 1.4
Labor 3	− 2.3	− 6.9	− 0.2	− 0.9
Land	0	− 1.8	0	2.2
390 Other				
Capital	0.1	0.2	0.2	2.2
Labor 1	3.2	0.1	10.5	1.4
Labor 2	4.7	4.3	− 0.4	− 2
Labor 3	− 1.5	− 3.4	− 0.1	− 1.2
Land	0	− 0.3	0	2.3

substantial changes in technologies or relative prices across the two periods.

While the regression findings of tables 9.7–9.9 are broadly supportive of the even HO model, tests to distinguish between the even and uneven HO model provide strong support for the uneven version. The uneven HO model suggests factor price equalization among countries with similar relative factor endowments. This implies that subgroups of countries with similar relative endowments will satisfy equations (3), (4), and (5) for a given set of coefficients. As one shifts from one subgroup to another, however, the predicted coefficients will change.

Table 9.10 reports tests of structural differences in coefficients in the factor demands, output, and earnings regressions, where the sample of countries was split between the fifteen countries with the largest and the twelve with the smallest 1978 capital-labor ratios. The table provides both F statistics testing for structural differences as well as the posterior probabilities of structural breaks. The posterior probability is calculated using a prior probability that is diffuse with respect to coefficient values and specifies a 50% chance that there is a structural

Table 9.10   *F*-Values and Posterior Probabilities in Favor of Hypothesis of Structural Difference

ISIC	F-Values			Posterior Probabilities			
	Lab.	Cap.	Wage	Out.	Lab.	Cap.	Wage
311 Food	35.62	5.01	4.76	.89	1.00	.99	.99
313 Beverages	37.11	29.02	20.37	1.00	1.00	1.00	1.00
314 Tobacco	1.47	42.41	2.59	1.00	.02	1.00	.38
321 Textiles	2.10	1.34	5.26	.84	.13	.01	.99
322 Apparel	1.64	8.74	22.14	1.00	.04	1.00	1.00
323 Leather	10.76	25.51	17.60	1.00	1.00	1.00	1.00
324 Footwear	30.71	21.44	12.65	1.00	1.00	1.00	1.00
331 Wood	1.62	2.11	1.66	.02	.03	.14	.04
332 Furniture	5.17	21.31	9.02	1.00	.99	1.00	1.00
341 Paper	2.24	2.49	3.40	.99	.19	.32	.82
342 Printing	12.76	22.71	19.43	1.00	1.00	1.00	1.00
351 Ind. chem.	27.77	5.39	23.04	1.00	1.00	1.00	1.00
352 Other chem.	25.96	8.43	24.39	1.00	1.00	1.00	1.00
353 Petro. refin.	3.39	3.56	8.89	.98	.82	.87	1.00
354 Petro., coal prod.	1.00	3.20	4.91	.28	.00	.74	.99
355 Rubber prod.	3.11	8.63	24.63	.93	.70	1.00	1.00
356 Plastics	11.60	9.52	8.27	.96	1.00	1.00	1.00
361 Pottery	30.30	15.80	24.17	1.00	1.00	1.00	1.00
362 Glass	31.65	2.20	15.18	1.00	1.00	.17	1.00
369 Nonmetal prod.	48.97	0.45	7.95	1.00	1.00	.00	1.00
371 Iron and steel	22.74	10.33	9.95	1.00	1.00	1.00	1.00
372 Nonferrous metals	17.81	4.74	8.56	1.00	1.00	.99	1.00
381 Metal prod.	32.46	4.98	14.18	1.00	1.00	.99	1.00
382 Machinery	11.27	9.34	8.45	.98	1.00	1.00	1.00
383 Electrical mach.	7.32	14.18	16.16	1.00	1.00	1.00	1.00
384 Transport equip.	19.70	2.89	9.28	1.00	1.00	.57	1.00
385 Professional goods	2.44	26.81	15.72	1.00	.29	1.00	1.00
390 Other	2.13	9.75	38.30	1.00	.15	1.00	1.00

break (see Leamer 1978, chap. 4). The posterior probability is computed as $\delta/1 - \delta$, where δ is given by

$$\delta = \left(\frac{\text{ESS}}{\text{ESS}_D + \text{ESS}_U}\right)^{T/2} T^{-K/2},$$

and T is the number of observations, K is the number of parameter restrictions, ESS is the error sum of squares in the regression including the entire sample, and ESS_D and ESS_U are the respective error sums of squares from the separate regressions for the high- and low-capital-intensity country samples. Holding the sample size and parameter restrictions constant, the posterior probability of structural differences is an increasing function of the calculated F statistic.

The critical F-value at the 95% confidence level is 2.74. Virtually all of the F statistics in table 9.10 exceed this critical value; many exceed 15. The corresponding posterior probabilities of structural differences are also very large. Over three-quarters of these 112 probabilities are essentially unity. With the exception of the wood industry, there is a strong rejection of the structural equivalence of the two samples for at least one of the four dependent variables. The equally strong rejection of structural similarities in the case of the earnings and labor input regressions indicates that these tests are probably picking up more than differential measurement error.

The fact that significant structural differences are found for virtually each industry suggests that dividing the sample based on capital per worker is a fairly good proxy for distinguishing countries lying in different cones of diversification. However, since there are five factors in our data set rather than two, there is no theoretical rationale to split the sample on the basis of capital divided by the sum of the three types of workers. In a multifactor setting there appear to be no simple rules for segmenting the sample. In the absence of a theoretical guide to splitting the sample, we also tested for structural differences across countries by including higher-order terms in the regressions. More precisely, we added the squares of the country's endowments as well as the cross products of the country's capital and each of its three types of labor. Table 9.11 presents tests of the significance of these additional variables. Like table 9.10, the F-values as well as the posterior probabilities, which the regression properly includes, are typically quite large. They also constitute a fairly strong rejection of the linearity prediction of the even HO model.

Additional regression results are presented in table 9.12 that also contravene the even HO model but that are consistent with both the uneven HO and the adjustment cost models. The dependent variable here is earnings per worker in particular industry and country. According to the even HO model, earnings per worker in an industry should be unrelated to a country's endowment of capital per worker. In addition, given domestic labor mobility, an assumption of all three models, industrial wages should be unrelated to the capital in place in the particular industry.

The t-values in the second column of table 9.12 quickly dismiss the notion of wage equalization across countries within particular industries. If there is error in measuring labor input, such error apparently goes beyond industry-specific differences in skills. While high capital-

Table 9.11   ***F*-Values and Posterior Probabilities in Favor of Second-Order Model**

	F-Values				Posterior Probabilities			
ISIC	Out.	Lab.	Cap.	Wages	Out.	Lab.	Cap.	Wages
311 Food	3.55	30.02	6.47	4.47	.90	1.00	1.00	.99
313 Beverages	11.11	23.00	21.74	24.00	1.00	1.00	1.00	1.00
314 Tobacco	24.11	3.17	193.62	11.92	1.00	.76	1.00	1.00
321 Textiles	7.23	3.39	3.79	8.13	1.00	.85	.94	1.00
322 Apparel	13.68	2.42	6.73	17.20	1.00	.24	1.00	1.00
323 Leather	9.48	5.28	15.54	15.16	1.00	1.00	1.00	1.00
324 Footwear	17.11	23.15	19.38	17.42	1.00	1.00	1.00	1.00
331 Wood	1.11	2.20	0.79	0.87	.00	.13	.00	.00
332 Furniture	6.13	8.79	19.17	8.03	1.00	1.00	1.00	1.00
341 Paper	2.19	1.27	1.01	1.03	.12	.00	.00	.00
342 Printing	24.27	29.60	24.07	32.40	1.00	1.00	1.00	1.00
351 Ind. chem.	7.58	12.86	3.18	22.53	1.00	1.00	.76	1.00
352 Other chem.	26.35	27.08	4.45	38.64	1.00	1.00	.99	1.00
353 Petro. ref.	2.74	2.19	2.03	3.55	.47	.12	.07	.90
354 Petro./coal	2.93	4.67	3.14	11.34	.61	.99	.74	1.00
355 Rubber prod.	3.02	3.59	3.59	10.75	.67	.91	.91	1.00
356 Plastics	2.46	4.79	7.09	7.44	.26	.99	1.00	1.00
361 Pottery	46.42	34.37	28.33	27.43	1.00	1.00	1.00	1.00
362 Glass	8.64	14.46	1.59	19.30	1.00	1.00	.01	1.00
369 Nonmetal	13.47	21.42	0.52	8.57	1.00	1.00	.00	1.00
371 Iron, steel	4.49	13.83	12.24	10.49	.99	1.00	1.00	1.00
372 Nonfer. met.	6.74	10.62	3.38	4.48	1.00	1.00	.85	.99
381 Metal prod.	4.33	11.64	2.44	9.67	.98	1.00	.25	1.00
382 Machinery	3.13	5.63	6.81	8.28	.74	1.00	1.00	1.00
383 Elect. mach.	4.77	5.62	10.20	16.37	.99	1.00	1.00	1.00
384 Trans. eq.	5.20	9.08	2.77	9.07	1.00	1.00	.49	1.00
385 Prof. goods	62.93	2.07	28.70	22.58	1.00	.08	1.00	1.00
390 Other	29.71	4.30	16.78	36.65	1.00	.98	1.00	1.00

labor ratio countries have higher within-industry earnings per worker, the particular amount of capital in place in the industry typically has a negligible effect on this variable. Only five of twenty-eight industry-specific capital coefficients are significant explanatory variables in table 9.12. The evidence here is broadly supportive of the domestic labor mobility assumption.

Tables 9.13 and 9.14 provide two different tests of the adjustment cost model. In contrast to the even and uneven HO models, the assumption of adjustment costs implies that lagged industry-specific inputs should be significantly correlated with current input demand. To test this we added the industry's 1963 labor input to the list of country endowments in cross-industry regressions explaining 1978 labor demand. We also included 1963 output in the regression of 1978 output on national endowments. Lagged employment enters significantly for

Table 9.12   Regressions of ISIC Earnings per Worker on National Capital per
                    Worker and ISIC Capital per Worker, 1978

	Capital per Worker		ISIC Capital per Worker		
ISIC	Coef.	t-Value	Coef.	t-Value	R^2
311 Food	.31	7.90	.06	0.80	.83
313 Beverages	.34	5.30	.06	0.90	.81
314 Tobacco	.29	8.00	.05	3.80	.83
321 Textiles	.27	9.20	.08	0.90	.85
322 Apparel	.22	8.20	.31	1.40	.86
323 Leather	.27	10.10	.12	0.90	.85
324 Footwear	.25	8.40	.07	0.40	.84
331 Wood	.32	7.60	.05	0.60	.85
332 Furniture	.32	8.40	−.04	−0.40	.87
341 Paper	.35	7.40	.02	0.40	.80
342 Printing	.31	7.00	.33	2.10	.81
351 Ind. Chem.	.39	6.00	.03	1.40	.79
352 Other Chem.	.36	9.80	.02	0.60	.83
353 Petro refin.	.34	3.30	.06	13.00	.93
354 Petro., coal prod.	−.39	−1.00	.55	11.00	.88
355 Rubber prod.	.30	0.67	.10	1.00	.81
356 Plastics	.32	9.50	.06	0.60	.88
361 Pottery	.31	11.80	−.01	−1.00	.85
362 Glass	.35	7.60	.04	0.12	.81
369 Nonmetal prod.	.37	9.40	.00	0.00	.80
371 Iron and steel	.37	6.00	.02	0.50	.71
372 Nonferrous metals	.37	9.00	.00	0.00	.76
381 Metal prod.	.36	6.30	.09	0.50	.81
382 Machinery	.32	7.20	.22	1.50	.86
383 Electrical mach.	.34	6.10	.08	0.40	.82
384 Transport equip.	.37	6.60	.04	0.30	.75
385 Professional goods	.35	10.10	.25	2.10	.87
390 Other	.26	10.10	.21	1.10	.80

virtually all of the industries, but lagged output has a generally insignificant effect on output. This suggests that labor is rather immobile compared with capital, which is opposite to the mobility assumption that we have made so far.

A second prediction of the adjustment cost model, tested in table 9.14, is that current industrial labor demand is positively related to the amount of capital installed in the industry and negatively related to the economy's wage rate. In addition, given these variables, the adjustment cost model described in section 9.4 ascribes no explanatory power to national endowments in explaining current labor demand. The results shown in Table 9.14 provide some support for the adjustment cost model; seventeen of the twenty-eight industry-specific capital coefficients have t-values in excess of 2, and twenty-seven of the twenty-eight coefficients are positive. In contrast, the country's wage rate is

Table 9.13   **Regressions on Five Endowments and 1963 Value**

ISIC	1978 Labor Equation			1978 Output Equation		
	Coef.	t^a	Prob.	Coef.	t^a	Prob.
311 Food	.87	15.5	1.00	.002	0.2	.16
313 Beverages	.71	16.8	1.00	−.001	−0.05	.16
314 Tobacco	.82	5.4	1.00	−.001	−0.04	.16
321 Textiles	.21	2.6	.90	−.001	−0.1	.16
322 Apparel	−.06	−0.3	.17	.007	0.4	.17
323 Leather	.49	4.9	1.00	−.002	−0.2	.16
324 Footwear	.67	3.1	.9	−.001	−0.1	.16
331 Wood	.5	4.2	1.00	.003	0.1	.16
332 Furniture	.96	5.1	1.00	−.01	−0.2	.16
341 Paper	.7	7.8	1.00	.01	0.4	.17
342 Printing	.78	4.8	1.00	.02	0.5	.18
351 Ind. chem.	.93	9.3	1.00	−.003	−0.1	.16
352 Other chem.	1.1	13.1	1.00	.01	0.4	.17
353 Petro. refin.	.5	3.3	.98	.02	0.4	.17
354 Petro., coal production	.18	1.3	.36	−.001	−0.03	.16
355 Rubber prod.	.69	3.1	.97	−1e-4	−0.01	.16
356 Plastics	.76	4.9	1.00	.02	0.4	.17
361 Pottery	.77	10	1.00	−.006	−0.1	.16
362 Glass	.69	6.6	1.00	.004	0.3	.17
369 Nonmetal products	.69	5.8	1.00	−.003	−0.2	.16
371 Iron and steel	.63	23.2	1.00	.006	0.2	.16
372 Nonferrous metals	.56	11.8	1.00	.03	1.7	.53
381 Metal prod.	.69	8.3	1.00	.004	0.5	.18
382 Machinery	.67	9	1.00	.05	0.6	.19
383 Electrical machinery	.62	9.9	1.00	.005	0.1	.16
384 Transport equipment	.73	13	1.00	.04	0.9	.24
385 Professional goods	.33	1.8	.58	.1	1.1	.29
390 Other	.62	3.2	.98	.05	0.7	.21

Note: Probability refers to the posterior probability that the respective 1963 variable enters the equation.

[a]t = 1963 labor variable.

insignificant in all twenty-eight regressions. Furthermore, t-values for aggregate national endowments are typically quite large. While the posterior probabilities that the industry's capital and national wage influence labor demand exceed 50% for eighteen of twenty-eight industries, the small explanatory power of national wage rates and the significance, for numerous industries, of country-wide endowments in explaining labor demand weaken the case for the adjustment cost model.

9.7 Conclusion

These preliminary tests of three alternative models of transitional international growth provide partial support for each view of the evolution of international trade and factor prices. While we intend to ex-

Table 9.14   **Labor Regressions on Five Endowments**

	ISIC Capital		National Wage		Capital		Labor 1		Labor 2	
	Coef.	t	Coef.	t	Coef.	t	Coef.	t	Coef.	t
Food	11	0.4	4,060	1.1	0	−0.7	−21	−0.6	19	4.4
Beverages	27	10	262	0.6	0	−3.7	−5.6	−2.2	3	5.6
Tobacco	4.2	1.2	385	0.9	0	−1.5	7	1.4	.5	0.8
Textiles	80.8	0.5	1,975	0.9	−.16	−2.1	−47.4	−3.8	15.4	5.2
Apparel	112.4	2.3	−1,956	−1.3	−.15	−3	384	3.3	8	4.4
Leather	158.3	10.3	40.3	0.2	0	−2.5	−2.5	−2.7	1.2	5.7
Footwear	282	5	−85.4	−0.1	0	−3.6	−.1	0	2.7	3.4
Wood	21	2	143.2	0.1	.1	3.2	−39.3	−4.7	7.2	5.3
Furniture	32	1.1	225.3	0.2	0	−1.6	13.2	1.6	4	2.4
Paper	8	2.1	1,086	1	0	−0.7	25	3.3	2.4	1.8
Printing	48	1.9	205.1	0.1	0	−0.4	28	1.1	3.2	1.3
Ind. chem.	22	2.6	1,267	0.7	−.2	−2.4	−21	−1	6	2.4
Other chem.	171	5.3	1,189	0.8	−.2	−3.4	−68	−3.5	4.1	2.4
Petro. refin.	5.4	4.1	−9	−0.1	0	−2.4	2.3	1.6	.3	1.3
Petro., coal prod.	3.1	1.6	−23	−0.2	0	−2.7	3.4	.5	.3	1.7
Rubber prod.	107	4.2	1,449	2	−.1	−4.8	−15.4	−2.3	4	4.8
Plastics	39	2.6	270.3	0.4	0	1.3	−9	−1.6	3	4
Pottery	121	6.5	−13	0	0	−1.5	−7	−2.4	2	3.1
Glass	33	2.5	−118	−0.2	0	−2.3	4	0.8	1.5	2.3
Nonmetal prod.	1	0.3	553	0.3	0	0.7	−24.3	−3	8	4.3
Iron and steel	21.3	2.1	2,940	0.8	−.2	1.3	79	2.7	−.2	−0.4
Nonferrous metals	13	1	591.2	0.9	0	−0.5	13	3.7	.8	1.1
Metal Prod.	−23	−0.5	2,621	0.8	0	0.3	82	1.7	7	1.6
Machinery	61.4	4.6	3,419	0.8	−.2	−1.2	30	0.9	9.2	1.7
Electrical mach.	75	4.3	2,852	0.8	−.2	−1	−11	−0.5	12	2.9
Transport equip.	68	2.9	7,071	1.5	−.8	−2.8	121	4.5	5	0.9
Prof. goods	27.3	1.7	−521	−0.6	0	−0.5	27	2.8	1.1	1
Other	166	8.7	763	1.5	0	−2.3	−20	−4.7	4	6.5

plore these data more closely in the future, our current assessment is that each of the three models plays an important role in determining trade, growth, and factor returns.

References

Krueger, Anne O. 1968. Factor endowments and per capita income differences among countries. *Economic Journal* 78:641–54.

Leamer, Edward E. 1978. *Specification searches.* New York: Wiley.

———. 1980. An empirical study of changing comparative advantage. Technical report to the Bureau of International Labor Affairs, U.S. Department of Labor.

———. 1984. *Sources of international comparative advantage.* Cambridge, Mass.: MIT Press.

IV The Gang of Four: The Pacific Asian Newly Industrializing Countries

10 Export-Oriented Growth and Trade Patterns of Korea

Wontack Hong

10.1 Introduction

The first objective of this paper is to analyze the relationship between the export-oriented growth strategy and the high growth performance of the Korean economy, on the one hand, and the relationship between the shifting comparative advantage and the manufactures trade pattern of Korea, on the other. The second objective is to analyze the impact of subsidized credit rationing, which was adopted as one of the major policy measures to promote export expansion in Korea, upon the pattern of manufactures trade.

The four principal policy measures that have been adopted in Korea to pursue its export-oriented growth strategy consist of vigorous administrative supports for export promotion, a preferential tax system and subsidy allocation for export activities, and reduction of the import substitution biases in the Korean economy.[1] In general, the more severe the bias of commodity market distortions for import substitution activities, the stronger should be the first three measures to promote export activities. Since there already exists a vast amount of literature dealing with the details of the export promotion policies that have been followed by the Korean government (see Hong 1979; Frank, Kim, and Westphal 1975; Krueger 1979), this study concentrates on the subsidy allocation in the form of low-interest-rate bank loans in relation to the sectoral orientation of investments and the characteristics of the leading export sectors.[2] That is, this paper concentrates on capital market distortions and their impact on production and trade patterns.

Wontack Hong is professor of international economics, Seoul University, Seoul, Korea.

Section 10.2 analyzes the relationship between the export-oriented growth strategy and the high growth performance of the Korean economy in terms of the productivity-enhancing and savings-increasing effects of export promotion. Sections 10.3 and 10.4 examine the rising real wages, capital intensity, and changing patterns of manufactures production and trade over the period 1960–80. Section 10.5 examines credit rationing at low interest rates, and the last two sections examine the impact of subsidized credit rationing on the pattern of manufactures exports.

10.2   Export-Oriented Growth Strategy and the Growth Performance of Korea

As a result of significant distortions in commodity markets that were heavily biased toward import substitution activities, the labor-abundant Korean economy had not actively taken advantage of the gains from trade à la Heckscher-Ohlin in the 1950s and maintained a semiautarkic state until the beginning of the 1960s. Even after the initiation of its export-oriented growth strategy, Korea was not a free trade economy. However, the import substitution biases caused by import restrictions, though they could not be removed entirely, have been more than offset by the vigorous government policies promoting manufactured exports.

While the absolute magnitude of Korea's exports amounted to only about $20 million a year in the 1950s, exports expanded so rapidly in the 1960s and 1970s as to reach more than $21 billion by 1981. Furthermore, the proportion of commodities with SITC code numbers 5 through 8 (which are usually classified as manufactured goods) in total exports expanded from less than 15% in 1960 to 77% in 1970 and to about 90% in 1981.[3]

Prior to the initiation of vigorous export promotion, the comparative advantage of Korea in labor-intensive manufactures remained merely a potential one. In this sense, Korea's export-oriented growth in the 1960s and thereafter may be regarded as the process of opening up the Korean economy to semifree trade. According to Corden (1971), the opening up of an economy to trade generates a "static" efficiency gain, which is very similar to a "once-and-for-all" technical progress in raising the absorption possibility frontier of a country at the given factor supplies. Furthermore, with a given constant propensity to save, the static efficiency gain itself will induce the rate of capital accumulation to rise and consequently will raise the growth rate of the economy, which might be described as the "induced growth gain" from trade. If investment goods were mostly imported, then this induced growth gain will also include the effect of reduced prices of investment goods. On the other hand, the opening up to free trade may raise the "rate" of growth of an economy not only through the static efficiency gain and the associated induced growth gain but also by directly raising the propensity to save of the country.

If instantaneous structural adjustments are assumed, as Corden (1971) does, the static efficiency gains would materialize instantaneously. However, the opening up of a semiautarkic economy to semifree trade may occur over an extended period of time. Then, the static efficiency gains from the opening up to free trade may materialize year after year over a long period of time. Furthermore, the so-called static efficiency gains may be broadly interpreted to include the Keesing-Bhagwati-Krueger (Keesing 1967; Bhagwati and Krueger, 1973) type of positive effects of intensified international competition upon the quality of domestic entrepreneurship, the realization of internal scale economies, and the exploitation of external economies that arise from the ''infant'' export production activities.

In the 1950s, the imports of Korea were mostly financed by foreign aid, much of it on very concessional terms. The freeing of the Korean economy to trade (as measured by the ratio of exports to GNP) occurred over an extended period of time covering the 1960s and 1970s. The efficiency gains from trade have materialized partly in the form of rapidly increasing real wage rates and partly in the form of rising rates of return on investment. The average rates of return on investment in the Korean manufacturing sector increased from 13% in 1954–61 to about 23% in 1972–79 (see table 10.1). Over the period 1962–81, there also have been rapid increases in domestic savings, which, together with the productivity gains from trade, maintained nearly a 10% average annual growth rate of the GNP (table 10.2).

During the inward-looking growth period of 1953–61, the export share of Korea's GNP amounted to only about 3%. With the initiation of the outward-looking growth strategy in the early 1960s, the export GNP share rose rapidly from about 8% in 1962–66 to about 38% in 1977–81. The average annual growth rate of GNP rose from about 4% in 1953–61 to about 8% in 1962–66 and to about 10% in 1967–76. Because of the political turmoil associated with the assassination of President Park and a minus 6% growth in 1980, the average annual growth rate for 1977–81 fell to about 6%. However, if 1980 is excluded, the average growth rate for 1977–81 amounts to nearly 9%.

Domestic savings increased from about 4% of GNP in 1953–61 to about 24% of GNP in 1977–81. On the other hand, the proportion of gross investment in GNP rose from about 16% in 1962–66 to about 30% in 1977–81. Consequently, although domestic savings increased rapidly, Korea had to maintain substantial foreign capital inflows throughout the period 1962–81 because of the vigorous pace of investment activities.

Table 10.1   Average Annual Rates of Return on Investment in Manufacturing: Korea

	(A) Incremental Output-Capital Ratio	(B) Share of Capital in Value Added (I-O Data)	(C) Ratio of Net Working Capital to Fixed Assets	(D) Estimated Capital Gain (per annum)	Estimated Rates of Return (E) = (A × B)	(F) = E/(1 + C)	(G) = (F − D)
1954–61	0.345	0.520	0.300	−0.01	0.18	0.14	0.13
1962–66	0.448	0.520	0.300	−0.03	0.23	0.18	0.15
1967–71	0.441	0.517	0.183	−0.01	0.23	0.20	0.19
1972–76	0.679	0.592	0.268	−0.09	0.40	0.32	0.23
1977–79	0.594	0.546	0.112	−0.06	0.32	0.29	0.23
1980	−0.033	0.602	−0.017	−0.20	−0.02	−0.02	−0.22
1981	0.343	0.602	−0.069	−0.09	0.21	0.23	0.14
1982	0.199	0.602	−0.044	0.03	0.12	0.13	0.13

Sources: Bank of Korea, *Economic Statistics Yearbook*, *National Income in Korea*, various issues; and idem, *Input-Output Tables of Korea*, various issues.

Notes: (A) Gross incremental value-added/fixed-capital ratios were computed allowing a one-year time lag between the increase in value added (at a 1975 constant factor cost) and gross fixed capital formation.

(B) Imputed wages for unpaid family workers were excluded from the share of capital in value added.

(C) In order to take account of the fact that most firms also use (net) working capital in addition to fixed capital, the rates-of-return figures were deflated by the amount of net working capital.

(D) Capital loss was approximated by the differences between the rates of increase in average prices of capital goods and those of the wholesale price index for all commodities. Estimates (G) differ from those in Hong 1979 (p. 189): 12% in 1954–61, 17% in 1962–66, 26% in 1967–71, and 27% in 1972–75. Estimates in this table use income statistics of 1975 as base year and incremental-value-added/gross-investment ratios, while the estimates of Hong 1979 use income statistics of 1970 as base year and the inverse of ICOR (incremental-capital-output ratios) in computing output attributed to gross investment. For a more detailed discussion on the estimation of the rate of return on investment see Hong 1979, 176–96.

Table 10.2   **Growth, Savings, and Trade Balance in Korea** (percentages)

A. Growth Rate (annual averages)

	GNP	Manufacturing	ICOR
1953–61	4.0	10.5	1.3
1962–66	7.9	15.1	2.3
1967–71	9.7	21.8	2.8
1972–76	9.7	19.2	2.7
1977–79	9.6	15.9	3.8
1980	−5.2	−1.1	—
1981	6.2	7.2	4.4
1982	5.6	4.0	5.8
1983	9.5	10.8	3.8
1984	7.6	14.6	—

B. Ratio to GNP

	Gross Investment	Domestic Saving	Foreign Saving	Commodity Exports	Commodity Imports
1953–61	12.4	4.4	8.0	1.1	10.6
1962–66	16.3	7.7	8.6	4.4	15.3
1967–71	25.7	15.6	10.1	9.5	22.8
1972–76	27.0	20.3	6.7	23.7	31.0
1977–79	31.5	27.9	3.6	25.9	30.0
1980	31.3	21.9	9.4	29.8	36.9
1981	29.1	21.4	7.7	32.7	37.0
1982	27.0	22.5	4.5	31.5	33.9
1983	27.6	24.7	2.9	32.9	33.8
1984	29.9	27.6	2.3	34.4	34.4

Source: Bank of Korea, *National Income Accounts: 1984.*

During 1962–71, government savings amounted to about 5.8% of GNP on average, of which about 30% was generated by tariff revenue. Government savings amounted to 4.0% and 6.1% of GNP during 1972–76 and 1977–81, respectively, and the proportion contributed by tariff revenue expanded from 48% in 1972–76 to 95% in 1977–81.

During 1953–81, around 20% of total investment was allocated to the manufacturing sector, around 10% to the primary sectors, and the rest to the service and social overhead sectors. Throughout the period, the manufacturing sector grew approximately twice as rapidly as the whole economy. During 1963–79, the total number of employed persons increased by about 3.5% per annum, while the number of workers employed in manufacturing increased by about 10% per annum (table 10.3). As a result, the proportion of manufacturing output in GNP rose from about 9% in 1953 to about 14% in 1960, to about 21% in 1970, and to about 30% by 1981. The manufacturing sector absorbed only

Table 10.3   Rising Real Wages and Capital Intensity of Korean Manufacturing

	1960	1968	1980
Capital stock (in millions won)	$ 24,131	$332,790	$10,727,405
Employees' remuneration (in millions won)	$ 6,765	$ 77,058	$ 3,471,631
Number of workers	275,254	748,307	2,014,751
Per worker capital stock			
In millions current won	$ 0.088	$ 0.445	$ 5.324
In millions of 1980 dollars won[a]	$ 1.956	$ 2.853	$ 5.324
In thousands of 1980 dollars[b] (k)	$ 3.190	$ 4.650	$ 8.680
Wage rate			
In millions current won	$ 0.025	$ 0.103	$ 1.723
In millions of 1980 dollars won[c]	$ 0.373	$ 0.510	$ 1.723
In thousands of 1980 dollars[b] (w)	$ 0.608	$ 0.831	$ 2.809
Labor share in value added	31%	26%	29%
Elasticity of substitution[d]			
Av. annual $(dk/k)/(dw/w)$: 1960–80	(5.0%)/(8.0%) = 0.63		
Av. annual $(dk/k)/(dw/w)$: 1968–80	(5.5%)/(10.5%) = 0.52		

Sources: Economic Planning Board, *Report on Mining and Manufacturing Census;* and Bank of Korea, *Economic Statistics Yearbook.*

[a]Applying the GNP deflator for gross fixed capital formation in manufacturing. (Land is excluded from fixed assets.)

[b]Applying the exchange rate of 613.4 won per dollar.

[c]Applying the GNP deflator for value added in manufacturing.

[d]Point elasticities of capital-labor substitution estimated by assuming constant rental price for capital service over the period covered. If the rental price for capital service had actually been falling over the periods covered, the true point elasticities should be smaller than these estimates.

about 8% of total employment in 1963, but it absorbed about 13% of total workers in 1970 and 20% of the total by 1981.

The opening up of the Korean economy to trade was associated with rapid increases in the aggregate savings propensity, which resulted in continuous shifts of Korea's comparative advantage in international trade. Such a rise in the savings propensity may be explained by the high marginal propensity to save and rapid increases in per capita income, by the highly profitable export activities motivating larger savings (especially by entrepreneurs), or by a change in the basic time preference structure itself, making people more patient. The opening up to trade is equivalent to the discovery of new efficient production techniques and, hence, will raise the savings propensity.[4] The opening up to trade might also change thrift, foresight, self-control, and benevolence of individuals as well as the government so as to raise the aggregate savings.[5] Furthermore, the gains from trade might also stabilize political conditions and the purchasing power of money, reducing the overall risk elements in a society and raising the propensity to save (see Fischer 1961, 500–506).

10.3   Rising Real Wages and Capital Intensity of Korean Manufacturing

The very high rates of capital formation in Korea have not only generated high rates of growth in GNP and manufactured outputs but also resulted in rapid increases in real wage rates and significant rises in ICOR (incremental-capital-output ratios). During 1967–81, the average real wage rate in the manufacturing sector increased by about 7% per annum if deflated by the GNP deflator for the whole industry, and increased by about 10% if deflated by the consumer price index.[6] The ICOR rose from 1.3 in 1953–61 to 2.3 in 1962–66, to 2.75 in 1967– 76, and then jumped to 4.3 in 1977–81 (excluding 1980).

If we apply the GNP deflator for value added in manufacturing, the average real wage rate for workers employed in the manufacturing sector increased by only about 37% during 1960–68 (from $608 to $831), but it increased about 3.4 times during 1968–80 (from $831 to $2,809), implying an average annual growth rate of about 10.5%. On the other hand, the fixed capital stock per worker in manufacturing (excluding land) increased by about 87% during 1968–80, implying an average annual growth rate of about 5.5%. If we assume a constant rental price for capital service throughout the period 1968–80, the estimated point elasticity of capital-labor substitution becomes 0.52 for the period 1968– 80. However, it may be more reasonable to assume somewhat falling prices for capital service in Korea during this period, implying the likely upward biases in the above estimate of point elasticity.[7]

The share of wages in value added steadily fell from about 37% in 1958 to 31% in 1960 and to 23% in 1973. However, the labor share in value added started to increase steadily thereafter, reaching about 29% in 1980. These shifts in labor share are consistent with the estimated point elasticity of capital-labor substitution. In any case, one can conclude that there were rapid increases in real wage rates and the capital intensity of the manufacturing sector in Korea during the late 1960s and throughout the 1970s.

10.4   Changing Pattern of Manufactures Production and Trade

In 1960 less than 14% of Korea's GNP was contributed by the manufacturing sector, and furthermore, less than 3% of total manufactured products were exported. The only manufacturing sector which had a sizable export-output ratio (e) was fish processing (with $e = 0.27$).[8] The exports of various textile products (including wearing apparel) amounted to less than 3% of their ouputs. By 1970, however, more than 20% of Korea's GNP was contributed by the manufacturing sector, and about 13% of total manufactured products were exported. The following six sectors had been firmly established as Korea's major export sectors: footwear (with $e = 0.28$), wearing apparel (with $e = 0.35$), miscellaneous manufactures (with $e = 0.54$), fish products (with $e = 0.51$), veneer and plywood (with $e = 0.37$), and electronic products (with $e = 0.44$).[9] The export-output ratios of textile yarn and textile fabric also increased to 18% and 15% respectively by 1970.

In 1980 nearly 30% of Korea's GNP was contributed by the manufacturing sector, and about 19% of total manufactured products were exported. Four labor-intensive manufacturing sectors have been added to the list of Korea's major manufacturing export sectors: textile fabrics (with $e = 0.35$), metal products (with $e = 0.46$), precision instruments, consisting mostly of watches and optical instruments (with $e = 0.42$), and leather products (with $e = 0.46$). Textile yarns (with $e = 0.18$), electrical machinery (with $e = 0.16$), and nonmetallic mineral products excluding cement (with $e = 0.14$) also became important export sectors.

Throughout the period 1960–80, the electronic products, metal products, precision instruments, electrical machinery, and leather products sectors were heavily import dependent. However, electronic products became a major export sector by the end of the 1960s and each of the others by the end of the 1970s. All these sectors are classified as export-import sectors in the sense that they exported significant proportions of their outputs in the 1970s while also being significantly dependent on imports.

The total number of workers employed in manufacturing establishments with five or more employees increased 2.7 times during 1960–68 and also during 1968–80. Among the labor-intensive manufactured export sectors, electronics and communications equipment manufacturing contributed most of the labor absorption: from 0.3% of total manufacturing employment in 1960 to 1.2% in 1968 and to 7.8% in 1980. The proportion of labor employed in the clothing and footwear sectors (including leather products) also expanded from about 10% of total manufacturing employment in 1968 to 16% of it by 1980. Surprisingly, the proportion of labor employed in textiles declined steadily from about 30% in 1960 to about 25% in 1968 and to less than 20% in 1980. The proportion of labor employed in the wood and furniture sector also declined, from about 5.8% in 1968 to about 3.3% in 1980. However, the proportion of workers employed in labor-intensive export sectors, textiles, electronic products, and labor-intensive export-import sectors as a whole steadily increased from about 59% of total manufacturing employment in 1960 to about 61% of it in 1968 and to 65% in 1980.

The major labor-intensive manufactured export sectors of Korea may be divided into three different groups. The first group represents those which were the leading export sectors in the late 1960s and early 1970s but whose export growth rates became much lower in the late

1970s. This group consists of wearing apparel, miscellaneous manu-factures (mostly wigs), fish products, textile fabrics (including miscel-laneous textile products), natural fiber yarns, and veneer and plywood. The second group represents those which revealed high rates of growth in exports only at the end of the 1970s. This group consists of footwear, watches and optical instruments, radios and televisions (including phonographs and tape recorders), metal products, and nonmetallic min-eral products (excluding cement). The third group represents those which maintained more or less the same rates of growth throughout the 1960s and 1970s. This group consists of electronic products, wood products, and leather products. Apparently, the rise and fall of various labor-intensive manufactured exports over time do not occur strictly in relation to the order of capital intensity. That is, the magnitude of the adverse impact inflicted by the tripling of the real wage rate during 1968–80 does not seem to have been proportional to the capital intensity of the sectors.

In the 1970s there occurred a significant shift in the composition of Korea's commodity exports: the exports of capital-intensive manufac-tures increased significantly. Sugar refining (with $e = 0.29$), cement (with $e = 0.17$), fertilizer (with $e = 0.29$), and rubber products (with $e = 0.53$), (which are presented as capital-intensive export sectors in table 10.4) became important export sectors by 1980. Furthermore, synthetic resin, fiber and plastic materials, transport equipment, steel products, and iron and steel, which were heavily import-dependent sectors in the 1960s, became capital-intensive export-import sectors in the 1970s. However, their employment effect seems to have been very limited. The proportion of labor employed in capital-intensive export sectors and capital-intensive export-import sectors as a whole in-creased from about 7% of total manufacturing employment in 1960 to about 12% in 1968, but it was still 12% in 1980.

The major capital-intensive manufactured exports of Korea may be divided into two groups on the basis of employment effect. The first group represents extremely capital-intensive manufactures which ex-perienced a declining share of labor absorption in spite of increasing exports. This group consists of synthetic resin, fiber and plastic ma-terials, fertilizers, sugar refining, iron and steel, cement, and petroleum refining. The second group represents those sectors with relatively lower capital intensity which consequently had significant positive em-ployment effects. This group consists of machinery, ships, automobiles and parts, rubber tires and tubes, steel products, and nonferrous metal products.

The increasing exports of such capital-intensive manufactured goods may be explained mostly in terms of the rising relative labor costs and rapid capital accumulation in Korea during 1960–80. However, gov-

Table 10.4   Sectoral Capital Intensity and Trade Patterns: Korean Manufacturing

Sector	Capital Intensity (thousands of 1980 $)[a]			Export-Output Ratio (e) (%)			Import-Domestic Demand Ratio (m) (%)			Labor Allocation (%)		
	1960	1968	1980	1960	1970	1980	1960	1970	1980	1960	1970	1980
All primary sectors	—	—	—	3.1	3.7	5.6	12.8	17.2	42.1	—	—	—
All manufacturing sectors	4.0	5.8	10.4	2.5	13.0	19.1	18.2	23.2	20.1	100	100	100
L-intensive export[b]	2.4	2.8	4.4	5.2	35.6	43.1	10.2	4.4	5.7	23.0	27.0	28.0
K-intensive export[c]	12.8	50.1	32.3	0.6	5.4	30.2	61.5	2.8	5.1	1.7	2.7	2.1
Textile yarns and fabrics[d]	3.0	4.7	7.4	2.7	16.6	24.8	1.5	15.7	8.6	29.7	25.2	19.5
Electronic products[e]	2.0	3.6	4.5	2.7	44.2	43.8	57.4	52.3	39.6	0.3	1.2	7.8
L-intensive Export-import[f]	3.0	4.1	7.7	3.3	7.2	34.5	28.7	43.9	32.7	5.9	7.2	9.8
K-intensive Export-import[g]	4.7	6.8	28.2	4.3	3.6	20.2	26.1	39.2	23.8	5.4	9.6	9.9
N-intensive import[h]	3.4	10.9	20.8	1.8	7.4	3.6	61.0	15.4	16.6	3.5	3.3	3.7
Chemicals	9.7	6.0	16.7	2.8	1.0	7.0	38.9	39.5	30.0	4.7	4.0	5.0
Machinery	3.7	4.1	11.4	2.7	3.3	10.7	39.6	78.3	61.7	3.5	3.2	4.0
Other manufacturing[i]	5.0	4.7	11.4	0.9	3.4	2.3	3.3	6.3	9.7	22.3	16.6	10.2

Sources: Bank of Korea, *Input-Output Tables of Korea*; and Economic Planning Board, *Report on Mining and Manufacturing Census*.

[a]1980 prices were obtained by applying the GNP deflator for gross fixed capital formation in manufacturing and the 1980 exchange rate of 613.4 won per dollar. Capital stock includes land.

[b]Footwear, wearing apparel, miscellaneous manufactures, fish products, wood and furniture, and nonmetallic mineral products excluding cement.

[c]Rubber products, fertilizer, cement, and refined sugar.

[d]Includes miscellaneous textile products.

[e]Electronic products and communication equipment, including radios and televisions.

[f]Metal products, precision instruments, electrical machinery (excluding electronic products and communication equipment), and leather products.

[g]Synthetic materials (resins, fibers, and plastic material), transport equipment, steel products, and iron and steel.

[h]Nonferrous metal products, pulp and paper products, and petroleum products.

[i]Food products (excluding fish products and sugar), printing, and coal products.

ernment subsidy of capital in Korea has also played a role in this trend, especially in the case of increasing exports of highly capital-intensive goods.

In the 1960s the export-oriented growth of Korea was possible only through the expansion of manufactured exports to advanced countries such as the United States, Japan, and the European Community. Korea's exports to the newly affluent OPEC countries have recently increased greatly. Manufactured exports to non-OPEC developing countries steadily increased in the 1970s.[10] Since, in general, developing-country import restrictions against intermediate and investment goods are not as severe as those against consumer goods, and since Korea has been transforming its output and export pattern toward such products, it is expected that in the future export expansion to developing countries may become as important as that to advanced countries. Korea has imported almost all its intermediate and investment goods from advanced countries, especially from Japan, the United States, and the European Community. The resource-rich advanced countries such as Canada, Australia, and the United States have supplied most of the non-oil primary products to Korea. Also, Korea's import dependency on non-OPEC developing countries has continuously increased, mainly in primary products but also in some manufactures as well.[11]

10.5   Credit Rationing at Low Real Interest Rates

In addition to the full-fledged administrative support for export expansion, two major policy instruments were applied by the Korean government in carrying out the export-oriented growth strategy: the preferential tax system and the allocation of subsidies. The most important form of government subsidy allocation was, first, to maintain extremely low real interest rates on bank loans by applying fixed nominal interest rates along with high rates of inflation through expansionary monetary policy and, second, to ration these low real-interest-rate loans to preferred sectors for export expansion.

Total loans provided through the deposit money banks (DMB), Korea Development Bank (KDB), and Korea Export-Import Bank (EXIMB) have steadily increased from a magnitude equivalent to about 15% of GNP in 1962–66 to about 32% in 1967–71, to about 39% in 1972–76, and to about 46% of GNP in 1977–81.[12]

During 1962–66, EXIMB did not exist, but KDB alone provided more than one-third of total loans in the form of discretionary policy loans. During 1967–76 KDB and EXIMB provided only about 15% of total loans, but as a result of the rapidly expanding EXIMB activities since the late 1970s, their share in total loans expanded to about 18% during 1977–81. Discretionary policy loans provided through DMB (in the form of the machine industry promotion fund, the term loan fund, the medium industry fund, the export industry equipment fund, and the foreign currency loan fund, etc.) increased from about 10% of total loans in 1962–66 to about 20% in 1967–81. Therefore, the magnitude of loans formally designated as discretionary policy loans amounted to around 36% of total loans during 1967–81.

Short-term export credits and loans for agriculture, fisheries, and housing may be classified as nondiscretionary policy loans. These loans composed about 17% of total loans during 1967–81. Thus, formal policy loans slightly exceeded half of total loans (provided through DMB, KDB, and EXIMB) during 1967–81. However, discounted commercial bills and loans based on general banking funds were also rationed at the discretion of the government in Korea, and hence, these loans should be regarded as nonpolicy but discretionary loans. The number of such loans declined from about 30% of total loans in 1967–71 to about 20% in 1977–81.

Overdraft, loans based on installment savings deposits, personal loans, remunerations (Citizens National Bank loans based on installment savings deposits), and loans by branches of foreign banks may be regarded as nonpolicy loans free of government discretion, though they may still have been subject to favoritism and political influence. These nondiscretionary nonpolicy DMB loans amounted to around 22% of total loans during 1972–81.[13]

The real interest rate (i.e., difference between nominal interest rate and the rate of change in GNP deflator) on one-year time deposits amounted to about -10.7% per annum on the average in 1954–64, 10.0% per annum during the high-interest-rate era of 1965–71, and -3.4% per annum in 1972–81. The real interest rate applied to discounts of commercial bills amounted to -7.3% per annum on the average in 1954–64, 9.5% per annum in 1965–71, and -1.7% per annum in 1972–81.[14] If we estimate the real interest rates on all loans provided by all banking institutions in Korea by using the real interest rates applied to discounts of commercial bills (since the real rate of return on capital in manufacturing amounted to around 23% per annum on the average during 1972–79; as shown in table 10.1), the rate of the subsidy element associated with rationed low-interest loans in Korea seems to have amounted to about 24% per annum on the average during 1972–81.[15]

The weighted-average real interest rate on foreign loans amounted to 2.1% per annum during 1967–71 and -7.4% per annum during 1972–76 on the average (Hong 1979, 201). During 1977–79 Korea maintained a fixed exchange rate (at 484 won per dollar) in spite of the fact that domestic prices were rising at about 19% per annum, while the (weighted average) price level of its major trade partners (i.e., the United States and Japan) was rising at about 6% per annum (applying equal weights to both countries). Since the Euro-dollar interest rates amounted to about 11% per annum during 1977–79 on average, the real interest rates on Korea's foreign borrowing could not have exceeded -2% during 1977–79.[16] Therefore, there seems to have been as much of a subsidy element associated with foreign borrowing as there was with domestic bank loans. Naturally, the allocation of foreign borrowing has also been strictly controlled by the government.

The total volume of domestic loans provided through DMB, KDB, and EXIMB amounted to about 39% of GNP in 1972–76 and about 46% of GNP in 1977–81. On the other hand, the estimated average real rates of return on investment in the Korean manufacturing sector amounted to around 22% in the 1970s. If we take the difference between the real rate of return on investment and the real interest rate as the subsidy rate associated with domestic bank loan allocations (which exceeded 24% per annum), the annual provision of credit subsidies in Korea amounted to at least 10% of GNP each year on average in the 1970s.[17] At 10% of GNP, the domestic credit subsidy must be judged large enough to significantly affect the pattern of Korea's output and trade. Furthermore, there were also low-interest-rate foreign loans amounting to about 6% of GNP each year on average in the 1970s that were allocated directly to entrepreneurs. Indeed, the rationing of domestic and foreign loans provided the largest source of rents in Korea, helping to worsen the distribution of income in the 1970s (see Hong 1981).

We have so far ignored the nonmonetary financial markets. In Korea, a business group which gets preferential treatment in bank loan rationing either directly controls (owns) a significant portion of a nonmonetary financial institution or gets preferential treatment from them. The political and economic significance of getting preferential treatment in credit rationing in the highly regulated Korean economy is the vastly reduced possibility of bankruptcy in the eyes of lenders not only in nonmonetary financial markets but also in unorganized money markets. Hence, the size of bank loans rationed to a firm itself leads to substantial additional benefits from nonbank financial markets.

10.6 Manufacturing Output and Export with Factor Market Distortions

According to Krueger (1977), factor market distortions in the form of lower rental-wage rates applied to capital-intensive manufacturing sectors would result in production (and exports) of excessively capital-intensive manufactures. Furthermore, the lower rental-wage rates that would result for labor-intensive manufacturing sectors would make very labor-intensive sectors become profitable with excessively labor-intensive techniques of production. As a result, we would expect to observe more significant disparities in capital intensities among manufacturing sectors (as well as manufactured exports) of a country with substantial factor market distortions than in those of a country with moderate distortions in factor markets. If the government allocates subsidized loans to each manufacturing sector in proportion to sectoral value added, then the rates of subsidy (in the form of low rental price for capital service) provided per unit of each manufacturing activity will be identical. However, if the more capital-intensive sectors are allocated a larger proportion of subsidized credits per value added, then the rates of subsidy provided for these production activities will be higher than those for labor-intensive production activities. For instance, subsidized credits allocated in proportion to sectoral capital use rather than in proportion to sectoral value added will raise the relative rates of subsidies for capital-intensive sectors. This will be conducive to both output expansion and factor substitution toward more capital-intensive techniques of production in capital-intensive sectors.

In order to see what manufacturing sectors in Korea received more than proportionate amounts of subsidized loans per unit of value added, the ratio of year-end balances of outstanding (domestic and foreign) bank loans to value added of each manufacturing sector was computed (table 10.5). The "L-intensive I" group of labor-intensive manufacturing export sectors, consisting of clothing and footwear (including leather products), food products, textiles, and metal products, received subsidized bank loans much below the manufacturing average throughout the 1970s. The "L-intensive II" group of labor-intensive manufacturing sectors, consisting of miscellaneous manufactures (including precision instruments, telecommunications equipment, furniture, pottery, clay, and other miscellaneous nonmetallic mineral products) and wood products, received an above-average rate of subsidized loan allocations in the 1970s. In 1968 the shares of both groups in total manufacturing value added and exports were very similar (table 10.6). However, while the share of the L-intensive I group in manufacturing value added and exports expanded substantially during 1968–80, the share of the L-intensive II group declined significantly. In spite of the very unfavorable loan allocation, the L-intensive I group was the leading labor-intensive manufacturing export sector of Korea in the 1970s.[18]

In 1968 none of the capital-intensive manufacturing sectors contributed significantly to exports. In a relative sense, the K-intensive III group (consisting of cement, fertilizers, and petroleum products) contributed most to the exports in 1968. However, the K-intensive I group, consisting of basic chemicals (including refined sugar and synthetic

Table 10.5   **Sectoral Loan/Value-Added Ratios for Korean Manufacturing**

	Ratio of Year-end Domestic Loan Balance to Value Added			Ratio of Year-end Total Loan Balance to Value Added		
	1971	1976	1981	1971	1976	1981
L-intensive I	1.4	0.8	0.8	1.7	0.9	0.8
L-intensive II	2.2	1.6	1.2	3.1	2.0	1.6
K-intensive I	2.1	1.1	1.4	3.0	1.7	1.7
K-intensive II	2.4	1.5	1.4	4.7	3.2	2.7
K-intensive III	0.9	0.6	1.2	4.3	1.5	2.0
All manufacturing	1.5	1.1	1.1	2.5	1.6	1.5

Source: Table 10.A.5.
Note: "L-Intensive I" consists of clothing and footwear (including leather products), food products (excluding sugar refining), textiles, and metal products; "L-Intensive II" includes miscellaneous manufactures (including precision instruments), wood products, telecommunications equipment, and nonmetallic mineral products (excluding cement); "K-Intensive I" consists of basic industrial chemicals (including synthetic materials and sugar refining), electrical and nonelectrical machinery and equipment, and transport equipment; "K-Intensive II" consists of steel products, nonferrous metal products, and iron and steel; "K-Intensive III" consists of cement, fertilizers, and petroleum products.

fiber, resin, and plastic materials), electrical and nonelectrical machinery, and transport equipment), and the K-intensive II group, consisting of steel products, iron and steel, and nonferrous metal products, contributed most to the expansion of capital-intensive manufactured exports in the 1970s. Indeed, these two groups constituted the leading capital-intensive manufacturing sectors of Korea in the 1970s. On the other hand, the share of the K-intensive III group in total manufactured exports increased only slightly, while its shares in outputs and employment were significantly reduced. All the capital-intensive manufacturing sectors received very large amounts of subsidized loan allocations in the 1970s, but the K-intensive II group (especially the iron and steel sector) received the largest amount of subsidized loan allocations per value added and achieved the most rapid expansion in shares of exports and outputs during 1968–80.

Assuming a constant rental price for capital service, we estimated the sectoral point elasticities of capital-labor substitution (i.e., the ratio of average annual percentage change in capital intensity to average annual percentage change in real wages) during 1968–80 in each manufacturing sector (see also table 10.A.2). A high estimated elasticity may imply both the high substitutability between capital and labor in the sector and the decrease in actual rental price for capital service, contrary to our assumption of constant rental price during 1968–80. Because of aggregation, however, the capital-labor substitution within

Table 10.6   Shifts in the Pattern of Specialization and Capital Intensity of Korean Manufacturing

	Share in Total Manufactured Exports (%)		Composition of Value Added (%)		Sectoral Labor Allocation (%)		Import-Domestic Demand Ratio (%)	
	1968	1980	1968	1980	1968	1980	1968	1980
L-intensive I	43.0	51.3	20.9	31.7	34.8	46.0	8.4	14.3
L-intensive II	46.1	11.2	19.3	14.8	29.1	21.8	13.8	8.4
K-intensive I	2.7	14.1	14.1	16.6	12.6	14.6	42.5	39.7
K-intensive II	1.5	11.0	3.8	7.8	3.9	4.5	26.1	22.8
K-intensive III	3.4	4.4	11.5	7.3	2.1	1.1.1	16.1	10.5
All manufacturing	100	100	100	100	100	100	17.0	19.7

	Export-Output Ratio (%)		Capital Intensity (thousands of 1980 $)		Wage Rate (thousands of 1980 $)		Point Elasticity of Substitution 1968–80
	1968	1980	1968	1980	1968	1980	
L-intensive I	15.6	26.8	3.00	4.91	0.65	2.39	0.39
L-intensive II	24.1	22.5	4.79	7.61	0.69	2.39	0.36
K-intensive I	2.0	15.8	6.84	17.87	0.97	3.59	0.74
K-intensive II	3.4	21.0	5.33	40.08	0.99	3.85	1.54
K-intensive III	5.4	6.7	68.65	64.60	1.90	5.71	-0.05
All manufacturing	10.8	19.2	5.79	10.37	0.83	2.81	0.48

Sources: Bank of Korea, *Input-Output Tables of Korea*; and Economic Planning Board, *Report of Mining and Manufacturing Census.*

Note: 1980 prices were obtained by applying the GNP deflators for gross fixed capital formation and value added in manufacturing and the exchange rate of 613.4 won per dollar. Fixed capital includes land.

a sector might well imply mainly the introduction of new capital-intensive commodities rather than factor substitutions in existing lines of production in each sector.

The K-intensive II group of sectors revealed the highest point elasticity of substitution.[19] The share of this group in total manufacturing value added more than doubled, its share in total manufactured exports increased over sevenfold, and its average export-output ratio increased over sixfold during 1968–80. The K-intensive I group of sectors revealed the second-highest point elasticity of substitution. The share of this group in total manufacturing value added increased only moderately, but its export-output ratio increased nearly eightfold, and its share in total manufactured exports increased more than fivefold during 1968–80. Therefore, in terms of the rate of increase in absolute amounts of exports as well as export-output ratios, these two groups represent the leading export sectors of Korea in the 1970s. The high value of estimated elasticities for these groups may mostly reflect the lower rental price for capital service in these sectors resulting from the favorable credit rationing.

On the other hand, the K-intensive III group of sectors revealed the lowest elasticity, a substantial decline of shares in total manufacturing value added, and a slight increase in export-output ratio. The low estimated value of elasticity may reflect the facts that the capital intensity of this group was extremely high already by 1968, and hence there existed only a limited possibility for further factor substitutions, and also the sectors in this group were fairly narrowly defined and consequently there was not much room for the introduction of new commodities in any significant scale within these sectors.[20]

As can be observed in table 10.A.2, the real wage rates have also been rising in every labor-intensive manufacturing sector, and the response of each labor-intensive sector (in terms of capital intensity) to rising labor costs seems to have been more or less uniform, and the estimated elasticities were quite close to the manufacturing average as a whole. On the other hand, there have been wide disparities in the rates of increase in capital intensities of capital-intensive sectors.[21]

10.7 Intensity of Capital Market Distortions and the Trade Pattern

Among the four Asian advanced developing countries, Korea and Hong Kong seem to reflect opposite extremes in capital-market distortions and credit rationing in favor of capital-intensive manufacturing sectors. Taiwan and Singapore seem to fall somewhere between Korea and Hong Kong. Hence, one may expect Korea to have exported the largest amount of capital-intensive manufactures among the four countries, and Hong Kong the smallest. In 1980 commodity exports of these countries amounted to $13–$20 billion. Indeed, the capital-intensive goods (excluding petroleum products) exported by Korea amounted to about $4.1 billion, those by Taiwan about $3.4 billion, those by Singapore about $1.5 billion, and those by Hong Kong only about $1.4 billion.[22] Including petroleum products, the capital-intensive manufactures exported by Singapore amounted to about $6.9 billion, those by Korea $4.1 billion, those by Taiwan $3.7 billion, and those by Hong Kong $1.4 billion. The Singapore economy in the 1970s, which had the highest per capita income among the four, may be characterized by a semiinfinite supply of capital (owing to the Singapore dollar market and relatively high domestic savings) and low rates of growth in labor supply.[23] The Hong Kong economy may also be characterized by the relatively abundant supply of capital (owing to the Hong Kong dollar market) but has maintained relatively high rates of growth in labor supply (owing to its proximity to mainland China). Taiwan has maintained a more rapid growth of domestic capital supply than Korea because of higher domestic savings. Korea, which had the lowest per capita income and the lowest propensity to save among the four, exported the largest amount of capital-intensive manufactures, excluding petroleum products. If petroleum products are included, then Korea exported the second-largest amount of capital-intensive manufactures. This might well be explained by the significant capital market distortions in favor of capital-intensive sectors in Korea during the 1970s.

Compared with Korea, Taiwan has maintained fairly high rates of real interest on bank deposits and loans and hence seems to have suffered less from the adverse effects of arbitrary credit rationing. In Korea, the real interest rate on one-year time deposits amounted to 10.0% per annum on average during the high-interest-rate era of 1965–71. However, it amounted to − 10.7% per annum on average in 1954–64 and − 4.0% per annum in 1972–79, while in Taiwan it amounted to about 10.7% per annum in 1953–60, 6.4% in 1961–70, and 0.3% in 1971–79. In Korea, the real rate of interest applied to the discount of nonpreferential commercial bills amounted to about 9.5% per annum on average during 1965–71, but it amounted to only about − 7.3% per annum in 1954–64 and − 2.6% in 1972–79, while in Taiwan it amounted to about 10.4% per annum on average in 1953–60, 9.4% in 1961–70, and 2.3% in 1971–79. That is, except for the so-called high-interest-rate period of 1965–71 in Korea, real rates of interest on bank deposits and loans in Taiwan were on average higher than those in Korea by 4% or more.[24]

If we compare the sectoral export performance of Korea and Taiwan in 1981 (see table 10.7). Taiwan's exports of such labor-intensive manufactures as wood and furniture products and miscellaneous manufactures were about 2.4 times larger than those of Korea (i.e., $5.5 billion

Table 10.7   **Sectoral Export Performance in 1981: Korea and Taiwan**

	Exports (billions of dollars)		A/B	Capital Intensity[a] (thousands of 1981 $)		Wage Rate[a] (thousands of 1981 $)	
	Korea (A)	Taiwan (B)		Korea (1981)	Taiwan (1976)	Korea (1981)	Taiwan (1976)
Miscellaneous manufactures[b]	1.7	4.3	0.41	7.0	5.6	2.7	1.9
Wood products	0.5	1.2	0.42	9.0	6.4	2.6	2.0
Electronic and Telecommunications equipment	1.8	2.8	0.65	5.6	5.3	2.8	2.2
Metal products	1.1	1.0	1.09	8.3	5.8	3.1	2.0
Clothing and footwear	4.9	4.4	1.12	2.3	4.0	2.1	1.8
Textiles, natural[c]	1.3	1.2	1.09	7.9	8.8	2.4	2.0
Textiles, synthetic	1.2	0.9	1.36	9.6	29.7	2.5	2.5
Steel products	1.4	0.4	3.71	17.4	10.6	3.6	2.7
Transport equipment	2.0	0.8	2.39	20.6	20.9	4.3	2.4
Rubber products	0.5	0.2	2.82	12.6	7.3	3.7	2.3
Basic chemicals	0.36	0.3	1.19	53.1	55.5	4.7	3.3
Sugar refining	0.2	0.02	10.04	66.1	29.0	5.4	4.6
Fertilizers	0.2	0.0	94.00	48.2	64.2	5.8	4.3
Cement	0.34	0.07	5.21	69.4	101.2	5.5	5.1
Nonferrous metal products	0.1	0.04	2.44	28.6	35.7	3.8	2.8
Iron and steel	0.4	0.05	7.37	75.5	154.0	4.5	3.4
Machinery	0.9	2.2	0.42	13.5	11.2	3.3	2.4
Petroleum products	0.1	0.4	0.32	113.1	118.3	8.4	4.3
All manufacturing	21.0	22.5	0.93	11.7	12.0	3.0	2.2

Sources: Korean Traders Association, Foreign Trade Statistics; and Inspectorate General of Customs, Taiwan, The Trade of China (Taiwan District).

[a]1981 prices for Taiwan were obtained by applying the wholesale price index for all commodities (158.42) and the WPI for capital goods (143.35) with 1976 as base year and the exchange rate of NT $36.8 per dollar. (The exchange rate of 682.7 won per dollar was applied to Korea.)

[b]Including nonmetallic mineral products (except cement), precision instruments, and plastic products.

[c]Including natural fiber yarns and fabrics and other textile products except synthetic fiber yarns and fabrics.

versus $2.2 billion), and Taiwan's exports of electronic and telecommunications equipment were about 55% larger than those of Korea (i.e., $2.8 billion versus $1.8 billion). On the other hand, Korea's exports of such capital-intensive manufactures as steel products were about 3.7 times larger than those of Taiwan (i.e., $1.4 billion versus $0.4 billion) and its exports of transport equipment (including ships and containers) amounted to about 2.4 times those of Taiwan (i.e., $2.0 billion versus $0.8 billion). Furthermore, the exports of such capital-intensive manufactures as rubber products, basic industrial chemicals (including synthetic resin, fiber, and plastic materials), fertilizers, cement, refined sugar, nonferrous metal products, and iron and steel amounted to about $2.1 billion in Korea but only about $0.7 billion in Taiwan.

One might regard the case of machinery as an exception because, while the machinery sector was relatively capital intensive in Korea, Korea's exports of machinery in 1981 amounted to only about 43% of those of Taiwan. In 1981 Taiwan's exports of electric motors and generators, sewing machines, machine tools for particular industries, air pumps and gas compressors, lifting and loading machinery, electrical equipment for internal combustion engines, electromechanical domestic appliances with motors, apparatus for making or breaking electric circuits, and calculating and other office machines and parts amounted to about $1.1 billion, while Korea's exports of these items amounted to only about $0.25 billion (see table 10.A.7). In Korea the average capital intensity of these sectors amounted to about $9.2 thousand per worker, while that of the other electrical and nonelectrical machinery sectors amounted to about $16 thousand per worker. That is, although Taiwan's exports of electrical and nonelectrical machinery as a whole ($2.2 billion) were only 2.4 times larger than those of Korea in 1981 ($0.9 billion), Taiwan's exports of relatively labor-intensive machinery and equipment were as much as 4.6 times larger than those of Korea in 1981. After all, the machinery sector in Taiwan could be classified as relatively labor-intensive, while the machinery sector in Korea (excluding electronic and telecommunications equipment) had to be classified as relatively capital-intensive.[25]

10.8 Concluding Remarks

In Korea, the efficiency gains associated with the long process of the opening up of a semiautarkic economy to semifree trade have materialized not only in the form of rapidly rising real wage rates but also in the form of high rates of return on investment. These enhanced rates of return in turn seem to have kindled the "animal spirit" of Korean entrepreneurs and generated a vigorous pace of investment activities in Korea during the past twenty-year period. By the beginning of the 1980s, however, exports as a percentage of GNP already exceeded 40%. As of 1981, the raw materials and intermediate inputs imported for "direct" use in export production amounted to about 29% of total commodity imports. Hence, there is still substantial room to increase the net value-added content of exports even while maintaining the same export share of GNP. However, the large efficiency gains associated with the initial phase of the opening up of trade must now be more or less exhausted. In this sense, Korea might have to worry about the sagging animal spirit of entrepreneurs and the weakening vigor of their investment activities in the 1980s. However, with the vast amount of positive experience and kinetic energy accumulated during the past two decades, the gains from marginal structural adjustment can be amplified, as has been observed in Japan. To accomplish this, however, Korea may have to pay more attention to "marginal" efficiency and to the market mechanism in general.

Because of the increase in real wages in Korea and the worsening protectionist policies of advanced countries against labor-intensive manufactures, Korea does not have any alternative but to keep undertaking structural transformation of its production and exports toward the more skill- and technology-intensive and the somewhat more capital-intensive manufacturing sectors. The system of negative real interest rates, subsidies, and credit allocations has been maintained as one of the important policy instruments to promote export-oriented growth in Korea. The most serious problems associated with this "repressed" financial regime have been the slower growth in the magnitude of loanable funds of formal financial institutions and the increasing probability of inefficient and wasteful allocation of available investment funds. There was a rapid increase in aggregate savings propensity in Korea during 1962–81, and yet the savings/GNP ratio (especially the level of household savings) achieved by Korea is far below those achieved by Taiwan, Singapore, and Japan. The reason for this gap is often attributed to the repressed financial regime.

The mismanagement of credit rationing in favor of the arbitrarily selected heavy industries was most conspicuous in the late 1970s and is believed to have lowered the overall productivity of Korean industries. The notorious failures in Korea were the investments in nonferrous metal manufacturing, large petrochemical complexes, large fertilizer plants, capital-intensive armament factories, and a gigantic heavy-machine factory. The low rates of growth in industrial productivity, GNP, and commodity exports experienced by Korea since the beginning of the 1980s may readily be attributed to the second oil crisis, worldwide recession, and the prevailing high interest rates in international financial markets. However, the arbitrary system of credit rationing may also have to share some of the responsibility.

Furthermore, credit rationing seems also to have been, at least partly, responsible for the worsening distribution of income in Korea (see Hong 1981). Credit rationing has been concentrated on large company groups, and as a result, there occurred a concentration of export activities. In the beginning of the 1970s, the share of exports from the nine general-trading-company groups in Korea's total commodity exports amounted to only about 15%. By the early 1980s, however, these nine groups exported nearly half of the total of commodity exports.[26] Their expanding share in the 1970s was at the expense of the share of small- and medium-sized exporting firms.[27]

Considering the equity and efficiency aspects of credit rationing, one may be able to conclude that it is time for the Korean government to start reducing the excessiveness of credit rationing by enhancing the role of the market mechanism in resource allocation. If the governments succeeds in maintaining the past trend of an increasing propensity to save and in eliminating excessive distortions in factor and commodity markets, Korea will be able to improve the efficiency of its export-oriented economy and consequently will be able to maintain high rates of growth in the 1980s and thereafter.

Table 10.A.1   Output and Trade Patterns of Korean Manufacturing

	Value Added (Wage Share)		Output		Exports (Export-Output Ratio)		Imports (Import Dependency)	
	1968	1980	1968	1980	1968	1980	1968	1980
Clothing and footwear	156(37.2)	1,601(40.6)	756	6,709	187(24.7)	3,615(53.9)	7(1.2)	289(8.5)
Food products	151(25.2)	1,383(26.7)	1,408	12,015	106(7.5)	295(2.5)	83(6.0)	752(6.0)
Electronic products	25(40.0)	1,034(37.6)	118	3,835	32(27.1)	1,678(43.8)	27(23.9)	1,416(39.6)
Metal products	64(34.4)	629(40.4)	142	1,918	16(11.3)	877(45.7)	76(24.3)	275(20.9)
Miscellaneous manufactures	156(35.9)	1,480(37.2)	553	3,529	95(17.2)	1,193(33.8)	39(7.9)	648(21.7)
Textiles	404(34.4)	2,623(35.5)	1,541	6,157	309(20.1)	1,237(20.1)	161(11.6)	484(9.0)
Wood products	106(24.5)	237(51.1)	395	1,272	158(40.0)	431(33.9)	76(24.3)	42(4.8)
Basic chemicals	119(13.5)	904(17.6)	341	6,556	5(1.5)	769(11.7)	228(40.4)	2,178(27.4)
Machinery	126(32.5)	1,170(38.0)	453	3,991	18(4.0)	524(13.1)	418(49.0)	3,758(52.0)
Transport equipment	128(32.8)	1,141(39.7)	585	2,729	4(0.7)	805(29.5)	355(37.9)	1,424(42.4)
Steel products	34(29.4)	325(29.5)	287	3,987	4(1.4)	1,214(30.4)	101(26.3)	537(16.2)
Nonferrous metal products	13(38.5)	262(27.5)	58	937	11(19.0)	111(11.9)	30(39.0)	476(36.3)
Iron and steel	54(31.5)	920(19.3)	91	2,886	0(0.0)	311(10.8)	18(24.7)	813(24.0)
Cement	82(12.2)	452(12.4)	166	1,356	13(7.8)	231(17.0)	7(4.4)	2(0.2)
Fertilizers	114(15.8)	212(17.0)	108	1,098	4(3.7)	321(29.2)	75(41.9)	52(6.3)
Petroleum products	107(3.7)	749(4.1)	351	7,388	17(4.8)	106(1.4)	31(8.5)	1,022(12.3)
Rubber products	23(26.1)	244(34.4)	58	877	4(6.9)	464(52.9)	2(3.6)	47(10.2)
Other products	822(19.3)	3,965(19.8)	2,110	10,637	33(1.6)	757(7.1)	95(4.4)	1,231(11.1)
All manufacturing	2,642(25.6)	19,329(29.3)	9,404	77,877	1,014(10.8)	14,939(19.2)	1,718(17.0)	15,441(19.7)

Sources: Bank of Korea, *Input-Output Tables of Korea* (for output and trade data); and Economic Planning Board, *Report on Mining and Manufacturing Census* (for value-added and wage-share data). See also notes for table 10.3.

Note: Numbers are millions of 1980 dollars.

Table 10.A.2   Shifts in Wage Rates and Capital Intensity of Korean Manufacturing

	Capital (Capital-Labor Ratio)[a]		Wages (Per Worker Wage Rate)[a]		Number of Workers (Labor Allocation)[b]		Point Elasticity of Substitution 1968–80
	1968	1980	1968	1980	1968	1980	
Clothing and footwear	170(2.26)	682(2.12)	53(0.71)	650(2.02)	75.4(10.1)	321.3(16.0)	−0.06
Food products	258(4.26)	1,219(8.91)	35(0.58)	369(2.70)	60.6(8.1)	136.8(6.8)	0.48
Electronic products	32(3.60)	710(4.60)	9(1.03)	389(2.52)	8.9(1.2)	154.4(7.7)	0.25
Metal products	100(3.52)	645(7.24)	20(0.71)	254(2.85)	28.6(3.8)	89.1(4.4)	0.48
Miscellaneous manufactures	219(2.54)	1,287(5.73)	52(0.60)	551(2.45)	86.9(11.6)	224.6(11.2)	0.56
Textiles	875(4.71)	2,923(7.44)	128(0.69)	931(2.37)	186.4(24.9)	392.8(19.5)	0.36
Wood products	168(5.37)	423(9.16)	24(0.76)	121(2.62)	31.4(4.2)	46.2(2.3)	0.41
Basic chemicals	247(17.17)	1,775(45.95)	15(1.02)	159(4.12)	14.4(1.9)	38.6(1.9)	0.68
Machinery	185(4.30)	1,573(11.22)	38(0.87)	445(3.17)	43.1(5.8)	140.2(7.0)	0.74
Transport equipment	211(5.73)	1,918(16.56)	39(1.05)	453(3.91)	36.8(4.9)	115.8(5.8)	0.78
Steel products	45(5.65)	445(16.70)	9(1.16)	96(3.60)	7.9(1.1)	26.7(1.3)	0.95
Nonferrous metal products	26(6.52)	436(25.53)	5(1.18)	72(3.43)	3.9(0.5)	21.0(1.0)	1.26
Iron and steel	83(4.90)	2,621(62.07)	16(0.92)	178(4.22)	17.0(2.3)	42.2(2.1)	1.78
Cement	577(85.84)	683(63.49)	9(1.37)	56(5.21)	6.7(0.9)	10.8(0.5)	−0.21
Fertilizers	381(60.11)	306(51.35)	17(2.61)	36(6.05)	6.3(0.9)	6.0(0.3)	−0.18
Petroleum products	107(43.52)	403(83.45)	4(1.50)	31(6.42)	2.5(0.3)	4.8(0.2)	0.42
Rubber products	21(3.75)	302(12.38)	6(0.97)	84(3.44)	5.7(0.8)	24.4(1.2)	0.91
Other products	603(5.09)	2,291(11.44)	138(1.17)	721(3.60)	118.6(15.9)	200.3(9.9)	0.70
All manufacturing	4,337(5.79)	20,898(10.37)	621(0.83)	5,660(2.81)	748.3(100)	2,014.8(100)	0.48

Source: Economic Planning Board, *Report on Mining and Manufacturing Census.*

[a]In thousands of 1980 dollars. See notes for table 10.3. Fixed capital includes land.

[b]In thousands of persons.

Table 10.A.3   The Composition of Bank Loans in Korea (in billions won and percentages)

	Nondiscretionary Nonpolicy DMB Loans[a]		Discretionary Nonpolicy DMB Loans[b]	Nondiscretionary DMB Policy Loans		Discretionary Policy Loans		Total Loans (DMB, KDB, and EXIMB)
	Domestic Banks	Foreign Banks		Export Credit	Others[c]	DMB Loans[d]	EXIMB and KDB[e]	
1961	1(2)	—	11(21)	1(2)	14(26)	5(10)	20(39)	52(100)
1962	5(8)	—	15(22)	2(2)	14(20)	7(11)	24(36)	68(100)
1963	8(10)	—	15(20)	3(4)	15(20)	8(11)	28(36)	77(100)
1964	9(10)	—	16(19)	3(3)	16(19)	10(12)	32(37)	85(100)
1965	14(12)	—	26(24)	5(4)	17(16)	11(10)	37(34)	109(100)
1966	28(18)	—	38(25)	5(3)	20(14)	12(8)	47(31)	150(100)
1967	43(17)	—	70(27)	17(6)	30(11)	49(19)	52(20)	261(100)
1968	84(18)	2(0)	146(32)	25(5)	49(11)	80(18)	66(15)	452(100)
1969	158(20)	5(1)	246(31)	35(4)	79(9)	180(23)	96(12)	798(100)
1970	194(20)	10(1)	296(31)	56(6)	110(12)	157(16)	129(14)	953(100)
1971	224(18)	18(2)	398(32)	80(6)	130(11)	227(18)	158(13)	1,234(100)
1972	244(16)	29(2)	401(26)	108(7)	160(10)	358(23)	239(16)	1,540(100)
1973	383(19)	51(3)	475(23)	224(11)	186(9)	419(21)	319(16)	2,034(100)
1974	573(19)	71(2)	829(27)	360(12)	241(8)	549(18)	426(14)	3,048(100)
1975	820(21)	132(3)	893(23)	339(9)	291(8)	774(20)	608(16)	3,857(100)
1976	976(20)	184(4)	1,025(21)	462(9)	391(8)	1,033(21)	796(16)	4,867(100)

Table 10.A.3 (continued)

	Nondiscretionary Nonpolicy DMB Loans[a]		Discretionary Nonpolicy DMB Loans[b]	Nondiscretionary DMB Policy Loans		Discretionary Policy Loans		Total Loans (DMB, KDB, and EXIMB)
	Domestic Banks	Foreign Banks		Export Credit	Others[c]	DMB Loans[d]	EXIMB and KDB[e]	
1977	1,073(17)	409(7)	1,348(21)	567(9)	530(8)	1,189(19)	1,129(18)	6,345(100)
1978	1,433(15)	685(7)	1,995(21)	883(9)	763(8)	1,948(21)	1,608(17)	9,316(100)
1979	2,272(17)	943(7)	2,620(20)	1,126(9)	1,126(9)	2,513(19)	2,364(18)	13,064(100)
1980	2,654(14)	1,953(11)	3,635(20)	1,721(9)	1,646(10)	3,192(17)	3,617(18)	18,417(100)
1981	3,025(13)	2,236(9)	5,007(21)	2,197(9)	1,799(8)	4,466(19)	4,773(20)	23,503(100)
1982	3,777(13)	2,684(9)	6,805(23)	2,278(8)	2,444(8)	5,397(18)	6,234(21)	29,619(100)
1983								
1962–66	11.6%	—	22.0%	3.2%	17.8%	10.4%	34.8%	100.0%
1967–71	18.6%	0.8%	30.6%	5.4%	10.8%	18.8%	14.8%	100.0%
1972–76	19.0%	2.8%	24.0%	9.6%	8.6%	20.6%	15.6%	100.0%
1977–81	15.2%	8.2%	20.6%	9.0%	8.6%	19.0%	18.2%	100.0%

Source: Bank of Korea, *Economic Statistics Yearbook*, various issues.

[a]Consists of overdrafts, loans based on installment savings deposits, personal loans, remunerations (Citizens National Bank loans based on mutual installment funds), and loans by the branches of foreign banks (including foreign currency loans).

[b]Consists of discounted commercial bills and loans of general funds.

[c]Consists of loans for agriculture, fisheries, and housing with banking funds and government funds.

[d]Includes foreign currency loans by domestic DMBs. Foreign currency loans include a small amount of import usage (around 5%). The non-foreign currency loans are for specified projects.

[e]Includes foreign currency loans.

Table 10.A.4   Money Supply and Domestic Credit in Korea

	Reserve Money	M_1	M_2	M_3	Domestic Credit 1	Domestic Credit 2[a]	Loans by KDB, EXIMB, DMB
	Average Annual Growth Rates (percentages)						
1953–61	35.4	51.6	—	—	—	—	—
1962–66	48.4	19.4	32.3	—	28.1	—	24.0
1967–71	30.5	33.9	48.7	—	56.0	—	54.5
1972–76	38.2	34.2	31.2	—	33.8	—	31.9
1977–81	16.6	21.5	30.3	34.0	36.2	39.2	37.2
	Percentage Ratio to GNP						
1953–61	6.9	8.9	—	—	—	—	—
1962–66	6.4	8.5	12.3	—	12.7	—	14.9
1967–71	9.6	10.9	29.1	—	28.5	—	31.6
1972–76	11.0	12.7	34.2	38.5[b]	38.4	49.9[b]	38.9
1977–81	10.5	11.2	35.2	43.4	43.0	60.9	46.2

Source: Bank of Korea, *Economic Statistics Yearbook*, various issues.
[a]Including credits by nonmonetary financial institutions.
[b]Average for 1974–76.

Table 10.A.5   **The Sectoral Allocation of Domestic and Foreign Loans: Korean Manufacturing**
(in billions won)

	1971		1976		1981	
	Bank Loans	Total Loans	Bank Loans	Total Loans	Bank Loans	Total Loans
Clothing and footwear	15(1.1)	15(1.1)	175(0.9)	185(0.9)	566(0.8)	584(0.8)
Food products	37(2.2)	50(3.1)	174(1.2)	198(1.3)	272(0.6)	325(0.7)
Electronic products	8(1.1)	9(1.2)	57(0.4)	77(0.6)	495(0.7)	549(0.8)
Metal products	3(0.9)	3(0.9)	26(0.7)	29(0.7)	405(1.2)	446(1.3)
Miscellaneous manufactures	11(0.9)	11(0.9)	59(0.7)	63(0.8)	325(0.7)	339(0.8)
Textiles	86(1.9)	131(2.9)	463(1.4)	615(1.9)	1,527(1.1)	2,146(1.5)
Wood products	27(4.5)	28(4.7)	129(2.6)	134(2.7)	303(2.8)	310(2.9)
Basic chemicals	20(3.0)	31(4.6)	78(0.9)	140(1.6)	531(1.2)	764(1.7)
Machinery	16(1.3)	20(1.7)	117(0.8)	142(0.9)	741(0.9)	1,048(1.3)
Transport equipment	34(2.2)	50(3.3)	230(1.5)	404(2.6)	1,581(1.9)	1,816(2.2)
Iron and steel	15(2.6)	29(5.0)	233(1.6)	505(3.4)	1,039(1.2)	2,189(2.5)
Nonferrous metal products	1(1.8)	2(2.0)	49(1.4)	75(2.1)	393(2.8)	477(3.4)
Cement	25(1.7)	75(5.0)	66(1.1)	136(2.2)	213(1.0)	380(1.7)
Fertilizers	12(0.8)	40(2.8)	38(0.8)	66(1.4)	105(0.7)	257(1.7)
Petroleum products	3(0.2)	75(5.1)	7(0.1)	64(1.0)	585(1.5)	926(2.4)
All manufactures	371(1.5)	637(2.5)	2,149(1.1)	3,120(1.6)	10,105(1.1)	13,798(1.5)

Source: Bank of Korea, *Financial Statements Analysis*, various issues.

Notes: Total loans represent the sum of domestic bank loans and foreign loans. Figures in parentheses represent loan/value-added ratios. Miscellaneous manufactures include furniture, pottery, clay products, and miscellaneous nonmetallic mineral products. Electronic products include ratios and televisions.

Table 10.A.6   **Exports of Manufactures in Korea, Taiwan, Hong Kong, and Singapore**
(in billions of dollars)

	Korea		Taiwan		Hong Kong		Singapore	
	1970	1980	1970	1980	1970	1980	1971	1980
Clothing and footwear	0.2	3.7	0.2	3.8	0.7	4.8	—	0.4
Textiles	0.1	2.2	0.2	1.8	0.2	0.9	—	0.2
Elec. and telecom. equip.	—	1.6	0.2	2.5	0.2	1.3	0.1	2.0
Precision instruments	—	0.3	—	0.4	—	0.5	—	0.2
Misc. manufactures	0.1	1.0	0.2	2.9	0.6	2.6	—	0.2
Wood and furniture	0.1	0.4	0.1	1.1	—	0.1	—	0.3
Metal products	—	0.8	—	0.8	0.1	0.4	—	0.1
Food products	—	0.4	0.1	0.7	—	0.1	—	0.1
Nonmetallic mineral	—	0.4	—	0.5	—	0.1	—	0.1
Petroleum products	—	—	—	0.3	—	—	0.4	5.4
Chemicals	—	0.8	—	0.6	—	0.1	—	0.3
Steel products	—	1.3	0.1	0.3	—	—	—	0.1
Nonferrous metal	—	0.1	—	0.1	—	0.1	—	0.1
Machinery	—	0.8	0.1	1.8	0.1	1.2	—	0.8
Transport equip.	—	1.1	—	0.6	—	—	—	0.3
All manufactures	0.7	16.2	1.2	18.4	2.0	13.2	0.6	10.4
All commodities	0.8	17.5	1.4	19.7	2.0	13.7	0.8[a]	12.6[a]

Sources: United Nations, *Commodity Trade Statistics;* and Inspectorate-General of Customs, Taiwan, *The Trade of China* (*Taiwan District*).
[a]Including oil bunkers of $1,199 million in 1980 and oil bunkers of $78 million in 1971 (data from Department of Statistics, Singapore, *Yearbook of Statistics*).

Table 10.A.7   **Exports of Machinery and Equipment: Korea and Taiwan (1981)**

	Exports (millions of dollars)		Capital Intensity in Korea[a]
	Taiwan	Korea	
Electric motors, generators, and generating sets	100	14	10.42
Sewing machines and parts	202	16	6.23
Machine tools and parts for particular industries	97	17	6.68
Air pumps and gas compressors	34	2	5.78
Lifting and loading machinery and conveyors	59	19	8.62
Electrical equipment for internal combustion engines	29	2	9.24
Electromechanical domestic appliances	181	14	12.24
Apparatus for making or breaking electric circuits	158	67	10.15
Calculating and office machines and parts	271	94	9.97
Subtotal	1,131	245	9.23
Other machinery and parts	1,019	652	15.94
(Metal-cutting machine tools)	(183)	(28)	(17.22)
All manufacturing	—	—	11.74

Sources: Korean Traders Association, *Foreign Trade Statistics;* Economic Planning Board, *Report on Mining and Manufacturing Census;* and Inspectorate-General of Customs, Taiwan, *The Trade of China* (*Taiwan District*).
[a]Capital stock per worker in thousands of dollars in 1981.

Notes

1. By allowing tariff-exempt free imports of raw materials, intermediate inputs, and investment goods for export production activities, the Korean government has tried to prevent its own protectionist import-restrictive regime from adversely affecting the incentives for export activities. Furthermore, it has tried to reduce the degree of overall import restrictions as Korea's ability to earn foreign exchange becomes enhanced through export promotion.

2. In effect, this is an example of a general pattern of subsidized capital formation in fast-growing economies discussed by Bradford in chapter 7 of this volume.

3. According to the input-output data (Bank of Korea, *Input-Output Tables of Korea*), the proportion of manufactured goods in total commodity exports was 47% in 1960, rising to 86% in 1970 and to 95% in 1980. Apparently, the input-output tables regarded many primary products, which are only slightly processed, as manufactured goods. The fact that these types of commodities composed a relatively large portion of Korea's exports in the 1950s causes the differences between the SITC and input-output table classifications of manufactured goods exports as a percentage of total exports in the early period.

4. According to Hirschman (1958, 37), "In underdeveloped countries, . . . a readiness to save and invest exists, but is being frustrated. . . . [T]he total supply of savings is highly responsive to the appearance of new investment opportunities."

5. As a result of the exposure to the affluent living standards of advanced countries after the opening up to trade, the people in a poor country may desire a more rapid rate of economic growth, and consequently the structure of time preference changes in such a fashion as to make the savings propensity higher in the poor country than in the rich country.

6. The increase in real wages during 1962–66 was negligible: -4% per annum if the GNP deflator for the whole industry is applied, and 1% per annum if the wholesale price index is applied. (The consumer price index for the period 1962–66 is not available.)

7. The 1980 prices for capital stock were obtained by applying the GNP deflator for gross fixed capital formation in manufacturing, and those for wages by applying the GNP deflator for value added in manufacturing (instead of the consumer price index, because we are concerned with the cost aspect rather than with the workers' welfare aspect). Since the estimated point elasticity depends crucially on price deflators, the absolute magnitude of an estimated elasticity itself may not be very meaningful.

8. According to the I-O statistics, there were also significant exports of light electrical machinery and automobiles and parts in 1960. However, these exports might well have been listed as occasional reexports: exports of these items became negligible in the I-O statistics for 1963, 1966, and 1968.

9. In 1970 about 90% of miscellaneous manufactures exports consisted of wigs, and the rest consisted of toys, sporting goods, musical instruments, and travel goods.

10. In 1970 about 47% of Korea's exports went to the United States, about 28% to Japan, and about 10% to the European Community. Exports to OPEC countries expanded from less than 2% of total exports in 1970 to more than 10% by 1980. Exports to other developing countries expanded from about 11% of total exports in 1970 to about 22% in 1980. Exports to the European Community also expanded to about 19% of total exports in 1980, but the shares of the United States and Japan fell drastically to about 28% and 18% respectively.

11. In 1970 about 52% of Korea's imports of nonfuel primary products were from the United States, about 4.2% from Canada, New Zealand, and Australia, and about 24% from developing countries. In 1980 the share of the developing countries increased to about 31%, and the share of Canada, New Zealand, and Australia to about 12.4%. The share of the developing countries in Korea's manufactures imports increased from about 2.4% in 1970 to about 4.4% in 1980. As of 1981 about 30% of Korea's imports were mineral fuels, 27% were other primary products, about 22% were machinery and transport equipment, and 21% were other manufactures.

12. In the 1970s total domestic credits increased from a magnitude equivalent to about 50% of GNP (1974–76) to about 60% (1977–81). The proportion of securities in domestic credits increased from about 5% to about 8%. The proportion of domestic credits provided through nonmonetary financial institutions excluding KDB and EXIMB (i.e., provided through investment companies, savings institutions, life insurance companies, and the Korea Long-Term Credit Bank) steadily increased from a magnitude equivalent to about 3% of GNP in 1969 to about 12% of GNP by 1981.

13. They amounted to only about 12% of total loans in 1962–66 and about 19% in 1967–71.

14. The real interest rate applied to discounts of commercial bills amounted to −5.6% per annum on average in 1954–61, −3.2% in 1962–66, 9.4% in 1967–71, −2.5% in 1972–76, and −0.9% in 1977–81.

15. The weighted-average real interest rate on all loans provided by all banking institutions in Korea amounted to −14.4% per annum in 1962–64, 4.1% in 1965–71, and −6.2% in 1972–76, while the real interest rate applied to discounts of commercial bills amounted to −7.1%, 9.5%, and −2.5% in each period. This implies that the rates on discounts of commercial bills overestimate the real interest rates on total bank loans by 4%–7% (see Hong 1979, 162–201).

According to the IMF *World Economic Outlook* (Washington, D.C., 1983, 204), the (weighted average) long-term "real" interest rates in major industrial countries amounted to about 1.2% per annum in 1976–79, and those in Japan, which is believed to practice an extensive credit-rationing system, amounted to about 2.6% per annum.

16. Since 1980, there were significant devaluations and high interest rates worldwide, which effectively terminated the era of low-cost foreign borrowing for Korean businessmen.

17. The M_2 statistics of Korea include a substantial amount of corporate time and savings deposits. These are mostly forced savings extracted by the banks from corporations as a condition for bank loans. Their effect is to raise the statistics of both bank credits and time and savings deposits simultaneously. If we subtract these corporate time and savings deposits both from the aggregate time and savings deposit figures and from the aggregate domestic credit figures, the volume of total domestic credits provided through DMB, KDB, and EXIMB would be reduced by around 7% of GNP on average, and consequently, the magnitude of subsidies associated with domestic bank loan allocations would be reduced by about 1.6% of GNP per annum on average in the 1970s. Even in Japan, "traditionally banks offer loans to the firm on the condition that some proportion of the loan be deposited into time deposit balances. This implies a reduced availability from a given size, or equivalently, a higher effective rate of return to the bank."

18. In a relative sense, textiles and wood products (mostly plywood) were the leading export sectors of Korea only in the 1960s. In the 1970s Korea's

competitive power in synthetic fiber yarn seems to have been rather limited because of the expensive domestic supply of synthetic fiber materials. Korea's competitive power in synthetic fiber fabrics was limited by the requirement of sophisticated advanced technologies, and Korea's natural fiber yarn industry had to compete with other, less-developed countries (such as China). The plywood industry suffered from export restrictions on timber by resource-rich countries (such as Indonesia and the Philippines).

19. Among the three sectors included in this group, iron and steel revealed the highest elasticity (1.78). This reflects the construction of a large-scale integrated steel mill in the 1970s.

20. The export-output ratios of fertilizers and cement amounted to 29% and 17% respectively in 1980; however, the more important aspect of this group may be the drastic fall in the import dependence of fertilizers.

21. Some capital-intensive sectors revealed extremely high rates of elasticities. However, the increasing capital intensity of some of these sectors was mainly due to the introduction of new capital-intensive production within each sector, such as an integrated steel mill, petrochemical complexes, a modern shipyard, and automobile assembly lines. Therefore, unless there occur continual additions of extremely capital-intensive production, one may expect that the rates of increase in capital intensities of these sectors will significantly slow down in the 1980s and that the possible continuing allocation of subsidized loans will impact mostly the output-expanding effect rather than the factor-substitution effect.

22. Capital-intensive manufactures consist of chemicals, steel products, nonferrous metal products, electrical and nonelectrical machinery, and transport equipment.

23. Unlike the other advanced developing countries, clothing and footwear (including leather products) have never been a leading export sector in Singapore. The export of other labor-intensive products such as textiles, wood and furniture, metal products, and miscellaneous manufactures was also relatively insignificant. The leading export sector of Singapore was petroleum refining, and the second leading export sector was assembling of electronic products (see table 10.A.6). On the other hand, the distinct feature of Korean exports was the importance of steel products and transport equipment (especially ships) and the relative insignificance of electrical and nonelectrical machinery.

24. A low rate of inflation coupled with high real rates of interest on deposits in Taiwan seem to have been conducive to a rapid increase in the supply of loanable funds in Taiwan. The money/GNP ratio in Taiwan increased from about 16% in 1953 to 35% in 1962, to 65% in 1973, and to 83% in 1978. On the other hand, the money/GNP ratio in Korea jumped from about 12% in 1965 to 34% in 1970, but the ratio was still 34% in 1979.

25. In Korea the capital intensity of the (electrical and nonelectrical) machinery sector amounted to about $13.5 thousand, while that of all manufacturing amounted to about $11.7 thousand per worker in 1981. In Taiwan the capital intensity of the machinery sector amounted to about $11 thousand per worker, while that of all manufacturing amounted to about $12 thousand per worker in 1976 (in 1981 prices). In Taiwan steel products and rubber products could also be classified as relatively labor-intensive sectors, while in Korea these sectors had above-average capital intensities and, hence, could be classified as capital-intensive sectors.

26. General trading companies were formally introduced in 1976, but those companies had been actively exporting even before they were officially christened with the ''general trading'' title. All the firms which are owned by the same owner of a general trading company were grouped together here and then

regarded as a general-trading-company group. Approximately half of the exports of these groups consist of manufactures directly produced by the groups themselves. Small export producers who exported through the general-trading-company groups obtained loan allocations through these groups in the form of local loans and credits.

27. The share of the next forty-one largest groups of exporting firms did not change much in the 1970s. However, the share of the next 103 groups in total commodity exports declined from about 22% in 1970 to about 8% in 1981. Furthermore, the share of the remaining small firms that were not included among the 153 groups of exporting firms declined from about 45% of Korea's total commodity exports in 1970 to about 25% by 1981.

References

Bhagwati, Jagdish N., and Anne O. Krueger. 1973. Exchange control, liberalization, and economic development. *American Economic Review* 63 (2): 419–27.

Corden, W. Max. 1971. The effects of trade on the rate of growth. In *Trade, the balance of payments, and growth,* ed. Jagdish Bhagwati, R. W. Jones, R. A. Mundell, and J. Vanek. Amsterdam: North-Holland.

Fischer, Irving. 1961. *The theory of interest.* New York: Augustus M. Kelley (original edition, 1930).

Frank, C. R., K. S. Kim, and L. Westphal. 1975. *Foreign trade regimes and economic development: South Korea.* New York: NBER.

Hirschman, Albert O. 1958. *The strategy of economic development.* New Haven: Yale University Press.

Hong, Wontack. 1979. *Trade, distortions and employment growth in Korea.* Seoul: Korean Development Institute Press.

———. 1981. Trade, growth and income distribution: The Korean experience. In *Trade and growth of the advanced developing countries in the Pacific Basin,* ed. Wontack Hong and Lawrence B. Krause. Seoul: Korean Development Institute Press.

Keesing, Donald B. 1967. Outward-looking policies and economic development. *Economic Journal* 77:303–20.

Krueger, Anne O. 1977. *Growth, distortions and patterns of trade among many countries.* Princeton Studies in International Finance, no. 40. Princeton: International Finance Section, Dept. of Economics, Princeton University.

———. 1979. *The development role of the foreign sector and aid.* Cambridge: Harvard University Press.

11   Trade Patterns and Trends of Taiwan

Chi Schive

Over the past two decades, Taiwan's successful export-led economic development has been documented in many studies (Scott 1979; Lee and Liang 1980; Stein 1981). Trade has expanded Taiwan's domestic market and has provided necessary capital goods and much needed materials. More importantly, many industries established during this period have flourished with trade, have been directly in line with the comparative advantage of Taiwan, and have created a large amount of employment. This development strategy has not only alleviated Taiwan's heavy population burden[1] but has also improved its income distribution situation. The so-called Kuznets trap has been rather successfully avoided in the case of Taiwan.

The export-led development process in Taiwan can be summarized as in table 11.1. In 1960 the trade dependence index (the ratio of the total amount of trade to the GNP) was 27.4%. The ratio doubled during the following ten years, exceeded 100 percent in 1980, and reached 103.12% in 1983. Only a few other countries (e.g., Hong Kong and Singapore) have had higher trade dependence ratios than Taiwan. We might also hope that Taiwan has not been involved in reexport activities. Given this situation, in order to assess Taiwan's growth in the 1980s, we first have to foresee its trade prospects, and then we will be in a position to analyze the probable links between trade and the domestic economy. Within the international economic setting, Taiwan's strong position as a big supplier to the United States and to some European countries may already have demonstrated Taiwan's potential as a future buyer. Oddly enough, during the past decade Taiwan has

Chi Schive is professor of economics at National Taiwan University, Taiwan, Republic of China.

Table 11.1   Trade Dependence Index of Taiwan

	Trade/GDP[a] (%)	GNP (billions of U.S. $)
1960	27.45	1.55
1965	37.57	2.80
1970	54.85	5.64
1975	74.08	14.61
1980	102.36	39.52
1981	104.48	44.84
1982	98.19	45.60
1983[b]	103.12	48.56

Source: Council of Economic Planning and Development (CEPD), *Taiwan Statistical Data Book 1983.*
[a]The difference between GNP and GDP in Taiwan is negligible.
[b]Estimated by assuming a 6.5% growth rate of GNP and a 10% growth rate of trade in 1983.

accumulated a substantial trade surplus, in spite of having also had to contend with two bouts of stagflation. This accumulated foreign exchange reserve has made Taiwan (and it may be the only non-oil-exporting newly industrializing country in such a position) a net lender rather than a borrower on the international monetary market.

This paper, focusing on the trade patterns and trends of Taiwan, begins with a presentation of the trade structure of Taiwan in the past. It then analyzes the determinants underlying the changes that have been implemented in the trade structure. Three questions are discussed: (1) Can the trade patterns in Taiwan be explained by its vested comparative advantage? (2) Should the trade fluctuations of the 1970s be largely attributed to a lack of foreign demand, or should the rigid domestic monetary system, in particular the fixed exchange rate, share some of the blame? (3) Did the industrial structural change that occurred when Taiwan entered into a post-labor-surplus development stage in the 1970s (called "secondary import substitution," i.e., the establishment of the materials and capital goods industries) affect the commodity composition of trade? Knowledge gained from this part of the analysis will be extremely useful to us when we examine the 1980s in the last section of the paper.

11.1   Trade Structure, 1960–80

11.1   The Growth of Trade

Though Taiwan's industrial and export sectors had already been partially developed during the colonial period, World War II destroyed much of it. It was not until the early 1950s that agricultural production returned to the prewar level. In the 1950s, Taiwan's economic policy was inward-looking, with top priority given to producing enough consumer nondurables and construction materials for basic needs. Exports in this period were traditional export items; sugar, rice, tea, and canned and tropical fruits accounted for the bulk of exports (87.4% in 1953 and 67.7% in 1960). Manufactured exports, mainly textiles, were minimal during the period but did start picking up near the end of the period. The average annual growth rate of total trade in U.S. dollars in the 1950s was 5.7%.

At the end of the 1950s, by which time the domestic economy had gradually become saturated, as evidenced by stable prices and low utilization rates of industrial capacity (Tang and Liang 1975),[2] the economy seemed to have reached a turning point, requiring change. A set of policy reforms was therefore initiated around 1960, including two devaluations that brought the New Taiwan dollar to its market value, the unification of the multiple exchange systems, and the promulgation of the investment law, which provided various incentive schemes for investment (Lee and Liang 1980; Lin 1973). These policy measures created a favorable environment for encouraging exports. Nonetheless, it is still unclear whether these decisions, made during a critical period, were based upon careful calculations or were simply based on a belief that a market-oriented and more liberal policy should be put into effect. We mention this because during the policy reform period no one predicted the rapid expansion of trade that followed in the next decade, and exports grew only at a moderate rate, 7.5% during the policy transition period, 1958–61.

In the 1960s, the so-called export promotion, export substitution period, nominal trade grew at an average annual rate of 21.57%, which was about the growth rate of trade in real terms. In the 1970s, though nominal trade grew at an even higher rate, 30.73%, inflation accounted for more than half of it. During the export promotion stage, even though exports did increase much faster than imports, 25.32% compared with 18.40%, the trade balances were still negative in 1970. They have turned positive since 1971. If there had not been an energy crisis, Taiwan would have stored up a handsome trade surplus back in the first half of the 1970s. In the second half of the 1970s, when exports were boosted again, a total trade surplus of $4.48 billion was recorded. The trade surplus has continued to mount through 1981 and 1982. This time the important factor is not export expansion but is the shrinking of imports (see table 11.2).

11.1.2 The Commodity Composition of Trade

Taiwan's export trade commodity composition has changed significantly over the past two decades. At present, Taiwan exports mostly manufactured goods in exchange for materials and capital goods. In

Table 11.2   **Growth Rates of Trade in Taiwan (percentages)**

	Imports		Exports		Total		
	Value	Quantum	Value	Quantum	Value	Balance[a]	GNP
1961–65	14.01	24.06	23.46	17.20	18.43	–0.34	9.5
1966–70	22.69	20.90	27.18	23.70	24.71	–0.57	9.8
1971–75	35.46	13.02	30.82	17.88	32.58	–0.59	8.9
1976–80	27.36	12.32	30.79	19.88	28.87	4.48	10.4
1981–82	–1.74	–1.80	6.17	4.35	2.29	4.73	4.4
1961–70	18.40	22.48	25.32	20.45	21.57	–0.91	9.6
1971–80	31.41	10.26	30.81	16.46	30.73	3.89	9.6
1961–82	22.48	15.81	26.07	18.27	23.98	7.71	9.2

Source: CEPD, *Taiwan Statistical Data Book, 1983.*
Note: Value is in terms of U.S. dollars. Quantum is based on 1976 prices.
[a]In billions of dollars.

1982, 92.4% of total exports were accounted for by manufactures, 1.9% by agricultural products, and 5.7% by processed agricultural products. In 1970 nonagricultural products accounted for 78.6% of Taiwan's total exports, but the figure was only 32.3% in 1960.

While Taiwan has exported increasingly many manufactured goods, in both the relative and the absolute sense, the export composition of manufactures has also changed rapidly (see table 11.3). Over the past two decades, textiles have obviously been in the forefront of Taiwan's exports, although their importance has declined since 1970, and they have now been replaced by electrical equipment and electronics. Plywood has followed basically the same pattern as textiles, but with an even shorter life cycle. Exports of metals and metal products with scraps from ship-breaking increased faster than total exports in the 1960s and were further augmented by a modern steel complex established in the late 1970s. Another industry that demonstrated a remarkably stable increasing trend in total exports, albeit slowly, was machinery.

On the import side, in 1982 raw materials and manufactured intermediates comprised 67.3% of Taiwan's total imports, capital goods 24.8%, and consumption goods only 7.9%. Looking backward for comparison, we note that raw materials and intermediates were 62.8% of total imports in 1970 and 64.0% in 1960, and that the shares of capital goods and consumption goods in total imports were 32.3% and 4.9% in 1970 and 27.9% and 8.1% in 1960, respectively. Thus, during the past two decades Taiwan's import composition has remained relatively stable, though some changes can still be identified. For instance, the proportion accounted for by consumption goods declined slightly in the 1960s and then rose gradually in the 1970s. The capital goods share in total imports displayed an opposite movement, having first an increasing trend in the 1970s and then a declining one in the 1980s.

Table 11.3   The Trade Commodity Structure of Taiwan (percentages)

A. Exports

	Agric. Products	Processed Agric. Products			Textiles	Plywood	Plastic Products	Manufactured Products				Total Exports
		Sugar	Canned Food	Total				Metals & Metal Products	Machinery	Elect. Eq., Electronics, & Appliances	Total	
1960	12.0	44.0	4.79	55.7	14.2	1.7	—	3.99	0.20	0.59	32.3	100.0
1965	23.6	13.1	10.47	30.4	15.8	5.9	—	4.75	1.30	2.67	46.0	100.0
1970	8.6	3.1	5.73	12.8	31.7	5.3	—	6.31	3.27	12.32	78.6	100.0
1975	5.6	5.0	2.90	10.8	27.6	3.3	6.5	4.79	3.62	14.72	83.6	100.0
1980	3.6	1.2	1.42	5.6	22.6	2.1	7.4	6.35	3.75	18.17	90.8	100.0
1982	1.9	0.4	0.90	5.7	21.6	1.5	6.8	7.58	3.80	17.60	92.4	100.0

B. Imports

	Capital Goods		Crude Oil	Materials and Intermediates			Consumer Goods	Total Imports	Elect. Eq. & Electronics	Trans. Vehicles
	Machinery	Total		Iron & Steel	Chemicals	Total				
1960	15.5	27.9	6.4	9.5	6.7	64.0	8.1	100.0	5.3	6.3
1965	12.4	29.3	2.3	11.9	10.5	65.5	5.1	100.0	6.3	10.3
1970	13.3	32.3	3.1	7.8	11.0	62.8	4.9	100.0	11.7	10.7
1975	16.2	30.6	10.5	6.6	12.1	62.6	6.8	100.0	8.5	5.3
1980	12.14	23.4	20.8	6.8	7.8	70.8	5.8	100.0	9.8	3.7
1982	10.40	24.8	20.5	8.7	8.0	67.3	7.9	100.0	10.6	5.5

Source: CEPD, *Taiwan Statistical Data Book 1983.*

A further breakdown of the capital goods and materials categories reveals more information on changes in the import shares of certain commodities. Crude oil imports, which were not a major item at all in the 1960s, accounted for 10.5% of Taiwan's total imports after the first oil crisis. In 1980, right after the second oil crisis, around one-fifth of Taiwan's total imports consisted of oil. Because of the significant rise in oil imports, most of the other major import commodities have shown a declining trend in import shares after 1970. If we excluded oil from total imports, the import shares of machinery, iron and steel, and chemicals would become more stable in the 1980s. However, there are two industries that show clearer trends in import shares. Electrical equipment and electronics (E&E) increased two percentage points in import shares between 1975 and 1982, even with oil included in total imports. Part of the increase in E&E items in total imports was due to the import of more consumer durables after 1975. Imports of transportation vehicles, on the other hand, decreased significantly after 1970, which was not due to the rise of oil imports either. In view of these changes in import composition, it can be inferred that import substitution for consumer goods continued in the 1960s and that for certain materials and capital goods (transportation vehicles in particular), was more gradual in the 1970s.

11.1.3   Trade Partners

Taiwan's major contemporary trade partners are developed countries (DCs), which account for about two-thirds of exports and supply about the same ratio of imports. In the past, the DCs were not as important as buyers as they are at present, but they sold more to Taiwan. Less-developed countries (LDCs) have enjoyed favorable trade balances with Taiwan since the first energy crisis. The newly industrializing countries (NICs)—Korea, Singapore, and Hong Kong—have never been major recipients of Taiwan's exports (see table 11.4).

Among the DCs, the United States has been the most important trade partner of Taiwan, especially as a buyer, over the past decade. In 1970 the United States absorbed 39.70% of Taiwan's total exports; the figure was 21.87% in 1961. However, the picture is different on the import side. The United States used to be Taiwan's largest supplier in the early 1960s but has gradually been replaced by Japan. In 1970 Japan provided 41.46% of all imported commodities. This figure has also decreased in the 1970s, mainly because of the rise in oil imports. If we excluded oil from total imports, we would find that the U.S. position as a supplier of Taiwan's imports has improved significantly since the 1970s. Simply from these figures, we would expect that Taiwan had amassed a large

Table 11.4   **Taiwan's Trade Partners by Country Classification** (percentages)

		DCs				
	U.S.	Japan	EC	Total	LDCs	NICs
			Exports			
1961	21.87	28.81	8.35	60.14	21.76	18.16
1965	21.54	30.17	9.86	65.44	25.51	10.05
1970	39.70	15.19	9.83	70.64	15.16	14.18
1975	34.28	13.04	13.67	68.61	19.50	11.81
1980	34.08	10.96	13.21	65.98	22.13	11.89
			Imports			
1961	40.95	30.50	8.12	83.52	14.48	2.00
1965	31.52	39.16	7.09	84.06	13.54	2.40
1970	23.18	41.46	8.07	78.60	16.68	4.72
1975	27.50	30.16	11.32	75.03	22.07	2.90
1980	23.58	26.99	8.04	65.52	31.00	3.48

Sources: Commodity Trade Statistics of the Republic of China (SITC Revised) Research, Development and Evaluation Commission, Executive Yuan, (1976). Data after 1975 are from Ministry of Finance, *Trade Statistics of the Republic of China.*

Note: NICs include Hong Kong, South Korea, and Singapore. Row summation may not equal 100 because of rounding.

trade surplus with the United States but a trade deficit with Japan. On the other hand, there have been recent signs indicating some encouragement for the closing of these two trade gaps. The European Community (EC) countries have become a much more important market for Taiwan. In 1970 the EC countries received 9.83% of Taiwan's total exports, up from 8.35% in 1961. However, by 1980 their share was over 13%. On the import side, the EC has continued to supply a roughly consistent share of Taiwan's total imports during the last two decades. But if oil is again excluded, imports from the EC would increase beyond former levels.

Table 11.5 gives a breakdown of the commodity composition of Taiwan's foreign trade by country groups. In general, machinery (SITC 7), chemicals (SITC 5), products from materials (including iron and steel) (SITC 6), and nonedible materials (SITC 2) were imported from the DCs. Fuel (SITC 3) and some nonedible materials (SITC 2) came from the LDCs. The DCs were most interested in Taiwan's food items in the 1960s, but in the 1970s the demand of the DCs was more for miscellaneous items, including footwear, furniture, etc. The DCs' purchase of machinery and materials accounted for 25.40% and 17.27% of Taiwan's total exports in 1981. The LDCs and NICs were also large buyers of these goods.

Table 11.5   Commodity Composition of Taiwan's Foreign Trade (percentages)

	SITC 0	SITC 1	SITC 2	SITC 3	SITC 4	SITC 5	SITC 6	SITC 7	SITC 8	SITC 9	Total
						Imports					
1961											
DCs	10.18	2.09	23.19	1.03	1.58	15.21	13.95	28.78	3.76	0.23	100.00
LDCs	14.66	0.02	30.17	50.97	0.11	0.37	1.57	0.55	0.23	1.35	100.00
NICs	8.55	—	60.02	0.32	0.10	8.16	2.91	12.20	4.78	2.95	100.00
1966											
DCs	5.99	0.86	17.83	1.01	1.01	13.76	20.43	35.59	3.40	0.12	100.00
LDCs	9.64	0.15	44.95	39.96	0.14	1.15	1.83	1.14	0.04	1.00	100.00
NICs	15.35	1.00	65.41	0.33	1.07	1.96	5.21	4.67	4.29	0.71	100.00
1971											
DCs	6.21	0.77	16.05	0.60	0.75	12.28	18.92	40.06	4.29	0.07	100.00
LDCs	14.52	0.05	44.53	29.16	0.17	1.20	2.12	5.30	0.90	2.05	100.00
NICs	4.79	2.53	29.42	1.30	0.84	3.90	34.84	17.41	4.78	0.18	100.00
1976											
DCs	8.47	0.50	11.22	1.28	0.33	15.45	15.90	40.85	5.84	0.15	100.00
LDCs	7.27	0.09	22.73	62.81	0.13	1.12	2.44	2.45	0.29	0.68	100.00
NICs	5.97	3.64	18.19	4.14	1.75	5.33	21.54	22.35	10.91	6.18	100.00
1981											
DCs	9.21	0.51	10.15	4.56	0.27	13.00	15.05	40.07	7.05	0.13	100.00
LDCs	2.28	0.25	15.99	70.56	—	1.97	2.36	5.74	0.52	0.32	100.00
NICs	3.89	1.09	22.13	9.10	1.61	6.08	26.04	20.80	6.04	3.22	100.00

Exports

	SITC 0	SITC 1	SITC 2	SITC 3	SITC 4	SITC 5	SITC 6	SITC 7	SITC 8	SITC 9	Total
1961											
DCs	66.95	1.57	6.07	1.50	0.07	6.09	12.71	0.03	5.00	—	100.00
LDCs	37.99	0.60	2.17	4.83	0.02	6.22	41.99	4.59	1.57	0.02	100.00
NICs	37.19	0.26	2.91	2.87	0.02	3.66	50.10	1.52	1.47	—	100.00
1966											
DCs	54.94	0.78	8.23	0.64	0.02	1.43	15.74	5.34	12.83	0.06	100.00
LDCs	19.91	0.11	1.96	0.97	0.07	6.35	53.84	12.54	4.25	0.01	100.00
NICs	33.13	0.62	3.99	0.93	0.16	7.04	41.63	2.76	9.71	0.03	100.00
1971											
DCs	17.19	0.14	2.91	0.16	—	0.73	17.86	17.37	43.57	0.06	100.00
LDCs	8.70	0.21	2.44	1.32	0.01	6.59	47.79	19.20	13.36	0.01	100.00
NICs	21.90	0.08	3.43	1.02	—	2.57	47.67	14.62	8.71	0.02	100.00
1976											
DCs	12.86	0.12	1.82	0.22	0.01	1.40	15.88	20.78	46.89	0.02	100.00
LDCs	8.61	—	1.52	5.70	0.01	3.44	34.27	22.28	24.16	0.01	100.00
NICs	9.47	0.22	2.23	0.84	0.01	4.13	53.88	19.65	9.56	—	100.00
1981											
DCs	7.79	0.05	1.52	0.74	0.01	1.86	17.27	25.40	45.35	0.01	100.00
LDCs	5.24	0.05	2.22	5.40	—	3.73	26.08	26.53	30.74	0.01	100.00
NICs	7.31	0.15	2.40	2.50	0.02	3.22	46.59	24.82	12.97	—	100.00

Sources: Data before 1971 are from *Commodity Trade Statistics of the Republic of China (SITC Revised)* (Executive Yuan, Research, Development and Evaluation Commission, 1976); data after 1971 are from Ministry of Finance, Republic of China, *Monthly Statistics of Exports and Imports,* various issues.

Notes: NICs include Hong Kong, South Korea, and Singapore.

SITC (Revised) 0: foods and animals. SITC 1: beverages and tobacco. SITC 2: nonedible materials. SITC 3: mineral fuels, lubricants, and related materials. SITC 4: animal and vegetable oils. SITC 5: chemicals. SITC 6: manufactured goods classified chiefly by material. SITC 7: machinery and transport equipment. SITC 8: miscellaneous manufactured articles. SITC 9: commodities and transactions not classified according to kind.

11.2   Determinants of Trade

11.2.1   Comparative Advantage

Comparative advantage can explain the trade pattern of Taiwan. Taiwan is not rich in natural resources. Except for a few coal mines, which are thousands of feet underground, and limestone for cement plants, there are almost no valuable mineral deposits in Taiwan. The availability of arable land is also a problem. The existing amount of cultivated land, around one-third of Taiwan's total area, cannot be increased. Thus agricultural production has been raised, but at a decreasing rate, in the past only via improvements in land productivity, not through cultivation of more land. Moreover, Taiwan's population density is extremely high. Taiwan will continue to export labor-intensive products, as the neoclassical trade doctrine asserts.

The results of studies on both the industrial level and the firm level confirm the predictions of neoclassical theory. Table 11.6 classifies all manufacturing industries into four trade categories according to their import and export ratios: export, import-competing, export-and-import-competing, and non-import-competing industries. Export industries refer to those industries that export more than 10% of their output and import less than 10%. Import-competing industries are just the opposite. If an industry exports more than 10% of its production and imports more than 10% of its total supply (domestic production plus imports), then this industry is classified as an export-and-import-competing industry. If both the export and import ratios are less than 10%, then this industry is called a non-import-competing one.

Table 11.6   **Capital Intensity and Skilled-Labor Intensity by Trade Category**

	Capital-Labor Ratio (NT $1,000 per worker)			Skilled-Labor to Total Labor Ratio		
	1966	1971	1976	1966	1971	1976
Export industries	64.73	124.08	734.76	.3387	.4253	.1306
Export- and import-competing industries	60.81	146.56	1,527.49	.4755	.5067	.3650
Import-competing industries	96.10	356.22	1,400.30	.4738	.5350	.4245
Non-import-competing industries	46.52	52.85	1,353.90	.3715	.2152	.1873
All industries	69.99	154.15	1,239.63	.4292	.4823	.2691

Sources: 1966 and 1971 figures are from Lee and Liang 1980, 343. 1976 figures are calculated from CEPD, *Taiwan Input and Output Table 1976, The Republic of China.* Capital and labor (skilled and unskilled) data for each industry are from CEPD.

With the total capital (measured by fixed assets only) and labor requirement data for producing one unit of final product, we can calculate an average capital-labor ratio for each group of industries by using the production volume of each industry as a weight. In 1966 each worker in the exporting industries used NT $64.73 thousand worth of capital; the figure for the import-competing industries was NT $96.10 thousand. For non-import-competing industries (consisting mainly of foods, printing and publishing, etc.) the average capital-labor ratio was NT $46.52 thousand, the lowest among the four groups. The average capital-labor ratio for export-and-import-competing industries with no clear market sign was NT $60.81 thousand. In 1971 the average capital-labor ratio of all manufacturing industries increased to NT $154.15 thousand from NT $69.99 thousand in 1966, with a good deal of the increment the result of capital deepening in the import-competing industries. In short, the export industries in the 1960s used a slightly more labor-intensive technology than the export-and-import-competing ones. Both categories of industry were characterized by a much lower capital-labor ratio than that of the import-competing industries. Thus, the results for 1966–71 are in accord with the theoretical prediction that Taiwan would export high-labor-content products in exchange for high-capital-content goods.

An interesting question is whether Taiwan's trade patterns changed in the first half of the 1970s (a different period when Taiwan experienced for the first time real wage growth that equaled or exceeded productivity growth) or remained the same as the pattern outlined above.[3] In 1976 the export industries were still the most conservation-oriented group in terms of using capital, while the export-and-import-competing and non-import-competing industries had been continuing the process of capital deepening at a fast clip and had succeeded in raising their capital-labor ratios to about the same level as those of the import-competing industries. Part of the change in the non-import-competing industries was due to industry reclassification—for instance, cement was classified as an export industry in 1971, but it became a non-import-competing one in 1976 and hence raised the average capital-labor ratio of the non-import-competing industries significantly. However, reclassification was not a factor in raising the ratio for the export-and-import-competing industries. Thus, a large amount of investment was directed during the period to the export-and-import-competing industries. In addition to this, we might also point out that the capital-labor ratio difference between the export industries and the other three industry categories lessened in the relative sense. Without more recent data for further comparison,[4] the results reached here tend to suggest that the capital deepening was a general phenomenon for the manufacturing sector in response to the labor-shortage pressure constantly felt in the post-labor-surplus stage in the 1970s, though the doctrine of comparative advantage still influenced Taiwan's trade pattern.

The Hecksher-Ohlin hypothesis, usually focusing on capital and labor only, can be viewed from another perspective. That is, if a country has abundant unskilled labor, then the country will export those products having a higher unskilled-labor content than that of its imports. Table 11.6 presents the ratio of skilled labor to total labor requirement for four industry groups. Export industries again were the most unskilled-labor-intensive ones during the period from 1966 to 1976. In 1976 a much lower average skilled-labor ratio was observed for the non-import-competing industries. Part of the change was due to the fact that different definitions were adopted for skilled labor.[5] Another explanation, which has not yet been proved with detailed data, might be that automation polarized the labor requirement, which is to say that when labor was replaced by highly automated machinery, only a handful of technicians or operators were needed (the jobs that could not be performed by machinery were certain packaging and delivery tasks, for which minimum training was required). Sectors adopting automation were flour mills and edible oil and cement plants; all are non-import-competing industries.

A serious obstacle to analyzing the capital-labor ratio at the industry level is that an industry may simultaneously be involved in both import and export activities, and these different activities may quite likely employ different types of technology. In fact, the import-and-export-competing industry group in table 11.6 is the largest one of the four trade categories. But with reliable industry data we may be able to solve the problem. The figures presented in table 11.7 are for this purpose.

In 1975 a foreign-firm survey (foreign firm is defined as a company with any amount of foreign capital in it) including 607 companies in the manufacturing sector provided the needed data. Assuming that the company in the sample used similar technology for its products sold in both the domestic and the foreign markets, we may then weigh each company's capital-labor ratio by its exports to take into account the size of export activity and by its domestic sales to take into account its domestic sales activity. We will thus obtain the industry's average capital-labor ratios for both exports and domestic sales.

In 1975 exports resulted from foreign manufacturing firms with an average of U.S. $9.00 thousand worth of fixed assets per worker, whereas domestic sales were produced from foreign firms with an average of U.S. $18.18 thousand worth of fixed assets per worker. Apparently, foreign firms as a whole tended to use different technologies for products with different market orientations. In industry, the foreign firms that predominated in the domestic sales in the foods and beverages,

Table 11.7   **Capital-Labor Ratios of Foreign Firms Weighted by Export and Domestic Sales, 1975** (in thousands of U.S. dollars)

Industry	Fixed Assets per Worker	
	Exports	Domestic Sales
Foods and beverages	3.11	12.26
Textiles	26.84	19.95
Apparel	1.26	2.34
Wood, bamboo, and rattan products	1.92	2.74
Paper and paper products	12.00	11.42
Leather and leather products	1.61	2.76
Plastic and rubber products	2.29	10.76
Chemicals	16.24	17.61
Nonmetallic products	24.58	50.79
Basic metals and products	3.89	5.24
Machinery	3.32	10.47
Electrical equipment and electronics	2.89	3.95
Total	9.00	18.18

Source: Foreign Firm Survey primary data, Investment Commission, Ministry of Economic Affairs, 1975.

apparel, wood, bamboo, and rattan products, leather and leather products, plastic and rubber products, nonmetallic products, basic metals and basic metal products, machinery, and electrical equipment and electronics categories all used a much more capital-intensive technology than the firms which predominated in exports. The differences were extremely large in the foods and beverages, plastic and rubber products, and the machinery industries, of which the capital-labor ratios for local market sales were more than three times those for exports. In two industries, paper and paper products and chemicals, foreign firms did not greatly differentiate their production techniques with regard to market orientations. There was only one industry, textiles, in which export activities were more capital-intensive than in domestic market activities. A closer look at this particular industry, however, revealed that a few artificial fiber makers with a large amount of committed capital were active in exporting.

By using the same set of data, we may easily verify a corollary proposition that foreign firms located in the export-processing zones would use less capital per unit of worker than those outside the zones. In view of the fact that some companies in the zones rented their buildings and land, a better measure here would be the value of machinery and equipment per unit of direct worker, instead of fixed assets per unit of worker. In 1975 foreign firms in three zones used a total of

U.S. $789 worth of machinery and equipment per unit of direct worker, which is only 38.46% of the average figure for foreign firms in the electrical equipment and electronics industry limited to exporting activities (Schive 1982; Ranis and Schive 1985).

11.2.2   Trade Fluctuations and Fixed Exchange Rates

Trade in Taiwan has experienced two dips over the past ten years. One was in 1975 when exports decreased 5.7% in value, or remained barely the same as the previous year in real terms, and imports dropped 16.8% in value, or 11.0% in real terms. The other was in 1982 when exports climbed only 4.2% in value, or actually decreased 1.1% in real terms, and imports shrunk both in value and in real terms by 5.4% and 2.6%, respectively. These trade fluctuations were commonly attributed to the energy crisis followed by two worldwide recessions. These explanations have been readily accepted by economists (who have believed in the absorption approach) and have even been welcome among government officials charged with managing trade promotion affairs. However, in the case of Taiwan, when we recognize that the economy has been maintaining a fixed exchange rate system with tight controls on foreign exchange, especially in the sense that the exchange rate has not varied in response to wild fluctuations of relative (domestic and foreign) prices, then we may look for other determinants, rather than blindly accepting the simplistic explanation given above.

In analyzing Taiwan's trade fluctuations, and the balance of trade in particular, we may look at its purchasing-power-parity effective exchange rates (NT dollar per U.S. dollar). First, before 1972 the official exchange rate was pegged at U.S. $1 to NT $40. In 1973 a 5% appreciation of the Taiwan dollar shifted the official exchange rate to 1:38. The currency appreciated further in 1978 to 1:36 (this rate was effective for three years). In 1981, when Taiwan joined the mainstream and adopted a flexible exchange rate system, the Central Bank still exercised its power over the financial market and depreciated the Taiwan dollar by 5.5%.

In a free economy without price distortions, either against or in favor of trade, the exchange rate will vary in accordance with the balance of trade and changes in relative prices between foreign and domestic markets. In Taiwan, as pointed out earlier, a variety of incentive schemes were formulated to promote trade around 1960, including customs duties and indirect tax rebates and lower-interest-rate loans. This meant that in 1971, for example, an exporter, on average, would have received NT $5.71 extra beyond the official exchange rate for every U.S. $1 worth of exports owing to the export incentives mentioned above (see table 11.8). These incentives have declined since 1971 and by 1981 amounted to NT $1.53 for each U.S. $1 worth of exports. By adding

Table 11.8   Purchasing-Power-Parity Effective Exchange Rates on Exports

	1970	1971	1972	1973	1974	1975	1976	1977	1978	1979	1980	1981
A. Official exchange rate for exports[a] (NT $ per U.S. $)	40.00	40.00	40.00	38.16	37.90	37.95	37.95	37.95	35.95	35.98	35.98	37.79
B. Incentives (NT $) per U.S. $ of exports												
Interest subsidy[b]	0.09	0.1	0.095	0.074	0.083	0.083	0.076	0.057	0.05	0.058	0.059	0.097
Customs duties rebate[c]	4.06	4.27	3.68	2.82	2.47	2.70	2.14	2.11	1.65	1.569	1.348	1.185
Indirect tax rebate[d]	1.36	1.34	1.24	0.98	0.87	1.12	0.89	0.89	0.77	0.62	0.50	0.25
Subtotal	5.51	5.71	5.015	3.874	3.423	3.903	3.106	3.057	2.49	2.247	1.907	1.532
C. Nominal effective exchange rate (A + B)	45.51	45.71	45.02	42.03	41.32	41.85	41.06	41.01	38.44	38.23	37.88	39.32
D. Taiwan's WPI (1960 = 100)	121.46	121.67	127.08	156.04	219.38	208.33	214.17	220.00	227.71	259.29	315.15	339.17
E. Average WPI of major trade partners[e]	121.74	125.67	130.16	146.34	180.76	193.95	198.59	211.85	223.25	244.48	290.29	320.47
F. Exchange rate index[f]	96.03	96.92	101.45	109.33	103.63	104.65	106.89	106.95	113.30	116.15	121.29	113.43
G. Purchasing-power-parity effective exchange rate on exports (C·E·F/D)	43.80	45.76	46.78	43.09	35.28	40.77	40.70	42.24	42.69	41.86	42.33	42.14

Sources: DGBAS, Republic of China, *Commodity-Price Statistics Monthly, Taiwan District*; International Monetary Fund, *International Financial Statistics*; Economic Research Department, Central Bank of China, Republic of China, *Taiwan Financial Statistics Monthly*; Department of Statistics, Ministry of Finance, *Yearbook of Financial Statistics of the Republic of China*; Census and Statistics Department, Hong Kong, *Consumer Price Index Report*. Figures before 1978 are from Liang and Liang 1981.

[a]Where the rates fluctuated over a period of time, the mean of the range was taken. The rate up to 14 April 1958 was that applicable to exports by private enterprises. Therefore, until 30 September 1963, it was the rate applicable to all exports other than a few commodities (e.g., sugar, rice, salt, bananas) for which lower rates applied. The same rate applied to all exports after 30 September 1963 (see Scott 1979, 326).

[b]The difference in the interest on export loans and that on unsecured loans is treated as an export subsidy.

[c]Includes defense surtax and harbor dues.

[d]Includes commodity tax, salt tax, and flood rehabilitation surtax.

[e]An average of wholesale price indexes in Australia, Canada, West Germany, Hong Kong, Japan, Korea, the Netherlands, Singapore, the United Kingdom, and the United States, weighted by Taiwan's annual export value with the respective countries. When the WPI was not available, the consumer price index was used.

[f]An average of exchange rate index weighted by Taiwan's annual export value with the respective major trade partners. The exchange rate is expressed in terms of U.S. dollars per unit of the currencies of Taiwan's trading partners.

the subsidies for exports to the official exchange rate, we derive the nominal effective exchange rate.

Two other adjustments must be made before we reach the purchasing-power-parity effective exchange rates. In 1974 Taiwan experienced an inflation rate of 40.6% in wholesale prices, which was much higher than the average inflation rate (23.5%) of its major trade partners. Surprisingly enough, the government failed to act to correct the over-valued NT dollar, which definitely weakened the export incentives and the international competitiveness of Taiwan exports in that year. During the four-year period from 1974 to 1978, the wholesale price index rose by only 3.8%, or less than 1% annually. Nonetheless, in 1979 and 1980 the WPI increased by 12.1% and 21.5%, respectively, increases that were higher than the average inflation rates of Taiwan's ten major trading partners (see note e of table 11.8)) in the corresponding years (9.5% and 18.7%). These changes in relative prices again put Taiwan's products at a disadvantage in the international market. Finally, we have calculated the effective exchange rate to take into account the U.S. dollar situation in the international market.

Figure 11.1 depicts three curves, two representing Taiwan's balance of trade for commodities and commodities plus services, respectively, and one for the real effective exchange rate on exports in the 1970s. From figure 11.1, first we observe a close movement between the two balance-of-trade curves and a parallel movement between these two curves and that for the real effective exchange rate. These are four turning points on the balance of trade which matched nicely with the real effective exchange rate either simultaneously or with a one-year lag. Second, the movements of the three curves were more in tandem before 1975 than afterwards; the magnitude of fluctuations has decreased for the real effective exchange rate since 1975 but not for the trade surplus. Third, the trade balance curves reveal roughly an increasing trend, while the real effective exchange rate shows a declining trend.

The first observation reminds us that the trade fluctuations in Taiwan in the 1970s could not be attributed completely to external factors. The varying real effective exchange rate, caused mainly by unstable domestic prices, was also relevant. Looking again at the situation in 1974, in that single year the real effective exchange rate deteriorated about NT $8 for U.S. $1 worth of exports, or appreciated 18% annually, or 23% when compared with the 1972 figure. It is very difficult to accept that there was trade inertia when the exchange rate moved so radically. The second finding is probably due to the inflationary effect, resulting in larger trade balance variations. For the third finding, an increasing trade surplus, to a large degree, reflects a long-term improvement of Taiwan's international competitiveness, while the declining effective

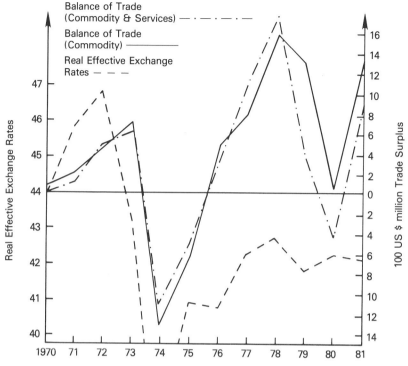

Fig. 11.1   Trade balance and the real effective exchange rates, 1970–
80

exchange rate was mainly caused by the gradual lifting of the export
incentives.

To focus on the turning points of the curves, if the appreciations of
the NT dollar did result in a weak competitive position for Taiwan's
exports, then the factors underlying the appreciations deserve further
attention. As pointed out earlier, both appreciations could be attributed
mainly to higher inflation in Taiwan and abroad. It would be superficial
to say that the quadrupling of oil prices in 1973 and the later tripling
of oil prices in 1979 were absolutely responsible for Taiwan's inflation.
A multiple-regression analysis showing that import prices can explain
domestic inflation quite satisfactorily would not be surprising, because
Taiwan has imported around half of what it produced, and hence import
prices are weighted heavily in calculating the domestic WPI. Further
questions should be asked: Has inflation in Taiwan been higher than
in neighboring countries (Japan, Hong Kong, or Singapore) that have
depended on imported energy? Is there any way to calculate the impact
on domestic prices of the rise in oil prices?

To answer the first question, in 1974 the inflation rate was 31.4% in Japan in WPI, 22.33% in Singapore in CPI, and 15.0% in Hong Kong in CPI (all much lower than the WPI inflation rate of 40.7% in Taiwan). In 1979 and 1980, when Taiwan experienced an average 17.7% rise in WPI, rates were 12.5% in Japan, 17.0% in Singapore, and 13.9% in Hong Kong in CPI.[6] For the second question, we assume full-cost pricing that reflects the oil price surge by using input and output tables and estimate that 52.19% of domestic inflation in 1973 and 1974 and 70.35% in 1979 and 1980 were attributable to the price surge of imported materials, mainly the external oil price shocks.[7] With this information, Taiwan's inflation during the two periods coinciding with the two oil crises was not completely the result of higher imported-oil prices, even taking all imported materials into account.[8] In other words, a strong demand increase in these two periods was also relevant, or we can state that demand-pull inflation coexisted with cost-push inflation in the 1970s.

On the demand side, we found that the money supply increased at the unusually high rates of 42.2% and 31.9% annually during 1972–73 and 1976–78, but at much lower rates during the rest of the 1970s (table 11.9). A very rapid expansion in the money supply in both subperiods, much more than the economy could have absorbed, built up inflationary pressure, which inevitably raised the domestic price in the following subperiods. In examining the sources of monetary increase, we find that 98.72% of the increase in the money supply between 1972 and 1973 came from the accumulation of foreign assets that had resulted directly from the trade surplus. An equally high percentage contribution to the increase of the money supply from the same sources took place in the 1976–78 subperiod.

In short, Taiwan experienced wild fluctuations in GNP growth, trade expansion, and the price level in the 1970s, though the trend toward economic growth remained basically the same as during the earlier

Table 11.9   **Factors Affecting the Money Supply in Taiwan** (percentages)

	Annual Changes in Money Sup.	Percentage Contributed by:				
		Claims on Gov. & En- terprises	Net For. Assets	Saving & Gov. Dep.	Others[a]	Total
1972–73	42.2	188.4	98.7	−142.9	−44.2	100.0
1974–75	19.6	351.1	−73.1	−148.8	−29.2	100.0
1976–78	31.9	182.2	89.8	−156.1	−15.9	100.0
1979–80	15.2	362.7	−8.1	−171.8	−82.8	100.0

Source: CEPD, *Taiwan Statistical Data Book 1983.*

[a]Others include presettlement requirements for imports and other items (net).

decades. The trade variation, or that of the balance of trade, was caused to a certain extent by the changing position of the real effective exchange rate, for which unstable domestic prices were also responsible. The sources of domestic inflation can be traced to the fixed exchange rate system, in addition to external factors. Under the fixed exchange rate system the undervalued NT dollar encouraged exports and allowed the stockpiling of a large trade surplus, which, in turn, increased the money supply and the domestic price level later. Thus, Taiwan in the 1970s had a monetary system that was too rigid and a price level that was too flexible. All this meant that when the fixed exchange rate system failed to correct the undervalued local currency, the correction was made in the process of a higher domestic inflation rate, which resulted in an appreciation of the local currency anyway. The impact on trade of the readjustment of exchange rates was that the undervalued NT dollar boosted trade first, but then the appreciation later dampened it, and the magnitude of the trade fluctuations increased accordingly.

11.2.3 Secondary Import Substitution

Loosely used, import substitution refers to the augmentation of domestic production to replace imports. More strictly defined, import substitution occurs during a certain period only if the import share (imports over total supply) decreases. However, in measuring the import substitution effect, either at the industry level or at the aggregate level, most existing studies suffer from two limitations. First, imports are improperly compared with "gross" domestic production (Morley and Smith 1970);[9] i.e., the production of an industry usually includes not only the final product but also a number of different kinds of intermediates for that product. Therefore, the total production of the industry is not strictly comparable with the imported goods, which are final products. Second, the studies do not distinguish between imports for final and intermediate usages. The first limitation is purely due to the data problem, which can be solved by excluding all intermediates when measuring a product or by using an input-output table to convert imports into the "gross" measure of imports for comparison. The second limitation has conceptual significance and deserves further elaboration.

LDCs prefer the inward-looking, import substitution strategy because it protects the domestic market against foreign competition and therefore is easier to implement. Furthermore, by protecting the domestic market it facilitates the decision-making process for investment. Given the fact that a developing country is often in short supply of the entrepreneurial talent for decision making, this approach is not without merit. As to which industry is to be developed, in the earlier phase of the import substitution period this strategy focuses on consumer goods, and nondurables in particular, since consumer goods usually account for a large share of imports and the technology required to manufacture nondurable consumer goods is most likely not too sophisticated. This approach is also in line with Hirschman's linkage concept, i.e., the notion that backward linkages are better thought out than are the forward ones (Hirschman 1958). However, when the domestic market gradually becomes saturated, whether it is wise to continue the same inward-looking policy (i.e., to develop certain upstream industries after the downstream industries have already been established) or to pursue an outward-looking policy becomes debatable.

The appropriate policy response may seem rather obvious for a small economy like Taiwan or Korea, based either upon the empirical evidence of their past performance or upon the theoretical reasoning that exports can alleviate the constraints of scale economies just as they reduce the inefficiencies in resource allocation produced by the protectionism of the inward-looking policy. Nonetheless, after years of successful export-led growth—now that exports have greatly expanded Taiwan's markets and increased the volume of domestic production in certain industries, now that the economy has had to contend with rapidly rising wages because of previous labor shortages, produced by the fast-growing export sector, and now that the nation's technological base is sufficiently high to support the development of some relatively high-technology industries—is the time perhaps right for the economy to develop certain intermediate and capital goods industries? It is from this line of reasoning that the secondary import substitution strategy can be justified and the distinction between imports for final consumption and those for intermediate uses in measuring the import substitution effect becomes relevant.

For the manufacturing sector as a whole, the results shown in table 11.10 indicate that the ordinary import substitution measure as well as the revised measure both had negative signs in the 1960s. In the first half of the 1970s, although the ordinary Chenery measure became positive, the sign for the revised measure remained negative. Furthermore, we also want to notice that the revised import substitution measure had a much larger negative value than the Chenery index. Thus, Taiwan was still in the import substitution stage when the export-led growth strategy was put into effect.

This finding, which may look puzzling and which differs from the general impression that Taiwan had terminated its import substitution stage by the end of the 1950s, is in fact quite logical. The majority of Taiwan's first manufactured exports were consumer goods with very high import content or products that were assembled and packaged from imported parts. It was actually the increasing amount of imports that facilitated the rapid expansion in exports. Further breakdown of

Table 11.10   **Import Substitution Coefficients of the Manufacturing Sector in Taiwan** (percentages)

	Chenery Formula (IS)	Revised Formula		
		First (IS*f)	Secondary (IS*i)	Total (IS*)
1964–66	−17.33	−19.09	−8.90	−17.99
1966–71	−2.54	1.44	−10.17	−8.73
1971–76	1.12	2.31	−4.01	−1.70

Source: See relevant issues of the input-output tables of the Republic of China (published by CEPD).

Notes: The import substitution formulas are derived as follows:

$$IS = Z_0 (m_0 - m_1)/\Delta X,$$

where X = domestic production (vector), M = imports (vector), $Z = X + M$, $m = M/Z$, and 0 and 1 represent the beginning and ending of a year. IS = import substitution index.

$$IS^* = Z^* (m_0^* - m_1^*)/\Delta X,$$

where $M^* = (1 - A)^{-1}M$, A is the input-output matrix, $Z^* = (1 - A)^{-1}$, F = final demand vector, $m^* = M^*/Z^*$.

$$IS^{*i} = Z_0^* (m_0^{*i} - m_1^{*i})/\Delta X,$$
$$IS^{*f} = Z_1^* (m_0^{*f} - m_1^{*f})/\Delta X,$$
$$M^{*i} = (1 - A)^{-1}M^i,$$

M^i = intermediate imports vector, M^f = final goods imports vector, $m^{*f} = (1 - A)^{-1}M^f$, $M = M^i + M^f$.

the revised import substitution index verifies this because the secondary import substitution index became worse in the second half of the 1960s, precisely at the time when exports grew at the highest rate. The secondary import substitution index even remained negative during the first half of the 1970s, though the import substitution for final goods index had been positive since the middle 1960s.

The overall picture we have painted above for Taiwan's import substitution is not necessarily representative of each separate industry. Using the same technique, table 11.11 presents those industries that have become significantly self-sufficient (that is, the replacement of imported intermediates and capital goods by domestic substitutes has contributed more than 10% to their growth). In the 1960s, some materials industries (petrochemical raw materials, steel and iron, artificial fibers) increased production, and a part of the increase has been used to substitute for previous imports, thereby lowering the import ratios of these industries. The capital goods industry, including machinery, electrical equipment and electronics, steel and iron products, and transportation equipment, performed equally well during the same period.[10] In the first half of the 1970s, the artificial fibers, artificial fabrics, steel and iron, and transportation equipment industries continued the previous import substitution development pattern. The "other industrial chemicals" category also joined the secondary import substitution group

Table 11.11   **Industries with Significant Import Substitution Effects**

	Materials Industry	Capital Goods Industry
1964–66	Cotton, wool, and fabrics; artificial fiber fabrics; petrochemical raw materials; artificial fibers; steel and iron	Steel and iron products; machinery
1966–71	Rubber and rubber products; artificial fibers; miscellaneous manufactures	Steel and iron products; machinery; electrical equipment and electronics; transportation equipment
1971–76	Artificial fabrics; artificial fibers; other industrial chemicals; steel and iron	Transportation equipment

Source: See relevant issues of the input-output tables of the Republic of China (published by CEPD).

Note: Industries with significant import substitution effects refer to those industries with $IS^{*i} \geq 10\%$ (or $IS^{*f} \geq 10\%$ for capital goods industries).

for the first time in the 1970s. These industry data clearly reveal that some material and capital goods industries had already been developed in the 1960s and early 1970s that have increasingly supplied domestic needs and moreover have reduced domestic reliance on imports.

11.3   Trade Patterns and Trends of Taiwan in the 1980s

Before predicting Taiwan's future trade patterns and trends, we should first lay the groundwork by making the following points:

1. Taiwan's trade dependence index has already exceeded 100%. Though a further increase in trade dependence is not impossible, more emphasis will probably be placed on the net contribution of trade to the domestic economy, i.e., the development of secondary import substitution industries.

2. Over the past decade Taiwan has experienced wild fluctuations in growth, trade, and the price level. Nonetheless, the basic increasing trends of economic growth and trade have not changed. In fact, Taiwan has performed relatively better than Korea and Japan in exports, and even in growth, during the last recession period.

3. The government must have learned a hard lesson from its mismanagement of monetary policy in the 1970s, which was at least partly responsible for the domestic inflation that hurt Taiwan's exports. After moving into a flexible exchange rate system, price instability could be avoided to some extent.

4. According to the revised secondary import substitution index, Taiwan might have already entered into this phase in the second half

of the 1970s. Several materials and capital goods industries that were established in the 1960s and continued to grow through the 1970s reveal significant import substitution effects. This group of industries is expected to expand both in its coverage and in the size of individual industries.

5. Taiwan has exported basically labor-intensive or unskilled-labor-intensive products. However, in view of rising wages, export industries and export-and-import-competing industries have been employing increasingly capital-intensive techniques to raise labor productivity.

6. For the time being, Taiwan has a large trade surplus with the United States and the EC countries as a whole, but it also has a large deficit with Japan. The accumulated trade balances have created difficulties for both Taiwan and its major trade partners.

7. In spite of the gradual lifting of the export incentives, the New Taiwan dollar is getting stronger and stronger as a result of the accumulation of foreign exchanges from trade surplus.

On the basis of the circumstances outlined above, we expect the following:

1. Trade will continue to grow in the 1980s but at a slightly slower rate than before, owing to the development of the secondary import substitution industries.

2. As the result of the successful development of the local materials and capital goods industries, the commodity composition of imports will change, with consumption goods increasingly imported (the comsumption goods share in total imports has already shown an increasing trend). On the export side, Taiwan will become a strong competitor in the international markets for machinery and several intermediate products: steel and iron products, petrochemical raw materials, artificial fibers, etc.

3. Taiwan's traditional exports (textiles, garments, rubber and plastic products) will maintain an important share of Taiwan's total exports. Modernization efforts in these industries should help recapture, at least partly, the competitive position of these product types, which has recently been lost.

4. With a more cautious monetary policy, it is hoped that Taiwan will not repeat the same mistake it made in the 1970s. We expect a moderate appreciation of the NT dollar resulting from the stockpiled volume of foreign exchange. An appreciation of the local currency will be healthy for the domestic economy in the long run because by lowering the cost of imported materials, appreciation helps stabilize domestic prices and generates pressure for further improving efficiency.

5. The United States and Japan will still be the top two trade partners of Taiwan in the near future. The trade ties between Taiwan and the EC countries will be further improved.

6. Though the trade imbalances between Taiwan and Japan and between Taiwan and the United States (and even including the EC countries) cannot be corrected overnight, there is one area of hope. That is, Taiwan has been receiving more technology from the United States and the EC countries.[11] If the technology flow leads the trade flow, then trade between Taiwan and the United States will increase faster than that between Taiwan and Japan.

Notes

1. In the 1950s and 1960s the population of Taiwan grew, respectively, by 3.5% and 2.7% annually. In the 1970s the growth rate remained high, at 1.9%. The population density of 512 persons per square kilometer in Taiwan in 1982 was the second highest in the world, behind Bangladesh.

2. We should, however, exercise some caution in accepting the low-utilization argument because unless the utilization was higher before, which has not been proved yet, the lower utilization rate alone does not imply market saturation.

3. In the 1960s labor productivity in the manufacturing sector increased at a higher rate than the growth rate of the money wage, which implies a declining unit labor cost. In the first half of the 1970s, wages rose on the average of an annual rate of 22.58% in money terms, or 9.93% in real terms, compared with a 6.07% rise in labor productivity.

4. We do have input-output tables for 1979. Nonetheless, these tables are extensions of the 1976 tables. Moreover, the 1979 tables contain ninety-nine industries, roughly one-half of the number of industries contained in the 1976 tables. Thus distortion would be unavoidable if the two sets of tables were used for comparison.

5. In the 1966 and 1971 data, skilled labor refers to those workers with more than three years' work experience. This definition classifies almost all farmers as skilled laborers and obviously raises the skilled-labor ratios for those relevant agricultural products industries when a total labor requirement instead of a direct one is used in estimating the skilled-labor ratio. In the 1976 data, farmers are excluded from the skilled-labor group.

6. Inflation rates for the four regions were taken from CEPD, *Taiwan Statistical Data Book 1983;* and Federal Reserve Bank of San Francisco, *Pacific Basic Economic Indicators.*

7. Internal report of the Council for Economic Planning and Development, 1981.

8. Ibid.

9. For the measurement of the "gross" product, see note to table 11.10.

10. It should be noted that some industries cover both consumption and capital goods. Because of data limitations, however, it is impossible to separate them.

11. In three major industries (electrical equipment and electronics, machinery, and chemicals) that are receiving foreign technology through formal technical collaboration, Japan's contribution to the technology flow declined during the 1970s. For instance, Japan accounted for 89% of the total technical col-

laboration cases in the electrical equipment and electronics industry in 1970, but only 75% in 1979; 93% in the machinery industry in 1972, but only 72% in 1980; and 53% in the chemicals industry in 1973, but 43% in 1981 (Schive 1980, 1981, 1983).

References

Hirschman, A. 1958. *The strategy of economic development.* New Haven: Yale University Press.

Lee, T.H., and Kuo-shu Liang. 1980. Taiwan. In *Development strategies in semi-industrial economies,* ed. B. Balassa. (Baltimore: Johns Hopkins University Press.

Liang, Kuo-shu, and Ching-in Ho Liang. 1981. Trade strategy and the exchange rate policies in Taiwan. In *Trade and growth of the advanced developing countries in the Pacific Basin,* ed. Wontack Hong and Lawrence B. Krause. Seoul: Korean Development Institute Press.

Lin, Ching-yuan. 1973. *Industrialization in Taiwan, 1946–72: Trade and import substitution policies for developing countries.* New York: Praeger.

Morley, S. A., and G. W. Smith. 1970. On the measurement of import substitution. *American Economic Review* 60 (September): 728–35.

Ranis, Gustav, and Chi Schive. 1985. Direct foreign investment in Taiwan's development. In *Foreign trade and investment: Economic development in newly industrializing Asian countries,* ed. Walter Galenson. Madison: University of Wisconsin Press.

Schive, Chi. 1980. *A report on technical collaboration in the electricals and electronics industry.* Taipei: Investment Commission, Ministry of Economic Affairs, Government of Taiwan.

———. 1981. *A report on technical collaboration in the machinery industry.* Taipei: Investment Commission, Ministry of Economic Affairs, Government of Taiwan.

———. 1982. Direct foreign investment and technology transfer: A factor proposition approach in Taiwan. *Economic Essays* 10:211–27.

Scott, Maurice F. 1979. Foreign trade. In *Economic growth and structural change in Taiwan,* ed. Walter Galenson. Ithaca: Cornell University Press.

Stein, L. 1981. The growth and implications of LDC manufactured exports to advanced countries. *Kyklos* 34:36–69.

Tang, Anthony M., and Kuo-shu Liang. 1975. Agricultural trade in the economic development of Taiwan. In *Trade, agriculture, and development,* ed. G. S. Tolley and P. A. Zadrozny. Cambridge: Ballinger.

12 Foreign Trade and Economic Growth in Hong Kong: Experience and Prospects

Edward K. Y. Chen

12.1 Introduction

Hong Kong is one of the world's fastest growing economies in the postwar period. Rapid economic growth in Hong Kong began with its economic transformation from an entrepôt to an industrial city in the 1950s. What is worth noting is that such an economic transformation was achieved without planning or even premeditation. In the 1960s and early 1970s, Hong Kong experienced a process of rapid industrialization accompanied by a high rate of income growth. During all this time, the role of the government was relatively unimportant, and the entire experience of rapid industrialization represented a series of successful self-adjustments to changes in the internal and external economic environment. Limited by its small internal market, Hong Kong had to adopt an outward-looking policy of export-oriented industrialism from the very beginning. This outward-looking policy has proved to be successful not only in Hong Kong but also later in other Asian economies such as South Korea, Singapore, and Taiwan and at one time in Brazil and Mexico.

Basic statistics for the macroeconomic performance of the Hong Kong economy in the past twenty years or so are given in the Appendix (tables 12.A.1–12.A.4). Table 12.1 shows the average annual growth rates of GDP and GDP per head during the period 1961–82. It can be seen that the rate of economic growth in Hong Kong as measured by GDP or GDP per head has been extremely high by any standard during the past fifteen years. The average annual growth

Edward K. Y. Chen is director of the Centre of Asian Studies and reader in economics at the University of Hong Kong.

The author is grateful to Miss Teresa Wong for computational assistance.

Table 12.1   **Average Annual Growth Rates of GDP and GDP per Head (at constant prices of 1973): Hong Kong** (percentages)

	GDP	GDP per Head
1961–66	10.9	8.0
1966–71	7.6	5.4
1971–76	8.8	6.8
1976–81	12.4	9.5
1961–81	9.9	7.4
1961–82	9.5	6.9

Sources: Hong Kong, Census and Statistics Department, *Estimates of Gross Domestic Product* (1983). Hong Kong Government, *1983 Economic Prospects* (1983).

rate of real GDP was 9.5%, and even in terms of GDP per head, the growth rate was 6.9% per annum on average. If we exclude 1982, the year of slow growth, the average GDP and GDP per head growth rates were 9.9% and 7.4% respectively for the period 1961–81. Owing to changes in the world trade situation and internal events (such as the banking crisis in 1965 and the riots in 1967), the Hong Kong economy has experienced considerable fluctuations in the level of economic activities. Nevertheless, the recovery after an economic setback has always been rapid and remarkable. For instance, the economy recovered quickly from the relatively slow growth in the years 1966, 1968, and 1971. Like everywhere else, Hong Kong suffered from the world economic recession during 1974–75, but Hong Kong recovered remarkably well in 1976. It would seem that there is some kind of "well-behaved" automatic mechanism which regulates the economy. Since late 1979, the world has suffered from the second oil crisis. Owing to the strong internal demand and the increased importance of the financial sector, the growth rates of Hong Kong were still at the high level of 11.7% and 10.9% in 1980 and 1981 respectively. The world recession had its impact on Hong Kong in 1982, during which the economy grew at only 2.4%. But, once again, taking full advantage of the U.S. recovery in 1983, Hong Kong achieved a 6% growth in that year.

The process of economic growth is almost invariably accompanied by structural changes involving the intersectoral shift of resources. There have been two phases of structural changes in Hong Kong in the past thirty years. The first phase occurred in the 1950s and 1960s, during which there was a shift of resources to the manufacturing sector. The second phase began in the early 1970s, and the direction has been toward the development of financial services.[1] In 1980, for the first time, the contribution of financial services to GDP (26%) surpassed that of manufacturing (25%).

12.2   Commodity Patterns of Export

Hong Kong has an area of just over 1,036 km²; moreover, most of the land is hilly and therefore not arable. Hong Kong lacks not only arable land but also other kinds of natural resources. There are no important mineral reserves such as coal or petroleum and hardly any raw material supplies.[2] Thus, because of its shortage of arable land, Hong Kong has to depend on imports for its food supply, and because of the lack of mineral reserves, Hong Kong has to import virtually all raw materials and fuels required by the various industrial activities. In addition, as Hong Kong is a small place, the domestic market is not large enough to absorb all the manufactured products produced locally by the rapidly expanding industries. The major manufacturing industries in Hong Kong are therefore export oriented.

It is frequently said that the rapid growth in Hong Kong is export-led; i.e., the rapid economic growth is initiated and sustained by a rapid expansion in exports. Although this proposition is largely true for Hong Kong, it may not necessarily be true for other countries in which a strong positive association between growth and export expansion exists. In the case of Hong Kong, industrialization can take place only if the manufactured products produced can find overseas markets. In this sense, export expansion makes it possible to industrialize, and industrialization gives rise to higher rates of economic growth. Export earnings enable a country to import capital goods, which have the effect of raising the level of productivity and therefore the rate of growth.[3] For some other countries cause and effect may not be as simple as this. It is equally possible for export expansion to be the result rather than the cause of economic growth; the export expansion of Japan is often said to be growth-led.

This paper will study changes in the product composition of Hong Kong's exports and imports in the past twenty years. Such changes will be explained on the demand side in terms of the changing conditions in the overseas markets and on the supply side in terms of the changing comparative advantages within the domestic economy. This paper will also deal with the direction of Hong Kong's foreign trade. Hong Kong's trade with its major trading partners (the United States, Japan, and Western Europe) will be analyzed in some detail. Lastly, the prospects of the Hong Kong economy and thus its foreign trade will be assessed, with special attention given to its attempts to diversify the economy and the political uncertainty caused by the 1997 issue.

It is necessary to distinguish between domestic exports and reexports in the total export figures for Hong Kong. Before the mid-1950s, the major source of income in Hong Kong was entrepôt trade, and reexports were much larger than domestic exports. For example, in 1950 it was estimated that reexports constituted 89% of total exports. There has been a drastic fall in the share of reexports in total exports since the mid-1950s, but in recent years, there has been a revival of the importance of entrepôt trade as a result of China's new economic policy since 1977. By 1981 and 1982, reexports constituted some 35% of total exports, which was a drastic increase when compared with a figure of about 20% in the early 1970s. In this section, we confine ourselves to the analysis of domestic exports; reexports will be dealt with briefly in a later section. Unless stated otherwise, domestic exports are referred to as exports.

The economy of Hong is highly industrialized and export oriented. It can be seen from table 12.2 that manufactured exports accounted for over 90% of Hong Kong's total exports in the past twenty years. In fact, since the late 1960s, only 3%–4% of Hong Kong's exports have been nonmanufactured products. At the SITC one-digit level, it seems that Hong Kong has experienced a considerable change in the composition of its exports. Specifically, there have been a significant decline in section 6, manufactured goods classified by materials, and a signif-

Table 12.2   **Share of Manufactured Exports in Total Exports** (percentages)

	SITC 5	SITC 6	SITC 7	SITC 8	Total
1963	1.4	23.1	5.1	62.0	91.6
1964	1.2	21.5	5.1	64.5	92.3
1965	1.1	22.0	6.8	63.5	93.4
1966	0.9	21.3	9.3	62.9	94.4
1967	0.9	19.0	10.0	65.0	94.9
1968	1.0	17.2	10.4	66.8	95.4
1969	1.0	15.4	11.2	68.2	95.8
1970	0.8	15.1	11.8	68.3	96.0
1971	0.9	14.2	12.2	69.0	96.3
1972	0.9	14.4	14.0	67.4	96.7
1973	0.9	16.5	14.5	64.4	96.3
1974	0.8	16.5	16.0	63.1	96.4
1975	0.8	13.5	14.6	68.1	97.0
1976	0.7	13.2	14.7	68.4	97.0
1977	0.8	11.8	16.0	68.0	96.6
1978	0.8	11.4	15.7	68.3	96.2
1979	0.8	11.2	16.7	67.1	95.8
1980	0.8	11.3	18.1	65.7	95.9
1981	0.9	10.7	18.7	66.4	96.7
1982	0.9	10.0	18.2	67.5	96.6

Source: Hong Kong Census and Statistics Department, *Hong Kong Trade Statistics,* various issues.

Note: SITC 5 = chemicals; SITC 6 = manufactured goods classified chiefly by material; SITC 7 = machinery and transport equipment; SITC 8 = miscellaneous manufactured articles.

icant increase in section 8, machinery and transport equipment. A further analysis at the SITC two-digit level reveals that this shift at the one-digit level is principally due to the decline of the textile (spinning, weaving, dyeing, and finishing) industry and the rise of the electronics industry. Changes in the other divisions were relatively insignificant. Miscellaneous manufactured articles, which are principally labor-intensive products, accounted for two-thirds of Hong Kong's exports, indicating the very high labor intensity of Hong Kong's manufactured exports even in recent years. An analysis at the two-digit and three-digit levels shows that there have been some changes in the composition of exports within the section of miscellaneous manufactured articles. Throughout the last twenty years, clothing consistently accounted for 35%–45% of Hong Kong's exports. On the other hand, the relative importance of footwear has been declining and that of watches and clocks rising very rapidly. At the same time, the decrease in the relative importance of plastic flowers and household goods was compensated for by the rapid increase in the relative importance of toys and dolls. In the mid-1980s, Hong Kong is the world's number one exporter of toys and dolls in value terms and the world's number three exporter of watches and clocks.

It is perhaps more revealing to look at the changing composition of Hong Kong's exports by types of industry. Table 12.3 shows the percentage shares of the exports of Hong Kong's major industries. These industries accounted for about three-quarters of Hong Kong's total exports. So far clothing remains the single most important industry, accounting for more than one-third of Hong Kong's total exports. While textiles, footwear, and plastic articles (excluding plastic toys) are declining industries, toys and dolls, electronics, and watches and clocks are the industries enjoying rapid growth. The rise of the watches and clocks industry in the past few years has been particularly noteworthy.

For some of these major industries, it is necessary to undertake a more disaggregate analysis in order to examine the changes in their product composition.

12.2.1 Clothing

A better idea of the product composition of Hong Kong's exports of clothing can be obtained by breaking down the exports by type of material, kind of wear, and method of manufacture, as shown in tables 12.4–12.6. Owing to the import restrictions imposed on cotton products at an early stage, there was a marked trend of diversification into clothing of man-made fibers. This trend has however reversed since the mid-1970s. This switching back to cotton was partly due to the extension of trade restrictions on noncotton products by many importing countries, and partly because of the coming back into fashion

Table 12.3   Percentage Share of Major Industries in Exports

	Clothing	Textiles	Toys & Dolls	Electronics	Footwear	Watches & Clocks	Plastic Articles[a]
1964	36.6	16.0	6.7	2.4	3.9	—	6.6
1970	35.1	10.3	7.1	9.5	2.4	—	4.1
1971	39.7	10.2	7.6	10.1	2.6	—	3.4
1973	38.3	12.1	8.6	12.4	1.4	1.5	3.5
1974	38.2	11.9	8.0	12.0	1.4	2.2	2.5
1975	44.6	9.4	7.0	10.7	1.1	2.8	1.8
1976	43.8	9.4	7.4	11.4	1.0	3.7	1.8
1977	39.7	7.6	8.8	12.7	1.0	4.8	2.1
1978	38.6	7.1	8.3	12.7	1.0	6.7	2.1
1979	36.0	7.3	9.3	12.9	0.9	8.3	1.9
1980	34.1	6.7	8.8	13.9	0.9	9.6	2.4
1981	35.2	6.6	9.2	13.5	1.0	9.2	2.3
1982	35.0	4.0	11.1	10.7	0.9	9.0	2.3

Source: Hong Kong Census and Statistics Department, *Hong Kong Trade Statistics*, various issues.

[a]Excluding toys.

Table 12.4   **Exports of Clothing by Type of Material** (in millions of HK $ and percentages)

	Cotton	Man-made Fibers	Wool	Silk[a]	Other	Total
1969	1,339 (35.0)	1,114	1,008 (26.3)	—	365 (9.6)	3,826
1970	1,283 (29.6)	(29.1)	990 (22.8)	—	477 (11.1)	4,334
1971	1,724 (31.6)	1,584	906 (16.6)	—	633 (11.5)	5,464
1972	1,997 (32.7)	(36.5)	915 (15.0)	—	675 (11.0)	6,109
1973	2,431 (32.5)	2,200	857 (11.5)	—	952 (13.1)	7,426
1974	3,352 (38.6)	(40.3)	729 (8.4)	—	1,046 (12.1)	8,678
1975	4,605 (45.7)	2,522	773 (7.7)	—	1,109 (11.0)	10,677
1976	6,965 (49.3)	(41.3)	968 (6.9)	—	1,418 (10.0)	14,114
1977	6,490 (47.4)	3,186	1,352 (9.9)	—	1,409 (10.3)	13,678
1978	7,251 (47.4)	(42.9)	1,414 (9.2)	—	1,686 (11.1)	15,295
1979	9,341 (48.1)	3,551	1,520 (7.8)	—	2,320 (12.0)	19,406
1980	10,779 (48.0)	(40.9)	2,179 (9.7)	—	2,561 (11.4)	22,453
1981	12,863 (47.3)	3,591	2,898 (10.7)	1,258 (4.6)	1,720 (6.3)	27,191
1982	13,644 (49.2)	(35.6)	2,519 (9.1)	1,345 (4.8)	1,716 (6.2)	27,734
		4,764				
		(33.8)				
		4,428				
		(32.4)				
		4,944				
		(32.3)				
		6,226				
		(32.1)				
		6,934				
		(30.9)				
		8,451				
		(31.1)				
		8,510				
		(30.7)				

Source: Hong Kong Census and Statistics Department, *Hong Kong Trade Statistics,* various issues.

[a]Classified under Other before 1981.

of clothing made of cotton. At present, about one-half of Hong Kong's exports of clothing and about two-thirds of Hong Kong's exports of nonknitted outerwear are made of cotton. In the case of underwear the use of cotton is also greater than the use of man-made fibers. As can be seen from table 12.4, the exports of wool clothing have declined in relative importance. This is of course a result of the clothing industry's attempt to diversify into higher-quality and more sophisticated products to overcome nontariff trade restrictions.

The major clothing exports of Hong Kong are outerwear, the relative importance of which has in fact increased from two-thirds of the total clothing exports in 1969 to almost three-quarters in 1982. The produc-

Table 12.5   **Exports of Clothing by Kind of Wear** (in millions of HK $ and percentages)

	Outerwear	Underwear and Nightwear	Other
1969	2,562 (67.0)	938 (24.5)	326 (8.5)
1970	2,852 (65.8)	1,065 (24.6)	417 (9.6)
1971	3,610 (66.1)	1,336 (24.5)	518 (9.4)
1972	4,133 (67.7)	1,462 (23.9)	514 (8.4)
1973	5,132 (69.1)	1,610 (21.7)	684 (9.2)
1974	5,848 (67.4)	2,024 (23.3)	806 (9.3)
1975	7,062 (70.1)	2,264 (22.5)	751 (7.4)
1976	10,066 (71.3)	3,035 (21.5)	1,013 (7.2)
1977	9,569 (70.0)	2,976 (21.8)	1,133 (8.2)
1978	10,835 (70.8)	3,453 (22.6)	1,007 (6.6)
1979	13,711 (70.7)	4,261 (22.0)	1,434 (7.3)
1980	16,073 (71.6)	4,930 (22.0)	1,450 (6.4)
1981	20,295 (74.6)	5,416 (20.0)	1,480 (5.4)
1982	20,618 (74.3)	5,609 (20.2)	1,507 (5.5)

Source: Hong Kong Census and Statistics Department, *Hong Kong Trade Statistics,* various issues.

Table 12.6   **Exports of Clothing by Method of Manufacture** (in millions of HK $ and percentages)

	Nonknitted	Knitted	Other
1969	2,029 (53.0)	1,510 (39.5)	287 (7.5)
1970	2,198 (50.7)	1,756 (40.5)	380 (8.8)
1971	2,714 (49.7)	2,278 (41.7)	472 (8.6)
1972	3,001 (49.1)	2,536 (41.5)	571 (9.4)
1973	3,675 (49.5)	2,834 (38.2)	915 (12.3)
1974	4,628 (53.3)	3,016 (34.8)	1,034 (11.9)
1975	5,433 (53.9)	3,597 (35.7)	1,048 (10.4)
1976	8,116 (57.5)	4,641 (32.9)	1,357 (9.6)
1977	7,549 (55.2)	4,829 (35.3)	1,301 (9.5)
1978	8,895 (58.2)	5,121 (33.5)	1,279 (8.3)
1979	11,700 (60.3)	6,094 (31.4)	1,612 (8.3)
1980	13,238 (59.0)	7,662 (34.1)	1,553 (6.9)
1981	16,272 (59.8)	9,352 (34.4)	1,567 (5.8)
1982	16,976 (61.2)	9,338 (33.7)	1,421 (5.1)

Source: Hong Kong Census and Statistics Department, *Hong Kong Trade Statistics,* various issues.

tion of outerwear offers greater opportunities for product sophistication and diversification. Recently, Hong Kong has moved into the area of fashion designs, which have won Hong Kong some prizes in international shows. Exports of nonknitted outerwear have increased since the mid-1970s, following the return to fashion of cotton apparel, which are mostly nonknitted. On the other hand, in the case of underwear and nightwear, the relative importance of knitted products has increased over time. Today, the export value of knitted underwear and nightwear is almost as great as that of nonknitted.

In sum, there have been considerable changes in Hong Kong's clothing industry in the past ten years or so, which are, however, not revealed at the two- or three-digit level of product classification.

12.2.2 Textiles

Hong Kong's exports of textile yarns, fabrics, and made-up articles have declined since as early as the beginning of the 1960s. The relative decline in the production of textiles was to a large extent the result of the increasing trade restrictions imposed on our textile products by the importing countries. The first severe blow to the rapid growth of textiles came in 1959 when the United Kingdom imposed restrictions on our textile exports under the Lancashire Pact. In 1961 Hong Kong had to agree to the General Agreement on Tariffs and Trade (GATT) Long Term Cotton Textile Agreement (CTA), by which textile exports to the United States and the European Community (EC) were limited by a quota. At first, only textiles were restricted under this agreement. Later, clothing was also included. In 1974 the CTA was replaced by the Multi-Fiber Arrangement (MFA), which also covered noncotton textiles. Both the CTA and the MFA laid down the basic principles under which bilateral agreements between Hong Kong and the importing countries were to be negotiated. In general, these agreements specified certain initial maximum quantities of textiles and clothing that might be exported from Hong Kong, allowing an annual percentage increase thereafter.

Like the clothing industry, the textile (spinning, weaving, dyeing, and finishing) industry has been responding to trade restrictions by a process of product diversification and sophistication, although perhaps at a less rapid rate than that in the clothing industry. In addition, the textile industry has increasingly turned to Hong Kong's internal market as a substitution for exports. In 1971, 45.3% of textiles produced in Hong Kong were exported; in 1978, the corresponding figure dropped to 23.5%.

Table 12.7 indicates that the major item of textiles exports is fabrics. The exports of yarn and thread are relatively small because most of the yarn and thread are used locally for the manufacture of fabrics. Of the various types of fabrics exported, there has been a gradual shift in relative importance from cotton to noncotton fabrics. One reason is that an increasing proportion of cotton fabrics produced is used by the local clothing industry, which, as noted earlier, has in recent years

Table 12.7   Exports of Textile by Item (in millions of HK $ and percentages)

	Yarn & Thread	Made-up Articles & Related Products	Fabrics Total	Cotton	Noncotton	Other[a]
1963	68 (12.2)	59 (10.6)	434 (77.2)	—	—	—
1964	85 (14.0)	61 (10.0)	463 (76.0)	—	—	—
1965	93 (13.0)	81 (11.3)	540 (75.7)	—	—	—
1966	94 (11.6)	123 (15.2)	592 (73.2)	—	—	—
1967	88 (9.4)	164 (17.5)	685 (73.1)	610	51	24
1968	88 (8.5)	199 (19.2)	749 (72.3)	654	63	32
1969	114 (10.1)	198 (17.6)	815 (72.3)	685	91	39
1970	140 (11.0)	208 (16.3)	929 (72.7)	772	121	36
1971	157 (11.2)	243 (17.4)	998 (71.4)	786	173	39
1972	187 (12.1)	237 (15.3)	1,127 (72.6)	765	317	45
1973	412 (17.5)	212 (9.0)	1,728 (73.5)	1,178	506	44
1974	483 (17.6)	277 (10.1)	1,978 (72.3)	1,384	538	56
1975	299 (13.9)	234 (10.9)	1,612 (75.2)	1,175	384	53
1976	407 (13.3)	292 (9.6)	2,352 (77.1)	1,763	519	70
1977	426 (16.1)	291 (11.0)	1,931 (72.9)	1,397	448	86
1978	345 (12.0)	331 (11.5)	2,192 (76.5)	1,521	573	98
1979	450 (11.1)	504 (12.4)	3,110 (76.5)	2,144	819	147
1980	490 (10.8)	603 (13.3)	3,442 (75.9)	2,399	842	201
1981	553 (10.4)	633 (11.9)	4,116 (77.7)	2,740	1,117	259
1982	584 (11.6)	570 (11.3)	3,898 (77.1)	2,510	1,092	296

Source: Hong Kong Census and Statistics Department, Hong Kong Trade Statistics, various issues.
[a]Special textile fabrics, lace, ribbons, embroidery, and small wears.

emphasized the production of cotton apparel. Yet in terms of absolute values, the exports of cotton fabrics are still more than twice those of noncotton fabrics.

12.2.3   Electronics

There has been no clear-cut classification of products into electronics. Electronics has increasingly become a technology used in all kinds of industries. In the trade statistics of Hong Kong's electronics exports, two ambiguous sectors are toys and watches and clocks. With the introduction of electronic LED/LCD watches and clocks and electronic toys such as hand-held games and toys with electronic controls, a problem of classification arises because these products were earlier classified as electronics and later as toys and watches and clocks. Even today, some degree of ambiguity exists. For example, in the case of a multiproduct electronics firm producing toys and watches and clocks as sidelines, such products are most likely grouped under electronics rather than watches and clocks or toys. Owing to the process of rapid product diversification within the electronics industry, there has also been a frequent reclassification of electronics products within the industry itself.

Hong Kong's electronics industry started with the manufacture of transistor radios and gradually branched into components and parts (see table 12.8). Even today the exports of radios constitute almost one-half of the export earnings of Hong Kong's electronics industry. Hong Kong started to manufacture electronic parts and components relatively early but for a long time confined itself mostly to assembly work. It is only in recent years that Hong Kong has begun to produce semiconductors and integrated circuits from the raw material stage. There are at present a few firms designing and manufacturing home and commercial computers. Hong Kong is a latecomer in the production of telephones and related products, but the growth in this area has been very fast in the past two years. So far, Hong Kong is not an important producer of television sets, especially color sets. Generally speaking, the Hong Kong electronics industry has been flourishing on

Table 12.8   **Exports of Electronics Products** (in millions of HK $)

	Computer Components and Parts	Elec. Mach. Components and Parts	Calc. Mach.	Trans. Radios and Parts[a]	Semi-conductors, Integrated Circuits	Transistors and Diodes
1963				68		
1964				95		
1965				128		
1966				185		
1967		64		210		
1968		98		329		136
1969		134		472		232
1970	197	77		549		259
1971	285	9		712	5	225
1972	279	73		919	48	276
1973	399	65		1,230	91	388
1974	465	137		1,422	229	387
1975	340	79		1,377	163	259
1976	467	149		2,001	266	351
1977	683	171	213	2,259	251	382
1978	678	160	388	2,462	303	431
1979	787	215	549	3,483	442	594
1980	1,465	258	464	4,300	522	643
1981	2,126	187	321	4,351	584	506
1982	1,694	234	308	4,131	541	549

Source: Hong Kong Census and Statistics Department, *Hong Kong Trade Statistics,* various issues.

[a]Includes nontransistor radios and parts from 1978 on.

the basis of what has been called the "three-year cycles." This means that Hong Kong electronics firms quickly spot opportunities in the world market and produce the fashionable products for about three years. At the end of three years, firms will shift to other products because of declining demand or increasing competition from other Asian exporters. Most of these products are, as expected, consumer electronics, the production of which does not require very sophisticated technology.

12.2.4 Toys and Dolls

For some years Hong Kong has been the world's number one exporter of toys and dolls, followed at some distance by Taiwan, Japan, and the United States, in that order. In both toys and dolls, there has been a shift from the use of nonplastic materials to plastic. Miscellaneous toys include stuffed and rubber toys and the electronic games recently come into fashion (table 12.9).

12.2.5 Plastics

Besides plastic toys and dolls, Hong Kong also produces plastic flowers and other articles for export (table 12.10). The exports of plastic flowers were an important foreign exchange earner for Hong Kong in the 1960s. Today, Hong Kong is still the world's number one exporter of plastic flowers, followed by Taiwan, West Germany, and South Korea. Since the early 1970s, the industry has diversified rapidly into the production of plastic household and related products. In the past few years, the relative importance of plastic flowers has become smaller than that of other plastic articles.

Table 12.9   **Exports of Toys and Dolls** (in millions of HK $)

	Plastic Toys	Metal Toys	Misc. Toys	Plastic Dolls	Nonplastic Dolls	Elec. Motors for Toys	Carnival Articles
1973	1,160	71	27	158	88	31	74
1974	1,249	103	34	192	82	41	56
1975	1,114	94	49	155	55	40	39
1976	1,651	146	80	215	85	84	59
1977	2,155	178	75	277	101	107	90
1978	2,327	193	83	268	81	127	117
1979	3,192	286	168	405	123	199	141
1980	3,578	409	162	451	124	185	200
1981	4,710	600	511	475	181	207	222
1982	5,814	415	1,153	489	187	230	223

Source: Hong Kong Census and Statistics Department, *Hong Kong Trade Statistics,* various issues.

Table 12.10   **Exports of Plastic Products, Excluding Plastic Toys** (in millions of HK $)

	Artificial Flowers and Fruits	Other Articles
1963	216	21
1964	271	20
1965	266	20
1966	258	23
1967	288	31
1968	308	41
1969	366	54
1970	416	88
1971	354	111
1972	418	133
1973	479	209
1974	344	233
1975	200	205
1976	291	306
1977	375	355
1978	435	436
1979	448	622
1980	873	786
1981	895	952
1982	889	1,053

Source: Hong Kong Census and Statistics Department, *Hong Kong Trade Statistics,* various issues.

12.2.6 Watches and Clocks

With the assistance of the electronics industry, the production of watches and clocks has experienced a phenomenal growth in the past five years as a result of the application of electronic devices to watches and clocks. In the past two years, Hong Kong has been the world's number one exporter of watches in terms of quantity and the world's number three exporter in terms of value (after Switzerland and Japan). But, Hong Kong has so far by and large confined itself to the assembly of imported parts of watches. The watches produced in Hong Kong therefore either have relatively low value-added content or are largely for the lower price range of the market.

12.2.7 Value Added in Manufacturing Industries

Many developing countries serve as subcontracting centers for foreign firms or at most undertake assembly work of imported semimanufactures. In these cases, the value-added content of manufactured exports is generally low.

In the case of Hong Kong, detailed data on manufacturing are available for the two years 1973 and 1978. These data show that value added constituted about one-third of the gross output of Hong Kong's manufactured industries as a whole. In fact, there was a slight decline in value-added content from 36.7% in 1973 to 34.4% in 1978, indicating that the process of product sophistication was quite slow. Table 12.11 gives the percentages of value added in gross output at the three- or four-digit SITC level of classification. Only in nonelectrical machinery, tobacco manufacturing, and clothing (especially leather and fur) did the value-added content increase considerably. Most of Hong Kong's major exporting industries have relatively low value-added content.

Table 12.11   Value Added as Percentage of Gross Output in Hong Kong Manufacturing

	1973	1978
Food manufacture	28.68	29.89
Beverages	65.50	61.58
Tobacco manufacture	41.24	59.90
Textiles	34.21	29.39
Clothing	33.03	36.28
Leather products	25.94	31.84
Footwear	43.97	44.21
Wood products	35.29	35.47
Furniture	46.62	45.39
Paper and paper products	31.32	33.27
Printing and publishing	50.42	46.89
Chemical and chemical products	43.00	35.58
Rubber products	42.82	36.60
Plastic products	42.13	41.39
Plastic flowers	47.45	50.15
Plastic toys	43.17	43.70
Nonmetallic mineral products	35.22	30.82
Basic metal	25.50	23.38
Fabricated metal	44.58	40.40
Nonelectrical machinery	36.38	46.36
Electrical machinery	31.78	30.05
Sound equipment	28.42	22.13
Transistorized radios	26.26	26.36
Electrical appliances	34.80	32.08
Transport equipment	61.83	52.08
Professional and scientific equipment	37.10	22.02
Photographic and optical goods	56.81	36.17
Watches and clocks	30.01	20.87
Other manufacturing industries	22.97	35.43
Jewelry and related goods	11.94	28.80
All manufacturing industries	36.69	34.42

Sources: Hong Kong Census and Statistics Department, *1973 Survey of Industrial Production and 1978 Survey of Industrial Production.*

12.3   Geographic Distribution of Exports

While Hong Kong's exports are mainly from the products of a few industries, the direction of Hong Kong's exports is even more narrowly confined to a few countries. Table 12.12 shows that the United States is by far Hong Kong's most important export market, accounting for over one-third of Hong Kong's domestic exports. The relative importance of the United Kingdom market has been steadily declining, and West Germany for some years (1975–80) became the second-largest market for Hong Kong's exports. Australia, Japan, and Canada are the other important markets of Hong Kong. Hong Kong's exports to Canada began to pick up only in the late 1970s. In 1982, 3.3% of Hong Kong's exports went to Canada. The increasing importance of China as a market is even more recent. In 1982 China became the fourth-largest market of Hong Kong. But it is important to note that many of Hong Kong's exports to China consist of parts and semimanufactures representing intraindustry or intrafirm trade only. This is largely the result of the opening up of China, especially its Special Economic Zones, for foreign investment and participation. At present there are many Hong Kong firms which have subsidiaries in China and/or subcontracting arrangements with factories in China.[4]

The six countries listed in table 12.12 imported about two-thirds of Hong Kong's domestic exports. Nonetheless, the problem of market concentration is perhaps not as serious as many people think. As long as the right products are produced to satisfy the needs of overseas markets, certainly these countries can maintain or even expand their existing level of importation of Hong Kong products. After all, these

Table 12.12   **The Direction of Trade: Exports** (as percentages of totals)

	United States	United Kingdom	West Germany	Australia	Japan	China
1964	27.7	21.9	6.6	2.6	2.7	0.9
1968	41.4	15.9	5.9	2.9	2.8	0.1
1972	40.2	14.4	10.0	2.9	3.1	0.1
1974	32.4	12.1	10.7	5.7	4.6	0.4
1976	34.4	10.1	12.2	4.2	4.3	0.1
1977	38.7	8.7	10.5	3.6	4.0	0.1
1978	37.2	9.5	10.9	3.7	4.6	0.2
1979	33.6	10.7	11.4	3.2	4.8	1.1
1980	33.2	10.0	10.8	2.9	3.4	2.4
1981	36.3	9.6	8.8	3.4	3.7	3.6
1982	37.6	8.7	8.5	3.4	3.8	4.6

Sources: Hong Kong Census and Statistics Department, *Hong Kong External Trade,* various issues.

countries are all large countries with sizable markets. Hong Kong's existing level of exports to each of these countries represents only a relatively small share of their markets. Table 12.13 shows Hong Kong's exports as a share of total imports into Hong Kong's major overseas markets. It must however be noted that for some individual products such as clothing and toys, the shares of Hong Kong's exports in the total imports of some countries (such as the United States, Germany, and the United Kingdom) can be substantial. The comparative share of Hong Kong's principal export commodities in main overseas markets is given in the Appendix (Tables 12.A.5–12.A.7). Hong Kong has always been very responsive to the U.S. market; for example, we usually increase (decrease) our exports by more than 10% if demand in the United States increases (decreases) by 10%. A similar relationship exists between Hong Kong and the United Kingdom. The relative importance of Hong Kong's exports in West Germany's imports has increased from 0.6% in the early 1970s to a leveling off at 0.9% in recent years. Australia has been steadily increasing its imports from Hong Kong. In theory the Japanese market has a great potential for Hong Kong products, but it is difficult in practice to penetrate the Japanese market because of the existence of many economic and institutional barriers. In the past three years, for example, in the cases of clothing, watches and clocks, radios, footwear, toys and dolls, and electronic components and parts for computers, the United States, the United Kingdom, and West Germany are generally the three largest markets for Hong Kong. In the case of textile fabrics and manufactures of metal, China, the United Kingdom, and the United States are the largest markets.

12.3.1   United States

The United States is Hong Kong's largest market for almost all its major exports. But in the past ten years or so, the leading position of Hong Kong in the U.S. market in some products has been increasingly challenged by the other Asian newly industrializing countries (NICs)—South Korea, Singapore, and Taiwan. Today, Hong Kong is still the largest exporter of clothing, the second-largest exporter of watches and clocks, and the second-largest exporter of dolls and toys to the U.S. market. The first position in the export of toys and dolls to the U.S. market was lost to Taiwan in 1981. In the exports of electronics and textile products, the relative importance of Hong Kong in the U.S. market has been decreasing over time. However, Hong Kong has become the third-largest exporter of office machines and automatic data-processing equipment to the United States in recent years.

Table 12.13   Hong Kong's Exports in Main Overseas Markets (percentage share)

	1970	1971	1972	1973	1974	1975	1976	1977	1978	1979	1980	1981	1982
United States	2.4	2.2	2.2	2.1	1.6	1.6	2.0	2.0	2.1	2.0	2.0	2.1	2.3
United Kingdom	1.4	1.7	1.7	1.7	1.3	1.3	1.4	1.2	1.3	1.4	1.7	1.7	1.5
West Germany	0.6	0.6	0.8	0.8	0.7	0.9	1.0	0.9	0.9	0.9	0.9	0.9	0.9
China	—	—	—	—	—	—	—	—	—	—	7.0	5.3	—
Japan	0.5	0.5	0.5	0.7	0.4	0.4	0.5	0.5	0.6	0.6	0.4	0.5	0.5
Australia	1.4	1.5	1.9	2.3	2.5	2.3	2.6	2.4	2.5	2.4	2.2	2.2	2.3
Canada	0.6	0.5	0.5	0.5	0.4	0.5	0.8	0.6	0.6	0.7	0.8	0.8	1.0
Singapore	2.5	2.3	2.5	2.8	2.3	2.2	2.4	2.6	2.9	2.2	2.1	1.9	2.1
Taiwan	1.8	2.1	2.4	2.6	1.7	1.3	1.3	2.4	1.4	1.4	1.3	1.5	1.6

Source: Hong Kong Census and Statistics Department, *Hong Kong Trade Statistics.*

12.3.2   West Germany

Hong Kong has been for many years the second-largest exporter of clothing to West Germany. Hong Kong also exports a significant share of West Germany's imports of watches and clocks, toys and dolls, and travel goods. In 1981 Taiwan replaced Hong Kong as the second-largest exporter of travel goods to West Germany. Hong Kong's shares of textiles and manufactures of metal in the West Germany market have also declined in recent years.

12.3.3   United Kingdom

Hong Kong has always been the largest exporter of clothing to the U.K. market. The position of Hong Kong in this case seems much more secure than in the U.S. market, where Taiwan, South Korea, and, more recently, China have been keen competitors. Hong Kong is also the leading exporter of toys and dolls, electronics products, and watches and clocks to the U.K. market. The United Kingdom is also an important market for Hong Kong's exports of metal products, textile fabrics, plastic flowers and other plastic articles, and heating and lighting fixtures and fittings, though these products are not among Hong Kong's leading exports.

12.3.4   Japan

None of Hong Kong's exports make up a significant share of Japan's imports. Hong Kong's major exports to Japan are clothing, watches and clocks, toys and dolls, metal products, travel goods, jewelry, artificial flowers, and metal scrap. There have been various attempts by Hong Kong to penetrate the Japanese market to a greater extent, but success has so far been limited. The problems facing Hong Kong are believed to be similar to those facing other exporters, especially other developing countries. It is believed that Japan imposes a number of administrative (invisible and yet effective) protective measures on imports. The Japanese yen has been thought to be deliberately undervalued. The multilayered distribution network is difficult for exporters to break into. Also, Japanese consumer tastes are difficult to satisfy. A special problem for Hong Kong is that its lower-end products are more expensive than the products of lower-wage countries and its higher-end products cannot compete with the name-brand products of Europe, for which Japanese consumers have a uniquely strong preference.

12.4   The Determinants of Export Growth

Table 12.14 shows the value index, unit value index, and quantum index of Hong Kong's exports for the period 1969–82. It is evident

Table 12.14   Trade Indices of Hong Kong's Exports

	Value Index	Unit Value Index	Quantum Index
1969	13	33	39
1970	15	36	43
1971	17	38	45
1972	19	40	47
1973	24	48	50
1974	28	61	47
1975	28	61	47
1976	41	67	61
1977	44	69	64
1978	51	72	70
1979	70	84	83
1980	85	92	92
1981	100	100	100
1982	103	106	97

Source: Hong Kong Census and Statistics Department, *Hong Kong Review of Overseas Trade,* various issues.

that Hong Kong's exports have grown at a very fast rate. Exports increased 7.9 times in terms of value (at current prices), 3.2 times in terms of unit value, and 2.5 times in terms of quantity, when we compare the beginning and ending years. As we have seen, about 95% of Hong Kong's exports are manufactured products. This high rate of export growth must therefore reflect an equally high rate of growth in Hong Kong's manufacturing sector. Most of the major manufacturing industries in Hong Kong are highly export oriented. According to the industrial surveys, some 75% of the output of the major industries in Hong Kong was for export. The figures are in fact much higher for many individual industries, such as consumer electronics, watches, clothing, and toys and dolls, all of which export over 90% of their output. The textile (spinning and weaving) industry is the notable exception, exporting only about one-quarter of its output in recent years. There is evidence that Hong Kong's growth is export-led (see Chen 1980). The issue here is how the rapid growth of Hong Kong's manufactured exports in the past two decades can be explained.

An often-used technique to analyze the sources of export growth is the constant-market-share method, first developed by Tyszynski (1951)and later widely applied to many country and regional studies (for a more recent review and extension see Richardson 1971). Essentially, this constant-market-share method uses a simple conceptual framework to decompose export growth into four components:

1. The effect of the increase in total world trade
2. The effect of the changes in the commodity composition of world trade; this effect will be greater the greater the more-than-

proportionate growth in world trade of the commodities which Hong Kong exports in the base year

3. The effect of the changes in the market distribution of world trade; this effect will be greater the greater the more-than-proportionate growth in demand in the markets which Hong Kong exports to in the base year

4. The effect of a country's increased competitiveness and therefore its ability to capture a larger share of its markets in the base year

This decomposition method is presented by the following formula:

$$\frac{dX}{dt} = \left(s\frac{dQ}{dt} \right) + \left(\sum_i s_i \frac{dQ_i}{dt} - s\frac{dQ}{dt} \right) + \left(\sum_i \sum_j s_{ij}\frac{dQ_{ij}}{dt} \right.$$
$$\left. - \sum_i s_i\frac{dQ_i}{dt} \right) + \left(\sum_i \sum_j Q_{ij}\frac{ds_{ij}}{dt} \right).$$

The quantity X is Hong Kong's total exports; s is Hong Kong's share in world trade; Q is the world's total trade; s_i is Hong Kong's share in the total world trade of commodity i; Q_i is the world's total trade in commodity i; s_{ij} is Hong Kong's share in the total world trade of commodity i to market j; Q_{ij} are the total exports of commodity i to market j; and t is time.

The constant-market-share analysis is simple to operate but also subject to a number of shortcomings (see Richardson 1971; Ooms 1967). For example, the method is arbitrary in that the share, or competitiveness, effect is nothing but an unexplained residual and the ordering of the terms in the actual computation affects the results. More importantly, this approach concentrates on the demand side. The supply factors are only implicitly considered in the competitiveness effect, which is only a residual. Also, this model treats commodity and market distributions in a static sense, with reference to only the base year. Nonetheless, such a decomposition analysis should be useful as a partial and preliminary analysis, especially when it is supplemented by other evidence. We will consider later an analysis of Hong Kong's export growth in terms of Hong Kong's changing comparative advantage.

Table 12.15 gives the sources of Hong Kong's export growth in 1976–81 using the constant-market-share technique. Commodity exports are divided into eight groups. Markets are divided into five regions: ASEAN (Association of South East Asian Nations) and Australia, East Asia, North America, Western Europe, and others. For all exports, it is shown that 93% of Hong Kong's export growth in 1976–81 was accounted for by increases in world demand. The dominance of the world trade effect is true in fact for all commodity groups. The commodity composition effect is unimportant except in footwear, and the market distribution effect is unimportant except in the category "other." Over-

Table 12.15   **Sources of Hong Kong's Export Growth by Commodity Groups, 1976–81** (percentages)

	World Trade Effect	Commodity Composition Effect	Market Distribution Effect	Competitiveness Effect
Textiles	119.81	6.30	3.11	− 29.21
Metal	85.59	1.20	10.76	2.45
Clothing	96.51	− 150.45	− 48.47	202.40
Electrical machinery	72.34	− 7.02	− 8.89	43.58
Plastic products	69.21	− 316.68	− 115.13	462.59
Sci. instr., watches, clocks	65.88	− 8.08	− 0.54	42.74
Footwear	104.75	177.93	− 12.24	− 170.37
Other	90.67	− 2.15	37.24	− 25.76
Total	93.27	− 7.35	− 10.06	24.15

Sources of data for computation: Hong Kong Census and Statistics Department, *Hong Kong Trade Statistics,* 1976 and 1981; State Statistical Bureau, People's Republic of China, *Statistical Yearbook of China,* 1981; Directorate-General of Budget, Accounting, and State, Republic of China, *Statistical Yearbook of the Republic of China,* 1982; United Nations, *Yearbook of International Trade Statistics,* vols. 1–2, 1981.

all, about one-fourth of export growth can be explained by the increased competitiveness of Hong Kong products. It is in this sources of export growth that we find considerable differences among commodity groups. Increased competitiveness was the major source of export growth in clothing and plastic products. These are the two industries which have gone through a relatively rapid process of product sophistication and diversification. In electrical machinery (mainly electronics products) and scientific instruments and watches and clocks, the effect of increased competitiveness is also significant. It is of course not a surprise to find that in such declining industries as textiles and footwear, increased competitiveness was not a source of export growth.

The constant-market-share analysis has in fact been applied to Hong Kong for an earlier period and to other Asian NICs as well.[5] Table 12.16 gives the computations for Hong Kong, South Korea, Singapore, and Taiwan for two time periods (except for Singapore). The table is constructed from three sources, yet the computed results are largely comparable. All the sources used a three-digit SITC classification of commodities, but they categorized markets differently. Two observations can be made. First, there has been a trend of increasing dependence on the growth of world trade, while there has been at the same time a decrease in the relative importance of the competitiveness effect. These trends are particularly notable in the case of South Korea and

Table 12.16   **Sources of Export Growth in the NICs** (percentages)

	World Trade Effect	Commodity Composition Effect	Market Distribution Effect	Competitiveness Effect
Hong Kong				
1965–70[a]	50.2	5.4	−4.4	48.9
1976–81[b]	93.3	−7.4	−10.1	24.2
South Korea				
1965–69[a]	26.2	−2.7	−1.5	78.0
1977–81[c]	92.0	−3.5	−1.8	13.3
Singapore				
1977–81[c]	65.0	7.1	2.8	25.1
Taiwan				
1965–70[a]	30.6	−6.5	3.2	72.7
1977–81[c]	70.9	−1.1	−0.1	30.3

[a]Kuo 1983.
[b]Computed by the author.
[c]Cha et al. 1983.

Taiwan, when we compare the periods 1965–70 and 1977–81. The reasons for this are probably (1) that the protective measures taken by developed countries in recent years have prevented the Asian NICs from capturing a larger share of their existing markets and (2) that many more developing countries (such as Mexico, Brazil, Malaysia, and Thailand) have switched to an export-oriented development strategy, thus competing with the Asian NICs in the developed-country markets. Thus, to a large extent, the Asian NICs in recent years could expand their exports only at a rate corresponding to the growth in world trade.

The second observation is that, with perhaps the exception of Singapore, the effects of commodity composition and market distribution have not been important factors explaining export growth. What is implied by these results is that the commodities and markets that the Asian NICs concentrate on in the base year do not experience more than proportionate growth during the period under construction. There is, however, no indication as to whether commodity and market diversifications have taken place.

It is of interest to examine how much diversification of products was undertaken by Hong Kong manufacturing in the past twenty years. One simple method to achieve this is to calculate the concentration ratios of Hong Kong's commodity exports at the, say, three-digit level. This is given in table 12.17. The computation of these ratios is based on the "H" concentration measure, which is defined as the square root of the sum of the percentage share of different commodities (or commodity groups) in total exports (Hirschman 1945; Adelman 1969; Naya 1973). When multiplied by 100, the ratio will vary between 0 and 100; the more diversified the commodity pattern, the smaller the ratio. The

Table 12.17   Commodity Concentration Ratios of Hong Kong's Exports

Year	Concentration Ratio	Year	Concentration Ratio
1964	40.52	1973	41.33
1965	42.66	1974	40.88
1966	39.68	1975	46.09
1967	39.09	1976	45.50
1968	39.96	1977	42.00
1969	40.84	1978	41.39
1970	40.09	1979	41.26
1971	43.08	1980	41.82
1972	43.15		

Source: Computed from data in Hong Kong Census and Statistics Department, *Hong Kong External Trade,* various issues.

commodity concentration ratios of Hong Kong's exports indicate that there has not been much diversification in Hong Kong manufacturing at the three-digit level. There are in fact indications that the commodity pattern was more concentrated in the 1970s than in the 1960s.

Nonetheless, it is unlikely that Hong Kong was able to respond to the increase in world trade so well without having diversified. At a more disaggregate level, it can be shown that, within individual industries such as clothing, textiles, plastics, and electronics, very rapid processes of product diversification have been taking place. This has been discussed above in connection with the patterns of Hong Kong's exports. Hong Kong industrialists are extremely flexible and adaptable in coping with changes in consumers' tastes within a particular subsector or product group. On the other hand, Hong Kong industrialists are more reluctant to diversify into new industries, the establishment of which requires much longer term investment and greater risk. This reluctance is reinforced by the fact that there has been no definite government industrial policy.

Very much in line with our expectations, market diversification has been of no importance in explaining Hong Kong's export growth. As we have seen, in the past two decades Hong Kong has continued to rely on a few markets, whose growth was generally relatively slow, with perhaps the exception of West Germany. Some diversification into the Middle Eastern and African markets has been achieved, but the overall significance of this is understandably limited.

Let us now turn to a consideration of the supply factors affecting Hong Kong's export growth. Owing to data limitations, we can examine only the two years 1973 and 1978, during which large-scale surveys of industrial production were performed.

Table 12.18 shows the relationship between export performance and changes in capital intensity. Two interesting observations emerge from these data. First, the major exporting industries of Hong Kong were

Table 12.18   **Export Performance and Capital Intensity of Principal Commodities**

	Exports[a]	Export Share (%)	Export Growth 1973–78 (%)	Capital-Labor Ratio[b]
Clothing: outerwear				
1973	4,724	24.3		4.02
1978	10,306	25.3	118.2	4.72
Clothing: underwear				
1973	1,604	8.2		2.04
1978	3,330	8.2	107.6	3.49
Footwear				
1973	273	1.4		2.54
1978	407	1.0	49.1	2.83
Textile yarn & thread				
1973	412	2.1		9.02
1978	345	0.8	− 16.3	10.05
Textile fabrics				
1973	1,728	8.9		22.83
1978	2,192	5.4	26.9	17.77
Textile made-up articles				
1973	212	1.1		11.42
1978	331	0.8	56.1	7.96
Toys & dolls				
1973	1,669	8.6		5.15
1978	3,373	8.3	102.1	6.80
Artificial flowers				
1973	479	2.5		5.94
1978	435	1.1	− 9.2	7.05
Plastic articles[c]				
1973	209	1.1		10.47
1978	436	1.1	108.6	10.66
Iron & steel utensils				
1973	91	0.5		6.60
1978	190	0.5	108.8	7.91
Metal lanterns				
1973	56	0.3		6.80
1978	151	0.4	169.6	10.51
Electric torches				
1973	81	0.4		5.86
1978	127	0.3	56.8	6.89
Handbags, etc.				
1973	288	1.5		2.66
1978	611	1.5	112.2	3.30
Watches & clocks				
1973	293	1.5		5.84
1978	2,734	6.7	833.1	7.90
Cameras				
1973	75	0.4		6.03
1978	297	0.7	296.0	5.91

Table 12.18   (continued)

	Exports[a]	Export Share (%)	Export Growth 1973–78 (%)	Capital-Labor Ratio[b]
Nonelectric machinery & parts				
1973	213	1.1		8.40
1978	353	0.9	65.0	8.20
Electronic components & parts				
1973	464	2.4		3.85
1978	838	2.1	80.6	7.24
Transistor radios & parts				
1973	1,230	6.3		2.65
1978	2,247	5.5	82.7	3.67
Electric heating equipment & parts				
1973	36	0.2		4.77
1978	404	1.0	1,022.2	9.30

Sources: Hong Kong Census and Statistics Department, *1973 Survey of Industrial Production* and *1978 Survey of Industrial Production;* idem, *Hong Kong External Trade.*
[a]In millions of HK dollars.
[b]HK $1,000 per worker, at 1973 prices.
[c]Excluding flowers.

quite labor-intensive in 1973, and many of them remained so in 1978. Clothing, radios, and handbags are notable examples.[6] This is perhaps because Hong Kong exports are relatively human-capital-intensive rather than physical-capital-intensive. Secondly, over the period 1973–78, the capital intensity of most of the major industries nonetheless increased substantially. In fact there is some evidence that those industries which performed better are also those with more significant increases in capital intensity. Examples are clothing, metal lanterns, watches and clocks, and electric heating equipment and parts. The capital intensity of electronic parts and components increased significantly, but this sector did not capture an increasing share in total exports. There was perhaps a time lag in this case. In later years, after 1978, this sector grew at a phenomenal rate. The manufacture of textiles is an interesting case. The capital intensity of this sector is high, and the technology used is very modern. The severe trade restrictions imposed on textiles have initiated two kinds of changes: (1) production catering to the local market and (2) reduction in the rate of investment, resulting in a lower capital intensity, which may be more appropriate for Hong Kong's factor endowment considering that Hong Kong is perhaps more human-capital abundant than physical-capital abundant.

If export performance is an indicator of revealed comparative advantage (Balassa 1965), our findings indicate that the comparative advantage of Hong Kong is gradually changing toward more capital-intensive products. This is surely a natural and expected phenomenon in the process of economic development; a study of this process has been called the "stages" approach to comparative advantage (Balassa 1979; Heller 1976). It implies that countries will gradually change their trade structure in the course of economic growth and development. There are of course good reasons to believe that the comparative advantage of Hong Kong has been changing. With the accumulation of experience and knowledge over time, levels of both labor skills and technology have increased. However, it is important to note that the change in Hong Kong's comparative advantage toward higher technology and capital intensity has not been as rapid as in other Asian NICs. First, Hong Kong has traditionally been a laissez-faire economy, with the government playing very little part in building up a technological infrastructure for the promotion of the level of technology. Second, though the absolute wage rate of Hong Kong manufacturing is second to only Japan in Asia, the increase in wage rate in the past twenty years has most likely been smaller than productivity increases. For example, for the period 1964–82, the real wage rate in Hong Kong manufacturing increased at an average annual rate of only 3.7% (see Appendix table 12.A.3). In addition, during the period 1978–81, about half a million people came to Hong Kong from China; almost all of them are in the working-age group (for population statistics see table 12.A.2). This huge supply of unskilled and semiskilled workers certainly had an unfavorable effect on Hong Kong's moving up the comparative advantage ladder.

Unlike most other developing countries, the upgrading of industries in Hong Kong is not constrained by a shortage in the supply of capital. Capital is not a problem inasmuch as the private saving rates are high and the amount of foreign direct investment has been substantial. Multinational corporations in Hong Kong have also played a positive role in technology transfer and the promotion of manufactured exports.[7]

12.5   The Patterns of Imports

The lack of arable land and natural resources in Hong Kong means that Hong Kong has to import foodstuffs, raw materials, and fuels from other countries. With rapid industrialization, the need to import these products increases. Nowhere else in the world can we find a closer link between imports and exports than in Hong Kong.

Foodstuffs accounted for a quarter of total imports in 1964 but declined to about 10% in recent years (see table 12.19). This is an expected

Table 12.19   **Imports Classified by End Use** (as percentages of totals)

	Foodstuffs	Consumer Goods	Fuels	Raw Materials	Capital Goods
1964	24.7	19.7	2.8	44.3	8.5
1968	20.7	23.9	3.1	43.8	8.6
1970	17.9	25.5	2.7	41.7	12.2
1972	17.5	25.8	2.8	41.0	12.8
1974	18.4	22.3	5.9	40.9	12.6
1976	16.0	21.4	5.9	44.1	12.6
1977	15.5	23.5	5.8	41.9	13.3
1978	13.6	26.6	4.7	42.2	12.9
1979	11.6	25.1	5.4	43.7	14.2
1980	10.8	26.4	6.8	41.6	14.4
1981	10.6	26.7	7.7	40.4	14.6
1982	11.8	27.0	7.8	39.5	13.9

Source: Hong Kong Census and Statistics Department, *Hong Kong External Trade,* various issues.

trend because when the level of income increases, the demand for foodstuffs will normally increase less than proportionately. The increase in the percentage of fuels in total imports since 1974 is a reflection of the drastic increase in crude oil prices. In recent years, the quantity of crude oil imports has actually fallen, indicating that the demand for crude oil has become much more price-elastic over time. The percentage of capital goods has also been increasing moderately over time, and to some extent this reveals the rapid process of industrialization in Hong Kong and a movement toward more capital-intensive methods of production. It is of interest to note that Hong Kong does produce many of the consumer goods we currently import, such as radios, television sets, cameras, domestic electrical equipment, clothing, and footwear. We have continued to import these goods while at the same time exporting similar products to overseas markets. This indicates the snobbish behavior of many Hong Kong people and also how highly export oriented the Hong Kong economy is. On the one hand, owing to the small size of the domestic market, manufacturers are not interested in making the effort to develop the domestic market. On the other hand, with rapid increases in income, consumers prefer higher-quality and more sophisticated imported goods in many cases.

China has always been the major supplier of foodstuffs to Hong Kong and was the largest trading partner with regard to imports up to 1968, when Japan became the largest supplier of products to Hong Kong (see table 12.20). With the opening up of China and the recent closer economic ties between China and Hong Kong, China in 1982 once again became Hong Kong's largest supplier. The importance of the United

Table 12.20   **Sources of Hong Kong's Imports** (as percentages of totals)

	Japan	China	United States	United Kingdom	Singapore	Taiwan
1964	18.1	23.0	11.5	9.8	3.0	2.2
1968	21.8	19.5	13.8	8.7	2.1	3.3
1972	23.3	17.7	11.9	6.6	3.1	6.0
1974	20.9	17.6	13.5	5.7	5.5	5.2
1976	21.6	17.9	12.3	4.2	7.7	7.1
1977	23.7	16.6	12.5	4.5	5.9	6.7
1978	22.8	16.7	11.9	4.7	5.1	6.8
1979	22.5	17.6	12.1	5.1	5.6	7.0
1980	23.0	19.7	11.8	4.9	6.6	7.1
1981	23.2	21.3	10.4	4.5	7.7	7.8
1982	22.1	23.0	10.8	4.8	7.1	7.1

Source: Hong Kong Census and Statistics Department, *Hong Kong External Trade,* various issues.

States and the United Kingdom has generally been declining, while Singapore (for its supply of petroleum) and Taiwan have emerged as important sources of supply to Hong Kong. Hong Kong imports a wide range of products from Japan and the United States, including both capital and consumer goods. Hong Kong imports mainly foodstuffs from China; but the import of textile goods, clothing, and some manufactured articles has become increasingly significant. The major imports from the United Kingdom and West Germany are machinery, electrical appliances, fruits and vegetables, and plastic materials. Table 12.A.8 in the Appendix gives detailed information on the main sources of imports by end-use category in recent years.

12.6   The Patterns of Reexports

As mentioned above, there has been a strong revival of Hong Kong's entrepôt trade following China's much more open economic policy after 1977. Hong Kong has once again become an important port of China trade. Traditionally, textile products were the major reexport items and they still remain of importance (see table 12.21). Since the early 1970s, the relative importance of watches and machinery increased while that of medical and pharmaceutical products declined. Another notable feature of the changes in the commodity composition of reexports is the rapid growth of Hong Kong into a world trading center for diamonds and other precious stones during 1968–79. With a recent drop in the prices of precious stones, the importance of diamonds in Hong Kong's reexports has decreased drastically.

Table 12.21   Reexports by Principal Commodities (as percentages of totals)

	1964	1968	1970	1972	1974	1976	1977	1978	1979	1980	1981	1982
Textiles	15.0	19.5	13.4	14.1	13.1	10.7	12.1	13.7	13.8	14.3	16.7	14.5
Diamonds	6.3	13.1	17.8	14.8	10.0	8.7	7.5	9.2	7.1	4.7	3.8	2.6
Watches	2.7	3.8	4.5	5.0	7.1	6.2	6.3	6.6	6.2	6.9	6.2	5.1
Articles of apparel and clothing accessories	1.6	1.9	1.8	2.5	2.9	3.2	3.1	3.5	4.7	5.2	5.3	6.8
Electrical machinery, apparatus, and appliances	1.7	1.9	3.7	5.2	6.8	7.1	8.3	8.0	8.2	8.7	10.5	10.2
Nonelectrical machinery	2.3	3.5	4.8	4.5	5.0	5.5	6.2	7.0	8.1	7.6	7.2	7.9
Medical and pharmaceutical products	5.2	8.2	8.7	5.7	3.9	3.9	3.7	3.2	2.7	2.0	1.8	1.8

Sources: Hong Kong Census and Statistics Department, *Hong Kong External Trade*, various issues.

Table 12.22   The Direction of Reexports (as percentages of totals)

	Japan	Singapore	Taiwan	Indonesia	United States	China
1964	14.7	13.9	4.1	15.3	3.4	3.4
1968	16.4	10.8	4.7	15.7	6.4	1.7
1972	20.1	10.5	8.4	7.8	8.8	2.0
1974	14.4	12.1	9.7	8.6	7.2	2.8
1976	16.8	10.5	9.1	7.9	9.6	1.4
1977	13.6	10.8	8.9	9.0	10.8	1.8
1978	17.3	10.5	9.3	9.9	9.3	1.6
1979	12.4	9.0	8.6	8.4	10.0	6.6
1980	7.3	8.3	7.4	9.2	10.3	15.4
1981	6.7	7.8	5.8	10.2	11.5	19.3
1982	5.8	8.2	6.0	10.4	12.7	18.0

Source: Hong Kong Census and Statistics Department, Hong Kong External Trade, various issues.

Table 12.22 gives the major reexport markets of Hong Kong. It is of interest to note that the relative importance of the markets has been changing. In general, the relative importance of Japan and Singapore has been declining and that of the United States and China has been increasing very rapidly. China has once again become by far the most important reexport market of Hong Kong. Taiwan's and Indonesia's shares in Hong Kong's reexports have fluctuated. It is also of interest to note that, while there is as yet no direct trade between China and Taiwan and between China and South Korea, there has been indirect trade with Hong Kong as the middleman between China on the one hand and Taiwan and South Korea on the other, and this indirect trade has been growing in the past few years. In 1982 Hong Kong reexported 3.8% of its total reexports to South Korea.

12.7 Balance of Trade and Payments

In Hong Kong, it is not only true that the import value of merchandise is always much greater than its export value but also that this imbalance exists from time to time even after allowing for the exports and imports of services. Such imbalances occurred in the period 1961–66 and have occurred since 1978. Thus, even with Hong Kong's prosperous tourist industry and financial and transportation services, the current account in the balance of payments is still generally unbalanced. Table 12.A.4 in the Appendix shows the huge imbalance in merchandise trade and the net exports of goods and services. After two years' rapid recovery and growth, domestic consumption began to increase very rapidly, and this was especially apparent in 1978, during which aggregate demand tended to increase at a more rapid rate than that of aggregate supply.

This increased drastically our import of goods and led to huge imbalances in our net exports of goods and services. The imbalance reached an unprecedented figure of HK $8337 million in 1981 and has been reflected in the rapidly falling exchange rate of the Hong Kong dollar since late 1977.

Does this imbalance in the *current* account mean that Hong Kong has suffered from an *overall* imbalance in the balance of payments? Unlike most other countries, Hong Kong does not yet have any official balance-of-payments accounts, which means that a definite answer to the question cannot be given. However, it must be true that for most of the years in the postwar period Hong Kong did not have a balance-of-payments deficit, because the deficit in the current account was offset by the surplus in the capital account. Owing to the relative social and political stability, sound financial structure, low taxation, and free foreign exchange market, Hong Kong has always attracted a large inflow of capital, both long term and short term. It is reasonable to believe that such an inflow of capital each year can well offset the deficit in the current account.

Nevertheless, the situation has become less clear because of the uncertainties created by the 1997 issue. Since mid-1982, Hong Kong has suffered from a kind of confidence crisis: local capital has become much more hesitant to stay in Hong Kong, and there is evidence of a significant amount of outflow of local Hong Kong capital. But to a large extent, this outflow of local capital has been offset by an increase in the inflow of foreign capital, particularly the long-term capital in productive activities. This can perhaps be explained by the fact that in the global strategies of foreign multinational corporations Hong Kong is considered relatively politically stable and profitable to invest in.

In terms of trade balances with individual countries and regions, Hong Kong has a substantial favorable balance with North America, a small favorable balance with Western Europe, but a huge trade deficit with Asia. Our exports to the United States are more than double our imports from it. Hong Kong has a favorable balance of trade with West Germany, the Netherlands, and the United Kingdom, and an unfavorable balance with Switzerland, France, and Italy. In Asia, we have huge deficits in our trade with Japan, China, and Singapore.[8] Hong Kong's trade with Africa, Australia, the Middle East, and Central and South America is limited, but there is favorable balance in all these cases.

12.8 Prospects

After two decades of rapid growth, the Hong Kong economy has now come to a point where future rapid growth of the economy depends on the success of undertaking some structural transformation. As we have analyzed above, two important reasons for Hong Kong's rapid growth of exports and therefore income are a high growth rate in world trade in the past two decades and the ability of the Hong Kong economy to undertake product diversification within say the three-digit classification of industries. In sum, the rapid growth of Hong Kong in the past twenty years was largely demand determined in the sense that Hong Kong was able to take advantage of the favorable international economic environment prevailing in the 1960s and 1970s, during which trade liberalization took place under the Kennedy Round and Tokyo Round negotiations. On the supply side, Hong Kong was able to produce in accordance with its comparative advantage those labor-intensive products for which there was a tremendous increase in world demand. Unfortunately, this international economic environment favorable to developing countries has changed since the mid-1970s. Increasing measures of trade restriction, often in the form of nontariff protection, were imposed by developed countries against imports from developing countries. Protectionism is certainly detrimental to the export-led growth of developing countries, but it is not fatal. Recent studies indicate that developed countries in fact do not import many manufactured goods from developing countries (Keesing and Wolf 1981; Hughes and Waelbroeck 1981). This is true even for textiles and clothing, not to mention other more technology- and capital-intensive products. Thus, there is in fact plenty of room for developing countries to penetrate developed-country markets. Trade restrictions imposed by developed countries can normally be overcome by industrial or product diversification and sophistication. This means that as long as a developing country can maintain its flexibility and dynamism, export-led growth is still feasible in the 1980s. Also, although the competition among the NICs will continue to be keen, that between the NICs and other developing countries will not be severe for some time to come. It is unlikely that a new group of NICs will emerge in the 1980s.[9]

Our conclusion is therefore that Hong Kong in theory should be able to maintain a reasonably high growth rate, say 6%–8%, in the 1980s irrespective of the greater uncertainties in the increase in world demand and the rise of protectionism, if Hong Kong can continue to diversify its products. However, any further diversification in Hong Kong manufacturing has to be at a less aggregate level than before. In other words, Hong Kong has to begin both diversification toward new industries at the two- or three-digit level and diversification toward much more capital- and technology-intensive products within the existing industries, such as clothing and electronics. In the years to come, this means that the export growth of Hong Kong will be more supply determined than demand determined. Technological intensity and capital intensity are slowly increasing in Hong Kong manufacturing, but the speed does not seem to be adequate for the maintenance of Hong Kong's economic position. For two reasons, it is difficult for Hong Kong to transform its economy and move up the comparative advantage ladder swiftly and therefore to continue a rapid growth of exports in the 1980s.

First, in terms of technological capability Hong Kong is now somewhat behind the other NICs. Unlike the other NICs, Hong Kong does not enjoy the benefits of government long-term industrial policies. The Hong Kong government is still hesitant in providing technical support and backup services to industries, despite the fact that it is quite clear that some form of centralized effort for technological promotion is necessary for the present direction of industrial development toward products with greater capital and technological intensity. While the laissez-faire system was undoubtedly a contributing factor to Hong Kong's success in the last two decades, there is no reason to insist that this system without modification will also be the best policy for Hong Kong in the forthcoming Second Industrial Revolution.

Second, the economic future of Hong Kong is of course very much dependent on the final settlement of the 1997 lease issue. Since 1981, the question of 1997, when the lease of a part of Hong Kong runs out, has become the issue of the day, culminating in Prime Minister Thatcher's visit to China in September 1982. China has since insisted on regaining sovereignty over Hong Kong and allowing Hong Kong "persons" to govern Hong Kong as a special administrative zone of China after 1997. At present, negotiations are taking place between the British and the Chinese governments. Meanwhile, a great deal of uncertainty has been created, and this is surely detrimental to Hong Kong's economic transformation, which requires a longer-term political and economic stability. In 1983 the growth of domestic capital formation was negative. Capital flight from local investors has been significant, though for the time being the gaps are being filled by increased investment from China and continued investment from overseas. The exchange rate of the Hong Kong dollar fell from HK $6 to U.S. $1 in September 1982 to almost HK $10 to U.S. $1 on 24 September 1983, resulting in the government's decision to link the Hong Kong dollar to the U.S. dollar at a fixed rate of HK $7.8 to U.S. $1. In addition, owing largely to the cooling off of the real estate market, many banks and finance companies are in trouble because of their heavy commitments in real estate loans. The government had to take over a private commercial bank in one case.

It is however of interest to note that with the recovery of the American economy in the latter part of 1983, the export sector of Hong Kong has been able to respond quickly to the increased demand in the U.S. market, notwithstanding all the difficulties facing Hong Kong. It seems that Hong Kong's export growth can still be sustained for some time on the basis of its traditional exports if markets become available. But one certainly cannot be optimistic about the long-term economic growth of Hong Kong in the 1980s unless a truly amicable settlement of the 1997 issue can be reached soon.

If the export growth of Hong Kong does eventually decline, Taiwan and South Korea will of course derive benefits regarding their exports of labor-intensive products such as clothing, textiles, dolls and toys, and plastic products. But Taiwan and South Korea have in fact already diversified into other products and have become less dependent on such traditional exports. Greater benefits may therefore fall to the next-tier NICs such as Thailand and Malaysia, which have embarked on export substitution policies. When Hong Kong's export growth declines, its import capability will necessarily be lower, and under such circumstances Japan and China as the main sources of supplies to Hong Kong will of course suffer. It is therefore understandable that Japan has been watching very carefully what is happening to Hong Kong. Hong Kong's trade with Southeast Asia is limited and is not expected to grow significantly in the foreseeable future. It is unlikely that Hong Kong will join or play a significant role in the Asia-Pacific club of economic integration. The future of Hong Kong as it affects Southeast Asia will largely be related to the role of Hong Kong as an entrepôt of the region. On the other hand, it is expected that the Hong Kong-China economic nexus will continue to be a key factor in Hong Kong's future development before and after 1997.

Appendix

Table 12.A.1   **Hong Kong's Gross Domestic Product**

	At Current Market Prices		At Constant (1973) Market Prices	
	GDP in Millions of HK $	% Change	GDP % Change	GDP per Capita % Change
1966	11,219	—	—	—
1967	12,591	12.2	7.7	5.1
1968	13,669	8.6	4.7	2.5
1969	16,274	19.1	14.8	13.0
1970	19,214	18.1	6.2	3.7
1971	21,873	13.8	5.0	2.7
1972	25,854	18.2	9.7	7.8
1973	33,796	30.7	15.8	13.1
1974	38,786	14.2	1.8	−0.7
1975	40,574	4.6	2.2	0.5
1976	51,973	28.1	18.8	17.5
1977	59,615	14.7	10.2	8.6
1978	69,557	16.7	10.3	8.2
1979	89,473	28.6	12.8	6.2
1980	112,981	26.3	11.7	8.1
1981[a]	137,377	21.6	10.9	8.4
1982[b]	157,302	14.5	2.4	0.8

Sources: Hong Kong Census and Statistics Department, *Estimates of Gross Domestic Product 1966 to 1981* (1983); Hong Kong Government, *1982 Economic Background* (1983).

Note: Estimates for 1966 to 1973 have not been adjusted for changes in stock.

[a]Provisional estimates.

[b]Preliminary estimates.

Table 12.A.2   **Population of Hong Kong**

	Midyear Population	Crude Birth Rate per 1,000	Crude Death Rate per 1,000	Natural Increase (%)	Population Growth Rate (%)
1946	1,550,000	20.1	10.8	0.9	—
1947	1,750,000	24.3	7.6	1.7	12.9
1948	1,800,000	26.4	7.5	1.9	2.9
1949	1,857,000	29.5	8.8	2.1	3.2
1950	2,237,000	29.5	8.3	1.9	20.5
1951	2,015,300	27.1	10.2	2.4	−9.9
1952	2,125,900	33.9	9.2	2.5	5.5
1953	2,242,200	33.7	8.2	2.6	5.5
1954	2,364,900	35.2	8.2	2.7	5.5
1955	2,490,400	36.3	7.7	2.9	5.3
1956	2,614,600	37.0	7.4	3.0	5.0
1957	2,736,300	35.8	7.1	2.9	4.7

(continued)

Table 12.A.2   (continued)

	Midyear Population	Crude Birth Rate per 1,000	Crude Death Rate per 1,000	Natural Increase (%)	Population Growth Rate (%)
1958	2,854,100	37.4	7.2	3.0	4.3
1959	2,967,400	35.2	6.8	2.8	4.0
1960	3,075,300	36.0	6.2	3.0	3.6
1961	3,168,100	35.0	6.1	2.9	3.0
1962	3,305,200	34.0	6.3	2.8	4.3
1963	3,420,900	33.5	6.0	2.8	3.5
1964	3,504,600	30.7	5.3	2.5	2.4
1965	3,597,900	28.1	5.0	2.3	2.7
1966	3,629,900	25.3	5.3	2.0	1.0
1967	3,722,800	23.7	5.4	1.8	2.6
1968	3,802,700	21.7	5.1	1.7	2.1
1969	3,863,900	21.4	5.0	1.6	1.6
1970	3,959,000	20.0	5.1	1.5	2.5
1971	4,045,300	19.7	5.0	1.5	2.2
1972	4,078,400	19.7	5.4	1.4	1.0
1973	4,159,900	19.8	5.1	1.5	2.0
1974	4,319,600	19.3	5.1	1.4	3.8
1975	4,395,800	18.2	4.9	1.3	1.8
1976	4,443,800	17.7	5.1	1.3	1.1
1977	4,513,900	17.7	5.2	1.3	1.6
1978	4,606,300	17.5	5.2	1.2	2.1
1979	4,878,600	17.0	5.2	1.2	5.9
1980	5,038,500	17.1	5.0	1.2	2.3
1981	5,154,100	16.9	4.8	1.2	2.3
1982	5,232,900	16.5	4.8	1.2	1.5

Source: Hong Kong Government, *Hong Kong Annual Report,* various years.

Table 12.A.3   **Average Daily Wages in Manufacturing Industries and Consumer Price Changes**

	Nominal Wage[a] (HK $)	Nominal Wage Index[a]	Real Wage Index[a]	Increase of Consumer Prices over Previous Year (%)[b]
1964	8.60	100	100	—
1965	9.50	110	109	—
1966	10.20	118	113	2.6
1967	10.90	127	119	6.2
1968	11.50	134	117	2.5
1969	12.20	142	122	3.6
1970	14.20	165	134	7.1
1971	16.70	194	146	3.4
1972	18.40	214	157	6.1
1973	20.80	241	160	18.2
1974	22.50	261	141	14.4

Table 12.A.3   (continued)

	Nominal Wage[a] (HK $)	Nominal Wage Index[a]	Real Wage Index[a]	Increase of Consumer Prices over Previous Year (%)[b]
1975	22.90	266	135	1.3
1976	26.49	308	152	2.4
1977	29.50	343	160	5.9
1978	32.69	382	168	6.0
1979	39.07	458	181	11.6
1980	43.78	513	175	15.5
1981	50.14	587	174	15.4
1982	58.63	686	184	10.6

Sources: Labour Department, Hong Kong Government, *Wage Statistics,* various issues; Hong Kong Government, *Hong Kong Annual Report,* various years.
[a]Wage statistics are calculated from March wages and exclude fringe benefits.
[b]A new series of consumer price indexes has been used since 1976.

Table 12.A.4   **Hong Kong's Foreign Trade** (in millions of HK $)

	Imports	Domestic Exports	Reexports	Total Exports	Net Exports of Goods and Services
1947	1,550	—	—	1,217	—
1948	2,077	—	—	1,583	—
1949	2,750	—	—	2,319	—
1950	3,788	—	—	3,715	—
1951	4,870	—	—	4,433	—
1952	3,779	—	—	2,899	—
1953	3,872	—	—	2,734	—
1954	3,435	—	—	2,417	—
1955	3,719	—	—	2,534	—
1956	4,566	—	—	3,210	—
1957	5,150	—	—	3,016	—
1958	4,594	—	—	2,989	—
1959	4,949	2,282	996	3,278	—
1960	5,864	2,867	1,070	3,937	—
1961	5,970	2,939	991	3,930	− 1,234
1962	6,657	3,318	1,070	4,388	− 1,463
1963	7,412	3,831	1,160	4,991	− 1,602
1964	8,550	4,428	1,356	5,784	− 1,907
1965	8,965	5,027	1,502	6,529	− 1,645
1966	10,097	5,730	1,833	7,563	− 836
1967	10,499	6,700	2,081	8,781	253
1968	12,472	8,428	2,142	10,570	343
1969	14,893	10,518	2,679	13,197	1,053
1970	17,607	12,347	2,892	15,239	1,030
1971	20,256	13,750	3,414	17,239	244
1972	21,764	15,245	4,154	19,399	1,430

(*continued*)

Table 12.A.4   (continued)

	Imports	Domestic Exports	Reexports	Total Exports	Net Exports of Goods and Services
1973	29,005	19,474	6,525	25,999	1,266
1974	34,120	22,911	7,124	30,005	711
1975	34,472	22,859	6,973	29,832	920
1976	43,293	32,629	8,928	41,557	4,392
1977	48,701	35,004	9,829	44,833	2,096
1978	63,056	40,711	13,197	53,908	− 2,343
1979	85,837	55,912	20,002	75,934	− 2,467
1980	111,651	68,171	30,072	98,243	− 5,448
1981	138,375	80,423	41,739	122,162	− 8,337
1982	142,893	83,032	44,353	127,385	− 6,985

Sources: Hong Kong Government, *Hong Kong Annual Report,* various years; Hong Kong Census and Statistics Department, *Estimates of Gross Domestic Product* (1977 and 1983); Hong Kong Government, *1982 Economic Background* (1983).

Table 12.A.5   **Comparative Share of Hong Kong's Principal Export Commodities in Main Overseas Markets: United States**

Principal Commodities and Selected Suppliers	Percentage Share of Total Imports to the United States		
	1980	1981	1982
Articles of apparel and clothing accessories			
Hong Kong	25.9	25.2	24.3
Taiwan	19.6	17.8	18.7
Republic of Korea (South Korea)	15.9	17.1	17.1
China	3.9	5.5	7.6
Philippines	3.5	3.7	3.4
Japan	3.1	3.7	3.1
Italy	2.7	2.5	2.5
Mexico	3.6	3.1	2.2
Singapore	2.1	2.0	2.1
India	2.4	3.3	1.9
France	1.6	1.2	1.1
Baby carriages, toys, games, and sporting goods			
Taiwan	23.9	26.7	26.1
Hong Kong	26.3	25.2	25.5
Japan	13.9	14.5	16.6
Republic of Korea (South Korea)	9.7	8.9	9.2
Canada	2.7	3.5	2.6
Haiti	2.0	1.9	1.7
United Kingdom	2.1	1.8	1.5
France	2.3	1.5	1.3
Italy	2.1	1.6	1.2
Singapore	1.1	1.0	1.0

Table 12.A.5   (continued)

Principal Commodities and Selected Suppliers	Percentage Share of Total Imports to the United States		
	1980	1981	1982
Electrical machinery, apparatus, and appliances, and electrical parts thereof			
Japan	20.8	21.4	21.4
Mexico	9.7	10.9	9.8
Singapore	8.8	8.3	7.9
Canada	7.3	7.7	7.1
Taiwan	5.3	5.4	5.8
Federal Republic of Germany	6.8	5.2	5.4
Hong Kong	4.7	4.9	4.9
Republic of Korea (South Korea)	3.9	3.8	4.8
United Kingdom	3.7	2.7	2.5
Photographic apparatus, equipment, and supplies and optical goods, watches, and clocks			
Japan	44.4	47.3	45.9
Hong Kong	11.6	12.1	10.4
Taiwan	5.9	6.5	7.7
Switzerland	7.6	6.3	5.7
Federal Republic of Germany	6.3	5.4	5.6
Belgium and Luxembourg	4.0	3.7	4.5
Canada	3.0	2.8	3.2
France	3.3	2.7	3.1
United Kingdom	2.6	2.5	3.0
Republic of Korea (South Korea)	2.5	2.5	2.1
Singapore	1.5	1.3	0.7
Office machines and automatic data processing equipment			
Japan	40.4	46.8	48.9
Canada	15.1	14.3	12.4
Hong Kong	8.2	7.3	5.2
Singapore	1.9	1.9	4.9
Federal Republic of Germany	6.6	5.2	4.7
Taiwan	2.2	3.7	3.9
Mexico	3.1	3.1	3.1
United Kingdom	6.0	3.6	3.0
Republic of Korea (South Korea)	1.4	1.6	1.8
Textiles			
Japan	14.8	16.6	18.8
China	5.7	8.1	8.5
Italy	8.1	8.1	8.4
Taiwan	6.1	7.4	7.1
Republic of Korea (South Korea)	4.5	5.2	6.3
Hong Kong	6.2	6.4	5.2
India	8.6	6.2	4.9
United Kingdom	5.0	4.0	4.1

(*continued*)

Table 12.A.5   (continued)

Principal Commodities and Selected Suppliers	Percentage Share of Total Imports to the United States		
	1980	1981	1982
France	3.4	2.8	3.4
Federal Republic of Germany	3.6	2.9	3.4
Pakistan	2.9	3.2	2.8
Iran	1.2	1.1	0.7
Singapore	0.7	1.0	0.4

Source: Hong Kong Review of Overseas Trade.

Table 12.A.6   **Comparative Share of Hong Kong's Principal Export Commodities in Main Overseas Markets: United Kingdom**

Principal Commodities and Selected Suppliers	Percentage Share of Total Imports to the United Kingdom		
	1980	1981	1982
Articles of apparel and clothing accessories			
Hong Kong	26.0	24.8	23.6
Italy	8.7	8.9	10.5
Republic of Korea (South Korea)	7.2	10.2	8.7
Portugal	5.4	4.2	4.7
Irish Republic	5.7	4.4	4.5
France	3.8	3.7	4.1
Taiwan	2.6	3.2	3.3
Singapore	1.1	1.2	1.1
Japan	0.5	0.5	0.5
Miscellaneous manufactured articles			
United States	20.7	20.9	20.8
Federal Republic of Germany	10.1	9.6	10.7
Japan	6.8	9.0	8.7
Italy	8.4	7.3	7.8
France	10.3	8.8	7.6
Hong Kong	5.9	6.8	7.2
Switzerland	6.1	5.5	6.0
Netherlands	4.9	4.9	4.6
Taiwan	1.9	2.6	2.1
Singapore	0.8	1.1	0.9
Republic of Korea (South Korea)	0.9	0.9	0.8
Textiles			
Federal Republic of Germany	10.7	12.5	14.6
Italy	10.2	10.9	11.3
Belgium and Luxembourg	8.5	9.6	10.1

Table 12.A.6   (continued)

Principal Commodities and Selected Suppliers	Percentage Share of Total Imports to the United Kingdom		
	1980	1981	1982
Irish Republic	8.3	7.5	6.7
France	6.2	6.4	6.7
United States	10.9	8.6	5.6
Switzerland	4.0	4.3	4.2
Japan	2.8	3.3	3.7
Hong Kong	3.2	3.1	2.8
China	1.6	1.9	1.9
India	3.7	2.3	1.7
Republic of Korea (South Korea)	1.2	1.5	1.4
Taiwan	0.5	0.4	0.7
Singapore	0.2	0.2	0.1
Electrical machinery, apparatus, and appliances, and electrical parts thereof			
United States	22.4	22.5	23.5
Federal Republic of Germany	17.6	16.8	18.2
Japan	7.6	10.2	9.2
Hong Kong	2.3	2.8	2.5
Singapore	1.7	1.7	1.7
Taiwan	1.1	1.2	0.8
Republic of Korea (South Korea)	0.5	0.3	0.2
Photographic apparatus, equipment, and supplies and optical goods, watches, and clocks			
United States	18.1	18.6	19.9
Federal Republic of Germany	16.6	16.9	16.4
Japan	12.9	13.5	15.0
France	9.9	10.7	9.4
Netherlands	7.0	9.2	7.0
Hong Kong	8.7	6.7	6.5
Switzerland	6.5	5.8	6.2
Taiwan	1.1	1.1	1.1
Republic of Korea (South Korea)	0.7	0.7	0.7
Singapore	0.9	0.4	0.2
Telecommunications and sound recording and reproducing apparatus and equipment			
Japan	35.7	40.9	45.9
United States	11.8	10.6	9.8
Federal Republic of Germany	8.8	8.0	8.7
Netherlands	5.2	4.1	3.4
Hong Kong	6.0	5.8	3.2
Taiwan	2.9	2.9	2.4
Singapore	3.4	2.8	2.1
Republic of Korea (South Korea)	2.3	1.6	1.8

Source: *Hong Kong Review of Overseas Trade.*

Table 12.A.7   **Comparative Share of Hong Kong's Principal Export Commodities in Main Overseas Markets: Federal Republic of Germany**

Principal Commodities and Selected Suppliers	Percentage Share of Total Imports to Federal Republic of Germany		
	1980	1981	1982
Articles of apparel and clothing accessories			
Italy	21.8	20.6	21.4
Hong Kong	11.6	12.1	11.2
Greece	9.0	8.6	7.4
Republic of Korea (South Korea)	5.5	6.7	6.3
France	5.9	4.8	5.6
Yugoslavia	5.1	5.1	5.2
Taiwan	2.8	3.4	3.2
Netherlands	2.0	1.8	3.1
India	1.8	2.3	2.0
China	1.6	2.1	1.6
Philippines	1.0	1.2	1.0
Photographic apparatus, equipment, and supplies and optical goods, watches, and clocks			
Japan	21.7	24.8	29.1
United States	13.1	14.0	13.4
Switzerland	11.3	10.3	8.9
United Kingdom	6.9	6.3	8.3
Netherlands	6.5	6.2	7.4
France	9.0	8.0	7.1
Hong Kong	8.0	7.1	4.9
Taiwan	1.2	1.0	0.6
Singapore	1.8	1.5	0.5
Republic of Korea (South Korea)	0.8	0.7	0.5
Baby carriages, toys, games, and sporting goods			
Italy	11.3	10.9	12.3
Japan	11.2	13.7	10.2
Austria	8.0	7.9	9.8
Hong Kong	7.9	8.4	8.3
United States	10.2	9.4	7.4
United Kingdom	6.2	5.7	6.4
Taiwan	11.9	8.0	6.0
France	5.8	5.4	5.9
Netherlands	4.5	4.1	3.9
Republic of Korea (South Korea)	3.5	3.2	3.5
Telecommunications and sound recording and reproducing apparatus and equipment			
Japan	36.6	43.2	42.0
United States	6.5	7.0	6.9
Austria	6.3	5.5	6.8

Table 12.A.7   (continued)

Principal Commodities and Selected Suppliers	Percentage Share of Total Imports to Federal Republic of Germany		
	1980	1981	1982
Netherlands	3.6	5.0	5.8
Belgium and Luxembourg	4.4	4.2	4.7
France	6.7	5.1	4.6
Taiwan	5.9	5.4	4.4
Italy	4.3	3.6	3.3
Hong Kong	3.2	2.8	3.0
United Kingdom	4.9	3.5	3.0
Republic of Korea (South Korea)	3.3	3.0	2.1
Singapore	2.3	1.8	1.7
Travel goods, handbags, and similar containers			
Italy	36.3	32.1	33.1
Taiwan	13.0	17.3	16.9
Hong Kong	13.8	12.4	11.7
Republic of Korea (South Korea)	8.8	10.5	10.1
Netherlands	3.1	3.0	3.3
France	3.7	3.2	2.6
Japan	1.5	2.0	1.4
Belgium and Luxembourg	0.9	1.0	0.6
Spain	1.2	0.9	0.6

Source: *Hong Kong Review of Overseas Trade*.

Table 12.A.8   **Main Sources of Hong Kong's Imports by End-Use Category**

End-Use Category and Source	Imports in Millions of HK $		
	1980	1981	1982
Raw materials and semimanufactures	*46,489*	*57,235*	*56,444*
Japan	12,790	15,180	15,134
China	6,685	9,315	10,010
Taiwan	5,613	7,728	7,113
United States	4,196	4,886	4,912
Republic of Korea (South Korea)	2,865	3,720	3,129
United Kingdom	1,798	2,064	2,249
Singapore	1,165	1,563	1,709
Federal Republic of Germany	1,212	1,533	1,606
Switzerland	1,433	1,275	887
Canada	465	573	726
Australia	670	813	698
Thailand	605	655	697
Pakistan	801	551	685
Malaysia, West	627	694	650

(continued)

Table 12.A.8   (continued)

End-Use Category and Source	Imports in Millions of HK $		
	1980	1981	1982
Consumer goods	*29,469*	*37,070*	*38,614*
China	6,883	9,727	11,423
Japan	6,931	9,001	8,603
United States	3,111	3,418	3,827
Taiwan	1,219	1,650	1,721
Switzerland	1,200	1,305	1,478
France	921	1,128	1,233
United Kingdom	1,134	1,230	1,232
Italy	731	963	1,155
Belgium and Luxembourg	841	700	987
Singapore	807	1,124	895
Israel	1,114	1,052	860
Federal Republic of Germany	760	885	859
Republic of Korea (South Korea)	582	1,370	764
India	578	548	687
Capital goods	*16,055*	*18,822*	*19,943*
Japan	4,987	6,733	6,582
United States	4,373	4,229	4,451
United Kingdom	2,344	2,815	3,207
China	582	989	1,054
Federal Republic of Germany	883	927	1,003
Taiwan	698	787	850
Singapore	308	321	434
Italy	211	264	242
Switzerland	226	214	229
Sweden	134	134	209
Foodstuffs	*12,065*	*14,660*	*16,785*
China	5,624	7,240	7,941
United States	1,530	1,909	2,152
Japan	892	974	1,125
Thailand	675	799	844
Australia	550	663	789
Taiwan	397	389	469
Vietnam	89	140	407
Singapore	203	283	340
Republic of Korea (South Korea)	270	281	319
Macau	117	125	265
New Zealand	146	199	225
Netherlands	133	163	210
United Kingdom	181	174	204
Fuels	*7,573*	*10,588*	*11,107*
Singapore	4,901	7,335	6,829
China	2,175	2,239	2,507
Bahrain	64	126	735
Republic of Korea (South Korea)	15	3	243
Australia	43	a	180

Table 12.A.8 (continued)

End-Use Category and Source	Imports in Millions of HK $		
	1980	1981	1982
Republic of South Africa	54	154	175
United States	a	a	118
Japan	44	142	96
United States of Oceania	—	—	56

Source: *Hong Kong Review of Overseas Trade.*
aLess than HK $0.5 million.

Notes

1. For the development of Hong Kong as a financial center see Jao 1979.
2. A variety of minerals can be found in Hong Kong—namely, iron and tungsten ores, graphite, kaolin, quartz, and feldspar—but none of them occur in large quantities.
3. For an export-led growth model applied to Hong Kong and some other Asian countries, see Chen 1980.
4. For discussions on the economic interdependence of Hong Kong and China, see Youngson 1983.
5. Lin, Mok, and Ho (1980) find that both the world trade effect and the commodity composition effect were the major sources of Hong Kong's export growth in 1964–74. They, however, simply divide markets into developed and developing.
6. Balassa (1979) states that "the exports of Hong Kong are less capital-intensive than expected."
7. For a study of the role of multinational corporations in Hong Kong's industrial development see Chen 1983.
8. Hong Kong imports a large proportion of its fuels from Singapore.
9. Some elaborations of this view can be found in McMullen 1982, pp. 23–28, based on work by Bradford.

References

Adelman, M. A. 1969. Comment on "H" concentration measure as a number-equivalent. *Review of Economics and Statistics,* February.

Balassa, Bela. 1965. Trade liberalization and revealed comparative advantage. Manchester School of Economic and Social Studies.

———. 1979. The changing pattern of comparative advantage in manufactured goods. *Review of Economics and Statistics,* May.

Cha, D. S., et al. 1983. *A comparative study of the export competitiveness of Korea, Japan, Taiwan and Singapore.* Seoul: Korea Institute of Industrial Economics and Technology. (In Korean.)

Chan, W. C. 1974. International trade in manufactures: A comparative study of the export performance of Hong Kong, the Republic of China, and the Republic of Korea, 1962–71. M.A. thesis, Chinese University of Hong Kong.

Chen, E. K. Y. 1980. Export expansion and economic growth in some Asian countries: A simultaneous-equation model. In *Measurement, history, and factors of economic growth*, ed. R. C. O. Matthew. London: Macmillan.

———. 1983. *Multinational corporations, technology, and employment*. London: Macmillan.

Heller, Peter S. 1976. Factor endowment change and comparative advantage: The case of Japan, 1956–69. *Review of Economics and Statistics*, August.

Hirschman, Albert. 1945. *National power and the structure of foreign trade*. Berkeley: University of California Press.

Hughes, Helan, and J. Waelbroeck. 1981. Can developing-country exports keep growing in the 1980s? *World Economy*, June.

Jao, Y. C. 1979. Hong Kong's rise as a financial centre. *Asian Survey.*

Keesing, Donald B., and Martin Wolf. 1981. Questions on international trade in textiles and clothing. *World Economy*, March.

Kuo, Shirley W. Y. 1983. *The Taiwan economy in transition*. Colorado: Westview Press.

Lin, Tzong-biau, V. Mok, and Y. P. Ho. 1980. *Manufactured exports and employment in Hong Kong*. Hong Kong: Chinese University Press.

McMullen, Neil. 1982. *The newly industrializing countries: Adjusting to success*. London: British-North American Committee.

Naya, Seiji. 1973. Fluctuations in export-earnings and economic patterns of Asian countries. *Economic Development and Cultural Change*, July.

Ooms, V. D. 1967. Models of comparative export performance. *Yale Economics Essays*, Spring.

Park, Ungsuh K. 1980. Export competition between and comparative advantages of newly industrializing countries. *Korean Journal of International Business*, July.

Richardson, J. D. 1971. Constant-market-shares analysis of export growth. *Journal of International Economics.*

Tyszynski, H. 1951. World trade in manufactured commodities, 1899–1950. *Manchester School of Economic and Social Studies*, September.

Youngson, A. J., ed. 1983. *China and Hong Kong: The economic nexus*. Hong Kong: Oxford University Press.

13   Trends and Patterns of Singapore's Trade in Manufactures

Chung Ming Wong

In recent years Singapore has achieved a satisfactory record of economic growth together with relative price stability (table 13.1). Because Singapore is a small and very open economy,[1] the growth of Singapore's exports of manufactured goods and services is expected to have a significant influence on its overall rate of economic growth. This paper examines the trends and changes in composition of Singapore's trade in manufactures in the last two decades and attempts to relate them to the nation's industrial development and shifts in government policies.[2] Also included is a discussion of how Singapore's comparative advantage—and therefore the pattern of trade—may be expected to change in the future. Finally, the paper examines the problems that need to be overcome in view of current world economic conditions if Singapore's export-led growth is to continue.

13.1   Singapore's Industrial Development, 1959–82

Because of its favorable location, Singapore developed initially as an entrepôt, serving as a center for the collection and distribution of goods to the neighboring countries. The industries at that time produced simple types of consumer manufactures and intermediate inputs. The goods produced were based on easy access to raw materials (e.g., processing of rubber and coconut and vegetable oils), or enjoyed natural protection because of high transport costs (e.g., beverages, clay products, and furniture).

When Singapore became a self-governing state in 1959, entrepôt trade was showing signs of stagnation. The neighboring countries were in-

Chung Ming Wong is lecturer, Department of Economics and Statistics, National University of Singapore.

379

Table 13.1 Singapore: Selected Economic Indicators

Year	Unemployment Rate (%)	Gross Domestic Product At Current Factor Cost Value	Annual Change	At 1968 Factor Cost Value	Annual Change	(M¹) at End Period Value	Annual Change	CPI (annual change in %)	GDP Defl.	Current Acct. Bal. (million U.S. $)	Overall Balance	Official Foreign Reserves at End of Year (million U.S. $)	Year
1960	—	1,985.3	—	2,122.3	—	—	—	—	—	−79.9	45.7	—	1960
1961	—	2,153.3	8.5	2,305.5	8.6	—	—	0.4	0.0	−91.0	22.7	—	1961
1962	—	2,327.5	8.1	2,466.2	7.0	783.6	—	0.4	0.9	−65.0	43.3	—	1962
1963	—	2,594.0	11.5	2,724.3	10.5	832.8	6.3	2.3	1.0	−108.5	32.1	377.1	1963
1964	—	2,504.3	−3.5	2,607.0	−4.3	842.3	1.1	1.4	0.7	−54.2	−3.9	371.8	1964
1965	—	2,707.1	8.1	2,780.3	6.6	890.5	5.7	0.3	1.4	−49.0	−4.6	349.1	1965
1966	8.9	3,037.4	12.2	3,074.6	10.6	996.6	11.9	2.1	1.3	1.1	49.9	394.4	1966
1967	8.1	3,444.6	13.4	3,475.2	13.0	972.7	−2.4	3.2	0.6	−68.4	99.4	495.6	1967
1968	7.3	3,970.8	15.3	3,970.8	14.3	1,172.3	20.5	0.7	1.1	−133.3	216.7	712.4	1968
1969	6.7	4,609.5	16.1	4,501.8	13.4	1,341.7	14.5	−0.2	2.3	−191.2	95.5	826.6	1969
1970	6.0	5,319.9	15.4	5,107.0	13.4	1,574.3	17.3	0.3	1.7	−571.9	184.5	1,012.0	1970
1971	4.8	6,279.4	18.0	5,747.4	12.5	1,759.9	11.8	2.0	4.5	−723.6	319.8	1,343.5	1971
1972	4.7	7,523.9	19.8	6,514.1	13.3	2,384.8	35.5	2.1	5.4	−495.7	336.4	1,754.9	1972
1973	4.5	9,437.8	25.4	7,247.2	11.1	2,632.7	10.4	19.5	12.1	−521.8	411.4	2,373.6	1973
1974	3.9	11,738.2	24.4	7,737.1	6.8	2,858.8	8.6	22.4	15.6	−1,021.6	294.8	2,668.5	1974
1975	4.6	12,507.2	6.6	8,043.5	4.0	3,472.2	21.5	2.6	2.4	−584.2	407.5	3,156.9	1975
1976	4.5	13,586.2	8.6	8,621.2	7.2	4,000.0	15.2	−1.9	1.4	−567.3	298.4	3,343.7	1976
1977	3.9	14,846.7	9.3	9,290.3	7.8	4,412.1	10.3	3.2	1.6	−295.1	312.9	3,698.8	1977
1978	3.6	16,474.9	11.0	10,088.6	8.6	4,925.9	11.6	4.8	2.3	−452.5	664.7	5,045.6	1978
1979	3.4	18,904.9	14.7	11,030.9	9.3	5,706.1	15.8	4.0	5.3	−735.8	523.0	5,776.9	1979
1980	3.5	22,381.7	18.4	12,160.5	10.2	6,134.6	7.5	8.5	7.3	−1,564.2	669.6	6,425.2	1980
1981	2.9	26,196.3	17.0	13,369.3	9.9	7,241.1	18.1	8.2	6.6	−1,382.3	917.5	7,332.4	1981
1982	2.6	28,906.7	10.3	14,217.9	6.3	8,156.8	12.6	3.9	3.9	−1,279.1	1,176.4	8,372.9	1982

Sources: Singapore, Department of Statistics, *Economic and Social Statistics: Singapore 1960–1982*; Singapore, Ministry of Finance, *Economic Survey of Singapore, 1975.*

^aIn millions of Singapore dollars.

^bIn percentages.

^cCalculation is based on consumer price index (June 1977–May 1978 = 100).

^dCalculated from GDP deflator based on 1968 = 100.

creasingly trading directly with countries who needed their materials and had begun developing their manufacturing industries. Moreover, population growth had been rapid, and in 1960 the unemployment rate was 13.5%. To solve the unemployment problem, Singapore embarked on an industrialization strategy. In that year, the Economic Development Board (EDB) was set up as the government agency to foster industrial development. But achievements during 1960–65 were modest because of political uncertainty and labor unrest.

The separation of Singapore from Malaysia in 1965 meant the loss of a well-protected market. To protect the domestic market, protective duties were imposed. But as Tan and Ow (1982) have pointed out, nominal and effective rates of protection were low compared with those of other developing countries.[3] Although import-competing activities were generally favored during that period, discrimination against exports was low and was finally eliminated after 1967, when imports were liberalized and additional export incentives were provided. Moreover, since the import substitution phase (1965–67) was short, interest groups did not develop. Thus when Singapore later shifted to an export-oriented strategy, the transition was eased by the absence of entrenched interests.

Singapore's export-oriented industrialization was remarkably successful, and with it came significant transformation of the economy. In terms of gross domestic product at constant prices the share of the manufacturing sector has increased significantly in the last two decades (table 13.2). In 1960 the trade sector accounted for one-third of GDP, and it is still the largest sector despite the decline in importance of entrepôt trade. The manufacturing sector is now the second-largest sector in terms of share in GDP and the largest sector in terms of

Table 13.2   **Singapore's GDP by Industry at 1968 Factor Cost for Selected Years** (percentages)

Industry	1960	1970	1980	1982
Agriculture and fishing	4.1	2.5	1.3	1.0
Quarrying	0.4	0.4	0.4	0.5
Manufacturing	13.2	19.7	23.9	21.2
Utilities	2.5	2.8	2.9	2.8
Construction	3.7	6.7	5.0	6.9
Trade	33.6	30.1	25.8	24.4
Transport and communication	14.0	11.6	19.2	20.7
Financial and business services	11.7	14.0	17.8	20.8
Other services	18.5	14.2	11.0	10.9
Less imputed bank charges	1.7	2.1	7.3	9.2
Total	100.0	100.0	100.0	100.0

Sources: Singapore, Ministry of Trade and Industry, *Economic Survey of Singapore, 1982;* Singapore, Department of Statistics, *Monthly Digest of Statistics, March 1983.*

employment. At the same time Singapore has also emerged as the region's financial center, as evidenced by the increase in the share in GDP of financial and business services. The construction sector has grown since 1960 (mainly the result of public housing and other projects), and so have transport and communication.

The recent experience of Singapore provides a classical example of export-led growth. Since the turn toward export-oriented industrialization, not only the growth of exports but the growth of manufacturing output and value added in general have become tied to world conditions. The growth rates of output, value added, and direct export of the manufacturing sector are closely related (table 13.3). In 1960–68 and especially during the import substitution phase (1965–68), the growth rate of direct export lagged behind those of manufacturing output and value added. In 1968–74, with the turn to export-oriented industrialization, the growth rate of direct export was almost twice those of value added and output. During this period there were significant increases in the degree of export orientation of most industries. Singapore, like many other developing countries, was hit by the 1974–75 recession, and despite its recovery since 1976, growth rates in 1974–81 were significantly lower than in the earlier period.

Singapore is essentially a free enterprise economy, and the government has relied mainly on private enterprise and initiative while employing fiscal incentives and other measures to attract investors. Fiscal incentives were first used in 1959 with the granting of relief from the prevailing 40% company profit tax to designated pioneer companies. Under the Economic Expansion Incentives (Relief from Income Tax) Act of 1967, the existing incentives were consolidated and new ones were added.

Table 13.3   **Compound Growth Rates of Singapore's Manufacturing Sector at Constant Prices[a]** (percentage per year)

		Subperiod			
	1960–81	1960–65	1965–68	1968–74	1974–81
Output[b]	17.06	15.56	24.35	24.92	8.89
Value added[b]	16.26	16.70	19.02	23.65	8.88
Direct export[b]	20.14	13.42	18.06	41.68	9.49

Source: Singapore, Department of Statistics, *Report on the Census of Industrial Production*, various issues.

[a]Computed using GDP deflator for manufacturing (1968 = 100) in all cases.

[b]Data on output, value added, and direct exports obtained from the *Report on the Census of Industrial Production* include only firms with ten or more workers. (The share in output of firms with less than ten workers is, however, very small.) Figures on direct exports are underestimates of domestically produced exports since goods sold in Singapore may subsequently be exported. All figures are for total manufacturing excluding rubber processing.

The rapid growth of export-oriented industries since 1967 was accompanied by increasing participation by foreign enterprises. In general, no limits were placed on foreign participation: local participation, though encouraged, was not required. Foreign firms could freely repatriate profits and were allowed to import workers with skills not available in Singapore. The major sources of capital at present are the United States, Western Europe, and Japan. Compared with local firms, foreign establishments are characterized by larger size, higher value added and output per worker, and higher degree of export orientation. In 1981 wholly foreign firms accounted for 16.7% of the total number of manufacturing establishments but 42.8% of total employment, 55.9% of output, 54.3% of value added, and 67.0% of direct export. The ratio of direct export to total sales was 73.5% for wholly foreign firms and 26.0% for wholly local firms.[4] Recent figures indicate that foreign investments are concentrated in highly capital-intensive industries like petroleum refineries or rapidly growing export-oriented industries like electronic and electrical machinery and appliances.

Although Singapore has relied mainly on private enterprise, the government has tried to influence resource allocation in various ways— such as providing incentives to industries regarded as desirable for the country. In fact, Pang and Tan (1981, 151) single out the government as the most important factor behind Singapore's economic success. Government intervention was perhaps especially significant in the labor market. The Employment Act and Industrial Relations (Amendment) Act of 1968 limited the negotiating power of unions by making matters such as promotion, internal transfer, and dismissal nonnegotiable and cut down labor costs by limiting bonuses and annual paid leave and by increasing the number of hours in the work week. While some may regard such stringent labor laws as unnecessary infringements of workers' rights, they were seen at the time to be necessary to correct the image of an undisciplined work force, and they paid off very well by attracting foreign capital to Singapore.

The policy of wage restraint by the government was an important factor responsible for the success of Singapore's labor-intensive export-oriented industrialization strategy. By 1970 unemployment was largely overcome (table 13.1), and Singapore became instead a labor-short economy. Immigration laws were relaxed to allow firms short of labor to bring in foreign workers. The tripartite National Wage Council (NWC) was formed in 1972 to recommend orderly wage changes. The wage guidelines, though not mandatory, were to a great extent adopted by the unionized sectors and the public sector. In 1972–74 the NWC recommended high wages to offset inflation, but from 1976 to 1979 it recommended only moderate wage increases in order to maintain Singapore's competitiveness in the world market. As a result labor-intensive firms were encouraged and employment opportunities increased. In

1979, however, the NWC shifted to a high-wage policy in view of widespread labor shortages to encourage firms to upgrade and use labor more efficiently. The high-wage policy was in fact part of a long-term strategy to restructure the economy in recognition of the fact that Singapore's future comparative advantage might not lie in labor-intensive industries, and thus Singapore would need to move upstream toward more skill-intensive, capital-intensive, and higher-technology industries.

At present the "pioneer" status (entitling tax relief for five to ten years from the 40% tax on profits) and the investment allowance incentive (with tax deduction equal to up to 50% of new fixed investment in plant, machinery, and factory buildings) are the main incentives used in investment promotion. Pioneer certificates are now mainly awarded to projects manufacturing new and high-technology products, while the investment allowance incentive is increasingly being used to promote the upgrading and mechanization of existing operations. Tax incentives are also given to encourage manufacturers to undertake research and development activities. Projects believed to be of strategic importance to Singapore's industrial development can obtain long-term fixed-rate loans at favorable interest rates under the Capital Assistance Scheme (CAS) administered by the Economic Development Board. Lastly, on realization that the restructuring of the Singapore economy with emphasis on high-technology industries and higher productivity through automation would create demand for new skills, the Skills Development Fund (SDF) was established in 1979 to provide financial assistance to employers for the training of employees in skills needed for Singapore's economic restructuring effort.[5]

13.2 Commodity Composition of Singapore's Trade and Relation to Domestic Development

The examination of Singapore's trade structure is complicated by the presence of entrepôt trade. To give some idea of the importance of entrepôt trade, in 1960 the value of reexports was ten times that of domestic exports, and the value of reexports of manufactured goods (SITC 5–8) was about five times that of domestically manufactured exports. The value of entrepôt trade has shown a rising trend, although its relative importance has declined. It was not until 1972 that the value of domestically manufactured exports exceeded that of manufactured reexports for the first time, and only in 1974 did total domestic exports exceed reexports.

Table 13.4 shows the changing composition of Singapore's trade (imports and exports), and table 13.5 shows the change in composition of its domestically produced exports.[6] In 1960 food, beverages, crude materials, and animal and vegetable oils and fats (SITC 0, 1, 2, and 4)

Table 13.4   Commodity Composition of Singapore's Imports and Exports for Selected Years, 1960–80 (in millions of U.S. Dollars)

SITC Rev. 1	Commodity	1960 Import	1960 Export	1965 Import	1965 Export	1970 Import	1970 Export	1975 Import	1975 Export	1980 Import	1980 Export
0	*Food and live animals*	**220.93** (16.59)	**150.78** (13.27)	**242.82** (19.52)	**142.35** (14.51)	**307.31** (12.49)	**178.21** (11.47)	**694.07** (8.53)	**383.24** (7.13)	**1,362.93** (5.68)	**938.66** (4.84)
1	*Beverages and tobacco*	**23.24** (1.74)	**23.01** (2.03)	**22.98** (1.85)	**15.11** (1.54)	**41.78** (1.70)	**23.38** (1.50)	**55.02** (0.68)	**17.25** (0.32)	**129.02** (0.54)	**73.46** (0.38)
2	*Crude materials except fuels*	**496.83** (37.30)	**509.08** (44.82)	**229.59** (18.46)	**267.68** (27.28)	**283.75** (11.53)	**468.55** (30.16)	**523.25** (6.43)	**716.81** (13.33)	**1,599.13** (6.66)	**2,200.11** (11.36)
231	Crude rubber (incl. synthetic and reclaimed)	444.33	467.73	181.69	221.14	184.92	383.29	316.39	556.64	1,101.41	1,539.69
24	Wood, lumber, cork	—	—	15.94	—	39.66	36.21	71.51	64.80	198.04	273.43
3	*Mineral fuels*	**193.17** (14.50)	**128.09** (11.28)	**166.04** (13.35)	**140.83** (14.35)	**331.52** (13.47)	**360.07** (23.18)	**1,998.49** (24.57)	**1,808.73** (33.64)	**6,882.14** (28.67)	**4,882.18** (25.20)
331	Petroleum, crude and partly refined	5.75	4.10	34.29	0.00	142.71	—	1,518.46	21.87	5,681.56	—
332	Petroleum products	187.24	123.88	131.25	140.37	188.16	358.60	478.50	1,768.53	1,196.05	4,809.40
4	*Animal and veg. oils and fats*	**12.79** (0.96)	**16.42** (1.45)	**18.73** (1.51)	**19.59** (2.00)	**41.15** (1.67)	**45.80** (2.95)	**102.16** (1.26)	**103.45** (1.92)	**467.96** (1.95)	**512.07** (2.64)
4222	Palm oil	—	—	12.28	11.70	29.64	28.32	66.61	73.18	52.86	304.17
5	*Chemicals*	**44.41** (3.33)	**28.18** (2.48)	**62.06** (4.99)	**36.45** (3.71)	**126.87** (5.16)	**42.36** (2.73)	**472.63** (5.81)	**200.49** (3.73)	**1,341.28** (5.59)	**1,374.84** (7.10)
51	Chem. elements and compounds	8.37	6.37	9.99	5.92	23.06	6.03	86.25	30.40	337.49	132.09
541	Medicinal products	8.58	—	11.97	5.95	20.21	7.23	63.42	73.31	96.68	151.13
581	Plastic materials	—	—	6.20	2.34	19.71	4.38	69.43	54.94	306.05	103.72
6	*Basic manufactures*	**153.25** (11.50)	**102.74** (9.05)	**204.48** (16.44)	**116.56** (11.88)	**539.31** (21.91)	**138.24** (8.90)	**1,481.87** (18.22)	**457.94** (8.52)	**3,367.61** (14.03)	**1,601.58** (8.2727)
63	Wood and cork manuf. n.e.s.	—	—	2.85	3.31	9.73	18.32	30.24	84.61	119.30	256.69
64	Paper, board, and manuf.	12.75	—	17.60	6.22	36.07	7.24	72.08	18.75	235.11	60.85
65	Textile yarn, fabrics, etc.	72.75	46.18	87.71	45.89	264.63	53.71	374.40	130.20	846.92	366.65
66	Nonmetallic mineral manuf. n.e.s.	9.63	7.43	19.05	13.55	37.28	14.43	149.67	38.55	422.69	133.98

(*continued*)

Table 13.4 (continued)

SITC Rev. 1	Commodity	1960 Import	1960 Export	1965 Import	1965 Export	1970 Import	1970 Export	1975 Import	1975 Export	1980 Import	1980 Export
67	Iron and steel	22.52	13.11	38.16	16.70	102.03	12.79	542.01	86.82	866.97	212.33
68	Nonferrous metals	4.79	2.87	8.98	4.83	22.22	3.76	61.87	16.89	258.26	316.62
69	Metal manuf. n.e.s.	14.63	14.11	21.67	18.48	52.46	20.77	210.01	66.74	491.96	204.48
7	*Machinery and transport equip.*	**93.94** (7.05)	**76.63** (6.75)	**179.71** (14.45)	**102.88** (10.48)	**561.34** (22.81)	**170.15** (10.95)	**2,130.28** (26.19)	**1,220.00** (22.69)	**7,053.09** (29.38)	**5,105.49** (26.35)
71	Machinery other than elec.	39.01	34.28	62.01	35.17	275.46	61.93	990.35	375.01	2,511.16	1,157.67
714	Office mach.	0	0	—	—	10.86	13.25	55.40	87.55	212.00	153.35
715	Metalworking mach.	0	0	—	—	11.76	—	46.05	—	109.44	—
717	Textile and leather mach.	0	0	3.85	—	15.11	—	22.38	—	74.69	—
718	Mach. for special industries	0	0	11.39	9.79	96.83	19.65	278.30	96.38	544.99	295.13
719	Mach. and appliances (other than elec.) and mach. parts n.e.s.	0	0	—	—	102.39	15.96	416.11	113.22	1,207.86	485.02
72	Elec. mach., apparatus, appliances	17.36	10.73	50.88	16.69	160.33	62.10	793.29	620.36	2,894.55	3,120.61
722	Elec. power mach. and switchgear	0	0	14.04	2.38	26.85	5.29	152.94	54.14	476.23	286.29
723	Equip. for distributing elec.	0	0	7.09	—	18.82	—	56.68	—	120.03	—
724	Telecommunications apparatus	0	0	14.16	3.91	35.66	11.69	164.79	168.82	645.77	1,259.15
725	Domestic elec. equip.	0	0	6.02	—	8.38	1.94	18.62	14.68	78.30	113.45
729	Other elec. mach. and apparatus	0	0	—	—	70.35	42.29	398.20	374.80	1,567.72	1,428.65
73	Transport equip.	37.53	31.07	66.73	50.21	125.55	46.12	346.64	224.64	1,647.38	827.21
732	Road motor vehicles	29.97	26.42	60.45	46.93	90.41	39.52	140.56	80.44	559.80	211.24
734	Aircraft	0	0	—	—	9.41	0.85	65.77	10.70	529.34	158.48
735	Ships and boats	0	0	—	—	20.15	5.13	125.98	130.21	521.08	435.20
8	*Misc. manufactures*	**70.08** (5.26)	**32.46** (2.86)	**91.26** (7.34)	**49.33** (5.03)	**175.49** (7.13)	**80.69** (5.19)	**562.00** (6.91)	**371.07** (6.90)	**1,487.50** (6.20)	**1,283.10** (6.62)
84	Clothing	15.58	8.44	20.21	16.47	23.16	30.94	60.62	117.07	146.67	426.26
86	Instruments, watches, clocks	21.17	—	26.72	6.19	62.56	10.12	207.60	124.52	553.29	257.88
9	*Unclassified*	**26.40** (1.98)	**68.44** (6.03)	**26.01** (2.09)	**90.54** (9.23)	**52.53** (2.13)	**46.10** (2.97)	**115.21** (1.42)	**98.09** (1.82)	**311.99** (1.30)	**1,403.99** (7.25)
Total	*All commodities*	1,332.05	1,135.84	1,243.68	981.34	2,461.06	1,553.55	8,134.98	5,377.08	24,002.67	19,375.48

Source: United Nations, *Yearbook of International Trade Statistics,* various issues.

Note: Percentage shares of SITC one-digit sections shown in parentheses; . . . = not available or negligible.

Table 13.5   **Composition of Singapore's Domestic Exports in Selected Years, 1960–82** (percentages)

		Share of Domestic Exports of Commodity							
		1960		1969		1975		1982	
SITC	Commodity	Total	SITC 5–8	Total	SITC 5–8	Total	SITC 5–8	Total	SITC 5–8
0	*Food and live animals*	**22.29**		**5.34**		**3.69**		**1.54**	
1	*Beverages and tobacco*	**9.63**		**0.73**		**0.34**		**0.46**	
2	*Crude materials except fuels*[a]	**4.15**		**2.09**		**0.60**		**0.43**	
3	*Mineral fuels*[b]	**—**		**53.74**		**42.88**		**47.49**	
4	*Animal and vegetable oils and fats*	**9.35**		**1.75**		**0.74**		**1.66**	
5	*Chemicals*	**12.30**	22.53	**2.60**	11.63	**2.76**	6.83	**2.37**	6.41
	Medicinal products			0.58	2.59	1.80	4.45	0.89	2.42
	Plastic materials			0.18	0.80	0.31	0.77	0.37	1.01
6	*Manufactured goods classified by materials*	**22.31**	42.70	**8.39**	37.50	**6.45**	15.95	**4.16**	11.27
	Wood, simply shaped	n.a.	n.a.	1.99	8.91	1.92	4.75	0.99	2.69
	Textiles, yarn, thread	n.a.	n.a.	—	—	0.58	1.44	0.26	0.71
	Cotton fabrics, woven	n.a.	n.a.	0.81	3.63	0.58	1.43	0.25	0.67

(*continued*)

Table 13.5 (continued)

		Share of Domestic Exports of Commodity							
		1960		1969		1975		1982	
SITC	Commodity	Total	SITC 5–8	Total	SITC 5–8	Total	SITC 5–8	Total	SITC 5–8
7	*Machinery and transport*	**7.65**	**14.01**	**4.87**	**21.77**	**22.37**	**55.31**	**23.87**	**64.61**
	Office machines	n.a.	n.a.	0.01	0.05	2.32	5.75	1.31	3.55
	Other nonelectric machines	n.a.	n.a.	0.38	1.71	1.15	2.84	1.49	4.03
	Electric generators	n.a.	n.a.	0.04	0.19	1.16	2.87	2.10	5.67
	Telecommunications apparatus	n.a.	n.a.	0.22	0.99	4.62	11.42	5.91	16.00
	Other electric machinery	n.a.	n.a.	3.15	14.06	7.85	19.42	7.75	20.99
	Ships and boats and oil rigs	n.a.	n.a.	0.50	2.24	2.38	5.88	2.62	7.10
8	*Miscellaneous manufactured articles*	**11.33**	**20.76**	**6.51**	**29.10**	**8.86**	**21.92**	**6.54**	**17.70**
	Clothing	n.a.	n.a.	3.41	15.26	3.13	7.75	2.58	6.99
	Scientific instruments	n.a.	n.a.	0.03	0.13	1.75	4.32	0.56	1.52
	Watches and clocks	n.a.	n.a.	0.02	0.11	1.12	2.77	0.51	1.39
	Printed matter	n.a.	n.a.	0.56	2.51	0.56	1.38	0.38	1.03
	Toys and sporting goods	n.a.	n.a.	0.13	0.56	0.31	0.78	0.52	1.41
9	*Miscellaneous transactions n.e.s.*	—		**13.98**		**11.32**		**11.48**	
	Oil bunkers			13.51		11.14		11.37	
5–8	*Total manufactures*	**54.58**	**100.00**	**22.38**	**100.00**	**40.44**	**100.00**	**36.95**	**100.00**

Sources: Singapore, Department of Statistics, *Economic and Social Statistics: Singapore 1960–1982*; Singapore, Ministry of Trade and Industry, *Economic Survey of Singapore, 1982*.

Note: — = nil or negligible; n.a. = not available.

[a]Excludes processed rubber and sawn timber.

[b]Figures from 1975 include petroleum naphtha, which was previously included under chemicals.

made up about 60% of total trade, but their share declined to less than 20% in 1980. In the early 1960s, trade consisted mainly of transshipments of primary commodities such as rubber, tin, coconut and palm oil, and timber to industrial countries, and reexports of manufactures from the rest of the world to neighboring countries. In recent years crude materials like rubber are still important in entrepôt trade, but since the relative importance of rubber has declined in general, the share of SITC 0, 1, 2, and 4 has fallen. On the other hand, the shares of manufactures (SITC 5–8) and mineral fuels (SITC 3) have significantly increased. This reflects the changing nature of entrepôt trade as well as Singapore's successful export-oriented industrialization. While reexports of raw materials from Southeast Asian countries (and also petroleum from West Asian countries) to industrialized countries are still important, entrepôt trade is increasingly dominated by manufactures—e.g., the reexport of machinery and capital equipment from industrialized countries to the Asian region. At the same time (as will be seen) Singapore's domestic exports of manufactures have increased significantly as a result of successful industrialization. Domestic exports consist not only of labor-intensive manufactures like clothing but also increasingly of capital goods like machinery (especially electrical machinery and appliances) and transport equipment (including ships and boats, oil rigs, and aircraft). With industrialization, Singapore in turn requires increasing imports of raw materials, intermediate inputs, and machinery and capital goods. The effect of Singapore's industrialization on the trade pattern is once again clearly seen in the case of mineral fuels. In 1960 export of crude petroleum and petroleum products was mainly entrepôt trade. With the development of domestic refinery facilities, in the last decade exports of crude petroleum became insignificant, while exports of petroleum products (mostly to Japan) greatly exceeded imports (table 13.4). It can be seen from table 13.5 that domestic exports of mineral fuels were negligible in 1960 but accounted for more than half of domestically produced exports by 1969.

The shares of food, beverages, tobacco, crude materials, and animal and vegetable oils and fats in domestically produced exports have declined (table 12.5). The share of manufactures (SITC 5–8) in domestically produced exports declined from 1960 to 1969, but this was mainly due to the rapid expansion of domestically produced exports of petroleum products; more recently the share in the total has increased. Within manufacturing itself the share of machinery and transport increased tremendously—from 14% in 1960 to 65% in 1982—at the expense of other major categories. Increases in shares were especially spectacular for telecommunications apparatus and other electrical machinery.

The change in composition of Singapore's direct exports during industrial development and its relation to changes in composition of output and value added can be seen in table 13.6. In 1960 most industries with large shares of output and value added were those which enjoyed considerable degrees of natural protection (food and beverages, printing and publishing) or were based on materials from nearby countries (rubber and wood products). In 1960 these industries together with tobacco accounted for 54% of output, 58% of value added, and 48% of direct export. The shares of the same industries have, however, declined consistently so that by 1981 their respective shares in output, value added, and direct export were 10%, 12%, and 7%. Since the shift to an export-oriented industrialization strategy, the shares of chemical and petroleum products, electrical machinery, and transport equipment have increased tremendously so that by 1981 they accounted for almost 80% of direct export. The shares of textiles, clothing, and footwear increased until the early 1970s and then declined—apparently a result of the move to the higher-skill, higher-technology phase of export-oriented industrialization.

Also presented in table 13.6 are annual growth rates for the manufacturing sector and the Schiavo-Campo (1978) measure of structural change calculated at three-year intervals.[7] It can be seen that in terms of output and value added structural changes are the greatest in 1960–63 and the two subperiods between 1966 and 1972. Growth rates of the manufacturing sector are also the highest in the same periods. As for direct export, both structural changes and growth rates are the highest in the years between 1966 and 1975, when there was a significant turn toward export-oriented industrialization.[8] As can be seen from the last row of the table, while the ratio of direct export to total sales fell from 36% in 1960 to 31% in 1966, it increased sharply to almost 60% in 1975.

Not only had there been increasing trade in manufactures relative to primary commodities, but trade in the former had become increasingly concentrated in capital goods at the expense of intermediate goods. This can be seen clearly in table 13.7, which shows the change in composition of Singapore's trade in manufactures according to broad categories of goods. Only goods under SITC 5–8 are included; thus food and beverages and petroleum products, etc., do not enter the calculation. Figures on reexports are not generally available before 1975 and those for retained imports have to be estimated; thus they may be subject to considerable inaccuracy.[9] The figures nevertheless show a clear tendency for the shares of capital goods in both exports and imports to increase and the shares of intermediate goods to decline. These trends are especially evident when one looks at domestic exports and retained imports, where the shares of capital goods have increased from about one-fourth in 1960 to over two-thirds in 1982. The shares of consumer goods in export, reexport, and domestic export fluctuated, showing some tendency to increase up to the early 1970s and then

Table 13.6   Composition of Singapore's Manufacturing Output, Value Added, and Direct Exports (percentages)

SIC	Industry[a]	1960	1963	1966	1969	1972	1975	1978	1981
	A. Output	100.00	100.00	100.00	100.00	100.00	100.00	100.00	100.00
20	Food	16.18	13.80	13.62	12.48	9.65	6.69	6.25	4.60
21	Beverages	8.45	5.04	4.27	1.85	1.28	1.04	1.04	0.89
22	Tobacco	8.36	7.09	6.23	2.82	1.79	1.15	0.87	0.53
23+24+29	Textiles, clothing, footwear, leather products	3.27	2.51	4.51	5.10	7.73	4.74	5.45	3.95
25	Wood and cork products	7.67	5.91	6.35	4.99	4.56	2.47	2.78	1.74
26	Furniture and fixtures	0.83	1.05	1.05	0.89	0.51	0.39	0.59	0.75
27	Paper and paper products	1.11	0.74	1.08	1.01	1.06	0.77	0.81	0.82
28	Printing and publishing	9.17	6.32	4.94	2.44	2.50	1.79	1.91	1.83
30	Rubber products	3.90	1.76	2.11	1.46	0.98	0.59	0.44	0.28
31+32	Chemicals, chemical products, petroleum	13.67	26.44	26.91	40.12	32.25	41.01	41.07	42.08
33	Nonmetallic mineral products	3.72	7.30	4.61	2.41	2.33	2.77	2.08	2.38
34	Basic metal products	1.06	1.31	3.41	2.24	1.65	1.48	1.24	1.29
35	Metal products	6.53	6.62	7.07	4.95	4.29	3.88	3.74	4.06
36	Nonelectrical machinery	3.61	1.87	1.94	1.55	2.24	5.17	4.26	3.83
37	Electrical machinery	3.67	2.49	2.52	3.82	12.95	11.79	15.82	17.45
38	Transport equipment	6.81	5.86	5.99	8.08	9.67	10.60	7.79	9.95
39	Misc. manufacturing industries	2.02	3.89	3.40	3.79	4.56	3.70	3.86	3.57
	Structural change[b]	18.80	6.38	17.59	14.92	13.05	5.65	5.64	
	Growth rate at constant prices (% per yr.)	19.22	13.22	32.86	15.59	14.51	13.26	12.04	

(*continued*)

Table 13.6 (continued)

SIC	Industry[a]	1960	1963	1966	1969	1972	1975	1978	1981
	C. Direct exports	100.00	100.00	100.00	100.00	100.00	100.00	100.00	100.00
20	Food	14.21	14.93	14.04	11.54	6.00	4.41	4.79	3.92
21	Beverages	10.99	5.21	3.65	1.01	0.55	0.43	0.33	0.43
22	Tobacco	0.19	1.52	1.04	0.27	0.13	0.03	0.04	0.10
23+24+29	Textile, clothing, footwear, leather products	2.49	2.48	9.61	7.26	10.93	5.06	5.48	3.99
25	Wood and cork products	10.48	9.22	9.37	5.75	5.25	2.72	2.72	1.45
26	Furniture and fixtures	0.76	1.26	0.61	0.25	0.10	0.18	0.35	0.62
27	Paper and paper products	0.84	0.59	0.91	0.50	0.44	0.15	0.17	0.16
28	Printing and publishing	4.38	4.78	2.49	0.67	0.89	0.63	0.53	0.51
30	Rubber products	7.82	3.32	2.79	1.64	0.94	0.46	0.29	0.22
31+32	Chemicals, chemical products, petroleum	17.70	19.46	29.16	50.17	32.53	45.63	48.14	45.41
33	Nonmetallic mineral products	9.10	9.10	1.82	1.31	0.55	1.10	0.70	0.73
34	Basic metal products	1.81	2.52	3.15	1.47	0.31	0.47	0.64	0.60
35	Metal products	7.88	8.18	6.20	3.21	1.93	2.07	1.49	1.83
36	Nonelectrical machinery	2.44	1.86	1.42	0.47	2.40	6.63	4.25	3.94
37	Electrical machinery	8.31	5.68	4.40	6.69	23.79	17.43	20.68	24.00
38	Transport equipment	0.42	6.82	8.62	5.76	8.57	9.32	6.57	9.46
39	Misc. manufacturing industries	0.20	0.33	0.73	2.03	4.68	3.26	2.83	2.63
	Structural change[b]		13.63	18.76	24.61	28.39	19.02	6.92	7.01
	Growth rate at constant prices (% per yr.)		8.39	18.66	44.60	21.90	22.92	17.79	10.02

C. Direct exports

	100.00	100.00	100.00	100.00	100.00	100.00	100.00	100.00
20 Food	14.21	14.93	14.04	11.54	6.00	4.41	4.79	3.92
21 Beverages	10.99	5.21	3.65	1.01	0.55	0.43	0.33	0.43
22 Tobacco	0.19	1.52	1.04	0.27	0.13	0.03	0.04	0.10
23+24+29 Textile, clothing, footwear, leather products	2.49	2.48	9.61	7.26	10.93	5.06	5.48	3.99
25 Wood and cork products	10.48	9.22	9.37	5.75	5.25	2.72	2.72	1.45
26 Furniture and fixtures	0.76	1.26	0.61	0.25	0.10	0.18	0.35	0.62
27 Paper and paper products	0.84	0.59	0.91	0.50	0.44	0.15	0.17	0.16
28 Printing and publishing	4.38	4.78	2.49	0.67	0.89	0.63	0.53	0.51
30 Rubber products	7.82	3.32	2.79	1.64	0.94	0.46	0.29	0.22
31+32 Chemicals, chemical products, petroleum	17.70	19.46	29.16	50.17	32.53	45.63	48.14	45.41
33 Nonmetallic mineral products	9.10	9.10	1.82	1.31	0.55	1.10	0.70	0.73
34 Basic metal products	1.81	2.52	3.15	1.47	0.31	0.47	0.64	0.60
35 Metal products	7.88	8.18	6.20	3.21	1.93	2.07	1.49	1.83
36 Nonelectrical machinery	2.44	1.86	1.42	0.47	2.40	6.63	4.25	3.94
37 Electrical machinery	8.31	5.68	4.40	6.69	23.79	17.43	20.68	24.00
38 Transport equipment	0.42	6.82	8.62	5.76	8.57	9.32	6.57	9.46
39 Misc. manufacturing industries	0.20	0.33	0.73	2.03	4.68	3.26	2.83	2.63
Structural change[b]	13.63	18.76	24.61	28.39	19.02	6.92	7.01	
Growth rate at constant prices (% per yr.)	8.39	18.66	44.60	21.90	22.92	17.79	10.02	
Ratio of direct export to total sales (%)	35.95	26.75	30.82	38.87	46.51	58.07	64.60	61.23

Source: Singapore, Department of Statistics, *Report on the Census of Industrial Production,* various issues.

[a]See Appendix table 13.A.1.

[b]The Schiavo-Campo (1978) measurement of structural change. Over the entire period 1960–81, the indices for output, value added, and direct exports are respectively 48.03%, 40.56%, and 57.88%.

Table 13.7 Singapore's Trade in Manufactures Divided into Consumer Goods (C), Intermediate Goods (I), and Capital Goods (K)

		Value (in thousands of U.S. dollars)					Trade in C, I, and K as Percentage of Total				
Year	Type of Good	Total Exports	Total Imports	Domestic Exports[a]	Reexports[b]	Retained Imports[c]	Total Exports	Total Imports	Domestic Exports[a]	Reexports[b]	Retained Imports[c]
1960	*Total*	*240,023*	*358,685*	*38,710*	*201,313*	*157,372*					
	C	32,465	70,085	8,036	24,429	45,655	13.53	19.54	20.76	12.13	29.01
	I	100,846	152,721	20,050	80,796	71,925	42.02	42.58	51.80	40.13	45.70
	K	106,711	135,879	10,624	96,087	39,791	44.46	37.88	27.44	47.73	25.28
1966	*Total*	*317,015*	*558,614*	*80,423*	*236,592*	*322,021*					
	C	53,152	98,060	14,050	39,103	58,958	16.77	17.55	17.47	16.53	18.31
	I	115,426	212,744	34,905	80,521	132,223	36.41	38.08	43.40	34.03	41.06
	K	148,437	247,810	31,468	116,969	130,841	46.82	44.36	39.13	49.44	40.63
1970	*Total*	*431,438*	*1,403,018*	*226,404*	*205,034*	*1,197,984*					
	C	80,979	175,986	26,487	54,492	121,494	18.77	12.54	11.70	26.58	10.14
	I	143,025	488,989	71,066	71,959	417,030	33.15	34.85	31.39	35.10	34.81
	K	207,434	738,044	128,851	78,583	659,461	48.08	52.60	56.91	38.33	55.05
1975	*Total*	*2,250,781*	*4,641,930*	*1,292,092*	*958,690*	*3,683,240*					
	C	321,276	561,409	282,399	88,877	472,532	16.50	12.09	21.86	9.27	12.83
	I	488,269	1,139,426	240,633	247,636	891,790	21.69	24.55	18.62	25.83	24.21
	K	1,391,236	2,941,096	769,060	622,177	2,318,919	61.81	63.36	59.52	64.90	62.96
1980	*Total*	*8,650,274*	*13,160,265*	*4,937,966*	*3,712,309*	*9,447,957*					
	C	1,201,386	1,378,224	883,391	317,995	1,060,229	13.89	10.47	17.89	8.57	11.22
	I	1,534,032	3,014,647	712,873	821,160	2,193,487	17.73	22.91	14.44	22.12	23.22
	K	5,914,856	8,767,394	3,341,702	2,573,154	6,194,241	68.38	66.62	67.67	69.31	65.56
1982	*Total*	*9,317,202*	*15,079,255*	*5,186,249*	*4,130,953*	*10,948,301*					
	C	1,323,146	1,800,131	893,886	429,260	1,370,871	14.20	11.94	17.24	10.39	12.52
	I	1,685,540	3,179,457	695,329	990,211	2,189,246	18.09	21.08	13.41	23.97	20.00
	K	6,308,516	10,099,667	3,597,034	2,711,482	7,388,185	67.71	66.98	69.36	65.54	67.48

Sources: Singapore, Department of Statistics, *Singapore Trade Statistics: Imports and Exports*, various issues; idem, *Report on the Census of Industrial Production*, various issues.

Note: Manufacturers are defined as SITC 5 to 8 and are subdivided as follows: consumer goods (SITC 8), intermediate goods (SITC 5 + 6, excluding 67 + 68 + 69), and capital goods (SITC 67 + 68 + 69 + 7) . See Appendix tables 13.A.1 and 13.A.2 for correspondence with Singapore industrial codes. Industrial codes 311 to 314 and 353 to 355 do not belong to SITC 5 to 8 and are not included in the calculation.

[a]Estimates for 1960, 1966, and 1970 are based on direct exports.

[b]Estimated by total exports minus direct exports for 1960, 1966, and 1970.

[c]Estimated by total imports minus reexports.

decline. For reexport, capital goods always had the largest share. Their share has increased further in recent years, while the share of intermediate goods has declined. Table 13.7 also shows the changing importance of entrepôt trade in manufactures. In 1960 the value of reexports was five times that of domestic exports, but by 1970 domestic manufactured exports exceeded reexports. The share of reexports in total exports fell from 84% in 1960 to 43% in 1975 but then increased slightly, reaching 44% in 1982. Retained imports as a fraction of total imports increased from 44% in 1960 to 85% in 1970 but fell gradually to 73% in 1982. This may reflect in part the change in nature of entrepôt trade, which has come to consist increasingly of reexport of capital goods to neighboring countries. The pattern of change also differs according to the type of good. For instance, even in 1982, reexport of intermediate goods continued to exceed domestic export.

The changes in export orientation and the growth and export performance of Singapore's major industry groups are shown in table 13.8. Between 1970 and 1981, the export orientation of Singapore's manufacturing sector increased from 40% to over 61%. Most industries have become more export oriented, although there are exceptions (e.g., leather, paper, plastic, and nonmetallic mineral products). Several industries which are highly export oriented (e.g., petroleum products, radios, televisions, and electrical machinery) or have significantly increased their export orientation (e.g., transport equipment, oil rigs, professional and scientific equipment, calculators, and industrial machinery) have experienced high rates of growth and their shares of direct exports have increased. On the other hand, some industries that have increased their export orientation have experienced declines in shares (e.g., food and beverages).

Singapore's manufacturing industries are characterized by high degrees of import content. In 1973 direct and total (direct and indirect) import requirements per unit of commodity output were 58% and 65% respectively.[10] In 1978 the corresponding figures were 64% and 73%.[11] This characteristic of Singapore's industries is apparent from the ratio of value added to output for the manufacturing sector (excluding rubber processing), which in 1978 was 26% (table 13.9). Owing to high import requirements, the ratio for petroleum refineries and petroleum products is among the lowest, even though this industry group has the highest value added per employee. However, ratios of value added to output are considerably higher for most other industries.

13.3 Factor Intensity of Singapore's Trade in Manufactures

Until the late 1960s, Singapore was abundant in unskilled labor; her comparative advantage was in low-technology, unskilled, labor-intensive

Table 13.8   Export Orientation and Growth and Export Performance of Singapore's Major Industry Groups

SSIC, 1969	Industry	Compound Annual Growth Rate at Current Prices, 1970–81 (% per yr.)			Ratio of Direct Exports to Total Sales (%)		Share in Direct Exports (%)	
		Output	Value Added	Direct Exports	1970	1981	1970	1981
311 + 312	Food	10.73	14.60	15.17	33.22	50.25	12.19	3.92
313	Beverages	15.60	13.46	19.85	19.78	29.21	0.86	0.43
314	Cigarettes, other tobacco prod.	6.43	9.64	16.71	4.20	11.58	0.27	0.10
321	Textiles, textile manuf.	15.76	17.20	15.52	50.02	47.51	2.68	0.89
322	Wearing apparel except footwear	24.09	26.22	25.13	64.71	71.16	3.64	2.92
323	Leather and leather prod.	11.70	16.37	9.20	54.40	41.14	0.55	0.10
324	Footwear	10.71	10.47	15.08	22.30	34.63	0.27	0.09
331	Sawn timber, other wood prod., except furniture	11.88	10.17	12.96	46.27	51.14	5.57	1.45
332	Furniture and fixtures except primarily of metal	24.89	22.82	44.20	10.24	50.71	0.16	0.62
341	Paper, paper prod.	20.81	21.24	17.74	15.51	11.76	0.39	0.16
342	Printing and publishing	19.13	18.87	21.64	13.78	17.06	0.87	0.51
351	Industrial chemicals and gases	23.75	20.03	36.89	15.03	45.80	0.34	0.73
352	Paints, pharmaceuticals, other chem. prod.	21.52	23.47	29.61	28.41	58.11	1.45	1.72
353 + 354	Petroleum refineries and petroleum prod.	25.18	20.97	29.08	47.74	66.88	38.09	42.96

Code	Industry							
355	Processing of jelutong and gum dammar	6.17	7.73	4.80	72.90	61.92	0.71	0.08
357	Plastic prod.	6.16	5.53	7.14	36.68	42.06	0.98	0.14
361 + 362	Pottery, china, earthenware, glass prod.	15.88	12.72	16.76	48.40	56.24	0.55	0.21
363	Bricks, tiles, other structural clay prod.	13.79	12.05	19.96	1.55	2.49	0.01	0.00
364 + 365	Cements, cement additives, structural cement, concrete prod.	26.24	27.22	44.55	3.08	13.85	0.10	0.38
369	Asbestos, stone, other non-metallic mineral prod.	21.33	23.05	6.36	64.42	21.68	1.00	0.13
371	Iron and steel	19.03	20.93	36.13	3.64	14.74	0.12	0.24
372	Zinc and other nonferrous metals	16.21	15.78	17.23	57.48	63.80	0.93	0.36
381	Metal grills, cans, pipes, other fabricated prod.	19.11	20.07	20.86	24.15	27.37	3.35	1.83
382	Calculators, refrigerators, air conditioners, indust. mach.	30.61	32.66	43.23	24.60	63.14	1.11	3.94
383	Radios, TVs, semiconductors, other elec. mach.	32.81	27.56	34.15	77.27	82.90	13.92	24.00
384	Transport equip. and oil rigs	24.46	24.97	32.15	31.32	61.80	6.47	9.46
385	Professional and sci. equip., photog. and optical goods	33.14	36.86	40.97	48.04	90.15	0.39	1.15
390	Other manuf. industries (jewelry, toys, umbrellas, etc.)	14.05	15.63	17.47	31.94	42.90	2.38	0.95
	Total manufacturing (excl. rubber processing)	22.66	21.97	27.67	39.60	61.23	100.00	100.00

Source: Singapore, Department of Statistics, *Report on the Census of Industrial Production*, various issues.

Table 13.9   The Ratio of Value Added to Output and the Capital and Skill Intensities of Singapore's Major Industry Groups

SSIC, 1969	Industry	Ratio of Value Added to Output, 1978 (%)	Net Value of Fixed Assets per Employee (thousands of S$)		Value Added per Employee (thousands of S$)		Skill Index[a]	
			1970	1978	1970	1978	1970	1980
311 + 312	Food	16.8	10.98	22.25	9.14	22.21	0.0639	0.1378
313	Beverages	39.6	18.20	18.09	14.95	31.38	0.0439	0.1199
314	Cigarettes, other tobacco prod.	24.0	13.28	12.91	23.76	32.53	0.0715	0.1006
321	Textiles, textile manuf.	32.7	9.35	19.72	3.35	11.81	0.0547	0.0736
322	Wearing apparel except footwear	32.6	1.34	3.28	2.45	7.21	0.0091	0.0403
323	Leather and leather prod.	26.3	2.68	4.69	3.81	10.23	0.0470	0.1079
324	Footwear	36.3	2.38	6.64	3.27	8.48	0.0251	0.0662
331	Sawn timber, other wood prod. except furniture	32.8	5.80	13.33	6.74	18.24	0.0335	0.0662
332	Furniture and fixtures except primarily of metal	37.5	2.57	4.71	6.12	9.40	0.0197	0.0603
341	Paper, paper prod.	34.2	3.82	12.93	5.03	14.52	0.0569	0.1122
342	Printing and publishing	50.8	5.55	9.44	7.53	17.62	0.1978	0.2773
351	Industrial chemicals and gases	36.7	34.35	50.62	19.67	40.66	0.2104	0.3955
352	Paints, pharmaceuticals, other chem. prod.	54.9	7.53	26.52	11.09	60.40	0.1643	0.3982
353 + 354	Petroleum refineries and petroleum prod.	10.5	130.45	610.11	95.63	255.35	0.4125	0.7573
355	Processing of jelutong and gum dammar	9.2	2.72	21.51	6.81	13.13	0.0277	0.0585
356	Rubber prod. except footwear	42.1	11.57	15.51	11.78	18.13	0.0718	0.1360

Code	Industry							
357	Plastic prod.	34.1	6.17	12.75	5.43	12.82	0.0757	0.1204
361 + 362	Pottery, china, earthenware, glass prod.	50.4	6.63	12.91	5.54	32.25	0.0566	0.1061
363	Bricks, tiles, other structural clay prod.	66.3	10.79	32.15	5.09	19.75	0.0534	0.0764
364	Cements, cement additives	20.8 ⎫	13.28	42.73	11.04	36.16	0.1134	0.1352
365	Structural cement, concrete prod.	39.7 ⎭						
369	Asbestos, stone, other non-metallic mineral prod.	44.5	11.38	14.45	7.57	28.42	0.0686	0.1537
371	Iron and steel	47.7	18.85	53.86	16.22	63.29	0.0684	0.1464
372	Zinc and other nonferrous metals	24.0	6.33	13.99	12.20	21.82	0.0655	0.2602
381	Metal grills, cans, pipes, other fabricated prod.	35.1	6.78	16.34	8.41	18.20	0.0716	0.1296
383	Radios, TVs, semiconductors, other elec. mach.	31.9	2.40	6.84	9.40	16.70	0.0946	0.1166
382	Calculators, refrigerators, air conditioners, indust. mach.	47.3	3.14	17.84	7.64	21.12	0.1266	0.1495 ⎫
384	Transport equip. and oil rigs	47.7	10.80	29.75	9.88	25.88	0.0815	⎭
385	Professional and sci. equip., photog. and optical goods	52.1	4.75	13.20	3.99	15.15	0.1444	0.1090
390	Other manuf. industries (jewelry, toys, umbrellas, etc.)	29.8	1.32	7.68	3.64	13.77	0.0334	0.0784
	Total manufacturing (excl. rubber processing)	26.3	9.05	21.64	9.24	21.38	0.0731	0.1254

Sources: Singapore, Department of Statistics, *Report on the Census of Industrial Production*, various issues; idem, *Report on the Census of Population, 1970*, vol. 2; idem, *Census of Population 1980: Singapore* (Release no. 4).

[a]A modification of the Keesing (1965) skill ratio made by Nyaw (1979):

$$index = \frac{(professional,\ technical,\ and\ related\ workers\ +\ administrative\ and\ managerial\ workers)}{production\ and\ related\ workers}.$$

manufactures.[12] Since 1970 Singapore has moved into a skill-intensive, higher-technology, and possibly more capital-intensive phase of industrial development, and it is interesting to see how this shift is reflected in her trade in manufactures. Three different measures of factor intensity calculated for the years 1970 and 1978 are presented in table 13.9.[13] The net value of fixed assets per employee is used as an indicator of (physical) capital intensity. Its main disadvantage is that it does not allow for differences in skill. Skill differences can be taken into account in two main ways: redefining capital to include both physical and human capital or introducing skill as a separate factor. Lary (1968) used the value added per employee as an index of total (physical plus human) capital intensity. Lary (1968, 19) argued that this measure provides an "integrated treatment of the flows of services rendered by capital and labor," whereas previous measures of capital intensity neglect skill differences and tend to treat capital as a stock rather than as a flow of services. Keesing (1965, 1968), on the other hand, preferred to treat skill as a factor separate from unskilled labor and physical capital. He argued that, since capital is fairly mobile internationally, it is the ratio of skilled to unskilled labor that determines comparative advantage in trade in manufactures. The skill index presented in table 13.9 is a modification of Keesing's skill ratio made by Nyaw (1979).[14]

It can be seen from table 13.9 that the rankings of various industry groups according to the three indices do not change very much in the course of eight to ten years. Moreover, there is a fairly close relationship between the indices. The petroleum refinery and products industry is the most capital-intensive and also has the highest skill ratio and value added per employee. Several other capital-intensive industries (e.g., industrial chemicals and gases, iron and steel, and transport equipment) also rank high in terms of skill intensity and value added per employee. At the lower end, industries such as clothing, footwear, and leather are characterized by low value added, low skill intensity, and low capital intensity. The relationship is of course not perfect, as can be seen from the Spearman rank correlation coefficients in table 13.10. Value added per employee reflecting total (physical plus human) capital intensity is strongly correlated with physical capital intensity and skill intensity. But, as might be expected, the relationship between skill intensity and physical capital intensity is weaker. The same table shows the relationship between factor intensity and growth and export performance as measured by growth rates and changes in shares between 1970 and 1981. As shown in row 3, industries with high skill intensities tend to have high growth rates of output, value added, and direct exports and have experienced increases in shares in the total. The relationship between value added

Table 13.10 Spearman Rank Correlation Coefficients between Indices of Factor Intensity and Indicators of Growth and Export Performance of Singapore's Major Industry Groups

	Net Value of Fixed Assets per Empl., 1975 (1)	Value Added per Employee, 1975 (2)	Skill Index, 1970 (3)	Dir. Exp./ Tot. Sales Ratio, 1975 (4)	Change in Dir. Exp./ Tot. Sales Ratio, 1970–81 (5)	Compound Annual Growth Rate 1970–81			Change in Share over 1970–81 in:		
						Output (6)	Value Added (7)	Direct Export (8)	Output (9)	Value Added (10)	Direct Export (11)
(1)	1.0000	0.6429[a]	0.4167[b]	−0.0345	0.2256	0.0606	−0.0315	0.1828	0.0734	−0.1409	0.1764
(2)		1.0000	0.6882[a]	−0.1330	0.3754[b]	0.2187	0.1355	0.3236[c]	0.1404	−0.0611	0.3754[b]
(3)			1.0000	0.0616	0.2852	0.5409[a]	0.4709[d]	0.4857[d]	0.4054[b]	0.1847	0.5296[a]
(4)				1.0000	0.1271	0.2714	0.2897	−0.0340	0.3483[c]	0.3729[b]	0.0764
(5)					1.0000	0.3744[b]	0.2882	0.6409[a]	0.2507	0.1069	0.5498[a]
(6)						1.0000	0.9443[a]	0.8251[a]	0.8207[a]	0.6936[a]	0.6704[a]
(7)							1.0000	0.7458[a]	0.7522[a]	0.7837[a]	0.5571[a]
(8)								1.0000	0.6236[a]	0.5281[a]	0.7631[a]
(9)									1.0000	0.7818[a]	0.7828[a]
(10)										1.0000	0.5562[a]
(11)											1.0000

[a]Significant at 1% level.
[b]Significant at 5% level.
[c]Significant at 10% level.
[d]Significant at 2% level.

per employee and growth and export performance is much weaker, while no significant relationship is observed for physical capital intensity. It can be seen that the growth rates of output, value added, and direct exports of various industries (and changes in their shares) are highly correlated. Moreover, row 5 of table 13.10 indicates that industries that have significantly increased their export orientation during the period tend to have higher growth rates of exports (and, to a lesser extent, of value added and output) and experience increases in shares. This reinforces the notion of export-led growth. Moreover, as we have seen, in the most recent decade, skill-intensive industries have performed better than the average. It can be seen from table 13.9 that skill intensities for the manufacturing sector as a whole, and for all industry groups other than professional and scientific equipment, have increased over the period. All these reflect the shift to the skill-intensive phase of industrial development. (Similar conclusions cannot be drawn for the other two indices for want of an adequate deflator.)

To provide estimates of the comparative advantage of Singapore's trade in manufactures in the most recent decade, we have computed in table 13.11 the weighted averages of factor intensities of Singapore's exports and imports.[15] To allow for differences between trade with industrialized countries and trade with other countries, for the year 1978 weighted-average factor intensities are also calculated separately for trade with the two country groups. One serious problem encountered in examining Singapore's comparative advantage as revealed by the factor intensity of its trade in manufactures is that export and import figures include, respectively, reexports and entrepôt imports. The volume and direction of entrepôt trade are determined by an entirely different set of factors, and there is no reason why its commodity structure should reflect Singapore's comparative advantage in production. Thus in table 13.11 calculations have also been made for domestically produced exports and retained imports. As noted earlier, we have only rough estimates for retained imports, and, hence, our results are subject to some inaccuracy.[16]

It is to be noted that the factor intensity figures used in the calculation refer only to direct requirements of capital, labor, and skill. Moreover, the use of factor requirements of Singapore's industries to study factor requirements of exports and imports assumes that there are broad similarities between Singapore's structure of production and that of other countries in general.[17] These facts, together with the fact that only twenty-nine major industry groups are distinguished, imply that our figures should be regarded as only rough estimates.

In table 13.12 the ratios of factor intensities of Singapore's exports of manufactures to those of manufactured imports are presented.

Table 13.11   Factor Intensity of Singapore's Imports and Exports of Manufactures (SITC 5–8), 1970 and 1978

Singapore's Trading Partners	Net Value of Fixed Assets per Employee[a]	Value Added per Employee[a]	Skill Index[b]
		1970	
All countries			
Total exports	6.9054	7.7557	0.0868
Total imports	7.7440	7.9836	0.0923
Domestic exports[c]	5.8262	7.9979	0.0767
Retained imports	7.6539	8.0659	0.0911
		1978	
All countries			
Total exports	15.5818	21.1113	0.1354
Total imports	19.8279	23.5969	0.1425
Domestic exports	13.0134	19.9082	0.1263
Retained imports	20.0134	23.8612	0.1404
Industrialized countries[d]			
Total exports	11.3223	18.2068	0.1234
Total imports	20.8314	24.9168	0.1488
Domestic exports	10.3274	17.7141	0.1188
Retained imports	21.1204	25.1771	0.1485
Other countries			
Total exports	19.7379	23.9432	0.1471
Total imports	16.3529	19.0127	0.1208
Domestic exports	18.9164	24.7255	0.1428
Retained imports	15.3545	14.3432	0.0863

Sources: Table 13.9; Singapore, Department of Statistics, *Singapore Trade Statistics: Imports and Exports,* various issues.

Note: The figures shown are weighted averages, with the shares of major industry groups in total exports, total imports, domestic exports, and retained imports as weights. See Appendix table 13.A.2. Industrial codes 311 to 314 and 353 to 355 do not belong to SITC 5 to 8 and are not included in the calculations.

[a]In thousands of Singapore dollars.

[b]Calculations for 1978 are based on the skill index of 1980.

[c]Direct exports.

[d]Following the United Nations classification, countries in this group are United States, Canada, Japan, Australia and New Zealand, EC (Belgium and Luxembourg, Denmark, France, Federal Republic of Germany, Ireland, Italy, Netherlands, United Kingdom), European Free Trade Association (Austria, Finland, Iceland, Norway, Portugal, Sweden, Switzerland), Greece, Malta, Spain, and Yugoslavia.

When trade with all countries is considered, the ratios are all less than unity for both 1970 and 1978. Thus, in general, Singapore's manufactured exports have lower (physical and total) capital and skill intensities than its imports. The exceptional case is that of value added per employee in 1970, where the ratios are very close to one.

Table 13.12   **Ratios of Factor Intensities of Singapore's Manufactured Exports to Manufactured Imports, 1970 and 1978**

Singapore's Trading Partners	Net Value of Fixed Assets per Employee	Value Added per Employee	Skill Index
		1970	
All countries			
Total exports/total imports	0.8917	0.9715	0.9404
Domestic exports[a]/retained imports	0.7612	0.9916	0.8419
		1978	
All countries			
Total exports/total imports	0.7859	0.8947	0.9502
Domestic exports/retained imports	0.6502	0.8343	0.8996
Industrialized countries			
Total exports/total imports	0.5435	0.7307	0.8293
Domestic exports/retained imports	0.4890	0.7036	0.8000
Other countries			
Total exports/total imports	1.2070	1.2593	1.2177
Domestic exports/retained imports	1.2320	1.7238	1.6547

Source: Table 13.11.
[a]Direct export.

In general the ratios fall so that the contrast is greater when one relates factor intensities of domestically produced exports to those of retained imports. From 1970 to 1978, the ratios have risen for skill intensity but fallen for physical and total capital intensities. The latter result may be partly explained by the fact that in 1978 a higher proportion of Singapore's exports went to developed countries. On the whole, despite the fact that recently Singapore has shifted its attention to skill-intensive and high-value-added industries, its exports are still relatively labor-intensive (less capital- and skill-intensive) compared with its imports. When Singapore's trading partners are divided into industrialized countries and other countries, the ratios are significantly less than one for industrialized countries and greater than one for other countries. When one looks at factor intensities of domestic exports compared with retained imports, the ratios become still lower for trade with industrialized countries and still higher for trade with other countries. Thus, as might be expected from comparative advantage, in its trade with industrialized countries Singapore's exports are labor-intensive compared with imports, while in its trade with other countries its exports are capital- and skill-intensive compared with imports.[18]

13.4   Geographic Patterns of Trade in Manufactures

There have been significant changes in the geographic pattern of Singapore's trade in manufactures (table 13.13). In general, trade in manufactures with developed countries has grown greatly in importance compared with trade with developing countries. There are, however, differences among countries. The shares of the United Kingdom have declined greatly, because of the loss of colonial ties and the gradual phasing out of Commonwealth preferences with Britain's entry into the Common Market. On the other hand, the importance of the United States, Japan, and West Germany as trading partners has increased.

For manufactured imports into Singapore the relative shares of developed countries and developing countries have not changed much in the last two decades, with the greater part (about 80%) continuing to come from the former group of countries. There have been significant changes, however, in the shares of individual countries. The share of the United Kingdom fell from 23% in 1960 to only 5% in 1980, while those of the United States and Japan increased.

For manufactured exports the change in trade pattern has been remarkable. In 1960 less than 4% of Singapore's exports went to developed countries, but by 1980 the latter's share reached 45%. (It should be noted that the share of developed countries in Singapore's domestic exports is higher than their share in total exports because a higher percentage of exports of manufactures to developed countries consists of domestic exports.) The share of developing countries fell correspondingly from 94% in 1960 to 52% in 1980. This was partly due to the decline in entrepôt trade. Moreover, since the 1960s, neighboring developing countries have begun their industrialization based on import substitution, leading to reduced imports of labor-intensive types of manufactures (textiles, clothing, footwear, etc.) from Singapore. Malaysia is the clearest example of this trend, and as can be seen from table 13.13, its share of total manufactured exports from Singapore fell from almost 60% in 1960 to 20% in 1980. Among developed countries, increases in shares have been particularly great for the United States and West Germany. The shares of manufactured exports going to Asian newly industrializing countries (NIC) and centrally planned economies have also increased somewhat.

For all commodities together, the shares of developed countries and developing countries in Singapore's exports remained relatively stable, while for imports the share of developing countries increased. In 1960 manufactured exports made up 21% of exports to all countries and less than 2% of exports to developed countries; in 1980 the corresponding percentages were 45% and 49%. In 1960 Singapore's trade was dominated by trade in primary commodities (a large part of which was

Table 13.13   **Composition of Singapore's Trade in Manufactures: By SITC One-Digit Codes and by Countries and Regions** (in thousands of U.S. dollars)

		1960			
		Imports		Exports	
SITC	Trading Partner[a]	Value	%	Value	%
5	*Chemicals*	41,414	100.00	28,185	100.00
	Developed economies	**31,374**	**75.76**	**2,005**	**7.11**
	United States	4,909	11.85	143	0.51
	Japan	2,847	6.87	50	0.18
	Western Europe	21,977	53.07	1,498	5.31
	EC (9)	21,135	51.03	1,493	5.30
	France	811	1.96	76	0.27
	Fed. Rep. of Germany	3,929	9.49	21	0.07
	Italy	372	0.90	6	0.02
	United Kingdom	13,533	32.68	1,110	3.94
	Australia	719	1.74	276	0.98
	Developing economies	**7,578**	**18.30**	**25,463**	**90.34**
	ASEAN[b]	3,071	7.42	18,053	64.05
	Malaysia	2,927	7.07	16,847	59.77
	Philippines	1	0.00	240	0.85
	Thailand	143	0.35	966	3.43
	Asian NICs[c]	2,941	7.10	801	2.84
	Centrally planned economies	**2,238**	**5.40**	—	—
6	*Basic manufactures*	152,343	100.00	102,127	100.00
	Developed economies	**109,982**	**72.19**	**5,322**	**5.21**
	United States	7,252	4.76	590	0.58
	Japan	58,337	38.29	158	0.15
	Western Europe	41,753	27.41	3,489	3.42
	EC (9)	37,296	24.48	2,938	2.88
	France	1,805	1.18	—	—
	Fed. Rep. of Germany	4,905	3.22	282	0.28
	Italy	1,777	1.17	—	—
	United Kingdom	23,545	15.46	2,484	2.43
	Australia	1,696	1.11	354	0.35
	Developing economies	**22,834**	**14.99**	**94,198**	**92.24**
	ASEAN[b]	7,587	4.98	63,508	62.19
	Malaysia	6,566	4.31	57,927	56.72
	Philippines	559	0.37	133	0.13
	Thailand	462	0.30	5,448	5.33
	Asian NICs[c]	6,211	4.08	2,946	2.88
	Centrally planned economies	**19,091**	**12.53**	—	...
7	*Machinery and transport equipment*	96,016	100.00	77,575	100.00
	Developed economies	**86,649**	**90.24**	**1,454**	**1.87**
	United States	16,307	16.98	7	0.01
	Japan	8,890	9.26	11	0.01
	Western Europe	56,387	58.73	762	0.98
	EC (9)	55,402	57.70	758	0.98
	France	1,629	1.70	—	—
	Fed. Rep. of Germany	9,711	10.11	8	0.01

| 1971 | | | | 1980 | | | |
| Imports | | Exports | | Imports | | Exports | |
Value	%	Value	%	Value	%	Value	%
143,366	100.00	60,619	100.00	1,255,973	100.00	663,029	100.00
117,407	**81.89**	**6,342**	**10.46**	**1,039,059**	**82.73**	**106,907**	**16.12**
26,904	18.77	324	0.53	316,774	25.22	4,180	0.63
26,883	18.75	659	1.09	207,062	16.49	74,145	11.18
52,720	36.77	603	0.99	449,400	35.78	19,474	2.94
47,528	33.15	348	0.57	398,930	31.76	15,998	2.41
4,452	3.11	113	0.19	57,234	4.56	1,421	0.21
10,462	7.30	143	0.24	118,904	9.47	1,482	0.22
2,232	1.56	—	—	13,627	1.08	302	0.05
22,204	15.49	—	—	144,917	11.54	4,451	0.67
4,354	3.04	4,076	6.72	28,676	2.28	8,207	1.24
18,809	**13.12**	**54,270**	**89.53**	**143,920**	**11.46**	**538,775**	**81.26**
10,163	7.09	41,415	68.32	53,011	4.22	327,499	49.39
9,500	6.63	37,505	61.87	44,656	3.56	262,638	39.61
414	0.29	894	1.47	3,361	0.27	19,115	2.88
249	0.17	3,016	4.98	4,994	0.40	45,746	6.90
4,316	3.01	4,395	7.25	37,846	3.01	37,332	5.63
7,150	**4.99**	—	—	**72,994**	**5.81**	**17,348**	**2.62**
603,975	100.00	174,673	100.00	3,383,255	100.00	1,608,697	100.00
423,867	**70.18**	**34,184**	**19.57**	**2,161,503**	**63.89**	**444,076**	**27.60**
30,813	5.10	10,282	5.89	268,168	7.93	177,523	11.04
287,913	47.67	2,174	1.24	1,191,414	35.22	33,417	2.08
83,580	13.84	14,383	8.23	501,322	14.82	164,417	10.22
70,240	11.63	13,685	7.83	404,008	11.94	147,842	9.19
3,596	0.60	372	0.21	44,087	1.30	8,246	0.51
16,552	2.74	877	0.50	105,140	3.11	28,363	1.76
6,268	1.04	304	0.17	68,298	2.02	11,123	0.69
35,137	5.82	10,289	5.89	117,803	3.48	50,677	3.15
15,868	2.63	3,209	1.84	109,408	3.23	47,831	2.97
111,884	**18.52**	**140,076**	**80.19**	**1,000,051**	**29.56**	**1,091,388**	**67.84**
35,515	5.88	89,598	51.29	323,634	9.57	476,447	29.62
29,341	4.86	86,450	49.49	262,881	7.77	424,110	26.36
2,779	0.46	471	0.27	10,578	0.31	25,251	1.57
3,395	0.56	2,677	1.53	50,175	1.48	27,086	1.68
30,522	5.05	8,721	4.99	328,604	9.71	104,657	6.51
68,223	**11.30**	**413**	**0.24**	**221,701**	**6.55**	**73,233**	**4.55**
721,641	100.00	241,889	100.00	7,154,221	100.00	5,183,407	100.00
670,758	**92.95**	**88,164**	**36.45**	**6,180,842**	**86.39**	**2,637,632**	**50.89**
233,054	32.30	65,632	27.13	2,234,466	31.23	1,522,022	29.36
159,266	22.07	2,621	1.08	2,358,905	32.97	132,946	2.56
256,255	35.51	14,335	5.93	1,517,704	21.21	844,046	16.28
233,902	32.41	13,938	5.76	1,221,450	17.07	749,424	14.46
8,912	1.23	1,089	0.45	117,467	1.64	160,773	3.10
64,976	9.00	1,341	0.55	457,837	6.40	293,562	5.66

(continued)

Table 13.13   (continued)

		1960			
		Imports		Exports	
SITC	Trading Partner[a]	Value	%	Value	%
	Italy	2,381	2.48	9	0.01
	United Kingdom	37,888	39.46	728	0.94
	Australia	2,939	3.06	385	0.50
	Developing economies	**8,375**	**8.72**	**75,497**	**97.32**
	ASEAN[b]	7,309	7.61	50,874	65.58
	Malaysia	7,274	7.58	49,177	63.39
	Philippines	26	0.03	61	0.08
	Thailand	9	0.01	1,636	2.11
	Asian NICs[c]	827	0.86	740	0.95
	Centrally planned economies	**892**	**0.93**	**9**	**0.01**
8	*Miscellaneous manufactured goods*	68,900	100.00	32,128	100.00
	Developed economies	**44,537**	**64.64**	**420**	**1.31**
	United States	5,534	8.03	53	0.16
	Japan	11,143	16.17	14	0.04
	Western Europe	27,412	39.79	179	0.56
	EC (9)	13,555	19.67	171	0.53
	France	138	0.20	—	—
	Fed. Rep. of Germany	4,090	5.94	17	0.05
	Italy	519	0.75	84	0.26
	United Kingdom	7,984	11.59	61	0.19
	Australia	279	0.40	31	0.10
	Developing economies	**19,806**	**28.75**	**30,507**	**94.95**
	ASEAN[b]	3,933	5.71	18,137	56.45
	Malaysia	3,752	5.45	17,680	55.03
	Philippines	—	—	104	0.32
	Thailand	181	0.26	353	1.10
	Asian NICs[c]	12,862	18.67	986	3.07
	Centrally planned economies	**4,448**	**6.46**	**2**	**0.01**
5–8	*Total manufactures*	358,673	100.00	240,015	100.00
	Developed economies	**272,542**	**75.99**	**9,201**	**3.83**
	United States	34,002	9.48	793	0.33
	Japan	81,217	22.64	233	0.10
	Western Europe	147,529	41.13	5,928	2.47
	EC (9)	127,388	35.52	5,360	2.23
	France	4,383	1.22	76	0.03
	Fed. Rep. of Germany	22,635	6.31	328	0.14
	Italy	5,049	1.41	99	0.04
	United Kingdom	82,950	23.13	4,383	1.83
	Australia	5,633	1.57	1,046	0.44
	Developing economies	**58,593**	**16.34**	**225,665**	**94.02**
	ASEAN[b]	21,900	6.11	150,572	62.73
	Malaysia	20,519	5.72	141,631	59.01
	Philippines	586	0.16	538	0.22
	Thailand	795	0.22	8,403	3.50
	Asian NICs[c]	22,841	6.37	5,473	2.28
	Centrally planned economies	**26,669**	**7.44**	**11**	**0.00**

| 1971 | | | | 1980 | | | |
| Imports | | Exports | | Imports | | Exports | |
Value	%	Value	%	Value	%	Value	%
23,940	3.32	3,256	1.35	104,463	1.46	82,663	1.59
107,604	14.91	7,204	2.98	372,413	5.21	135,051	12.61
14,949	2.07	3,386	1.40	45,338	0.63	81,627	1.57
40,666	**5.64**	**153,310**	**63.38**	**913,681**	**12.77**	**2,415,207**	**46.59**
19,631	2.72	101,095	41.79	517,722	7.24	1,251,218	24.14
18,794	2.60	88,854	36.73	365,565	5.11	938,897	18.11
372	0.05	6,513	2.69	32,408	0.45	103,044	1.99
465	0.06	5,728	2.37	119,749	1.67	209,277	4.04
8,853	1.23	20,512	8.48	165,445	2.31	220,100	4.25
10,216	**1.42**	**415**	**0.17**	**59,698**	**0.83**	**130,567**	**2.52**
210,018	100.00	111,844	100.00	1,379,559	100.00	1,202,379	100.00
143,791	**68.47**	**51,808**	**46.32**	**947,792**	**68.70**	**725,655**	**60.35**
25,924	12.34	22,234	19.88	201,147	14.58	254,869	21.20
52,383	24.94	4,314	3.86	362,223	26.26	35,764	2.97
60,088	28.61	19,770	17.68	351,115	25.45	368,473	30.65
43,421	20.67	16,737	14.96	229,402	16.63	309,021	25.70
3,132	1.49	3,442	3.08	42,777	3.10	63,250	5.26
14,921	7.10	5,486	4.91	62,555	4.53	111,130	9.24
1,818	0.87	216	0.19	28,135	2.04	12,486	1.04
16,427	7.82	4,491	4.02	78,464	5.69	70,077	5.83
4,802	2.29	3,149	2.82	29,321	2.13	44,869	3.73
46,589	**22.18**	**57,709**	**51.60**	**374,284**	**27.13**	**469,237**	**39.03**
13,868	6.60	32,507	29.06	112,451	8.15	150,011	12.48
13,371	6.37	31,284	27.97	89,488	6.49	127,263	10.58
185	0.09	387	0.35	9,703	0.70	9,791	0.81
312	0.15	836	0.75	13,260	0.96	12,957	1.08
23,291	11.09	9,693	8.67	169,010	12.25	79,020	6.57
19,638	**9.35**	**2,326**	**2.08**	**57,483**	**4.17**	**7,487**	**0.62**
1,679,000	100.00	589,025	100.00	13,173,008	100.00	8,657,512	100.00
1,355,823	**80.75**	**180,498**	**30.64**	**10,329,196**	**78.41**	**3,914,270**	**45.21**
316,695	18.86	98,472	16.72	3,020,555	22.93	1,958,594	22.62
526,445	31.35	9,768	1.66	4,119,604	31.24	276,272	3.19
452,643	26.96	49,091	8.33	2,819,541	21.40	1,396,410	16.13
395,091	23.53	44,708	7.59	2,253,790	17.11	1,222,285	14.12
20,092	1.20	5,016	0.85	261,565	1.99	233,690	2.70
106,911	6.37	7,847	1.33	744,436	5.65	434,537	5.02
34,258	2.04	3,776	0.64	214,523	1.63	106,574	1.23
181,372	10.80	21,984	3.73	713,597	5.42	260,256	3.01
39,973	2.38	13,820	2.35	212,743	1.63	182,534	2.11
217,948	**12.98**	**405,365**	**68.82**	**2,431,936**	**18.46**	**4,514,607**	**52.15**
79,177	4.72	264,615	44.92	1,006,818	7.64	2,205,175	25.47
71,006	4.23	244,093	41.44	762,590	5.79	1,752,908	20.25
3,750	0.22	8,265	1.40	56,050	0.43	157,201	1.82
4,421	0.26	12,257	2.08	188,178	1.43	295,066	3.41
66,982	3.99	43,321	7.35	700,905	5.32	441,109	5.10
105,227	**6.27**	**3,154**	**0.54**	**411,876**	**3.13**	**228,635**	**2.64**

(continued)

Table 13.13   (continued)

SITC	Trading Partner[a]	1960 Imports Value	%	1960 Exports Value	%
0–9	*All commodities*	1,332,058	100.00	1,135,849	100.00
	Developed economies	**404,584**	**30.37**	**470,487**	**41.42**
	United States	50,964	3.83	79,101	6.96
	Japan	97,326	7.31	51,173	4.51
	Western Europe	210,403	15.80	248,871	21.91
	EC (9)	187,164	14.05	205,852	18.12
	France	9,454	0.71	29,861	2.63
	Fed. Rep. of Germany	24,172	1.81	25,685	2.26
	Italy	5,649	0.42	26,896	2.37
	United Kingdom	118,543	8.90	93,665	8.25
	Australia	34,594	2.60	44,218	3.89
	Developing economies	**874,770**	**65.67**	**574,593**	**50.59**
	ASEAN[b]	326,157	24.49	321,688	28.32
	Malaysia	277,884	20.86	267,798	23.58
	Philippines	663	0.05	18,878	1.66
	Thailand	47,610	3.57	35,012	3.08
	Asian NICs[c]	29,213	2.19	19,569	1.72
	Centrally planned economies	**51,087**	**3.84**	**82,099**	**7.23**

Source: United Nations, *Commodity Trade Statistics,* Statistical Papers, series D, various issues.
[a]Classification of countries into developed, developing, and centrally planned follows the source cited.
[b]Excluding Indonesia.
[c]Hong Kong and Republic of Korea (Taiwan is not included).

entrepôt trade); since then, trade in manufactures has grown tremendously in importance. This reflects partly the change in nature and importance of entrepôt trade and partly Singapore's successful industrialization: there has been increasing demand by industrialized countries for Singapore's labor-intensive (and, at a later stage, more skill- and capital-intensive) types of manufactures.

The composition of Singapore's trade in manufactures differs significantly across countries, as can be seen from tables 13.13–13.17. For chemicals and basic manufactures (SITC 5 and 6) the great majority of Singapore's exports continued to go to developing countries. By 1980, however, over half of Singapore's exports of machinery and transport equipment (SITC 7) and 60% of exports of miscellaneous manufactures (SITC 8) were to developed countries. Manufactured imports from developing countries continued to be dominated by basic manufactures, over half of which consisted of textile yarns and fabrics in recent years. The share of machinery and transport equipment in

1971				1980			
Imports		Exports		Imports		Exports	
Value	%	Value	%	Value	%	Value	%
2,827,286	100.00	1,754,610	100.00	24,002,667	100.00	19,375,478	100.00
1,591,853	**56.30**	**721,120**	**41.10**	**11,677,760**	**48.65**	**8,058,148**	**41.59**
360,087	12.74	207,370	11.82	3,383,235	14.10	2,464,185	12.72
555,202	19.64	124,077	7.07	4,283,232	17.84	1,560,357	8.05
520,140	18.40	270,778	15.43	3,199,597	13.33	2,738,738	14.14
457,858	16.19	229,933	13.10	2,589,238	10.79	2,259,540	11.66
30,712	1.09	28,260	1.61	326,778	1.36	423,528	2.19
111,018	3.93	37,132	2.12	783,999	3.27	582,968	3.01
36,788	1.30	20,799	1.19	226,333	0.94	249,118	1.29
206,878	7.32	108,995	6.21	827,980	3.45	499,743	2.58
120,129	4.25	84,035	4.79	543,333	2.26	780,938	4.03
1,078,686	**38.15**	**955,365**	**54.45**	**11,594,624**	**48.31**	**10,583,838**	**54.62**
543,875	19.24	465,789	26.55	3,877,654	16.16	4,026,036	20.78
471,595	16.68	401,298	22.87	3,326,420	13.86	2,906,380	15.00
15,296	0.54	12,370	0.70	74,871	0.31	273,955	1.41
56,984	2.02	52,121	2.97	476,363	1.98	845,701	4.36
76,657	2.71	109,622	6.25	766,585	3.19	1,784,484	9.21
156,746	**5.54**	**78,125**	**4.45**	**730,284**	**3.04**	**733,491**	**3.79**

Source: United Nations, *Commodity Trade Statistics*, Statistical Papers, series D, various issues.

[a]Classification of countries into developed, developing, and centrally planned follows the source cited.

[b]Excluding Indonesia.

[c]Hong Kong and Rupublic of Korea (Taiwan is not included).

imports increased, while that of miscellaneous manufactures fell. Machinery and transport equipment have the largest share in exports to developing countries and also dominate trade in manufactures with developed countries. About 60% of machinery and transport equipment exports (SITC 7) are domestically produced exports, reflecting Singapore's industrialization.

Japan was Singapore's largest trading partner (in terms of exports plus imports) in 1981 and second-largest after Malaysia in 1982. For trade in manufactures (SITC 5–8) it was Singapore's second-largest trading partner after the United States. In recent years, Singapore's exports and domestically produced exports to Japan have been dominated by mineral fuels. In 1982 about one-quarter of Singapore's domestic exports of mineral fuels (mostly petroleum products) went to Japan and accounted for 75% of domestic exports to Japan. Imports from Japan have been dominated by machinery and transport equipment in recent years, followed by basic manufactures. It can be seen

Table 13.14   Commodity Composition of Singapore's Trade in Manufactures with Individual Countries and Regions in Selected Years (percentages)

Destination of Export/ Origin of Import	1960		1971		1980	
	Imp.	Exp.	Imp.	Exp.	Imp.	Exp.
All countries						
SITC 5	11.55	11.74	8.54	10.29	9.53	7.66
SITC 6	42.47	42.55	35.97	29.65	25.68	18.58
SITC 7	26.77	32.32	42.98	41.07	54.31	59.87
SITC 8	19.21	13.39	12.51	18.99	10.47	13.89
Developed economies						
SITC 5	11.51	21.79	8.66	3.51	10.06	2.73
SITC 6	40.35	57.84	31.26	18.94	20.93	11.35
SITC 7	31.79	15.80	49.47	48.84	59.84	67.39
SITC 8	16.34	4.56	10.61	28.70	9.18	18.54
United States						
SITC 5	14.44	18.03	8.50	0.33	10.49	0.21
SITC 6	21.33	74.40	9.73	10.44	8.88	9.06
SITC 7	47.96	0.88	73.59	66.65	73.98	77.71
SITC 8	16.28	6.68	8.19	22.58	6.66	13.01
Japan						
SITC 5	3.51	21.46	5.11	6.75	5.03	26.84
SITC 6	71.83	67.81	54.69	22.26	28.92	12.10
SITC 7	10.95	4.72	30.25	26.83	57.26	48.12
SITC 8	13.72	6.01	9.95	44.16	8.79	12.95
Western Europe						
SITC 5	14.90	25.27	11.65	1.23	15.94	1.39
SITC 6	28.30	58.86	18.46	29.30	17.78	11.77
SITC 7	38.22	12.85	56.61	29.30	53.83	60.44
SITC 8	18.58	3.02	13.27	40.27	12.45	26.39
Developing economies						
SITC 5	12.93	11.28	8.63	13.39	5.92	11.93
SITC 6	38.97	41.74	51.34	34.56	41.12	24.17
SITC 7	14.29	33.46	18.66	37.82	37.57	53.50
SITC 8	33.80	13.52	21.38	14.24	15.39	10.39

Source: Table 13.13.

from table 13.13 that while Japan accounted for almost one-third of Singapore's manufactured imports in 1980, exports of manufactures to Japan accounted for only 3% of Singapore's total manufactured exports. Table 13.14 indicates that basic manufactures accounted for a higher percentage of manufactured imports from Japan than from the United States and Western Europe; in fact they accounted for over half of manufactured imports from Japan in 1971. In 1982, 64% of Singapore's imports of iron and steel originated from Japan. In addition, Singapore has been Japan's main customer of textile manufactures (SITC 65) in the Asian region. On the export side, chemical products

Table 13.15   **Singapore's Trade Balance in Manufactures with Country Groups in Selected Years** (in thousands of U.S. dollars)

	1960	1971	1980
	Manufactures (SITC 5–8)		
All countries	**– 118,658**	**– 1,089,975**	**– 4,515,496**
SITC 5	– 13,229	– 82,747	– 592,944
SITC 6	– 50,216	– 429,302	– 1,774,558
SITC 7	– 18,441	– 479,752	– 1,970,814
SITC 8	– 36,772	– 98,174	– 177,180
Developed economies	**– 263,341**	**– 1,175,325**	**– 6,414,926**
SITC 5	– 29,369	– 111,065	– 932,152
SITC 6	– 104,660	– 389,683	– 1,717,427
SITC 7	– 85,195	– 582,594	– 3,543,210
SITC 8	– 44,117	– 91,983	– 222,137
Developing economies	**167,072**	**187,417**	**2,082,671**
SITC 5	17,885	35,461	394,855
SITC 6	71,364	28,192	91,337
SITC 7	67,122	112,644	1,501,526
SITC 8	10,701	11,120	94,953
Centrally planned economies	**– 26,658**	**– 102,073**	**– 183,241**
SITC 5	– 2,238	– 7,150	– 55,646
SITC 6	– 19,091	– 67,810	– 148,468
SITC 7	– 883	– 9,801	70,869
SITC 8	– 4,446	– 17,312	– 49,996
	All Commodities (SITC 0–9)		
All countries	**– 196,209**	**– 1,072,676**	**– 4,627,189**
Developed economies	65,903	– 870,733	– 3,619,612
Developing economies	– 300,177	– 123,321	– 1,010,786
Centrally planned economies	31,012	– 78,621	3,207

Source: Table 13.13.

accounted for a much higher percentage of exports of manufactures to Japan than to the United States and Western Europe. In recent years, domestic export of medicinal products to Japan has grown greatly in importance. As shown in table 13.14, the share of chemicals in exports to Japan grew tremendously from 1971 to 1980. In 1980, 70% of Singapore's exports of chemicals to developed countries went to Japan.

Machinery and transport equipment have recently dominated Singapore's manufactured exports to and imports from developed countries. The United States has recently become Singapore's largest trading partner in manufactures. In 1982, 80% of Singapore's manufactured exports and 83% of manufactured domestic exports to the United States were in this category. Although ASEAN (Association of South East Asian Nations) exports to the United States under the Generalized System of Preferences (GSP) were rather small, because of its export

Table 13.16   **Singapore's Trade Balance with Selected Countries in Manufactures Divided into Consumer (C), Intermediate (I), and Capital (K) Goods** (in thousands of U.S. dollars)

	1975	1978	1982
	Manufactures (SITC 5–8)		
All countries	**−2,391,149**	**−2,758,573**	**−5,762,052**
C	− 190,132	− 152,341	− 476,985
I	− 651,158	− 863,947	− 1,493,916
K	− 1,549,859	− 1,742,285	− 3,791,151
EC (9)	**−552,696**	**−712,266**	**−1,408,269**
C	16,663	30,521	− 42,463
I	− 167,202	− 250,600	− 485,606
K	− 402,157	− 492,187	− 880,200
United States	**−741,793**	**−377,388**	**−984,363**
C	12,284	99,726	10,523
I	− 129,873	− 168,901	− 403,922
K	− 624,204	− 308,213	− 590,964
Japan	**−1,215,617**	**−2,202,467**	**−4,456,353**
C	− 131,393	− 238,052	− 464,805
I	− 222,771	− 318,989	− 608,263
K	− 861,453	− 1,645,426	− 3,383,285
	All Commodities (SITC 0–9)		
All countries	**−2,746,363**	**−2,909,326**	**−7,369,996**
EC (9)	− 333,905	− 304,259	− 1,043,641
United States	− 526,577	− 38,377	− 1,019,640
Japan	− 903,035	− 1,513,704	− 2,779,011

Source: Singapore, Department of Statistics, *Singapore Trade Statistics: Imports and Exports,* various issues.
Note: Consumer goods are defined as SITC 8; intermediate goods as SITC 5 + 6, excluding 67 + 68 + 69; and capital goods as SITC 67 + 68 + 69 + 7.

orientation Singapore was probably the chief beneficiary among ASEAN countries. Since the early 1970s, Singapore's exports of electrical and electronic products and transport equipment to the United States have grown quickly partly as a result of inflow of American investment into these industries. In the last recession, resentment against the NICs and (especially) Japan gave rise to new protective measures. Although they were aimed mainly against products of technologically advanced countries, Singapore was also affected to some extent. Machinery and transport equipment have also dominated trade in manufactures with Western Europe and Japan in recent years, though to smaller extents.

For miscellaneous manufactures (SITC 8), which are mainly labor-intensive types of manufactures, Singapore had a trade surplus with the United States, Western Europe, and the developing countries as a group but a large deficit with Japan. Some of the main imports from

Japan in this category are scientific instruments, photographic apparatus, watches, and clocks. Singapore is also a net importer of clothing from Japan (and from Asian NICs and developing countries as a group). In the mid-1960s, almost all of Singapore's clothing exports to developed countries were to the United Kingdom. Recently clothing exports have gone mainly to the United States and West Germany (table 13.17). In 1982 almost 80% of Singapore's domestic exports of clothing went to the United States and the European Community (EC), but only 13% of imports of clothing came from these countries. Table 13.14 shows that the percentage share of miscellaneous manufactures tends to be higher in exports of manufactures to Western Europe than to other developed countries.

In the last two decades Singapore consistently has had negative trade balances in manufactures with developed countries and positive balances with developing countries; this has been true for all major SITC categories (table 13.15). Most of the deficits with the former group of countries can be accounted for by the net imports of machinery and transport equipment, followed by basic manufactures and chemicals. The overall trade deficits with developed countries have been less than those for manufactures because of exports (mostly reexports) of primary commodities and fuels to these countries. The trade surpluses in manufactures with developing countries have been more than offset by net imports of primary commodities and fuels, so that Singapore also has trade deficits with this group of countries. Singapore's trade surpluses in manufactures with developing countries were mainly due to the machinery and transport equipment category. All this shows the role played by Singapore in distributing primary commodities and fuels from developing countries to developed countries, and in distributing machinery and transport equipment from the latter to the former group of countries. It may be noted, for example, that in 1982, 80% of Singapore's exports of SITC 7 manufactures to Southeast Asia (mainly Malaysia) were reexports.

In table 13.16, Singapore's balance in manufactures has been broken down into consumer, intermediate, and capital goods for major developed-country trading partners. It can be seen that for consumer goods Singapore's trade balances with the United States (and with the EC until 1982) have been positive.[19] For Japan, trade balances in all three categories have been negative, with capital goods contributing most to the deficit. What is remarkable is the size of the deficit with Japan in manufactures. In 1982 this deficit was equal to 60% of Singapore's trade deficit, 77% of Singapore's trade deficit in manufactures, and 160% of Singapore's trade deficit with Japan.

Tables 13.17–13.20 may be examined together. Tables 13.17 and 13.18 present detailed analyses of exports and imports of manufactures in

Table 13.17   Singapore's Trade in Manufactures by Commodity Groups and Selected Countries (in thousands of U.S. dollars)

SITC	Trading Partner	1975 Exports	1975 Domestic Exports	1975 Reexports	1975 Imports	1982 Exports	1982 Domestic Exports	1982 Reexports	1982 Imports
5	*Chemicals*	200,606	88,138	112,469	472,139	804,851	327,317	477,534	1,304,053
	EC (9)	2,578	1,867	711	144,897	29,494	25,041	4,453	390,579
	France	178	54	124	15,661	1,331	899	432	56,020
	Fed. Rep. of Germany	479	103	376	24,835	9,651	8,518	1,113	98,662
	Italy	20	13	6	4,166	2,737	2,689	49	13,294
	Netherlands	143	50	93	32,947	1,197	263	934	38,781
	United Kingdom	491	380	110	56,421	6,714	5,525	1,189	148,579
	United States	1,096	1,028	67	109,758	5,448	3,657	1,792	333,258
	Japan	37,508	36,876	632	74,805	87,678	79,243	8,436	204,943
6	*Basic manufactures*	458,204	207,315	250,889	1,480,325	1,793,786	597,828	1,195,958	3,928,671
	EC (9)	60,928	45,101	15,828	169,653	146,749	91,558	55,191	488,103
	France	4,029	2,995	1,033	26,445	10,907	10,431	475	59,712
	Fed. Rep. of Germany	7,903	5,246	2,657	37,390	21,831	18,800	3,031	121,631
	Italy	1,203	1,057	146	21,339	5,475	3,979	1,496	82,641
	Netherlands	6,262	3,959	2,302	6,514	49,445	18,857	30,588	33,032
	United Kingdom	34,086	24,866	9,220	61,683	44,972	32,755	12,217	132,580
	United States	20,480	12,587	7,893	159,817	145,888	38,684	107,204	306,827
	Japan	9,219	7,301	1,918	633,072	114,565	19,255	95,310	1,523,671
67	Iron and steel	86,865	15,296	71,569	541,444	330,585	63,911	266,674	1,213,083
	EC (9)	533	—	533	43,181	13,241	7,972	5,268	131,533
	France	7	—	7	12,791	7,117	7,117	—	17,352
	Fed. Rep. of Germany	217	—	217	13,986	411	261	150	32,798
	Italy	—	—	—	3,622	6	—	6	7,591
	Netherlands	10	—	10	1,627	3,165	529	2,637	12,413
	United Kingdom	299	—	299	9,551	918	66	852	34,811
	United States	1,227	164	1,063	73,975	10,801	4,186	6,615	60,443
	Japan	1,459	1,168	291	371,759	6,086	3,093	2,993	776,421

68	Nonferrous metals	16,903	5,842	11,061	61,803	340,985	46,022	294,963	212,050
	EC (9)	3,158	560	2,598	7,789	37,277	12,328	24,949	29,612
	France	—	—	—	162	203	203	—	2,736
	Fed. Rep. of Germany	122	116	6	2,225	97	97	—	12,136
	Italy	54	54	—	364	161	161	—	1,784
	Netherlands	1,595	1	1,594	224	36,586	11,765	24,821	917
	United Kingdom	1,319	322	997	3,832	215	102	113	9,260
	United States	1,040	996	43	6,008	89,793	1,039	88,754	12,664
	Japan	643	568	74	16,748	87,463	425	87,037	60,452
69	Metal manufactures	66,774	33,682	33,092	209,791	241,526	119,883	121,643	628,134
	EC (9)	3,616	3,250	366	40,178	21,875	20,029	1,845	128,079
	France	381	378	3	3,573	1,321	1,169	152	10,990
	Fed. rep. of Germany	600	475	125	8,601	13,182	12,270	912	39,243
	Italy	1	1	11	4,845	1,477	1,457	20	19,958
	Netherlands	374	369	5	2,305	1,994	1,733	261	13,874
	United Kingdom	2,105	1,885	219	19,403	3,386	3,117	269	38,809
	United States	5,218	4,253	965	45,628	11,685	8,656	3,029	123,997
	Japan	1,121	907	214	53,095	6,396	3,992	2,404	181,178
7	*Machinery and transport equip.*	1,220,695	714,240	506,456	2,128,058	5,395,420	3,367,218	2,028,201	8,046,400
	EC (9)	197,073	180,678	16,395	515,389	769,675	716,312	53,363	1,433,043
	France	27,628	26,089	1,539	43,341	159,586	151,346	8,240	291,317
	Fed. Rep. of Germany	80,986	75,084	5,902	165,007	241,016	230,795	10,221	541,935
	Italy	13,089	12,001	1,088	44,309	95,857	91,403	4,455	121,812
	Netherlands	20,495	18,111	2,384	38,377	112,923	107,936	4,987	79,477
	United Kingdom	51,283	46,206	5,077	209,246	131,713	109,535	22,179	353,511
	United States	317,902	297,246	20,656	823,979	1,718,807	1,530,695	188,113	2,224,945
	Japan	38,718	27,712	11,006	461,791	191,900	142,806	49,095	2,657,078

(*continued*)

Table 13.17 (continued)

SITC	Trading Partner	1975				1982			
		Exports	Domestic Exports	Reexports	Imports	Exports	Domestic Exports	Reexports	Imports
8	*Misc. manufactures*	371,276	282,399	88,877	561,409	1,323,146	893,886	429,260	1,800,131
	EC (9)	109,200	99,935	9,265	92,537	234,883	196,948	37,936	277,346
	France	16,163	12,986	3,177	9,249	57,707	47,525	10,183	53,582
	Fed. Rep. of Germany	60,043	57,486	2,557	30,062	69,660	58,379	11,281	77,841
	Italy	3,142	3,035	107	7,456	6,656	4,913	1,743	51,458
	Netherlands	10,054	9,189	865	9,682	19,344	15,021	4,323	9,811
	United Kingdom	15,006	12,861	2,145	32,825	64,190	55,105	9,085	75,139
	United States	80,854	78,744	2,110	68,570	299,385	267,812	31,573	288,862
	Japan	10,287	7,357	2,930	141,680	36,037	27,780	8,257	500,842
84	Clothing	117,140	99,610	17,530	60,558	457,797	351,789	106,008	253,797
	EC (9)	37,735	31,127	6,608	4,334	131,406	104,144	27,262	26,348
	France	7,634	5,003	2,631	2,031	33,083	25,245	7,838	7,495
	Fed. Rep. of Germany	13,739	11,650	2,089	166	45,012	36,400	8,612	2,136
	Italy	819	749	70	603	1,706	776	929	12,848
	Netherlands	7,176	6,636	540	40	13,893	10,335	3,558	115
	United Kingdom	4,963	3,990	973	1,468	28,152	23,010	5,143	3,699
	United States	45,168	44,783	385	3,234	183,429	166,631	16,798	7,747
	Japan	663	450	213	4,210	2,558	1,269	1,290	26,847
0–9	*All commodities*	5,380,132	3,334,263	2,045,869	8,126,496	20,781,677	13,927,743	6,853,934	28,151,672
	EC (9)	720,771	518,337	202,434	1,054,677	1,849,282	1,375,921	473,362	2,892,923
	France	94,751	71,957	22,794	112,532	313,625	239,642	73,983	525,513
	Fed. Rep. of Germany	203,048	160,611	42,437	268,276	455,444	348,983	106,461	893,643
	Italy	52,022	31,250	20,772	89,267	168,965	123,656	45,309	275,470
	Netherlands	102,421	75,446	26,976	118,279	354,767	257,344	97,423	211,240
	United Kingdom	227,649	150,150	77,498	403,159	422,757	314,495	108,262	798,297
	United States	748,688	503,903	244,786	1,275,265	2,613,714	2,055,022	558,692	3,633,353
	Japan	469,329	387,866	81,463	1,372,364	2,263,500	1,998,538	264,961	5,042,511

Source: Singapore, Department of Statistics, *Singapore Trade Statistics: Imports and Exports*, various issues.

Table 13.18   **Shares of the United States, Japan, and the European Community in Singapore's Trade in Manufactures** (percentages)

	1975			1982		
	Imp.	Exp.	Dom. Exp.	Imp.	Exp.	Dom. Exp.
SITC 5–8						
United States	25.04	18.67	30.15	20.92	23.29	35.49
EC (9)	19.87	16.43	25.35	17.17	12.67	19.86
Japan	28.25	4.25	6.13	32.41	4.62	5.19
Total	73.16	39.35	61.63	70.50	40.58	60.54
SITC 5						
United States	23.25	0.55	1.17	25.56	0.68	1.12
EC (9)	30.69	1.29	2.12	29.95	3.66	7.65
Japan	15.84	18.70	41.84	15.72	10.89	24.21
Total	69.78	20.54	45.13	71.23	15.23	32.98
SITC 6						
United States	10.80	4.47	6.07	7.81	8.13	6.47
EC (9)	11.46	13.30	21.75	12.42	8.18	15.32
Japan	42.77	2.01	3.52	38.78	6.39	3.22
Total	65.03	19.78	31.34	59.01	22.70	25.01
SITC 7						
United States	38.72	26.04	41.62	27.65	31.86	45.46
EC (9)	24.22	16.14	25.30	17.81	14.27	21.27
Japan	21.70	3.17	3.88	33.02	3.56	4.24
Total	84.64	45.35	70.80	78.48	49.69	70.97
SITC 8						
United States	12.21	21.78	27.88	16.05	22.63	29.96
EC (9)	16.48	29.41	35.39	15.41	17.75	22.03
Japan	25.24	2.77	2.61	27.82	2.72	3.11
Total	53.93	53.96	65.88	59.28	43.10	55.10

Source: Table 13.17.

1975 and 1982 showing the importance of commodity subgroups and trading partners, with domestic exports and reexports distinguished. Table 13.19 gives some idea about the shares of manufactures and primary products and their major subgroups in Singapore's exports and domestic exports to and imports from the world and selected countries. Finally, table 13.20 provides a finer breakdown of Singapore's domestic manufactured exports in 1982, with the major markets for individual commodities indicated.

It can be seen from table 13.17 that while for chemicals and manufactured goods classified by material reexports had been more important than domestically produced exports, much higher proportions of manufactured exports to advanced countries (EC, United States, and Japan) consisted of domestic exports. Thus, for chemicals, domestic

Table 13.19 Composition of Singapore's Imports, Exports, and Domestic Exports, 1982 (percentages)

	SITC 0	SITC 1	SITC 2	SITC 3	SITC 4	SITC 5	SITC 6	SITC 7	SITC 8	SITC 9	All Commodities
Imports (total)	*5.98*	*0.56*	*3.83*	*33.99*	*1.11*	*4.63*	*13.96*	*28.58*	*6.39*	*0.96*	*100.00*
United States	4.81	1.28	1.20	4.86	0.09	9.17	8.44	61.24	7.95	0.96	100.00
EC[a]	3.41	2.71	0.47	1.57	0.16	13.48	16.85	49.47	9.60	2.28	100.00
Japan	1.28	0.03	0.47	0.10	0.06	4.06	30.22	52.69	9.93	1.15	100.00
Exports (total)	*5.37*	*0.49*	*6.25*	*32.87*	*1.75*	*3.87*	*8.63*	*25.96*	*6.37*	*8.43*	*100.00*
United States	4.76	0.04	4.59	4.71	0.00	0.21	5.58	65.76	11.45	2.90	100.00
EC[a]	4.03	0.04	13.97	2.33	0.11	1.52	7.65	39.83	12.13	18.39	100.00
Japan	2.97	0.33	2.45	66.13	0.06	3.87	5.06	8.48	1.59	9.05	100.00
Domestic exports (total)	*1.65*	*0.45*	*1.31*	*46.46*	*1.63*	*2.35*	*4.29*	*24.18*	*6.42*	*11.27*	*100.00*
United States	1.26	0.04	0.78	5.98	0.00	0.18	1.88	74.49	13.03	2.36	100.00
EC[a]	1.21	0.02	2.16	3.10	0.10	1.72	6.31	49.32	13.54	22.52	100.00
Japan	1.25	0.32	0.90	74.89	0.01	3.97	0.96	7.15	1.39	9.18	100.00

Source: Singapore, Department of Statistics, *Singapore Trade Statistics: Imports and Exports, December 1982.*
[a]Figures include Greece.

exports to these countries greatly exceeded reexports. For manufactured goods classified by material, although domestic exports to these countries were smaller than reexports, they nevertheless represented a higher proportion of total exports to these countries than of exports to other countries. In fact, for iron and steel and metal manufactures, domestic exports to these countries were more important than reexports in 1982. Exports of machinery and transport equipment and miscellaneous manufactures were mostly domestically produced.

Table 17.18 shows that manufactured imports from the United States, Japan, and the EC together accounted for more than 70% of the total in 1982 and over 59% for all individual SITC one-digit categories. The countries' shares differed, however: imports of basic manufactures and miscellaneous manufactures were mostly from Japan, imports of chemicals were mostly from the EC and the United States, and imports of machinery and transport equipment were mainly from Japan and the United States. The share of these countries in manufactured domestic exports was about 60% in 1982. Their shares in domestically produced exports from Singapore were in general higher than those in total exports, reflecting the fact that much higher percentages of exports of manufactures to these countries were domestically produced exports. Their shares were higher for machinery and transport equipment, followed by miscellaneous manufactures. For chemicals and manufactured goods classified by material their shares were less than half since most of Singapore's exports were to developing countries. Again, there are differences among countries. Domestic exports of chemicals were mostly to Japan, and those of manufactured goods by material mainly to the EC. Over 45% of domestic exports of machinery and transport equipment and 30% of domestic exports of miscellaneous manufactures were to the United States, with the EC taking over another 20% in each case. The shares of Japan in these two categories were less than 4%.

Table 13.19 shows the importance of manufactures in Singapore's trade with all countries and with individual countries. In 1982 manufactured imports made up 54% of Singapore's imports. They made up 97% of total imports from Japan and close to 90% of imports from the United States and the EC. Machinery and transport equipment alone made up 50%–60% of total imports from these countries. Manufactures accounted for 90% of domestic exports to the United States and 71% of domestic exports to the EC. Machinery and transport equipment account for three-quarters of domestic exports to the United States and half of domestic exports to the EC, with miscellaneous manufactured articles contributing another 14% in both cases. Mineral fuels—especially petroleum products—accounted for three-quarters of domestic exports to Japan, with manufactures contributing only about 13%.

Table 13.20   **Commodity Composition and Geographic Distribution of Singapore's Domestic Exports and Domestic Manufactured Exports, 1982**

SITC Rev. 2	Commodity	Share (%) of Dom. Exp. in: Total	SITC 5–8	U.S.	EC[b]	Japan	Malaysian Peninsula	Others
0	*Food*	*1.65*		*11.33* (2)	*7.70*	*10.86* (3)	*9.88*	Hong Kong *13.60* (1)
1	*Beverages and tobacco*	*0.45*		*1.17*	*0.42*	*10.06*	*2.93*	Hong Kong *23.06* (1), Brunei *20.98* (2), Democratic Kampuchea *19.49* (3)
2	*Crude materials*	*1.31*		*8.77* (3)	*17.23* (1)	*9.82* (2)	*7.55*	Hong Kong *14.15* (3)
3	*Mineral fuels*	*46.46*		*1.90*	*0.70*	*23.13* (1)	*16.25* (2)	Saudi Arabia *32.05* (1), Nigeria *15.70* (2), Bangladesh *8.34* (3)
4	*Animal & veg. oils & fats*	*1.63*		*0.01*	*0.65*	*0.12*	*2.75*	
5	*Chemicals*	**2.35**	**6.31**	**1.12** (3)	**7.65** (3)	**24.21** (1)	**13.89** (2)	
51	Organic chem.		0.82					
52	Inorganic chem.		0.22					
53	Dyes and colors		0.41					
54	Medicinal prod.		2.35	0.38	2.53	54.13 (1)	3.60	Hong Kong 4.30 (2), Saudi Arabia 3.91 (3)
55	Perfumed toilet preps.		0.69					
56	Fertilizers mfd.		0.00					
57	Explosives		0.00					
58	Plastic materials		0.98	1.22	0.93	0.47	21.34 (1)	Australia 10.64 (2), United Arab Emirates 6.75 (3)
59	Chemical prod. n.e.s.		0.85					
6	*Basic manufactures*	**4.29**	**11.53**	**6.47**	**15.38** (2)	**3.22**	**17.02** (1)	Hong Kong **7.28** (3)
61	Leather prod. n.e.s.		0.02					
62	Rubber manuf. n.e.s.		0.39					
63	Wood and cork manuf.		2.61	2.32	28.65 (1)	2.66	5.61	Saudi Arabia 9.87 (2), Hong Kong 6.89 (3)
64	Paper manuf.		0.63					
65	Textile manuf.		1.87	18.99 (1)	6.26	5.00	9.50	Hong Kong 14.90 (2), Australia 9.63 (3)
66	Nonmetal mineral manuf.		1.58	1.43	0.32	2.36	33.42 (1)	China 14.23 (2), Hong Kong 8.06 (3)
67	Iron and steel		1.23	6.55	12.47 (2)	4.84	26.58 (1)	Brunei 11.11 (3)
68	Nonferrous metals		0.89					
69	Metal manuf.		2.31	7.22 (3)	16.71 (2)	3.33	18.43 (1)	

7	*Machinery and transport*	**24.18**	**64.93**	**45.46** (1)	**21.32** (2)	**4.24**	**4.72**	Hong Kong **5.29** (3)
71	Power-generating mach.		1.65	69.09 (1)	7.01 (3)	8.50 (2)	3.31	Australia 11.97 (2), Brunei 11.44 (3)
72	Industrial mach.		1.46	16.81 (1)	7.97	7.38	9.97	
73	Metalworking mach.		0.48					
74	General indust. mach.		3.89	28.92 (1)	11.46 (3)	16.79 (2)	9.17	Canada 2.61 (3)
75	Office and data mach.		4.43	58.60 (1)	27.31 (2)	1.14	1.73	
76	Telecommunications apparatus		16.75	37.74 (1)	33.62 (2)	1.98	3.35 (3)	Australia 4.83 (3)
761	Television receivers		4.47	12.49 (2)	51.93 (1)	0.55	4.27	
762	Radio-broadcast receivers		7.13	36.34 (2)	38.67 (1)	3.02 (3)	0.80	
763	Gramophones		1.22	61.37 (1)	18.98 (2)	3.56	0.59	Taiwan 5.01 (3)
764	Telecomm. equip.		3.93	61.63 (1)	8.16 (2)	1.24	7.77 (3)	Hong Kong 9.91 (3)
77	Elec. mach. n.e.s.		28.98	47.07 (1)	17.44 (2)	4.25	5.76	
771	Elec. power mach.		0.56					
772	Elec. circuit apparatus		4.95	65.10 (1)	15.19 (2)	3.60	4.30 (3)	
773	Electricity-distributing equip.		0.28					
774	Elec. medical apparatus		0.00					
775	Household goods		2.25	51.77 (1)	13.70 (2)	0.98	1.09	Saudi Arabia 5.31 (3)
776	Electronic valves		18.18	48.64 (1)	17.96 (2)	4.73	5.59	Hong Kong 13.08 (3)
778	Elec. mach. n.e.s.		2.75	8.89 (3)	23.52 (1)	3.61	5.63	Hong Kong 10.54 (2)
78	Road vehicles		0.24					
79	Transport equip.		7.04	60.09 (1)	17.56 (2)	0.03	1.83 (3)	
8	*Misc. manufactured articles*	**6.42**	**17.24**	**29.96** (1)	**22.06** (2)	**3.11**	**3.10**	Saudi Arabia **7.97** (3)
81	Sanitary lighting manuf.		0.12					
82	Furniture		1.27	41.80 (1)	10.80 (2)	5.31	1.50	Saudi Arabia 10.20 (3)
83	Travel goods		0.20					
84	Clothing		6.78	47.37 (1)	29.60 (2)	0.36	0.58	Sweden 3.60 (3)
85	Footwear		0.38					
87	Scientific instruments		1.06	40.64 (1)	10.52 (3)	11.16 (2)	3.51	Hong Kong 47.00 (1)
88	Photographic apparatus		1.83	14.89 (2)	9.79 (3)	7.37	4.27	Saudi Arabia 17.91 (2)
89	Misc. manuf. articles n.e.s.		5.59	12.32 (3)	23.16 (1)	3.36	5.66	Liberia **15.39** (2), Panama **14.58** (3)
9	*Misc. transactions n.e.s.*	**11.27**	**3.09**	**20.88** (1)	**11.68**	**2.30**		
5–8	*Total manufactures*	**37.24**	**100.00**	**35.49** (1)	**19.90** (2)	**5.19**	**6.44** (3)	
0–9	*All commodities*	**100.00**	**100.00**	**14.75** (1)	**10.45**	**14.35** (2)	**10.53** (3)	

Source: Singapore, Department of Statistics, *Singapore Trade Statistics: Imports and Exports, December 1982.*

[a]Ranks of the three most important markets are shown in parentheses. Geographic distributions are shown for all SITC one-digit categories and for individual manufactured goods whose shares in domestic exports of manufactures (SITC 5–8) exceed 1%.

[b]Figures include Greece.

Table 13.20 gives a detailed classification of Singapore's domestic exports of manufactures in 1982 and lists the major country destinations for individual commodities. The largest markets for Singapore's domestically produced exports of manufactures and their shares in the total are as follows: United States, 35.5%; EC, 19.9%; Malaysian Peninsula, 6.4%; Hong Kong, 5.8%; and Japan, 5.2%. For domestically produced exports of all commodities from Singapore, however, Japan's share (14.4%) ranks just behind the U.S. share (14.8%) owing to the importance of petroleum products. In 1982 Singapore's domestic exports of manufactures were dominated by machinery and transport equipment, which accounted for 65% of the total, followed by miscellaneous manufactured articles (17%), manufactured goods classified by material (12%), and chemicals (6%). Within machinery and transport equipment (SITC 7), electrical machinery not elsewhere specified (n.e.s.) (SITC 77) and telecommunications apparatus (SITC 76) together accounted for 46% of total domestically manufactured exports, while transport equipment (SITC 79) contributed another 7%. The single most important SITC three-digit group was SITC 776, electronic valves (mostly integrated circuits), which alone accounted for 18% of domestically manufactured exports. For SITC 7, the United States was by far the largest market for Singapore, with a share of 45%, followed by the EC (21%) and Hong Kong (5%). For miscellaneous manufactured articles (SITC 8, with clothing being the most important), the United States was also the largest buyer. For manufactured goods by material (SITC 6), the Malaysian Peninsula provided the largest market; for chemicals (SITC 5), especially medicinal products, Japan was the most important.

13.5 Prospects for Singapore's Exports of Manufactures

In the last two decades the Singapore economy has grown at a high and sustained rate as a result of its successful export-oriented industrialization. During that period, emphasis has shifted from entrepôt trade to domestic exports of manufactures, and export orientation has increased in most industries. The same period has witnessed significant changes in the commodity composition and geographic pattern of Singapore's trade. While twenty years ago trade was mainly concentrated in primary commodities, manufactures and fuels now make up the greater part of Singapore's trade. Within trade in manufactures, there have been declines in the shares of consumer and intermediate goods and increases in the share of capital goods. All these reflect the changing nature of entrepôt trade as well as Singapore's industrial development. In 1960 practically all manufactured exports (mainly reexports) were to developing countries; by 1982 over 60% of domestic exports of manufactures went to developed countries. Recently, there has also been increasing emphasis on high-value-added, skill-intensive, and capital-intensive industries. At present, however, Singapore's manufactured exports are still labor-intensive relative to its imports.

In recent years Singapore has run balance-of-trade deficits, partly as a result of its industrialization drive necessitating imports of intermediate inputs and capital goods. However, the trade deficits have been more than offset by foreign capital inflows, especially through the nonmonetary private sector in the form of foreign direct investment, giving rise to overall balance-of-payments surpluses (table 13.1). There is little doubt that Singapore's liberal policy with respect to foreign investment has been an important factor contributing to its success in developing the manufacturing sector. At the same time, it may be noted that a large supply of national savings is available, partly through contributions to the Central Provident Fund (CPF), a compulsory savings scheme for workers' retirement. The funds are mainly used to buy government securities and finance government expenditures on infrastructure such as public housing. Since a large part of Singapore's own capital is invested abroad, one might question why Singapore has not relied more on domestic capital in financing industrial development, thereby reducing "dependence" on foreign investment.[20] Tan and Ow (1982) pointed out that in addition to bringing in capital, foreign investment brings in new technology, entrepreneurship, and technical skills. Others have, however, noted that this might have an inhibiting effect on the development of local entrepreneurship in industry, and whether this has been more or less important than beneficial spillover effects is perhaps debatable (see, for example, Chia 1980). Nevertheless, from a macroeconomic point of view foreign investment provided the capital inflow necessary to offset the trade deficits that accompanied rapid industrialization.

Although Singapore's outward-looking strategy has been remarkably successful, difficulties have to be faced in the future. One is that of protectionism on the part of developed countries. The deepening of recession in 1982 and increasing unemployment led to increased pressured from domestic industries in advanced countries to curb imports, and the use of nontariff barriers (e.g., quotas and voluntary export restraints) became more widespread. Although attempts were made to halt rising protectionism (for example, at the General Agreement on Tariffs and Trade [GATT] meeting in Geneva in November 1982), there is not much hope for freer trade in the near future. This would be so even if there is a world economic recovery, since the fundamental issue is whether advanced countries are willing to restructure their economies and phase out certain (mainly low-technology and labor-intensive) declining industries.

Singapore has been a beneficiary under the U.S., EC, and Japanese Generalized System of Preferences. But protectionism is likely to affect GSP exports as well because of safeguard provisions if domestic industries are adversely affected by imports. Moreover there is the possibility that Singapore and other newly industrializing countries may soon lose their developing-country status and thus be excluded from preferential tariff treatment in developed countries. Closer economic cooperation among developing countries may be thought to be the solution, but the creation of a preferential regional market inevitably results in a loss of gains from specialization at the global level, which must be weighed against the possible benefits.

During a recession, labor-intensive manufactures like textiles are especially vulnerable to protectionist measures.[21] This provided further impetus for Singapore to move upstream toward higher-technology and higher-value-added industries. Another reason is the growing labor shortage.

Until the late 1960s, Singapore's high rates of industrial growth had been accomplished by rapid absorption of labor into labor-intensive industries. This "easy" phase of industrialization has come to an end. In the coming years it is labor shortage and not labor surplus that presents the problem. In the case of Singapore, it can be solved only by technological upgrading, since the import of foreign labor has obvious social and other costs and can hardly be regarded as a long-term solution. In a labor-shortage situation, improvements in productivity are essential for a high and sustainable rate of GNP growth. Unfortunately, productivity performance in manufacturing in the 1970s was less than satisfactory. Pang and Tan (1981) found that labor force expansion from 1975 to 1979—not growth of the capital stock or productivity improvement—was the dominant factor explaining output growth. They suggested that importation of foreign labor, together with the National Wage Council policy of emphasizing small wage increases during that period, might have delayed the needed structural adjustment in manufacturing of decreasing the number of industries and processes whose viability depends on an abundance of unskilled labor. In fact, as pointed out earlier, a high-wage policy was resumed in 1979 to encourage substitution of capital for unskilled labor. Singapore is now following a deliberate policy of phasing out unskilled-labor-intensive industries and restructuring the economy through the provision of fiscal and other incentives to move into high-technology and skill-intensive activities.

In its further industrialization, Singapore faces what has appropriately been described as a "sandwich problem" (Tan and Ow 1982, 308). Singapore is destined to lose its comparative advantage to other developing countries in the low-value-added, low-technology types of manufactures (e.g., textiles and plastic products). On the other hand, it may be some time before it can compete successfully with developed countries in those requiring high technology (e.g., precision and engineering products). The attraction of foreign investment into these high-technology and skill-intensive industries will also prove to be more difficult than attracting investment in labor-intensive operations through low wages. In addition to fiscal incentives, the development of a highly skilled local work force and trained professional and engineering manpower, among other things, will be crucial.

The restructuring of the manufacturing sector is likely to be a slow and expensive process. Because of Singapore's size there may be limits to its further industrialization. This leads some to suggest that areas other than manufacturing—such as modern traded services, e.g., banking and finance, professional and management services—may merit attention (see Tan and Ow 1982; Chia 1980). In the past they have developed rapidly without direct government support, and they may be the activities in which Singapore's future comparative advantage lies. Regardless of whether the future emphasis is on high-technology manufacturing or on high-value-added services, economic restructuring as a dynamic response to external conditions and internal development, the upgrading of the work force, and the improvement of productivity present the main challenges to Singapore in the coming years.

Appendix
Singapore's Industrial Classification and Relation to International Trade Data

Many of the analyses in this paper are based on time series comparisons of compositions of output, value added, and direct export. Many of the analyses also require relating production to trade data. Since published census data on industrial production in various years are sometimes based on different classification systems, an attempt has been made to make them comparable. Table 13.A.1 shows the relations between the three industrial classification systems on which the data in the study have been based. Table 13.A.2 shows the relation between Singapore's industrial classification and the United Nations' standard international trade classification (SITC), revision 1. The conversions given in the two tables should of course be regarded as approximate rather than exact.

Table 13.A.1   **Singapore's Industrial Classifications**

Industry	SIC[a]	SSIC, 1969[b]	SSIC, 1978[c]
Food	20	311 + 312	311 + 312
Beverages	21	313	313

(continued)

Table 13.20   (continued)

Industry	SIC[a]	SSIC, 1969[b]	SSIC, 1978[c]
Tobacco	22	314	314
Textiles	23	321	321
Footwear, wearing apparel, made-up textile goods	24	322 + 324	322 + 324
Wood and cork prod.	25	331	331
Furniture and fixtures	26	332	332
Paper and paper prod.	27	341	341
Printing, publishing, allied prod.	28	342	342
Leather, leather prod.	29	323	323
Rubber prod. (incl. footwear but excl. rubber proc.)	30	355 + 356	355 + 356
Chemicals and chem. prod.	31	351 + 352	351 + 352
Petroleum refineries, petroleum and coal prod.	32	353 + 354	353 + 354
Nonmetallic mineral prod.	33	361 + 362 + 363 + 364 + 365 + 369	361 + 362 + 363 + 364 + 365 + 369
Basic metal prod.	34	371 + 372	371 + 372
Metal prod. (except mach. and transport equip.)	35	381	381
Nonelect. mach.	36	382	382 + 38411 + 38412 − 38231 + 38239
Elect. mach.	37	383	383 + 38421 − 38429 + 3843 − 3849 + 38413
Transport equip.	38	384	385 + 38231 + 38239
Misc. manuf. industries	39	{ 385 390	386 390
Plastic products	3995	357	357

Sources: Nyaw 1979; Singapore, National Statistical Commission, *Singapore Standard Industrial Classification, 1973*; Singapore, Department of Statistics, *Singapore Standard Industrial Classification, 1978*.

[a]Singapore Industrial Classification, two-digit.

[b]Singapore Standard Industrial Classification of all economic activities, revised 1969.

[c]Singapore Standard Industrial Classification, 1978.

Table 13.A.2   **Relation between Singapore Standard Industrial Classification (Revised 1969) and United Nations' Standard International Trade Classification (Revised)**

Industry	Type[a]	SSIC, 1969	SITC (Rev. 1)
Food	C	311 + 312	013 + 022 + 032 + 046 + 048 + 053 + 0612 + 081
Beverages	C	313	111 + 112
Cigarettes, other tobacco prod.	C	314	122
Textiles, textile manuf.	I	321	65
Wearing apparel except footwear	C	322	84
Leather, leather prod.	I	323	61 + 83

Table 13.20   (continued)

Industry	Type[a]	SSIC, 1969	SITC (Rev. 1)
Footwear	C	324	851
Sawn timber, other wood prod. except furniture	I	331	63
Furniture and fixtures except primarily of metal	C	332	821
Paper and paper prod.	I	341	64
Printing and publishing	C	342	892
Industrial chemicals and gases	I	351	51 + 52+ 531 + 532 + 571
Paints, pharmaceuticals, other chem. prod.	I	352	541 + 533 + 55
Petroleum refineries, petroleum prod.	I	353 + 354	332
Processing of jelutong and gum dammar	I	355	231 + 232 + 233
Rubber prod. except footwear	I	356	62
Plastic products	I	357	893 + 581
Pottery, china, earthenware, glass prod.	I	361 + 362	666 + 664 + 665
Bricks, tiles, other structural clay prod.	I	363	662
Cements, cement additives	I	364	661
Structural cement and concrete prod.	I	365	
Asbestos, stone, other nonmetallic mineral prod.	I	369	663
Iron and steel	K	371	67
Zinc, other nonferrous metals	K	372	68
Metal grills, cans, pipes and other fabricated prod.	K	381	69
Calculators, refrigerators, air conditioners and indust. mach.	K	382	71
Radios, TVs, semiconductors, other elect. mach.	K	383	72
Transport equip. and oil rigs	K	384	73
Professional and sci. equip., photog. and optical goods	C	385	86
Other manuf. industries (jewelry, toys, umbrellas, etc.)	—	390	—

Source: Nyaw 1979, with modifications.
[a]C = consumer goods, I = intermediate goods, K = capital goods.

Notes

1. In 1982 total merchandise trade (sum of exports and imports) was 362% of gross domestic product. The calculation is based on figures from Singapore, Ministry of Trade and Industry, *Economic Survey of Singapore, 1982*.

2. A good description of Singapore's industrial development and its relation to trade can be found in Tan and Ow 1982, Pang 1981, and Pang and Tan 1981.

3. The average nominal and effective rates of protection to the whole manufacturing sector in 1967 were estimated to be 3% and 6% respectively. In addition, Tan and Ow (1982) calculated "effective subsidy rates" that also quantify the additional incentives provided by differential corporation tax rates and preferential loans. The average rate of effective subsidy for the whole manufacturing sector was 6%. The figures for predominantly export-oriented industries and predominantly import-competing industries were 7% and 15% respectively.

4. Singapore, Department of Statistics, *Report on the Census of Industrial Production, 1981.*

5. The SDF is financed through a levy on employers amounting to 4% of the payroll of all employees earning less than S $750 per month. See Singapore, Economic Development Board, *Annual Report 1982/83,* for details of the various schemes described in this paragraph.

6. Tables 13.4 and 13.5 have not been constructed on a comparable basis, since before 1975 official published data on domestic exports are available only for selected commodities—and only for certain years.

7. The Schiavo-Campo (1978) index of structural change (SC) between years t and $t + k$ is SC $= 50 \Sigma |s_i(t + k) - s_i(t)|$, where s_i is the share of subgroup i in the total.

8. Schiavo-Campo (1978) also suggested the following "index of consistency" of structural change (C) for years 1 through n: C $=$ SC$(1,n)/\Sigma$SC(i,j), $0 \le$ C ≤ 1, where $i = (1, k, 2k, \ldots, n - k)$ and $j = (k, 2k, 3k, \ldots, n)$ so that each subperiod has k years and the number of subperiods is n/k. The indices of consistency for output, value added, and direct export are respectively 0.59, 0.51, and 0.49, indicating that compositions do fluctuate considerably and the changes often reverse themselves.

9. Total exports (X) consist of domestically produced exports (X_d) and reexports (X_r), while total imports (M) consist of retained imports (M_r) and entrepôt imports (M_e). Thus we have $X = X_d + X_r$ and $M = M_r + M_e$. Since reexport figures are unavailable before 1975, they are estimated by subtracting direct export (see note to table 13.3) from total export. If one can further assume that $X_r = M_e$, then retained import can be estimated by $M_r = M - M_e = M - X_r$. However, M_e may differ considerably from X_r for two reasons. First, the two are not the same because of differences in valuation (Singapore's exports are valued f.o.b. and imports are valued c.i.f.) and because of the margin on entrepôt trade. Second, there is the timing problem: entrepôt imports may not be reflected in reexports of the same year.

10. Singapore, Department of Statistics, *Singapore Input-Output Tables 1973,* pp. 17–18.

11. Singapore, Department of Statistics, *Singapore Input-Output Tables 1978,* pp. 21–22.

12. See, for example the Rahman (1973) study, which suggests that developing countries are in the strongest competitive position if they concentrate their manufactured exports in labor-intensive products.

13. The skill index is computed for 1970 and 1980 since it requires population census data.

14. See also Chow 1975, in which Keesing's procedures are employed to study the skill intensity of Singapore's trade in manufactures.

15. The weighted-average factor intensity (physical capital, total capital, or skill intensity) F is given by

$$F = \sum_{i=1}^{n} w_i f_i ,$$

where f_i is the factor intensity in the production of commodity i and w_i is the share of commodity i in total exports or total imports.

16. See n. 9. Because of the timing problem (and possibly other reasons), the estimate of retained imports for a commodity group can be negative. When Singapore's trading partners are divided into industrialized and other countries, the estimate of retained imports for a commodity can also be negative because of the pattern of entrepôt trade: the commodity may be imported from, say, developed countries and then reexported to developing countries. In the few cases where estimates of retained imports are negative, they are assumed to be zero, and the commodities are therefore given zero weights in the computation of average factor intensities.

17. Chow (1975) in studying the skill intensity of Singapore's trade argued that, since Singapore is in between the advanced and less advanced industrialized countries, the skill requirements of Singapore's industries may reflect the "average" skill requirement in world trade. Moreover, although Singapore is a small country, it is not so specialized as to make its skill requirements inappropriate as a measurement yardstick.

18. It should be noted that "other countries" in tables 13.11 and 13.12 include both developing countries and centrally planned economies. If calculations are made for developing countries alone, the contrast would probably be even more marked.

19. In 1982 exports of clothing to the EC were more than offset by net imports of scientific instruments and other miscellaneous manufactured articles.

20. Forced savings in the form of contributions to CPF are also believed to help siphon off excessive purchasing power and to exert a deflationary influence on the economy. See Wong 1981 for a related discussion. It may be noted that during the 1974–75 inflation following the oil crisis, Singapore, unlike some other developing countries, chose to accept a lower rate of growth by deflationary domestic policies for the sake of limiting indebtedness and lowering the rate of inflation. External financing continued to take the form of direct foreign investment. Balassa (1981) noted that Singapore's gross debt service ratio declined from 9% in 1973 to 7% in 1978; and while the ratio of gross external debt to GNP rose from 13% to 15%, net reserves continued to exceed its gross external debt by almost three times.

21. See Singapore, Ministry of Trade and Industry, *Economic Survey of Singapore, 1982,* for a discussion of protectionist measures introduced in that year. In the case of textiles, more restrictions were introduced in the new Multi-Fiber Arrangement and in the Singapore EC Textile Agreement concluded in November 1982.

References

Balassa, Bela. 1981. The newly-industrializing developing countries after the oil crisis. *Weltwirtschaftliches Archiv* 117, no. 1:142–94.

Chia Siow Yue. 1980. Singapore's trade and development strategy and ASEAN economic co-operation, with special reference to the ASEAN common approach to foreign economic relations. In *ASEAN in a changing Pacific and world economy,* ed. Ross Garnaut. Canberra: Australian National University Press.

Chow Kit Boey. 1975. Human capital intensity of Singapore's trade in manufactures. *Malayan Economic Review* 20, no. 2:71–97.

Keesing, Donald B. 1965. Labor skills and international trade: Evaluating many trade flows with a single measuring device. *Review of Economics and Statistics* 47, no. 3:287–94.

———. 1968. Labor skills and the structure of trade in manufactures. In *The open economy: Essays in international trade and finance,* ed. Peter B. Kenen and Roger Lawrence. New York: Columbia University Press.

Lary, Hal B. 1968. *Imports of manufactures from less developed countries.* New York: National Bureau of Economic Research.

Nyaw Mee-kau. 1979. *Export expansion and industrial growth in Singapore.* Hong Kong: Kingsway International Publications.

Pang Eng Fong. 1981. Economic development and the labor market in a newly industrializing country: The experience of Singapore. *Developing Economies* 19, no. 1:3–16.

Pang Eng Fong and Augustine Tan. 1981. Employment and export-led industrialization: The experience of Singapore. In *The development of labour intensive industry in ASEAN countries,* ed. Rashid Amjad. Geneva: International Labour Organization.

Rahman, A. H. M. Mahfuzur. 1973. *Exports of manufactures from developing countries: A study in comparative advantage.* Rotterdam: Rotterdam University Press.

Schiavo-Campo, Salvatore. 1978. The simple measurement of structural change: A note. *Economic Record* 54, no. 146:261–63.

Tan, Augustine H. H., and Ow Chin Hock. 1982. Singapore. In *Development strategies in semi-industrial economies,* ed. B. Balassa. Baltimore: Johns Hopkins University Press for The World Bank.

Wong, Kum Poh. 1981. The financing of trade and development in the ADCs: The experience of Singapore. In *Trade and growth of the advanced developing countries in the Pacific basin,* ed. Wontack Hong and Lawrence B. Krause. Seoul: Korean Development Institute Press.

V The ASEAN Four: Next-Tier Newly Industrializing Countries?

14 Changes in the Malaysian Economy and Trade Trends and Prospects

Chee Peng Lim

14.1 Introduction

The Malaysian economy has experienced a relatively rapid growth rate during the last twenty years and has also undergone a structural transformation. From a largely agriculture-based economy, diversification has proceeded to the extent that manufacturing is slowly emerging as a leading sector. Needless to say, this structural transformation has affected the product composition of Malaysia's trade as well as the structure of its trade with the United States, Japan, and Western Europe.

The main purpose of this paper is to focus on the trade trends and prospects of Malaysia following the economic changes described above. The paper will also focus on how the product composition of trade in manufactures has changed as development occurred in Malaysia over the last twenty years and will examine the salient determinants of those changes. The analysis of trade will be linked to an analysis of domestic development in Malaysia; the growth of manufactured exports and the changing structure of trade with Malaysia's leading trade partners will be discussed. Finally the paper will assess whether the pattern of rapid growth, expansion of manufactured exports, and increased industrial imports will continue; a discussion of the implications of this assessment will conclude the paper.

The main problem encountered in this study is the lack of adequate, accurate, and up-to-date data. Some of the data required for this study, especially data on specific manufacturing industries, are not available. Other data, such as the Index of Manufacturing Prcduction, are not accurate because the 1968 weights used in the current production index

Chee Peng Lim is chairman of the Division of Analytical Economics at the University of Malaya, Kuala Lumpur, Malaysia.

do not represent the structure of production reflected by the 1973 manufacturing census. Finally, the 1978 manufacturing census has still not been published, so in many cases data from the 1973 census have to be used. Trade data are much better. Still there are some problems. A major problem is created by the changes in the SITC classification. Because of these changes there were some problems in comparing changes in the composition of exports and imports during the period under study. Another problem is the separation of the trade data of Sabah and Sarawak from those of Peninsular Malaysia.[1] Consequently in some cases we are able to present trade data only for Peninsular Malaysia and not the whole country.

The study is divided into eleven sections. Following the Introduction, section 14.2 discusses the rapid growth in the Malaysian manufacturing sector during the last two decades. Section 14.3 traces the structural changes which took place in the manufacturing sector during its rapid period of growth, and section 14.4 tries to distinguish the two stages of growth in the manufacturing sector. These discussions set the stage for the analysis of external trade patterns, which begins in section 14.5. Sections 14.6 and 14.7 examine the composition of and changes in Malaysian exports, while sections 14.9 and 14.10 do the same for imports. Section 14.8 focuses on the growth of manufactured exports. The concluding section tries to anticipate further changes in the Malaysian economy and to evaluate trade prospects for the rest of this decade and includes some implications of the assessment.

14.2   Growth of the Manufacturing Sector

Since its independence in 1957, the Malaysian government has promoted the manufacturing sector with the aim of diversifying its agriculture-based economy and as a means of generating employment opportunities. More recently, industrialization has become an important vehicle to achieve the aims of the New Economic Policy, namely, the restructuring of employment and ownership of assets as well as the alleviation of poverty.[2]

Considering the various important objectives which the Malaysian government has laid down for the manufacturing sector, it is not surprising that this sector has received the policymakers' special attention. As early as 1958, the Pioneer Industrial Ordinance was introduced to provide fiscal incentives for industrial investments. This was replaced a decade later by the broader Investment Incentives Act.[3] In addition, the Malaysian Industrial Development Finance (MIDF) was set up in 1960 and the Malaysian Industrial Development Authority (MIDA) was established in 1965 to provide financial and other facilities for investors in the manufacturing sector. Also, in line with the New Economic

Policy, the Malaysian government began to participate more actively and directly in the industrialization process by investing in industries.

In 1975 the Industrial Coordination Act was introduced to accelerate the pace of industrialization and achieve the New Economic Policy objectives. Pragmatic changes in industrial sector policies reinforced by sustained political and price stability, a buoyant balance of payments, a favorable investment climate, abundant natural resources, and a fairly well-educated labor force have helped the Malaysian manufacturing sector achieve substantial industrial growth over the last two decades. The average annual growth rate in this sector of 12% has been consistently higher than that of any other sector in the economy during the last two decades. This growth rate is twice the 6% rate of average annual growth of GDP in the 1960s and one and a half times the high 7.5% per annum GDP growth in the 1970s (Chee 1982a).

The increase in value added is also another good indicator of the very rapid growth in manufacturing activity. Between 1959 and 1973, total value added arising from the manufacturing sector grew from M $204 million to M $2,060 million—an increase of more than tenfold.[4] This increase represents an average annual growth rate in the region of 18%. More significantly, the increase in gross value added exceeded the increase in gross output in the last twenty years. The result is a continuously rising ratio of value added to gross output during this period and indicates Malaysia's success in increasing the domestic value added content of its manufacturing gross output. In addition, when growth rates are calculated over different time periods, we observe that there was an acceleration in the increase in value added, particularly after 1968 (Chee 1982a). This spurt appears to coincide closely with the Malaysian government's increasing use of tariff protection as an instrument to advance industrial development. However, it was also during this period that manufactured exports began to achieve some measure of success.

In terms of number of establishments and employment, in the last twenty years, the total number of manufacturing establishments has more than doubled, while the total number of employees has increased from 61,597 to 377,719 (about six times).

In short, all indicators show that manufacturing has been by far the fastest growing economic activity on a sustained basis in the Malaysian economy. Available evidence shows that the sources for the substantial growth in the manufacturing sector in the past may be traced to the growth in domestic demand and import substitution (accounting for about 90% of industrial development during the 1960s (Hoffmann and Ee 1980, chap. 5). By the late 1960s and early 1970s, the scope of the "easy" or first, stage of import substitution was substantially reduced. Further, beginning around the mid-1960s, manufactured exports gradually became an important direct source of growth, accounting for about a fifth of industrial growth. In more recent years, 1974–78, manufactured exports have maintained their contribution to growth at about 20%, and additional import substitution appears to have contributed 12%–13% to growth in those years.

The rapid growth in the Malaysian manufacturing sector has enabled it to make a significant contribution to the growth in the country's GDP (see table 14.1). This contribution of manufacturing to the growth in GDP has increased from nearly 20% in the early 1960s to nearly 26% in the late 1970s. Consequently the share of manufacturing in GDP has risen from less than 8% in 1960 to more than 20% two decades later, compensating for the declining share of the primary sectors (agriculture, forestry, and fishing).

Apart from the above, the rapid growth in the Malaysian manufacturing sector has also generated significant employment opportunities. The two leading contributors to direct employment creation were the wood-processing and electrical machinery industries—each providing 25,000–28,000 jobs during the decade 1963–73 (when the total increase in employment amounted to about 190,000 persons). The next in line were food products and textiles, each contributing about 21,000 jobs. Thus, these four subsectors together were responsible for almost half of the total jobs created in the entire manufacturing sector during 1963–73. Other leading industrial groups in generating direct manufacturing employment were fabricated metal products, followed by wearing apparel (excluding footwear), rubber products, machinery (except electrical and transport), and plastic products. These five groups together generated electrical and transport), and plastic products. These five groups together generated the majority of jobs created in the entire manufacturing sector.

14.3   Structural Changes in the Manufacturing Sector

Apart from a rapid growth in output, the manufacturing sector also experienced a structural change which is reflected in its pattern of production during the period under study. The shares of intermediate and capital goods industries in total value added have increased steadily at the expense of the food and wood products and printing industries, in particular (table 14.2). More specifically, in 1959 the food, wood products, and printing industries accounted for 26.0%, 16.1%, and 8.3% of total value added respectively, while the electrical machinery and basic metals industries accounted for less than 1% of total value added in manufacturing. By 1978 the shares of the food, wood products, and printing industries had declined to 20.8%, 9.7%, and 3.9% respectively, while those of the electrical machinery and basic metals industries had increased to 10.8% and 3.1% respectively.

Table 14.1 Malaysia: Gross Domestic Product by Sector of Origin

Sector	Gross Domestic Product					Average Annual Growth Rate (%)				Share of GDP (%)				
	1961	1965	1970	1975	1980	1961–70	1971–75	1976–80	1971–80	1961	1965	1970	1975	1980
Agriculture, forestry, and fishing	2,684	2,675	3,797	4,804	5,809	5.3	4.8	3.9	4.3	38.5	31.0	30.8	27.2	22.2
Mining and quarrying	424	537	778	792	1,214	1.8	0.4	8.9	4.6	6.0	8.6	6.3	4.6	8.6
Manufacturing	591	655	1,650	2,850	5,374	10.9	11.6	13.5	12.5	8.5	10.2	13.4	16.4	20.5
Construction	235	294	475	654	1,186	7.3	6.6	12.6	9.6	3.4	4.1	3.9	3.8	4.5
Electricity, gas, and water	88	97	229	365	592	—	9.8	10.2	10.0	1.3	1.6	1.9	2.1	2.3
Transport, storage, and communications	343	366	581	1,071	1,696	—	13.0	9.6	11.3	4.9	5.0	4.7	6.2	6.5
Wholesale and retail trade, hotels and restaurants	1,338	1,399	1,633	2,219	3,295	5.1	6.3	7.3	13.3	19.2	18.2	13.3	12.8	12.6
Finance, insurance, real estate, and business services	—	—	1,036	1,468	2,155	—	7.2	8.0	7.6	—	—	8.4	8.5	8.2
Government services	1,269	1,299	1,367	2,210	3,398	—	10.1	9.0	9.5	18.2	21.3	11.1	12.7	13.0
Other services	—	—	306	478	657	—	9.3	6.6	7.9	—	—	2.5	2.8	2.5
Less: imputed bank service charges	—	—	117	211	308									
Plus: import duties	1,053	1,088	573	665	1,120									
Equals: GDP at purchasers' value	5,919	6,234	12,308	17,365	26,188	5.5	7.1	8.6	7.8					

Sources: Young et al. 1980, 322; Malaysia, *Fourth Malaysia Plan 1981–85* (Kuala Lumpur: Government Press, 1982), 11.

Note: 1961–65 at current prices. 1970–80 at 1970 prices.

Table 14.2   Peninsular Malaysia: Value Added by Industry

Industry	Value Added (millions of ringgits)										Annual Growth Rate (%)				
	1959	%	1963	%	1968	%	1973	%	1978	%	1959–63	1963–68	1968–73	1963–73	1973–78
Food	53	26.0	65	17.5	140	17.6	239	11.6	1,101.4	20.8	5.2	16.6	11.3	13.9	16.6
Beverages	10	4.9	13	3.5	36	4.5	61	3.0	131.7	2.5	6.8	22.6	11.1	16.7	19.3
Tobacco	11	5.4	28	7.5	57	7.2	131	6.4	147.5	2.8	26.3	15.3	18.1	16.7	2.1
Textiles	a		4	1.0	20	2.5	104	5.0	346.2	6.5		38.0	39.1	38.5	38.8
Footwear and clothing	a		4	1.0	7	0.9	36	1.7	77.1	1.5		11.8	38.8	24.6	19.0
Wood products	33	16.1	49	13.2	94	11.8	304	14.8	514.3	9.7	10.4	14.0	26.5	20.0	11.5
Furniture	3	1.5	8	2.2	10	1.3	19	0.9	36.7	0.7	27.8	4.6	13.7	9.0	15.5
Paper	a		3	0.8	6	0.8	18	0.9	46.6	0.9		14.9	24.6	19.6	26.5
Printing	17	8.3	29	7.8	53	6.7	115	5.6	206.8	3.9	14.3	12.8	16.8	14.8	13.3
Leather	a		1	0.2	1	0.1	3	0.1	4.6	0.1		0	24.6	11.6	8.9
Rubber	15	7.4	23	6.2	51	6.4	82[b]	4.0	526.4	9.9	11.3	17.3	9.7	13.4	90.3
Chemicals	15	7.4	42	11.3	79	9.9	175	8.5	302.1	5.7	29.4	13.5	17.2	15.3	12.1
Petroleum products	a		a		41	5.1	52	2.5	176.4	3.3			4.9		39.8
Nonmetallic minerals	13	6.4	28	7.5	62	7.8	122[c]	5.9	208.6	3.9	21.1	17.2	14.5	15.9	11.8
Basic metals	a		9	2.4	21	2.6	135	6.5	166.4	3.1		18.5	45.0	13.1	3.9
Metal products	9	4.4	18	4.8	39	4.9	66	3.2	199.2	3.8	19.0	16.7	11.1	13.9	33.6
Machinery (except electrical)	6	2.9	15	4.0	25	3.1	87	4.2	153.9	2.9	25.7	10.8	28.3	19.2	12.8
Electrical machinery	a		5	1.3	21	2.6	189	9.2	572.2	10.8		33.2	55.2	43.8	33.8
Transportation equipment	8	3.9	6	1.6	19	2.4	62	3.0	160.7	3.0	– 0.7	25.9	26.7	26.3	26.5
Miscellaneous[d]	11	5.4	23	6.2	14	1.8	62	3.0	223.5	4.2			34.7	10.4	43.4
Total/average[e]	204	100.0	371	100.0	797	100.0	2,060	100.0	5,302.3	100.0	16.1	16.5	20.9	18.7	26.2

Source: Department of Statistics, *Census of Manufacturing Industries*, various issues.

[a]Included in Miscellaneous.

[b]Excluding rubber remilling, latex processing, and smokehouses.

[c]Including pottery, china, and earthenware.

[d]The category Miscellaneous has included different industries during different census periods.

[e]Excluding off-estate processing.

Basic metals and electrical machinery increased their shares substantially because of the very rapid rate of growth achieved since 1959. This change reflects, on the one hand, the relative success of the early import substitution strategy and, on the other, the advent of the strong drive toward a greater export orientation in manufacturing activities. The increase of value added in the electrical machinery industry, for example, is the direct result of the encouragement of such industries in specially established Free-Trade Zones.[5] Among the first firms to be established within the Free Trade Zones were the electronic assembly firms, which still represent one of the largest components of Malaysia's nontraditional, non-resource-based exports. However, the net export earnings of the electronic industry are low compared with gross export earnings because of the large imports of component inputs that invariably take place in such industries.

Among the more serious criticisms of these industries, such as the electronics assembly industries, is the absence of substantial exploitation of backward linkages, which could contribute to the improvement of the quality of labor as well as raise the level of employment. The electronics subassembly industry has, in particular, been criticized for this shortcoming in a review of the Progress of the Second United Nations Development Decade in the Asian and Pacific Regions by the Economic and Social Commission for Asia and the Pacific (ESCAP) Secretariat.[6] The answer would lie, it seems, in an incentive system and an investment climate which would persuade transnational corporations to develop closer links with the Malaysian economy and involve greater transfers of technology than presently experienced.

The structural change which took place in the Malaysian manufacturing sector can also be seen by regrouping the twenty-seven industrial groups into two types: (1) consumer- and producer-oriented industries (which are further divided into two categories: consumer durables and nondurables) and (2) intermediate and capital goods industries. During 1963–68, the per annum growth rates of consumer durable, consumer nondurable, and intermediate goods were about the same (17% in current prices), with capital goods lagging behind but still growing at an impressive rate of 14% per annum. During the second half of the period consumer durables were increasing at a very high rate of 34% per annum, compared with about 20% annual growth registered in consumer nondurable and intermediate goods and 28% in capital goods. But it is important to look at the contribution that these various categories have made to increased overall value added because of their different initial bases. In this respect the contribution of nondurable consumer goods and intermediate goods declined from 37.3% to 33.7% and from 49.9% to 41.1% respectively from the 1963–68 period to the 1968–73 period. Over this decade the contribution of durable consumer goods increased from 10.0% to 20.4% and that of capital goods from 2.8% to 4.8%. The smallness of the capital goods' contribution is as conspicuous as the substantial contribution made by intermediate products. Throughout the period, the production of consumer durable and intermediate products continued to account for about 60% of the total increase in value added in the manufacturing sector. This indicates that, despite the sluggish growth of the capital goods sector, some deepening of the manufacturing sector in the Malaysian economy has been achieved.

Yet another way of looking at the structural shift in the Malaysian manufacturing sector is to analyze the growth performance and the magnitude of the contribution made by the resource-based and non-resource-based industries. Given the rich resource base of Malaysia and the policymakers' natural preference for harnessing these resources, the resource-based industries (both agricultural and mineral) expanded rapidly during 1963–68 and contributed about 60% to the sector's overall growth during this period. This contribution fell to about 50% during the 1968–73 period. But most prominent is the increase in the contribution made by the so-called footloose industries (electronics, 36% during 1968–73). By the mid-1970s, the contribution made by these industries was catching up fast with the overall contribution made by the resource-based, agro-processing industries. It is clear that during the late 1960s and early 1970s the government shifted its emphasis from domestic-oriented, import substitution activities to export-oriented industrial development (Chee 1983c). Consequently, not only did the structure of manufacturing production shift in favor of non-resource-based industries, but among them it also shifted in favor of the export-oriented (even if footloose) industries mainly in the Free Trade Zones.

To sum up, we find that the structural changes that have taken place in the Malaysian manufacturing sector have been rather typical of the experience of other developing nations: at the initial stages of industrialization, import substitution was the primary objective, which in turn gradually gave way to the export growth targets of the present. The development of industries to supply the domestic market was nurtured primarily by the provision of attractive fiscal incentives to both indigenous and nonindigenous investors. The export growth anticipated in the eighties will have to rely upon additional incentives directed at export-oriented manufacturers.

14.4 Stages of Growth

As stated earlier, one can distinguish two stages in the growth of the manufacturing sector in Malaysia. The first stage centered on import substitution and was the dominant source of industrial growth up to the end of the 1960s. The second stage depended on the export of manufactured goods and started in the mid-1960s.

The initial industrial development strategy in Malaysia stressed the primary role of import-substituting activities. Changes in the values of the output-demand and trade ratios can usefully reflect the progress of import substitution within the economy. The output-demand ratio measures the extent to which domestic demand, defined as domestic production plus total imports minus total exports, is met by domestic production in each industry or group of industries. The trade ratio, which measures the foreign trade balance within the industry, is defined as (exports − imports) ÷ (exports + imports). The range of values which the trade ratio can take varies from + 1 to − 1. When the ratio is + 1, it means that the industry or group of industries is exporting and there are no competitive imports. When the ratio is − 1, there are no exports and only competitive imports are present. These two measures are complementary in their emphasis.

Production of all manufactured goods composed 43.8% of the domestic market in Malaysia in 1963 (table 14.3). By 1973 the proportion had increased to 75.3%. The trade ratio was − 0.87 in 1963 but had declined to − 0.41 in 1973 (table 14.4). By 1973 import substitution had almost been completed in the case of consumer and intermediate goods, although there was still wide scope for import substitution in the case of capital goods.

Resource-based industries appear to have progressed much faster in terms of import substitution than non-resource-based industries. For instance, as early as 1963, tobacco, furniture, rubber and rubber products, and wood and cork products accounted for more than 80% of domestic demand. By 1973 the ratio of domestic production to domestic market had risen in all four industries to well over unity.

Areas where import substitution has also been successful are food, beverages, wearing apparel, printing and publishing, motor vehicles, bicycles, plastics, leather and leather products, nonmetallic mineral products, and electrical machinery. We notice that those industries that produce more than 70% of market demand are those that produce consumer and intermediate goods.

The reason for this pattern is clear. There is an obvious and relatively large domestic market for finished consumer goods already in existence, and the cost disadvantages are normally less than for either intermediate or capital goods. This is particularly true where the manufacturing process consists primarily of the assembly of imported parts and components. It is clear that by 1973 the first easy period of import substitution was nearly completed; 89.5% of consumer nondurables,

Table 14.3   **Peninsular Malaysia: Production as a Percentage of Domestic Market**

	1963	1968	1973
Consumer nondurables	**50.7**	**70.5**	**89.5**
Foods	45.3	69.3	98.6
Beverages	48.9	77.5	104.6
Tobacco	83.7	91.3	101.7
Textiles	11.7	32.7	55.8
Wearing apparel and made-up goods	17.1	54.4	169.5
Footwear	a	a	a
Chemicals	74.5	77.4	73.2
Pottery, china, and earthenware	25.5	31.5	49.5
Printing and publishing	69.9	82.6	92.3
Plastics	a	a	104.2
Consumer durables	**21.1**	**47.1**	**94.8**
Furniture	96.0	100.0	106.6
Automobiles	5.9	42.5	98.4
Bicycles	2.8	8.8	52.8
Intermediate goods	**46.4**	**77.9**	**86.5**
Wood and cork	96.4	108.5	242.0
Paper and paper products	15.9	23.8	31.7
Leather and leather products	64.3	81.5	87.2
Rubber and rubber products	86.4	105.7	107.5
Industrial chemicals	23.8	48.6	46.1
Petroleum	b	84.1	45.5
Nonmetallic mineral products	53.4	84.6	86.3
Capital goods	**22.1**	**34.0**	**47.7**
Basic metals	22.3	28.9	54.8
Metal products	40.1	50.3	63.4
Nonelectrical machinery	16.3	22.3	25.9
Electrical machinery	10.7	34.0	63.5
Transport equipment	36.8	24.2	1.7
Miscellaneous	a	a	a
Total	43.8	162.4	75.3

Sources: Department of Statistics, *Census of Manufacturing Industries, Peninsular Malaysia, 1959, 1963, 1968, 1973* (Kuala Lumpur); idem, *External Trade of Malaya, 1959* (Kuala Lumpur, 1960); idem, *Annual Statistics of External Trade, 1964* (Kuala Lumpur, 1965); idem, *Monthly Statistics of External Trade, December 1968* (Kuala Lumpur, 1969); idem, *Annual Statistics of External Trade, 1973* (Kuala Lumpur, 1974).

Note: 1959 percentages cannot be calculated, because it is not possible to separate reexports from either imports or exports, and ratios based on available data are therefore inflated. Furthermore, in some cases, categorizations of production, import, and export data are not comparable.

[a]Ratio cannot be calculated, because production, import, and export data are not comparable.

[b]Ratio cannot be calculated, because production has been included in Miscellaneous category.

Table 14.4   **Peninsular Malaysia: Trade Ratios**

	1963	1968	1973
Consumer nondurables	**−0.79**	**−0.68**	**−0.26**
Foods	−0.78	−0.62	−0.13
Beverages	−1.00	−0.69	−0.36
Tobacco	−1.00	−0.99	0.07
Textiles	−0.93	−0.86	−0.64
Wearing apparel and made-up goods	−0.95	−0.55	0.48
Footwear	0.19	0.19	0.86
Chemicals	−0.35	−0.48	−0.38
Pottery, china, and earthenware	−0.95	−0.96	−0.93
Plastics	a	a	a
Consumer durables	**−0.93**	**−0.96**	**−0.17**
Furniture	−0.10	−0.29	0.36
Automobiles	−0.99	−0.98	−0.06
Bicycles	−1.00	−1.00	−0.76
Intermediate goods	**−0.89**	**−0.55**	**−0.18**
Wood and cork	−0.61	0.67	0.98
Pulp and paper products	−0.96	−0.92	−0.85
Leather and leather products	−0.78	−0.67	−0.49
Rubber and rubber products	−0.32	−0.07	0.23
Industrial chemicals	−0.92	−0.85	−0.74
Petroleum	−0.97	−0.25	−0.78
Nonmetallic mineral products	−0.95	−0.58	−0.45
Capital goods	**−0.97**	**−0.94**	**−0.79**
Basic metals	−0.98	−0.92	−0.77
Metal products	−0.93	−0.89	−0.64
Nonelectrical machinery	−0.99	−0.98	−0.85
Electrical machinery	−0.95	−0.91	−0.76
Transport equipment	−0.99	−0.85	−0.23
Miscellaneous	**−0.94**	**−0.85**	**−0.23**
Total	−0.87	−0.75	−0.41

Source: Table 14.3.

Note: The trade ratio is calculated as follows: $\dfrac{\text{exports} - \text{imports}}{\text{exports} + \text{imports}}$. 1959 ratios cannot be calculated, because it is not possible to separate reexports from either imports or exports, and ratios based on available data are therefore inflated. Furthermore, in some cases, categorizations of production, import, and export data are not comparable.

aRatio cannot be calculated, because import and export data are not available.

94.8% of consumer durables, and 86.5% of intermediate goods were being produced domestically.

The annual growth rates of the domestic market over selected periods are presented in table 14.5. Among the fastest growing are the markets for capital and intermediate goods. Though the growth in demand for consumer durables and nondurables has not been sluggish, their rates of growth are well below the average for the sector between 1968 and 1973. This tends to confirm our view that the possibilities of further

Table 14.5   Peninsular Malaysia: Annual Growth Rate of Domestic Market

	1959–63	1963–73	1968–73
Consumer nondurables	**12.6**	**9.1**	**11.1**
Foods	10.1	7.4	7.5
Beverages	11.4	10.5	11.5
Tobacco	10.4	5.4	7.1
Textiles	25.6	15.1	18.8
Wearing apparel and made-up goods	10.9	3.9	7.5
Footwear	n.a.	n.a.	n.a.
Chemicals	14.8	10.2	12.0
Pottery, china, and earthenware	15.1	15.0	23.0
Printing and publishing	15.3	12.1	15.2
Plastics	n.a.	n.a.	n.a.
Consumer durables	**12.3**	**9.1**	**6.9**
Furniture	15.4	11.1	16.2
Automobiles	11.6	9.4	4.3
Bicycles	12.0	5.2	10.3
Intermediate goods	**14.5**	**13.0**	**15.7**
Wood and cork	10.0	9.5	8.1
Paper and paper products	18.7	14.6	17.6
Leather and leather products	16.9	10.7	15.4
Rubber and rubber products	10.2	10.4	11.8
Industrial chemicals	16.5	14.8	19.2
Petroleum	17.8	16.3	20.1
Nonmetallic mineral products	15.5	10.6	14.7
Capital goods			
Basic metals	26.0	19.5	28.0
Metal products	14.9	9.0	13.9
Nonelectrical machinery	22.1	14.9	22.8
Electrical machinery	20.9	18.7	30.8
Transport equipment	17.0	15.8	22.3
Miscellaneous	*n.a.*	*n.a.*	*n.a.*
Total	14.6	11.7	15.3

Source: Table 14.3.
Note: n.a. = not available.

expansion of import substitution in Malaysia are becoming increasingly limited. The fastest growing market is for capital goods, at 24.6% per annum; within this group, basic metals, nonelectrical machinery, electrical machinery, and transport equipment experienced increases in domestic demand of more than 22% each year between 1968 and 1973. This fact combined with the finding that domestic production is still less than 50% of domestic demand for these products suggests that future import substitution has to take place to a larger extent in the capital goods sector.

Trade ratios computed for 1963, 1968, and 1973 give us a clear indication of the direction in which import substitution has been taking place and the growth of exports (table 14.4). There are only six industries with positive ratios: tobacco, wearing apparel and made-up goods, footwear, furniture, wood and cork, and rubber and rubber products. The very high negative ratios indicate that many industries were not exporting very much in 1973. This picture is confirmed by the export-output ratios contained in table 14.6. Only two industries exported

Table 14.6   **Peninsular Malaysia: Exports as a Percentage of Domestic Production**

	1963	1968	1973
Consumer nondurables	**13.2**	**11.4**	**17.3**
Foods	16.8	13.4	14.7
Beverages	0.0	6.4	15.4
Tobacco	0.0	0.0	12.4
Textiles	27.8	17.0	21.3
Wearing apparel and made-up goods	13.9	38.3	63.2
Footwear	a	a	a
Chemicals	34.5	21.9	30.0
Pottery, china, and earthenware	7.1	4.0	3.6
Printing and publishing	2.3	4.0	3.5
Plastics	a	a	11.2
Consumer durables	**11.2**	**2.5**	**13.3**
Furniture	18.2	5.3	11.8
Automobiles	2.0	1.4	13.7
Bicycles	0.0	0.0	14.0
Intermediate goods	**7.1**	**12.7**	**35.5**
Wood and cork	1.2	9.3	59.2
Paper and paper products	11.1	14.8	19.7
Leather and leather products	11.1	5.7	3.4
Rubber and rubber products	17.0	10.8	18.4
Industrial chemicals	14.2	10.5	14.7
Petroleum	b	23.7	16.5
Nonmetallic mineral products	2.3	8.3	9.5
Capital goods	**5.6**	**6.6**	**14.4**
Basic metals	2.8	6.9	6.7
Metal products	5.2	6.3	16.5
Nonelectrical machinery	3.1	3.9	25.2
Electrical machinery	22.6	9.5	9.2
Transport equipment	1.2	4.8	40.8
Miscellaneous	a	a	a
Total	10.4	10.9	23.7

Note: 1959 percentages cannot be calculated, because it is not possible to separate reexports from either imports or exports, and ratios based on available data are therefore inflated. Furthermore, in some cases, categorizations of production, import, and export data are not comparable.

aRatio cannot be calculated, because production and export data are not comparable.

bRatio cannot be calculated, because production has been included in Miscellaneous category.

more than 50% of output in 1973. These were wearing apparel and made-up goods and wood and cork.

For the manufacturing sector as a whole, the export-output ratio changed little between 1963 and 1968. However, by 1973 the ratio had more than doubled. The intermediate industry group had a higher ratio than the other three product groups in 1973 primarily because of the wood and cork industry, which was mainly import-substituting until 1973. However, for the older established consumer goods industries there appears to be a tendency for their export-output ratios to increase as the limits of the domestic market are reached. Examples of such industries are beverages, tobacco, and wearing apparel.

Between 1963 and 1968 the export-output ratio fell or remained unchanged for twelve industries. This is indicative of an increasing bias against exporting that was probably fostered by protection (which tended to encourage production for the domestic market at the expense of exports) during that period. Notable drops in the ratio were evident in the cases of textiles, chemicals, electrical machinery, and furniture. Thus, there appears to be room for further expansion of these industries if they can reorientate themselves to the export market. In 1973 the situation had changed: seventeen industries had experienced a rise in domestic output of less than 20%. At present, with much of the import substitution potential utilized, particularly among consumer and intermediate goods, future growth will have to take place through export expansion.

Another good measure of the possibility of future import substitution is the import-demand ratio (table 14.7). For the sector as a whole, the import-demand ratio has been falling steadily since 1963, indicating the success of the import-substituting manufacturing industries. When we examine this ratio by individual industries, we notice that it has been falling for all industries except chemicals, rubber and rubber products, industrial chemicals, petroleum, nonelectrical machinery, and transport equipment. In the case of petroleum this development is not surprising. Because of the quality of her oil resources, it pays Malaysia to export her output and import what she needs for domestic consumption. The other industries for which the import-demand ratio has been rising are mainly within the intermediate and capital goods groups. Such an increase in the import-demand ratio for capital goods is not unexpected during a period of rapid industrial growth in an economy with a small capital goods sector.

We conclude this section by looking at the growth scenario in the Malaysian manufacturing sector in recent years, during the period 1974–78. According to the Index of Industrial Production, the manufacturing sector grew at an annual real rate of 13% in the second half of the 1970s, showing a growth elasticity with respect to GDP of over 1.5.

Table 14.7   **Peninsular Malaysia: Imports as a Percentage of Domestic Market**

	1963	1968	1973
Consumer nondurables	**56.0**	**41.9**	**25.9**
Foods	62.3	40.2	18.4
Beverages	51.3	2.2	27.6
Tobacco	16.3	13.6	11.0
Textiles	91.6	73.4	56.1
Wearing apparel and made-up goods	85.3	71.8	37.6
Footwear	a	a	a
Chemicals	53.3	47.6	48.8
Pottery, china and earthenware	76.4	69.6	52.3
Printing and publishing	31.7	21.3	11.0
Plastics	a	a	7.5
Consumer durables	**82.0**	**54.9**	**17.7**
Furniture	21.5	9.6	6.0
Automobiles	94.3	58.2	15.1
Bicycles	97.2	92.1	54.4
Intermediate goods	**69.8**	**33.9**	**44.2**
Wood and cork	4.8	2.0	1.3
Paper and paper products	86.0	80.3	74.6
Leather and leather products	50.0	23.1	15.8
Rubber and rubber products	28.4	12.1	12.3
Industrial chemicals	79.8	60.9	63.1
Petroleum	b	33.4	62.0
Nonmetallic mineral products	47.8	26.1	21.9
Capital goods	**79.2**	**69.7**	**59.2**
Basic metals	78.3	65.7	52.0
Metal products	62.2	54.4	47.1
Nonelectrical machinery	84.3	79.5	80.6
Electrical machinery	91.8	71.2	42.3
Transport equipment	63.6	77.8	91.9
Miscellaneous	a	a	a
Total	62.7	46.6	41.0

Note: 1959 percentages cannot be calculated, because it is not possible to separate reexports from either imports or exports, and ratios based on available data are therefore inflated. Furthermore, in some cases, categorizations of production, import, and export data are not conparable.

[a]Ratio cannot be calculated, because production, import, and export data are not comparable.

[b]Ratio cannot be calculated, because production has been included in Miscellaneous category.

During this period manufacturing activities contributed 26% to GDP growth, twice the contribution of the primary sector. The main sources of growth sustaining this expansion during 1974–78 were domestic demand expansion (contributing about two-thirds to overall growth), an increase in manufactured exports (about one-fifth), and additional import substitution (about 12%–13%). With sustained rapid growth of the domestic market and a widening of the industrial base, the manufacturing sector appears to have acquired during the last five to six years a favorable environment for the next phase of import substitution.

At the disaggregated level, the fastest growing manufacturing industries during the 1974–78 period were electrical machinery and electronics, textiles, and rubber products. The slowest growing industries (some of which even declined) were remilling and latex processing of rubber and the food industries (mainly estate processing/refining of coconut oil, rice milling, and canning of pineapples). Other industries which showed considerable deceleration in growth rates were the plywood, hardboard, and particle board industries and, to a lesser extent, the food, beverage, and tobacco industries. Most of these are resource-based manufacturing or processing activities.

14.5   External Trade Pattern

The discussion so far has been aimed at providing the background to describe and analyze the development and changes in Malaysia's external trade pattern during the last twenty years. Briefly, we have described the rapid growth and structural changes in Malaysia over the last two decades. We have seen how the first stage of import substitution was quickly achieved and how the manufacturing sector subsequently moved on to the export market and the second stage of import substitution. In recent years the main sources of growth have been largely domestic demand expansion followed by manufactured exports and additional import substitution.

Obviously changes in the manufacturing sector would be reflected in Malaysia's external trade pattern. In this and the following sections we will try to analyze the impact of the above changes. We begin by noting the steady increase in the volume of Malaysia's external trade over the last twenty years. In 1960, total gross exports and imports were valued at M $6,419.0 million (table 14.8). In 1980 the figure had increased to more than M $50,000 million, or an eightfold increase in twenty years. Another interesting point to note is that Malaysia enjoyed a favorable trade balance every year during this twenty-year period.

We will now take a closer look at the pattern of Malaysia's external trade, beginning with the composition of exports.

14.6   Composition of Exports

In the last twenty years, Malaysian exports of merchandise have been equal to about 40% of GNP. This percentage has increased slightly in recent years, and it shows that Malaysia's heavy dependence on

Table 14.8   **Malaysia: External Trade** (in millions of ringgits)

Year	Gross Exports (f.o.b.)	Gross Imports (c.i.f.)	Sum of Gross Imports and Exports	Trade Balance
1960	3,632.6	2,786.4	6,419.0	846.2
1961	3,238.3	2,815.7	6,054.0	422.5
1962	3,259.6	3,056.3	6,315.9	203.3
1963	3,330.0	3,192.6	6,522.6	137.4
1964	3,381.9	3,205.3	6,587.2	176.6
1965	3,782.5	3,356.1	7,138.6	426.4
1966	3,845.8	3,379.9	7,225.7	465.9
1967	3,723.7	3,235.0	6,958.7	398.7
1968	4,122.6	3,551.6	7,674.2	571.0
1969	5,045.7	3,605.0	8,650.7	1,449.7
1970	5,162.4	4,323.3	9,485.7	839.1
1971	5,016.8	4,413.4	9,430.2	603.4
1972	4,854.2	4,461.9	9,316.1	393.2
1973	7,373.3	5,938.5	13,311.8	1,434.9
1974	10,194.7	9,891.2	20,085.9	303.5
1975	9,231.1	8,530.4	17,761.5	700.5
1976	13,442.9	9,721.8	23,164.7	3,721.1
1977	14,959.1	11,164.7	26,123.9	3,794.5
1978	17,073.9	13,645.9	30,719.8	3,428.0
1979	24,222.0	17,161.1	41,383.1	7,060.9
1980	28,171.6	23,451.0	51,622.6	4,720.6

Source: Department of Statistics, unpublished data; Bank Negara Malaysia, *Quarterly Economic Bulletin,* various issues.

Notes: Data have been adjusted to exclude intraregional trade. Data on gross imports from 1970 on, published beginning with the March/June 1978 *Quarterly Economic Bulletin,* are a revised series. They exclude military imports and imports for offshore installations of the petroleum industry. Quarterly totals may not necessarily add up to annual totals because of revisions and rounding.

merchandise exports has not lessened over the last two decades. What has changed has been the composition of exports.

Inedible crude materials accounted for nearly 68% of Malaysia's total gross exports in 1960, but by 1980 the percentage had been reduced by half to 32% (table 14.9). Inedible crude material exports are comprised mainly of rubber, tin, sawlogs, and sawn timber. Among these, rubber and tin declined drastically in relative terms, while the reverse was true of sawlogs and sawn timber (table 14.10).

Two other primary products registered relative increases in export earnings, and these were animal and vegetable oils and fats and mineral fuels (table 14.9). The exports of oils and fats are mostly palm oil. Malaysia became the largest producer of palm oil in the midseventies; this probably helped to increase the contribution of animal and vegetable oils and fats from 2.3% in 1960 to 11.1% in 1980.

Table 14.9   Malaysia: Gross Exports by Commodity Groups (in millions of ringgits)

Year	Food & Live Animals	Bev. & Tobacco	Inedible Crude Materials	Mineral Fuels	Animal & Veg. Oils & Fats	Chemicals	Manufactured Goods	Mach. & Trans. Equip.	Misc. Manuf. Articles	Other Exports	Total	Annual Growth Rate (%)
1960	129.5	13.6	2,462.3	290.1	87.1	18.5	546.8	34.2	17.9	32.6	3,632.6	—
	(3.6)	(0.4)	(67.8)	(8.0)	(2.3)	(0.5)	(15.1)	(0.9)	(0.5)	(0.9)		
1961	148.0	21.3	2,017.4	225.2	91.3	20.8	613.4	44.2	20.9	36.5	3,238.2	−10.9
	(4.6)	(0.7)	(62.3)	(7.0)	(2.8)	(0.6)	(18.9)	(1.36)	(0.6)	(1.1)		
1962	151.8	34.4	1,944.9	237.3	90.2	21.6	669.4	53.4	22.2	34.4	3,259.6	0.7
	(4.7)	(1.0)	(59.7)	(7.3)	(2.8)	(0.7)	(20.5)	(1.6)	(0.8)	(1.0)		
1963	146.9	43.7	1,999.8	209.8	93.0	28.9	686.5	53.6	25.9	41.9	3,330.0	2.2
	(4.4)	(1.3)	(60.0)	(6.3)	(2.8)	(0.9)	(20.6)	(1.6)	(0.8)	(1.3)		
1964	163.5	27.3	1,921.2	235.7	95.2	35.1	779.0	57.8	27.0	40.1	3,381.9	1.6
	(4.8)	(0.8)	(56.8)	(7.0)	(2.8)	(1.1)	(23.0)	(1.7)	(0.8)	(1.2)		
1965	198.8	41.5	2,067.0	244.1	125.7	37.1	931.4	65.7	26.9	44.3	3,782.5	11.8
	(5.3)	(1.1)	(54.6)	(6.5)	(3.3)	(1.0)	(24.6)	(1.7)	(0.7)	(1.2)		
1966	203.7	19.2	2,177.3	275.5	142.2	35.2	854.3	67.4	24.1	46.9	3,845.8	1.7
	(5.3)	(0.5)	(56.6)	(7.2)	(3.7)	(0.9)	(22.2)	(1.8)	(0.6)	(1.2)		
1967	207.5	21.5	2,061.2	295.5	141.7	34.3	827.2	56.5	29.6	48.7	3,723.7	−3.2
	(5.6)	(0.6)	(55.4)	(7.9)	(3.8)	(0.9)	(22.2)	(1.5)	(0.8)	(1.3)		
1968	220.5	11.0	2,259.7	351.0	165.4	37.5	918.3	73.6	31.3	54.3	4,122.6	10.7
	(4.6)	(0.3)	(54.8)	(8.5)	(4.0)	(0.9)	(22.3)	(1.8)	(0.8)	(1.3)		
1969	233.7	16.9	3,004.4	339.4	177.6	38.7	1,071.0	83.7	33.8	55.5	5,054.7	22.6
	(4.6)	(0.3)	(59.4)	(6.7)	(3.5)	(0.8)	(21.2)	(1.7)	(0.7)	(1.1)		

Year											Total	%
1970	284.0 (5.5)	21.7 (0.4)	2,777.5 (53.8)	365.6 (7.1)	309.8 (6.0)	36.4 (0.7)	1,182.8 (22.9)	84.1 (1.7)	43.4 (1.0)	57.8 (1.4)	5,163.1	2.1
1971	315.9 (6.3)	23.4 (0.5)	2,392.2 (47.7)	502.5 (10.0)	422.8 (8.4)	38.7 (0.8)	1,111.8 (22.2)	83.6 (1.7)	48.5 (1.0)	77.4 (1.4)	5,016.8	−2.8
1972	360.8 (7.4)	27.7 (0.6)	2,249.1 (46.3)	319.5 (6.6)	411.5 (8.5)	46.4 (1.0)	1,217.5 (25.0)	90.9 (1.9)	72.3 (1.5)	58.3 (1.2)	4,854.0	−3.2
1973	440.9 (6.0)	21.3 (0.3)	4,156.7 (56.4)	371.5 (5.0)	559.6 (7.6)	66.7 (0.9)	1,317.6 (17.9)	142.0 (1.9)	225.7 (3.0)	70.1 (1.0)	7,372.1	51.9
1974	513.7 (5.0)	24.4 (0.2)	4,515.8 (44.3)	832.9 (8.2)	1,370.0 (13.4)	79.8 (0.8)	1,966.2 (19.3)	399.4 (3.9)	395.9 (3.9)	96.6 (1.0)	10,194.7	38.3
1975	593.1 (6.4)	27.7 (0.3)	3,231.4 (35.0)	967.1 (10.5)	1,508.5 (16.3)	79.4 (0.9)	1,624.3 (17.6)	573.0 (6.2)	529.3 (5.7)	97.1 (1.1)	9,230.9	−9.5
1976	799.1 (5.9)	27.9 (0.2)	5,668.3 (42.2)	1,905.4 (14.2)	1,378.2 (10.3)	82.0 (0.6)	2,132.7 (15.9)	739.6 (5.5)	608.5 (4.5)	100.3 (0.7)	13,442.0	45.6
1977	826.9 (5.5)	23.4 (0.2)	5,975.7 (40.0)	2,101.1 (14.0)	1,979.4 (13.2)	86.8 (0.6)	2,324.3 (15.5)	1,001.2 (6.7)	545.4 (3.7)	95.0 (0.6)	14,959.2	11.3
1978	872.3 (5.1)	15.7 (0.1)	6,360.1 (37.3)	2,342.7 (13.7)	2,105.7 (12.3)	102.3 (0.6)	2,825.4 (16.6)	1,816.1 (10.6)	495.5 (2.9)	138.1 (0.8)	17,073.9	14.1
1979	1,081.9 (4.5)	20.9 (0.1)	9,024.9 (37.2)	4,345.8 (17.9)	3,016.4 (12.5)	131.0 (0.5)	3,314.5 (13.7)	2,535.4 (10.5)	603.8 (2.5)	147.4 (0.6)	24,222.0	41.9
1980	1,013.2 (3.6)	29.1 (0.1)	9,105.3 (32.3)	6,898.4 (24.5)	3,131.3 (11.1)	171.5 (0.6)	3,690.7 (13.1)	3,238.4 (2.6)	737.7 (2.6)	156.0 (0.6)	29,171.6	16.3

Source: Bank Negara Malaysia, *Quarterly Economic Bulletin,* December 1982.
Note: Figures in parentheses are percentages.

Table 14.10   **Composition of Malaysian Exports by Commodity or Group of Commodities** (percentages)

Commodity or Group of Commodities	Average 1960–64	Average 1965–69	Average 1970–74	Average 1975–79	Average 1980–81
Rubber	47	37	30	21	15
Palm oil products	2	3	8	10.8	10
Sawlogs	5	11	12	10.4	9
Sawn timber	2	3	5	5.1	14
Tin	18	20	17	11.1	8
Petroleum and petroleum products[a]	3	3	5	13.5	25
Subtotal, principal commodities	77	77	77	71.9	71
Manufactures	4	6	10	19.9	22
All other merchandise	19	17	13	8.2	7
Total merchandise	100	100	100	100	100

Source: Bank Negara Malaysia, *Quarterly Economic Bulletin,* various issues.
[a]Includes reexports of crude petroleum imported from Brunei and exports of liquefied natural gas.

An even more significant increase was shown by mineral fuels, comprised largely of crude petroleum, which increased its share of total exports from 8% in 1960 to 24.5% in 1980. This increase can be attributed largely to the discovery of offshore oil along the northeast coast of Peninsular Malaysia. The oil discovery and buoyant prices for crude petroleum enabled mineral fuels to become one of Malaysia's leading exports in the last few years. (Since 1980 crude petroleum has been the leading single export commodity in Malaysia, topping rubber, which has traditionally been the top export earner.)

However, the most significant change in the composition of Malaysia's exports is in manufactured products. If we take all manufactured products (i.e., manufactured goods, machinery and transport equipment, and miscellaneous manufactured articles—SITC 5–8), the share of these products totaled less than 17% in 1960 but increased to more than 27% of total exports in 1980, an increase of nearly 60%. Given the importance of manufactured exports in view of Malaysia's small domestic market and also in view of the country's objective of becoming an industrialized country by the end of this decade, the growth in manufactured exports will be discussed further in the following section.

14.7 Growth in Manufactured Exports

One of the most important features of the changing trade structure in Malaysia is the steady increase in the share of manufactured exports and the corresponding decline in the share of nonmanufactured exports during the last twenty years. Manufactured exports, as a percentage of total merchandise exports, have increased, from an average of 4% in 1960–64 to 22% in 1980–81 (a more than fivefold increase) (table 14.10). Equally significant is the export of items, virtually nonexistent in the 1960s, such as textiles, clothing, electronics, and electrical machinery and appliances. On the other hand, Malaysia's traditional non-manufactured exports, namely, rubber and tin, registered a significant decline in terms of percentage contribution to total merchandise exports (table 14.10).

Most of the growth in Malaysian manufactured exports took place between 1970 and 1975. Before 1970 the growth of Malaysian manufactured exports was slightly below the average for all developing countries, but between 1970 and 1975, manufactured exports increased more than 24% a year in real terms (table 14.11), and the share in total exports of merchandise increased from 7% in 1970 to 17% in 1975 (Young et al. 1980, 287).

The remarkable rate of growth in Malaysian manufactured exports during the 1970–75 period may be largely attributable to the establishment of Free-Trade Zones in the country in 1970. These zones persuaded multinational corporations from many developed countries to set up offshore processing plants to manufacture various goods for exports and thus helped to boost the value of Malaysia manufactured exports.

Four industries—wood products, textiles and clothing, rubber products, and electronics components and assembly—were responsible for nearly all the growth in manufactured exports. These four industries have two things in common. First, they are relatively labor-intensive, a highly desirable characteristic, since they were established at a time when Malaysia urgently required greater job opportunities for its expanding labor force. Secondly, the four industries are non-resource-based, a contrast to traditional Malaysian exports, which were generally resource-based. Thus the rapid growth in these four industries

Table 14.11   **Rates of Growth of Manufactured Exports from Malaysia and from All Developing Countries, 1960–75, and Projections for 1975–85**
(average annual percentage rates)

Exporting Country or Group of Countries	1960–70	1970–75	1960–75	1975–85
Malaysia	10.6	24.5	15.1	12.2
All developing countries	11.0	14.9	12.3	12.2

Source: Young et al. 1980, 288.

has changed the composition of Malaysian exports from the resource- to the non-resource-based. Obviously this has also affected the pattern of imports—particularly, the import content of manufactured exports.

Table 14.12 shows the present composition of manufactured exports in Malaysia. The table shows that of the four industries which had been responsible for most of the growth in manufactured exports during the period 1970–75, textiles and clothing, electronics components (classified under electrical machinery, appliances, and parts), and wood products still compose a significant proportion of total manufactured exports. In fact, in 1980 these three groups accounted for more than

Table 14.12   Malaysia: Gross Exports of Manufactures

	1980	
	Millions of Ringgits	%
Food	422.0	7.1
Canned pineapple	55.0	0.9
Animal feed	69.1	1.2
Other	297.9	5.0
Beverages and tobacco	35.0	0.6
Textiles and footwear	787.0	13.3
Textiles, cotton fabrics, and yarn	365.5	6.0
Clothing	321.3	5.4
Footwear	86.5	1.5
Other	22.7	0.4
Wood products	443.0	7.5
Veneer	26.5	0.5
Plywood	268.0	4.5
Chipwood	24.0	0.4
Wooden moldings	62.0	1.0
Other	62.5	1.1
Rubber	83.2	1.4
Chemicals and petroleum	323.0	5.4
Nonmetallic mineral	55.0	0.9
Manufactures of metal	265.0	4.4
Electrical machinery, appliances, and parts	2,790.0	47.0
Other machinery and transport equipment	312.8	5.3
Other manufactures	419.1	7.1
Subtotal	5,935.0	100.0
Palm oil and other oil products	3,183.0	
Total	9,118.0	

Source: Bank Negara Malaysia, *Annual Report 1980*, p.1.

60% of all manufactured exports. Only the rubber products industry lost its significant position, accounting for only 1.4% of total manufactured exports, well behind food (7.1%), chemical and petroleum products (5.4%), and other machinery and transport equipment (5.3%).

14.8 Changes in Export Market

Changes in the composition of Malaysian exports were accompanied by changes in the direction of exports in the last two decades. Briefly, efforts were made to diversify the Malaysian export market, but despite these attempts, Malaysia is now even more dependent on its three leading trade partners, namely, the United States, Singapore,[7] and Japan. These three countries still continue to take about 55% of Malaysia's exports.

In the early sixties, Malaysia's three leading export markets were Singapore (21.5%), Japan (17.3%), and the United States (11.7%). These three countries accounted for 50.5% of Malaysian exports. In 1981 these three countries still topped the list of Malaysian exports, with their positions unchanged. All three countries increased their share of Malaysian exports, with Japan accounting for the largest relative increase (nearly 4%). These increases were made largely at the expense of Western Europe and the rest of the world. In short, despite the change in export composition and Malaysia's efforts to diversify its export market, the country is now even more dependent on its three leading export markets.

While Japan has registered the largest increase in the Malaysian export market during the last twenty years, the United Kingdom has registered the sharpest decline. In 1961 the United Kingdom accounted for more than 16% of Malaysia's exports, but in 1981 its share had fallen to less than 3%. This may be attributed to the erosion of Commonwealth preferential tariffs on trade with the United Kingdom and the increasing competitive pressure from Japan, the United States, and other countries.

But although Japan is one of the leading customers of Malaysia's merchandise exports (buying more than one-fifth of its total exports), most of the exports to Japan are nonmanufactured goods. More specifically, manufactured products composed only 15.1% of total Japanese imports from Malaysia in 1980. The percentages were much higher in the case of Malaysia's two other leading importers. For example, manufactured products accounted for 44.4% of U.S. imports, while in the case of Singapore, they accounted for 18.8%. Netherland's manufactured imports from Malaysia accounted for 51.2% of its total imports, making it the country with the largest percentage of Malaysian manufactured imports in 1980.

In terms of region, more than half of Malaysia's exports go to the OECD countries (Organization for Economic Cooperation and Development) (table 14.13). Within the OECD market, Western Europe remains the principal trading partner of Malaysia, but it is significant to note that Western Europe's share of Malaysian exports has declined from 24.1% in 1961–64 to 16.4% in 1981. Still, Western Europe remains one of Malaysia's leading export markets. More important, considering that more than half of Malaysia's exports moved into OECD markets, the economic situation and policies in these countries have a strong influence on Malaysian exports. Finally, because Malaysia depends heavily on exports, changes in the OECD demand for imports affect all sectors of the Malaysian economy.

In view of the heavy dependence of Malaysian exports on the OECD countries, the government has tried to find new export markets, especially in other Asian countries. Unfortunately most Asian countries (except Japan) have similar resources and exports, so the diversification policy has not been very successful. Nevertheless, Malaysian exports to other Asian markets have increased from 4.2% in 1961–64 to 19.2% in 1981 (an almost fivefold increase). Most of the increase was accounted for by India and the other ASEAN (Association of South East Asian Nations) countries (excluding Singapore).[8]

14.9   Composition of Imports

Table 14.14 shows the pattern of Malaysian imports over the last twenty years. In 1960 the three most important imports were food (23.4%), manufactured goods (15.2%), and mineral fuels (14.9%). These three items accounted for more than 53% of total imports. By 1980 the pattern had changed. Food was no longer the leading import item. It

Table 14.13   The Direction of Malaysian Exports (percentages)

Country or Region	1961–64	1965–69	1970–74	1975–80	1981
United States	11.7	14.4	12.9	17.0	13.1
Western Europe	24.1	18.0	21.9	20.4	16.4
Japan	17.3	18.3	17.7	21.5	21.2
Australia and New Zealand	3.0	2.8	2.4	2.3	2.0
Canada	a	2.0	1.9	0.7	0.6
Total, OECD countries	56.1	55.5	56.8	61.9	53.3
Singapore	21.5	22.6	22.4	17.8	22.8
Other Asian markets	4.2	4.4	8.5	15.2	19.2
Total, Asia, excluding Japan	25.7	28.0	30.9	33.0	42.0
Rest of the world	18.2	16.5	12.3	5.1	4.7

Source: Bank Negara Malaysia, *Quarterly Economic Bulletin,* various issues.
aZero or negligible.

Table 14.14 Malaysia: Gross Imports by SITC Group

SITC Group	Import Share[a]					Average Annual Growth Rate (%)			
	1960	1965	1970	1975	1980	1960–65	1965–70	1970–75	1975–80
Food	651.9 (23.4)	613.9 (23.5)	786.7 (18.3)	1,401.5 (16.4)	2,444.3 (10.4)	6.6	−2.6	18.4	5.9
Beverages and tobacco	109.3 (3.9)	60.7 (2.3)	92.9 (2.1)	119.4 (1.4)	221.3 (1.0)	1.7	−4.2	6.5	10.7
Inedible crude materials	378.7 (13.6)	229.4 (8.8)	322.1 (7.5)	554.1 (6.5)	1,052.8 (4.5)	−14.9	9.3	14.3	9.8
Mineral fuels, lubricants, etc.	416.2 (14.9)	174.2 (6.7)	517.5 (12.0)	1,021.1 (12.0)	3,554.4 (15.2)	−3.0	6.1	28.4	16.6
Animal and vegetable oils and fats	15.4 (0.6)	14.8 (0.6)	23.8 (0.5)	26.0 (0.3)	29.7 (0.1)	0	7.1	19.9	−4.1
Chemicals	164.9 (5.9)	208.3 (8.0)	312.5 (7.3)	711.8 (8.3)	2,022.4 (8.6)	5.3	6.3	27.9	16.8
Manufactured goods	423.7 (15.2)	510.2 (19.6)	770.2 (18.0)	1,389.4 (16.3)	3,849.2 (16.4)	6.6	2.9	26.0	11.4
Machinery and transport equipment	395.8 (14.2)	580.2 (22.2)	1,197.3 (27.9)	2,774.1 (32.5)	9,105.3 (38.8)	12.6	6.2	33.2	15.4
Misc. manufactured articles	150.1 (5.4)	165.3 (6.3)	199.9 (4.7)	465.3 (5.5)	975.0 (4.2)	6.3	−0.8	28.9	8.1
Other imports	80.4 (2.9)	51.3 (2.0)	65.5 (1.5)	66.9 (0.8)	196.6 (0.8)	−4.3	−1.4	9.7	22.0
Total	2,786.4 (100.0)	2,608.3 (100.0)	4,288.4 (100.0)	8,530.4 (100.0)	23,451.0 (100.0)	3.6	2.4	24.4	12.4

Source: Department of Statistics, *Annual Statistics of External Trade*, various years.
[a]In millions of ringgits and (in parentheses) percentages.

had been replaced by machinery and transport equipment. This item (38.8% of total imports), together with manufactured goods (16.4%), and mineral fuels (15.2%), accounted for more than 70% of total imports.

Food imports declined during the period 1965–70, coinciding with the initial phase of import substitution (see section 14.4 above). On the other hand, there was a dramatic increase in the annual rate of growth of the importation of machinery and transport equipment, averaging 33.2% during the period 1970–75. This was the period when investment activities were intensified and the manufacturing sector was gearing production toward the export market.

Another way of analyzing the changing composition of Malaysian imports is to classify the imports by economic function. Using this classification, in 1961 consumption goods accounted for 46.7% of total imports, while intermediate and investment goods accounted for 44.9% (table 14.15). By 1980 the share of consumption goods had dropped to 18.4%, and the share of intermediate and investment goods had risen to nearly 80%. In short, the data in table 14.15 confirm that Malaysia has more or less completed the first stage of its industrial development and is now preparing for the second stage of industrialization.

14.10   Changes in Import Market

Along with the changes in the composition of imports over the last twenty years we can also perceive corresponding changes in the direction of imports. In the initial period, 1961–64, Western Europe (11.0%), especially the United Kingdom, Japan (8.6%), and Singapore (9.2%) were the main sources of Malaysian imports (table 14.16). Since then the ranking and sources have changed slightly. Thus in the last period, 1975–80, Malaysian imports came mainly from Japan (22.4%), Western Europe (19.5%), and the United States (13.8%). The emergence of Japan as Malaysia's leading source of imports is not surprising in view of the competitiveness of Japanese products.[9] Similarly, it is not surprising that Western Europe should lose its top position following the withdrawal of Commonwealth tariff preference for British goods. Also losers in the Malaysian market are the other Asian countries, excluding Japan. In the initial period, imports from these other Asian countries were valued at nearly 60% of total imports. In the last period, these imports had fallen to less than 25%, a drastic decline of more than 50%. The other Asian countries include the other ASEAN countries, and these, too, showed a significant decline in their exports to Malaysia. Finally it should also be noted that imports from the OECD countries as a whole showed a steady increase, from 30.2% in the 1961–64 period to 64.0% in the 1975–80 period. This trend may be expected to continue in view of Malaysia's continued efforts to develop the economy and upgrade the manufacturing sector.

Table 14.15   Malaysia: Imports by Economic Function

End Use	Import Share (millions of ringgits)						Import Share (%)					Average Annual Growth Rate (%)		
	1961	1964	1969	1974	1975	1980	1961	1964	1969	1974	1980	1964–69	1969–74	1974–80
Consumption goods	**1,315**	**1,484**	**1,139**	**2,160**	**1,720**	**4,325.4**	**46.7**	**46.3**	**31.6**	**21.6**	**18.4**	**– 5.2**	**13.7**	**16.7**
Food	594	723	461	925	615	1,177.0	21.1	22.6	12.8	9.2	5.0	08.6	11.7	4.5
Beverages and tobacco	128	136	71		85	a	4.5	4.2	2.0		a	–12.1		a
Consumer durables	169	227	133	295	260	992.3	6.0	7.1	3.7	2.9	4.2	–10.1	17.3	39.4
Other	424	398	474	940	760	2,156.1	15.1	12.4	13.1	9.4	9.2	3.6	14.7	21.6
Investment goods	**480**	**582**	**742**	**3,370**	**2,740**	**7,169.6**	**17.1**	**18.2**	**20.6**	**33.6**	**30.6**	**5.0**	**35.4**	**18.8**
Machinery	127	182	290	1,170	950	2,577.9	4.5	5.7	8.0	11.7	11.0	9.8	32.2	20.1
Transport equipment	117	91	64	195	250	919.4	4.2	2.8	1.8	1.9	3.9	–6.8	25.0	61.9
Metal products	122	155	203	920	550	1,906.4	4.3	4.8	5.6	9.2	8.1	5.5	35.3	17.9
Other	114	154	185	1,085	990	1,765.9	4.1	4.8	5.1	10.8	7.6	3.7	42.5	10.5
Intermediate goods	**784**	**885**	**1,357**	**4,056**	**3,726**	**11,550.0**	**27.8**	**27.6**	**37.6**	**40.5**	**49.3**	**8.9**	**24.5**	**30.8**
For manufacturing	220	309	725	2,373	2,017	6,531.0	7.8	9.6	20.1	23.7	27.8	18.6	26.8	29.2
For construction	87	116	73	185	170	580.4	3.1	3.6	2.0	1.8	2.5	–8.9	20.4	35.6
For agriculture	80	118	146	375	330	892.9	2.8	3.7	4.0	3.7	3.8	4.4	20.8	23.0
Petroleum	190	183	228	518	665	1,890.3	6.7	5.7	6.3	5.2	8.1	4.5	17.8	44.2
Other	207	159	185	605	544	1,655.4	7.4	5.0	5.1	6.0	7.1	3.6	26.7	28.9
Imports for reexport	**237**	**235**	**340**	**429**	**405**	**406.0**	**8.4**	**7.3**	**9.4**	**4.3**	**1.7**	**7.7**	**4.8**	**–0.9**
Tin ore	—	105	127	231	265	—	—	3.3	3.5	2.3	—	3.9	12.7	—
Natural rubber	—	53	74	58	40	—	—	1.7	2.1	0.6	—	6.9	–4.8	—
Petroleum	—	77	139	140	100	—	—	2.4	3.9	1.4	—	12.5	0.1	—
Total	**2,816**	**3,205**	**3,605**	**10,015**	**8,591**	**23,451.0**	**100.0**	**100.0**	**100.0**	**100.0**	**100.0**	**2.4**	**22.7**	**22.4**

Source: Bank Negara Malaysia, *Quarterly Economic Bulletin*, March 1982.

aIncluded in Other.

Table 14.16   **The Direction of Malaysian Imports** (percentages)

Country or Region	1961–64	1965–69	1970–74	1975–80
United States	4.8	6.8	8.9	13.8
Western Europe	11.0	16.9	20.1	19.5
Japan	8.6	14.6	21.6	22.4
Australia and New Zealand	5.4	7.1	7.5	7.2
Canada	0.5	0.8	1.1	1.1
Total, OECD countries	30.2	46.2	59.2	64.0
China	5.0	7.1	5.1	3.1
Hong Kong	n.a.	2.0	1.8	1.7
Singapore	9.2	9.7	7.8	9.5
Other Asian markets	59.7	42.8	29.6	24.3
Other ASEAN markets	n.a.	10.8	7.0	5.5
Total, Asia, excluding Japan	68.9	52.5	37.4	33.8
Rest of the world	0.9	1.3	3.4	2.2

Source: Department of Statistics, *Annual Bulletin of Statistics,* various years.
Note: n.a. = not available.

14.11   Conclusion

The available statistics show that the Malaysian manufacturing sector made considerable progress over the last two decades, in terms of both overall growth rate and structural changes. The manufacturing sector grew at an accelerated pace of 12% during the last two decades. Apart from its rapid growth, the Malaysian manufacturing sector has also undergone a structural change. After beginning mainly with the production of consumer nondurables for the domestic market during the initial phase of import substitution, the manufacturing sector has now entered a new phase of production aimed at the export market. At the same time there has also been a perceptible growth in the production of consumer durables and intermediate goods. It would thus appear that industrial policy should aim at strengthening the above developments, namely, export promotion and secondary import substitution.

However, it should be remembered that Malaysia's success in achieving an accelerated growth rate was facilitated to a considerable extent by a favorable world economic environment owing to a buoyant demand for Malaysia's commodity exports (petroleum, timber, rubber, palm oil, etc.), a rapidly expanding market for non-resource-based footloose manufactured exports (textiles, clothing, electronics, etc.) from developing economies, a ready access to an urban, easy-to-train labor force, and ample natural resources. These favorable factors can no longer be taken for granted. The present recession has put an end to the buoyant demand for Malaysia's commodity exports, while protectionism in the developed countries has reduced the market for Malaysia's manufactured exports. Even if the world economy were to recover by the end of this year, the volatile and uncertain economic situation as well as the vulnerability in the present set of export-oriented manufacturing industries makes one wonder whether Malaysia should continue to depend on the export of non-resource-based footloose manufactured goods. Many of these goods are low-value items and are the favorite targets of protectionist groups in the developed countries. For this reason it may be better for Malaysia to encourage the manufacturers concerned to develop their products for the high-value end of the market. For example, instead of simply producing textiles, manufacturers should be encouraged to go into fashion-designed clothing.

Another alternative is to encourage backward and forward linkages in the electronics and other industries located in the Free-Trade Zones instead of allowing these industries to develop in segregated enclaves isolated from the rest of the domestic economy. An appropriate incentive system should be designed to encourage the transfer of technology from these relatively technologically sophisticated industries.

As for the production of consumer durables and intermediate goods, top priority must be given to the question of competitiveness. Unlike the labor-intensive manufactured exports such as textiles and electronics for which Malaysia has a comparative advantage, there are very few consumer durables and intermediate goods which Malaysia can produce at competitive world prices. This means that such goods have to be sold in the domestic market. Because of the limited size of this market, production will only be viable if it is heavily protected. If this is the price for secondary import substitution, it is certainly not worth paying.

Instead of blindly pursuing a policy of secondary import substitution to the limit, a suitable policy should be formulated to encourage the development of the capital goods industry. Malaysia is one of the largest producers of several primary commodities, such as rubber, tin, and palm oil. The production and processing of these commodities require a variety of machinery and equipment. Some of this machinery and equipment is produced locally. Why not encourage the production of more of this machinery and equipment locally and subsequently the export of these items? The production of this machinery and equipment does not require a high level of skill or technology, and given the relatively large domestic market, Malaysia should have some comparative advantage in their production. In short, with suitable government encouragement and incentives, Malaysia can become a leader in the manufacture of agricultural machinery.

Another suggestion is to pursue the policy of promoting resource-based industries with greater effort and enthusiasm. These are also industries in which Malaysia has some comparative advantage, so they should be given greater priority than heavy industries in which Malaysia has absolutely no comparative advantage. A good example of the latter type of industry is the proposed made-in-Malaysia car. At a time when Japan has already revolutionized and dominated the motor vehicle industry, it is folly for Malaysia to think about producing its own cars, especially when the proposed industry will always require a relatively high level of protection to survive (see Chee 1983a, b).

Instead of paying so much attention to "prestigious" industries, Malaysia should concentrate on the resource-based industries. But apart from lip service, nothing much has been done to promote such industries. Not surprisingly, as our study pointed out earlier, resource-based industries have failed to establish a firm foothold in the Malaysian manufacturing sector. More aggressive policies should be pursued to develop resource-based industries not only because such industries increase value added but also because they stimulate the demand for primary commodities. Thus even if firms are reluctant to set up such industries in Malaysia, we should explore the possibility of investing in such industries abroad. In this connection, the proposed Malaysian *sogo shoshas* should consider investing in existing natural-resource-based industries in the developed countries (see Chee 1980a).

The Malaysian manufacturing sector has reached a crucial stage in its development. The current recession has exposed some of the weaknesses in the structure of the manufacturing sector. In this sense the recession may be a blessing in disguise, especially if it alerts policymakers to the dangers of fostering vulnerable or noncompetitive industries. In short, there is a need to chart new directions for the further development of the Malaysian manufacturing sector. We have suggested the new directions which the manufacturing sector should follow. With a rational industrial policy and suitable incentives, Malaysia should be able to join the ranks of the newly industrialized countries well before the end of this decade.

As for its external trade pattern and prospects it may be assumed that the present trend will continue. Malaysia will continue to export relatively more manufactured goods and less primary products. On the other hand, imports of consumption goods will continue to decline, while imports of intermediate and investment goods may be expected to increase even further. These developments will naturally favor Japan, which is already Malaysia's leading trade partner, but there is no reason why they should diminish the trade prospects of other countries, especially those in the OECD group. The complementary nature of the OECD and Malaysian economies will continue to foster closer mutual trade relationships. However, given a higher level of industrialization in the Malaysian economy, the country's efforts to diversify its export market may be more successful. At present, nontraditional export markets in the Pacific region, West Asia, Latin America, and Africa are still at a minimal level of development. The production of a wider range of manufactured products should help Malaysian exporters in their efforts to penetrate these markets.

Notes

1. Malaysia was formed in 1963 and comprises the eleven states in Peninsular Malaysia, together with the Borneo states of Sabah and Sarawak. Although Peninsular Malaysia constitutes a little less than 40% of the total land area, it has over 80% of the population and GNP and an even greater proportion of the manufacturing activities. Thus, although some data are restricted to Peninsular Malaysia because many statistical series cover only this area, the exclusion of Sabah and Sarawak is not too damaging.

2. For further details of the New Economic Policy, see Malaysia 1971. For a critical analysis of the New Economic Policy, see Young et al. 1980, chap. 3.

3. For further details of the Malaysian government's policies to promote industrialization, see Young et al. 1980, chap. 7, and Hoffmann and Ee 1980, chap. 3.

4. The Malaysian ringgit (M \$) is approximately equal to U.S. \$0.45 (U.S. \$1.00 equals M \$2.20).

5. For further details of the Free Trade Zones in Malaysia, see Chee 1980b.

6. See also Datta-Chaudhuri 1982.

7. Since Singapore is a free port and a regional trade center, most of Malaysia's exports to the republic are reexported to other countries.

8. On the whole, intra-ASEAN trade is at a relatively low level, accounting for less than 15% of the region's total trade. See Wong 1979, chap. 2.

9. Japan has managed to capture not only the Malaysian but also the ASEAN market, mainly at the expense of the Western countries, especially the United States. See Chee 1982b.

References

Chee, Peng Lim. 1980a. Does Malaysia need general trading corporations? *Malaysian Business,* September, 21–24.

———. 1980b. Export processing zones in Malaysia. *Malaysian Business,* November, 16–18.

———. 1982a. From import-substitution to export promotion: A study of changes in Malaysia's industrial policy. In *Trade and industrial policies of Asian countries,* ed. K. Yoneda. Tokyo: Institute of Developing Economies.

———. 1982b. International rivalry: U.S.-Japanese competition in the ASEAN countries. *Contemporary Southeast Asia* 4, no. 1:35–57.

———. 1983a. Ancillary firm development in the Malaysian motor vehicle industry. (With Fong Chan Onn.) In *The motor vehicle industry in Asia: A study of ancillary firm development,* ed. K. Odaka. Singapore: Singapore University Press.

————. 1983b. The Malaysian motor vehicle industry at the crossroads: Time to change gear? Paper presented at the Seventh Malaysian Economic Convention, organized by the Malaysian Economic Association, Kuala Lumpur, January.

————. 1983c. Manufactured export incentives in Malaysia. (With Mohammad Ariff.) Study prepared for the Council of Asian Manpower Studies, Manila. Mimeo.

Datta-Chaudhuri, M. 1982. The role of Free Trade Zones in the creation of employment and industrial growth in Malaysia. Asian Employment Programme Working Papers, ARTEP (ILO), Bangkok. Mimeo.

Hoffmann, L., and Tan Siew Ee. 1980. *Industrial growth, employment and foreign investment in Peninsular Malaysia*. Kuala Lumpur: Oxford University Press.

Malaysia. 1971, *Second Malaysia Plan 1971–75*. Kuala Lumpur: Government Press.

Wong, John. 1979. *ASEAN economies in perspective*. London: Macmillan.

Young, Keven, et al. 1980. *Malaysia: Growth and equity in a multiracial society.* Baltimore: Johns Hopkins University Press.

15   Trade Patterns and Trends of Thailand

Juanjai Ajanant

15.1   Introduction

Thailand's recent growth performance has been impressive, with GDP growth rate averaging almost 8% per annum over the previous decade. The high growth rate occurred in all sectors of the economy. Exports have grown at an average annual growth rate of over 14%, and per capita income in current value has increased from U.S. $110 in 1960 to U.S. $670 in 1980. Primary exports, which used to be 85% of total exports, declined to 70%, reflecting the emergence of manufactured exports. At present 30% of total export value comes from manufactured exports. This paper will examine (*a*) factors that contributed to the growth of the economy, based on the record of the previous two decades; (*b*) prevailing factors that will contribute to the growth of the economy and exports in the coming years; and (*c*) the notions of export-led growth and growth-led exports.

15.2   Factors Contributing to Growth

From 1960 to 1976 Thailand implemented an import substitution industrialization policy. Despite the pros and cons of this policy, Thailand is said to be a successful case. The economy was able to grow rapidly during implementation of the first three national plans (1960–76). The success of the economy can be attributed to several factors, but it suffices to mention only four important ones: (*a*) the availability of

Juanjai Ajanant is assistant professor of economics at Chulalongkorn University, Bangkok, Thailand.

Comments by Dr. David Grove and Professors Branson and Baldwin are deeply appreciated by the author.

cheap, resource-based raw materials, (*b*) the supply of low-wage un-skilled labor, (*c*) tax exemption on capital machinery imported into the country, and (*d*) the realization of managerial acumen.

During the first decade of development (1961–70) the policy toward the industrial sector was actually biased toward raw material processing industries (e.g., food, rubber, and basic metals). With an area of 540,000 km² and long coastal lines encompassing 24 provinces, Thailand is quite rich in terms of resources. Tropical crops can be grown in most parts of the country; marine life can be found in abundance within the Gulf of Thailand; mineral ores are found in the southern isthmus. Most of these resources were exported in unprocessed form. Because of the abundance of cheap raw materials, the processing industries dominated the industrial scene before the textile industry began to emerge as a major industry.

Today, Thai industrial workers must be paid their legal minimum wage. The early years of industrialization saw a different labor market situation. Then, the labor market was one of free competition in which the wage rate was determined by market forces. As the economy had surplus labor, the wage bill was relatively small in the total cost of production. The low wage attracted many foreign investors, especially the Japanese. The textile industry, which was founded in Thailand through the Thai-Japanese joint ventures, flourished because of the low wage bill. Of course, the low wage signifies that labor is unskilled and of low productivity. This is not at all surprising, since most workers had never experienced modern working conditions before; high absen-teeism was noted. Over the years the socialization process has been smooth and workers have acclimatized to the routine. The enactment of the minimum wage law in 1973 has surely lifted the standard of living of laborers, but the prevailing wage may not reflect the marginal product of labor. In sum, the low wage was a significant variable for industrial growth, which in turn led to the growth of the economy.

As a labor-surplus economy à la Lewis, Thailand would be better off with labor-intensive techniques. The government, mainly through the Investment Promotion Act of 1960, supported industry by ex-empting taxes on capital machinery imported into the kingdom. Thai industrialists were encouraged to employ modern machines to produce consumer goods. Had tariffs been imposed on capital machinery or the tax exemption not been applied, the growth of Thai industries un-doubtedly would have been retarded. Therefore, the tax exemption on capital machinery facilitated industrialization even though it may have biased it toward greater capital intensity.

It would be misleading to conclude that the growth rate was due only to the above factors without paying tribute to entrepreneurial and man-agement skills. Before 1960 the only group of people with some business experience were the Chinese or people of Chinese origin. These people were, however, denied the opportunity to demonstrate their skills by means of various restrictions. The government even passed a law reserving certain occupations for the indigenous Thais. The fear of Chinese domination in business began to subside in the 1960s, enabling this group to make its impact by investing and organizing business on a large scale. Most of the important branches of Thai business are today owned or managed by Thais of Chinese origin.

15.3   Growth and Trade

Despite the bias toward the industrial sector, the other sectors of the economy did not perform poorly. We examine here three broad sectors: agriculture, minerals, and manufactures. The average annual growth rate of agriculture for the period 1960–80 was 5.1% (see table 15.1). This growth rate is small when compared with those of the other two sectors. But it should be emphasized that the value of agricultural production was substantially larger than those of the other sectors, and thus a low percentage growth still represents substantial incremental agricultural output.

The sporadic pattern of growth of the mining sector is due to the importance of tin production. The cyclical movement of the sector is determined largely by the fluctuations of world tin prices. Hence, its growth rate, which was at 16.9%, dropped sharply to −0.77% during the third plan but, with the commodity boom in 1974, bounced back to 11.6% in the fourth plan period.

The manufacturing sector enjoyed the highest growth rate during the period 1960–80. The overall growth rate for the four plans stood at

Table 15.1	GDP and Growth of Production by Sectors (in billions of baht and percentages)				
Sector	1961–66	1967–71	1972–76	1977–80	1960–80
Agriculture	34.33	45.89	58.22	71.70	
	(6.26)	(5.88)	(6.74)	(3.53)	(5.1)
Mining	1.36	2.54	2.78	4.38	
	(16.9)	(5.35)	(−0.77)	(11.66)	(7.76)
Manufacturing	12.21	21.49	34.45	56.90	
	(11.42)	(9.17)	(10.49)	(8.64)	(10.59)

Source: Calculated from the National Income Accounts.

Notes: GDP value has been calculated using the simple average; GDP is at 1972 prices. Growth is expressed as average annual growth for the period in question. 1961–66 = first national plan; 1967–71 = second national plan; 1972–76 = third national plan; 1977–80 = fourth national plan.

10.59%, with relatively even growth rates per plan period compared with mining.

Looking at the import side of the foreign sector, Thailand's pursuit of import substitution of finished products has resulted in a heavy concentration in a few categories of imports, notably raw materials (including oil), capital machinery, and chemicals. In table 15.2 we show the structure of imports classified according to one-digit SITC codes for 1960–80, along with the percentage shares by commodities. The combined share of chemicals, manufactured goods, and machinery (SITC 5, 6, and 7) was almost 69% of the total import value in 1960. The share dropped to roughly 50% by 1980. The share of manufactured goods imports (SITC 6) shows a gradual declining trend from 34% in 1960 to 15% in 1980. Machinery imports dropped from 35% to 23% between 1975 and 1980. The chief reason why the share of these com-

Table 15.2   **Value of Imports of Thailand by Commodity Groups**

SITC Categories	1960	1965	1970	1975	1980
	In Millions of Baht				
All commodities	9,622	16,185	27,009	66,835	188,686
0. Food and live animals	784	891	1,091	1,951	5,763
1. Beverages & tobacco	108	201	303	753	1,518
2. Crude materials	143	477	1,400	3,977	10,755
3. Mineral fuels & lubricants	1,025	1,364	2,329	14,233	58,733
4. Animal & vegetable oils & fats	20	33	35	108	1,458
5. Chemicals	974	1,674	3,505	9,122	22,352
6. Manufactured goods	3,289	5,016	6,458	10,560	28,152
7. Machinery & transport equipment	2,390	4,924	9,536	23,125	43,102
8. Miscellaneous manufactured goods	522	923	1,350	2,145	10,959
9. Misc. transactions & commodities (incl. gold)	367	682	1,002	860	5,894
	Percentage of Total				
All commodities	100.00	100.00	100.00	100.00	100.00
0. Food and live animals	8.15	5.51	4.02	2.92	3.05
1. Beverages & tobacco	1.12	1.24	1.12	1.13	0.81
2. Crude materials	1.49	2.95	5.18	5.95	5.70
3. Mineral fuels & lubricants	10.65	8.43	8.62	21.30	31.13
4. Animal & vegetable oils & fats	0.21	0.20	0.13	0.16	0.77
5. Chemicals	10.12	10.34	12.98	13.65	11.85
6. Manufactured goods	34.18	30.99	23.91	15.80	14.92
7. Machinery & transport equipment	24.84	30.42	35.31	34.60	22.84
8. Miscellaneous manufactured goods	5.43	5.70	5.00	3.21	5.81
9. Misc. transactions & commodities (incl. gold)	3.81	4.21	3.71	1.29	3.12

Source: Bank of Thailand, *Monthly Bulletin,* various issues.

modity categories dropped is that the percentage share of fuel imports jumped more than two times in 1975 and rose to 31.13% in 1980. Excluding fuels and lubricants, the import share of SITC 5, 6, and 7 would have actually increased.

The growth rate of total imports was 15.34% for all commodities for the period 1960–80 (table 15.3). Fuels and lubricants (SITC 3) had a 56.4% and 41.3% growth for the third and fourth plans. Chemicals (SITC 5) had a rapid growth during the same period but averaged 17.71% for the twenty-year span. Crude materials (SITC 2) had a rapid growth in the first two plans but began to decline in the early 1970s.

Table 15.4 illustrates the sources of imports from selected countries. Japan leads the group as the single largest supplier of all commodities to Thailand over the twenty-year period. The United States ranked second during the same period. Other countries tend to have a small share in total imports. In 1960 and 1965 Saudi Arabia had 0.26% and 0.07% shares respectively. With the oil price hikes during the 1970s the import share of this country went up by leaps and bounds to become the third largest supplier to Thailand by the mid-1970s.

As for the type of product supplies by Thai trading partners, table 15.4 shows that the United States was the leading supplier of food, beverages, and tobacco (SITC 0 and 1). The United States also held the top spot as far as imports of crude materials and oils and fats (SITC 2 and 4) were concerned. Saudi Arabia, as mentioned earlier, was the main supplier of crude oil (SITC 3). For chemicals and machinery and transport equipment (SITC 5 and 7) Japan and the United States were the main suppliers. In the early part of the 1960s the United States was

Table 15.3   **Average Annual Growth Rates of Imports of Thailand by Commodity Groups** (percentages)

SITC Categories	1961–66	1967–71	1972–76	1977–80	1960–80 Average
All commodities	12.32	5.03	24.33	26.86	15.34
0. Food and live animals	5.23	−0.22	17.57	13.96	12.55
1. Beverages & tobacco	9.62	5.77	7.65	32.53	8.95
2. Crude materials	23.47	33.38	32.75	16.94	25.89
3. Mineral fuels & lubricants	10.79	13.11	56.42	41.31	22.07
4. Animal & vegetable oils & fats	17.28	0.23	31.76	71.21	19.89
5. Chemicals	14.66	9.40	20.87	21.17	17.71
6. Manufactured goods	8.02	−1.37	14.96	24.14	10.17
7. Machinery & transport equipment	17.95	3.78	23.26	15.16	15.39
8. Miscellaneous manufactured goods	14.39	3.63	8.81	44.53	14.22
9. Misc. transactions & commodities (incl. gold)	5.51	7.71	6.68	50.43	11.01

Source: Calculated from Bank of Thailand's statistics.

Table 15.4   **Sources of Imports of Thailand for Selected Commodity Groups**
(percentages)

	1960	1965	1971	1975	1980
			All Commodities		
World	100.00	100.00	100.00	100.00	100.00
Japan	25.24	32.53	37.70	41.55	20.65
United States	18.16	17.30	14.24	14.37	16.65
Fed. Rep. Germany	10.57	9.07	7.75	5.21	4.25
United Kingdom	10.53	9.12	7.68	4.53	2.60
Australia	1.10	2.04	3.23	2.30	1.83
Saudi Arabia	0.26	0.07	2.81	8.99	9.87
Italy	1.19	2.37	1.60	1.83	1.38
Netherlands	4.32	3.46	1.18	1.02	2.42
Hong Kong	6.48	2.86	1.17	0.96	0.93
Rest of the world	22.16	21.18	22.64	29.22	39.44
			SITC 0 + 1		
World	100.00	100.00	100.00	100.00	100.00
Japan	6.02	1.35	3.06	4.29	3.07
United States	13.43	25.11	40.61	41.02	24.36
Fed. Rep. Germany	0.15	0.86	1.22	1.30	3.70
United Kingdom	3.45	3.64	5.11	4.52	5.38
Australia	5.85	8.57	12.91	13.80	4.50
Saudi Arabia	—	—	—	—	—
Italy	5.95	—	0.17	0.16	0.15
Netherlands	27.61	31.49	10.88	4.57	3.40
Hong Kong	17.38	0.56	0.64	0.33	0.44
Rest of the world	10.15	28.42	25.40	30.00	54.99
			SITC 2 + 4		
World	100.00	100.00	100.00	100.00	100.00
Japan	6.99	9.27	12.67	11.78	6.11
United States	33.75	46.90	37.69	29.34	26.13
Fed. Rep. Germany	1.87	0.67	4.44	1.76	2.24
United Kingdom	11.41	4.42	4.72	1.61	0.88
Australia	7.91	2.18	2.06	4.90	3.03
Saudi Arabia	—	—	—	—	—
Italy	0.14	0.74	0.39	0.16	3.12
Netherlands	0.88	—	0.57	0.85	0.25
Hong Kong	18.37	1.10	1.84	3.32	3.31
Rest of the world	18.68	34.71	35.63	46.28	54.93
			SITC 3		
World	100.00	100.00	100.00	100.00	100.00
Japan	0.74	3.80	2.57	1.18	0.35
United States	6.45	8.96	4.63	0.96	0.78
Fed. Rep. Germany	0.10	0.28	0.18	0.04	0.02
United Kingdom	2.45	11.58	1.14	0.08	0.05
Australia	—	—	—	—	0.76
Saudi Arabia	2.57	0.66	26.90	41.66	32.38

Table 15.4 (continued)

	1960	1965	1971	1975	1980
Italy	—	—	—	—	1.06
Netherlands	4.65	0.88	0.95	0.25	0.38
Hong Kong	0.22	—	—	—	—
Rest of the world	82.82	73.84	63.62	55.83	64.22
			SITC 5 + 7		
World	100.00	100.00	100.00	100.00	100.00
Japan	16.92	33.26	46.19	44.08	35.76
United States	26.01	19.67	12.28	16.89	25.51
Fed. Rep. Germany	18.68	15.80	11.51	8.45	8.75
United Kingdom	15.48	12.10	10.34	6.79	4.76
Australia	0.44	1.52	2.08	1.38	0.85
Saudi Arabia	—	—	—	—	—
Italy	2.25	4.01	2.45	3.19	1.88
Netherlands	3.35	2.17	1.37	1.08	1.89
Hong Kong	2.62	1.08	0.64	0.43	0.52
Rest of the world	14.24	10.38	13.13	17.70	20.07
			SITC 6 + 8		
World	100.00	100.00	100.00	100.00	100.00
Japan	45.16	49.65	53.74	49.44	40.70
United States	11.68	8.51	7.73	10.04	8.73
Fed. Rep. Germany	6.33	6.49	5.16	4.60	3.17
United Kingdom	8.22	7.03	6.58	4.84	2.69
Australia	0.24	1.72	4.17	4.02	5.27
Saudi Arabia	—	—	—	—	—
Italy	0.97	1.43	1.24	1.41	0.91
Netherlands	1.00	0.58	0.52	0.99	0.60
Hong Kong	10.77	6.33	2.47	2.78	2.82
Rest of the world	15.63	18.25	18.37	21.89	35.11

Source: United Nations, *Commodity Trade Statistics.*

the most important, with a 26.01% share, but Japan surpassed the United States by the mid-1960s and has held this position ever since. The preeminence of Japan is also exhibited in the imports of manufactured products and other manufactured goods (SITC 6 and 8). During 1960–80 Japan had about a 45% share in any given year, with the United States remaining second at some distance.

Between 1960 and 1965 Thai exports consisted mainly of food and crude materials (SITC 0 and 2) (see table 15.5). In 1960, for example, these two classes of products combined to produce 95% of the total export value. The share of crude materials (SITC 2) began to plummet by the early 1970s; this was partly offset by an increase in manufactured exports (SITC 6) at the same time. In 1975 the export of food (SITC

Table 15.5   Value of Exports of Thailand by Commodity Groups

SITC Categories	1960	1965	1970	1975	1980
		In Millions of Baht			
All commodities	8,614	12,980	14,722	45,007	133,197
0. Food and live animals	3,912	6,786	6,957	26,599	59,338
1. Beverages & tobacco	25	92	206	579	1,393
2. Crude materials	4,303	4,966	4,262	6,804	19,095
3. Mineral fuels & lubricants	—	46	45	249	86
4. Animal & vegetable oils & fats	2	7	14	43	222
5. Chemicals	8	15	33	243	936
6. Manufactured goods	96	599	2,188	6,419	19,474
7. Machinery & transport equipment	1	10	15	573	7,618
8. Miscellaneous manufactured goods	14	27	59	1,582	8,467
9. Miscellaneous transactions & commodities	61	133	471	983	3,777
Reexports	192	299	522	933	2,791
		Percentage of Total			
All commodities	100.00	100.00	100.00	100.00	100.00
0. Food and live animals	45.41	52.28	47.26	59.10	44.55
1. Beverages & tobacco	0.29	0.71	1.40	1.29	1.05
2. Crude materials	49.95	38.26	18.95	15.12	14.34
3. Mineral fuels & lubricants	—	0.35	0.31	0.54	0.07
4. Animal & vegetable oils & fats	0.23	0.05	0.10	0.10	0.17
5. Chemicals	0.09	0.12	0.22	0.54	0.70
6. Manufactured goods	1.11	4.62	14.86	14.26	22.13
7. Machinery & transport equipment	0.01	0.08	0.10	1.27	5.72
8. Miscellaneous manufactured goods	0.16	0.21	0.04	3.52	6.36
9. Miscellaneous transactions & commodities	0.71	1.03	3.20	2.18	1.84
Reexports	2.23	2.30	3.54	2.07	2.10

Source: Bank of Thailand, *Monthly Bulletin,* various issues.

0) recorded the highest value because of the commodity boom in the preceding year. Crude materials and manufactured products (SITC 2 and 6) represented 30% of the total export value during the early 1970s. It therefore can be stated that for the period 1960–75 food, crude materials, and manufactured goods were the main exports. By 1980 the exports of food items had declined, but the exports of manufactured products rose beyond the 20% level for the first time.

Table 15.6 illustrates the average annual growth of exports of Thailand. When we compare the figures of this table with table 15.3, it can be concluded that the overall export value grew slightly more slowly than the overall import value. The only exception is the period of 1972–76, when the growth rate of exports was higher than that of imports. High-growth products can be found in chemicals, manufactured products, machinery and transport equipment, and miscellaneous manufactured products (SITC 5–8).

Table 15.6   **Average Annual Growth Rates of Exports of Thailand by Commodity Groups** (percentages)

SITC Categories	1961–66	1967–71	1972–76	1977–80	1960–80 Average
All commodities	8.61	4.82	26.15	23.90	14.55
0. Food and live animals	8.86	1.36	34.55	14.74	14.43
1. Beverages & tobacco	47.65	9.96	26.90	13.71	23.08
2. Crude materials	3.55	6.66	12.35	22.32	7.53
3. Mineral fuels & lubricants	361.96	22.39	–19.13	68.76	37.07
4. Animal & vegetable oils & fats	–6.18	88.29	37.27	79.25	15.77
5. Chemicals	10.90	30.82	34.35	47.99	29.26
6. Manufactured goods	57.69	5.74	22.97	35.02	32.50
7. Machinery & transport equipment	65.87	26.86	135.56	62.51	54.34
8. Miscellaneous manufactured goods	7.60	32.23	56.78	45.53	41.06
9. Miscellaneous transactions & commodities	11.98	49.92	–3.19	36.20	23.44
Reexports	2.88	7.13	–8.37	45.73	11.64

Source: Calculated from Bank of Thailand's statistics.

Table 15.7 shows the direction of exports. During the 1970s Japan and the United States bought about 35% of Thai exports. The Netherlands ranked second, slightly ahead of Japan in 1980. This is expected since the Netherlands alone imported one-half of Thai tapioca products. In terms of product classification, Thailand exported food, beverages, and tobacco (SITC 0 and 1) chiefly to Japan and the Netherlands. Japan was the largest buyer of commodities, but the Netherlands concentrated on one single product (tapioca). Within the categories of crude materials and oils and fats (SITC 2 and 4), Japan was the most important buyer. Japan's imports consisted of rubber sheet, block rubber, and unwrought tin metal. There is no clear-cut pattern for mineral fuels and lubricants (SITC 3). The export pattern for chemicals and machinery and transport equipment was unsettled before 1975. From that year on, Singapore was the largest purchaser. The role of Singapore must be interpreted with some caution. Since Singapore is an entrepôt, she acts as an intermediary for countries which have no direct trade relations with Thailand, particularly the socialist countries in Indochina. Thailand exported a substantial proportion of manufactured products (SITC 6 and 8) to the United States, Japan, and the Netherlands. Among these are textile yarns, garments, and canned food (Ajanant 1984).

Thus far, the supply side of production and trade has been emphasized. The demand side of trade was also important to the growth of the Thai economy. A recent World Bank report (1982) which focused on manufactures found that domestic demand was the primary source of growth in manufacturing output throughout the past decade in Thailand. Import substitution was also important in the period 1966–72 and

Table 15.7   **Direction of Exports of Thailand for Selected Commodity Groups**
(percentages)

	1960	1965	1971	1975	1980
			All Commodities		
World	100.00	100.00	100.00	100.00	100.00
Japan	16.95	19.64	25.30	26.04	15.31
United States	5.37	5.28	12.86	9.92	12.81
Netherlands	3.04	3.53	8.25	9.56	13.51
Singapore	—	8.02	7.03	8.24	7.36
Hong Kong	13.92	9.74	6.77	12.71	4.96
Malaysia	0.25	10.25	3.93	4.29	4.50
Fed. Rep. Germany	5.69	4.86	3.80	2.32	4.20
United Kingdom	4.51	2.07	2.45	1.05	1.89
Rest of the world	50.27	39.31	29.60	25.87	35.46
			SITC 0 + 1		
World	100.00	100.00	100.00	100.00	100.00
Japan	10.16	15.14	22.44	18.69	9.64
United States	3.87	3.29	3.49	5.93	4.90
Netherlands	2.34	3.29	10.14	14.24	17.41
Singapore	—	9.67	10.23	9.60	5.88
Hong Kong	0.01	12.00	11.18	7.00	4.48
Malaysia	0.00	12.18	5.25	5.16	5.72
Fed. Rep. Germany	3.52	4.44	2.31	1.41	3.04
United Kingdom	1.61	0.83	1.32	0.42	0.91
Rest of the world	78.49	39.06	33.63	27.55	48.04
			SITC 2 + 4		
World	100.00	100.00	100.00	100.00	100.00
Japan	33.83	25.32	41.24	38.16	47.80
United States	6.72	9.79	9.06	10.47	15.00
Netherlands	4.87	4.84	1.98	2.97	6.58
Singapore	—	1.36	4.29	8.78	7.89
Hong Kong	3.92	2.30	1.58	2.14	1.63
Malaysia	5.45	3.50	4.08	6.17	4.44
Fed. Rep. Germany	10.71	6.64	7.40	3.23	4.30
United Kingdom	10.61	4.58	4.35	1.49	0.48
Rest of the world	23.89	41.68	26.02	26.58	11.89
			SITC 3		
World	100.00	100.00	100.00	100.00	100.00
Japan	—	9.99	—	—	7.53
United States	—	—	—	—	—
Netherlands	—	—	—	—	—
Singapore	—	54.16	23.79	—	9.01
Hong Kong	—	—	4.70	10.87	6.53
Malaysia	—	35.21	—	—	14.78
Fed. Rep. Germany	—	—	—	—	—
United Kingdom	—	—	—	—	—
Rest of the world	—	0.63	71.51	89.13	62.16

Table 15.7   (continued)

	1960	1965	1971	1975	1980
			SITC 5 + 7		
World	100.00	100.00	100.00	100.00	100.00
Japan	—	—	21.12	13.54	3.28
United States	24.00	—	—	4.94	19.60
Netherlands	—	—	—	0.79	0.39
Singapore	—	—	12.69	34.77	36.77
Hong Kong	25.14	—	3.73	9.87	8.45
Malaysia	43.43	—	8.08	11.51	12.72
Fed. Rep. Germany	—	—	—	2.17	1.33
United Kingdom	—	—	—	—	1.56
Rest of the world	7.43	100.00	54.38	22.42	15.89
			SITC 6 + 8		
World	100.00	100.00	100.00	100.00	100.00
Japan	0.59	1.82	5.55	14.44	10.79
United States	36.79	18.85	49.95	19.13	21.70
Netherlands	—	—	15.95	3.89	15.11
Singapore	—	8.33	2.75	3.51	3.18
Hong Kong	16.66	11.45	2.27	33.78	6.43
Malaysia	11.60	5.19	0.45	0.99	0.99
Fed. Rep. Germany	6.36	2.11	1.89	3.41	6.22
United Kingdom	9.49	10.96	1.85	1.84	4.04
Rest of the world	18.50	41.30	19.35	19.01	31.54

Source: United Nations, *Commodity Trade Statistics.*

before, when a number of consumer goods industries were established in Thailand. These were principally in consumer durables, transport equipment, and the production of some intermediate and final products such as textiles, rubber products, and wood products.

Table 15.8 is reproduced from that World Bank report. Overall, there was no net import substitution during 1972–75; there was even some "negative substitution" in sectors where demand outpaced the growth of domestic capacity and the import share grew. However, exports made an increasing contribution to the growth of output. The beginning of a shift toward greater export orientation is evident in some sectors, including intermediate products such as textiles, rubber products, and wood products.

In the most recent period, 1975–80, export demand has become much more important in its direct contribution to the growth of manufacturing. Import substitution did not contribute to growth during 1975–80. In fact, on the average, there was negative impact. The transport equipment sector did enjoy some net import substitution in this period as higher local content laws began to have an effect. Almost all other

Table 15.8   **Foreign Trade: Sources of Growth of Manufacturing Output** (percentage contribution to increase)

Sector	DE[a]	IS	EX	DE[a]	IS	EX
	1966–72			1972–75		
Processed foods	107.3	0.5	−7.8	89.3	0.6	10.0
Beverages & tobacco	73.6	26.4	−0.1	87.9	0.1	11.9
Construction materials	69.5	19.6	10.9	89.5	0.3	10.2
Intermediate products I	65.8	23.7	10.5	96.3	−2.1	5.8
Intermediate products II	33.6	50.6	15.9	89.7	−9.5	23.6
Consumer nondurables	51.8	35.6	12.6	80.8	14.9	4.3
Consumer durables	31.7	66.7	1.6 ⎤			
Machinery	48.3	49.0	2.7 ⎬	107.3	−7.7	0.4
Transport equipment	24.7	75.2	0.1 ⎦			
Total	64.1	29.4	6.5	91.0	0.5	8.5
	1975–78			1977–80		
Processed foods	46.9	−4.6	57.7	72.3	−7.5	35.2
Beverages & tobacco	101.6	−219.9	0.6	110.6	−11.2	0.5
Construction materials	103.6	−1.0	−2.6	130.1	−28.6	−1.5
Textiles & clothing	65.8	3.4	30.8	74.5	10.4	15.0
Leather & leather products	−420.2	−18.5	538.6	51.6	−3.0	51.4
Wood & wood products	107.2	−16.0	8.8	96.8	−1.2	4.4
Paper & paper products	102.6	−4.0	1.5	70.6	2.7	26.7
Chemicals & petroleum	130.2	−29.5	−0.6	72.1	−10.7	38.6
Rubber & rubber products	31.8	16.4	51.7	−11.8	−9.2	121.0
Metals & metal products	64.1	−1.0	36.9	70.3	−3.6	33.3
Machinery	60.8	4.4	34.8	81.8	−60.5	78.8
Transport equipment	81.1	18.2	0.5	81.9	16.1	1.9
Other	89.0	−33.5	44.5	64.7	13.9	21.4
Total	79.5	−7.7	28.2	74.3	−7.0	32.2

Source: World Bank 1982.

Note: DE = domestic demand effect; IS = import substitution; EX = export demand.

[a]Domestic demand effects greater than 100 indicate that domestic demand grew faster than production and either the import share increased (negative import substitution) or surpluses available for export were reduced (negative export expansion) or both to meet the higher domestic demand in excess of domestic supply capacity.

sectors continued to show net negative impact from import substitution. Since 1980, exports have become critical to the Thai economy.

15.4   The Future

The recession in the 1980s has brought numerous problems for Thai exports. First, terms of trade have turned against leading exports such as rubber, tin metal, and sugar. Second, in the attempt to restructure their economies in general and some industries in particular, industrialized countries have resorted to restrictive trade and nontrade measures. Though these measures were nondiscriminatory, Thai products felt the effect. The resultant trade deficit of 89,000 million baht in 1983 is a testimony to this struggle.

The degree to which the Thai economy can rebound and continue to grow at the fast pace achieved during the previous decade will depend to a large extent on the degree to which the world economy recovers. Thailand cannot grow without the external demand from the industrialized world. Given the world economy, the following factors should indicate the possible outcome. These are (*a*) the wage rate, (*b*) the new breed of entrepreneurs, (*c*) energy, (*d*) foreign debt, and (*e*) government policy.

Though the minimum wage has gradually risen over the past ten years (see table 15.9), the real wage has not kept up with inflation. The CPI increase averaged 11.5 for the period 1977–81; the increase was about 20% for 1979 and 1980. This clearly denotes a fall in real wage in recent years. The wage issue has been accepted by union leaders as a fait accompli. The union leaders accepted the stagnant situation and compromised on a fractional increase in 1983. In order to gain a share in the international market, Thai products must be price-competitive,

Table 15.9   **Minimum Wage** (in baht per day[a])

Year	Bangkok and Surrounding Provinces	Central Plains and Southern Regions	Northern and Northeastern Regions
1973	12	—	—
1974	16	—	—
1975	20	—	—
1976	25	18	16
1977	28	21	19
1978	35	28	25
1979	45	38	35
1980	54	47	44
1981	61[b]	52[c]	52[c]
1982	64[d]	61[e]	52[f]
1983	66[d]	63[e]	56[f]

Source: Labour Department.

[a]20.40 baht equals U.S. $1.00 during the period 1960–80; 23.00 baht equals U.S. $1.00 since July 1981.

[b]Bangkok, Samutprakan, Nonthaburi, Prathumthani, Nakornprathom, Samut-sakorn, Cholbury, Saraburi, Nakornrachasima, Chiangmai, Phuket, Panga, and Ranong.

[c]Provinces other than those mentioned in note b.

[d]Bangkok, Samutprakan, Nonthaburi, Prathumthani, Nakornprathom, Samut-sakorn, Phuket, Panga, and Ranong.

[e]Cholburi, Saraburi, Nakornrachasima, and Chiangmai.

[f]Provinces other than those mentioned in notes d and e.

and the wage rate can be the deciding factor. The Thai wage rate is lower than rates in the newly industrializing countries (NIC). But it is higher than wages paid in the Philippines, Sri Lanka, and Indonesia. Provided the wage restraint can be maintained, Thai labor-intensive products will remain competitive with products of her rivals.

Unlike the 1960s, there is no shortage of qualified people to manage the public and private sectors. There are hundreds of M.B.A.-trained individuals plus a few hundred engineers waiting to be promoted. One stumbling block is the older generation of businessmen. The older generation has not fully realized the potential of these qualified people. They continue to apply their skills to old-fashioned family businesses. The process of accepting the professionals as valuable assets to a firm is beginning, and within five years we shall witness the contribution of a new corps of professionals. Beyond 1990, the prospect is even brighter, because most of the older generation will be reaching retirement age.

The oil shock of the 1970s has left its mark on Thailand. Thailand is sensitive to oil price changes since about one-third of her export earnings went back to the Gulf states as payments for crude oil. At present the rate of crude oil consumption stands at about 200,000 barrels per day. The discovery of crude oil in the northeastern region and natural gas in the Gulf of Thailand will reduce oil imports by one-fifth to one-seventh in two years. There has been a deliberate switching from oil to other sources of energy. The electricity authority of Thailand has used natural gas, lignite, and hydroelectric dams to product electricity in various parts of the country. Looking into the near future, the prospect of reducing dependence on imported oil is promising, though the country will have to import some crude oil well beyond 1990.

At the outset of the last recession many developing countries resorted to debt rescheduling and/or increased indebtedness to stave off short-term economic problems. Thailand, on the other hand, relied more upon fiscal austerity coupled with prudential borrowing. As a result Thailand remains one of the few countries in the world undisturbed by the liquidity problem. There are two basic reasons for this. First, there is a law limiting the government's borrowing so that the debt-service ratio remains within a limit of 9% of exports. The government has not sought fresh loans to roll over the impending debt. It has also searched for cheaper sources of funds. Second, many officials still remember the treaties with the Western nations dating back to 1856 which took away the right to levy import duties over 3% for seventy years. The Ministry of Finance, following the old tradition of the early years, has been adamant and refuses to borrow to buttress the economy. In all likelihood, this trend will continue, and the debt service burden experienced by other countries and dampening their growth will not be an issue for Thailand.

As we have seen, the government has been active in promoting industries through granting incentives. The government has drawn up and implemented policy measures to encourage industrial restructuring and agricultural development. One hard fact is that increased production in the last decade hinged upon the expansion of cultivated areas. Thai agricultural production, however, remains the most primitive among countries of the region. Fertilizer application per hectare is probably the lowest among grain-exporting countries. Furthermore, farm mechanization is not widespread. The acreage expansion has reached its ecological limits. There is no marginal land which the farmer can use except by encroaching upon the dwindling forested land. The forested area has shrunk so much that some parts of the country may soon become deserts. A recent Food and Agriculture Organization report (1984) states that Thailand is losing her forests at a rate of 16% of the estimated forested land per annum. Only Indonesia loses her forested land faster than Thailand. The government has reacted by stopping logging in several areas. In addition a 1% export tariff is placed on all wood products exported, and a ban has been placed on the export of all unprocessed woods. Farmers are encouraged to stop slash-and-burn farming and to apply new techniques of farming, some of which are the use of chemical fertilizers, pesticides, herbicides, and high-yield seeds. The real incentive in agriculture can be found in economic measures. The government has introduced several measures to move the local markets closer to the market signals. It has previously kept the domestic price below the world market price through intervention. Recent trends indicate that the market mechanism is being allowed to replace the interventionist measures. As long as agricultural policy follows this line of thinking, agriculture will continue to be a dominant sector for several decades.

On industrial policy, the government has gradually initiated measures to liberalize trade. For example, there is an ongoing industrial restructuring program to increase the efficiency of industries through reducing tariff protection, developing the financial market, streamlining the export procedure, and so on. The transition from a restrictive trade regime to a more outward-oriented type may take three to four years to accomplish. By then it is envisaged that Thailand can make a bid for NIC status.

15.5 Export-Led Growth or Growth-Led Exports

This retrospective examination of Thai economic performance in the last two decades provides evidence both that exports led to growth and that growth contributed to exports. This paper argues that the notions are two sides of the same coin in the context of Thailand.

In the early 1960s Thailand had a savings gap which was filled by foreign savings. Later in the decade increases in investment were financed largely with increases in domestic savings. Nevertheless, the savings gap was a binding constraint during the last twenty years, because domestic savings were insufficient to finance investment, despite their increase, and were supplemented by foreign funds (table 15.10). Investment expenditure depends then on the balance-of-payments position as well as the savings propensity. As a leading rice exporter to the world, the economy can rely on the earnings of this staple crop, which contributes about one-eighth to one-tenth of the total export revenue in any given year. Thus, the economy can save out of the export earnings. This type of saving has been advanced by Maizels (1968) as a contributor to the economic growth of Malaysia. Therefore, if export earnings are up, the investment program can be funded from that source. In a recent work by Ajanant, Chunanuntathum, and Meenaphant (1984) it was found from an analysis of domestic resource costs that export sectors can earn the foreign exchange necessary for such an investment program. Without the exports the economy cannot mobilize the investment funds, and it cannot grow as rapidly as it has been. By the same token, it can be equally stated that a shortfall of export earnings represents a major setback to economic growth. The recent shortfall of export earnings in 1983 has presented the government with economic problems.

While the above argues for the export-led growth in a static fashion, akin to the Harrod-Domar growth theorem, the exports of the country can also be viewed as the direct result of the growth process. this aspect is interesting since it posits that the growth of GDP generates exports. One way to examine this process is through intersectoral investigation. When the manufacturing sector was promoted by many

Table 15.10   Investment and Saving Ratios

Year	I/Y	S_d/Y	S_f/Y
1960	0.1569	0.1153	0.0413
1965	0.2018	0.1980	0.0037
1970	0.2462	0.2101	0.0361
1975	0.2555	0.2136	0.0413
1980	0.2705	0.2057	0.0647

Source: National Income Accounts.

Note: I = gross domestic investment (1972 prices). Y = GDP (1972 prices). S_d = gross domestic saving (1972 prices). S_f = gross foreign saving (1972 prices).

incentives and privileges in the early 1960s, the output of industry was far below its potential. This implies an economic loss to society apart from the usual deadweight loss. The strength of the whole economy rested on the growth of the traditional sectors, agriculture and minerals. The products of the two traditional sectors not only generate export revenue earnings but are used in the processing industries. Thus, while the manufacturing sector was developing, the nourishment came from the other sectors. Finally, when the manufacturing sector became mature, it could export to the world market. The export possibilities of the manufacturing sector, given demand conditions, depended largely on the revenue generated by the two traditional sectors. This type of argument, however, cannot be generalized to cover every economy. Thailand was fortunate to have large resources to rely upon, and the primary exports were sufficiently diversified not to be trapped in the export instability problem (Roemer 1983).

15.6 Conclusion

From 1960 to 1975 Thailand pursued an import substitution policy. The shift toward export promotion was a long-felt need and materialized during the fourth plan (1976–80). Import substitution in retrospect is judged to have been a correct policy. Despite problems in the allocation of resources and income distribution, the growth of the economy has been rapid. The growth of the manufacturing sector depended on the two traditional sectors. Both traditional sectors—agriculture and minerals—had to create sufficient surpluses in terms of export revenues and raw materials to boost the industry through the fiscal linkage. The growth of the manufacturing sector relied upon several factors: the availability of low-wage labor, the abundance of resource-based inputs to be used in processing industries, the incentives given by the government, and the business acumen of the Chinese Thais during the early years of industrialization. Though the supply side is crucial, we have not overlooked the demand side. Both domestic and external demand stimulated the growth of the manufacturing sector. Even while the economy was undergoing the import substitution process, foreign demand was a major force leading to export promotion by the mid-1970s.

In the final analysis, Thailand can be an equally good example of both export-led growth and growth-led exports. At the macroeconomic level, the export-led notion explains how Thailand relies on export earnings to boost its growth. At the sectoral level, in a dynamic setting, it can be observed that growth of the traditional sectors facilitates the industrial development of the country.

References

Ajanant, J. 1984. Export promotion of processed food and textile products. UNIDO/UNDP/NESDB. March.

Ajanant, J., Supote Chunanuntathum, and Sorrayuth Meenaphant. 1984. Trade and industrialization in Thailand, phase I. International Development Research Centre, Ottawa, Canada. April.

Food and Agriculture Organization. 1984. *Yearbook of forest products*. Rome: FAO.

Maizels, A. 1968. *Exports and economic growth of developing countries*. Cambridge: Cambridge University Press.

Roemer, Michael. 1983. Primary exporting countries: Problems of poverty and plenty. Paper presented at the Arne Ryde Symposium on the Primary Sector in Economic Development, University of Lund, Sweden, August.

World Bank. 1982. *Thailand industrial and sector background report*. Washington, D.C.

16 Manufactured Exports and Industrialization: Trade Patterns and Trends of the Philippines

Florian A. Alburo

16.1 Introduction

This paper examines (1) the recent Philippine experience in trade and industrial development, including changes and adjustments arising from economic disturbances, and (2) the prospects for future economic growth in terms of present discernible trends. First, I present contextual scenarios through which industrial development may be interpreted. The second section reviews the historical background of trade and industrialization. In the third section, industrial growth in the seventies will be further expounded upon, especially the role of manufactured exports in the process. A fourth section develops the notion of structural change and its evidence. The prospects of the changes in the pattern of trade and industrialization, especially in terms of long-term sustainability, are considered in the fifth section.

Industrial growth may be stimulated in large part by the vigor of the internal markets, whose buoyancy in turn springs from productivity increases. Excess labor from agriculture, foreign exchange earnings from traditional export markets, and relatively low internal terms of trade allow the industrial sector to proceed unhampered in its development, acquiring economies and efficiencies in response to eventual international competition. Trade in this picture takes on a more passive

Florian A. Alburo is associate professor of economics, University of the Philippines, Diliman, Quezon City, Philippines.

This paper was written while visiting with the Overseas Development Council, Washington, D.C., in 1982–83 as an Asian Visiting Scholar under a Henry A. Luce Foundation Fellowship. Revisions were made at the Institute of Southeast Asian Studies, Singapore, while on a research fellowship. Thanks are due to these institutions for support in the preparation and revision of this paper as well as to Professor Romeo M. Bautista for comments on an earlier draft.

485

role, feeding the industrial process, which in turn is determined by industry-agriculture interactions. During the early stages of this development scenario one outcome is the emergence of a system protecting industrial formation. Later, sufficient markets must evolve within the economy to prop up industries and propel them toward greater economies.

In this context, trade is essentially supportive of the industrialization process and not a direct stimulant of it. Via productivity improvements in agriculture and export products (in part from technological breakthroughs) trade provides the exchange resources for pursuing industrial growth.

This scenario, crudely summarized here, is not of course unfamiliar to students of development. It is often associated with the doctrines espoused by Prebisch (1959) and Nurkse (1953).[1]

In contrast to this scenario is an industrial growth that is "outward-looking" or "export-led," and is exemplified by experiences in a number of developing countries but most prominently in East Asian countries. In this context, trade is a determinant of the industrialization process. The growth and strength of industry are paced by the degree to which international trading of industrial products takes place in open systems. The country's resource endowments dictate the directions of comparative advantage and thus industrial change itself. Resource allocation in industry and associated factor rewards respond to (in a small-country assumption) trade signals. Indeed, trade takes an active role.

Within the tradition of international trade theory, this scenario does not necessarily imply the delegation of developing countries to the status of primary producers and exporters. Dynamic comparative advantages, the mobility of resources, and improvements in technology contribute to the development of an industrial base.

The extent to which developing countries take either route in their development processes is perhaps constrained by their initial resource endowments. Quite naturally small city-states are quicker to look toward external trade to fuel growth than large economies which have a bigger domestic base to exhaust.

There is no direct evidence that these scenarios are completely adequate for describing the basis for industrialization. Most of the assertions are in fact ad hoc rationalizations for a variety of policy initiatives rather than descriptions arising out of a systematic, neat schema for industrial drive. Baldwin (1975, 67) indirectly alludes to how the "inward-looking" path influences policy in the Philippines.

16.2 Philippine Industrialization: A Historical Review

There is an array of studies on Philippine industrial development, most treating the subject with sufficient depth and rigor. A postwar analysis of trade and industry was undertaken by Power and Sicat (1971). Industry analyses were performed by Sicat (1968) and Williamson and Sicat (1968) that were mainly concerned with tracing sources of growth. Baldwin (1975) investigated industrial development within a framework of trade regimes characterized by control and liberalization of international transactions. The World Bank (1976, 1980) and the International Labor Office (1974) have addressed industrial perspectives in a policy context. Bautista et al. (1979) have documented the process of industrial promotion policies in the Philippines.

All these studies contain data and analytical tracks that are exhaustive and sufficiently disaggregated to allow specific explanations of industrial growth and specific descriptions of policy implications. Although the studies are somewhat dated in the sense of the period covered, it is noteworthy that an analytical series can be constructed with respect to industrialization in the postwar era. For example, the Power and Sicat volume explores the process during the sixties. Baldwin discusses the period up to 1971. Bautista et al. document the experiences of the midseventies.

16.2.1 Postwar Protection and Development

Philippine industrialization is usually described as a cumulative record of controls, protection, exchange overvaluation, and distorted domestic policies. In the immediate postwar period a combination of an early boom, institutional constraints, subsequent trade deficits, trade controls, and biased monetary and fiscal policies created the setting for a protective system conducive to consumer goods industries and finishing stages of production and biased against export industries. One outcome was a continuing drain on exchange resources and reserves and a penalty on export development.

Because of a limited domestic market, the need to arrive at more realistic exchange regimes, and the desire for correcting export biases, the country began to plan a gradual process of decontrol in the late fifties and implemented a four-phase program in April 1960. The features included (*a*) an increasing proportion of exports to be exchanged at market rates (beginning with one-quarter of export earnings of traditional exports and ending with 100% in 1962), (*b*) free mobility of capital, and (*c*) a "free market" determination of exchange rates.

The gradual dismantling of controls such as import licenses, deposit margins, and import bans did not happen without tradeoff. With an industrial base fashioned by the trade protection of the fifties, it was expected that industries would demand support to continue their growth. Thus while decontrol was taking place and exchange rates approaching market signals (and thus benefiting exporters), the country's tariff structure retained the essential pattern of protection encouraged in the immediate postwar era.[2] Monetary policies were likewise geared to the promotion of new and necessary industries and did not differ significantly from those used during the control period.[3] Despite the appearance of removing exchange and physical controls to trade, decontrol was thus more nominal than real. The protective structure remained the same even after complete decontrol in 1965.

The seventies is thought to be the time when a drift, if not a real shift, is visible in the industrial path of the Philippines.[4] Indeed, the hypothesis is advanced that during this period the country took its first steps away from an inward-looking drive to an outward-looking drive in terms of (a) the absolute values and shares of manufactured exports in aggregate trade, (b) the expansion of industries more consistent with the country's resource endowments, (c) the absorption of more employment in industry than ever before, and (d) the broad incidence of benefits through factors shares.

16.2.2   Some Causes and Consequences

Table 16.1 shows the average yearly growth rates of the Philippine GNP and selected sectors from 1946 to 1980, divided into quinquenniums (except the first period), and from 1980 to 1982, on a more preliminary basis. By most accounts, the performance of the economy during the immediate postwar reconstruction was an aberration, a "catching up" of lost prewar capacity. What would be more useful to look at is the three-decade period 1950–80. While it is interesting to include consideration of the more recent years, it would seem that the prolonged recession in the West probably had its full effect after 1980 and would tend to distort the picture. Where data for 1981 and 1982 are available, they are included in the appropriate tables.

The controls of the fifties created an economic environment favorable to full-scale import substitution as consumer industries profited from liberal inflows of capital goods imports and the high domestic price of finished products engendered by the system. Thus the types of manufacturing industries began to proliferate in the fifties, from a concentration on food, beverages, and tobacco in 1948 to such industries as textiles, paper and paper products, chemical and chemical products, nonmetallic mineral products, and machinery. (See table 16.2 for the distribution of value added in manufacturing.)

The balance-of-payments problems that plagued the country toward the end of the sixties necessitated another round of adjustment, culminating in the floating of the exchange rate and currency depreciation of nearly 50% in 1970. Bautista (1980) has adequately analyzed the consequences of the floating exchange rates in terms of balance of payments and its major components, domestic economic activities and trade flows and directions.[5]

Table 16.1   **Average Annual Growth Rates of GNP and Net Domestic Product of Selected Sectors** (in percentages at constant 1972 prices)

	1946–50[a]	1950–55	1955–50	1960–65	1965–70	1970–75	1975–80[b]	1980–82[b]
Agriculture	12.4	7.0	2.9	4.8	3.5	3.8	5.4	3.6
Manufacturing	50.5	12.1	7.7	4.5	6.1	6.0	7.0	2.9
Services	16.9	9.0	5.0	4.5	4.8	4.8	5.3	3.0
GNP	19.9	7.7	4.9	5.6	4.8	6.5	6.2	3.2

Sources: Baldwin 1975, 3, for 1946–50; National Economic and Development Authority, *1983 Philippine Statistical Yearbook.*

[a]Rates at 1955 prices.

[b]Gross value added except GNP.

Table 16.2   Distribution of Value Added by Industry (percentages)

Industry	1948	1956	1960	1965	1970	1975	1980	1982
Food, Beverages, Tobacco	60.6	43.8	41.2	40.1	41.8	40.0	43.9	44.6
Textiles	2.6	3.7	4.6	4.7	5.9	5.6	4.5	4.3
Footwear, wearing apparel	6.6	5.1	3.0	7.0	3.8	3.6	4.4	5.0
Wood and cork products	9.7	5.0	4.0	4.6	4.2	2.8	2.9	2.9
Furniture and fixtures	1.8	1.3	0.9	1.4	0.7	0.4	0.6	0.6
Paper, paper products	0.0	1.7	2.3	2.1	2.9	2.9	0.8	0.7
Publishing, printing	3.7	3.1	3.2	4.1	2.2	2.7	1.4	1.5
Leather, leather products	0.0	0.2	0.3	0.3	0.2	0.2	0.3	0.3
Rubber products	0.6	0.9	3.2	2.9	1.4	1.6	1.3	1.3
Chemicals, chem. products	2.9	9.9	10.0	9.1	7.9	13.1	16.1	14.4
Nonmetallic mineral prod.	2.1	4.7	3.7	4.4	4.2	3.6	2.5	2.3
Basic metals, metal products	1.9	4.7	8.0	8.5	7.4	6.0	8.2	8.0
Machinery	0.5	2.1	4.2	4.8	4.5	3.8	8.1	9.2
Transport equip.	1.0	2.2	2.2	2.8	4.2	5.1	3.8	3.6
Misc. manufactures	5.7	11.2	8.2	5.2	8.7	8.7	1.1	1.3
Total	100	100	100	100	100	100	100	100

Sources: Bautista et al. 1979 for 1948–65; National Economic Development Authority, *1983 Philippine Statistical Yearbook.*

Overall, there seems to be a convincing argument that industrialization in the Philippines was fashioned in the fifties and sixties to be inward looking, an import substitution strategy. The system of protection and tariff structure created the pattern of manufacturing industries. There is further evidence that even, in 1974, the structure had perhaps remained the same (Tan 1979).

What this means in terms of results is widely known and appreciated. Industries are invariably capital using and labor saving. Capital-labor ratio indices increased over 20% in the sixties. The share of labor in manufacturing to total employment increased by only 4.4% over much of the same period (with the share virtually remaining constant at 12%).

Repercussions from the trade problems were not conducive for industrial growth either. Export prices (in U.S. dollar values) were fairly stable in the sixties and erratic in the seventies, while import prices (in U.S. dollar values) continued their upward climb throughout the two decades (see table 16.3). Consequently the terms of trade deteriorated. This had profound effects on overall growth but more so on the industrial sector in the sense of marginal ability to generate foreign exchange and broadening of internal markets. Moreover, consumer price indices exhibited wild fluctuations. The recent 1981 and 1982 data show declines in export prices similar to the midseventies, which, with a sharp increase in input prices in 1980 and 1981, reflect continued terms of trade deterioration. While the increase in consumer price index was less in 1982, the most recent (1983) economic crisis will undoubtedly lead to an escalated index.

Manufacturing development therefore suffered from the type of process that the Philippines experienced in the sixties for at least three

Table 16.3   **Percentage Change in Philippine Export, Import, and Consumer Price Indices**

	Export[a]	Import[a]	Consumer
1960	−1.46	2.22	4.66
1961	−8.00	1.45	1.27
1962	−1.07	1.85	5.65
1963	5.31	6.72	5.74
1964	−0.81	0.79	8.24
1965	1.73	1.69	2.42
1966	0.90	1.66	5.40
1967	1.78	2.27	6.41
1968	6.23	9.11	2.41
1969	0.37	1.81	1.91
1970	1.46	3.66	14.00
1971	−4.95	2.14	15.06
1972	−5.30	4.71	10.01
1973	45.90	28.80	14.00
1974	66.07	64.29	33.51
1975	−20.43	3.78	8.15
1976	−12.45	−1.09	6.20
1977	1.48	11.05	7.90
1978	13.08	1.95	7.60
1979	21.94	9.89	18.80
1980	4.15	32.76	17.83
1981	−2.19	11.15	n.a.
1982	−16.04	−9.78[b]	10.25

Sources: Bautista 1980 for 1960–76; Central Bank of the Philippines, *Statistical Bulletin 1981* (1981); National Economic and Development Authority, *1983 Philippine Statistical Yearbook.*

[a]Based on U.S. dollar values.

[b]Average of first three quarters 1982.

reasons. First, the manufacturing sector was insulated from international competitiveness by protection and could not profit from the exuberance of export prices on the one hand nor avoid the sting of rising import prices (which directly affected it via intensity of input use) on the other. Second, the transmission of import prices into the movements of the consumer prices meant real incomes were deteriorating. In fact real wages of unskilled labor in industrial establishments in metropolitan Manila fell by 13.8% between 1959 and 1964 (though recovering by 13.2% between 1964 and 1970) and by 53.7% between 1970 and 1974. Finally, the broad-based potential of import substitution hinged on the spread of internal markets. On the basis of income distribution, it appears that this potential was not realized in the sixties and early seventies.

16.2.3   From Inward- to Outward-Looking Industrialization

Table 16.4 presents the changing composition of Philippine exports in the two decades 1960–80. A striking change is noticeable between 1970 and 1980, when nontraditional manufactured exports increased in share from 8.3% to 36.4% of the total.[6] The marked distributional change reflects a more outward-looking path of industrial development.

Even though traditional exports are still a dominant share, the fact that nontraditional manufactures imply processing would seem to augur well for industrial development. An examination of table 16.5, which breaks down nontraditional manufactured exports into specific commodities, indicates that for many products the seventies (especially after 1975) was the time for breaking out into world markets. The trend remained strong in the face of serious disturbances occasioned by the oil shocks of 1973 and 1979, the recessions in the major trading partners, and the competition from other newly industrializing countries.

Whether or not the redirection is significant will in part be determined by the net effect of positive and negative influences. The former includes active promotion policies that favor export growth, while the latter encompasses the constraints imposed by past developments.

Table 16.4   **Philippine Exports** (percentage share)

Sector	1960	1970	1980
Traditional primary	49.3	40.0	7.8
Traditional manufactured	48.4	49.8	47.2
Nontraditional primary	—	1.1	8.0
Nontraditional manufactured	1.2	8.3	36.4
Reexports	1.1	0.8	0.6
Total	100.0	100.0	100.0

Source: National Census and Statistics Office, *Foreign Trade Statistics,* various years.

Table 16.5   Philippine Exports of Nontraditional Manufactures (in millions of U.S. dollars)

	1970	1971	1972	1973	1974	1975	1976	1977	1978	1979	1980	1981	1982
Electrical & electronic equip. & components	—	0.3	0.4	11.3	27.1	47.3	85.0	124.3	253.4	412.5	671.0	837.7	1,000.1
Garments	36.2	35.7	38.8	58.0	94.0	107.0	184.7	249.7	326.3	404.2	500.0	616.5	539.3
Handicrafts	6.5	9.2	12.9	27.4	46.0	78.2	94.9	84.1	100.1	133.6	154.3	133.7	121.6
Chemicals	5.4	7.0	6.3	10.6	15.9	22.1	27.0	54.1	59.9	112.8	94.9	106.7	96.8
Food products & beverages	8.2	9.0	11.2	15.0	17.5	14.7	28.7	43.7	46.8	57.0	170.4	309.9	214.5
Furniture & parts	1.1	1.2	1.5	3.3	6.1	5.2	9.8	21.7	26.6	54.9	77.2	87.4	71.6
Footwear	1.1	0.9	1.2	2.1	3.7	3.0	5.0	10.2	32.2	50.3	67.1	73.1	62.0
Machinery & trans. equip.	1.1	2.1	2.1	3.4	5.5	9.5	16.1	26.1	36.9	47.3	46.5	51.3	50.6
Textile yarn, fabrics & related prod.	2.8	5.3	3.5	17.3	7.2	8.7	15.1	12.4	23.6	31.4	49.3	43.3	38.9
Builders' woodwork & other wood manuf. excl. plywood, veneer & lumber	4.0	5.7	7.7	17.2	24.8	16.9	15.5	13.8	20.7	31.4	23.8	38.8	30.9
Nonmetallic mineral manuf., particularly cement	3.0	11.0	10.0	25.2	36.4	32.2	28.1	38.6	42.2	30.3	58.9	47.3	39.5
Cordage, cable, ropes & twines	1.9	2.1	3.1	4.6	9.7	7.6	10.3	12.4	12.5	16.8	18.5	20.5	55.8
Other	24.4	20.2	19.9	36.8	43.3	30.1	53.5	78.2	95.0	137.1	175.00	205.5	139.1
Total exp. of nontrad. manuf.	96.7	109.7	118.6	232.2	337.2	382.5	573.7	769.3	1,076.2	1,519.6	2,106.9	2,571.7	2,460.7
Total exports	1,142	1,136	1,106	1,837	2,752	2,294	2,574	3,151	3,425	4,601	5,788	5,722	5,020

Source: National Economic and Development Authority, *1983 Philippine Statistical Yearbook.*

Some factors prevent a detailed technical assessment of the redirection hypothesis. One is lack of recent transactions data for a comprehensive input-output analysis. The 1974 input-output data would obviously be inadequate to capture any profound changes associated with structural adjustments after the 1974 oil crisis.[7] Another is paucity of information on technical characteristics of firms in the manufactured exports industries. The classification of table 16.5 is fairly recent. Finally, a number of policy changes (e.g., tariff reforms) reinforcing the outward-looking trend were implemented only recently. Nevertheless, the following sections attempt to pursue the argument.

16.3   Trade and Industrial Growth in the Seventies

Manufacturing increased its share of gross domestic product from 23.2% in 1970 to 25.3% in 1980. The increase in share of 2.1% is matched only by the 3.9% increase in the share of construction in GDP over the same period, whereas most of the other sectors show declining shares. But even more important was the increase in the share of manufactures in total exports between 1970 and 1980.

Manufacturing is often characterized as dualistic. Large factories—fairly productive, capital-intensive, and possessing up-to-date technologies—coexist with small, household-type, unorganized production units. Each subsector provides critical components of the aggregate manufacturing picture. The World Bank (1980), for example, estimated that the small- and medium-sized firms employ almost 80% of labor but provide only 25% of value added. For a time, large-scale establishments were relied upon to create additional output, and the unorganized sector was depended upon to absorb additional employment.

It seems, however, that a reverse pattern has emerged in the seventies. Large establishments (with more than twenty workers) employed 24.5% of labor in manufacturing in 1971. The proportion increased to 32% in 1976, the latest year for which data are consistent. In terms of value added, the same group accounted for 94.5% in 1971 but only about 56% in 1976.

More interesting perhaps than these static figures are the rates of growth of employment and value added in the sector during the decade. They reveal changes that help explain the overall performance of manufacturing. Table 16.6 shows the rates of growth for both employment and value added for all of manufacturing, establishments with 20 or more workers, and those with less. The last has been calculated as a residual and must be viewed with the usual caution when dealing with indirect figures.

The annual average growth rate of manufacturing employment was 3.9% in 1968–76, falling to 3.1% during 1971–76 after peaking at 5.2%

Table 16.6   **Manufacturing Value Added and Employment Annual Average Growth Rates** (percentages)

Employment	1968–76	1968–71	1971–76
Total	3.9	5.2	3.1
Establishments with more than twenty workers	6.2	2.1	8.7
Establishments with less than twenty workers	3.0	6.3	1.0
Value added (*current prices*)			
Total	n.a.	n.a.	24.0
Establishments with more than twenty workers	n.a.	n.a.	12.0
Establishments with less than twenty workers	n.a.	n.a.	17.5[a]

Sources: National Census and Statistics Office, *Annual Survey of Establishments,* various years; National Economic and Development Authority, *1983 Philippine Statistical Yearbook.*

Notes: Labor force data are based on October 1968, November 1971, and August 1976 surveys. n.a. = not available.

[a] 1971–74.

in 1968–71. When broken down into the two subsectors, it is clear that large establishments experienced a high employment growth rate compared with the unorganized sector (8.7% versus 1.0% in 1971–76). Because of the absolute weight of the latter sector, however, the average growth rate was in fact lower. In terms of value added, establishments with less than twenty workers had a slightly higher growth rate than large-scale firms.

Of course, these differences are not revealed when looking at the aggregate behavior of manufacturing in the seventies. The reduction in labor absorption between the late sixties and the middle seventies masks the vigor of employment growth among large establishments and the stagnation of the small firms.

This reversal in the pattern of employment and value added between the late sixties and the seventies implies a decline in labor productivity during the period at least for the organized factory level sector. The data come from surveys covering large establishments, i.e., employing twenty or more workers.

Between 1960 and 1970, value added per employee grew at an annual average rate of 3.4% in real terms.[8] From 1970 to 1976 the rate declined to 1.1% per year. There was a further decline by 1977 in absolute terms. One notes sharp declines especially in 1977 for all industries, but with particular severity in textiles, leather products, rubber, chemicals, non-metallic mineral manufacturers, basic metals, electrical machinery, and transport equipment.

Falling value added per worker is in part associated with a falling capital-worker ratio, and both may reflect a transitional change in technology. The amount of new investment per worker fell between 1970 and 1977, mirroring the general reduction in capital in newly registered business organizations in 1970–80 and a sustained reduction in paid-in capital per organization—despite a threefold increase in the number of new organizations between the sixties (an increase of 4.6% per year) and the seventies (an increase of 14.1% per year).[9] It is difficult to examine this more thoroughly because of data constraints.

Nevertheless, a number of factors suggest the fluid state of manufacturing development in the seventies, a period of significant adjustments. First, the evidence seems to point to the growing importance of the formal sector in terms of employment generation and the growing importance (though less pronounced) of the informal, or household, sector in terms of value added. By all indications a diffusion process may have taken place toward medium-scale industries more consistent with relevant factor proportions. Second, the industrial structure has broadened, reflected in the changes in the distribution of value added during the decade. Indeed, combined with growth of the industries producing manufactured exports, industrial growth appears also to have deepened. Third, capital-labor ratios, both average and incremental, declined across the entire manufacturing sector. This is not surprising given the ability of the industrial structure to respond to differential factor pricing. What is worth noting is that during the decade, the floating of the peso, the flexible policies that did not liberally shelter industry, and the incentives promoting manufactured exports allowed a smoother industrial adjustment.

How much of the industrial growth and change in the seventies was triggered by manufactured exports or vice versa is hard to untangle. Where the growth of manufactured exports is exogenous, it obviously induced industrial responses that partly shaped the structure in the seventies. Where the macroeconomic and trade policies appropriately accommodated this growth they also partly shaped the structure. These policies, however, simply corrected the distortions of the earlier inward-looking decade. In short, trade has had a significant role in shaping the industrial patterns of the seventies.

16.4 Structural Change: Search for Evidence

A loose interpretation of structural change is followed here. More specifically, the notion is investigated in terms of output and input. On the output side, patterns of manufactured exports are analyzed relative to other sectors or to aggregate trade. On the input side, various technical characteristics such as factor proportions, productivity, value added are considered as clues to understanding changes. Table 16.7 recasts table 16.5 in constant terms.[10]

Although exports were beginning to pick up in the early seventies, it was not until after 1974 that more than one-half of the thirteen sectors

Table 16.7   Philippine Exports of Nontraditional Manufactures (in millions of U.S. dollars)

	1970	1971	1972	1973	1974	1975	1976	1977	1978	1979	1980	1981	1982
Electrical & electronic equip. & components	—	0.3	0.4	7.7	11.2	24.5	50.4	72.6	130.8	174.6	272.8	348.2	495.1
Garments	32.6	33.8	38.8	39.7	38.8	55.5	109.4	145.8	168.5	171.1	203.2	256.2	267.0
Handicrafts	5.9	8.7	12.9	18.8	19.0	40.6	56.2	49.1	51.7	56.6	62.7	55.6	60.2
Chemicals	4.9	6.6	6.3	7.3	6.6	11.5	16.0	31.6	30.9	47.8	38.6	44.3	47.9
Food products & beverages	7.4	8.5	11.2	10.3	7.2	7.6	17.0	25.5	24.2	24.1	69.3	128.8	106.2
Furniture & parts	1.0	1.1	1.5	2.3	2.5	2.7	5.8	12.7	13.7	23.2	31.4	36.3	35.4
Footwear	1.0	0.8	1.2	1.4	1.5	1.6	3.0	5.9	16.6	21.3	27.3	30.4	30.7
Machinery & trans. equip.	0.9	2.0	2.1	2.3	2.3	4.9	9.5	15.2	19.0	20.0	18.9	21.3	25.0
Textile yarn, fabrics & related prod.	2.5	5.0	3.5	11.9	3.0	4.5	9.0	7.2	12.2	13.3	20.0	18.0	19.2
Builders' woodwork & other wood manuf. excl. plywood, veneer & lumber	3.6	5.4	7.7	11.8	10.2	8.8	9.2	8.1	10.7	13.3	9.7	16.1	15.3
Nonmetallic mineral manuf., particularly cement	2.7	10.4	10.0	17.3	15.0	16.7	16.6	22.5	21.8	12.8	23.9	19.6	19.5
Cordage, cable, ropes & twines	1.7	2.0	3.1	3.1	4.0	3.9	6.2	7.2	6.4	7.1	7.5	8.5	27.6
Other	22.8	19.1	19.9	25.2	17.9	15.6	31.7	45.7	49.0	58.0	71.1	85.4	68.9
Total exp. of nontrad. manuf.	85.1	101.8	115.9	155.4	135.2	194.1	340.0	449.1	555.5	643.2	856.4	1,068.9	1,218.2
Total exports	1,028.0	1,075.8	1,106.0	1,259.0	1,135.8	1,189.8	1,524.9	1,839.5	1,768.2	1,948.0	2,353.0	2,378.0	2,485.0

Source: National Economic and Development Authority, *1983 Philippine Statistical Yearbook.*

covered in table 16.7 experienced peak growth rates. Moreover, furniture and footwear began to be exported at significantly greater rates. One can detect serious concentration on certain commodities from 1971 to 1980. In 1971 three product groups (garments, nonmetallic mineral manufactures, handicrafts) constituted half of the earnings, while in 1975 and 1980 half of export earnings were from only two groups (garments and handicrafts in 1975 and electrical equipment and garments in 1980). Despite the strong emergence of electronic equipment exports in 1974 and 1975, it was in 1979 and 1980 that their dominance was felt. In 1980 electronic equipment and garments exports composed 20.2% of total exports.

The growing share of these exports in total trade in a sense relieves the burden placed on the country's principal exports. Yet it can be seen that, even for the nontraditional manufactured exports, a similar excessive reliance is placed on only two or three commodity groups.

It has been estimated from the 1974 input-output tables that 14.2% of manufacturing output is exported, including traditional manufactures (World Bank 1980). Another way to measure the importance of manufactured exports is to examine the fraction of these exports to the total manufacturing value added and trace its pattern over time. The Central Bank of the Philippines regularly reports yearly exports of manufactured products classified chiefly by materials. By using this data source it is possible to trace manufactured exports over a longer time horizon than that in tables 16.5 and 16.7. In the aggregate these two sources are not directly comparable. In 1960 the proportion of these exports to the value added in the manufacturing sector of 1.5%, growing to 4.5% in 1965 and with a slight rise to 4.7% in 1970. By 1975 the proportion increased to 8.0% and by 1980 to about 13%. The corresponding proportion of manufactures to total exports is 8.3% in 1970, 16.3% in 1975, and 36.4% in 1980 (49% in 1982). Thus the proportion of manufactures to total exports was growing faster than the proportion of manufacturing output being exported. These figures seem to suggest that changes in the structure of the manufacturing sector would be slower than changes in the structure of exports.

Table 16.8 illustrates the annual growth rates of exports for selected manufacturing sectors from 1960 to 1980. The annual growth rates are in general relatively high across most of these industries and over the twenty-year time period. This is not a surprising finding, however, given the fact that especially in the sixties manufactured exports were absolutely low. The low absolute base would therefore imply high growth rates. For example, in the early sixties footwear exports were less U.S. $100 thousand; exports of leather manufactures, paper and paper products, and nonmetallic mineral manufactures were minimal. What is significant in the table is the growth rate for some of the industries

Table 16.8   **Annual Growth Rates of Selected Manufactured Exports**
              (percentages)[a]

Industry	1960–65	1965–70	1970–75	1975–80
Food[b]	2.4	6.6	24.9	11.0
Textile yarn	7.6	2.3	32.3	27.7
Footwear	32.5	87.4	23.6	86.1
Clothing	58.9	−9.8	236.8	53.3
Wood and cork	23.2	23.2	7.1	25.6
Furniture and fixtures	2.8	28.8	29.4	71.7
Paper and paper products	67.0[c]	90.9	16.4	−1.1
Rubber products	53.9	19.2	33.3	−5.1
Chemicals[d]	−0.4	21.6	32.3	80.7
Nonmetallic mineral manufactures	14.9[e]	89.6	57.6	12.2
Metal products	82.3[f]	41.3	26.9	40.9
Machinery, except electrical	−2.7	88.2	30.5	38.2
Electrical machinery	—	201.5[g]	243.5	87.1
Transport equipment	74.1	30.7	86.3	68.7
Misc. manufactured goods				
Total manufactured articles	20.1	14.5	34.1	27.6

Source: Central Bank of the Philippines, *Statistical Bulletin* (1978, 1980).
[a]Export values in thousand U.S. dollars.
[b]Includes meat, dairy products, and food processing.
[c]1961–65.
[d]Includes crude chemicals, chemical products, and pharmaceuticals.
[e]1960–64.
[f]1962–65.
[g]1967–70.

producing nontraditional manufactured exports. Export growth accelerated in the seventies for such products as furniture, chemicals, electrical machinery, and transport equipment.

Structural change may also be examined using an approach taken by Lary (1968). Here industrial exports are classified according to factor proportions content and then traced in terms of changes over time. Products have either high or low capital intensities and high or low skill intensities as measures of labor content.[11]

Table 16.9 lists industries according to a four-way classification. This classification of the Philippine industrial exports is intuitively appealing—garments, furniture, and footwear products, for example, require low capital and low labor skills, whereas the electronics industry, while of low capital intensity, needs highly skilled labor. Nonmetallic mineral products use high capital inputs but not highly skilled labor when compared with chemicals.[12]

The record of nontraditional manufactured exports for the seventies reveals that about 71% have been products requiring low capital and

Table 16.9 **Classification of Manufactured Exports by Factor Intensity**

Low Skill Intensity	High Skill Intensity
Low Capital Intensity	
Garments Handicrafts Furniture Footwear Textile yarn Builders' woodwork Cordage	Electrical machinery and transport equipment
High Capital Intensity	
Nonmetallic mineral manufactures Food products	Chemicals

Source: Lary 1968.

Table 16.10 **Value and Distribution of Nontraditional Manufactured Exports** (in millions of 1972 U.S. dollars and percentages)

Factor Content	1971	1975	1980	1982
Low capital–low skill	56.8	117.6	361.8	455.4
	(67.4)	(74.3)	(80.6)	(78.1)
Low capital–high skill	2.0	4.9	18.9	25.0
	(2.4)	(3.1)	(3.7)	(4.3)
High capital–low skill	18.9	24.3	93.2	54.9
	(22.4)	(15.3)	(18.2)	(9.4)
High capital–high skill	6.6	11.5	38.6	47.9
	(7.8)	(7.3)	(7.5)	(8.2)

Source: Tables 16.7 and 16.9.
Note: Figures do not include nontraditional manufactured exports classified under Other in previous tables.

low skill, 3% requiring low capital but high skill content, 18% requiring high capital and low skill, and the rest requiring high capital and high skill. Note, however, that exports of electrical products in the seventies are not necessarily comparable to similar exports in the sixties in terms of skill content. (The figures in table 16.10 exclude the value of exports of electrical equipment and electronic components.)

Changes in the factor intensity of exports occurred during the seventies (see table 16.10). At the start of the decade products with low capital and labor intensities composed more than two-thirds of new exports, with the other significant share composed of those with high capital but low skill intensities. During the decade the share of low-capital exports increased from 69.8% to 84.3% (dropping slight!y in

1982). The share of products requiring high capital content decreased at the end of the decade (with the high-capital, low-skill products sharply decreasing and about a constant share maintained by high-capital, high-skill products). The data suggest that there has been a trend toward exporting goods from less capital-intensive and more labor-intensive (both skilled and unskilled) industries. Low-capital- and high-skill-intensive exports had the highest growth rates (especially between 1971 and 1975).

In summary, a search for structural changes associated with the recent growth of manufactured exports leads to several specific conclusions. First, data are available only for a relatively short period, and thus it is too early to determine whether the manufacturing sector has undergone a permanent adjustment (to new equilibria) in terms of output mix, factor proportions, productivity, and technology. The adjustments are too recent to allow a rigorous causal analysis of the surge of manufactured exports. On the other hand, the evidence explored here tends to suggest that the manufacturing sector experienced some structural change, though not highly visible, over the period of high growth of manufactured exports. It is perhaps necessary to measure the changes more precisely than has been done here.

Although the growth in the value of nontraditional manufactured exports during the decade is quite phenomenal, it is also true that is has been mostly concentrated among two or three product groups. Thus the influence on the manufacturing sector as a whole is probably shallow and not as widespread as it would be with a broader growth pattern.

Third, the movement of manufactured exports has been consistent with an outward-looking industrial path. For one, while the types of exports have a wide range of factor content, it is apparent that most are from industries with low capital intensities. For another, the growth rates of the various exports appear to indicate a trend toward less capital-intensive exports and more labor-intensive ones. And then, even in the manufacturing sector as a whole, this change is perceptible only beginning with the midseventies.

Finally, these are aspects of change emanating from the supply side. Demand factors, intraindustry and interindustry relations, and even institutional arrangements equally affect structure. Any assessment therefore of the prospects for sustained growth or continued structural change must take account of these larger perspectives.

16.5 Prospects

An appropriate assessment of prospects will have to consider such important factors as product diversification and market penetration, competition from other developing countries, and trade barriers as well as the factors reviewed in the previous section (factor responsiveness, efficiency, and capacity).

The share of developing-country imports in the apparent consumption of manufactured goods in industrial countries was barely 1% at the end of the sixties. In 1980 the share was 3.4%. What is more, the growth rate of the shares was 7.2% per year, ranging from 1.4% going into Belgium to 11% into Australia. Even more interesting than this implied dynamism is the fact that the growth in the shares of imports from industrial countries was 3.6% per year (Hughes and Krueger 1982).

Hughes and Krueger (1982) have argued that despite increases in the protective measures employed by the industrialized countries during the seventies, the developing countries performed respectably. The fall in the penetration rate in the latter half of the seventies reflects the deepening recession more than the effect of protection. This penetration success came about in part from product diversification and offshore production, aided by the apparent ineffectiveness of growing protectionism.

What is relevant to Philippine prospects are (a) the volume of the industrialized countries' imports in comparison with the degree of Philippine trade intensity, (b) the direction of diversification, (c) the relative experiences of other (especially the Association of South East Asian Nations [ASEAN]) developing-country manufactured exports, and (d) the scale of expected protection in these markets.

Traditional exports declined in importance between 1970 and 1980. In addition, trade with the United States and Japan (which imported 81.1% of Philippine exports) significantly declined (to 53.7%). Commensurately, trade with the European Community, Australia and New Zealand, and the rest of Asia accelerated, taking up most of the slack left by the United States and Japan. In sum, aside from the continued strength of trade with traditional sources, the Philippines gained firmer ground in those countries with high growth in the shares of manufactured imports from developing countries.

With the exception of basic metals, nonmetallic mineral products, and paper, the ASEAN group of countries had the highest growth rates of manufactured exports to industrial countries (see Table 16.11). One must, of course, single out Singapore as primarily the source of such rates, with some help from Malaysia in a number of industries. Yet the Philippines does fare equally well in a number of the high-import-growth industries, e.g., floor coverings, tapestries, footwear.

What does this mean in terms of the prospects for exports of nontraditional manufactures? Much depends on the strength of the economic recovery in the industrial countries and the degree of protec-

Table 16.11   Manufactured Exports of Developing Countries to Industrial Countries by Origin and Product Groups

ISIC	All Developing Countries (billions of U.S. $)	Southern Europe	Far East[a]	Latin America	Other Developing Countries	(ASEAN)[a]
31 Food, beverages, and tobacco						
1970	7.5	9.5	2.7	50.0	37.8	(8.0)
1980	27.6	8.4	4.4	49.1	38.1	(12.1)
Growth rate: 1970–80	15.2	11.7	19.3	±5.1	15.9	(20.1)
32 Textiles, wearing apparel, and leather industries						
1970	3.4	19.7	41.8	7.7	30.7	(2.5)
1980	31.4	18.6	44.5	9.0	27.9	(5.4)
Growth rate: 1970–80	24.5	22.9	25.6	27.4	23.0	(36.3)
33 Manufacture of wood and wood products, including furniture						
1970	0.8	20.3	29.9	13.7	36.2	(22.5)
1980	5.6	20.0	31.2	10.0	38.8	(31.3)
Growth rate: 1970–80	21.1	20.1	22.4	16.2	22.1	(25.4)
34 Manufacture of paper and paper products: printing and publishing						
1970	0.2	57.9	14.2	10.7	17.2	(2.9)
1980	1.6	39.1	21.0	32.0	7.8	(2.8)
Growth rate: 1970–80	26.4	21.7	32.6	39.7	16.0	(23.7)
35 Manufacture of chemicals and chemical, petroleum, coal, rubber, and plastic products						
1970	3.6	10.4	10.9	54.4	24.2	(4.9)
1980	37.5	9.5	13.3	37.7	40.0	(10.4)
Growth rate: 1970–80	25.8	23.7	29.9	21.5	31.4	(33.9)

(continued)

Percentage Share of Exports from:

Table 16.11 (continued)

ISIC	All Developing Countries (billions of U.S. $)	Percentage Share of Exports from:				
		Southern Europe	Far East[a]	Latin America	Other Developing Countries	(ASEAN)[a]
36 Manufacture of nonmetallic mineral products, except products of petroleum and coal						
1970	0.1	50.2	17.0	27.5	5.3	(1.0)
1980	1.4	39.4	36.4	13.5	10.6	(2.3)
Growth rate: 1970–80	27.9	23.8	40.2	20.2	48.0	(41.7)
37 Basic metal industries						
1970	4.0	7.3	0.7	30.9	61.1	(7.4)
1980	15.1	16.2	8.2	32.9	42.7	(13.2)
Growth rate: 1970–80	14.7	22.7	41.5	15.4	10.7	(22.0)
38 Manufacture of fabricated metal products, machinery, and equipment						
1970	1.6	25.8	35.5	16.5	22.2	(4.1)
1980	28.5	22.9	43.7	14.9	18.5	(16.8)
Growth rate: 1970–80	32.8	28.9	34.6	31.0	37.2	(48.5)
39 Miscellaneous manufacturing industries						
1970	0.5	4.5	85.2	3.3	6.9	(8.1)
1980	3.1	4.7	79.7	4.5	11.1	(5.6)
Growth rate: 1970–80	22.8	21.6	22.1	25.2	28.5	(32.2)
3 All manufactured products						
1970	21.7	13.1	15.5	35.3	36.1	(6.6)
1980	151.9	15.2	25.7	27.1	32.0	(11.7)
Growth rate: 1970–80	21.8	22.1	27.9	18.9	20.5	(28.7)

Source: Hughes and Krueger 1982, 26.

[a]The category Far East includes Korea, Taiwan, Hong Kong, and Singapore, and the category (ASEAN) includes Indonesia, Malaysia, Philippines, Thailand, and Singapore. Singapore is thus included in both groups. The other ASEAN countries are also included in Other Developing Countries. The ASEAN group is duplicative.

tionism imposed. It may be true that the protective measures undertaken so far have not had a perceptible effect on export performance. Yet the time of approaching limits on exports may not be far away, especially with a drag in growth and reluctance to open up markets. On the other hand, there is a danger that simultaneous export expansion may drive penetration ratios to some limit prompting the erection of strong barriers (Cline 1982).

Also, while it may be expected that more restraints will be asked of countries for which penetration ratios are already high, it is likely that opportunities for increasing the shares of the Philippines will materialize. Thus while the overall import limits are low, the distribution occasioned by selective protectionism will allow expansion of Philippine nontraditional exports.[13]

In terms of the supply potential of the manufacturing sector, the previous section examined a number of parameters associated with changes in manufacturing output in general and manufactured exports in particular. In the final analysis the ultimate and critical question with respect to the supply side is whether the scale and composition of incremental output are consistent with the country's factor endowments. It is not so much whether manufactures are absorbed in domestic or international markets as whether policies create perverse movements one way or the other.

The partial and aggregate evidence seems to support the hypothesis that (a) the recent surge of nontraditional manufactured exports is along the lines of the country's comparative advantage, (b) the changes in product composition during the seventies favor the relatively greater use of the country's abundant resources, (c) factor proportions used in the manufacturing sector have declined in capital intensities, and (d) emerging policies and programs have recognized past distortions and consequently either compensated for them or explicitly favored labor-using incentives.

These trends and developments must be verified by firmer data than those presented here. In particular, input-output analysis is necessary to measure protection of industries, factor proportions, export intensity, and other behavior in order to substantiate the notion of sustained structural change and adjustment.[14]

On balance, however, the prospects for active participation in the growing international trade of industrial products appear encouraging. In the first place, opportunities for increasing market penetration in developed countries are available to the Philippines, given its relatively low share among developing nations. With continued diversification of trading partners (especially those countries where penetration growth rates have been high), the opportunities are even greater. In the second place, even in the face of rising protectionism the likely effect on the country's exports will probably be less than on those that have gained substantial shares of markets. And with the preferences for bilateral trade negotiations, there would seem to be greater scope for marginal access.[15] In the third place, economic growth has been consistent with indigenous resource proportions. If development spreads faster in consonance with the recent past, the medium-term outlook will conform to directions mapped out by policy changes instituted as reactions to previous industrial growth. Finally, while the changes (and prospects) have not been without difficult problems, such as excessive product concentration and declines in value added, productivity, and new capital investments in manufacturing, these problems may be minimized with appropriate policies (outlined below) so as to sustain further economic progress.

The record and prospects can be captured in a rough way by looking at the role of Philippine manufactured exports vis-à-vis the rest of the developing countries. Table 16.12 shows the shares of the Philippines in the sixty-four leading commodity exports of developing countries at the three-digit SITC level for which the country's share exceeds 0.05%. In more than half of the products in the table the country's share was

Table 16.12   **Share of the Philippines in Leading Commodity Exports of Developing Countries** (percentages)

SITC	1970	1975	1980
512 Organic chemicals	a	a	3.90
631 Veneers, plywood	15.81	6.29	8.93
653 Textiles	a	a	0.57
657 Floor covering	a	1.05[b,c]	—
674 Iron and steel plates	a	a	3.01
719 Machinery, nonelectrical	0.02	0.69	—
729 Electrical machinery	a	a	1.10
732 Motor vehicles	a	a	1.05
831 Travel goods	a	a	0.67
841 Clothing	0.04	0.75	2.02
851 Footwear	a	a	2.08[b]
864 Watches and clocks	a	a	1.02
893 Plastic	a	a	0.87
894 Toys	0.07	0.77	1.05
899 Other manufactures	0.94	11.18	6.72[b]
931 Special transactions	0.37	18.12	22.43

Source: UNCTAD, *Handbook of International Trade and Development Statistics* (New York: United Nations), various issues.

Note: SITC 0–4 not included.

[a]Value less than 0.05%.

[b]Value higher than Singapore's share.

[c]1978.

insignificant. SITC 631 really belongs to the traditional exports in the sense that it is not included in table 16.5. Clearly these shares (which account for 76% of exports of nontraditional manufactures) are small in comparison to other countries, particularly Singapore, Korea, Hong Kong, and Taiwan. There is substantial scope for further, if not accelerated gains.

The dangers that may thwart these prospects must, however, be recognized and anticipated, and those that are policy sensitive must be countered by effective policies. The realization of the expectations for manufactured exports necessitates a resilient and flexible approach within the scope of domestic policies. However,such an approach has not been exhibited in the recent past.

Resiliency is reflected in the country's ability to look toward both the domestic market and the external market. What constrains this ability is the growth of incomes and more critically the income distribution associated with manufactured export growth. On this score the country has consistently fared poorly. Section 16.2.2 noted the declines in real incomes of industrial workers throughout the sixties and the seventies. Figure 16.1 traces the movements of real wages of skilled and unskilled industrial workers during the decade of rising manufactured exports. A secular deterioration is obvious for both types of workers.[16] In terms of income distribution, there is no apparent broad improvement in shares between 1965 and 1975 (the latest year for which data are available). In short, the necessary conditions for potential

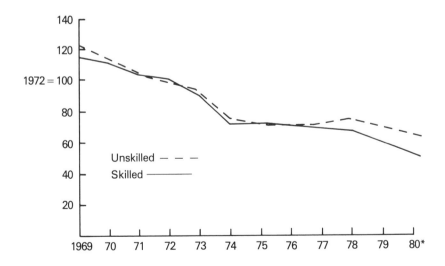

*JANUARY-SEPTEMBER

Fig. 16.1   Index of real wages of labor. 1972 = 100.

market redirection appear to be lacking. Not only do these circum-stances go against the traditional Heckscher-Ohlin expectations,[17] but there is a tendency to extol low labor prices as a virtue when competing for comparative advantage (World Bank 1980, 26).The route of com-petitiveness via improved productivity rather than wage deterioration is often neglected.[18]

The message that this lack of resiliency imparts is evident: if failure to export manufactures slowed industrial development during the im-port substitution era of the sixties (because of the limited demand of the domestic market), it is likely that failure to expand and widen domestic markets will likewise weaken industrial resurgence in the eighties (should world trade in manufactures fail to actively recover).

Lack of flexibility is demonstrated in the implied manner of supply responses to trade in manufactures. Notice in table 16.12 that the sector in which the Philippines has a large share of developing-country exports is SITC 931, "special transactions not classified according to kind." This is also the category with the highest growth, increasing in share 91-fold between 1970 and 1980. Whereas in 1970 this type of transaction was only 0.05% of all exports, in 1980 this had reached 14%.

These transactions are defined as those exports of products manu-factured from imported materials on a consignment basis. In the Phil-ippines, most belong to electrical and electronic equipment and gar-ments. The former includes semiconductor devices, diodes, and finished electrical and electronic machinery, while the latter includes gloves and mittens, handkerchiefs, women's and men's wear, children's and in-fants' wear, and embroideries. Some 38.5% of the 1980 manufactured exports were in these categories.

It is probably necessary to adjust the export contribution of nontra-ditional manufactures to determine *net* values rather than gross figures. This is not pursued here. However, assuming that most of SITC 931 transactions belong to electrical and electronics exports, aggregate im-port values for SITC 931 are likewise large. Consequently, the net exports (or value added) of these items are low—less than 1% of exports in 1980 and even negative in some years. A finer analysis is necessary but the implications are quite evident. For this reason the calculations made in table 16.10 would have been heavily biased had the exports of electrical and electronic equipment and components been included.

The nature of this behavior while disturbing may simply be a product of policies (e.g., the creation of free trade zones).[19] What is unfortunate is perhaps its implications for a more widespread industrial growth and deeper manufactured exports development. First, the smaller linkage engendered by special transactions generates fewer, if any, interindus-try relations. Production on consignment means labor is the only ef-fective link between the production process and the rest of industry.

Second, there is an inherent bias against domestic input suppliers in terms of increased value added. Indeed, exports under this category contribute less to value added than other products.[20] Finally, although one may argue that markets are assured under these arrangements, they do not adequately test Philippine marketing capacities through exposure of production decisions to more external and global factors. These do not spell greater flexibility in market penetration or widespread manufacturing development.

The message that this lack of flexibility imparts is similarly evident: if simple packaging was considered a weakness of import substitution, the pattern of export growth behind these special transactions is no more than packaging either. One may of course argue that the labor intensiveness of the latter (and its ability to absorb surplus labor) makes a difference. But the broader question is, first, whether this alternative is an optimal one and, second, whether within the system changes can be made to improve interactions with the rest of the economy.

The Philippines seems to be the only country with the given scale of export (in terms of shares with respect to total country trade and to developing-country exports) in SITC 931. Both Brazil and Singapore experienced rising export shares in this category in the late sixties to midseventies, but it has since declined in importance. Indeed, it may be instructive to draw comparisons with other countries' experiences with these transactions; such a comparison may throw light on the process of export-led development at least to the extent of achieving some consistency of definition among countries.

These weaknesses serve to qualify the prospects for expansion of manufactured exports spelled out earlier, not invalidate them. Moreover, they appear to be amenable to policy changes. In fact the broad structural adjustment reforms currently being adopted address certain aspects of these weaknesses directly. For instance, tariff reform will allow domestic input suppliers an equal footing with imported inputs. Modernization in certain industries will raise productivities and increase comparative advantage. Dismantling of domestic distortions (e.g., interest rate structure) will strengthen manufacturing development and encourage greater savings as well as capital formation. A concomitant drive to enlarge domestic market potentials requires a broad-based agricultural growth, which, combined with serious attempts to improve factor rewards and income equities, can create a more resilient outward-looking industrialization.

Aside from these kinds of measures fostering the prospects shaped by recent trends, one assumes the ability of the country to cushion the transition process.[21] The Philippines has increasingly relied on external debt to provide much of this cushion, evident in its increase from $2 billion in 1970 to $17 billion in 1980 and more than $25 billion in 1983.[22]

While there may be questions about the effective use of debts in the country, it is important to remember that this cushion prevents drastic cuts in imports (in critical components of manufactures), sustains development infrastructure, and facilitates structural adjustments.

In view of declining sources for this cushion, it becomes even more imperative to aim for a more selective and judicious use of external resources. In the final analysis, global recovery and the thrust of export expansion are interdependent. In the same vein, the expansion of manufactured exports and industrial restructuring and development are interdependent.

The beginnings of industrial change are evident from the parameters explored in this paper. These changes have obviously been helped along by a more conscious outward-looking policy even amidst a continuing protectionist situation. In other words, the policy thrust of the seventies has occured on top of the vestiges of an import substitution era, rather than in lieu of it. The Philippines, as pointed out, must depart fully from its past regime.

The external exuberance of the growth of manufactured exports also helped industrial restructuring. The redirection of supply responses to correct their structural defects, evident from the experience of the seventies, will likewise lead to more manufacturing growth. Internal policy activism and external resurgence are mutually reinforcive of the interaction between trade and industrial growth.

Notes

1. There is a temptation, in this context, to narrowly view the seminal Lewis and Ranis and Fei models of development along these lines. This is partly because of the static nature of the analysis as well as the secondary importance given to manufactured exports. See also Lewis 1980 and Ranis and Fei 1964.

2. See Baldwin 1975, 39, passim, for more details on the evolution of the tariff system in the Philippines.

3. Rather than relying on moral suasion, the kinds of policies used were particularly those with proven effectiveness in influencing financial flows, such as deposit margins, selective and differential discount rates, and reserve ratios.

4. The World Bank (1980, 1) identifies a number of major points in this shift.

5. Bautista (1980) makes a strong case for the currency realignments of 1971 having had an influence on the trading system between the Philippines and the United States and Japan. In the postrealignment period, however, one can surmise that cross-currency adjustments would have less impact than real factors (Bautista 1980).

6. The best way of defining nontraditional manufactures is to define the composition of traditional manufactures and then say that those which do not belong to the latter are nontraditional. Traditional manufactures are associated

with the intermediate processing of traditional exports, viz., sugar, wood products (excluding furniture), coconut and food products, and mineral products (excluding nickel).

7. There is a 1978 I-O table, but it is not based on a new transactions matrix but is in fact collapsed from the larger matrix (from a 128-sector to a 68-sector) and adjusted proportionally for prices.

8. Calculations of census value added divided by total employees were made from National Census and Statistics Office, *Annual Survey of Establishments,* from 1956 to 1977, adjusted for prices.

9. This is based on the number of newly registered business organizations (corporations plus partnerships plus single proprietorships) and the total initial paid-in capital (converted in real terms through the GNP deflator).

10. The appropriate weight to use for the adjusted figures of Table 7 should be a price index series for manufactured exports. However, since there is no readily available set of indices for the Philippines, the export price index has been used.

11. See Tuong and Yeats 1980 for an analysis that argues for this classification scheme as a basis for measuring comparative advantage. World-wide, a test is found in UNCTAD 1982.

12. Capital intensity is measured in terms of fixed capital assets per worker, while labor intensity is measured by wages per worker.

13. However, this may not be as easy as it seems. For a detailed analysis of trade barriers and penetration into the EC by the ASEAN countries, see Langhammer 1981.

14. Bautista (1982) has calculated protection rates in Philippine manufacturing resulting from the ongoing tariff reform program and concludes that the postreform protective structure would be the same. A serious qualification here is that structural parameters are assumed to remain the same between 1974 and 1985 (Alburo 1982).

15. This is not necessarily a beggar-thy-neighbor notion (in contrast to combating protectionism through regional solidarity) but simply a recognition of nonglobal approaches to trade negotiations (e.g., the Multi-Fiber Arrangement).

16. The index of real wages apples only to laborers in industrial establishments in metropolitan Manila and does not include government-decreed allowances (cost of living, thirteenth-month pay, food supplement, among others). For this reason the government discounts the trend as capturing actual returns. On the other hand, the metropolitan Manila rates are presumably on the high side because of great compliance with labor laws.

17. The prediction of the model that labor-using exports lead to an absolute and relative rise of labor's share is of course static. The dynamic results depend on the relative growth rates of capital and labor as well as trade itself.

18. This is a practical statement not a technical assertion. Under competitive conditions the value of the marginal product of labor determines the wage rate.

19. The export processing zones in 1980 accounted for a small portion of the 931 transactions (3.4% of electronics and 24% of garments). The major source is through another export-incentive scheme, the bonded warehouse, wherein imported inputs on consignment are stored in designated customs warehouses where processing takes place for eventual export.

20. For example, handicraft exports (SITC 899) enhance value added as well as generate more interindustry transactions.

21. For example, Krueger (1981) argues that the role played by multilateral and aid agencies in this process is much smaller than what seems required to push the transformation.

22. External debt growth rates have been rising faster after 1975, when the growth of exports increased (compared with the annual average rate for 1970–75) and import growth fell.

References

Alburo, Florian A. 1982. Discussion of "The recent tariff reform and effective protection of manufacturing industries" by Romeo M. Bautista. Paper presented at 4th Annual Scientific Meeting of the National Academy of Science and Technology, July.

Baldwin, Robert E. 1975. *Foreign trade regimes and economic development: The Philippines*. New York: National Bureau of Economic Research.

Bautista, Romeo M. 1980. Structural change in the Philippines. In *Economic interaction in the Pacific Basin* ed. Lawrence B. Krause, and Sueo Sekiguchi. Washington, D.C.: Brookings Institution.

———. 1982. The recent tariff reform and effective protection of manufacturing industries. University of the Philippines School of Economics Discussion Paper 8213.

Bautista, Romeo M., John H. Power, et al. 1979. *Industrial promotion policies in the Philippines*. Manila: Philippine Institute for Development Studies.

Cline, William R. 1982. Can the East Asian model of development be generalized? *World Development,* February, 81–90.

Hughes, Helen, and Krueger, Anne O. 1982. Effects of protection in developed countries on developing countries' exports of manufactures. Paper presented at the NBER Conference on the Structure and Evolution of Recent U.S. Trade Policy, 3–4 December.

International Labor Office. 1974. *Sharing in development: A programme of employment, equity and growth for the Philippines*. Geneva.

Krueger, Anne O. 1981. Loans to assist the transition to outward looking policies. *World Economy,* September.

Langhammer, Rolf. 1981. ASEAN manufactured exports in the EEC markets. Paper presented at the ASEAN Economic Research Unit Conference on ASEAN-EEC Economic Relations, Singapore, 6–8 August.

Lary, Hal. 1968. *Imports of manufactures from less developed countries*. New York: National Bureau of Economic Research.

Lewis, W. Arthur. 1980. The slowing down of the engine of growth. *American Economic Review* 70, no. 4.

Nurkse, Ragnar. 1953. *Problems of capital formation in underdeveloped countries*. New York: Oxford University Press.

Power, John H., and Gerardo P. Sicat. 1971. *The Philippines: Industrialization and trade policies*. London: Oxford University Press.

Prebisch, Raul. 1959. Commercial policy in the underdeveloped countries. *American Economic Review,* May.

Ranis, Gustav, and John C. H. Fei. 1964. *Development of the labor surplus economic: Theory and policy*. Homewood, Ill.: Irwin.

Sicat, Gerardo P. 1968. Industrial production functions in the Philippines. University of the Philippines IEDR Discussion Paper 68-18.

Tan, Norma A. 1979. The structure of protection and resource flows in the Philippines. In Bautista et al. 1979.

Tuong, Ho Dac, and Alexander Yeats. 1980. On factor proportions as a guide to the future composition of developing country exports. *Journal of Development Economics,* September.

UNCTAD (United National Conference on Trade and Development). 1982. *Trade and development report, 1982.* New York: UN.

Williamson, Jeffrey G., and Gerardo P. Sicat. 1968. Technical change and resource allocation in Philippines manufacturing, 1957–1965. University of the Philippines IEDR Discussion Paper 68-21.

World Bank. 1976. *The Philippines: Prospects and priorities for development.* Washington, D.C.: World Bank.

———. 1980. *The Philippines: Industrial development strategy and policies.* Washington, D.C.: World Bank.

17　　Trade Patterns and Trends of Indonesia

Ralph E. Beals

17.1　Introduction

Indonesia is a vast nation with a population of more than 150 million persons (the fifth largest national population in the world). With an average income per capita of $530 in 1981 she is not a rich country; the World Bank places Indonesia among its "lower middle-income economies." Yet, she surely plays a significant role in the international trade of East and Southeast Asia and beyond. Her size is one factor: Indonesia's GDP is larger than that of any other nation in the region except China and Japan. Oil is another: largely because of oil, Indonesia's total exports in 1981 were approximately equal to those of Korea, Hong Kong, or Singapore, and were second only to Japan among nations of the region (Appendix, table 17.A.1).

Also of great importance is the rapid growth the Indonesia economy has accomplished since the change in government and economic policy in 1966. According to World Bank estimates, Indonesia's GDP grew at an average annual rate of 7.8% over 1970–81. This is a point or two below the growth rates of Korea, Taiwan, Hong Kong, and Singapore but markedly higher than the 2.9% growth rate of the United States or even Japan's 4.5% rate. Compared with middle-income economies generally, Indonesia's growth rate for the decade was about 40% above average, and it was 25% higher than the average rate achieved by middle-income oil exporters.[1]

The manufacturing sector in Indonesia has had comparatively even more rapid growth. Manufacturing output increased at 13.9% per an-

Ralph E. Beals is Clarence Francis Professor of Economics at Amherst College. He has been associated with the Harvard Institute for International Development as consultant and adviser in Indonesia.

515

num for 1970–81 and was outpaced only by Korea (Appendix, table 17.A.2). Of course, this growth in manufacturing started from a very small base, so that even now the manufacturing sector accounts for a comparatively small fraction (12% in 1981) of GDP. More important from the point of view of trade, and in considerable contrast to other nations of the region, it will be seen below that manufacturing has been aimed largely at the domestic market. Manufactured goods certainly account for no more than 5% of merchandise exports; for 1981 the World Bank's estimate of the share is 2% (Appendix, table 17.A.1).

The plan of this paper is to examine in subsequent sections (1) the growth and sectoral composition of output and expenditures over the past fifteen to twenty years and (2) the growth in trade along with its structure by product group and by origin and destination. Government development policy will be discussed with particular emphasis on its consequences for industrialization and the observed patterns of trade. Finally, trends and prospects for the future will be assessed in view of recent policy initiatives.

The data used throughout this paper come from publications of the Central Bureau of Statistics (BPS) in Jakarta. The reliability of BPS import data, in particular, has been questioned in view of the fact that they are generally below alternative import estimates made for balance-of-payments purposes. The figures used here are also used by the International Monetary Fund (*International Financial Statistics*) and, in any event, are the only series for which product composition breakdowns are available. In several cases more recent data are available in Jakarta but were not yet available to the author.

17.2   Economic Growth and Structure

The growth of Indonesia since 1966 contrasts sharply with the immediately preceding period. Between 1958 and 1965, under ill-defined principles of "guided economy," planning and mismanagement of the economy by a government distrustful of markets resulted in disastrous inflation (100% and more per annum from 1962 through 1966), virtually stagnant production, and rapidly deteriorating levels of transport and other public services. Export earnings declined, and imports had to be severely restricted in the face of rising foreign debt. Real GDP growth did not keep up with population growth.

The present government, under President Suharto, came to power in 1966. The "New Order" undertook quickly a program of fiscal restraint and financial reform, plus trade and foreign exchange liberalization. Foreign aid began to flow in after 1966 and foreign investment was encouraged again. The policies had enormous and swift success. Hyperinflation was eliminated,[2] investment picked up strongly, real growth accelerated, and the share of manufacturing in GDP, after having declined in the early 1960s, began to increase. Also, trade was increasing rapidly by the end of the decade.

So strong was the spurt of growth begun after 1966 that even the "oil boom" dating from late 1973 does not show up as a marked increase in the growth rate of the Indonesian economy. Growth of real GDP continued during the late 1970s at approximately the same rate that had been established in the late 1960s and early 1970s.

These changes in the level and structure of output can usefully be examined in more detail. In table 17.1, growth rates of real GDP, real investment, and the level of manufacturing output are reported for various periods between 1960 and 1981 and annually for 1970 through 1982. Looking at the decade averages, real GDP growth appears to

Table 17.1   **Average Percentage Growth in Real GDP, Gross Domestic Investment, and Output of the Manufacturing Sector, and the Inflation Rate in Indonesia** (percentages)

Year	Real GDP	Real GDI	Real Manufacturing Output	Rate of Inflation[a]
1960–65	2.0	3.4	1.7	—
1965–70	7.0	13.5	7.5	—
1970–75	8.0	17.3	12.3	21.2
1975–80	7.9	11.9	15.0	14.7
1960–70	3.9	4.6	3.3	—
1970–81	7.8	14.0	13.9	—
1970	7.5	33.0	3.1	8.9
1971	7.0	21.2	15.1	2.6
1972	9.4	19.0	15.1	25.7
1973	11.3	17.1	15.2	27.4
1974	7.6	19.2	16.2	33.3
1975	5.0	14.6	12.3	19.7
1976	6.9	6.0	9.7	14.2
1977	8.9	15.9	13.8	11.8
1978	7.7	15.0	16.8	6.7
1979	6.3	4.4	12.9	24.6
1980	9.9	17.7	25.4	17.1
1981	7.9	17.7	7.3	7.3
1982	2.2	13.0	1.2	10.0
1983	4.2[b]	7.8[b]	2.2[b]	11.9

Sources: For the periods 1960–65 and 1965–70: World Bank, *World Tables* (1980) (data in constant 1976 prices). For the periods 1960–70 and 1970–81: World bank, *World Development Report 1983*. All others: BPS, Jakarta (real data in constant 1973 prices). BPS = Biro Pusat Statistik (Central Bureau of Statistics).

[a]Through 1979, inflation rate based on changes in year-end cost-of-living index for Jakarta; for 1980 and since, rate based on consumer price index for Indonesia (seventeen cities).

[b]Preliminary

have doubled in the 1970s as compared with the 1960s. But as has been previously noted, the change in regime and, correspondingly, the change in growth rate did not come at 1970 but earlier. The data for five-year periods confirm that the early 1960s were truly dismal and that growth increased sharply in the late 1960s to a rate that was sustained very well until 1982. Real investment and real manufacturing output have grown more rapidly than GDP, indicating structural shifts in the composition of output and expenditure.

Table 17.2 shows first a shrinking of all sectors except agriculture during the early 1960s as the economy languished. Then, it reveals a remarkable transformation of the industrial structure over the next fifteen years of growth and development. In 1965 agriculture and domestic trade accounted for more than 70% of industrial output, but by 1975 they accounted for less than 50%, and by 1980 for less than 40%. These declines were offset by increases in construction, manufacturing, and, most importantly, mining.

Viewed from the expenditure side, there is impressive growth in the share of GDP going to investment. As measured, the share doubled between 1965 and 1970 and tripled between 1965 and 1975, when it reached 20.3%. Although the investment share did not rise appreciably from 1975 to 1980, when it still remained at 20.9%, below the average level of 25% reported for middle-income economies (World Bank 1983, table 5), its opposite number—the savings ratio—was 29.2% in 1980 as compared to 21.0% in 1975. This difference reflects, of course, a surplus on the trade balance. The government could have allowed or forced greater domestic investment. Yet changes in the oil market, and the related trade balance, after 1980 suggest that it may have been only prudent not to increase investment spending in response to the rising oil prices in 1979 and 1980. Note that in 1982 the trade balance had turned substantially negative.

Table 17.3, which evaluates the changing distributions of output and expenditures derived on the basis of constant 1973 prices, allows one to see some sizable effects that oil price increases have had. With sectoral outputs evaluated in constant prices, there is little growth in mining's share of GDP; most of the growth in the mining sector's importance as shown in table 17.2 is due to the higher prices realized for crude oil and petroleum products rather than to greater quantities of production. In table 17.3 a sectoral share increases only when its real growth rate is high relative to the economy-wide average. Thus, in table 17.3 the manufacturing industry shows a pronounced increase in share, because most of its increase in output value was attributable to greater quantity produced and not to a higher price. Construction output, concealed within services, also attains a larger share in table 17.3, where prices are held constant at the 1973 level. Meanwhile the

Table 17.2   **The Percentage Distribution of GDP by Industrial Origin and by Expenditure Category in Indonesia (based on current market prices)** (percentages)

	1960	1965	1970	1975	1980	1982
Industrial origin						
Agriculture	53.9	58.7	47.2	31.7	24.8	26.3
Mining	3.7	2.5	5.2	19.7	25.7	19.6
Manufacturing	8.4	7.6	9.3	8.9	11.6	12.9
Services	34.0	31.2	38.3	39.7	37.8	41.2
Construction	2.0	1.8	3.0	4.7	5.6	5.9
Wholesale & retail trade	14.3	12.4	18.5	16.6	14.1	14.9
Transport & communications	3.7	2.1	2.9	4.1	4.3	4.7
Other services	14.0	14.9	13.9	14.3	13.8	15.7
GDP	100.0	100.0	100.0	100.0	100.0	100.0
Expenditure category						
Private consumption	79.8	88.2	80.6	69.1	60.5	69.9
Government consumption	11.5	5.5	8.8	9.9	10.3	11.5
Gross domestic investment	7.9	6.3	13.6	20.3	20.9	22.6
Net exports	0.8	−0.4	−3.0	0.7	8.3	−3.9
Exports	13.3	5.1	12.8	22.9	30.5	22.4
Imports	−12.5	−5.5	−15.8	−22.2	−22.2	−26.3
GDP	100.0	100.0	100.0	100.0	100.0	100.0

Sources: BPS, *National Income of Indonesia,* various issues; BPS, *Statistical Pocketbook of Indonesia,* various issues.

Table 17.3 **The Percentage Distribution of GDP by Industrial Origin and by Expenditure Category in Indonesia** (percentages)

	Based on Constant 1960 Prices			Based on Constant 1973 Prices			
	1960	1965	1970	1971	1975	1980	1982
Industrial origin							
Agriculture	53.9	52.4	47.4	44.0	36.8	30.7	29.8
Mining	3.7	3.7	5.6	9.9	10.9	9.3	7.6
Manufacturing	8.4	8.3	9.0	8.8	11.1	15.3	15.4
Services	34.0	35.6	38.0	37.3	41.2	44.8	47.2
GDP	100.0	100.0	100.0	100.0	100.0	100.0	100.0
Expenditure category							
Private consumption	79.8	82.8	79.5	73.7	74.7	79.4	86.8
Government consumption	11.5	6.7	8.6	9.3	11.0	13.3	14.4
GDI	7.9	8.4	12.2	15.6	21.6	25.9	29.5
Net exports	0.8	2.0	−0.3	1.3	−7.3	−18.6	−30.7
Exports	13.3	13.0	14.4	17.0	18.5	15.4	11.7
Imports	−12.5	−11.0	−14.7	−15.7	−25.7	−34.0	−42.4
GDP	100.0	100.0	100.0	100.0	100.0	100.0	100.0

Sources: BPS, *National Income of Indonesia*, various issues; BPS, *Statistical Pocketbook of Indonesia*, various issues.

relative decline of agriculture, because of price effects, is moderated when table 17.3 is compared with table 17.2.

Investment growth also shows up more visibly when the distribution of expenditures is calculated on the basis of constant 1973 prices. The most striking changes occur in the export and import shares, however. The oil price increases of 1973 and later obviously represent a large improvement in the terms of trade of Indonesia. Even though the number of units, or quantity, of oil exports increased relatively little, the value of exports increased greatly. These extra foreign exchange earnings were what allowed the quantity of relatively stably priced imports to be increased.

One might hope and expect that the ability to finance an expanded flow of materials and capital goods from abroad would produce an acceleration of economic growth. Yet, as was seen in the data of table 17.1, there was no acceleration of GDP growth in the late 1970s, and the growth rate of GDI declined. Increases in imports during the period tended to be concentrated on intermediate goods and materials.

17.3   Trade and Its Product Composition

17.3.1   Exports

Indonesia has long been an exporter of agricultural and mineral products. Many different crops and products have been exported and are still exported, but their number cannot gainsay the fact that the bulk of export earnings has always been concentrated on a very short list of primary commodities. At one time—during the 1930s and the 1950s— rubber was Indonesia's most important export. It regularly accounted for a third or more of total export earnings (Sievers 1974, 343 and 356). In view of things to come, it may be of some interest to note that the second most important export of the period was oil.

The oil industry is not a newcomer to Indonesia. Production and export had already begun before 1900. It has been reported that in 1911 Indonesia produced 13 million barrels, equal to about 3.4% of world production (Ooi 1982, 3). More recently, Indonesia has accounted for only about 2%–2.5% of world production. By 1940 Indonesia was producing at a rate of 61.5 million barrels per year, precisely one-tenth the peak production level achieved in 1977. About half of 1940 oil production was exported, accounting for 20.6% of the total value of Indonesian exports (Ooi 1982, 7 and 125; Sievers 1974, 343). The industry was greatly disrupted by World War II and the subsequent struggle for independence, but nevertheless, in 1951 oil production reattained the 1940 level and then continued to increase. During the rest of the 1950s petroleum exports accounted for a rising share of total exports, averaging about 25% of total value (Ooi 1982, 9; Sievers 1974, 356).

Table 17.4 charts total exports and the values of major export commodities from 1960 to 1983. One can pick up the story of developments in the oil industry and relate them to the table. During the renewed growth period of the late 1960s, oil maintained its already substantial share of total exports. With stable world oil prices, this came about through increases in oil production, which, of course, also contributed to the growth of GDP. Oil price increases in late 1971 and late 1973, along with continued increases in volume of production, raised oil's share in total export value to 50% for 1972 and 1973. Then the major price increase announced at the end of 1973 (amounting to a quadrupling of price in the space of a year) caused the huge 1974 jump in share from 50% to 70%. Since then, petroleum has been overwhelmingly the dominant Indonesian export.

Table 17.4 also gives the record of export earnings from five other commodities: timber, rubber, coffee, palm oil, and tin. As the data show, these commodities, plus oil and gas, account for more than 90% of export earnings in every year since 1974. And even in the early part

Table 17.4   **Principal Indonesian Exports** (values in millions of U.S. $ and percentages of total, by year)

Year	Total Exports	Oil and Gas	Wood	Rubber	Coffee	Palm Oil	Tin and Tin Ore
1960	841	221 (26)	—	377 (45)	14 (2)	21 (2)	51 (6)
1965	708	272 (38)	2 (—)	222 (31)	32 (5)	27 (4)	38 (5)
1966	679	204 (30)	4 (1)	223 (33)	33 (5)	33 (5)	31 (5)
1967	665	239 (36)	6 (1)	169 (25)	44 (7)	24 (4)	49 (7)
1968	731	298 (41)	12 (2)	176 (24)	44 (6)	20 (3)	26 (4)
1969	854	383 (45)	29 (3)	226 (26)	60 (7)	24 (3)	25 (3)
1970	1,108	446 (40)	104 (9)	253 (23)	69 (6)	35 (3)	54 (5)
1971	1,234	478 (39)	161 (13)	222 (18)	55 (4)	45 (4)	52 (4)
1972	1,778	913 (51)	229 (13)	189 (11)	77 (4)	41 (2)	64 (4)
1973	3,211	1,609 (50)	574 (18)	391 (12)	78 (2)	70 (2)	93 (3)
1974	7,426	5,211 (70)	725 (10)	479 (6)	98 (1)	157 (2)	175 (2)
1975	7,102	5,311 (75)	500 (7)	258 (4)	100 (1)	152 (2)	140 (1)
1976	8,546	6,004 (70)	780 (9)	530 (6)	238 (3)	136 (2)	165 (1)
1977	10,853	7,378 (68)	954 (9)	588 (5)	599 (6)	184 (2)	250 (2)
1978	11,643	7,985 (69)	995 (9)	716 (6)	491 (4)	209 (2)	286 (2)
1979	15,590	10,164 (65)	1,797 (12)	937 (6)	614 (4)	204 (1)	404 (3)
1980	23,950	17,781 (74)	1,852 (8)	1,165 (5)	658 (3)	255 (1)	510 (2)
1981	25,164	20,663 (82)	874 (3)	828 (3)	346 (1)	107 (0.4)	461 (2)
1982	22,328	18,399 (82)	548 (2)	602 (3)	342 (2)	96 (0.4)	379 (2)
1983	21,146	16,141 (76)	342 (2)	844 (4)	427 (2)	112 (0.5)	310 (1)

Sources: BPS, *Ekspor,* various issues; BPS, *Indikator Ekonomi,* various issues; BPS, *Statistical Pocketbook of Indonesia,* various issues.

of the period clear back to 1960, this same short list of commodities accounts for 80% or more of export earnings. The combination of an initial high concentration of exports in a few primary products and an improvement in terms of trade for the major initial export commodity would appear to create, owing to numerical considerations alone, an imposing barrier to achievement of a substantial share in exports by the manufacturing industry. Despite some gain in the export share achieved by Indonesian manufacturing, the share remains quite small.

Table 17.5 allows one to examine the distribution of exports by SITC sections for recent years, 1978, 1980, and 1982. If manufacturing is defined to consist of the one-digit SITC sections 5 through 8, then manufactured goods account for 4.2% of the total value of exports in 1978, 3.9% in 1980, and 5.4% in 1982. By this measure, exports of manufactured goods fill about half the gap remaining after the six commodities of table 17.4 have been taken into account. Relative to GDP, it would appear that manufactured exports have risen in importance only slightly since 1978 and are in any case a very small percentage of GDP.

Further examination of specific products makes the summary estimates appear more dubious as indicators of the importance of manufacturing for export. In particular, the major item under section 6 is

Table 17.5   **Indonesian Exports by SITC Sections** (values in millions of U.S. $ and percentages)

	1978		1980		1982	
SITC Section	Value	%	Value	%	Value	%
0. Food and animals	989	8.5	1,291	5.4	905	4.1
1. Beverages and tobacco	55	0.5	61	0.3	42	0.2
2. Crude materials, inedible	1,891	16.2	3,569	14.9	1,581	7.1
3. Mineral fuels, lubricants	7,986	68.6	17,783	74.2	18,408	82.4
4. Animal and vegetable oils	214	1.8	285	1.2	133	0.6
5. Chemicals	55	0.5	84	0.4	61	0.3
6. Manufactured goods	332	2.9	615	2.6	817	3.7
7. Machinery and transportation equip.	71	0.6	109	0.5	180	0.8
8. Misc. manufactured articles	34	0.3	120	0.5	141	0.6
9. Other	16	0.1	33	0.1	59	0.3
Total exports	11,643	100.0	23,950	100.0	22,328	100.0
Export of manufactures (5–8)	492	4.2	928	3.9	1,199	5.4
Addendum						
Exp. of manufactures as % of nonfuels total		13.5		15.0		30.6
Exp. of manufactures as % of GDP		1.0		1.3		1.3

Source: BPS, *Ekspor,* various issues.

"unwrought tin," or tin ingot. In 1980 it accounts for $423 million of the $615 million total value listed in section 6. Its inclusion there rather than in section 2, where "tin ore and concentrates" appears, is at best likely to be somewhat misleading. The main point is that the extent of manufacturing involved in turning tin concentrate into tin ingot (unwrought tin) is not great. It involves only smelting; and the value added in this process is small, probably accounting for no more than 2% of the ingot value (Gillis and Beals 1980, 270–71). Consistency is also a question: Smelting to produce ferronickel adds substantial value to nickel ore. Yet the data of table 17.5 include ferronickel under category 2 as a crude material. On balance, it seems desirable and reasonable not to consider unwrought tin a manufactured good and, accordingly, to adjust the total value of manufactured goods exports substantially downward.

For 1980 and 1982 the adjusted figures are shown in table 17.6. After adjustment, the total value of manufactured exports is reduced to $504.4 million in 1980, or 2.1% of the total value of exports.[3] Between 1980 and 1982 the adjusted value of manufactured exports increased, although total exports did not; thus the share of manufactured goods in exports rose fairly sharply to 3.7%.

Table 17.6 also shows export values for important manufactured goods exports. It lists every three-digit SITC division of manufacturing for which Indonesia was a net exporter in 1980. Under section 7, almost all 1980 exports are accounted for by the subcategory "diodes, transistors, etc." Yet, the majority of the increase in section 7 exports between 1980 and 1982 is accounted for by aircraft.

Many of the goods in table 17.6 may be classified as natural resource based: leather, plywood, other wood manufactures, pearls, cement, essential oils, and quinine. With the exception of plywood, hardly any of these show immediate potential for growth or are labor-intensive so as to offer much promise of accompanying employment expansion. Apart from natural resources, Indonesia's major resource is its large labor force, and thus, comparative advantage would appear to lie in labor-intensive activities. Among its major exports, clothing and textile products appear to be most labor-intensive, although production activity in Indonesia's transistor industry is at present also labor-intensive.

In any event, the list of important manufactured goods exports for 1980 is obviously not long. Further, it could reasonably be shortened to only three really significant product lines. Only plywood, transistors, and clothing exports are valued at more than $50 million. Collectively, these three product lines accounted for half of all manufactured goods exports in 1980. The 1982 data make the importance of these three product lines even more clear: in 1982 their share was almost two-thirds of the total. And, while overall manufactured goods

Table 17.6   **Important Manufactured Goods Exports** (values in millions of U.S. $)

	1980	1982	Change
Total exports, SITC sections 5–8	927.7	1,199.4	271.7
Less unwrought tin	423.3	367.4	−55.9
Adjusted value: total exports of manufactured goods	504.4	832.0	327.6
5. *Chemicals*	83.8	61.5	−22.3
* Fertilizer (urea, etc.)	34.9	10.1	−24.8
Essential oils (patchouli, citronella, etc.)	21.2	17.4	−3.8
* Medicinal products (quinine, etc.)	11.7	11.7	0
* Organic chemicals (alcohol, glycerol, etc.)	9.0	13.3	4.3
6. *Manufactured goods*	191.4	449.8	258.4
Veneers, plywood, sawn timber	68.5	316.1	247.6
* Woven fabrics	27.7	24.3	3.4
* Cement and products	25.5	8.5	−17.0
Floor coverings (rattan mats)	7.7	7.1	−0.6
Leather	6.5	7.4	0.9
Other wood manufactures	5.0	6.7	1.7
Pearls, worked and unworked	3.4	4.7	1.4
7. *Machinery and transport equipment*	109.0	179.6	70.6
* Other electrical machinery and apparatus	94.0	116.8	22.8
Diodes, transistors, etc.	90.6	114.3	23.7
Dry batteries	2.4	0.6	−1.8
* Aircraft	2.1	43.3	41.2
8. *Miscellaneous manufactured articles*	120.2	141.1	20.9
Clothing	98.3	116.4	18.1
* Music instruments and accessories	7.3	10.8	3.5
Tapes in cassettes	5.9	7.6	1.7

Source: BPS, *Ekspor* (1980 and 1982).
'Indicates Indonesia is a *net importer* of the product category.

exports increased by $328 million between 1980 and 1982, the three major items increased by $290 million, accounting for 88% of the total increase.

A further look shows that the values of transistor exports and clothing exports grew moderately between 1980 and 1982, while the value of plywood exports soared. Increased export earnings from plywood account for three-quarters of the entire increase over 1980–82. A still closer look takes price, or unit value, into account. Doing so makes performance in production of clothing for export look stronger. In the case of clothing, value of exports increased by 18%, but the weight of shipments was up by 82% while nominal unit values fell by 35%. In the case of transistors, etc., unit value increased, but the volume (weight) of shipments decreased. Despite a 22% drop in volume, the total value of shipments rose 26% between 1980 and 1982.

The growth in plywood exports looks less impressive on further examination. Calculated on the basis of unit values of exports, plywood prices rose about one-third between 1980 and 1982, while log prices were unchanged. This increase in plywood price suggests a somewhat less rapid growth of output and employment than might be inferred by looking at export values alone.

Further, one should recognize the costs of achieving the increases in exports of processed wood products. Government policy limiting log exports and tying them to plywood exports has resulted in a great deal of investment activity in plywood plants and sawmills. It has also, for the present, markedly reduced earnings from log exports. To a considerable extent, the growth of plywood exports represents a displacement of timber exports. This may, in a sense, always be true; only value added is true production. But the abrupt actions by the Indonesian government have gone beyond that simple truth by reducing log exports even when they cannot yet be processed domestically. In view of the recession it is virtually impossible to sort out the magnitudes of the various effects. Nonetheless, one should notice that the $248 million increase in manufactured plywood exports was accompanied by a decline of $1,304 million in earnings from timber exports (cf. table 17.4).

Finally, a word about one other new export: aircraft. The $43 million of export receipts from aircraft in 1982 represent sales by P. T. Nurtanio. This company, under the directorship and aegis of the Minister of Research and Technology, has been hailed as a source of pride and as evidence that high technology is the way to development. Although Nurtanio has shown it can produce airframes, it is extremely doubtful that it can sell them at a price and rate that will allow the company to cover its very substantial capital costs. So far, its sales have largely been to other public enterprises that have been given little or no choice about what to buy.

17.3.2   Imports

Indonesia's imports have grown rapidly as its export earnings have increased. The division of import demand among consumption goods, materials, and capital goods shifted at the beginning of the 1970s away from consumer goods and toward capital and intermediate goods (see table 17.7). The pattern has been relatively stable since then, although a large increase in government rice purchases in 1973 and subsequent large imports of fertilizer caused noticeable fluctuation in the percentage distribution. The capital goods share was about 5 percentage points lower in 1973 and 1974 than in 1972 and 1976. During the late 1970s the share of capital goods imports again declined a bit.

The price of petroleum products was kept low during the 1970s even as the number of motor vehicles increased rapidly. As a result, domestic

Table 17.7   **Indonesian Imports by Economic Groups** (values in millions of
U.S. $ and percentages of total, by year)

Year	Total Imports	Consumption Goods	Raw Material and Auxiliary Goods		Capital Goods
			Petroleum	Other	
1960	578	—	6 (1)	—	—
1965	695	231 (33)	13 (2)	230 (33)	221 (32)
1966	527	225 (43)	7 (1)	173 (33)	122 (23)
1967	649	232 (36)	12 (2)	226 (35)	179 (28)
1968	716	266 (37)	6 (1)	246 (36)	190 (27)
1969	781	221 (28)	11 (1)	310 (40)	239 (31)
1970	1,002	251 (25)	15 (1)	362 (36)	374 (37)
1971	1,103	210 (19)	20 (2)	408 (37)	465 (42)
1972	1,562	252 (16)	31 (2)	567 (36)	712 (46)
1973	2,729	649 (24)	44 (2)	929 (34)	1,107 (41)
1974	3,842	707 (18)	183 (5)	1,399 (36)	1,553 (40)
1975	4,770	678 (14)	254 (5)	1,707 (36)	2,131 (45)
1976	5,673	916 (16)	438 (8)	1,586 (28)	2,733 (43)
1977	6,230	1,105 (18)	732 (12)	1,720 (28)	2,673 (43)
1978	6,690	1,197 (18)	579 (9)	2,085 (31)	2,829 (42)
1979	7,202	1,182 (16)	793 (11)	2,535 (35)	2,692 (37)
1980	10,834	1,543 (14)	1,744 (16)	3,064 (28)	4,483 (41)
1981	13,272	1,399 (11)	1,722 (13)	3,979 (30)	6,173 (47)
1982	16,859	1,260 (7)	3,545 (21)	3,916 (23)	8,138 (48)
1983	16,352	1,295 (8)	4,144 (25)	3,875 (24)	7,038 (43)

Sources: BPS, *Indikator Ekonomi,* various issues; BPS, *Statistical Pocketbook of Indonesia,* various issues.

demand for gasoline and other refined products grew rapidly, so that petroleum began to take an increasing share of imports. In response to this, the government has raised domestic prices of petroleum products substantially in recent years.

The general pattern of table 17.7 is confirmed by the distribution of imports across SITC sections, as shown in table 17.8. Imports are concentrated in section 7 (machinery and transport equipment) and section 6 (manufactured goods), with the share of fuel imports rising very noticeably. Between 1978 and 1980 there was little change in the distribution except for shared reductions in sections 0 (food) and 7 (machinery) to offset the increases that raised fuel imports from a 9% share to a 16% share. Even as fuel imports continued to gain from 1980 to 1982, machinery imports also gained with most of the matching decline in shares being borne by food.

In view of government policy that encouraged capital-intensive investment in import-competing sectors, it is not surprising that capital goods and intermediate goods to be processed have gained and held a large share of imports.

Table 17.8   **Indonesian Imports by SITC Sections** (values in millions of U.S. $ and percentages)

SITC Section	1978 Value	%	1980 Value	%	1982 Value	%
0. Food and animals	1,042	15.6	1,285	11.9	1,074	6.4
1. Beverages and tobacco	27	0.4	42	0.4	51	0.3
2. Crude materials, inedible	295	4.4	491	4.5	609	3.6
3. Mineral fuels, lubricants	582	8.7	1,754	16.2	3,550	21.1
4. Animal and vegetable oils	65	1.0	9	0.1	13	0.1
5. Chemicals	756	11.3	1,255	11.6	1,804	10.7
6. Manufactured goods	1,263	18.9	2,053	18.9	2,732	16.2
7. Machinery and transportation equip.	2,434	36.4	3,634	33.5	6,260	37.1
8. Misc. manufactured articles	198	3.0	285	2.6	376	2.2
9. Other	28	0.4	27	0.2	390	2.3
Total imports	6,690	100.0	10,834	100.0	16,859	100.0
Import of manufactures (5–8)	4,651	69.5	7,227	66.7	11,172	66.3
Addendum						
Imp. of manufactures as % of nonfuels total		76.1		79.6		83.9
Imp. of manufactures as % of GDP		9.0		10.0		12.4

Source: BPS, *Impor,* various issues.

17.4   The Distribution of Trade by Destination and Origin

17.4.1   Exports

Table 17.9 summarizes the Indonesian export trade pattern from 1965 through 1982. Overall, Japan emerges as the largest customer, accounting for a slowly growing share equal to nearly half the total since 1970. Meanwhile, Europe appears to have been a steady loser of relative share.

A more useful picture is obtained, however, when petroleum is separated from other exports. The vast majority (more than 80%) of Japan's purchases from Indonesia are oil or, recently, liquified natural gas. The same holds for the United States. Europe, on the other hand, buys virtually no oil from Indonesia.

The market for nonpetroleum exports is more dispersed, and the shares are more constant. Japan's share is largest at 25%–30%. The U.S. share is 10%–15%, while the EC (European Community) accounts for 20%. The Association of South East Asian Nations (ASEAN) also

Table 17.9 Indonesian Exports and Distribution by Area or Country of Destination (values in millions of U.S. $ and percentages)

Area or Country of Destination	1965		1970		1975		1980		1982	
	Value	%	Value	%	Value	%	Value	%	Value	%
Total exports	708	100.0	1,108	100.0	7,102	100.0	23,950	100.0	22,328	100.0
Japan	123	17.4	452	40.8	3,132	44.1	11,833	49.4	11,193	50.1
USA	153	21.6	144	13.0	1,866	26.3	4,798	20.0	3,546	15.9
EC	168	23.7	156	14.1	405	5.7	1,388	5.8	896	4.0
ASEAN	27	3.8	234	21.1	732	10.3	3,265	13.6	3,499	15.7
Other	237	33.5	122	11.0	968	13.6	2,666	11.1	3,194	14.3
Petroleum exports[a]	272	100.0	446	100.0	5,311	100.0	17,781	100.0	18,399	100.0
Japan	71	26.1	314	70.4	2,600	49.0	10,074	56.7	10,287	55.9
USA	42	15.4	61	13.7	1,670	31.4	4,067	22.9	2,961	16.1
EC	10	3.7	1	0.2	41	0.8	42	0.2	107	0.6
ASEAN	24	8.9	31	7.0	385	7.2	2,057	11.6	2,578	14.0
Other	125	46.0	39	8.7	615	11.6	1,541	8.7	2,466	13.4
Nonpetroleum exports	436	100.0	662	100.0	1,792	100.0	6,169	100.0	3,929	100.0
Japan	52	11.9	138	20.8	532	29.7	1,759	28.5	906	23.1
USA	111	25.5	83	12.5	196	10.9	731	11.8	585	14.9
EC	158	36.2	155	23.4	331	18.5	1,346	21.8	789	20.1
ASEAN	3	0.7	203	30.7	283	15.8	1,208	19.6	921	23.4
Other	112	25.7	83	12.5	450	25.1	1,125	18.2	728	18.5

Sources: BPS, *Ekspor*, various issues; BPS, *Indikator Ekonomi*, various issues; BPS, *Statistical Pocketbook of Indonesia*, various issues.

[a]Includes liquefied natural gas.

appears to have about a 20% share, but this may be problematic. About 85% of the ASEAN total goes to Singapore. It is often claimed that much of this flow is simply reexported from Singapore to other markets. The residual Other category includes quite a variety of nations and probably represents no clear or persistent trade pattern.

Despite Japan's overall importance as a buyer of Indonesian goods, Japan is not generally a prominent destination for the traditional agricultural exports of Indonesia. Only small percentages of rubber, coffee, palm oil, tea, tobacco, pepper, and teak exports go to Japan. A major exception has been timber: Japan has regularly accounted for half or more of revenues from log sales. In 1980 Japan purchased a billion dollars worth of logs from Indonesia, amounting to 55% of export earnings from timber. Sharp curtailment of log exports, mentioned earlier, had much to do with Japan's 1982 log purchases being only $277 million, which still represented almost half of total log exports.

Increases in plywood exports have been absorbed in great measure by the so-called Gang of Four—Hong Kong, Singapore, South Korea, and Taiwan. Japan had not by 1982 made significant purchases of plywood, even though its timber supply from Indonesia had been reduced to a quarter of its earlier level.

Japan does buy Indonesian minerals: about 20% of tin exports and three-quarters of copper output, all of which is for export. Another substantial and new export from Indonesia to Japan is shrimp: recently exports of shrimp have amounted to about $180 million annually, of which about 85% goes to Japan.

Japan is a major investor in the Indonesian textile industry, the output of which is sold almost exclusively on the domestic market. Of the approximately 2% of fabric output that was exported in 1980, Japan took about one-sixth. Almost no clothing was shipped to Japan. A sizable fraction of fabric exports go officially to Singapore, and possibly elsewhere from there; the Middle East is also an important destination. Indonesia's markets for clothing are the EC and the United States. In 1981 they each accounted for about 40% of total clothing exports. Much of the remainder went to or through Singapore.

Diodes, transistors, and other electrical apparatus are shipped almost exclusively to Singapore, presumably to be used as components in various electronic manufactures. Plywood output is expanding rapidly and finding markets in Asia, the United States, and Europe.

17.4.2 Imports

Table 17.10 shows the distribution of imports by area of origin. The petroleum import pattern, not surprisingly, differs sharply from the petroleum export pattern. Indonesia sells oil to Japan, while importing refined products and lower-quality crude to meet domestic needs. These

Table 17.10   **Indonesian Imports and Distribution by Area or Country of Origin** (values in millions of U.S. $ and percentages)

Area or Country of Origin	1965 Value	1965 %	1970 Value	1970 %	1975 Value	1975 %	1980 Value	1980 %	1982 Value	1982 %
Total imports	695	100.0	1,102	100.0	4,770	100.0	10,834	100.0	16,859	100.0
Japan	159	22.9	295	29.4	1,477	31.0	3,413	31.5	4,279	25.4
USA	66	9.5	179	17.9	670	14.0	1,409	13.0	2,417	14.3
EC	126	18.1	219	21.9	885	18.6	1,445	13.3	2,653	15.7
ASEAN	52	7.5	76	7.6	412	8.6	1,350	12.5	3,302	19.6
Other	292	42.0	233	23.2	1,326	27.8	3,217	29.7	4,208	25.0
Petroleum imports	12.6	100.0	15	100.0	254	100.0	1,744	100.0	3,545	100.0
Japan	0.1	0.8	5	33.3	5	2.0	10	0.6	30	0.8
USA	5.4	42.9	2	13.3	10	3.9	29	1.7	28	0.8
EC	3.7	29.4	1	6.7	2	0.8	4	0.2	11	0.3
ASEAN	—	—	3	20.0	154	60.6	709	40.7	2,290	64.6
Other	3.4	27.0	4	26.7	83	32.7	992	56.9	1,186	33.5
Nonpetroleum imports	682	100.0	987	100.0	4,516	100.0	9,090	100.0	13,314	100.0
Japan	159	23.3	290	29.4	1,472	32.6	3,403	37.4	4,249	31.9
USA	60	8.8	177	17.9	660	14.6	1,380	15.2	2,389	17.9
EC	122	17.9	218	22.1	883	19.6	1,441	15.9	2,642	19.8
ASEAN	52	7.6	73	7.4	258	5.7	641	7.1	1,012	7.6
Other	289	42.4	229	23.2	1,243	27.5	2,225	24.5	3,022	22.7

Sources: BPS, *Impor,* various issues; BPS, *Indikator Ekonomi,* various issues; BPS, *Statistical Pocketbook of Indonesia,* various issues.

imports come largely from Singapore refineries and from the Middle East.

Examination of the origin of particular imports shows Japan to be a major supplier of capital goods: iron and steel pipe, industrial and commerical machinery, and motor vehicles. The United States and the EC have smaller shares in imports of these products. Except for the case of motor vehicles, where Japan's share has grown substantially, the share distribution for capital goods imports seems fairly stable.

A comparison of nonpetroleum imports and exports shows no geographic area to be dominant in trade. There is a rough balance of exports and imports in trade between Indonesia and the rest of ASEAN. For all other areas, Indonesia tends to have a substantial trade deficit when petroleum is ignored.

17.5 Manufacturing Growth and Industrial Policy

If manufacturing output has grown so rapidly in Indonesia, as indeed it has, why do exports of manufactured goods remain so limited? As has been seen, after adjustment exports of manufactured goods amounted to only about 2.1% of total exports in 1980 and 3.7% in 1982. Relative to GDP, the total value of manufactured goods exports was only 0.7% in 1980 and 0.9% in 1982.[4] The answer lies in the structure and composition of manufacturing output. Circumstances and government policies have steered investment and industrial growth away from areas of Indonesian comparative advantage and into import-competing sectors.

17.5.1 Manufacturing Output and Employment

Overall Estimates

There are no really good, or widely accepted, estimates of manufacturing employment in Indonesia; there are many conflicts and inconsistencies in the existing data. Yet there is general agreement that employment in manufacturing has grown quite slowly in comparison to growth in manufacturing output (value added) or even in comparison to growth in real GDP. Estimates reported by the World Bank (1982, 95) put employment in manufacturing at 4,540,000 in 1980 compared with 3,204,000 in 1971. These figures yield an average annual growth rate of 3.95%, in comparison to 2.65% for total employment and 13.80% for value added in manufacturing. BPS revisions[5] have since lowered the 1980 manufacturing employment estimate to 4,361,000 and imply a reduced average employment growth rate of only 3.5% for 1971–80. At the same time, the estimate of 1980 value added in manufacturing was increased, with the result of adding 1 percentage point to the 1971–80 average growth rate of output originating in manufacturing.

These figures represent poor performance for employment growth, especially so given the government's often-stated goal of increasing employment through promotion of labor-intensive industry. For 1971–80 the apparent elasticity of manufacturing employment with respect to manufacturing output was only about one-quarter. Fairly clearly, manufacturing growth has been rather capital-intensive.

Sectoral Estimates

There is a vast range of sizes among Indonesian manufacturing enterprises, and there are many, many tiny firms with fewer than five workers. These cottage enterprises account for about 60% of those employed in the manufacturing sector, but a much smaller fraction of total manufacturing output. The larger firms are categorized either as "small" (five to nineteen employees) or "large or medium" (twenty employees or more). Survey data are available annually for the latter category and periodically for "small-scale enterprises."

In 1979 the large and medium firms accounted for 870,000 workers with average measured productivity (value added per worker) of Rp 1,908,500, while the 827,000 employed in small-scale establishments had average productivity of only Rp 226,500 (11.9% of productivity in the large and medium firms). These huge differences make it imperative that not only product sector but establishment size be taken into account in analyses of manufacturing. Accordingly, table 17.11 shows employment and productivity by manufacturing sector and establishment size. Among the large and medium establishments, textiles, wood, paper, and the "other manufactures" sector appear to be relatively labor-intensive. Yet in each case, the small-scale firms appear to be much more labor-intensive; for no sector is labor productivity in the small establishments more than one-third that in the larger firms. The lowest average productivity is found among the small firms in non-metallic mineral processing, while the large, capital-intensive (cement and sheet glass) firms in that sector have very high value added per worker. The food, beverage, and tobacco sector also is bifurcated, with the larger firms tending to be much more capital-intensive.

There is a remarkable difference between the two groups of establishments in the way employment responds to increases in output. Table 17.12 shows that, overall, the employment elasticity for small-scale establishments was unity in the late 1970s, while for the large and medium establishments it was only about 0.4. The textile industry shows an especially small employment elasticity of only 0.10 for the larger firms. According to Hill (1980), changes in clothing preferences—away from traditional cloth toward Western-style garments—and the

Table 17.11   Employment and Value Added per Worker by Sector and Enterprise Size in the Manufacturing Industry, 1979

Sector	Large and Medium Establishments		Small-Scale Establishments	
	Employment (thousands)	Value Added per Worker (Rp 1000s/ year)	Employment (thousands)	Value Added per Worker (Rp 1000s/ year)
Food, bev., tobacco	299.4	2,289.4	403.5	204.4
Textiles and leather	227.8	909.2	91.4	302.9
Wood and wood products	51.2	1,224.2	110.9	263.7
Paper and printing	29.9	1,694.4	11.9	390.5
Chemicals and rubber	103.8	2,547.9	17.4	504.3
Nonmetallic minerals	43.0	2,675.3	133.7	138.7
Basic iron and steel	8.2	7,171.7	—	—
Metal products	105.7	2,116.5	49.5	285.7
Other manufactures	6.0	824.8	8.7	204.8
Total	870.0	1,908.5	827.0	226.5

Source: BPS, *Statistical Pocketbook of Indonesia* (1982), 153–64.

increased demand for synthetic cloth, difficult to produce on hand-looms, combined to cause consolidation and growth of output and employment in large firms in the early 1970s. But by the late 1970s incentives for greater capital intensity—in the form of negative real interest rates for the textile industry, fiscal incentives to foreign investors in textiles, low tariffs on textile machinery, and a ban on import of (usually less mechanized) second-hand machinery—produced a situation in which weavers could increase textile production without adding appreciably to employment. For the late 1970s the evidence of table 17.12 shows that low employment elasticity is not limited to the large textile firms; small-scale establishments exhibit a higher, but still low, elasticity of only 0.42.

In the food, beverage, and tobacco industry there is a marked difference between small and large firms. The large firms—cigarette, sugar, beer, and vegetable oil producers and processors, among others—tend to be capital-intensive, high-capacity firms with a low employment response to output growth. At the same time, in the small-scale establishments the employment elasticity is extraordinarily high, nearly 1.3. This might seem to indicate declining average product of labor for small-scale firms in this sector. But the high employment elasticity is almost certainly due to a changing product composition within the sector, with low-productivity activities proliferating, expanding much faster than other activities in the sector.

Table 17.12   Sectoral Employment Growth in Relation to Output Growth in the Manufacturing Industry

	Large and Medium Establishments, 1975–80			Small-Scale Establishments, 1974/75–79		
	Average Annual Growth Rate		Employment Elasticity	Average Annual Growth Rate		Employment Elasticity
Sector	Employment	Value Added		Employment	Value Added	
Food, bev., tobacco	2.4%	8.3%	0.29	21.7%	16.9%	1.28
Textiles and leather	0.8	7.7	0.10	10.5	24.8	0.42
Wood and wood products	11.6	30.2	0.38	21.6	23.5	0.92
Paper and printing	4.4	8.4	0.52	8.0	13.5	0.59
Chemicals and rubber	13.1	16.1	0.81	7.0	12.5	0.56
Nonmetallic minerals	7.1	17.7	0.40	23.3	23.1	1.01
Basic iron and steel	25.4	91.6	0.28	—	—	—
Machinery and equipment	14.8	21.6	0.69	17.5	20.0	0.88
Other manufactures	5.1	29.5	0.38	9.6	12.0	0.80
Total	5.1%	13.4%	0.38	19.2%	19.3%	0.99

Source: See Appendix, tables 17.A.3 and 17.A.4.

Important Manufactured Products

Even within sectors there is tremendous diversity of activities and enterprises. Productivity and inferred labor intensity range widely as do growth rates. In Appendix table 17.A.5 value added is shown in relation to employment for a sampling of major products and subsectors of large and medium manufacturing industries. Within sector 31 (food, beverage, and tobacco), for example, value added per worker varies from Rp 19.25 million per year for white cigarettes to Rp 2.72 million and Rp 2.21 million for the products of greatest employment significance (*kretek* cigarettes and sugar refining, respectively) to as little as Rp 0.22 million for tea processing. The chemicals sector includes the highly capital-intensive fertilizer industry along with relatively labor-intensive plastic ware, rubber product, and match industries.

Table 17.13 shows production levels and growth rates for selected items of industrial production. Again, there is a wide range of experience. Among the fastest-growing products are cement and fertilizer, both quite capital-intensive and both actively supported by substantial government investments through state-owned enterprises. Although

Table 17.13   **Production of Selected Industrial Goods in Indonesia**

Product	Unit	1970/71	1975/76	1980/81	Average Growth Rate, 1975/76–1980/81
Cigarettes	billion pieces	34	57	84	8.1%
Vegetable oil	1,000 tons	284	299	889	24.4
Textile yarn	1,000 bales	217	445	1,184	21.6
Fabrics	million meters	598	1,017	2,027	14.8
Paper	1,000 tons	22	47	232	37.7
Urea	1,000 tons	103	387	1,985	38.6
Car tires	1,000 pieces	401	1,796	3,320	13.1
Bicycle tires	1,000 pieces	2,164	7,129	7,596	1.3
Soap	1,000 tons	132	165	213	5.2
Matches	million boxes	322	780	586	−5.6
Toothpaste	million tubes	25	108	123	2.6
Cement	1,000 tons	562	1,241	5,852	36.4
Glass bottles	1,000 tons	11	32	68[a]	20.7
Reinforcing iron	1,000 tons	10	202	640	25.9
Steel pipes	1,000 tons	3	97	154	9.7
Sewing machines	1,000 pieces	14	520	525	0.2
Radio sets	1,000 pieces	393	1,101	1,111	0.2
TV sets	1,000 pieces	5	166	730	34.5
Automobiles	1,000 units	3	79	173	17.0
Motorcycles	1,000 units	31	300	410	6.4

Source: Supplement to the President's Report to Parliament, August 1982.
[a]1979/80.

small shares have been exported, these products both are aimed at the domestic market and have substituted for imports. Even though total consumption of cement increased substantially during the 1970s, the share of domestic production rose from about 45% in 1970 (and less in 1975) to virtual self-sufficiency at the end of the decade.

Other industrial products—including glass bottles, automobile tires, dry cell batteries, automobiles, and television sets—had rapid growth under the protection of bans against imports. The production gains are impressive in the short run but not likely to continue since few if any can compete in export markets. It is notable that smaller and "older" goods such as radios, motorcycles, and matches have already experienced a marked slowdown in growth despite imports being banned.

Paper, cooking oils, textile yarns, and fabrics also have grown behind high nominal tariffs and higher effective rates of protection. With few exceptions—such as textiles and clothing—the most protected items tend to be rather capital-intensive. Given Indonesia's abundant labor and low wages, her exportable goods are predominantly labor-intensive. This is confirmed in studies by Pitt (1981, 20) and by World Bank staff, who also show that the most protected areas are predominantly the relatively capital-intensive, import-competing sectors.

17.5.2   The Policy Determinants of Manufacturing Growth

As the growth patterns discussed above strongly suggest, Indonesia has pursued industrialization during most of the 1970s through import substitution. A consequence has been that despite substantial investment in manufacturing and rapid overall growth of manufacturing output, there has been little increase in export of manufactured goods. The industrial structure is biased toward capital intensity and away from comparative advantage.

The principal policy elements behind this pattern of industrial growth may be enumerated as follows:

First, following an early period of liberalization, the New Order government became more protectionist during the 1970s. This was accomplished most evidently by the application of bans and quotas but also by tariff adjustments and extensive use of restrictive licensing. Greatest protection tended to be given to capital-intensive processing of final goods for the domestic market. Tariffs on intermediate materials and on capital goods were kept low, and other restrictions were few.

Second, development of export markets for manufactured goods was hindered by the maintenance of a fixed exchange rate with the dollar for most of the decade (August 1971 to November 1978). Since Indonesian inflation was more rapid than that of its trading partners and competitors, the real effective exchange rate appreciated. The resulting higher costs and wages made it difficult for Indonesian producers to compete for export markets and, at the same time, encouraged capital intensity by making imported capital goods cheap.

The devaluation of 1978, which raised the rupiah price of a dollar by about 50% (from Rp 415 to Rp 625), was undertaken with the clear goal of improving the international competitiveness of Indonesian labor. By most accounts, even though it helped bring on 25% inflation in 1979, the action had a positive effect on manufactured exports. There was a further 28% devaluation in March of 1983.

A third factor in capital-intensive industrial growth related to controls on interest rates for domestic borrowing and the granting of generous fiscal incentives to approved investment. These incentives included investment tax credits, accelerated depreciation, and exemption from existing duties on capital goods imports. These subsidies to capital, while facilitating manufacturing growth, had predictable effects on capital intensity as well as on total investment.

Fourth, worth separate mention, is Indonesia's energy pricing policy. During the 1970s and indeed until 1982, domestic prices of petroleum fuel were kept below their opportunity cost by implicit and explicit subsidy. This obviously also encouraged use of machinery and equipment.

A final factor is the direct role of government as investor in public enterprises engaged in capital-intensive production of fertilizer, cement, steel, aluminum, petrochemicals, and aircraft.

17.6 Prospects

Indonesia's economy almost certainly will not grow in the 1980s at the pace set during 1966–80. Her prospects for the near future depend on worldwide economic recovery and, in particular, on the state of the world oil market. As officials have apparently realized, Indonesia's longer-run prosperity will require strengthening of the non-oil sectors of the industrial economy to reduce reliance on oil both for government revenues and for foreign exchange and to deal better with the employment problem. This will require restructuring of the industrial sector to increase production of manufactured goods for export.

To achieve such a shift will, of course, require access to world markets. This is not seen to be a major problem if the world economy recovers and trade continues to grow. The very smallness of Indonesia's present trade and the paucity of manufactured goods work in her favor. Growth can be very rapid relative to the existing base level without making much difference in the total volume of world trade.

The problem lies within Indonesia. For reasons enumerated in the preceding section and the additional factor that the "easy" import substitution phase seems to be near an end, prospects for a resumption of industrial growth fueled by rapid expansion of manufactured exports are not good. A change in strategy is needed, but it is by no means clear that it will come.

There are reasons for optimism, however. During 1983 the government put in place or took huge steps toward several major reforms of economic policy. These include a 28% devaluation in apparent recognition of the importance of the foreign exchange rate to successful promotion of non-oil exports; rephasing or cancellation of a number of government-sponsored, highly capital-intensive industrial projects; and a marked freeing of the banking system by elimination of sector-specific credit and interest rate controls so as to achieve better allocation of capital and reduce subsidy inducements to capital intensity. Also, a sweeping tax reform package was presented to Parliament last fall, and some tax changes have already been implemented. The purpose is to reduce reliance on oil company taxes but also to reduce further the bias toward capital intensity by ending tax holidays and investment allowances.

Nonetheless, so far, questions of tariff and nontariff barriers to trade and their relation to the structure of industry have not been addressed by decisive policy action. If nationalism and protectionism prevail in trade policy, prospects for continued industrial growth and expanded trade in manufactured goods are poor, despite the reforms already achieved in the other aspects of economic policy. Indonesia is an economy considerably less industrialized than its neighbors. Yet it has the potential for rapid expansion of manufactured exports in the future, even if it is not likely to match the dramatic growth of exports achieved by the East Asian newly industrialized countries.

Appendix

Table 17.A.1   Income, Production, and Merchandise Trade in 1981 in East and Southeast Asia and the United States

	GNP per Capita (U.S. $)	GDP (U.S. $ billions)	Merchandise Trade (U.S. $ billions and % of GDP)		Manuf. Output as % of GDP	Manuf. Goods as % of Total Exports
			Exports	Imports		
Indonesia	530	85.0	22.3 (26)	13.3 (16)	12	2
Thailand	770	36.8	6.9 (19)	10.0 (27)	20	29
Philippines	790	38.9	5.7 (15)	7.9 (20)	25	37
Rep. of Korea	1,700	65.8	21.3 (32)	26.1 (40)	28	40
Malaysia	1,840	24.8	12.9 (52)	13.1 (53)	18	19
Hong Kong	5,100	27.2	21.7 (80)	24.7 (91)	27[a]	93
Singapore	5,240	12.9	21.0 (163)	27.6 (214)	30	54
Japan	10,080	1,129.5	152.0 (13)	143.3 (13)	30	96
United States	12,820	2,893.3	233.7 (8)	273.4 (9)	23	68

Source: World Bank, *World Development Report 1983* (New York: Oxford University Press), tables 1, 3, and 9.
[a]1980 figure.

Table 17.A.2   **Average Annual Growth Rates in East and Southeast Asia and the United States, 1970–81** (percentages)

	GDP	Manufacturing	Exports	Imports
Indonesia	7.8	13.9	6.5	11.9
Thailand	7.2	10.3	11.8	4.9
Philippines	6.2	6.9	7.7	2.6
Rep. of Korea	9.1	15.6	22.0	10.9
Malaysia	7.8	11.1	6.8	7.1
Hong Kong	9.9	10.0	9.7	12.1
Singapore	8.5	9.7	12.0	9.9
Japan	4.5	6.5	9.0	3.9
United States	2.9	2.9	6.5	4.4

Source: World Bank, *World Development Report 1983* (New York: Oxford University Press), tables 2 and 9.

Table 17.A.3   **Growth in Value Added and Employment, Large and Medium Manufacturing Establishments**

Sector	1975	1980	1980R[a]	Annual Growth Rate (%)
Value added (Rp billions)				
31	270.9	939.1	404.5	8.3
32	88.8	298.8	128.7	7.7
33	19.0	166.2	71.2	30.2
34	18.0	62.4	26.9	8.4
35	78.3	384.2	165.5	16.1
36	26.8	140.5	60.5	17.7
37	1.2	71.9	31.0	91.6
38	66.0	407.3	175.4	21.6
39	1.1	9.3	4.0	29.5
Total	570.0	2,479.8	1,068.1	13.4
Employment (thousands)				
31	285.0	321.3		2.4
32	244.8	254.6		0.8
33	38.5	66.6		11.6
34	26.0	32.2		4.4
35	63.2	116.9		13.1
36	33.5	47.3		7.1
37	2.9	9.0		25.4
38	61.5	122.8		14.8
39	4.6	5.9		5.1
Total	760.0	976.6		5.1

Source: BPS, *Statistical Pocketbook of Indonesia,* various issues.

[a]Nominal value added for 1980 has been adjusted to a real basis at 1975 prices by means of the wholesale price index. Since WPI = 202 for 1975 and WPI = 469 for 1980, the 1980R figures are obtained by multiplying each 1980 nominal figure by 0.4307 (= 202/469).

Table 17.A.4   Growth in Value Added and Employment, Small-Scale Manufacturing Establishments

Sector	1974/75	1979	1979R[a]	Annual Growth Rate (%)
Value added (Rp billions)				
31	25.6	82.5	54.1	16.9
32	6.3	27.7	18.2	24.8
33	7.0	29.3	19.2	23.5
34	1.7	4.7	3.1	13.5
35	3.3	8.8	5.8	12.5
36	4.5	18.5	12.1	23.1
37	—	—	—	—
38	3.9	14.2	9.3	20.0
39	0.7	1.8	1.2	12.0
Total	53.0	187.3	122.9	19.3
Employment (thousands)				
31	151.2	403.5		21.7
32	55.4	91.4		10.5
33	41.7	110.9		21.6
34	8.1	11.9		8.0
35	12.4	17.4		7.0
36	46.9	133.7		23.3
37	—	—		—
38	22.1	49.5		17.5
39	5.5	8.7		9.6
Total	343.2	827.0		19.2

Source: BPS, Statistical Pocketbook of Indonesia (1982), 160–64.

[a]Nominal value added for 1979 has been adjusted to a real basis at 1974 prices by means of the wholesale price index. Since WPI = 189 for 1974 and WPI = 288 for 1979, the 1979R figures are obtained by multiplying each nominal figure by 0.65625 (= 189/288).

Table 17.A.5   Output, Employment, and Productivity for Important Manufacturing Industries within Sectors, 1979

	Gross Output (Rp billions)	Value Added (Rp billions)	Employment (thousands)	Value Added per Employee (Rp millions/yr.)
31. *Food, beverage, tobacco*				
Kretek (clove) cigarettes	632.4	284.8	104.6	2.72
White cigarettes	159.3	117.4	6.1	19.25
Drying tobacco	22.8	4.8	40.7	0.12
Sugar factories	245.2	149.2	67.6	2.21
Beer	38.1	26.6	1.9	13.86
Bakery products	13.5	3.8	11.1	0.34
Tea processing	7.2	0.8	3.5	0.22
Rice milling	16.8	2.0	4.1	0.49
Mfg. of coconut oil	63.0	7.1	5.4	1.31
Mfg. of other veg. oil	47.8	10.7	2.8	3.82

Table 17.A.5   (continued)

	Gross Output (Rp billions)	Value Added (Rp billions)	Employment (thousands)	Value Added per Employee (Rp millions/yr.)
32. *Textiles and leather*				
Weaving	307.8	94.9	115.0	0.83
Yarn	179.7	56.7	39.0	1.45
Batiks	211.0	7.1	15.4	0.46
Knitting	19.5	5.7	11.8	0.48
Gunny & plastic bags	17.5	6.7	10.3	0.65
Wearing apparel	9.9	4.6	5.8	0.79
Other wearing apparel	1.9	1.1	2.6	0.55
Footwear	22.3	12.8	6.0	2.13
Made-up textile goods	10.9	4.9	7.1	0.69
33. *Wood and wood products*				
Sawmills	112.5	39.5	25.5	1.55
Plywood mfg.	61.8	17.7	14.8	1.20
Furniture	5.8	2.6	5.1	0.50
Rattan products	6.9	1.7	3.3	0.52
34. *Paper and printing*				
Paper mfg.	46.4	13.1	6.7	1.97
Containers, boxes	19.7	9.9	2.3	4.30
Printing, publ.	51.5	23.2	18.1	1.28
35. *Chemicals and rubber*				
Fertilizer	136.3	68.2	5.5	12.40
Plastic wares	54.5	15.4	16.5	0.93
Crumb rubber	305.2	39.4	16.3	2.42
Remilling & smoking rubber	37.2	5.7	5.0	1.14
Rubber products, n.e.c.	9.9	2.2	4.4	0.64
Tires and tubes	72.7	27.9	8.4	3.32
Soap, etc.	63.0	9.3	5.5	1.69
Matches	3.9	1.4	5.3	0.26
Perfumes, cosmetics	17.6	6.5	3.7	1.76
Paints	29.1	9.7	3.5	2.77
Drugs & medicine	86.3	30.9	14.2	2.18
Native medicine	3.5	1.7	3.3	0.52
Basic chemicals	36.7	12.5	4.6	2.72
36. *Nonmetallic minerals*				
Cement	133.5	78.1	7.2	10.85
Goods of cement	21.1	10.4	8.7	1.20
Sheet glass	24.0	14.1	1.3	10.85
Mfg. of glass & products	16.1	7.5	7.3	1.03
Ceramics & porcelain	7.8	3.3	5.3	0.62
Roofing tiles	2.4	1.4	5.5	0.25
Other	3.0	1.0	2.7	0.37
37. *Basic iron and steel*	68.4	18.0	4.6	3.96

(continued)

Table 17.A.5   (continued)

	Gross Output (Rp billions)	Value Added (Rp billions)	Employment (thousands)	Value Added per Employee (Rp millions/yr.)
38. *Machinery and equipment*				
Electrical appar. & supplies	81.5	18.4	12.9	1.43
Struct. metal prod.	116.3	28.3	11.8	2.40
Sewing machines, etc.	48.0	27.5	11.0	2.40
Radio, TV assembly	114.5	29.7	9.4	3.16
Motor vehicle assembly	75.8	18.4	9.7	1.90
Motorcycle assembly	105.1	38.3	4.5	8.51
Ship bldg. & repair	24.0	14.5	6.9	2.10
Metal container mfg.	15.8	5.8	5.1	1.14
Kitchen apparatus	7.5	2.5	5.7	0.45
Dry cell batteries	35.8	16.8	4.9	3.43
Other metal products, n.e.c.	7.8	2.8	5.4	0.52

Source: BPS, *Statistik Industri* (1979).

Notes

1. According to World Bank 1983, the average 1970–81 growth rate of GDP for middle-income economies was 5.6%, and for middle-income oil exporters it was 6.2%. Also see Appendix, table 17.A.2.

2. As measured by the Jakarta cost-of-living index the rate of inflation was 10% in 1969 and less for the next two years. See table 17.1 for inflation rates after 1969.

3. This agrees with the World Bank estimate of 2% reported in table 17.A.1. The World Bank staff also treats tin ingot as a crude mineral product, not as a manufactured product.

4. Indonesian GDP was Rp 45,446 billion in 1980 and Rp 59,633 billion in 1982. Converting these figures to dollars using the corresponding average exchange rates of Rp 627 and Rp 661 yields dollar GDP estimates of $72,482 million and $90,216 million, respectively. The 1980 ratio of manufactured goods exports to GDP is 505.4/72,482 = 0.7%. Similarly, the 1982 ratio is 832.0/90,216 = 0.9%.

5. BPS, *Statistical Pocketbook of Indonesia* (1982), 44–45, 386.

References

Gillis, M., and R. E. Beals. 1980. *Tax and investment policies for hard minerals: Public and multinational enterprises in Indonesia.* Cambridge: Ballinger Publishing.

Hill, H. 1980. The economics of recent changes in the weaving industry. *Bulletin of Indonesian Economic Studies* 16:2.

Ooi Jin Bee. 1982. *The petroleum resources of Indonesia*. Kuala Lumpur: Oxford University Press.

Pitt, M. M. 1981. Alternative trade strategies and employment in Indonesia. In *Trade and employment in developing countries,* vol. 1, ed. A. O. Krueger, H. B. Lary, T. Monson, and N. Akrasanee. Chicago: University of Chicago Press.

Sievers, Allen M. 1974. *The mystical world of Indonesia*. Baltimore: Johns Hopkins Press.

World Bank. 1982. *Indonesia: Financial resources and human development in the eighties*. Report no. 3795-IND. Washington, D.C.: World Bank.

———. 1983. *World development report 1983*. London: Oxford University Press.

Contributors

Juanjai Ajanant
Faculty of Economics
Chulalongkorn University
Bangkok 10500
Thailand

Florian A. Alburo
School of Economics
University of the Philippines
Diliman, Quezon City
Philippines

Robert E. Baldwin
Department of Economics
University of Wisconsin
Madison, Wisconsin 53706

Ralph E. Beals
Department of Economics
Amherst College
Amherst, Massachusetts 01002

Colin I. Bradford, Jr.
Yale Center for International and
    Area Studies
Yale University
85 Trumbull Street
New Haven, Connecticut 06520

William H. Branson
Woodrow Wilson School
Princeton University
Princeton, New Jersey 08544

Edward K. Y. Chen
Centre of Asian Studies
University of Hong Kong
Pokfulam Road
Hong Kong

Wontack Hong
Department of International
    Economics
College of Social Sciences
Seoul University
Seoul 151
Korea

Lawrence R. Klein
Department of Economics
University of Pennsylvania
3718 Locust Walk CR
Philadelphia, Pennsylvania 19104

Laurence J. Kotlikoff
Department of Economics
Boston University
Boston, Massachusetts 02115

Lawrence B. Krause
The Brookings Institution
1775 Massachusetts Avenue, NW
Washington, D.C. 20036

Edward E. Leamer
Department of Economics
University of California
Los Angeles, California 90024

Chee Peng Lim
Division of Analytical Economics
Faculty of Economics and
    Administration
University of Malaya
Kuala Lumpur 22-11
Malaysia

J. David Richardson
Department of Economics
University of Wisconsin
Madison, Wisconsin 53706

Chi Schive
Department and Graduate Institute
    of Economics
National Taiwan University
21, Hsu Chow Road, Taipei 100
Taiwan, Republic of China

Jean L. Waelbroeck
Center for Econometrics and Mathe-
    matical Economics
Free University of Brussels
1050 Brussels
Belgium

Chung Ming Wong
Department of Economics and
    Statistics
National University of Singapore
Kent Ridge 0511
Singapore

Ippei Yamazawa
Faculty of Economics
Hitotsubashi University
Kunitachi, Tokyo
Japan

Author Index

549

Subject Index